Designing and Using
ActiveX Controls

Tom Armstrong

HENRY HOLT & COMPANY, INC.
NEW YORK

M&T Books
A Division of MIS:Press, Inc.
A Subsidiary of Henry Holt and Company, Inc.
115 West 18th Street
New York, New York 10011
http://www.mispress.com

First Edition—1997

ISBN 1-55851-503-8

MIS:Press and M&T Books are available at special discounts for bulk purchases for sales promotions, premiums, and fundraising. Special editions or book excerpts can also be created to specification.

For details contact: Special Sales Director
                         MIS:Press and M&T Books
                         Subsidiaries of Henry Holt and Company, Inc.
                         115 West 18th Street
                         New York, New York 10011

10 9 8 7 6 5 4 3 2 1

Associate Publisher: *Paul Farrell*

Executive Editor: *Cary Sullivan*   **Production Editor:** *Anthony Washington*
Editor: *Andrew Neusner*   **Technical Editor:** *Mark Bramer*
Copy Edit Manager: *Shari Chappell*   **Copy Editor:** *Betsy Hardinger*

Contents-in-Brief

Dedication

To Nicole, Jessica, and Eric. Your love and support empower me to achieve things I never dreamed possible.

Contents

Acknowledgments

Acknowledgments for Designing and Using ActiveX Controls

When the M&T gang decided that a new edition of *Designing and Using OLE Custom Controls* would be a good idea, I jumped at the chance. I said to myself, "a second edition will be easy." Well, it wasn't. In many ways, writing a second edition is harder than writing the first. With the software development industry changing so rapidly, second editions are nearly total rewrites, and rewriting is harder than just writing, at least for me. It was an arduous process, and I couldn't have done it without a lot of help. Thanks to my editor, Andy Neusner, for keeping me on schedule but being flexible when emergencies came up. Thanks to Anthony Washington for laying out these pages, and to Betsy Hardinger, who did a great job of transforming my prose into something a real writer would produce.

I'm most thankful for my wife, Nicole. She again allowed me to spend part (actually most) of my evenings writing. She's just about finished with dental school, so her evenings are busy, too. Thanks also to my children, Jessica and Eric, who, when I slipped into a TV-zone and spent too much time on the couch, reminded me to get to work on the book. I love you all dearly.

Thanks to my technical editor, Mark Bramer. Mark and I go way back. All the way back to our first job together when I interviewed him and didn't want to hire him. What a mistake. Smarter heads prevailed and Mark and I have been working together ever since. Mark is a talented developer, editor, and writer. One of these days, Mark, we'll co-author a book.

Thanks to Marc Ritterbusch, who has finally moved over to the Windows development side of our group (better late than never!), for designing the icons for the Chapter 10 tree view example. One of these days, Marc, you're going to catch something when you go fishing.

Thanks to Richard "Doogie" Clark. Doogie read through each chapter and provided a lot of valuable feedback. In particular, he kept me honest when I started getting lazy. Thanks also to Bruce Allen. Bruce, I'm going to need your help on my next book now that you're an expert on Internet Explorer and connection points. Don't forget.

Thanks to the students who helped work out some of the presentation bugs in the examples. Thanks to the members of the AWD development team, Chuck Reeves and Mark Clobes in particular, who spent the week of October 21 learning about COM, OLE, and ActiveX controls. Thanks also to Dan Weiss, President of Step 1 Training, where I teach an occasional ActiveX/MFC class.

Thanks to all the readers of the first edition, many of whom have provided valuable feedback that has been incorporated into this edition. Specifically, thanks to Stuart Bessler, John Wood, Rick Anderson, and Bob Wilkins. Bob provided a great example of using ActiveX controls within another ActiveX control (it's included on the CD-ROM).

Acknowledgments for Designing and Using OLE Custom Controls

I have to first thank my editor, Judy Brief, who took a chance on a first-time writer by responding to my proposal letter in a record three business hours. Thanks to the whole team at M&T Books: Stephanie Doyle who designed these pages (and spent her weekends doing it) and Karen Tongish who transformed my doggerel into something readable. Thanks also to my technical editor, John Elsbree of Microsoft.

I am thankful for the love and understanding provided by my beautiful wife, Nicole, and my wonderful children, Jessica and Eric. They endured my absence on the weekends, in the evenings, and even on the summer vacation while I pounded away on these pages. I promise to love and support each of them in whatever they choose to pursue.

To the members of the EnCorr development team: To Rob Alumbaugh, a brilliant young developer who reviewed some of the chapters and kept me from getting too "low-level." Thanks Rob. Thanks to Mark Bramer for his help with the design of the clock control and for providing his considerable editing prowess even when he had only a few hours to review a chapter. Thanks to Jim Crespino, who had many ideas and suggestions regarding the control examples, particularly the pipe control of Chapter 11. Thanks to Steve and Doris Stava for reviewing some of the chapters, providing control ideas, and the continual encouragement. And to Roy Lambright, Bob Rench, and Marc Ritterbusch: Thanks for your friendship and humor. When are you going to start developing for a real operating system and forget that OS/2 stuff?

Thanks to various individuals that I've had the pleasure to attend school with or work with in my career who have provided opportunities; stimulated intellectual growth through discussion; provided moral support, friendship, and encouragement; or a combination: Jim Phelan, Jim Kurtenbach, David Bridges, Chuck Reeves, Devin Sherry, Phil Brennaman, Steve Gray, Steve Luke, Danny Hughes, Mike Hudgins, and David Cloud.

To my mother Maureen, my late father Tom Sr., my mother-in-law Millie Koschmeder, my late father-in-law Fred Koschmeder, and my grandparents Cloyd and Josephine Jenkins: Thank you for the unconditional love and support that you have always provided.

To those teachers who have taught me more than the requisite material, in particular Graham Glass, an instructor at the University of Texas at Dallas: Graham you were the one teacher who affected my life profoundly. Your enthusiasm, voracious thirst for knowledge, and general love of life inspired me to approach learning (and life) in a different way. Thank you.

And finally, to that which inspires each of us to push beyond our sphere of contentment. We all have the ability, creativity, and stamina to change the world, but we must endeavor to do it. In the words of Gandhi: "We must become the change we seek in the world."

Preface

This book is for those software developers who want to participate in the burgeoning field of component software development. Software components, specifically those based on Microsoft's Component Object Model (COM), are having a broad impact on the development of Windows-based software. In order for developers to remain productive and competitive, it is imperative that they understand and apply this new technology.

Today, the Internet is having a major impact on the software development industry. To maintain its lead in PC-based environments, Microsoft has radically altered its approach to software development. Microsoft has embraced the new Internet-based development technologies and is moving rapidly to provide developers with state-of-the-art tools and techniques. ActiveX is at the center of this movement. This book covers one of the most important new technologies: ActiveX controls.

What Is Expected from the Reader

To build and understand the sample applications, the reader is expected to have a programming background that includes work in Windows software development, using C, C++, or visual tools such as Visual Basic. This book is not a complete tutorial on any of these languages or tools, but rather is about how to use Visual C++, MFC, COM, OLE, and ActiveX to build robust software components, particularly ActiveX controls. An understanding of object-oriented techniques is valuable but not necessary.

The reader is not expected to understand Microsoft's Component Object Model or ActiveX, but this book cannot cover every aspect of COM. Only those areas important to development of component software, automation, and specifically ActiveX controls are discussed. Other areas of COM will be discussed only as they pertain to the understanding of our primary topic: ActiveX controls.

Hardware and Software Required for the Sample Application

The examples were developed on a 90-MHz Pentium with 24 megabytes of memory running Windows NT 4.0. The software tools required to build and test the samples include: Microsoft's Visual C++ version 4.0 or higher running on Windows 95 or Windows NT 3.51 or higher. The screen shots are of Visual C++ 4.2.

Some control examples use features of Microsoft's ActiveX SDK and the August 1996 Win32 SDK, but by the time you read this, full support for these SDKs will be available in Visual C++ 5.0. If you have any questions as to the requirements to build the sample controls, check out my Web site at `http://www.widgetware.com`

Comments and Bug Reports

I welcome and encourage comments, suggestions, and bug reports at the email address given at the end of this Preface. The Visual C++ compiler is updated three times a year, and as it is changes, I update the example programs and controls. You can contact me via email or through my Web site URL. The site contains any updated examples, FAQs, pointers to other OLE/ActiveX sites, discussions, and other material concerning COM, MFC, and ActiveX technology.

email: `toma@sky.net` or `tom@widgetware.com`

URL: `http://www.sky.net/~toma/` or `http://www.widgetware.com`

Introduction

Software development is becoming more and more complex. New paradigms are needed to decompose this complexity so that the process of developing software can be improved. Large software applications must be broken down into smaller, more manageable pieces. During the last few years, object-oriented languages have helped reduce this complexity explosion. The C++ language in particular has garnered a lot of industry support and is currently enjoying healthy growth in many areas of software development. Smalltalk has become a viable development language in several environments as well, and Java, with the popularity of the Web driving its advance, is quickly becoming an important development language. However, even with these advancements in development paradigms and languages, software development is still a very complex task.

Examples of where software complexity has overwhelmed the development process are easy to find. Severe problems with the software that controlled the baggage system at Denver's new airport caused months of delays and cost billions of dollars. Microsoft's Windows 95 was delayed by nearly two years because (among other reasons) of the complexities of developing a robust operating system with more than 4 million lines of source code. While these examples are extreme, they illustrate the problems that exist in the software development industry today.

Object-oriented paradigms and their primary implementation language, C++, cannot solve this complexity explosion alone. Additional technologies and techniques are required. Microsoft's Component Object Model (COM), OLE, and ActiveX are the technologies that we will explore in this book. These technologies are having a major impact on the development of Windows software, specifically in the area of component software development.

Component Software

The concept of *component software* is not new. Software developers have long hoped for a technology that would enable them to assemble software in a manner similar to that used by hardware engineers. For more than 40 years, computer hardware designers have constructed complex hardware systems by combining off-the-shelf hardware components. These components, or integrated circuits (ICs), can be assembled in endless patterns to make practically anything (electronic) imaginable. When viewed independently, RAM, ASICs, JK flip-flops, and other chips perform rather insignificant functions, but when combined with other IC components, complex hardware systems can be built.

Each IC can be treated, from a design perspective, as a *black box*. The user provides the black box with a set of inputs, and depending on the behavior of the black box, a specific result will be provided as the output. The designer needs absolutely no understanding of *how* the black box performs its functions; he only needs an understanding of the input and output behavior. The inputs and outputs are stringently defined, and this rigid structure allows the easy combining of hundreds of IC components, working together to define complex hardware systems.

Component software is an effort to apply the hardware paradigm to software. This approach would provide software *ICs* that could be assembled in various configurations to quickly produce robust software systems. C++ and other OOP languages were supposed to provide this capability, but, for various reasons, they have not achieved this goal. Microsoft's Component Object Model and its companions, OLE and ActiveX, provide the technology to make component software a reality.

Twenty years ago, computer hardware was very expensive while software was relatively cheap. Today the reverse is true. The reason: Massive reuse of well-specified, discrete hardware components. This leap in productivity is currently occurring in software development, with Visual Basic custom controls providing the impetus.

Custom Controls

Visual Basic finally provided a platform that supported component development, not from the aspect of building software components (ICs), but by providing the *breadboard* on which to assemble the various components into usable applications. If we continue the hardware analogy, Visual Basic custom controls (VBXes) are the ICs and any Visual Basic source code is the *bus* or wires that connect these discrete components.

Custom controls provide specific, well-defined functionality. They do not provide all the advanced features of true OOP languages, such as inheritance and polymorphism, but this simplicity may explain their success. Custom controls cannot function independently and can only provide value when coupled with other custom controls by a controlling entity (usually Visual Basic). This controlling entity is called a *container* in OLE parlance; it provides the *glue* that ties the components together. It also provides the bus over which the controls can communicate.

Discrete hardware components and custom controls share many characteristics. They have a focused purpose, documented behavior, and a well-defined interface (the inputs and outputs). The user of a control only needs to understand its behavior and how to affect this behavior. Examples include simple entry fields that validate dates as they are entered or more complex controls that encapsulate the functionality of a complete editor. Industry-specific controls are also important. A vendor in the health care industry may provide a custom control that implements an interface to a medical device. Because the control hides any proprietary logic, he can freely distribute the control to end users. The examples and uses are myriad, as the healthy market for third-party controls demonstrates.

ActiveX Controls

While Visual Basic custom controls provided the stimulus that eventually validated component development, its VBX architecture has two major problems. The VBX architecture is inextricably tied to the Windows 16-bit environment, and Microsoft does not publish the details of how VBXes can be used within other applications or tools. Microsoft's Component Object Model, OLE, and ActiveX standards now provide a solid foundation on which to build software components. ActiveX controls have replaced the VBX and have added crucial functionality in the process. ActiveX controls can expect a much larger market, relative to that provided to VBX developers today, because ActiveX controls are supported by many more applications and software development tools. ActiveX controls have also been enlisted to become the central software element in Microsoft's new Web-based strategy.

ActiveX Controls and the Internet

On March 6, 1996, Microsoft unveiled its new ActiveX development strategy. Central to this new strategy is the ActiveX control: ActiveX controls can now be embedded in Web-based pages and accessed by browsers such as Internet Explorer. The component-based software revolution has now come to the Internet, and ActiveX controls are a major part of this new environment.

Automation

Another area of COM/OLE that enhances the viability of component software development is automation. Automation allows Windows applications to *expose*, or make available, their functionality to other Windows applications. In this way, applications like Microsoft Word become software components that can be used by other smaller, larger, or more complex applications. For example, say a developer is faced with the prospect of spending a few man-years developing a word processing package for his application. His users indicate their need for this capability and want him to "make it something like Word" if he can. Today, thanks to COM and OLE, he can choose either to spend the man-years developing a word processing package or to incorporate Microsoft Word directly into his existing application. His users gain the use of something familiar, and the developer can add Microsoft Word functionality with a minimum of work (measured in man-weeks). COM, OLE, and ActiveX, with their component and application integration technologies, make this possible.

Visual C++ and the MFC Libraries

Visual C++ and its Microsoft Foundation Class (MFC) libraries are today's most advanced development tools available for Windows. The MFC libraries provide an *application framework* that removes much of the tedious work involved with developing Windows and COM-based applications. While a lot of the tedium is removed, there is still a lot of complexity left behind. In particular, the incorporation of COM, OLE, and

ActiveX support within the MFC libraries adds another dimension that developers must assimilate. Nevertheless, Visual C++ and the MFC libraries help significantly in the development of COM-based components, as this book demonstrates.

The Chapters

The chapters in this book are probably best read in succession, although the first three chapters can be skimmed if you are already familiar with C++, Visual C++, and the MFC libraries. Chapter 1 discusses the issues facing software developers today: how to achieve reuse with today's software tools, why object-oriented development languages haven't solved more development problems, and the concept of component software. Chapter 2 provides an overview of the C++ language and how it can be used to effectively build software components. Chapter 3 introduces the Visual C++ development environment and details the workings of the Microsoft Foundation Class framework.

Chapters 4 focuses on Microsoft's Component Object Model and how this system-level technology enables the creation of robust software components. Chapter 5 builds on Chapter 4 by detailing the MFC implementation of COM and ActiveX. Chapter 6 covers the use of these technologies by wrapping C++ classes with automation.

The last half of the book focuses exclusively on the development of ActiveX controls. First the architecture is examined, and then various ActiveX control types are explored. Chapters 8, 9, 10, 11, and 12 each detail the development of a specific type of ActiveX control. A graphical clock control is developed in Chapter 9. Chapter 10 covers development of controls that subclass standard Windows controls and the new Windows 95 common controls. A nonvisual control that encapsulates the services provided by the Win32 named pipes API is developed in Chapter 11. Chapter 12 details what is required to develop and implement an Internet-aware control. And finally, Chapter 13 focuses on answering the most frequently asked questions concerning automation and ActiveX control development.

Chapter 1

Component-Based Development, the Web, and ActiveX

Component-based software development is changing the way Windows applications are developed. In this chapter we will look at what component software is and why it is having a tremendous impact on the software development industry. We will discuss the definitions of software objects and components as well as the benefits they can provide the application developer. We will also describe Microsoft's *Component Object Model* (COM), the primary technology we will use to construct and connect these components.

Within the past year, the popularity of the Internet has caused a major shift in the development of software. The way software is developed, deployed, and supported has been radically altered by this entity, called the Web. Component software—from ActiveX controls and Java applets to Netscape plug-ins—abounds in Web-based environments.

Web technologies are also changing the corporate software environment. Corporate *intranets,* a much larger and more lucrative market than the commercial Internet, are quickly moving to Web-based development tools and technologies. Microsoft's ActiveX is one of the most important new Web-based technologies.

ActiveX is a broad term that covers Microsoft's Web-based strategy. It covers a large number of applications, tools, and technologies, all of which use COM heavily in their implementation. For now, ActiveX can be thought of as the underpinning of Microsoft's Web-based technologies. In reality, the term *ActiveX* has basically replaced one that we all are familiar with: OLE. The term *OLE* now connotes a small subset of Microsoft's component technologies—specifically, the old compound document technology that has been available for several years. In this first chapter, we'll talk about COM and ActiveX in the context of component-based development.

This chapter is intended to whet your appetite by showing you the benefits that component-based software can provide the software industry and explaining why you, the software developer, should begin to study and adopt these methods. Trust me—component software is going to make our jobs much more fun.

If you don't really care how we got here or why and want to get your hands dirty, jump ahead to Chapter 2. But promise me that when you get time, you'll come back and read this chapter, because it explains why software components are going to change the world.

The Changing Development Landscape

Application development techniques have always changed rapidly, but within the last few years, for various reasons, profound changes have occurred. Users are more sophisticated and demanding, and business in general has become more competitive. And now, with the enormous growth in the popularity of the Internet, software is developed and deployed at a frenetic pace. Effective development and deployment of software systems is essential to the survival of most businesses. Only a few years ago, information technology was viewed as a back office requirement that meant little to the bottom line. Today, the opposite is true.

With the realization that information technology is crucial to the competitiveness of any business entity, there has been an increasing demand to develop and deploy mission-critical applications quickly and effectively. Business environments change more rapidly than they did only a few years ago, and competitiveness is difficult to maintain in this fast changing environment. Many books have been written on the information age, so I will not expound on it here. Suffice it to say that to be competitive, companies, business units, teams, and individuals must be willing to change and adapt.

In the Introduction, I described the concept of component software development. With its ability to support third-party, custom controls, the Visual Basic development environment has dramatically changed Windows software development. The practice of combining discrete software components into solid Windows applications has also increased the productivity of many software developers. Broad reuse of software components is one reason for this increase in productivity. Software reuse is of paramount importance if we, as developers, are to advance the state of software development. And now, with the addition of Web-based technologies, the job of making small, robust, and distributable components has become much easier.

Reuse Is What Counts

It's a waste of time to build various components if they are never reused. If a similar application needs to be built and if the components we've constructed are not generic enough or are not carefully delineated, they cannot be reused effectively. If there is no reuse, there is no saving of time in either the development or the building of other applications. Reuse is the primary focus of this book and the goal of component builders everywhere. Without it, component building would provide little benefit.

Reusable software has many forms and definitions. *Reuse,* for our purposes, means the ability to use a particular component many times, either within the same application or in various applications, *without modification* of the original component. Object-oriented programming languages, such as C++, profess to be replete with reuse. Although that may be true, there are other methods to obtain consistent reuse without resorting to building every piece of an application in C++.

Types of Reuse

There are many ways to reuse software when you're developing applications. I'll discuss two ways that are in wide use today: reuse through the inheritance mechanisms provided by object-oriented programming languages such as C++, and reuse through the development of discrete, language-independent components. The first method, reuse via inheritance, typically requires access to the implementing source code. Source code is required because few standards exist that allow the sharing of objects between language compilers (such as Watcom and Borland). Reuse with inheritance typically requires that the inheritor use the same language used in the original implementation. In other words, you cannot reuse, via inheritance, a C++ class in Smalltalk or Java. The second method, reuse by building and using components, does not depend on the implementing language, relying instead on component standards that allow sharing across languages and environments.

Inheritance allows a developer to extend an existing code module by augmenting the original base class code. A great amount of functionality may already be provided by the base class, so implementation of additional functionality requires only minor changes to the new subclass. This new class provides significant functionality with only a small change or augmentation. Inheritance used in this manner provides significant reuse of existing code. The principal problem with this approach is that to continue to augment and reuse, you must continue to use the same development language. Today's C++ compilers do not allow the sharing of C++ objects developed using different compilers, primarily because there is no standard method to mangle, or decorate, the exposed function points. *Mangling* is a method used by C++ compilers to construct unique names for public functions. C++ allows multiple definitions of functions using the same function name but different argument types. Mangling "mangles" these names (by attaching an encoding of the argument types) so that the linker can resolve the specific function at link time. This process is described in more detail in the next chapter. Smalltalk objects are similar in that no binary standard exists to describe the various Smalltalk language objects. You can overcome these problems by using one of the new *wrappering* technologies, which allow you to wrap an existing C++ or Smalltalk class with an external, language-independent interface. The two primary standards are IBM's System Object Model (SOM) and Microsoft's COM.

Reuse through inheritance is wonderful when the dynamics of a project allow for the building of applications using only one primary language, but in larger projects that require multiple languages and are staffed by individuals with diverse programming backgrounds, this arrangement can be difficult to implement. Another problem with inheritance-based reuse is that it is difficult to manage in large projects. Inheritance-based reuse creates a large hierarchical structure of classes that can complicate the process of code changes. If a change is made to a base level class, every class that derives from it will be affected. This can cause massive recompiles and relinks as the changes cascade through the project.

I'm not implying that inheritance-based languages are bad, just that they have their place and purpose. We will use C++ throughout this book to develop components. But the inheritance feature will be used internally by the components being developed and not as the primary reuse mechanism.

The other important type of reuse is that provided by software components. A component can be another application such as Microsoft's Word for Windows, a database management package, an ActiveX control, an Automation server, a Java applet, and so on. These components offer reuse on a different scale than that offered by language-based inheritance. This book focuses on building these types of components.

Software components can be built with various languages. The important characteristic that makes a component reusable is that it has a well-defined binary standard interface. A *binary standard* provides sharing, or interoperation, of objects developed using disparate languages and tools. We'll cover this in more detail soon. Components should also be generic and configurable. As mentioned earlier, the *interface*, or exposed functionality, is the most important aspect. Today the primary interface implementation mechanisms are IBM's SOM and Microsoft's COM. We will use COM (which includes OLE and ActiveX) because this book describes the development of Windows-based software and because COM is the de facto component technology on Windows machines.

Reuse and Portability

Another important aspect of reuse is portability. *Portability*, as used in this book, refers primarily to the easy movement of source code among the various Windows platforms: Windows 3.x, Windows NT, and Windows 95. Portability on a larger scale, including non-Microsoft platforms, is a valid goal, but we will touch on this topic only briefly.

Microsoft has recently stated that it will provide multiplatform support for most basic ActiveX technologies, including ActiveX controls. Versions of Internet Explorer 3 will be provided for 16-bit Windows, 32-bit Windows, the Macintosh, and certain flavors of UNIX. Portability among these operating systems will be provided with Visual C++ and the MFC libraries. Microsoft has also licensed the technology to other companies that are providing support on other platforms (such as IBM's MVS).

The code that we will develop will be portable across the various Microsoft Windows platforms. We will use the MFC libraries, an application framework that abstracts many of the complexities of Windows development and hides the differences among 16-bit Windows, 32-bit Windows, and Macintosh platforms. The 32-bit version supports Windows 95, Windows NT, and the Macintosh. Source code is portable among these operating environments with minor changes and a recompile and relink. Details and caveats will be discussed in later chapters as the various items are encountered.

New Development Methodologies

Many development methodologies have come and gone within the last few years. Some have confirmed their worth and enjoy broad acceptance. Examples include structured programming, client-server–based development, and the ubiquitous object-oriented analysis, design and development. Others, such as computer aided software engineering (CASE), expert systems, and artificial intelligence (AI), have proven useful only in well-defined, restrictive settings and do not yet show promise for broad application. Component software development is proving itself to be a viable and cost-effective method of developing applications for the Windows environment.

There are two primary methods of developing Windows applications. The first method is based on the visual combining of discrete software components. The most obvious example of this paradigm is Visual Basic, but there are many others, including Borland's Delphi, Computer Associates' Realizer, and IBM's Visual Age products. The more prevalent method is the use of object-oriented languages, typically C++.

Usually, an application framework (either supplied by a vendor, as with MFC, or developed in-house) is used to help manage complexity in large Windows applications. Because of the dynamics of the PC market, Windows developers must choose at least one of these methods to remain competitive. In reality, nearly all good development tools provide a mixture of both techniques.

Visual Programming

Initially, Windows development was done using the Windows Software Development Kit (SDK) and the C language. These tools were the only ones available to build professional, efficient Windows applications. Then, in 1991, Microsoft introduced Visual Basic, a radically different method of developing Windows applications. With Visual Basic you can write a "Hello World" program with zero lines of code. Even though there were certain deficiencies in Visual Basic development, it provided a truly *visual* development environment in which developers could drag-and-drop controls (or components), modify their properties, and have a fairly robust application with only a few hundred lines of Visual Basic code. Compare this to the thousands of lines of C/SDK code that would be required to provide similar functionality.

Visual Basic also provided a Control Development Kit (CDK) that allowed third parties to develop generic and specialized controls that could be incorporated seamlessly into the Visual Basic development environment. This proved to be a major event in the history of component software.

Visual Basic provided the genesis for software component building and combining. The use of the Visual Basic custom controls (VBX)—and now the incorporation of COM, OLE, and ActiveX support—has made Visual Basic the standard for building prototypes and commercial software. Even though the VBX specification did not provide an open standard for component development and was restricted to its 16-bit heritage, VBXs became the de facto "components" in many Windows development environments. Support for VBX controls is now included in most 16-bit C++ compilers and other visual development tools. Many vendors had to reverse-engineer the VBX architecture to enable it to work within their products, but the large number of VBX components made this a requirement. With ActiveX control, Microsoft now has an open standard for visual component development. Vendors can easily incorporate support for components developed with this standard, and today nearly all of them have done so.

The new Web-based technologies add another dimension to this environment. Web developers and designers must produce and publish material very quickly. Microsoft's ActiveX control technology makes it easy for these developers to incorporate dynamic content into their products. Design and development tools provide an efficient method of assembling these various components—HTML, ActiveX controls, and VBScript—to produce effective, dynamic Web pages.

Object-Oriented Languages

Object-oriented languages such as Smalltalk, Java, and C++ have recently received a great deal of attention (and use) within PC and workstation development environments. All of these languages greatly ease the task of building complex and reusable software. Various factors have contributed to the success of these languages. C++ is a superset of the widely used C language and lets developers progress to object-oriented methods as time permits. Smalltalk has taken longer to gain momentum primarily because its interpreted, run-time binding performance requirements make it slower. Smalltalk is a pure object-oriented language that started in academia for instructional purposes. Although Smalltalk has been around for more than 20 years, only now is the hardware sufficiently fast to allow its use in typical application development environments.

Smalltalk will not be used in this book; nevertheless, it is an important language of the future—many people believe it to be the COBOL of the '90s. Instead, we will use Visual C++ and the MFC libraries to develop COM-based software components. Visual C++ and MFC provide sufficient speed as well as a level of abstraction from the underlying complexities of both the Win32 and COM APIs.

Java is the newest object-oriented language, and its popularity has soared along with the popularity of the Web. Java is a product of the new component-based software model. Its initial purpose was to facilitate the development of small, portable *applets*, which are perfect for Web environments. Java removes most of the development difficulties and complexity of C++, and this is one of its main selling points. Unlike C++, Java is a new language unencumbered by a long history of modifications. It isn't perfect, however, because it still has some growing to do.

Although object-oriented languages provide significant help with software development problems, they are deficient in areas that are important to the broad application of the object-oriented technology. C++ and Smalltalk do not provide a binary standard that would allow the sharing of objects across languages or environments. Each language has *proprietary*, or nonstandard, methods of implementing specific features of the object-oriented paradigm. Because we're focusing on C++, let's review why it currently has such limitations.

C++

The C++ language was supposed to solve many of the problems caused by the increasing complexity of building large or complex applications, and to a large extent it has succeeded. C++ is useful when you're implementing large applications, frameworks, and systems. A good example is Microsoft's Foundation Class libraries. Visual C++, coupled with MFC, allows much of the complexity of Windows and COM software development to be hidden. Application frameworks such as MFC provide robust, well-tested application code. The developer doesn't have to initially understand all the underlying complexity. A developer can become productive quickly, gradually developing an understanding of the underlying architecture. There are problems with this approach (aren't there always?), and we'll discuss them in Chapter 3.

C++ has failed in its ability to provide a standard method of describing the produced objects in a binary fashion. For C++ objects to be effectively shared or reused across development platforms, hardware platforms, or even compilers, the original source code is required. There are no compiler-independent standards for decorating or mangling C++ function names, so to share these objects, the secondary user requires either the original source code or platform-specific (Windows, OS/2) and compiler-specific (Microsoft, Borland, Symantec) binaries (**.LIB** or **.OBJ** files). This doesn't mean that C++ isn't an effective language. It is. But more is required to take objects developed in C++ to the next level, where they can be shared and reused across environments and languages.

We're discussing only static objects; we haven't yet raised the issue of sharing actual run-time instantiations of these objects or components. There are major problems here as well, particularly in the sharing of objects across processes on local and distributed processors.

What is needed is a higher level of object orientation or a standard that encapsulates the underlying objects to allow many of the object-oriented features to be used across development environments. Such standards or technologies are described as object-oriented systems.

Object-Oriented Systems

Object-oriented languages provide significant leverage in the development of software, but to incorporate or share the developed objects across disparate languages, processes, and environments requires additional software. Object-oriented systems enable the sharing, or *distribution*, of these objects across the mentioned boundaries. Two primary standards address these requirements: Microsoft's COM, on which OLE and ActiveX are based, and IBM's SOM and Distributed SOM (DSOM). Each standard has strengths and weaknesses, but we will focus on what I feel is the de facto, Windows-based standard: Microsoft's Component Object Model.

A Binary Standard

If you haven't yet heard the phrase "provides a binary standard" (I've mentioned it a few times), you soon will. A *binary standard*, in the context of object and component sharing, provides the means by which objects and components, developed using various languages, from disparate vendors, running on heterogeneous platforms, can interoperate without any changes to the binary or executable. Whew. Let's try that again with pictures.

Figure 1.1 illustrates a hypothetical problem that we need to solve. We've written a wonderful text editor in Visual Basic, but we don't feel like implementing the spell checker, text search functions, or paragraph formatting in Visual Basic. So we locate specialized objects through our favorite object supplier or from a group within our organization. Great—this will save time. But wait—how are we going to get all the pieces to work together? Visual Basic knows nothing about the binary format of Borland's C++ objects, nor does it know about Visual C++ or Watcom binaries. In other words, there is no binary standard that describes how different languages should store the machine language representation of the implemented language algorithms that would allow other languages to access this implementation.

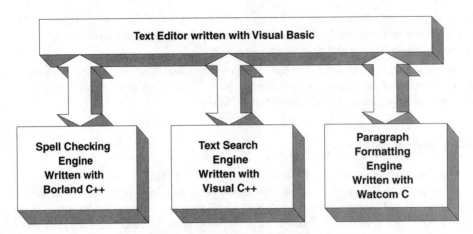

Figure 1.1 A hypothetical application.

Even without a binary standard, there are certain things we can do to solve this problem. If we have the source code to each module, we can determine which functions we would like to call from Visual Basic; then we remove the C++ mangling by declaring them extern "C" and recompile the source. To access these functions from Visual Basic, they must be implemented in a Windows DLL; they cannot exist in an executable (EXE).

Using a Windows DLL solves the initial problem by letting us use these functions within Visual Basic. We must, however, explicitly declare the functions from Visual Basic. Let's use something like the following:

```
Declare Function SpellCheck lib "spell.dll" (...) as long
Declare Function TextSearch lib "search.dll" (...) as long
```

Now we can access the various functions in the component "engines" to perform the needed tasks, and we complete the editor. This approach solves the problem, but only temporarily. Later, as enhancements and bug fixes are added to the C++ objects, we will be responsible for implementing them in our source code. Because we initially had to modify the source, we must also maintain any enhancements and bug fixes ourselves. As you can see, the C++ objects are no longer generic, but have become specific to our application.

Another problem with our approach is that the names of our DLLs are hard-coded within the Visual Basic Declare statements. Later if we want to plug in another DLL, possibly having a different name, we must touch the Visual Basic source and re-create the executable. A binary standard should allow a developer to plug in different components without modifying the original code.

This is a simple illustration of the problems with existing object-oriented language solutions. There are ways to get around interoperability problems in software development, but what we need is a standard way to do it, one that is prescribed and extensible so that vendors can build highly interoperable software. Microsoft's COM provides this binary standard.

Objects Versus Components

To help in the understanding of what objects and components are, we need to define identifying characteristics for the two types. The term *object* will be used for the traditional software module that is produced using object-oriented languages; the binary form of this module is typically an OBJ or LIB file. The term *component* will be used for items that have a binary standard wrapping, or interface, implemented around a language-dependent (usually C++) object, allowing the component to be reused across language environments. A component's binary form is either a DLL or EXE. Following are more detailed definitions.

SOFTWARE OBJECTS

In this book, the term *object* will primarily pertain to C++ or Smalltalk objects as they are used within their respective development environments. Object-oriented language objects have the following characteristics:

- **Reuse through inheritance**: As we've discussed, the primary method of reuse with object-oriented languages is through the use of inheritance.
- **Language dependency**: The objects produced are dependent on the language or compiler in which they are developed.
- Often, objects are dependent on other objects within their environment for part or most of their functionality.
- No current standard exists for use of objects outside of the programming language—that is, for proprietary methods of implementing certain object-oriented techniques.
- Reuse requires an understanding of the underlying or dependent objects.
- Objects are normally pieces of a particular application and can be difficult to extract for reuse.
- To reuse objects requires substantial knowledge of the underlying programming language.

SOFTWARE COMPONENTS

What is a software component? There are many definitions, but here I will define the components that we will build and use in this book. The type of component that we will build does not necessarily have all the traits of a normal object-oriented programming language object. *Component* objects typically will not have the popular characteristics of inheritance or polymorphism, but they will have what I think is the most important object-oriented characteristic of all: reusability. Inheritance and polymorphism are important but not nearly as important as the eventual reusability of the produced object. Purists will say that inheritance is important to—and basically provides for—reusable objects. I agree, but only when you are working within the framework of a single, inheritance-based language, such as C++. Few development organizations do this.

Our definition of a software component provides the following characteristics:

- **Internal implementation details are completely hidden**: Components *encapsulate*, or hide, to the fullest extent the details of how their functionality is implemented.

- **Independent of other components**: Components are self-contained and shouldn't depend on other components to provide supporting services.

- **A well-defined interface**: Components should provide a well-documented set of services.

- **Use of a binary standard to expose external services**: Components will use a language-independent, industry-standard method of exposing services. We will use Microsoft's COM, OLE, and ActiveX.

- Reusability is achieved through binary reuse of the discrete component and not through language-based inheritance.

- Components should not require *user* understanding of the implementing language and, if possible, should require minimal programming expertise to use.

- The component's behavior, and not its implementation, is what is important to the component user.

APPLICATIONS AS COMPONENTS

Given our definition of software components, you can see that a large Windows application such as Microsoft's Word or Corel's Quattro Pro can be a component of another application. The key is that these component applications provide a well-defined, external interface to their underlying application functions (sounds like a binary standard). By accessing these exposed functions, other applications can harness the built-in functionality and provide it to their users.

Today, many such applications provide functions that most client applications will not need. But in the future, smaller, more specialized applications (or components) will be developed for use by a broad range of component-based applications. In later chapters, we will build both business-specific and generic application-based components. As you can see, the distinction between applications and components can be hard to discern. It will eventually become subjective, significant only in the context of the specific development project.

THE COMPONENT INTERFACE

How a component implements what it does is of no concern to the component user. The component user asks, "What can this component do for me?" A component is completely described by its interface to the outside world. The interface details what the component can and cannot do under various conditions. That's the beauty of encapsulation. No one need know how the dirty work is done. The component user selects components solely by their advertised behavior. The only implementation detail that matters to the component user is performance: whether the component is fast enough.

Figure 1.2 depicts a simple component. Its primary capability or behavior is the evaluation of algebraic expressions. Its single interface provides four functions: `SetExpression`, `Verify`, `GetExpression`, and `Evaluate`. These functions encompass all the behavior this component exposes. Within the implementation, there are many other functions as well as internal structures to provide the external functionality, but the component user neither has nor needs any knowledge of these details.

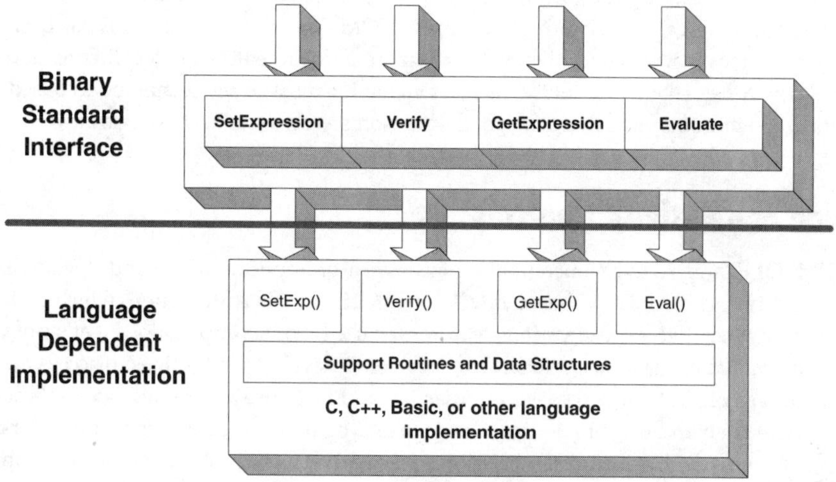

Figure 1.2 Component interface and implementation.

COM: The Facilitator

The technology that allows users to build component-based Windows software is Microsoft's Component Object Model standard. COM provides a system-level, well-defined set of services that standardizes the sharing of data and functionality. COM provides a language-independent way of exposing capabilities from your software, making software reusable at the binary level. COM and ActiveX provide an open, well-defined standard that applications can use to expose functionality to other applications or scripting languages such as Visual Basic.

A Brief Overview of OLE and ActiveX

The next few sections will briefly describe COM, OLE, and ActiveX. It would require more than one book to completely document COM in all its forms. If you need more information than this book provides, I recommend that you pick up a copy of Kraig Brockschmidt's book *Inside OLE* from Microsoft Press. It is required reading for anyone doing serious work with COM and OLE.

OLE is constructed as a layer above the Component Object Model and provides various services to application developers. The most familiar OLE concept is that of the *compound document*. OLE compound document services let you embed component objects created by other applications within an application's document. An example is embedding a Microsoft Excel spreadsheet within a Microsoft Word document. One of the most important OLE technologies for component development is *OLE automation*, or just *Automation*.

Like OLE, ActiveX is based on COM. Until April 1996, the term *ActiveX* did not exist; OLE was used to denote all the application-level services built on top of COM. Today, however, OLE has been relegated to use in those technologies that relate to Microsoft's compound documents (or object linking and embedding) services, and ActiveX has taken over as the primary name for most of the technologies based on COM. In particular, it refers to those services that are tied to Microsoft's Web-based technologies.

Automation and ActiveX Controls

Although COM, OLE, and ActiveX encompass a large area of application use and development, we will focus primarily on two areas of COM-based development. The first is Automation, which makes it easy for applications or components to expose various features for use by other applications. Let's say you're developing an application that needs to fax a document. You could develop the routines to access the fax modem, dial the phone, and so on, but a much easier approach would be to use an existing fax application to do the work for you. There are many ways to do this. One is to let Microsoft Word do most of the work (along with fax hardware and software that includes a Windows print driver). Using Automation, you can drive Word externally, tell it to load your document, perform a document conversion if necessary, and then print it directly to the fax modem. You're depending on software that you have no developmental control over, but it works well, and you need write only about 50 lines of code. That is reuse.

The other software component that we'll focus on is the ActiveX control. Although Automation is used primarily for nonvisual components, ActiveX controls provide the same type of reuse that Automation provides, but for visual components such as Windows entry fields, command buttons, and so on. ActiveX controls are also an important part of Microsoft's Web-based strategy. They play a major role in the majority of Microsoft's new technologies.

Monolithic versus Component-Based Applications

Most Windows applications can be called *monolithic* applications. A monolith is defined by the *Random House College Dictionary* as having a "uniform, massive, or intractable quality or character." When applied to software, this term describes applications that have grown massive with options and features, few of which the average user will ever use. The application is trying to be all things to all people. This type of Windows software will eventually become uncommon. It will be replaced by software based on combinations of individual, specific, and highly efficient components.

Figure 1.3 illustrates the differences between a monolithic application and a similar application built using COM-based components.

Almost every major Windows software package is currently implemented using the monolithic model. Microsoft Word, Excel, and Project are examples. Even though Microsoft Word and Excel may share various pieces, or software modules (maybe the spell checker), this sharing is implemented using closed, proprietary mechanisms. These mechanisms aren't meant to be proprietary, but the current C++ compilers do not intrinsically support interoperability standards. As I've mentioned, existing C++ compilers cannot share objects at the binary level.

Monolithic Application   **Component Based Application**

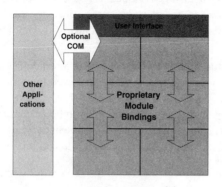 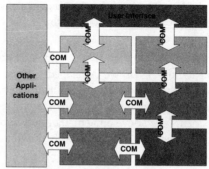

Figure 1.3 Monolithic versus component-based application.

There are also examples of small, highly functional software applications written using the new component-based approach. Microsoft's browser, Internet Explorer 3.0, is written using this approach. The main executable, **IEXPLORE.EXE**, is only 15KB in size. The majority of its functionality is provided by an ActiveX control.

What's in It for Me (the Developer)?

Why should software developers be excited about the future of component software? Many developers spend their days solving the same old problems. Sometimes they may solve the old problem in a new, creative way, but under normal circumstances, it's just the same old algorithm that we've used a hundred times. How many ways are there to implement a linked list? In a nutshell, components allow developers to solve new problems instead of continually solving the old ones.

With the advent of component software and object-oriented components, developers are free to tackle the real problems in software development. They can focus their creative energy on the combining of robust existing components into much more functional (and fabulous) applications. This technique is currently in use in pure C++ environments. In these C++ environments, experienced and astute developers are many times more productive than average programmers. Their productivity is enhanced through the use and understanding of the available C++ objects and tools. They never spend time writing a linked-list routine. Instead, they solve real problems.

Buy versus Build (or "Not Invented Here")

If we are to develop applications rapidly, it is important to use applications or components that are already available. Why spend ten worker-years developing a word processor when Microsoft Word is available for the price of a few hours' labor? Would you develop a database management system from scratch if your project required database services? Of course not—but that mentality is prevalent in many corporations. For whatever reasons, many organizations think that if a product isn't developed in-house, it's not worth using. In certain situations, proprietary development of software is necessary because it provides total control—you're not at the mercy of another vendor's bugs. But I bet these situations aren't nearly as common as most corporate developers think.

I once worked for a company that developed a Lotus 1-2-3 work-alike, because a certain client wanted spreadsheet capabilities. Later, we developed a messaging, or middleware, system even though a superior product—one that many developers were already familiar with—already existed. This "not invented here" mentality costs businesses millions of dollars each year. If they are to compete with other companies that embrace component-based development, they had better change. In today's environment of robust, inexpensive application frameworks, C++ source libraries, and components, it is ludicrous to continue to reinvent the wheel on a daily basis.

Component Builders versus Component Assemblers

Component development and assembly requires two types of application developers. There are those who create the components that can be assembled into various applications, and others who assemble these components into the finished applications. Many times these two development tasks are handled by one individual, but in the future these responsibilities will be assigned to separate developers, each focusing on the specifics of the job at hand. Each developer has a very important job, and in most cases these jobs are quite different.

The *component builder* focuses on building reusable components that provide either well-specified generic functionality, specific business functionality, or methods of gluing these components together effectively. Component builders will typically be computer science graduates with a low-level understanding of the problem and skills in various programming languages.

The *component assembler* focuses on the business problems to be solved. He or she analyzes the problem, chooses from the various components, and then assembles them using a high-level glue or scripting application. Typically a business major, the component assembler should have a business or analysis background in the field in which the program is being applied.

Although other individuals are also involved in building applications for the business environment, the focus of this book is to provide component builders and assemblers with techniques needed to put this process to work.

Component-Based Development and the Web

Development of Web pages and related software is a perfect application for component-based software techniques. The client-side Web browser is an ideal medium in which to use this technology. Small, easy-to-use components such as Java applets, ActiveX controls, and Netscape plug-ins make it easy to quickly add functionality to Web pages. The majority of the functionality will be encapsulated within these components, and a small amount of script coding such as VBScript will be used to tie the components together.

The Web server will benefit from the component-based paradigm as well. As we'll see in Chapter 12, ActiveX controls and VBScript can be used effectively here. The server-side architecture uses ActiveX controls to provide nonvisual services.

In short, the Web will hasten our move to the component-based model of development. The Web will be full of components. With the maturity of technologies such as Java and ActiveX, the Web page designer will become an assembler of discrete components: a Java applet here, a couple of ActiveX controls there, some HTML, and finally some VBScript to tie it all together. The Web user will be a downloader of components. As the user browses the Web, each page may install a number of small components on the local system. As all the pieces work together, a dynamic Web page is produced that not only is great to look at but also provides quite a bit of functionality.

Summary

There are two general methods of developing Windows software: object-oriented and visual. Both methods are effective, but visual programming enables quick and effective development by more individuals, including nonprogrammers. Our focus will be on developing software components (using the object-oriented method) that can be used and reused in both object-oriented and visual environments.

For corporations and developers to remain competitive, the reuse of newly developed and existing software is paramount. Reuse can be achieved in various ways. Inheritance, the principal method used in object-oriented languages, is a powerful feature, but isn't a requirement for reusable software. Software components achieve effective reusability without it. The primary difference between a well-written C++ object (or other language module) and a software component is the addition of a binary standard wrapper that allows its use across various languages. Figure 1.4 illustrates this concept. For our purposes, Microsoft's COM/OLE/ActiveX combination, particularly Automation and ActiveX controls, will provide these wrappering services.

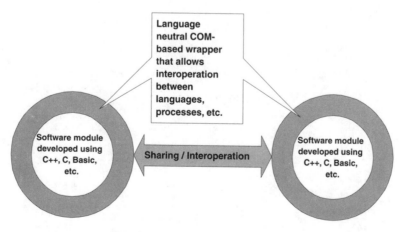

Figure 1.4 Binary standard wrapper.

Chapter 2

Designing Reusable Components with C++

In Chapter 1, we discussed the importance of reuse in software development. Software objects and their binary standard companions, software components, were offered as an effective method to achieve reuse in the development cycle, within both C++ and other development environments. In this chapter we'll begin the process of developing software components.

The first step is to create C++ classes that are themselves reusable or generic. These classes should not be specific to a particular task but instead should be general enough to be used in multiple areas of an application as well as across applications. This concept is far from new and has been used since the advent of structured programming. But C++ provides a fertile field in which to design and develop reusable modules or objects.

Not all classes can be designed to be widely reusable. Determining when a class might be reusable across the application and across projects is an art. In many cases, the added overhead of designing a class to be reusable is not worth the effort it requires. Designing reusable classes is like almost everything else in life: it's best not to have too much or too little of anything. Keep this in mind. Some organizations try too hard to make all the code they write reusable, and this added overhead can have a detrimental effect on the development process.

In this chapter, we'll go through the process of developing a general class that is composed of other general classes. Throughout this process, keep in mind that the potential user of the classes may not have access to the C++ language. If we design the classes with a multiple language focus, they can easily be adapted for use outside the C++ environment. In later chapters we will use these C++ objects to develop binary standard software components.

Before we begin developing C++ objects, we must be fairly proficient in the language, so this chapter begins with a quick tour of C++. This overview is far from comprehensive, because we focus only on those areas of C++ that we will use in the various projects and those that are necessary to understand various idioms used in Microsoft's Foundation Class (MFC) libraries. Use of MFC is described in more detail in Chapter 3, although minor references to certain MFC classes are made in this chapter. For a complete review

17

of the C++ language, several excellent books are listed in the Bibliography. (One of my favorites is the *Effective* C++ series by Scott Meyers.)

C++, the Language

This book uses the C++ language exclusively in the examples and sample programs. Although you may not need the quick refresher course provided here, you might as well plod through it, because I make a few comments on how MFC uses certain features of C++. The overview is by no means a course on C++; it only hits the high points and provides what is necessary to understand the C++ presented in this book. There isn't a long discourse on deep vs. shallow copies, and so on.

C++ is a supercharged version of the C language. C++ includes all the features of C and provides a way for C programmers to ease into the age of objects. I've programmed in C for more than eight years and in C++ for about three years. Daily, I become more aware of the power of C++. It is a profound language. It has many levels that developers can attain as they gain experience. An experienced C++ developer who is intimately familiar with a powerful framework and a solid class library (either self-built or commercial) is a programming machine. The productivity of such a developer is orders of magnitude greater than that of a beginning or slightly experienced C++ developer. This also can be said of developers who use other, non-C++ languages. Intimate knowledge of any good language and good supporting tools makes all of us productive.

This book will help you in your efforts to become a proficient C++ developer, but that's far from its main purpose. As component developers, our goal is to make our users—visual developers—as productive (although at a higher level) as seasoned C++ developers in much less time.

Classes (Encapsulation)

C++ endows the C language with the object-oriented characteristics of encapsulation, inheritance, and polymorphism. The primary device for these new features is the C++ class. Classes allow the encapsulation of data and of the functions that affect the data. The goal of a class is to capture and encapsulate the essence of a particular thing or object and then expose to users of the class only those items that are important for its use. The details of the internal implementation are encapsulated, or hidden, from the class user.

To make sure we're using the same terminology, let's go over some C++ terms. A *class* is a definition of a C++ object and is a compile-time construct. Once compiled, a class can be *instantiated* to create a run-time instance of the class definition. This run-time entity is typically deemed an *object*. There can be zero, one, or many of these instantiated objects during the execution of an application. They are quite dynamic.

Items within a class are referred to with several different terms. *Member variables* typically describe the class's internal variables. The MFC libraries, and programs written using them, regularly use the convention `m_variable`, where `variable` is the actual name used to identify member variables. Another widely used term for member variables is *property*. This term describes the relationship of member variables to the class; size and color are properties of a fruit. The terms *data members* and *attributes* are also used to describe member variables.

```
class Fruit
{
    // Member variables, or properties, or data members, or attributes
    CString   m_strName;
    long      m_lWeight;
    CString   m_strColor;
    ...
    // Member functions, or methods
public:
    Cstring   GetColor();
    long      GetWeight();
};
```

Member functions and *methods* are used to describe functions declared within a class. The term *method* comes from its use in Smalltalk, where objects respond to *messages*, or methods. When discussing C++ classes and objects, I'll use *member function* and *member variable*. Later, when we're discussing ActiveX components, the terms *property* and *method* will be used with a slightly different meaning. This is appropriate, because when we're discussing these items at the component level, a component property may be implemented as either a member variable or a member function.

Now let's talk about what encapsulation is and how it can help developers. Encapsulation is important for C++ developers as well as developers who use components. Software components provide rigid encapsulation of functionality. A component user cannot access the source code or any of the internal structures used to implement the component's functionality. They can use only what is exposed by the component developer.

C++ allows the encapsulation within a class of data and functions that operate on that data. The class can hide or protect many of these elements from external users. *Users* in this context and throughout this book refers to the class library user or component user and not the end user of an application. Encapsulation inside classes is implemented by the `public`, `protected`, and `private` keywords. We won't discuss the `protected` keyword until after the inheritance section. For now, `public` and `private` will suffice. Examine the following class declaration:

```
class Expression
{
private:
    CString   m_strExp;
    Stack     m_Stack;
    Tokenizer m_Tokenizer;

    void      InfixToPostFix();
    int       Precedence();

public:
    void      SetExpression( CString str );
```

```
CString  GetExpression();
BOOL     Validate();
long     Evaluate();
};
```

Here we have an `Expression` class. It appears to support expression conversion and evaluation, but the key is that the user of the class does not know how the conversion and evaluation occur. The class members and functions that follow the `private` keyword cannot be accessed by the class user. The user can access only those items designated as `public`. The implementation of the conversion and evaluation routines is hidden from the user. Later, if the class developer finds a more effective method of converting expressions, the developer can change the implementation without affecting the class user. We will use this example again later but, as you can see, encapsulation enables the hiding of implementation details. Other non–object-oriented languages can also do this. C functions, Fortran modules, and other language features allow encapsulation of functionality. But C++ provides additional features, such as the `public`, `private`, and `protected` keywords, that make encapsulation more effective.

NOTE As you've probably noticed, a C++ class declaration looks very similar to a C structure declaration. In C++, classes and structures are nearly identical. The C++ language adds all the capabilities of classes to C structures with one minor difference. C++ class members default to `private`, whereas C structure members default to `public`.

Constructors

When a C++ class is instantiated, or created, an instance of the class is created. An *instance* of a class is an actual chunk of memory in the address space of an executing application process. A class is the definition of the characteristics of that chunk of memory. A C++ class is of no use unless instances of the class (objects) are created and used at run time. Whenever a class is instantiated, its *constructor* is called. The constructor's primary purpose is to initialize member data. Contrast this with the C technique of initializing structured data.

```
struct Fruit

{

    char* pszName;
    long  lWeight;
    char* pszColor;
};
typedef struct Fruit Fruit;
```

If we need to create and use a `Fruit` structure, we use the following code:

```
void SomeFunction()
{
    // Let's create an apple on the stack
    Fruit Apple;

    // The structure contains members that must be
    // allocated and initialized. This memory is allocated on the heap.
    Apple.pszName = (char*) malloc( sizeof( "Apple" ) + 1 );
    strcpy( Apple.pszName, "Apple" );
    Apple.lWeight = 6;
    Apple.pszColor = (char*) malloc( sizeof( "Red" ) + 1 );
    strcpy( Apple.pszColor, "Red" );

    // Do something with Apple...

    // Now deallocate any non-stack allocated memory
    free( Apple.pszName );
    free( Apple.pszColor );

    // As the Apple structure goes "out of scope" only its memory
    // is deallocated
}
```

To do the same using C++ classes and constructors, you might do this:

```
class Fruit
{
private:
    CString m_strName;
    long    m_lWeight;
    CString m_strColor;

public:
    // Provide a default constructor that initializes
    // the class members. This cannot be done using the
    // C structure method above.
    Fruit()
    {
      m_strName = m_strColor = "";
      m_lWeight = 0;
    }

    // Overloaded constructor. This constructor takes parameters
    // that initialize the members of the new fruit object.
```

```
Fruit( CString strName, long lWeight, CString strColor )
{
  m_strName = strName;
  m_lWeight = lWeight;
  m_strColor = strColor;
}
};
```

Now when we need to create an instance of an apple, all we have to do is this:

```
void SomeFunction()
{

  // Let's create an apple on the stack.

    // We provide the parameters to initialize our
    // new apple. The constructor handles the allocations
    // for us. Contrast this with the C example.
    Fruit Apple( "Apple", 6, "Red" );

    // Do something with Apple...

    // As the Apple variable goes "out of scope"
    // C++ takes care of cleaning up any memory for us.
    // It does this with a destructor that we'll discuss
    // in a moment.

}
```

C++ makes the creation of user-defined types very easy. You code the logic in the constructor, and it is used whenever an object of that type is created, whether it is on the stack or on the heap. You could also do this in C by using a function that takes the particular parameters for the structure and a similar function for the deallocation of the dynamically allocated memory. In this case, you must ensure that you call the function for deallocation before the structure goes out of scope. As you will see in a moment, C++ provides for automatic deallocation ("destruction") of objects as they go out of scope.

Dynamic creation of structures and classes is a fundamental element of both C and C++ programming. Constructors allow the orderly initialization of dynamic elements as they are created. Constructors also remove much of the tedium involved in allocating dynamic objects. You code the constructor once, and it does the work from then on.

The syntax for declaring a constructor is the class name itself with zero or more parameters. If you do not specify any constructors for your class, the compiler will provide a default constructor that takes no arguments. On the other hand, if you specify any constructors at all, the compiler will not provide the default constructor. You must implement any constructors that you will need. Constructors can be *overloaded*, which provides the ability for a function to be multiply declared, and the compiler will determine, by matching the parameters, which function to call. Our previous example contained two constructors, each with the same function name. We will discuss overloading in more detail in a later section.

The new and delete Operators

In the previous example, which contrasted the dynamic creation of structures in C and C++, the objects were initially allocated on the stack. C++ provides two additional operators—new and delete—to help in the dynamic creation of objects on the heap. In C++, new should be used instead of the C malloc function, and instead of using the C free function you use the C++ delete operator.

```
// Instead of this
void TheCWay()
{
    char* pszColor;
    if ( ( pszColor = malloc( 128 )) == NULL )
    {
        // Error handling code...
    }
    // Do something with pszColor...

    free( pszColor );
}

// do this
void TheCppWay()
{
    char* pszColor = new char[128];

    // Make sure the new worked. We only need to do this
    // if we haven't installed a memory exception handler.
    assert( pszColor );

    // Do something with pszColor...

    delete [] pszColor;
}
```

The last example shows an important point to remember when you're using new and delete. When an array of objects (or intrinsic types) is allocated, it's important to append [] to the delete operator so that it knows whether one or multiple objects are being deleted.

There are other benefits of using new and delete instead of malloc and free. Instead of checking the return from new every time you allocate a new object, you can ignore it. Most compilers (including Visual C++) provide an exception mechanism to handle situations when memory is low. If new cannot allocate the needed memory, an exception is thrown. This technique allows developers to handle memory failures in one specific function instead of sprinkling their code with tests for a `NULL` return from `malloc`. However, the compiler's default behavior is to return 0 if `new` cannot allocate the memory. You must provide a simple exception handler to enable an exception thrown when an "out of memory" occurs. That's why I used the `assert` after the `new` in the preceding example.

Also, you can call `delete` on a `NULL` pointer. This is defined behavior, and `delete` will do nothing. There is no need to write code such as the following.

```
// During initialization (construction)
char *pszTemp = 0;
...
...// pszTemp may be used during execution
...
// Sometime later, during cleanup (destruction)
if ( pszTemp )
    delete pszTemp;
```

Because calling `delete` on a zero pointer is defined, the `if` is not needed, although some developers still do it just to be safe.

N O T E   The MFC libraries override the default `new` and `delete` operators when compiling and linking in debug mode. This enables MFC to keep track of all allocations and deallocations during the lifetime of your application. If your application terminates without deallocating all the memory allocated, MFC will dump (to the debug window) the memory address and allocating source line of each memory block that was not deallocated properly. This is a very useful debugging tool.

Destructors

Just as C++ provides a method to ensure the orderly creation of objects, it also provides for the orderly destruction of objects via a *destructor*. The syntax for a destructor is similar to that of a constructor except that destructors cannot take parameters. Like constructors, destructors also cannot return a value. Destructors are identified using the class name preceded by a tilde (~). Following is a destructor for our `Fruit` object:

```
class Fruit {
private:
    CString m_strName;
    long    m_lWeight;
    CString m_strColor;

public:
```

```
    // Provide a default constructor that initializes
    // the class members.
    Fruit() {
      m_strName = m_strColor = "";
      m_lWeight = 0;
    };

    // Overloaded constructor. This constructor takes parameters
    // that initialize the members of the new fruit object.
    Fruit( CString strName, long lWeight, CString strColor ) {
      m_strName = strName;
      m_lWeight = lWeight;
      m_strColor = strColor;
    }
    // Here's the declaration of the destructor
    ~Fruit() {
      cout << "Destructing Fruit object" << endl;
    }
};
```

Destructors don't normally do very much, and the compiler will provide one for you if you do not declare one within your class. User-declared destructors should be used, though, when your class dynamically allocates memory (that lives across method calls) from the heap during its lifetime. Here's an example:

```
// Declaration
// CobList is an MFC linked-list class, here we are
// inheriting the functionality of the linked-list.
// We will discuss inheritance in a moment. For now,
// just treat the FruitBasket class as a linked list.
class FruitBasket : public CObList {
public:
    FruitBasket();
    // Declaration of the destructor
    ~FruitBasket();
    ...
    void AddItem( Fruit* pItem );
};

// Implementation of the destructor
FruitBasket::~FruitBasket()
{
    // Get the position of the first element
```

```
POSITION pos = GetHeadPosition();
// Spin through and delete each element in the list
while( pos )
{
    // get the element, delete it, and increment to the next element
    delete GetNext( pos );
}
RemoveAll();
}
```

The destructor for the `FruitBasket` class ensures that the linked list of `Fruit` items is deallocated just before the object's final breath. If the compiler had provided a default destructor, any items in the list would not be properly destroyed. Here's another use for constructor and destructor implementations:

```
class Fruit {
    ...
    static int m_nCount;
    Fruit();
    virtual ~Fruit();
    ...
};
```

int Fruit::m_nCount = 0;

```
Fruit::Fruit()
{
    m_nCount++;
}
Fruit::~Fruit()
{
    m_nCount-;
}
```

We haven't talked about `static` items yet, but the preceding code enables us to keep a count of the number of `Fruit` objects that exist at any time during execution. As each `Fruit` object is constructed, a counter is incremented. During destruction, the counter is decremented.

Inheritance

In the last few sections we discussed the first element of object-oriented development: encapsulation. Now let's take a look at the object-oriented language characteristic that provides for our primary goal of software reusability. As discussed in Chapter 1, the object-oriented language characteristic of inheritance provides for the reusability of software modules. Inheritance is the primary mechanism for reuse and is one of the major strengths of C++. The MFC libraries also use inheritance extensively, so it's important that you understand what it's all about. Let's start with an example.

Figure 2.1 illustrates a hierarchical relationship between a set of collection classes. Class hierarchies are essential for organizing classes of similar capabilities. Hierarchies are usually depicted as in the illustration in a top-down manner. The top object is the most general and is usually abstract (we'll talk more about this in a minute). As you move down the hierarchy, the classes become more specific in their function. This element is important in the design of object-oriented software, where the goal is to program the exception. In other words, when you're developing new software, (new classes), it is desirable to derive from an existing, tested class.

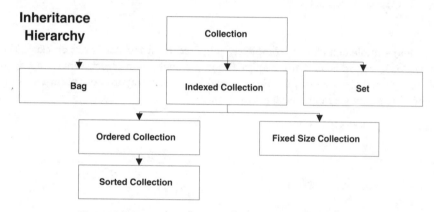

Figure 2.1 Example collection inheritance hierarchy.

The examples we discuss initially in this section are based on the Smalltalk implementation of collections. Smalltalk is a pure object-oriented programming environment and is useful for instructive purposes. The examples in this section use C++ syntax, but we won't concern ourselves much with how the functionality is provided. Our focus is on what inheritance is and what it can provide.

A *collection* is a group of disparate object instances. At the highest level in the hierarchy, there is no requirement for ordering or uniqueness of the collected elements. It's a loosely associated collection of objects. The top-level Collection class implements those functions (or methods) that are necessary for *all* collections. It strives to be general and thus provides only those functions that all collections need. At the next level are the Bag, Set, and IndexedCollection classes. These classes build on, or augment, that functionality provided by the base class, or superclass, Collection. Again, the purpose of aligning these classes in this way is to allow the reuse of base class code in the classes that derive from it. The Collection class might be declared this way in C++ (ignore the virtual keyword for now):

```
class Collection {

public:
```

```
    virtual void Add( CObject );
    virtual BOOL IsEmpty();
    virtual void Remove( CObject );
    virtual BOOL Has( CObject );
    virtual int  HowMany( CObject );
};
```

The `Collection` class encapsulates the basic behavior of a collection and implements the things that all collection classes should have. `Add`, `Remove`, `IsEmpty`, `Has`, and `HowMany` provide this basic functionality. For now, let's not concern ourselves with how the methods are implemented. Here's the definition of the `Bag` class.

```
class Bag : public Collection {

};
```

That's it—a `Bag`'s implementation is completely inherited from the `Collection` class. The functionality provided by `Collection` is all that is required to implement a `Bag` object. What is a `Bag`? It provides an unordered collection that allows duplicates and provides an easy way to count occurrences of objects. Pretty easy, isn't it? Here's how we might use the `Bag` class:

```
void SomeClass::SomeMethod()
{
    Bag aBag;

    for ( int i = 0; i <= 100; i++ )
    {
        // Add an integer that is the remainder
        // of the modulo division. This adds
        // integers in the range [0..9]
        // The Add member is from the base Collection class
        aBag.Add( i % 10 );
    }
    // How many 5s are in the bag?
    aBag.HowMany( 5 );
    // Are there any 14s in the bag?
    aBag.Has( 14 );
}
```

Now let's discuss the C++ syntax for declaring inheritance. In the `Bag` example, we are declaring a new class that is publicly derived from the `Collection` class. The colon following the class declaration (e.g., `Bag : public Collection`) signifies derivation, and the `public` keyword indicates public inheritance of the `Collection` class. Public inheritance is almost always used, and soon I'll explain why. With the syntax out of the way, let's look at the implementation of the `Set` class.

```
class Set : public Collection {

public:

   void Add( CObject);
};

void Set::Add( CObject obj )
{
   if ( Has( obj ) )
    return;
   // Call our parent's Add method
   Collection::Add( obj );
}
```

A `Set` is similar to a `Bag`, but it cannot contain duplicate elements. All we do is derive from the `Collection` class and override the `Add` member function. (We'll talk more about overriding functions in a minute. For now, overriding a member function means to re-implement, or hide, the implementation of the parent, or base, class.) As you can see, in the new `Add` method, we check to see whether the object being added already exists. If it exists, we simply return; otherwise, we call the base `Collection`'s `Add` method to add the item to the collection. This is what object-oriented development is all about. To add this new functionality, we wrote five lines of code.

The `IndexedCollection` class is a little more complicated. We need an additional member variable to help with the indexing, and it must be coordinated with the `Collection` class. We're talking in the abstract here, so don't worry about the details. Following is the definition for `IndexedCollection`. Indexed collections allow for iteration over the collection as well as direct access to specific elements via its index, but you can't specify the index when adding new elements. (It's basically a simple linked list.) Here's the definition for the `IndexedCollection` class.

```
class IndexedCollection : public Collection

{
public:

   // New Methods
   CObject   First();
   CObject   Last();
   CObject   Next( Position );
   long      IndexOf( CObject );
};
```

With this definition, the `FixedSizeCollection` is easy to implement:

```
class FixedSizeCollection : public IndexedCollection
```

```
{

private:
    long    m_lMaxSize;
    long    m_lCurrentSize;
public:
    long    Add( CObject );
};

long FixedSizeCollection::Add( CObject obj )
{
    if ( ++m_lCurrentSize > m_lMaxSize )
    {
        m_lCurrentSize--;
        return ERROR;
    }

    // Call the parent implementation to add the object.
    IndexedCollection::Add( obj );

    return NO_ERROR;
}
```

By now, you should see the effectiveness of reusing class code through inheritance. The goal is to build generic classes first and then proceed with inheritance to produce specific solutions. Inheritance won't solve all our problems, and we need to be careful not to abuse it. Let's look at what makes for good inheritance.

When should inheritance be used? This is a difficult question to answer. Typically, when we're deciding whether an object should be derived (or inherited) from an existing class, the new object should pass the "is-a" relationship test. In our simple example, a Bag "is-a" type of Collection. There is little ambiguity here, but in real development situations distinct delineations between objects seldom exist.

The MFC libraries use inheritance extensively. Almost all classes derive from the CObject class. Figure 2.2 shows a small part of the MFC hierarchy; in particular, this is a section of the visible objects hierarchy. The CWnd class encapsulates most of the Windows API functionality for generic window manipulation: SendMessage, ShowWindow, InvalidateRect, and all the others. And, thanks to inheritance, as you move down the hierarchy additional functionality is added. CListBox contains all the functionality of a standard window as well as the methods useful for listbox manipulation: AddString, GetCurSel, GetCount, SetItemHeight, and many others. Because CListBox is derived from CWnd, all the member functions implemented in CWnd are also available to the CListBox user.

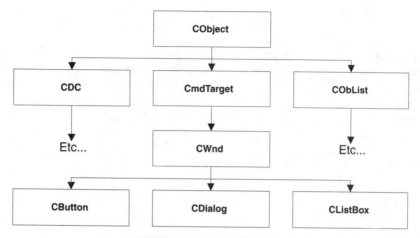

Figure 2.2 MFC visual object hierarchy.

Inheritance is only one of the methods that can be used to reuse code by building new classes. Other methods are equally effective. In a later section we will discuss class composition, another powerful method of reusing classes that have "has-a" type relationships.

The C++ keywords public, protected, and private allow class designers to tailor the inheritance capabilities of their classes. We'll discuss them next.

Public, Protected, and Private

As stated earlier, the concept of *data hiding*, or *encapsulation*, is an important characteristic of object-oriented development. C++ provides the public, protected, and private keywords to allow various degrees of visibility for class members.

Public is the easiest to understand. Anything declared public within a class, whether it is a member variable or a function, is visible to any user of the class. This is exactly the behavior if a structure is used instead of a class. The following declarations are equivalent:

```
struct Address {
    CString  m_strName;
    CString  m_strAddress;
    CString  m_strCityState;
};

class Address {
public:
    CString  m_strName;
    CString  m_strAddress;
```

```
   CString   m_strCityState;
};
```

Protected indicates that the members are private, or hidden, from class users, but are public to derived classes and their members. Private members of a class can be accessed only by other members of the same class. There is no visibility outside the class, even through inheritance. Determining when to use each of the three keywords is a design decision. Typically, class interfaces are declared public, and implementation members are declared protected or private. Here are some examples:

```
class Fruit {
// Private members, only Fruit members can access
private:
   CString   m_strName;
   void      DoSomethingPrivate() {}

// Protected members, only Fruit and other derived class members
//                    can access
protected:
   CString   m_strColor;
   long      m_lWeight;
   void      DoSomethingProtected() {}

// Public members - Everybody can access these
public:
   // Constructors
   Fruit() { m_strName.Empty(); }
   Fruit( CString str ) { m_strName = str; }

   void      DoSomethingPublic() {}
   void      SetWeight( long lWeight ) { m_lWeight = lWeight; }
   long      GetWeight() { return m_lWeight; }
   void      SetName( CString str ) { m_strName = str; }
   CString   GetName() { return m_strName; }
   void      SetColor( CString str ) { m_strColor = str; }
   CString   GetColor() { return m_strColor; }
};

//
// Publicly derive from Fruit
//
class Pear : public Fruit {
public:
   // Constructors
```

```
    Pear();
    Pear( CString strName );

    void  PearFunction();
}

Pear::Pear()
{
    // Can't do this because name is private

    m_strName.Empty(); // error

    // Must do this instead
    SetName( "" );
    // Protected member, OK
    m_strColor = "Green";
}

Pear::Pear( CString strName )
{
    // As above
    SetName( strName );
    m_strColor = "Green";
}

// Can access all of the public and protected members
// But can not access private members
void Pear::PearFunction()
{
    // We can directly access protected members
    m_strColor = "Green";

    // We can't to this, it's private
    DoSomethingPrivate();

    // We're derived so we can do this
    DoSomethingProtected();
}

main() {
    Fruit* pApple = new Fruit( "Apple" );

    // I'm a class user so this is illegal
    pApple->m_strColor = "Red";
```

```
// Even more illegal
pApple->m_strName = "Apple";
// Illegal
pApple->DoSomethingProtected();
// Illegal
pApple->DoSomethingPrivate();

pApple->SetColor( "Red" );      // OK
pApple->DoSomethingPublic();    // OK
delete pApple;
}
```

All these examples use public inheritance. The keyword preceding the base class indicates the specific type of inheritance. `Protected` and `private` inheritance are seldom used, primarily because they defeat or severely hamper the notion of inheritance.

When `private` inheritance is declared, the members inherited from the parent all become `private` in the newly derived class. Also, any pointers to this new class cannot be substituted for pointers of the base class. Nothing inherited from the base class is exposed to the user of the derived class. In other words, the purpose of inheritance, extending and augmenting a base class, is forfeited. `Protected` inheritance is similar to `private` inheritance. All `public` and `protected` members of the derived class become `protected`, and any `private` members remain `private`. Most often, derivation of new classes should use the `public` keyword. Only in rare cases should `private` and `protected` inheritance be used. Private and protected inheritance disable or hide the interface of the base class, but leave its implementation.

Function Overriding

Function overriding allows the hiding or re-implementation of a particular member function that is inherited from a parent class. Continuing our fruit example:

```
class Fruit {
    ...
    // Ignore the virtual keyword for now.
    // We'll cover it momentarily
    virtual void SayName() { cout << "My name is " << GetName() << endl; }
};

class FrenchFruit : public Fruit {
    ...
    virtual void SayName() { cout << "Je m'apelle " << GetName() << endl; }
    };
```

Although this is a contrived example, it illustrates the point. By declaring a function, SayName, in a derived class with the same name as one in the parent class, you hide, or override, its implementation. This technique provides a method to override the default behavior of the parent class. Even though you are overriding the behavior of the parent class, you need not completely hide the functionality. You can call the parent implementation at any time during your new implementation. Using the MFC libraries, you'll do this quite often. Here's a simple example using CObject, the base class for most of MFC.

```
// Abbreviated from afx.h
class CObject {
...
public:
   virtual void Dump( CDumpContext& dc );
...
}

class Fruit : public CObject {
protected:
   CString    m_strName;
   CString    m_strColor;

   virtual void Dump( CDumpContext& dc )
   {
      // Dump the parent's members
      CObject::Dump( dc );
      // Now dump our members
      dc << "Fruit contains\n";
      dc << "\tName is " << m_strName << "\n";
      dc << "\tColor is " << m_strColor << "\n";
   }
}

class Apple : public Fruit {
protected:
   long     m_lNumberOfSeeds;

public:
   virtual void Dump( CDumpContext& dc )
   {
      // Dump the parent's members
      Fruit::Dump( dc );
      // Now dump our members
      dc << "Apple contains\n";
      dc << "\tNumber of seeds is " << m_lNumberOfSeeds << "\n";
```

```
    }
}

// Do this to get a run-time dump of the objects
afxDump << pApple;

// produces this output
>
> a CObject at $2411
> Fruit contains
>       Name is Apple
>       Color is Red
> Apple contains
>       Number of seeds is 35
>
```

Dump is a member function of CObject, the top-level object of the MFC hierarchy, and provides debugging information for classes that derive from it. Dump provides a hierarchical dump of member variables of each object in the inheritance chain. Derived classes don't need to know and sometimes cannot know about all the members of the parent classes. The parent's Dump function is called in the implementation of the derived member's Dump function. This arrangement provides a useful, encapsulated way of dumping all of an object for debugging purposes.

It isn't a good idea to override functions of the parent class unless they've been declared virtual. We will discuss virtual functions in a moment. For now, remember that declaring functions in derived classes hides all functions with the same name in the base class.

Function Overloading

C++ allows functions, methods, and operators to be overloaded. *Overloading* is an object-oriented term that describes a type of polymorphism. C++ overloading allows you to implement a function (or method) with the same name multiple times, but each implementation must differ by the number or type of parameters, and it cannot differ by return type only. Here is an example from the MFC libraries:

```
class CRect {
    ...
public:
    void InflateRect( int x, int y );

    void InflateRect( SIZE size );

    ...
}
```

The MFC CRect class provides two methods for inflating a rectangle. To make it easy for the class user, InflateRect can be called with an x and y coordinate or a SIZE structure. This arrangement allows the developer to pass the most convenient parameter. The compiler determines which function to call by matching the type to the appropriate function. How does the linker resolve the ambiguity of two public methods having the same name?

In Chapter 1, I pointed out that C++ objects don't natively support sharing across languages or even across C++ implementations, because there is no standard way of mangling or decorating function and method names. Borland, Watcom, and Microsoft mangle C++ function names in proprietary ways. Mangling provides unique public names for each C++ function, solving the problem of link-time resolution. The mangling algorithm guarantees a unique name for all possible combinations of function names and parameters. Both the compiler and the linker must agree on the particular technique of mangling. Here are the mangled names generated by the Visual C++ compiler for the two InflateRect methods. To see them, compile and link with the proper command-line switches to produce a **.MAP** file.

```
// Mangled names for InflateRect
?InflateRect@CRect@@RECXHH@Z
?InflateRect@CRect@@RECXUtagSIZE@@@Z
```

One obvious use of overloading is in constructors. Class constructors are often overloaded to take various parameters during construction. This technique enables an object to be instantiated in various states depending on what is known about the object at the time of instantiation.

```
class CRect {
   ...
public:
   // Overloaded constructors for CRect class
   CRect();
   CRect( int l, int t, int r, int b );
   CRect( const RECT& srcRect );
   CRect( LPCRECT lpSrcRect );
   CRect( POINT point, SIZE size );
   ...
}

// Mangled names for the above CRect constructors
??0CRect@@REC@AFUtagRECT@@@Z
??0CRect@@REC@HHHH@Z
??0CRect@@REC@PFUtagRECT@@@Z
??0CRect@@REC@UtagPOINT@@UtagSIZE@@@Z
??0CRect@@REC@XZ
```

The MFC CRect class has five public constructors. The constructors are overloaded so that the class user has multiple methods to initialize a CRect object. This technique provides flexibility for class users who can use the constructor that best fits their needs.

NOTE When you're overriding an inherited function that is overloaded, all the parent member functions, and not just the particular one you have overridden, are hidden. Here's an example:

```
class Base {
public:
   virtual long  Sum( int i) { return i; }
   virtual long  Sum( int i, int i2 ) { return i + i2; }
   virtual long  Sum( int i, int i2, int i3 ) { return i + i2 + i3; }
};

class Derived : public Base {
public:
   // Overriding this function hides all implementations
   // in the base class.
   virtual long Sum( int i , int i2 ) { return SpecialSum( i, i2 ); }
};

main()
{
   Derived derived;
   // Error can't do this, the inherited overloaded members are gone
   derived.Sum( 1, 2, 3 );
}
```

Virtual Functions

Virtual functions allow C++ programs to resolve function calls dynamically (at run time) instead of statically at compile time. This powerful feature of C++ is what provides many of its object-oriented features. In *early-binding* languages such as C, the specific function to call in any particular instance is determined at compile time. C supports run-time binding, but the developer must do much of the work (using pointers to functions). C++ makes it much easier. *Virtual functions* allow the implementation of *polymorphism*, which is the ability of an object to respond differently to the same method or member function at run time depending on the object's type.

Virtual functions don't do much if you declare only one class. The strength of virtual functions is visible only as you augment existing base classes by creating subclasses of the original base class. The following example demonstrates the power of using virtual functions, which allow the dynamic determination of member function calls at run time instead of compile time.

```
class Fruit {
protected:
   CString    m_strName;
   CString    m_strColor;
public:
   virtual void    Draw() {};
   CString         GetColor();
};
```

The declaration for our Fruit class now contains a virtual function, Draw, that returns void and does nothing. The base fruit class does not have an implementation for Draw, because each particular type of fruit should implement its own Draw function. Let's derive some fruit from this base class.

```
class Apple : public Fruit {
   virtual void  Draw() { cout << "I'm an Apple" << endl; }
};
class GrannySmith : public Apple {
   virtual void  Draw() { cout << "I'm a Granny Smith Apple" << endl; }
};
class Orange : public Fruit {
   virtual void  Draw() { cout << "I'm an Orange" << endl; }
};
class Grape : public Fruit {
   virtual void  Draw() { cout << "I'm a Grape" << endl; }
};
```

Each class that is derived directly or indirectly from Fruit implements its own Draw function, which prints that particular fruit's type. In itself, this isn't anything spectacular but look at the following code:

```
int main()
{
   Fruit* pFruitList[4];
   pFruitList[0] = new Apple;
   pFruitList[1] = new Orange;
   pFruitList[2] = new Grape;
   pFruitList[3] = new GrannySmith;

   for( int i = 0; i < 4; i++ )
   {
      pFruitList[i]->Draw();
```

```
        delete pFruitList[i];
    }
}

// Produces this output
>
> I'm an Apple
> I'm an Orange
> I'm a Grape
> I'm a Granny Smith Apple
>
```

This code illustrates the power of virtual functions. We've declared an array of pointers of type `Fruit`, the base class, and have assigned to each element the address of an instance of a particular derived fruit type. As the line `pFruitList[i]->Draw()` is executed, the program dynamically determines which member function to invoke. This dynamic binding is implemented with a virtual function table, which we'll discuss in a moment.

Pure Virtual Functions and Abstract Classes

Abstract classes provide a model or template for all classes that derive from them. In our `Fruit` example, the base class `Fruit` is a very good abstract-class candidate. A "fruit" is itself an abstract thing. In real life, we cannot instantiate a "general" fruit object, something that has the broad characteristics of a fruit but isn't a specific kind of fruit. Abstract classes are used this way to categorize and classify things that have similar characteristics. Our base `Fruit` class contains the essence of all fruits but nothing specific. This makes it a perfect example of an abstract class.

```
class Fruit {
protected:
    CString    m_strName;
    CString    m_strColor;
public:
    void       SetColor( CString str ) { m_strColor = str; }
    CString    GetColor() { return m_strColor; }
    void       SetName( CString str ) { m_strName = str; }
    CString    GetName()  { return m_strName; }
    virtual    void Draw() = 0;
    virtual    long GetAvgWeight() = 0;
    };
```

Abstract classes provide those properties and actions that all fruits share. Abstract classes can choose not to implement specific member functions and require deriving classes to implement those functions. In the preceding example, the Draw function is declared as pure virtual by using the notation = 0. This notation indicates that all deriving classes must implement some form of the Draw function. By declaring a pure virtual function within a class, the class designer also makes the class abstract, meaning that the class cannot be instantiated. Although the class itself cannot be instantiated, pointers to the class can be used, and this proves to be an important characteristic. Recall the preceding example with the array of Fruit pointers.

```
int main()
{
    // Now we can't do this
    Fruit fruit;       // It doesn't make sense anyway, does it?

    // But we can still do this, and it produces the same output
    // as the example above.
    Fruit* pFruitList[4];
    pFruitList[0] = new Apple;
    pFruitList[1] = new Orange;
    pFruitList[2] = new Grape;
    pFruitList[3] = new GrannySmith;

    for( int i = 0; i < 4; i++ )
    {
        pFruitList[i]->Draw();
        delete pFruitList[i];
    }
}
```

The ability to determine object behavior at run time instead of only at compile time is a major improvement over C and provides the polymorphic behavior required by object-oriented development.

Understanding Vtables

Virtual functions allow C++ programs to invoke functions dynamically instead of statically. Other terms for dynamic and static function invocation are *late* binding and *early* binding, referring to binding the function address either at run time or at compile time. Whenever you declare a function as virtual, the compiler adds a pointer to your class structure called the *vptr*, or virtual pointer. The vptr points to a *Vtable* structure that contains the addresses of any virtual functions in your class including its base classes. Figure 2.3 depicts the vptr and the Vtable entries for the following class definition:

```
class Fruit {
protected:
    CString    m_strColor;
public:
```

```
    void      SetColor( CString str ) { m_strColor = str; }
    CString   GetColor() { return m_strColor; }
    virtual   void Draw() = 0;
    virtual   long AvgWeight() = 0;
}

class Apple : public Fruit {
protected:
    long      lAvgWeight;
public:
    // Constructor
    Apple() { lAvgWeight = 10; }
    virtual void Draw() { cout << "I'm an Apple" << endl; }
    virtual long AvgWeight() { return m_lAvgWeight; }
}

class GrannySmith : public Apple {
public:
    virtual void Draw() { cout << "I'm a Granny Smith Apple" << endl; }
}
```

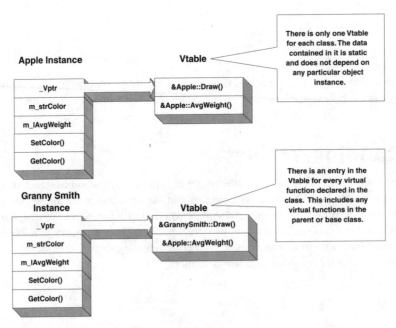

Figure 2.3 Vtable for fruit classes.

The Vtable provides the dynamic binding capability for C++. Examine the following example code:

```
main()
{
   Fruit* pFruit;
   Apple  apple;
   GrannySmith gsApple;

   pFruit = &apple;

   pFruit->Draw();
   cout << "Average weight for an Apple is " << pFruit->AvgWeight() << endl;

   pFruit = &gsApple;
   pFruit->Draw();
   cout << "Average weight for a Granny Smith is "
        << pFruit->AvgWeight()
        << endl;
}
```

This example produces the following output:

```
>I'm an Apple
>Average weight for an Apple is 10
>I'm a Granny Smith
>Average weight for a Granny Smith is 10
```

The example creates pFruit, a pointer to the Fruit abstract class, and then assigns to it the address of an Apple instance. Because Fruit is an abstract class, the compiler knows that pFruit will point to a dynamic (or polymorphic) type. When the statement pFruit->Draw() is encountered, the compiler generates instructions to access the vptr, look up the virtual function by position in the Vtable, and transfer execution to the address contained in the Vtable.

This late binding of function addresses at run time is important to object-oriented languages. Some object-oriented languages—Smalltalk and Java in particular—bind all functions late. Other languages, including C++, leave it up to the developer to decide which functions should bind late. C++ does this for performance reasons. There is overhead in providing the late binding necessary for polymorphic behavior. For every class that has at least one virtual function, a Vtable is needed for the class and a vptr is needed for each instance. The vptr must be initialized for each instance, and there is the run-time overhead of function lookup every time a virtual function is called.

That finishes our review of virtual function capabilities in C++. I've included it here because we will need this background as we begin to discuss COM and Automation in subsequent chapters.

Multiple Inheritance

Multiple inheritance (MI) is one of those philosophical topics that are best not discussed. There are those who say MI is an important part of object-oriented development and that certain problems can be solved (elegantly) only with MI. Others argue that anything you can do with MI can also be done using single inheritance. Indeed, many object-oriented languages, such as Smalltalk and Objective-C, support only single inheritance, but C++ supports multiple inheritance. We won't use multiple inheritance for our purposes, but in the Chapter 4 we will encounter it as we discuss the Component Object Model's concept of component interfaces.

We've discussed the wonderful things that inheritance can do. If inheritance is a wonderful thing, then multiple inheritance must be really impressive. You tell me. In the next example we have two classes: Speedometer and Tachometer.

```
class Speedometer {
protected:
    int    m_Speed;
    RECT   m_Position;
public:
    int    Mph();
    int    Kph();
    void   Display();
};

class Tachometer {
protected:
    int    m_Rpm;
    RECT   m_Position;
public:
    int    Rpm();
    void   Display();
};
```

Now, we create a new class, DashBoard, that combines the features of both classes.

```
class DashBoard : public Speedometer, public Tachometer {
    void   SpeedPos();
    void   TachPos();
    void   Display();
    void   SpeedDisplay();
    void   TachDisplay();
};
```

DashBoard now has "name ambiguity" within itself: both `Tachometer` and `Speedometer` have member variables named m_Position. In addition, there is a collision with the member function `Display`. This ambiguity is one of the primary problems with multiple inheritance. It can be overcome either by not using the ambiguous members or by directly addressing them using the class name:

```
void DashBoard::Display() {
  Speedometer::Display();
  Tachometer::Display();

  }
```

The MFC libraries do not use multiple inheritance at all, primarily because MFC is structured as a hierarchy in which almost every class derives from `CObject`. Multiple inheritance of MFC objects would imply the inclusion of multiple `CObject` objects, and this would cause name collisions, or ambiguity, with the MFC Dump function, among others. All this is explained in detail in MFC *TechNote 16*. If Microsoft developed MFC without resorting to multiple inheritance, I think we can infer that most C++ projects can do without it. Later, when we discuss COM interfaces, you'll be tempted to use multiple inheritance. It's a problem begging to be solved with MI, but MFC uses class nesting and class composition instead.

Class Composition

Instead of using single or multiple inheritance, a problem can also be solved by using *composition*, also called *containment* or *embedding*. Class composition involves including instances of other classes within the new class. This approach works best when there is a "has-a" relationship between the various classes. For example, an apple "is-a" type of fruit, so inheritance is appropriate. A fruit tree, on the other hand, "has-a" fruit, so composition is the better object-oriented approach. Instead of using multiple inheritance to combine the needed features, we create a new class by using a combination of inheritance and composition or by using composition alone.

Using the previous dashboard example, let's try to build a dashboard class by using class composition. A dashboard doesn't fit the "is-a" relationship required for inheritance. A dashboard is definitely not a speedometer, but it does fit the "has-a" relationship of class composition. A dashboard "has-a" speedometer and possibly a tachometer. So we implement a `DashBoard` class as follows:

```
class Speedometer {
public:
     int     Mph();
     int     Kph();
};
class Tachometer {
public:
     int     Rpm();
};
```

```
class DashBoard {
private:
   Speedometer    m_Speedometer;
   Tachometer     m_Tachometer;
public:
   void    SpeedPos();
   void    TachPos();
   void    SpeedDisplay();
   void    TachDisplay();
};
```

When using composition, we can obtain additional flexibility by storing only a pointer to the included class. This class can be an abstract base class and will allow us to "plug in" various derived classes. If we had two types of speedometers—say an analog and a digital type—we could implement the class as follows:

```
class Speedometer {
public:
   virtual void DisplayData() = 0;
};

class AnalogSpeedo : public Speedometer {
protected:
   void GetAnalogData();
public:
   virtual void DisplayData():
};

class DigitalSpeedo : public Speedometer {
protected:
   void GetDigitalData();
public:
   virtual void DisplayData():
};

class DashBoard {
   Speedometer* m_pSpeedometer;
   Tachometer    m_Tachometer;
   // Constructor that takes a speedometer as a parameter
   DashBoard( Speedometer* pSpeedo )
   {
      m_pSpeedometer = pSpeedo;
   }
};
```

```
...
// At run time, create a dashboard with a digital or analog speedometer
// Dynamic determination of created object
DigitalSpeedo* pDigitalSpeedo = new DigitalSpeedo;
AnalogSpeedo*  pAnalogSpeedo = new AnalogSpeedo;

// A digital dashboard

DashBoard* pDigitalDashBoard = new DashBoard( pDigitalSpeedo );
// A analog dashboard
DashBoard* pAnalogDashBoard = new DashBoard( pAnalogSpeedo );
...
```

At run time we can determine what type of speedometer we need for the particular dashboard that we are instantiating. Composition is an effective method of reusing existing classes and providing the flexibility needed to reuse code effectively.

The const **Keyword**

The C++ const keyword is useful for adding rigor to your class implementations. We don't have the space to go into much detail, so I'll hit the high spots with the next example:

```
BOOL Expression::IsNumber( const CString& strToken ) const;
```

Here are two examples of using const. Const prior to CString& indicates, that the strToken parameter is constant and cannot (or will not) be modified by the IsNumber function. Because we're passing by reference (we'll discuss this next) to increase efficiency, we want to ensure the class user that we will not modify the token that is being passed. The const following the function declaration ensures that the IsNumber function cannot modify any member variables of the Expression class. In other words, the const applies to the implicit this parameter passed to all member functions. Additionally, it ensures that IsNumber will not call any other member functions that can or might modify a member variable—that is, other member functions that aren't declared const.

References

The ampersand after CString in the IsNumber method above is called a reference. This new C++ feature causes much confusion, especially for old C programmers like me. Let's take a quick look at why references are useful when you're developing C++ applications. First, references clean up the syntax when you're working with pointers, and second, their use can greatly increase efficiency when you're passing objects to functions.

A reference behaves just like a constant pointer, but the compiler always provides the dereference operator for you.

```
CString strColor = "Blue Green";    // declare a CString
CString& rStrColor = strColor;      // declare a reference to strColor
CString* const pStrColor = &strColor // declare a const pointer to strColor

cout << "Reference " << rStrColor << endl;
cout << "Dereferenced Pointer " << *pStrColor << endl;
```

Both `cout` lines produce "Blue Green." References are like `const` pointers, because once a reference is initialized, it cannot be reassigned to point to a different object. In fact, a reference must be initialized when it is declared. The next example makes this clear:

```
CString strColor = "Blue Green";       // declare a CString
CString strAnotherColor = "Yellow";    // declare another CString
CString& rStrColor = strColor;         // declare a reference to strColor
CString* const pStrColor = &strColor   // declare a const pointer to strColor

// You can't do this
pStrColor = &strAnotherColor

// But you can do this, What do you think this does?
rStrColor = strAnotherColor;

cout << "rStrColor value is " << rStrColor << endl;
cout << "strColor value is " << strColor << endl;
cout << "strAnotherColor value is " << strAnotherColor << endl;

// Produces this output
> rStrColor value is Yellow
> strColor value is Yellow
> strAnotherColor value is Yellow
```

If `rStrColor` behaves like a `const` pointer, why can we assign `strAnotherColor` to it? We can't. The example produces an output of `"Yellow"` not because we were able to reassign the reference, but because the contents of `strAnotherColor` were assigned to `strColor`. In other words, the assignment statement behaves as if it were this:

```
*pStrColor = strAnotherColor;
// or
strColor = strAnotherColor;
```

The assignment operator for `CString` is called, and it copies the contents of `strAnotherColor` to `strColor`. Remember, wherever `rStrColor` occurs (outside of initialization) it really means `strColor`.

References are also useful for increasing the performance of object passing when you're calling functions. The following code must call the `CString` copy constructor and build a copy of the `CString` instance to pass to the `IsNumber` function:

```
// return TRUE if the string is a number
BOOL  Expression::IsNumber( CString strToken )
{
    int nLen = strToken.GetLength();
    for ( int i = nLen - 1; i >= 0 ; i- )
    {
        if (! isdigit( strToken[i] ))
            return FALSE;
    }
    return TRUE;
}
```

This may not seem too costly for `CString` objects, but it can get expensive on large objects. References allow you to use the same syntax as in the preceding example, but instead of a copy, a reference to the object is passed to the function. This technique can greatly increase the performance of an application that passes around large objects. Here's the new function:

```
// return TRUE if the token is a number
BOOL  Expression::IsNumber( const CString& strToken )
{
    int nLen = strToken.GetLength();
    for ( int i = nLen - 1; i >= 0; i- )
    {
        if (! isdigit( strToken[i] ))
            return FALSE;
    }
    return TRUE;
}
```

The syntax is exactly the same when you're accessing an object through a reference, but you must be careful. Because we're passing a reference instead of a copy of the string, the function can modify its contents. However, we're passing by reference for performance reasons. We don't want the function to be able to modify the contents of the parameter. That's why we've added the `const` keyword.

The this **Keyword**

C++ defines a keyword, `this`, that is a pointer to the instantiated object. This keyword is similar to the `self` keyword in Smalltalk and the me keyword in Visual Basic. The `this` pointer is in scope only within nonstatic member functions and is normally used when you're dealing with the copy constructor and when you're overloading operators. As stated earlier, `this` is available only within member functions and operators. In these cases, it is implicitly passed, and thus the following code is equivalent:

```
void SomeClass::SetValue( const short sNewValue )
{
    m_sValue = sNewValue;
}

void SomeClass::SetValue( const short sNewValue )
{
    this->m_sValue = sNewValue;
}
```

You'll use the `this` keyword when building copy constructors and when overriding the assignment (=) operator. We haven't discussed these two topics, so let's do that now.

Copy Constructors

We've discussed the role of class constructors in C++, but a particular type of constructor, called the *copy constructor*, is important in C++ class development. Whenever you develop a new class in C++, you should include a declaration for both a copy constructor and the assignment operator. The compiler's default implementations of the copy constructor and assignment operator are rarely what you want. The compiler performs a bit-wise copy of the instance members. If your class contains any pointers, this default will cause problems. We'll examine the assignment operator in the next section.

The copy constructor is used whenever a copy of an existing C++ object is needed. The class it constructs takes a parameter that is a reference to another instance of the class. Here is an example:

```
// Copy constructor for Apple class
Apple::Apple( Apple& x )
{
    // do the assignment
    m_strName = x.m_strName;
    m_strColor = x.m_strColor;
    ...
}

Apple* pApple = new Apple;
Apple Apple2( *pApple );      // Calls copy constructor
void PrintFruitName( Fruit fruit )
{
    cout << "fruit name is " << fruit.GetName() << endl;
}

PrintFruitName( Apple2 );    // Copy constructor called
```

Overloading Operators

Like member functions, C++ operators can be overloaded on either a class or global level. The assignment operator is similar to the copy constructor and should be declared in every class that you design and implement. The assignment operator is used whenever a instance assignment is performed.

```
Apple* pApple = new Apple;
Apple Apple2 = *pApple;
Apple Apple3, Apple4;

Apple3 = Apple2;      // Assignment operator
// If you return a reference to the left hand side (lhs) you can do this
Apple4 = Apple3 = Apple2;
```

The assignment operator implementation is similar to that of the copy constructor described in the last section. The primary difference is that you typically return a reference to the object being assigned. Here's its implementation.

```
Apple& Apple::operator=( const Apple& rhs )
{
   // Ensure we're not assigning to ourselves
   if ( &rhs == this )
      return *this;

   // do the assignment
   m_strName = rhs.m_strName;
   m_strColor = rhs.m_strColor;
   ...
   return *this;
}
```

I told you that we weren't going to get very deep in C++ details, but I'll give you a couple of sentences on deep versus shallow copies (because it's easy at this point). When making a copy of an object that contains pointers to other objects, what should you do? If you just copy the pointers to the new object, it's a shallow copy, but if you allocate additional memory and replicate any contained objects or data (for both) you've performed a deep copy. The choice is, of course, implementation-dependent. (Don't you hate that phrase?)

Static Class Members

In the constructors example, we encountered the use of `static` within a class declaration. The next example describes a method of keeping count of all instantiated objects of a particular class by using a static member variable. Static member variables are sometimes called *class variables* because they pertain to the class as a whole and not to any specific class instance (and because that's what Smalltalk calls them). The class variable is a single instance that is available to any and all instantiated objects of that class. Because class variables reside outside class instances, there isn't a constructor to initialize them. Like global variables, they must be initialized by a definition:

```
class Fruit {
    ...
private:
    static int m_nCount;
    Fruit();
public:
    virtual ~Fruit();
    ...
    int GetNumFruits() { return m_nCount; }
};

// Initialization (definition) of class variable (static member variable)
int Fruit::m_nCount = 0;

Fruit::Fruit()
{
    m_nCount++;
}
Fruit::~Fruit()
{
    m_nCount-;
}
```

This example also has a member function, GetNumFruits, that retrieves the number of outstanding instances of the Fruit class. We would use the function like this:

```
Fruit* pF1 = new Fruit;
cout << "There are "
    << pF1->GetNumFruits()
    << " Fruit objects"
    << endl;

Fruit* pF2 = new Fruit;
cout << "There are "
    << pF2->GetNumFruits()
    << " Fruit objects"
    << endl;
delete pF1;

cout << "There are "
```

```
      << pF2->GetNumFruits()
      << " Fruit objects"
      << endl;
delete pF2;

//  How do we get the number of objects?
```

As you can see, we have a problem determining when there are zero objects. How can we retrieve the number of objects when none is instantiated? Static member functions, or *class functions* or *class methods*, let us declare functions that operate on the class as a whole outside the scope of any particular instance, just like class variables. So if we declare the GetNumFruits function as follows, we can always determine the number of fruit objects.

```
class Fruit {
  ...
private:
  static int m_nCount;
  ...
public:
  static int GetNumFruits() { return m_nCount; }
};
```

Here's the syntax for invoking a class function. You can also append the call to a class instance, but it doesn't make sense.

```
Fruit* pF1 = new Fruit;
cout << Fruit::GetNumFruits(); // The preferred method, no ambiguity
cout << pF1->GetNumFruits();   // Also works, but seems a little silly
```

There are many cases when you need variables and functions that operate on the class and not on an instance of a class. The MFC library provides some good examples. Here's an abbreviated look at the MFC CFile class:

```
class CFile : public CObject
{
  ...
public:
  static void  Rename( const char* pszFileName, const char* pszNewName );
  static void  Remove( const char* pszFileName );
  BOOL         GetStatus( CFileStatus& rStatus ) const;
  static BOOL  GetStatus( const char* pszFileName, CFileStatus& rStatus );
  ...
};

main() {
```

```
// Let's rename a file
CFile::Rename( "c:\\oldname.txt", "c:\\newname.txt" );
// Now let's delete it
CFile::Remove( "c:\\newname.txt" );
};
```

The static member functions (class methods) can be used without an instance of the CFile class, and this approach is appropriate for functions such as Rename, Remove, and GetStatus. But as you can see, a member function is also provided that is specific to an instance of the CFile object. Remember, static member variables and functions should operate on the class as a whole and not on any particular class instance.

That ends our overview of the C++ language. Next, we'll design and develop a small class that we will use in later chapters.

The Problem

Our hypothetical expression evaluator application needs to allow its users to enter an expression in a standard Windows entry field in which they are currently allowed to enter only integer values. In short, we need to provide a simple integer calculator where they may need it, within the entry field itself. This is standard fare in a spreadsheet, but our users want something simple. To start, let's develop a C++ class that provides validation and evaluation of simple algebraic expressions such as these:

```
((1 + 2) * 100 / 5) - 12
5 * 17 - 3 + 3200
(1 + 22) * 7 / 10
```

Only integers and the binary operators +, -, *, /, and parentheses will be supported, but support for additional operators, user variables, and rational numbers shouldn't require much effort. We will use this example throughout the book as we move from a C++ class to an Automation component and eventually to an ActiveX control based on this expression functionality.

Solving the Problem with a Reusable Class

We have a problem statement, so let's design a C++ class that will provide the needed functionality. Designing reusable classes in C++ is a difficult task. In typical development environments, because of project time constraints, developers tend to solve the specific problem first. Then, if there's time, they go back and adapt the software (classes) to be more general so that it can be reused. There are valid reasons for doing it this way. If the problem to be solved is unclear or complex, only development of the specific solution will yield enough understanding to ultimately produce a general solution. Technology changes so rapidly that we really understand the problem only when we've finished solving it. But if we approach the problems as general problems, we will eventually gain the ability to solve them generally first and specifically second. In the long run, this is by far the best approach.

Designing reusable classes in C++ for use by C++ is best done by use of the inheritance mechanisms. The goal is to implement general behavior in a base (possibly abstract) class and then to override certain functionality through the use of virtual functions. Other approaches include designing the base class to allow other derived classes with their own specific behavior to be plugged in. The MFC libraries provide many good examples of these approaches, as you will see when we build components using MFC in later chapters.

As we discussed in Chapter 1, there are many ways to achieve reusability in software development. One approach is by using inheritance. The other technique—reuse by using discrete specialized components—is our primary focus, so we won't spend much time discussing how to design reusable classes for C++ developers. Instead, we will focus on designing C++ classes that can be easily converted into COM-based software components.

There are many books on object-oriented design, but this book is about component development. My purpose here is to help in the design of C++ classes that will eventually be used outside the C++ environment. In many ways, this minimalist approach makes the design process easier because binary standards provide only a subset of the object-oriented facilities provided by C++. We have less to work with, but it simplifies the design process. For example, a major aspect of C++ class design is to decide how, when, and why to overload operators. Binary standards are a long way from defining overloading capabilities at the function level, let alone the overloading of operators. Binary standards allow the standardizing only of the interface to a component and provide only limited (if any) inheritance capabilities. These restrictions require us to be specific in the way we design classes for use as components, and it is quite different from designing classes that will be reused within C++ development. With that said, let's design a class to solve the problem I've outlined.

When we're designing C++ classes that will be used as components, our focus should be on the interface of the class. It's important to focus on the member functions the user will use. These functions define the behavior of our class (and component) and will eventually be exposed through a binary standard interface. For the problem described, I've designed a simple C++ class as follows:

```
class Expression {
public:
    // Constructors and Destructor
    Expression();
    Expression( CString strExp );
    Expression( CString strExp, BOOL bInfix );
    ~Expression();

// Here's the interface
public:
    CString   GetExpression();
    void      SetExpression(CString strExp, BOOL bInfix );
    BOOL      Validate();
    long      Evaluate();
};
```

We're not worried about how to implement this yet. For now, we're interested in how we think the user should interact with our class. The user needs the ability to provide an expression string; `SetExpression` provides this capability. The user also needs to validate and at some point evaluate the expression, so we've provided `Validate` and `Evaluate` functions. We've also provided `GetExpression` in case the user expects us to maintain the storage for the expression (so that he or she doesn't have to). Here's how the class might be used:

```
main()
{

    Expression* pExp = new Expression;
    cout << "Enter an expression: ";
    cin >> strExp;
    pExp->SetExpression( strExp, TRUE );
    if ( pExp->Validate() )
        cout << "The result is " << pExp->Evaluate() << endl;
    else
        cout << "Invalid expression" << endl;

    delete pExp;
}
```

We could have designed the interface in other ways. One option is to have only one function:

```
class Expression {
public:
    // Returns False if Validate fails
    BOOL Evaluate( const CString strExp, BOOL bInfix, long& lResult );
}
```

This would work, but there is at least one problem. Binary standard wrappers, such as COM, don't necessarily support the use of C++ references or pointers. This design would preclude the use of this class as a component because of its use of references.

Next, we'll design the implementation, but first let's review interfaces and implementations.

Interface versus Implementation

It is important to distinguish between an interface and its implementation. We touched on this briefly earlier. The ability to insulate the class user from implementation details is a key advantage of C++. This ability is the essence of object-oriented encapsulation. The details of how an object implements its functionality are hidden or encapsulated from the class user. Thus, the implementation can change without affecting the user at all, although that isn't exactly true when C++ is used. When a C++ class library changes, it must be recompiled. If any users of the class also want these new features, they must at least relink or recompile their applications, depending on the nature of the changes. Binary standards overcome this limitation of C++ and allow dynamic changing of the method implementation without affecting the component user; there is no need to recompile or relink. Figure 2.4 illustrates the difference between the implementation and interface in the context of a C++ class.

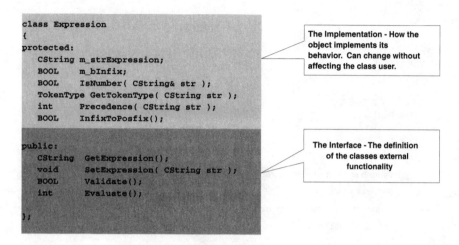

```
class Expression
{
protected:
    CString m_strExpression;
    BOOL     m_bInfix;
    BOOL     IsNumber( CString& str );
    TokenType GetTokenType( CString str );
    int      Precedence( CString str );
    BOOL     InfixToPosfix();

public:
    CString  GetExpression();
    void     SetExpression( CString str );
    BOOL     Validate();
    int      Evaluate();

};
```

The Implementation - How the object implements its behavior. Can change without affecting the class user.

The Interface - The definition of the classes external functionality

Figure 2.4 Class implementation and interface.

The public methods of a C++ class are what describe, to the external user, the capabilities and behaviors of the class. This public interface is also described as an interface *contract*. It's a contract in the sense that once it is defined and exposed for use by clients of the class, it shouldn't change. If the interface must change, it should be changed by augmentation; only new methods should be added. The old methods should not change. This arrangement ensures that users of the original interface will not be adversely affected by additions (upgrades) to the class interface. The idea of an interface contract is also important to component development. Additions and changes to a component interface should be handled in the same manner as they are in C++ implementations.

The Expression **Class Implementation**

We've defined how the class user will interact with our class, and now it's time to develop the implementation. Here's the complete declaration of the Expression class:

```
class Expression
{
protected:
    // Similar to a static, enum values are for the class as a whole
    enum TokenType
    {
```

```
        BogusToken,

        OperatorToken,

        OpenParenToken,

        CloseParenToken,

        NumberToken

    };

// Implementation variables
protected:
    CString        m_strExpression;
    BOOL           m_bInfix;

// Implementation functions
protected:
    BOOL           IsNumber( const CString& strToken );
    TokenType      GetTokenType( const CString& strToken );
    int            Precedence( const CString& strToken );
    BOOL           InfixToPostfix();

public:
    // Constructors
    Expression();
    Expression( CString str, BOOL bInfix );
    // Destructor
    ~Expression();

    // Copy constructor
    Expression( Expression& x );

    // Assignment operator
    Expression& operator=( Expression& rhs );

public:
    CString  GetExpression();
    void     SetExpression( CString strExp, BOOL bInfix );
    long     Evaluate();
    BOOL     Validate();
};
```

The Expression class also needs the services of a Tokenizer and a Stack class, which we will cover in detail later in the chapter. We're using the top-down approach to solve the problem. Our implementation contains four member functions. InfixToPostfix converts a standard infix expression to postfix for easier evaluation. IsNumber determines whether an expression token is a number. GetTokenType returns the type of the expression token, and `GetPrecedence` returns the evaluation precedence of the passed token. In the next section we'll describe each of these functions.

Infix and Postfix Expressions

We're all familiar with infix expressions (e.g., (1 + 2) / 3), but there are some difficulties in evaluating them. The problem with infix expressions is that they're more difficult programmatically to evaluate than their postfix equivalents. (Infix expressions require parentheses to remove ambiguity in the expression, but postfix expressions do not.) Table 2.1 shows some examples of infix and equivalent postfix expressions.

Table 2.1 Examples of Infix and Postfix Expressions

Infix	Postfix
(1 + 3) * 5 - 10	1 3 + 5 * 10 -
100 / 3 * 5 + 15 * 10	100 3 / 5 * 15 10 * +
900 - 45 + 10 / 5 * 10	900 45 - 10 5 / 10 * +

Postfix expressions place the binary operators after the two operands, removing any ambiguity in infix expressions. There is no need for parentheses. This technique also makes programmatic evaluation of the expression easy. This book isn't about expression evaluation, so we won't go into the details. If you're interested, complete coverage of this topic is available in *Intermediate Problem Solving and Data Structures*, by Helman and Veroff. (See the Bibliography.)

Here's our implementation of `InfixToPostfix`:

```
// Convert the expression from infix to postfix form.
// Use a local (on the stack) instance of the Tokenizer class
BOOL Expression::InfixToPostfix()
{
    CStringStack stack;
    Tokenizer tokenizer;
    CString strToken;
    CString strPostfix;
    CString strTop;
    CString strPop;

    tokenizer.SetString( m_strExpression );
    // Tokenize the expression
    tokenizer.Tokenize();
```

```
// while we have more tokens
while( tokenizer.GetToken( strToken ) )
{
    switch( GetTokenType( strToken ) )
    {
        // If we have a number, append it to the new postfix string
        case NumberToken:
            strPostfix += strToken;
            // Delimit the number tokens by appending an extra space
            strPostfix += " ";
            break;

        // If we encounter an open paren '(', push it on the stack
        case OpenParenToken:
            stack.Push( strToken );
            break;

        // If we encounter a close paren ')'
        case CloseParenToken:
            if ( stack.Peek( strTop ) )
            {
                // While we haven't found an open paren and
                // the stack is not empty
                while( strTop.Compare( "(" ) )
                {
                    stack.Pop( strPop );
                     // Pop the next element and append it to the postfix string
                    strPostfix += strPop;
                    if (! stack.Peek( strTop ) )
                        break;
                }
            }
            // Pop the paren off the stack, we don't need it
            stack.Pop( strPop );
            break;

        case OperatorToken:
            // While there is something in the stack
            while( ! stack.IsEmpty() )
            {
                // Peek at the next element on the stack
```

```
            stack.Peek( strTop );
            // If the top element on the stack is NOT an open paren, and its
            // precedence is greater than or equal to our current token, then
            // pop it off the stack and append it to our postfix string.
            // Exit the loop when the stack is empty, or we encounter an
            // element that is the open paren or whose precedence is lower
            // than our current token.
            if ( strTop.Compare( "(" ) &&
                 Precedence( strTop ) >= Precedence( strToken ))
            {
               stack.Pop( strPop );
               strPostfix += strPop;
               stack.Peek( strTop );
            }
            else
               break;
         }
         // Push the token that caused us to exit back
         // on the stack
         stack.Push( strToken );
         break;

      }
   }
   // Empty the stack and append the elements
   // to our postfix string.
   while(! stack.IsEmpty() )
   {
      stack.Pop( strPop );
      strPostfix += strPop;
   }

   // Everything is Ok
   m_strExpression = strPostfix;
   TRACE1( "New Postfix expression is %s\n", strPostfix );
   return FALSE;
}
```

Three other support functions are needed for the Expression class: IsNumber, GetToken, and Precedence. Here they are:

```
// Determine if the token is a number.
```

```
// Return TRUE if it is, else FALSE.
BOOL Expression::IsNumber( const CString& strToken )
{
    int nLen = strToken.GetLength();
    for ( int i = nLen - 1; i >= 0; i- )
    {
        if (! isdigit( strToken.GetAt(i) ))
            return FALSE;
    }

    return TRUE;
}

// Get the token type of the passed token
Expression::TokenType Expression::GetTokenType( const CString& strToken )
{
    if ( strToken.Compare( "(" ) == 0 )
        return( OpenParenToken );
    else if ( strToken.Compare( ")" ) == 0 )
        return( CloseParenToken );
    else if ( strToken.FindOneOf( "+-*/" ) != -1 )
        return( OperatorToken );
    else if ( IsNumber( strToken ) )
        return( NumberToken );
    else
        return( BogusToken );
}

// Return the precedence of the operator
// 2 is the highest precedence
int Expression::Precedence( const CString& strToken )
{
    if ( strToken.FindOneOf( "*/" ) != -1 )
        return( 2 );
    else if ( strToken.FindOneOf( "+-" ) != -1 )
        return( 1 );
    else
        return( 0 );
}
```

To finish, here are the member functions that implement the interface for the Expression class, the public constructors, and the assignment operator:

```cpp
// Constructors
Expression::Expression()
{
   // Default to infix
   m_bInfix = TRUE;
}

Expression::Expression( CString str, BOOL bInfix )
{
   m_strExpression = str;
   m_bInfix = bInfix;
}

// Copy constructor
Expression::Expression( Expression& x )
{
   m_bInfix = x.m_bInfix;
   m_strExpression = x.m_strExpression;
}

// The assignment operator
Expression& Expression::operator=( Expression& rhs )
{
    // If we're assigning to ourselves just return
    if ( this == &rhs )
       return *this;

    m_bInfix = rhs.m_bInfix;
    m_strExpression = rhs.m_strExpression;

    return *this;
}

// The destructor
Expression::~Expression()
{
}

// Get the current expression.
CString Expression::GetExpression()
{
   return m_strExpression;
}
```

```
// Set the expression to evaluate, set the bInfix flag to
// TRUE if it is an infix expression, FALSE for postfix
void Expression::SetExpression( CString strExp, BOOL bInfix )
{
    m_strExpression = strExp;
    m_bInfix = bInfix;
}

//
// Validate an infix expression by balancing the parentheses
// and checking for invalid tokens. Return TRUE if the expression
// is valid, else FALSE
BOOL Expression::Validate()
{
    CStringStack stack;
    Tokenizer tokenizer;
    CString strToken;
    CString strTop;

    tokenizer.SetString( m_strExpression );

    // Tokenize our expression
    tokenizer.Tokenize();

    // Check for validity
    while( tokenizer.GetToken( strToken ) )
    {
        switch( GetTokenType( strToken ) )
        {
            case NumberToken:
            case OperatorToken:
                break;

            case OpenParenToken:
                stack.Push( strToken );
                break;

            case CloseParenToken:
                if ( stack.IsEmpty() )
                {
                    TRACE0( "Too many closing parens\n" );
                    return FALSE;
                }
```

```
                else
                   stack.Pop( strTop );
                break;

            default:
                // Invalid operator type
                TRACE1( "Invalid Operator Type %s\n", strToken );
                stack.Clear();
                return FALSE;
        }
    }

    // If there's something on the stack, there's a paren mismatch
    if (! stack.IsEmpty() )
    {
        TRACE0( "Too many open parens\n" );
        return FALSE;
    }

    return TRUE;
}

//
// Actually evaluate the expression. If the expression is infix,
// convert it to postfix first. Return the result of the expression.
// You should call validate before calling this function.
long Expression::Evaluate()
{   .
    CStringStack stack;
    Tokenizer tokenizer;
    CString strToken;
    CString strOperand1;
    CString strOperand2;
    CString strResult;
    long lResult;
    char szTemp[32];

    if ( m_bInfix )
    {
        TRACE0( "Converting to postfix\n" );
        InfixToPostfix();
    }
```

```
tokenizer.SetString( m_strExpression );
tokenizer.Tokenize();

// While there are tokens to process

while( tokenizer.GetToken( strToken ) )
{
    switch( GetTokenType( strToken ) )
    {
        case NumberToken:
            stack.Push( strToken );
            break;

        // If we have an operator, pop the next two elements as they
        // will be the operands. Use the binary operands and evaluate
        // them. Push the result onto the stack for the next operator.
        case OperatorToken:
            stack.Pop( strOperand2 );
            stack.Pop( strOperand1 );
            if ( strToken.Compare( "+" ) == 0)
                lResult = atol( strOperand1 ) + atol( strOperand2 );
            else if ( strToken.Compare( "-" ) == 0)
                lResult = atol( strOperand1 ) - atol( strOperand2 );
            else if ( strToken.Compare( "*" ) == 0)
                lResult = atol( strOperand1 ) * atol( strOperand2 );
            else if ( strToken.Compare( "/" ) == 0)
            {
                // If division by zero is attempted
                // clear the tokens and continue. This
                // will exit the while
                if ( atol( strOperand2 ) == 0 )
                {
                    tokenizer.ClearTokens();
                    TRACE0( "Division by Zero\n" );
                    continue;
                }
                lResult = atol( strOperand1 ) / atol( strOperand2 );
            }
            sprintf( szTemp, "%ld", lResult );
            // Push the result onto the stack
            stack.Push( szTemp );
```

```
            break;

        default:
            TRACE1( "Invalid operator type %s\n", strToken );
        }
    }

    // When we're all finished, there is one element
    // on the stack and it is the final result
    stack.Pop( strResult );

    // Convert the result to a long and return it
    return atol( strResult );
}
```

A Tokenizer Class

To convert and evaluate algebraic expressions, we need a way to break the expression string into discrete expression elements, or *tokenize* it. Let's design a tokenizer class to do this. Remember, one way to achieve reusable classes is to break the problem into small pieces and implement each piece as an object. Small generic objects make reusability more attainable when you're using C++.

What follows is our `Tokenizer` class. It takes a string either during construction or later using `SetString`. When the user calls `Tokenize`, it parses the string into its tokens and stores them in a linked list (`CStringList` again). Then the user can iteratively retrieve (or peek at) the tokens.

```
/////
// Tokenizes an algebraic expression string
/////
class Tokenizer
{
protected:
    char        m_szBuffer[256];
    CStringList m_TokenList;

public:
    Tokenizer();
    Tokenizer( const CString& strString );
    ~Tokenizer();

public:
    void    SetString( const CString& str );
    short   Tokenize();
    BOOL    GetToken( CString& str );
```

```
    BOOL      PeekToken( CString& str );
    void      ClearTokens();

};

//////
// Tokenizer class members
//////
// Constructors
Tokenizer::Tokenizer()
{
}

// Construct a tokenizer with a default string
Tokenizer::Tokenizer( const CString& strString )
{
    strcpy( m_szBuffer, strString );
}

// When the tokenizer is destroyed, make sure
// that all of the strings are deallocated
Tokenizer::~Tokenizer()
{
    ClearTokens();
}

// Set the string to tokenize
void Tokenizer::SetString( const CString& str )
{
    strcpy( m_szBuffer, str );
}

// Tokenize the string into its discrete elements
short Tokenizer::Tokenize()
{
    char *pChar;
    short sCount = 0;
    char szTemp[128];
    char *pTemp;

    // Make sure the token list is empty
    ClearTokens();

    // Get a pointer into the string to tokenize
    pChar = m_szBuffer;
```

```cpp
// While we haven't encountered the
// NULL termination character
while( *pChar )
{
    // skip any spaces
    if ( *pChar == ' ' )
    {
        pChar++;
        continue;
    }

    // Get a pointer into a temp storage
    // for each token
    pTemp = szTemp;
    switch( *pChar )
    {
        // digit
        case '1':
        case '2':
        case '3':
        case '4':
        case '5':
        case '6':
        case '7':
        case '8':
        case '9':
        case '0':
            // While the char is a digit and
            // it's not the terminating NULL
            while( pChar && isdigit( *pChar ) )
            {
                *pTemp = *pChar;
                pTemp++; pChar++;
            }
            // Back up one char
            pChar-;
            // Terminate the number string
            *pTemp = '\0';
            break;

        default:
            // All other tokens are one character
```

```
                    // assign it to szTemp and NULL terminate it
                    *pTemp = *pChar;
                    pTemp++;
                    *pTemp = '\0';
                    break;

        }
        // Count the number of tokens
        sCount++;

        TRACE1( "Adding token %s\n", szTemp );

        // Add the token to the CStringList
        m_TokenList.AddHead( szTemp );

        // Move to the next character in the Token string
        pChar++;
    }

    // return the number of tokens found
    return sCount;

}

// Get the next token in the list. Return
// FALSE if the list is empty, TRUE otherwise.
BOOL Tokenizer::GetToken( CString& str )
{
    if ( m_TokenList.IsEmpty() )
        return FALSE;

    str = m_TokenList.RemoveTail();
    return TRUE;

}

// Clear all of the tokens in the list
void Tokenizer::ClearTokens()
{
    m_TokenList.RemoveAll();
}

// Peek at the top token
// Return FALSE if there are no tokens
BOOL Tokenizer::PeekToken( CString& str )
{
    if ( m_TokenList.IsEmpty() )
```

```
      return FALSE;

   str = m_TokenList.GetTail();
   return TRUE;
}
```

A Stack Class

The Expression class needs the services of a stack, so let's build a stack class. Stacks are normally implemented using arrays, but we want to build a stack that allows pushing of an arbitrary number of elements so that we have no intrinsic limit on the length of an expression. Using a static array would limit the number of elements that could be stored; in addition, the MFC libraries provide a linked-list class that we can reuse by inheriting its capabilities. Should we inherit this functionality from the CObList class? Let's take a look.

The following code shows a first attempt at building a CString stack. It's implemented by inheriting the methods from the MFC CStringList class. CStringList is like the CObList class, but it uses CStrings as the elements of the list. The "is-a" relationship seems to fit. A stack "is-a" kind of linked list, isn't it? Building a stack class that would support multiple data types would also be nice. The best way to do this would be to use C++ templates, but our purpose here is to illustrate the pros and cons of using inheritance or composition when building new classes.

```
class CStringStack : public CStringList
{
public:
   void    Push( CString );
   BOOL    Pop( CString& );
   BOOL    IsEmpty();
   BOOL Peek( CString& );
};

void CStringStack::Push( CString str )
{
   AddHead( str );
}

// Pop an element
BOOL CStringStack::Pop( CString &str )
{
   if (! IsEmpty() )
   {
      str = RemoveHead();
      return FALSE;
   }
```

```
      return TRUE;
}

BOOL CStringStack::IsEmpty()
{
      return CStringList::IsEmpty();
}
BOOL CString Stack::Peek( CString& Str )
{
      if(! IsEmpty() )
      {
         str = GetHead();
         return TRUE;
      }
      return FALSE;
}
```

This implementation works fine. In fewer than 40 lines of code, we've implemented a useful stack that supports an arbitrary number of CString elements. Inheritance is great! We've just reused hundreds of lines of MFC library code. But there's a problem. Here's how the class user might implement the code:

```
main()
{
      CStringStack stack;    // Get a stack

      stack.Push("One");     // OK
      stack.Push("Two");     // OK
      stack.Push("Three");   // OK

      POSITION pos = stack.FindIndex( 1 ); // Oh-oh, what's going on here?
      // Here's a way to get at any element in the stack!
      cout << "The middle element on the stack is " << stack.GetAt( pos ) <<
              endl;

      // Mess up the stack
      stack.RemoveAt( pos );
}
```

As you can see the user of the stack class can violate and corrupt our stack implementation. If we're going to provide a solid class implementation, we can't allow this. The encapsulation of the stack object is not complete. What happened? When we decided to use inheritance to build the stack class, we neglected to remember that all protected and public member functions of the base class are inherited. This means that all the linked-list functions—such as Find, FindIndex, InsertBefore, GetAt, and so on—are available to our CStringStack user. Somehow we must hide the linked-list–specific functions from CStringStack users so that they don't hurt themselves (or us). We could do something like the following to keep users from calling the linked-list functions:

```
class CStringStack : public CStringList
{
protected:                    // Override inherited member functions
   void    FindIndex() {}  // Not implemented
   void    GetAt()    {}   // Not implemented
   ...                        // For all linked-list function we want to hide
public:
   void    Push( CString& );
   BOOL Pop( CString& );
   BOOL IsEmpty();
   BOOL Peek ( CString& );
}
```

Now when stack users try to use the linked-list routines, they will get a parameter mismatch error from the compiler, because the linked-list functions expect and return specific parameters. But we've hidden them by effectively overriding them with do-nothing functions. This isn't the best solution; it requires additional code and is basically a kludge. Another approach is to use private inheritance, but this would also hide those functions that we want to expose publicly (such as IsEmpty). Let's try another approach.

Maybe a stack does not really have an "is-a" relationship with a linked list. It seems that it doesn't, because a linked list has functions that can violate the integrity of a stack. But a stack could have a "has-a" relationship with a linked list. We can implement a stack that "has-a" linked list. This means that we will use class composition instead of inheritance to implement our stack:

```
//
// A Stack class that supports CStrings
//
class CStringStack
{
protected:
   CStringList m_StringList;

public:
   // Default constructor
   CStringStack();
   // Copy constructor
   CStringStack( CStringStack& stack );
   // Destructor
   ~CStringStack();

   // Assignment operator
```

```
   CStringStack& operator=( const CStringStack& lhs );

// The interface
public:
   void     Push( Cstring& );
   BOOL     Peek( CString& );
   BOOL     Pop( CString& );
   BOOL     IsEmpty();
   void     Clear();
};

// Default constructor
CStringStack::CStringStack()
{
}

// Copy constructor
CStringStack::CStringStack( CStringStack& stack )
{
   // Copy the stack elements
   POSITION pos = stack.m_StringList.GetHeadPosition();
   while( pos )
   {
      CString strElement = stack.m_StringList.GetNext( pos );
      // Add them in the reverse order by using AddTail
      m_StringList.AddTail( strElement );
   }
}

// When we destroy the CStringStack, ensure
// that the linked list of strings is deallocated
CStringStack::~CStringStack()
{
   Clear();
}

// assignment operator

CStringStack& CStringStack::operator=( const CStringStack& rhs )
{
   // If we're assigning to ourselves just return
   if ( this == &rhs )
      return *this;
```

```cpp
    // remove the elements of the target stack
    m_StringList.RemoveAll();
    // Now move all of the elements
    POSITION pos = rhs.m_StringList.GetHeadPosition();
    while( pos )
    {
        CString strElement = rhs.m_StringList.GetNext( pos );
        // Add them in the reverse order by using AddTail
        m_StringList.AddTail( strElement );
    }
    return *this;
}

// Add an element to the top of the stack
void CStringStack::Push( Cstring& str )
{
    m_StringList.AddHead( str );
}

// Remove an element from the stack. If the
// stack is empty return TRUE, else FALSE
BOOL CStringStack::Pop( CString &str )
{
    if (! m_StringList.IsEmpty() )
    {
        str = m_StringList.RemoveHead();
        return FALSE;
    }
    else
        return TRUE;
}

// Return TRUE if the stack is empty
// This is easy, we defer to the CStringList
// IsEmpty method.
BOOL CStringStack::IsEmpty()
{
    return m_StringList.IsEmpty();
}

// Peek at the top element. If the stack
// is empty return TRUE, else FALSE
```

```
BOOL CStringStack::Peek( CString& str )
{
   if (! m_StringList.IsEmpty() )
   {
      str = m_StringList.GetHead();
      return TRUE;
   }
   else
      return FALSE;
}

// Remove any elements in the stack by
// clearing the strings in the CStringList
void CStringStack::Clear()
{
   m_StringList.RemoveAll();
}
```

There are only two differences between the implementations. The new `CStringStack` class has a member variable `m_StringList` of type `CStringList`, and all the member functions must explicitly access this variable when performing linked-list functions. Now that we have encapsulated the linked-list functionality within our stack class and expose only those functions that we deem appropriate, users can no longer access functions that violate our concept of a stack. Composition is just as important as inheritance to our goal of reusability.

NOTE

On the accompanying CD-ROM, there is an example for Chapter 2. It is a Win32 console application that uses the MFC libraries that we'll discuss in Chapter 3. The example is in the \EXAMPLES\CHAP2\EXPRESS subdirectory and contains the **EXPRESS.H** and **EXPRESS.CPP** files that we have developed in this chapter. The directory also contains the appropriate Visual C++ make file, so it is easy to modify. We will use this example in the next few chapters as we convert it to use the COM binary standard. It would be beneficial at this point to become familiar with the Expression example.

Summary

That wraps up our review of the C++ language and the various object-oriented methods used for designing reusable C++ classes. We also discussed how we might design C++ classes so that their functionality can be exposed, using a binary standard, to other languages and processes. In the next chapter, we'll review Visual C++ and the Microsoft Foundation Class libraries.

Chapter *3*

Visual C++ and the MFC Libraries

Throughout this book we will use Visual C++ and its application framework, the Microsoft Foundation Class (MFC) libraries, for the sample code and application examples. In this chapter we'll take a quick look at the Visual C++ environment, what the MFC libraries are, and how they can help with the building of COM-based components. We won't actually start using COM until the next chapter. This chapter will introduce the tools we will use as we explore Microsoft's COM, OLE, and ActiveX using MFC. We will get this experience by developing a simple MFC application to test the Expression class we developed in Chapter 2. For a more exhaustive treatment of Visual C++ and the MFC libraries, I recommend *The Revolutionary Guide to MFC 4 Programming with Visual C++* by Mike Blaszczak and *Inside Visual C++*, third edition, by David J. Kruglinski. Once you have a handle on MFC and you want to dig into the details, pick up a copy of *MFC Internals*, by Scot Wingo and George Shepherd.

Win16 versus Win32 Development

The decision whether to develop Win16 (Windows 3.x) or Win32 (Windows 95 and Windows NT) applications gets easier every day. By the time you read this, Microsoft's Windows 95 will have been generally available for more than a year. According to the latest sales figures I've heard, it is outselling Windows 3.x by a factor of five. I'm a big advocate for doing all new development in Win32. Windows 3.x applications will be replaced by more robust Win32-based ones, and the limitations of 16-bit development will eventually fade away. The future lies with the Win32 API, so the applications developed in this book use the 32-bit version of Visual C++. In the previous edition, we also provided 16-bit implementations of the controls, but Microsoft is no longer keeping the 16-bit and 32-bit versions of MFC in sync. Many of the new features of COM and ActiveX that we will explore in this book do not have an implementation in the 16-bit Windows environment, so we will focus purely on 32-bit development. There is a 16-bit version (1.52c) of Visual C++ and MFC that supports the development of COM and ActiveX-based applications, but it is lacking in several areas.

77

Visual C++

We will use the integrated development environment (IDE) of Visual C++, called Developer Studio, throughout this book. If you've been developing Windows software for a few years, as I have, you're probably skeptical of integrated development environments. If you're like most SDK developers, all you need is a good text-based editor, hand-coded make files, and the various command-line utilities to build solid Windows applications. I agree, but there are features of the Visual C++ IDE that can be a great help, particularly if you are using the MFC libraries. You don't have to use the IDE to use the MFC libraries, but by using it initially, you'll learn more quickly. Later, after you understand MFC inside and out, you can go back to using your favorite editor and the command-line utilities. But you'll soon miss the powerful **F1** key, the AppWizard, and the ClassWizard.

One of the reasons Visual C++ is such a powerful Windows development tool is its included application framework: the MFC libraries. Before we get started, let's look at what application frameworks can provide.

Application Frameworks

The MFC libraries can be described as an *application framework*. An application framework provides an abstracted, high-level view of the underlying operating system, or application environment (e.g., Windows). The primary purpose of application frameworks is to make the developer more productive. An application framework's goals are similar to those of C++: to hide the mundane details of programming within class libraries so that developers need not continually deal with trivial details. A second goal of application frameworks is to provide platform independence. An application framework can separate the details of a particular platform (Windows, OS/2) at an abstracted level within the framework. At the framework API or C++ class level, the details of the underlying target platform can be hidden. This arrangement allows the developer to *target* the application framework. If the developer adheres to the rules of the framework, the resulting source is portable among the various platforms supported by the framework. It also serves the first purpose of increasing developer productivity.

As with most tools, application frameworks have drawbacks. First, there is a significant learning curve involved in becoming familiar with an application framework. It takes time, and the knowledge is not directly transferable to other frameworks. Spending two years developing applications with Borland's OWL framework will not help you very much when your boss tells you to switch to Visual C++ and MFC.

Application frameworks also have *feature lag*. The implementation of new platform-specific features does not occur at the same time that it does for the underlying operating system. For example, MFC's ActiveX classes do not currently support the development of ActiveX controls that completely support the OLE Control 96 specification, but such development is supported via direct COM/ActiveX API calls. So when you're using a framework, be prepared either to wait for new features to be implemented in the framework or to go around the framework and implement needed features using the explicit API calls, possibly providing your own subclasses until the framework is updated.

The Microsoft Foundation Class Libraries

MFC's implementation provides only a thin layer of abstraction above the Windows API. This arrangement has caused some criticism within the industry, because it requires the programmer to understand many of the esoteric Windows constructs to use the libraries effectively. Depending on your perspective, this requirement can be a benefit or a stumbling block. Experienced Windows developers already understand the underlying Windows API, so the MFC libraries quickly enhance their productivity. Others who have used other application frameworks complain that MFC does not *hide*, or abstract, the details of Windows sufficiently. If you don't already have Windows development experience, the MFC libraries can be difficult to learn. Many developers moving from other platforms, such as OS/2, may get a triple whammy. To use MFC, they must also learn Windows, C++, and the libraries, and that is enough to cause many to consider a new career.

I think that Microsoft did it right when it developed the MFC libraries. The abstraction is at just the right level. It increases productivity but doesn't compromise application performance in the process. If you don't agree, there are other options.

Borland's application framework, Object Windows Library (OWL), which comes with Borland C++, provides a higher level of abstraction. This allows implementation of the framework on disparate GUI environments. Programs written using OWL can be ported among the various Windows environments and OS/2, but not the Macintosh platform, which MFC supports. IBM has its Open Class libraries, which are part of its Visual Age series of products. The Open Class framework is abstracted at a level that allows fairly direct movement between OS/2 and various Windows platforms. However, at the time of this writing, IBM's Open Class libraries provide very little support in the area of COM, OLE, and ActiveX.

Choosing a specific framework is difficult. The MFC libraries provide a great deal of functionality and support target platform features that other frameworks do not support. Specifically, other frameworks lack support for our primary goal: ActiveX controls. This is a very important difference, at least for our purposes.

In the scope of platform, or target, portability, the MFC libraries support easy movement of MFC source code among the various Windows platforms: Windows 3.x and Windows 95 on Intel hardware, and Windows NT on Intel, MIPS, Alpha, and PowerPC hardware. However, as I mentioned earlier, because of their differences, it is getting more difficult to move between the 16-bit and 32-bit Windows environments with MFC. Versions of MFC are also available for various flavors of UNIX as well as for Apple's System 7 operating environment. OS/2 is a target that the MFC libraries currently do not support.

The Internet—and its heterogeneous environment of Windows, UNIX, Solaris, OS/2, and Macintosh machines—makes multiplatform support very important. Microsoft has stated publicly that it is committed to providing the COM and ActiveX technologies on most of these platforms. It has also announced that the COM and ActiveX technologies will be handed over to an open standards body so that it will be available to all vendors that want to implement the technology on their platforms. Microsoft, however, is committed to providing the best implementation of the standard.

An MFC Application that Evaluates Expressions

Before we jump into the Component Object Model and ActiveX, let's build a quick MFC-based application to test the Expression class we developed in the last chapter. This application will give you a chance to get familiar with the Visual C++ IDE and introduce you to the use of the MFC libraries. We will augment this project as we move through the various chapters. For starters, we'll build a simple Windows single-document interface (SDI) application to try out our expression evaluator class. So fire up Visual C++ and let's get to work.

Using AppWizard

The Visual C++ AppWizard allows a developer to quickly build an MFC application from scratch. It provides a minimal application based on the options picked during the dialog with AppWizard. The resulting application will compile, link, and run, but not much else. Its purpose is to create the various source, resource, and project files necessary to build a Windows application using MFC. Once you run AppWizard to create a particular application, you cannot run AppWizard again to modify an existing application. The purpose of AppWizard is to quickly generate a template application on which to build. This aim is different from that of the usual application generators, which generate a complete application and allow subsequent modifications through the tool.

To start building the Chapter 3 example, start Visual C++ and invoke **New** from the File menu. The New dialog box will display; pick **Project Workspace** and click **OK**, and you will see the dialog box shown in Figure 3.1.

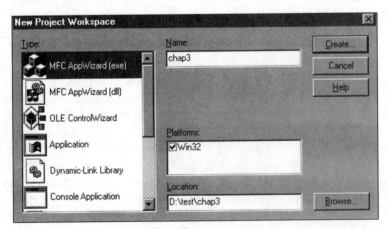

Figure 3.1 New Project Workspace dialog box.

Type **chap3** in the **Name** entry field as shown. Make sure that the **Type** is **MFC AppWizard (exe)** and then click **Create**. This action brings up the AppWizard dialog box shown in Figure 3.2.

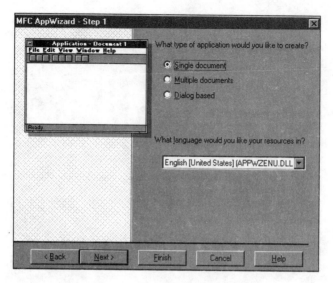

Figure 3.2 AppWizard dialog box, step 1.

For our initial projects we will use Windows single-document interface applications because they aren't as complex as their multiple-document interface (MDI) counterparts (remember, our focus is on COM-based components). The dialog box–based option produces an application that does not use the document/view architecture (we'll discuss this shortly) but instead uses a simple dialog box as the main window. We could have used this option for our simple example, but we will use the document/view architecture in several examples, and now is a good time to discuss it. Later, we will develop an example with MFC's dialog box–based support. Click the **Next** button to continue.

The next dialog box concerns MFC database support. We're not interested in that for now, so click **Next** again. The OLE Support dialog box is next. We're not going to include OLE support just yet, so choose **None** for OLE Compound Document support and **No, Thank you** for OLE (ActiveX) Automation support. Click **Next** again to move to the Application Features dialog box shown in Figure 3.3.

To reduce the complexity of the code that AppWizard will generate for us, we've turned off all the features except **Initial status bar** and **3D controls**. Once you've done this, click the **Advanced** button to get the dialog box shown in Figure 3.4.

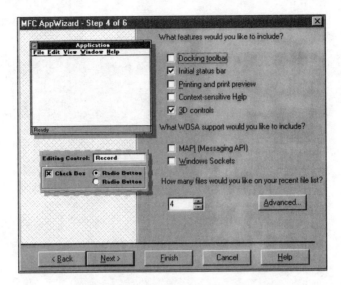

Figure 3.3 AppWizard dialog box, step 4.

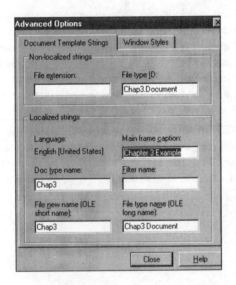

Figure 3.4 Advanced Options dialog box.

Change the caption and check the other features as shown in Figure 3.4, close the dialog box, and click **Next** to move to the Source Options dialog box shown in Figure 3.5.

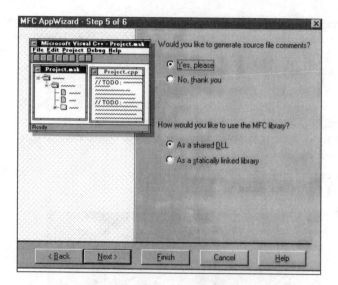

Figure 3.5 AppWizard dialog box, step 5.

I like comments in my code so I answer **Yes, please** to the first option. The next option, **How would you like to use the MFC library?**, allows you to either statically link with the MFC libraries or use the shared DLL version. The DLL option greatly reduces the size of your executable file, but you must distribute **MFC40.DLL** and any supporting files. This isn't a big deal, because most systems will already have these files present. We'll use the **shared DLL** option.

The final AppWizard step is shown in Figure 3.6.

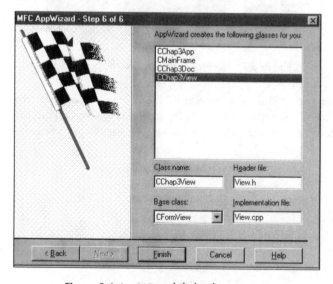

Figure 3.6 AppWizard dialog box, step 6.

There are a few things that must be done here. First, for consistency throughout the examples, select the **CChap3Doc** class and change the header file name to **DOCUMENT.H** and the implementation file to **DOC-UMENT.CPP**. Then change the CChap3View class header file to **VIEW.H** and the implementation file to **VIEW.CPP**. Finally, make sure that the base classes of the CChap3View class is CFormView instead of CView.

CFormView allows easy placement of controls on the client area of a view. This is similar to a dialog box–based application, because CFormView uses a dialog resource for the client area. Earlier versions of AppWizard required the developer to do some of the work to derive from CFormView, but the latest versions make this task painless, as you will see.

Click the **Finish** button, and you will see the dialog window shown in Figure 3.7. Make sure all the options are correct and then click the **OK** button.

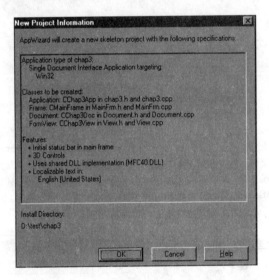

Figure 3.7 New Project Information dialog window.

As it says, the "skeleton project" has been generated, so let's go ahead and see whether it will compile and link before we add a line of code. Then we run it. The application doesn't do much, but in a few easy steps AppWizard has produced a fairly complete Windows application that can be enhanced with our intended functionality.

MFC Application Class Hierarchy

Our simple MFC SDI application contains the five highlighted classes in Figure 3.8. The interaction among these classes defines the behavior of the application. In a moment we will go through each class in detail. First let's examine how the classes interact.

CWinApp controls the application at its highest level. It is responsible for managing the relationships among the other classes. CDocument, CFormView, and CFrameWnd are responsible for managing and displaying the application user's data. You will add most of your application's functionality by augmenting the CView- and CDocument-derived classes. CFrameWnd is very functional as provided.

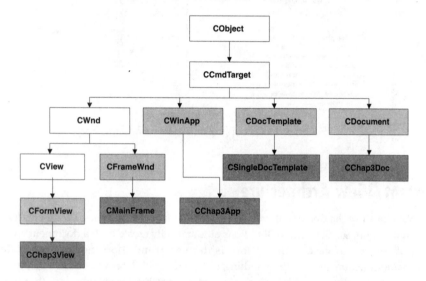

Figure 3.8 Abbreviated MFC application class hierarchy.

CDocument, CFormView, and CFrameWnd are collectively described as a *document template*. The document interacts with one or more views, and all views are contained inside a frame window. When the user selects **File/New**, CWinApp calls CDocTempate to create a new document/view/frame set. Applications can have more than one document type and thus would contain a list of document templates. This structure is illustrated in Figure 3.9.

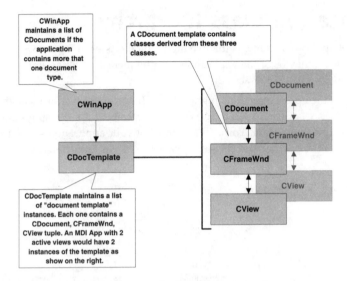

Figure 3.9 MFC application class relationships.

The Document/View Architecture

Most MFC applications use the document/view architecture that MFC supplies. When you use AppWizard to generate an application, the SDI and MDI options automatically create both a document and a view class. The document class (in our case, CChap3Doc) is derived from CDocument. Classes derived from CDocument provide functionality for the handling of "document" data. Whenever **File/New** is chosen, a new instance of CChap3Doc is created. CChap3Doc is responsible for storing data that our application should maintain when the user saves the document using **File/Save**. This data is loaded into the CChap3Doc class when the user reads a document from disk using **File/Open**. Of course, the concept of a *document* is different for every application. Microsoft Word's document is the internal representation of the characters, words, sentences, paragraphs, fonts, diagrams, and so on that the Word user creates. For Excel, the document is the internal representation of the spreadsheet and its figures and formulas.

The *view* part of the document/view architecture is responsible for rendering the document in the client area of the frame window or to a printer. Continuing the Word example, the view class will contain the code necessary to render the words, paragraphs, fonts, and so on of the document for presentation to the user. The view class provided by AppWizard for our application is CChap3View; it is derived from the CFormView class. The view is responsible for graphically displaying the data maintained in the CDocument-derived class. For our application, this view is actually a dialog resource that contains Windows controls. Our application has no associated data, so the document class is of little use. We will modify the CChap3View class to add the functions needed to test the Expression class.

The document/view architecture is important to most applications developed using MFC. For our purposes, though, it provides more functionality than we need. In Chapter 6, we will describe it in more detail as we develop an application that needs the architecture. ActiveX controls typically do not use the MFC document/view architecture, but the architecture can be used in the development of MFC-based ActiveX control containers, and, as we'll see in a later chapter, a view can contain instances of ActiveX controls.

AppWizard-Generated Files

Now that we've generated our first MFC application, let's look at the files that were produced by AppWizard. Table 3.1 briefly describes each file that AppWizard created. Next, we'll go through the classes and code that were generated for our application.

Table 3.1 AppWizard-Generated Files

Files	Purpose
chap3.h, chap3.cpp	CWinApp-derived class: CChap3App
mainfrm.h, mainfrm.cpp	Class for the main application window, CMainFrame
document.h, document.cpp	CDocument-derived class: CChap3Doc
view.h, view.cpp	CFormView-derived class: CChap3View
stdafx.h, stdafx.cpp	Application framework includes
chap3.def	Windows definition file
chap3.mak	Visual C++–maintained make file; you should not modify this file directly. Modifications should be made through the Visual C++ IDE
chap3.rc	Windows resource file; contains dialog definitions, string tables, and menu resources
resource.h	Include file with application and framework-defined IDs
res\chap3.ico	Icon for the application; used when minimized and shown in the default About box
res\document.ico	Icon representing the specific document type; this is useful when there are multiple document types within the application
res\chap3.rc2	User-editable resource file; Visual C++ will not touch this file. Maintains version information and so on

CDocument

The CDocument class and its derivatives encapsulate and maintain the data of a user document. This document is quite different from the one you are now reading. CDocument represents the way typical Windows applications handle the creating, saving, and retrieving of files from the Windows File menu. When the application user selects **File/New**, MFC creates a new CDocument object and, using the services of CView and CFrameWnd, displays the data contained in the document. The document class contains a pointer to the associated CView class. When data within the document is modified, CDocument is responsible for notifying the view that this modification has occurred. The view then determines whether the modified data is visible, and, if necessary, it updates the display.

The CDocument class stores data that needs to persist after the user closes the document. Temporary data that may be needed by the view when rendering should be maintained within the CView class. Think of an MFC document as a file (e.g., **TEST.DOC**) where you store your application data before, during, and after execution. How the data is stored is up to the developer, but MFC provides data serialization capabilities that simplify this process.

Our application does not require saving or retrieving data, so we don't actually need the CDocument-derived class, CChap3Doc. Table 3.2 contains useful members of the CDocument class. The functions that start with *On* are typically overridden in derived classes. Following are excerpts, with comments, from the **DOCUMENT.H** and **DOCUMENT.CPP** files. Our application will use the code as is.

```
//
// document.h
//
class CChap3Doc : public CDocument
{
...

    // Overrides
    // ClassWizard-generated virtual function overrides
    //{{AFX_VIRTUAL(CChap3Doc)
      public:
    // Override of the OnNewDocument function
    // Called when the user selects File/New or when the
    // framework initially displays the application
    virtual BOOL OnNewDocument();
    //}}AFX_VIRTUAL

// Implementation
public:
    virtual void Serialize(CArchive& ar);  // overridden for document i/o
...
};

//
// document.cpp
//
...
BOOL CChap3Doc::OnNewDocument()
{
    if (!CDocument::OnNewDocument())
        return FALSE;

    // TODO: add re-initialization code here
```

```
   // (SDI documents will reuse this document)

   return TRUE;
}

// CChap3Doc serialization
// You would add code here to save and restore
// any data maintained in CDocument
// This data defines the structure of the
// "document" when written to disk
void CChap3Doc::Serialize(CArchive& ar)
{
   if (ar.IsStoring())
   {
      // TODO: add storing code here
   }
   else
   {
      // TODO: add loading code here
   }
}
```

Table 3.2 Useful CDocument Functions

Member	Purpose
IsModified	Has the document been modified since last save?
SetModifiedFlag	Indicates that the document has changed since last save.
UpdateAllViews	Notifies each view that the document has changed.
DeleteContents	Called to clear a document (e.g., when the user opens a new document in an SDI application it must remove the previous document data).
OnCloseDocument	Called when the user selects **File/Close** or its equivalent.
OnNewDocument	Called when the user selects **File/New** or its equivalent.
OnSaveDocument	Called when the user selects **File/Save**.
OnOpenDocument	Called when the user selects **File/Open**.

CView

The MFC CView classes are responsible for the visual display of the document's data. The view class typi-cally handles Windows messages that relate to the rendering of information in the client area of a window and responds to command messages that may alter the display of the view. In our example application, the view class is defined in **VIEW.H** and **VIEW.CPP**.

We derived our view class from CFormView. CFormView associates a dialog resource with the client area of the frame window in an SDI application. Later, we will modify the dialog's resource file to add an entry field and two command buttons. Because CFormView uses a dialog resource as the view, we make sure that the client of the frame window is sized appropriately. The framework initially creates the frame window (and thus the client area) size using a default value stored in a static variable, rectDefault. For our purposes, we will override the OnInitialUpdate method and resize the frame window so that it is equal to our dialog resource. We'll do this in a moment, in our discussion of ClassWizard. Table 3.3 contains useful members of the CView class.

Table 3.3 Useful CView Members

Member	Purpose
GetDocument	Gets the CDocument instance associated with this view.
OnInitialUpdate	Called right after the view is attached to its associated document.
OnDraw	Called to render the document data within the view window.
OnPrint	Called to print or print preview the document.
OnUpdate	Called when the document data has changed, possibly requiring an update of the view.

CFrameWnd

The CFrameWnd class provides the functionality of a typical frame window in a Windows application. It contains and is responsible for the title bar, menu bar, status bar, and any control bars that are needed outside the client area. The frame window houses the application view, which in our application is an instance of CFormView. The frame creates the view and is responsible for many aspects of it. Our SDI application has only one frame window. It is the frame for both the application and our CDocument-derived class.

The CFrameWnd class provides much useful behavior that is standard for Windows applications. The menu bar contains the usual **File/New-**, **File/Open-**type commands and provides member functions that can be overridden to easily allow their implementation. The status bar and tool bars are easily maintained using methods provided within the CFrameWnd classes. I'm not going to show you the code generated by AppWizard for the CMainFrame class, because it is simple; however, it provides significant default functionality. There is one thing we should do for our CMainFrame: change its border so that it cannot be resized. We'll do this in a moment. Table 3.4 contains useful members of the CFrameWnd class.

Table 3.4 Useful CFrameWnd Members

Member	Purpose
Create	Creates a frame window.
LoadFrame	Creates a frame window based on a resource ID.
GetActiveDocument	Gets the active document.
GetActiveView	Gets the active view.

CDocTemplate

The CDocTemplate class manages the documents of an application. *Document* in this context includes the CFrameWnd-, CView-, and CDocument-derived classes. Information needed to instantiate the classes that form an application document is maintained in a CDocTemplate object. CWinApp contains a member variable, m_templateList, that maintains a list of all the valid document templates for the application. CDocTemplate is an abstract class with two standard MFC-derived classes: CSingleDocTemplate for SDI applications and CMultiDocTemplate for MDI applications. Following is the code that creates the document/view/frame template and adds it to the application's template list.

```
//
// chap3.cpp
//
...
BOOL CChap3App::InitInstance()
{
  ...
  // Register the application's document templates. Document templates
  // serve as the connection between documents, frame windows, and views.
  CSingleDocTemplate* pDocTemplate;
  pDocTemplate = new CSingleDocTemplate(
    IDR_MAINFRAME,
    RUNTIME_CLASS(CChap3Doc),
    RUNTIME_CLASS(CMainFrame),     // main SDI frame window
    RUNTIME_CLASS(CChap3View));
  // Update the list of valid "documents" for the application
  AddDocTemplate(pDocTemplate);
  ...
}
```

Table 3.5 Useful CDocTemplate Members

Member	Purpose
GetDocString	Retrieves document information from the resource file; examples include windowTitle, docName, filterName, etc.

CWinApp

Our main application class, CChap3App, is derived from CWinApp. CWinApp provides basic support for a Windows application. Except for one function, InitInstance, that has been overridden, CChap3App inherits all its functionality from CWinApp. The application instance is declared as a global object in

CHAP3.CPP. Global C++ objects are constructed *before* any application code is executed. This practice ensures that the application object is available before MFC enters `WinMain`. The standard Windows function `WinMain` is not provided within the `CWinApp` class but is provided by the framework. After MFC has set up its environment by registering window classes and initializing variables, including our already-constructed application instance, it calls the `InitInstance` member function, which is responsible for creating and displaying the main application window. `InitInstance`, as generated by AppWizard, is shown next:

```
// chap3.h
class CChap3App : public CWinApp {
  ...
  // Override of CWinApp InitInstance
  virtual BOOL InitInstance();
  ...
}

//
// chap3.cpp
//
...
// Global instance of CWinApp, constructed before WinMain() is called
CChap3App theApp;
...
BOOL CChap3App::InitInstance()
{
   // Standard initialization
   // If you are not using these features and wish to reduce the size
   //  of your final executable, you should remove from the following
   //  the specific initialization routines you do not need.

#ifdef _AFXDLL
   // Call this when using MFC in a shared DLL
   Enable3dControls();
#else
   // Call this when linking to MFC statically
   Enable3dControlsStatic();
#endif

   LoadStdProfileSettings();  // Load standard INI file options (including MRU)

   // Register the application's document templates.  Document templates
   //  serve as the connection between documents, frame windows and views.

   CSingleDocTemplate* pDocTemplate;
```

```
pDocTemplate = new CSingleDocTemplate(
    IDR_MAINFRAME,
    RUNTIME_CLASS(CChap3Doc),
    RUNTIME_CLASS(CMainFrame),          // main SDI frame window
    RUNTIME_CLASS(CChap3View));
AddDocTemplate(pDocTemplate);

// Parse command line for standard shell commands, DDE, file open
CCommandLineInfo cmdInfo;
ParseCommandLine(cmdInfo);

// Dispatch commands specified on the command line
if (!ProcessShellCommand(cmdInfo))
    return FALSE;

return TRUE;
}
```

InitInstance is called only once; its purpose is to set up the application environment and ultimately display the main window. Let's follow the preceding code.

Depending on the version of Windows that the application is running on, Enable3dControls either does nothing (Windows 95, Windows NT 4.0) or loads **CTL3D32.DLL** so that the standard Windows controls will appear three dimensional. LoadStdProfileSettings loads the MRU list of recently accessed files and attaches them to the File menu of the frame window if this feature has been enabled (in our case it has not). Next, a document template is created and our view/document/frame classes are associated with it. The application resource ID, IDR_MAINFRAME, is also included in the document template. This ID is used to load menus, toolbars, etc. for the application.

Every document type has certain resources. Typically, there are menu, string, accelerator, and icon resources associated with a document template. They are used in the creation of the frame window and child window areas. Pertinent sections of the **.RC** file are detailed next:

```
// chap3.rc - sections of the application resource file
...
// Icon
IDR_MAINFRAME        ICON  DISCARDABLE    "res\\chap3.ico"

IDR_CHAP3TYPE        ICON  DISCARDABLE    "res\\document.ico"

// Menu
IDR_MAINFRAME MENU PRELOAD DISCARDABLE
BEGIN
  POPUP "&File"
  BEGIN
    MENUITEM "&New\tCtrl+N",           ID_FILE_NEW
```

```
      MENUITEM "&Open...\tCtrl+O",    ID_FILE_OPEN
      MENUITEM "&Save\tCtrl+S",       ID_FILE_SAVE
   ...
END

// Accelerator
IDR_MAINFRAME ACCELERATORS PRELOAD MOVEABLE PURE
BEGIN
   ...
   "N",       ID_FILE_NEW,        VIRTKEY, CONTROL
   VK_F6,     ID_NEXT_PANE,       VIRTKEY
   ...
END

// This stringtable contains 7 substrings delimited by
// new lines (\n) that are used by the framework to define
// certain things.
STRINGTABLE PRELOAD DISCARDABLE
BEGIN
   IDR_MAINFRAME "Chapter 3 Example\n\nChap3\n\n\nChap3.Document\nChap3 Document"
END
```

The string table contains seven substrings that are used by the framework. The first item is the caption of the main window. The others contain the default document extension, document type name, and OLE type name (which we'll cover in the next chapter).

The RUNTIME_CLASS macro returns the run-time class structure that allows the document template to dynamically create instances of the document, view, and frame classes. Once the instance of CSingleDocTemplate is created, it is added to the list of application-supported document types by calling AddDocTemplate.

Next, an instance of the CommandLineInfo class is passed to ParseCommandLine, which parses the command line and updates the CommandLineInfo instance. By default, MFC provides seven command-line options, each of which is indicated by an enum and two Booleans maintained in the CommandLineInfo class shown next. Table 3.6 shows the syntax and actions provided by the default MFC implementation. The last two are OLE-specific; we'll have more to say about them in later chapters.

```
class CCommandLineInfo : public CObject
{
public:
   // Sets default values
   CCommandLineInfo();
   ~CCommandLineInfo();

   ...
```

```
enum{
    FileNew,
    FileOpen,
    FilePrint,
    FilePrintTo,
    FileDDE,
    FileNothing = -1
} m_nShellCommand;

BOOL m_bShowSplash;
BOOL m_bRunEmbedded;
BOOL m_bRunAutomated;
...
};
```

Table 3.6 MFC Default Command-Line Support

Command Line	Action
appname	Start with a new file.
Appname *filename*	Start and open the specified file.
Appnamne **/p** *filename*	Print the specified file to the default printer.
Appname **/pt** *filename* printer_port	Print the specified file to the specified printer.
Appname **/dde**	Start the application and await DDE command.
Appname **/Automation**	Start the application as an Automation server.
appname **/Embedding**	Start the application to edit an embedded OLE item.

Finally, ProcessShellCommand is called with the updated instance of CommandLineInfo. ProcessShellCommand then performs whatever action was specified on the command line. In most situations, this action will be a call to OnFileNew. In other cases, such as when the command line specifies the printing of a document, MFC will hide the application, print the document, and return FALSE from ProcessShellCommand. A return of FALSE forces the application to shut down.

In our case, OnFileNew starts everything. It calls OpenDocumentFile, which causes the creation of the document, which causes the creation of the frame window, which…. You get the idea. Figure 3.10 shows the process in fine detail. If everything works correctly, ProcessShellCommand returns TRUE to indicate that the main window has been created and processing should continue. Once this occurs, the framework invokes CWinApp::Run and starts processing the application's message loop.

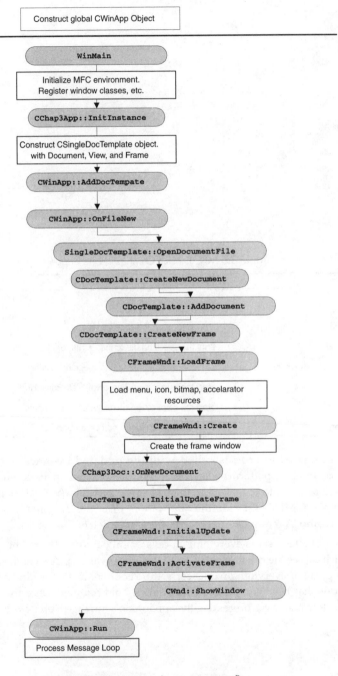

Figure 3.10 MFC application startup flow.

Table 3.7 describes some of the useful `CWinApp` members.

Table 3.7 Useful `CWinApp` Members

Member	Purpose
`m_hInstance`	Handle to the application instance.
`m_lpCmdLine`	Command line used to invoke the application.
`m_pMainWnd`	Pointer to application's main window.
`m_pszProfileName`	The application's INI filename.
`m_pszRegistryKey`	The complete registry key for the application; see the `SetRegistryKey`, `WriteProfileString`, and `GetProfileString` methods for details.
`AddDocTemplate`	Adds a document template, `CDocTemplate`, instance to the list of valid application documents.
`WriteProfileString`	Writes data to either the application's INI file or the system registry; the `SetRegistryKey` method determines which technique is used.
`ParseCommandLine`	Parses the command line that started the application; MFC provides default support for seven basic command-line options.
`ProcessShellCommand`	Opens a new file, prints a file provided on the command line, etc., depending on the state of the provided `CommandLineInfo` instance.
`InitInstance`	Initializes the application instance, used to define documents, views, and frames; sets up document templates and displays, initially, the main application window.
`Run`	Starts message loop, dispatches messages, etc.
`ExitInstance`	Called prior to exiting application.
`OnFileOpen`	Called when user selects **File/New**.

Editing and Adding Resources

We now have a simple MFC application that we can run, but it doesn't do much. Let's continue our quest to build an application that will use the `Expression` class from Chapter 2. We indicated to AppWizard that our view class should be derived from `CFormView`. This selection allows the client area to behave like a dialog box, which makes it easy to add controls. It isn't exactly a dialog box, but it does use a dialog resource to identify and position the controls.

To invoke the dialog editor, click the **Resource View** tab in the Project View window and then click the **chap3 resources** folder. This action brings up a list of the existing resource types in the application. Click the **Dialog** folder, and you should see two dialog resources: IDD_ABOUTBOX and IDD_CHAP3_FORM. AppWizard has created a default dialog resource for our `CChap3View` class. Double-click **IDD_CHAP3_FORM** and the dialog editor will look like Figure 3.11.

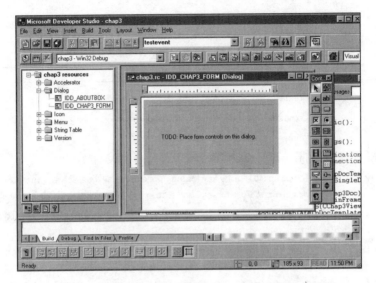

Figure 3.11 Editing the CChap3View dialog resource.

Resize the **To do** static field and change the text to **Enter an expression:**. Increase the size of the dialog box and add an entry field with an ID of IDC_EXPRESSION. Also, add two buttons: one with a caption of **Validate** and the other with a caption of **Evaluate**. Set the IDs for these buttons to IDC_VALIDATE and IDC_EVALUATE. When you're finished, it should look something like Figure 3.12.

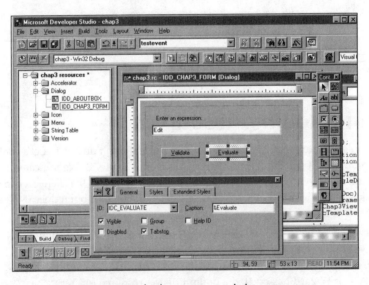

Figure 3.12 Finished CChap3View dialog resource.

Once we've modified the dialog resource and we recompile and relink, the application should have a working entry field and two push buttons. The dialog controls don't actually do anything yet. For that, we must tie a function to the specific control event using the Visual C++ ClassWizard.

ClassWizard

Even though you can't use AppWizard to change your application source once it has been initially generated, Visual C++ provides other tools to help with the management of various aspects of the application. ClassWizard performs many of these functions.

Visual C++ 2.0 added a useful feature to ClassWizard: ClassWizard now shows all the overridable (virtual) functions for the selected class in your application. This arrangement makes it easy to override the functions necessary to add functionality. In previous versions, you had to look up the function name, add the declaration to the header file, and implement the code in the **.CPP** file. ClassWizard now does everything except write the implementation code.

As I discussed earlier, we want the initial size of our frame window to be the same size as our CFormView dialog resource. The easiest way to do this is to override the OnInitialUpdate function of our view class, CChap3View. OnInitialUpdate is called right before the frame (and client) windows are displayed. This gives us time to resize the frame to match our dialog box. Start ClassWizard by pressing **Ctrl-W**. Click on the **Message Map** tab and select **CChap3View** from the drop-down list. Choose **CChap3View** in the **Object IDs** listbox. You should see a screen similar to Figure 3.13.

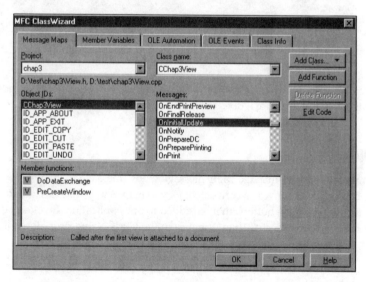

Figure 3.13 Overriding parent methods with ClassWizard.

Next, select the **OnInitialUpdate** method from the **Messages** listbox, click the **Add Function** button, and then click **Edit Code**. Add the following code:

```
void CChap3View::OnInitialUpdate()
{
    // TODO: Add your specialized code here and/or call the base class
    CFormView::OnInitialUpdate();

    // Set the frame window to the size of the Form (Dialog)
    GetParentFrame()->RecalcLayout();
    ResizeParentToFit( FALSE );
    ResizeParentToFit( TRUE );
}
```

While we're at it, we should ensure that our newly sized frame cannot be resized by the application user (now that it's the right size). We do this by removing the WS_BORDER window style just before the frame is created. Start ClassWizard again, choose the **CMainFrame** class, and override the PreCreateWindow method to do the following:

```
BOOL CMainFrame::PreCreateWindow(CREATESTRUCT& cs)
{
    // TODO: Add your specialized code here and/or call the base class

    // Don't include the WS_THICKFRAME style
    cs.style &= WS_THICKFRAME;

    return CFrameWnd::PreCreateWindow(cs);
}
```

Build the application to verify that its size is that of the dialog box we created for CFormView. You should be unable to resize the window, because it does not have a border.

Message Maps

ClassWizard also makes it easy to manage MFC message maps (message maps will be discussed in more detail in the next section), which provide a convenient way to map Windows messages to specific C++ functions. Let's do that for the two push buttons that we added to our application. Invoke ClassWizard (**Ctrl-W**) and click the **Message Map** tab. Select **CChap3View** from the **Class Name** drop-down list and you'll see a dialog box similar to Figure 3.14.

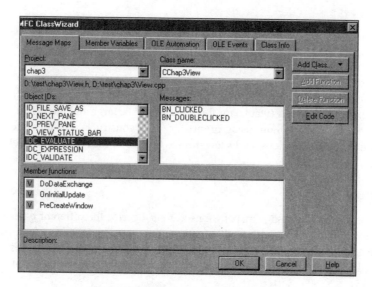

Figure 3.14 Message Maps dialog box.

Each of the custom IDs that we added through the dialog editor (e.g., IDC_EVALUATE) shows up under the **Object IDs**. When an ID is selected, the messages generated by the particular ID are displayed in the other listbox. We're interested in the BN_CLICKED message that is generated whenever a user clicks the push button. Click the **Add Function** button to add a member function for each button. This action should add two methods—OnValidate and OnEvaluate—to the CChap3View class. Now when the BN_CLICK message is generated from the IDC_VALIDATE push button, the OnValidate member function will be called. All this occurs through the magic of MFC message maps. Let's add one more message handler for instructional purposes. Select **CChap3View** in the **Object IDs** listbox and double-click on the **WM_LBUTTONDOWN** message to add a handler called OnLButtonDown.

Windows is a message-based operating environment. Everything that occurs does so because of a Windows or application *event* that is communicated through a Windows message. Anyone experienced in Windows programming understands this concept. The MFC libraries provide a mechanism called *message mapping* that hides somewhat the handling of these messages. Gone is the standard Windows GetMessage/DispatchMessage loop. Gone also are the enormous switch statements that SDK developers are used to. In their place are MFC message maps.

Microsoft implemented message mapping primarily because of the inherent inefficiencies of using the C++ virtual function mechanism. A good object-oriented solution would have been to provide a virtual function for each message that a particular object could handle. Here's an example of the how the CWnd class might have been implemented:

```
class CWnd : public CObject
{
    virtual int OnCreate( LPCREATESTRUCT& );
```

```
virtual void OnDestroy();
virtual void OnMove( int, int );
virtual void OnSize( UINT, int, int );

    ...
};
```

As you can imagine, the virtual table (vtable) for this class would be large and inefficient. MFC uses message maps to overcome this problem without using proprietary C++ constructs. The message map solution uses standard C++ notation and conventions (and a few macros to make things more readable).

Message Types

Before we take a look at MFC message maps, we need to categorize the different types of Windows messages. The ones we're most used to dealing with are those generated by Windows for a particular window. Examples include WM_PAINT, WM_LBUTTONDOWN, and WM_MOVE (basically, all the WM_ messages except WM_COMMAND). We'll classify these messages as *window messages*; they are, by their nature, destined to be handled by a window.

The WM_COMMAND message is used for two purposes. The first is for Windows control notification messages. These messages typically are sent from a child window to its parent. For example, in our application, the CFormView class contains an entry field and two command buttons. Each of these elements is a child window to the parent (the client window). When a command button is pressed, a WM_COMMAND message containing a BN_CLICKED notification code is passed to the parent.

The second use of WM_COMMAND messages is in the communication of menu selections and accelerator key presses. These messages aren't meant for a specific window, but they can be sent to various objects within the application as a whole. In our example application, the **File/New** selection generates a WM_COMMAND containing ID_FILE_NEW. This message could be handled by the frame object, the document object, or the view. Because WM_COMMAND messages need to be routed to various application objects, they are treated differently from standard Windows messages and control notification messages. Next, we'll detail how each message type is handled.

Window Messages and Control Notifications

Standard window messages and control window notifications are handled by a window. In MFC, all window objects derive from the CWnd class. CWnd has default message handlers for many of the standard window messages. If you were to look at the declaration for CWnd, you would see the following function declaration:

```
afxmsg void OnLButtonDown( UINT nFlags, CPoint point );
```

OnLButtonDown isn't virtual, but it provides a default implementation for the message mapping architecture. CWnd::OnLButtonDown calls the default window procedure if no window overrides or contains a message map entry for WM_LBUTTONDOWN.

We want to implement a message handler for the WM_LBUTTONDOWN message in our view class, so let's see how that works. Here's what ClassWizard added to the CChap3View class:

```
//
// view.h
//
...
class CChap3View : public CFormView
{
protected: // create from serialization only
    CChap3View();
    DECLARE_DYNCREATE(CChap3View)
...
// Generated message map functions
protected:
    //{{AFX_MSG(CChap3View)
    afx_msg void OnEvaluate();
    afx_msg void OnValidate();
    afx_msg void OnLButtonDown(UINT nFlags, CPoint point);
    //}}AFX_MSG
 DECLARE_MESSAGE_MAP()
};

// in view.cpp

BEGIN_MESSAGE_MAP(CChap3View, CFormView)
    //{{AFX_MSG_MAP(CChap3View)
    ON_BN_CLICKED(IDC_EVALUATE, OnEvaluate)
    ON_BN_CLICKED(IDC_VALIDATE, OnValidate)
    ON_WM_LBUTTONDOWN()
    //}}AFX_MSG_MAP
END_MESSAGE_MAP()
```

This code in **VIEW.H** and **VIEW.CPP** sets up a static array of message-map entries for the CChap3View class. The DECLARE_MESSAGE_MAP macro does most of the work. It creates a message map with three entries, each of which has its own unique signature (maintained by the framework). We're discussing the OnLButtonDown handler for now; we'll discuss the ON_BN_CLICKED entries next, but they are in the message map. The code in **VIEW.CPP** initializes the message map with the function addresses for our handler, CChap3View::OnLButtonDown, and initializes a pointer in the message map that points to our base class (CFormView) message map. The ON_WM_LBUTTONDOWN entry is a little tricky, because it doesn't contain the name of the function handler. When you added the WM_LBUTTONDOWN handler using ClassWizard, it didn't give you an opportunity to change the handler's name. The name of the handler must match that declared in the CWnd class. It's just like overriding a parent class member.

We know that CWnd has a default handler for OnLButtonDown, but we want *our* handler to be called instead. How does MFC do it? When the WM_LBUTTONDOWN message is generated by pressing the left button within the client area of our application, CWnd::WindowProc is called. If the message is not a command message, the message map for the "most derived" class (CChap3View) is checked for an entry that matches the message. If an entry in the map is not found in that class, the next class in the chain is checked, and so on. This continues until the inheritance hierarchy is exhausted. If no one handles the message, it is passed to DefWindowProc for default processing. If a handler is found, it is called and the search stops. Then it is important to call the parent's implementation of the handler if additional processing is required. In our example, once we process the OnLButtonDown event, we pass the message to our parent CFormView by directly calling its implementation.

Handling window messages is wonderfully easy using MFC, once you get the hang of it.

Command Messages

In the previous example, once we reached CWnd in the search for a handler and none was found, the framework called DefWindowProc. Command messages are treated differently. First, if command messages never find a handler, instead of calling a default hander, they're ignored. Second, command messages can be routed to various framework objects and not just to windows. A special class, CCmdTarget, provides the routing of command messages between the framework objects. Any class derived from CCmdTarget (including, of course, a CWnd-derived class; CWnd is derived from CCmdTarget) can participate in the receiving and routing of command messages.

What about our BN_CLICKED messages that are generated when a user clicks one of our command buttons? Well, technically, BN_CLICKED is a control notification message and it should be handled like the other standard Windows messages. But because command buttons can be used as tool bar buttons, the framework treats them as if they were command messages. They can be routed like all command messages.

NOTE In reality, all control notification messages, not just BN_CLICKED, can be routed like command messages. This capability is explained in detail in MFC Tech Note 21, but its use outside of BN_CLICKED, where it has a specific purpose, is not recommended because ClassWizard does not support this feature.

Command messages from menus or tool bars are typically first received by the application's frame window. Without the ability to *route* these messages using CCmdTarget and the message-mapping architecture, all commands would have to be handled in the CMainFrame class, which is not where you would typically want an MFC application. Command routing follows the course illustrated in Figure 3.15. When a frame window command message is received, it is routed first to the active view. If no handler is found, the routing continues all the way to the application object. If it is not processed by any object, it is discarded.

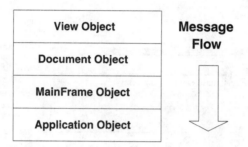

Figure 3.15 Command routing in an SDI application.

Command messages that contain control notifications (e.g., BN_CLICKED, EN_CHANGED) are received by their parent window, which is usually a dialog window. In our example, the button controls send their messages to the parent window—which is the view—and not to the application's frame window. This is the primary difference between command messages that are not actual control notifications and those command messages that are.

We have taken a quick look at the MFC library message maps for processing and routing Windows messages. Within the MFC libraries, this powerful concept of message routing is not confined to the handling of Windows messages. This concept is used in various MFC areas, including COM and OLE. So we've briefly stopped to ponder what message maps are and how they work. Later, understanding various concepts of COM, OLE, and ActiveX in the context of MFC will be easier.

Adding the Expression Class

We now have all the pieces in place to add the functionality from the Expression class that we developed in the last chapter. To do this, first copy the **EXPRESS.CPP** and **EXPRESS.H** files from the CD-ROM (**EXAMPLES\CHAP3**) to the working directory for your CHAP3 project. Then, from the Insert menu select **Insert Files into Project...** and add the file **EXPRESS.CPP** to the project (see Figure 3.16).

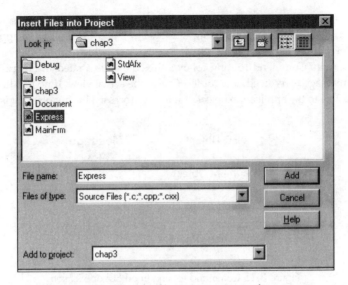

Figure 3.16 Adding the file **EXPRESS.CPP** to the project.

Add a forward declaration for the `Expression` class and add an `Expression` class pointer member variable to the `CChap3View` class as follows:

```
//
// view.h : interface of the CChap3View class
//
/////////////////////////////////////////////////////////////////////////////

// Forward declaration of Expression class
class Expression;
class CChap3View : public CFormView
{
...
protected:
  Expression*  m_pExpression;
...
};
```

Now we need to do something when the user clicks the `Validate` and `Evaluate` keys on the form view. Add the following code to **VIEW.CPP** to use the `Expression` class:

```
//
// view.cpp : implementation of the CChap3View class
//

#include "stdafx.h"
```

```
#include "chap3.h"

#include "document.h"
#include "view.h"

// Include our Expression class declarations
#include "express.h"

...
//////////////////////////////////////////////////////////////////////////////
// CChap3View construction/destruction
CChap3View::CChap3View()
    : CFormView(CChap3View::IDD)
{
   //{{AFX_DATA_INIT(CChap3View)
   // NOTE: the ClassWizard will add member initialization here
   //}}AFX_DATA_INIT

   // TODO: add construction code here
   m_pExpression = new Expression;
}

...

void CChap3View::OnEvaluate()
{
   // TODO: Add your message handler code here
   CString strExpression;
   char szTemp[128];

   // Get the expression from the entry field
   CWnd* pWnd = GetDlgItem(IDC_EXPRESSION);
   ASSERT( pWnd );
   pWnd->GetWindowText( strExpression );

   TRACE1( "OnEvaluate: Expression is %s\n", strExpression );

   // Set the expression to evaluate
   m_pExpression->SetExpression( strExpression, TRUE );
   long lResult = m_pExpression->Evaluate();
   sprintf( szTemp, "%ld", lResult );

   // Update the entry field with the result
   pWnd->SetWindowText( szTemp );

   // Set focus back to the entry field
   GetDlgItem( IDC_EXPRESSION )->SetFocus();
```

```
}
void CChap3View::OnValidate()
{
    // TODO: Add your message handler code here

    CString strExpression;

    // Get the expression from the entry field
    CWnd* pWnd = GetDlgItem( IDC_EXPRESSION );
    ASSERT( pWnd );
    pWnd->GetWindowText( strExpression );

    TRACE1( "OnValidate: Expression is %s\n", strExpression );

    m_pExpression->SetExpression( strExpression, TRUE );
    if (! m_pExpression->Validate() )
        AfxMessageBox( "Invalid Expression, try again" );

    // Set focus back to the entry field
    GetDlgItem(IDC_EXPRESSION)->SetFocus();
}
```

Once you've entered the code, compile, link, and run the application in debug. Everything should work. Figure 3.17 shows the finished application with a complex expression about to be evaluated. After you terminate the application, examine the **Debug** tab and see whether there are any problems with the application. There should be, so let's review some MFC debugging techniques.

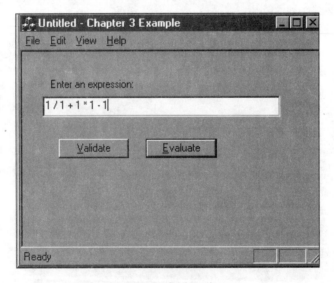

Figure 3.17 Finished application.

MFC Debugging Techniques

The MFC libraries provide a rich set of functions and classes for debugging applications. We'll look at a couple of the debugging features available to MFC developers. In later chapters, we'll use more-sophisticated techniques as we develop complex applications. Windows application debugging is a difficult task, but when you introduce COM into the equation—with multiple, interacting processes—it gets hairy. Luckily, MFC provides facilities to help with this process.

First, there are the TRACE macros which allow you to display messages as your code is executing. In the previous example, we used the TRACE1 macro to update the actual expression in the OnEvaluate and OnValidate methods. The TRACE macros work just like the old C-style printf functions, so you can format the output however you like. To see the trace output, however, you must compile and link your project in debug. This basically means defining the _DEBUG flag.

Second, there's the ASSERT macro, which is provided by MFC. It is a simple enhancement of the C-style assert function. The ASSERT macro is a convenient way of checking the validity of your program's variables; it provides a basic sanity check. The ASSERT macro is used like this:

```
// Get the expression from the entry field
CWnd* pWnd = GetDlgItem(IDC_EXPRESSION);
ASSERT( pWnd );
pWnd->GetWindowText( strExpression );
```

We're about 100 percent sure that we will get a valid, non-null pointer back from the GetDlgItem method, but just to be sure, we assert that it is nonzero. If this assertion fails, the ASSERT macro will pop up a dialog box informing us that it failed, and it will provide the file and line number where it failed. It is a good idea to sprinkle your code with assertions like this; it helps tremendously during the debugging phase of a project. You can't have too many, because they don't affect the size or performance of the release version of your program. If the _DEBUG flag is not set, the ASSERT macro is defined as nothing (i.e., the code is removed).

The MFC source code is a great example of this technique. There are thousands of ASSERTs throughout the MFC source code. There are also specialized versions. ASSERT_POINTER asserts that the parameter is a valid MFC-based pointer. ASSERT_KINDOF tests whether a class instance is a specific type of class. There are several other ASSERTs as well. Check out the MFC source code and the help files for more information.

Another nice feature provided by MFC is its tracking of every memory allocation (new) and deallocation (delete) that your application performs. If you somehow forget to delete something that you have allocated, MFC will dump (to the debug window) the source file and line number of the specific allocation that was not deallocated, assuming that you adhere to the following rules:

1. Derive your class directly or indirectly from CObject. Almost all the classes in MFC derive from CObject, so this shouldn't be a problem.

2. Within your class declaration, include the DECLARE_DYNCREATE(*classname*) macro and within the **.CPP** file for your class, include the IMPLEMENT_DYNCREATE(*classname*, *parentclass*) macro.

3. In your **.CPP** file, after any IMPLEMENT_DYNCREATE() macros, change the line: `#define` new to be DEBUG_NEW. This is added by default when you compile with _DEBUG defined.

In the example, we forgot to delete the `Expression` instance that we created in the constructor of the view class. When you terminate the application, you should see something similar to the following in the debug window:

```
Loaded symbols for 'C:\WINNT\system32\MFC42D.DLL'
Loaded symbols for 'C:\WINNT\system32\MSVCRTD.DLL'
  ...
Detected memory leaks!
Dumping objects ->
strcore.cpp(76) : {159} normal block at 0x004127A0, 20 bytes long.
 Data: <          2343> 01 00 00 00 07 00 00 00 07 00 00 00 32 33 34 33
D:\test\chap3\View.cpp(41) : {65} normal block at 0x004118B0, 8 bytes long.
 Data: < 'A      > AC 27 41 00 01 00 00 00
Object dump complete.
The program 'D:\test\chap3\Debug\chap3.exe' has exited with code 0 (0x0).
```

Because the AppWizard provided the DEBUG_NEW definition for us, we can immediately determine which line of code allocated memory but did not delete it. Line 41 of **VIEW.CPP** looks like this:

```
///////////////////////////////////////////////////////////////////////////
// CChap3View construction/destruction
CChap3View::CChap3View()
     : CFormView(CChap3View::IDD)
{
   m_pExpression = new Expression;
}
```

Just as we thought, we forgot to deallocate our `Expression` instance. MFC can do even more. If we derive our class from CObject and add the DECLARE_DYNCREATE and IMPLEMENT_DYNCREATE macros, MFC will display the class name of the object that wasn't deallocated. Classes derived from CObject inherit run-time type identification (RTTI) abilities. (This isn't the C++ standard RTTI, but it provides similar capabilities.) This arrangement allows the debugger to determine the type and name of the object that wasn't deallocated.

This behavior is provided by the DECLARE_DYNAMIC and IMPLEMENT_DYNAMIC macros as well as the DYNCREATE macros we are using. The DYNCREATE macros also allow MFC to dynamically create instances of classes at run time. We've used DYNCREATE instead of the more basic DYNAMIC macros here, because in the next chapter MFC will need the DYNCREATE feature to create instances of COM-enabled classes. Here's an example of adding the new macros to the `Expression` class:

```
// express.h
...
class Expression : public CObject
```

```
{
protected:
  DECLARE_DYNCREATE( Expression )
...
};

// express.cpp

...

#include <stdio.h>
#include <stdlib.h>
#include <string.h>
#include <ctype.h>

#include "express.h"
IMPLEMENT_DYNCREATE( Expression, CObject )
```

Now we get even more information about our memory leak. In addition to the line number, MFC informs us of the class name that caused the problem:

```
Loaded symbols for 'C:\WINNT\system32\MFC42D.DLL'
Loaded symbols for 'C:\WINNT\system32\MSVCRTD.DLL'
...
Detected memory leaks!
Dumping objects ->
strcore.cpp(76) : {401} normal block at 0x00411D00, 17 bytes long.
 Data: <            235 > 01 00 00 00 04 00 00 00 04 00 00 00 32 33 35 20
D:\test\chap3\View.cpp(41) :
        {65} client block at 0x004118B0, subtype 0, 12 bytes long.
a Expression object at $004118B0, 12 bytes long
Object dump complete.
The program 'D:\test\chap3\Debug\chap3.exe' has exited with code 0 (0x0).
```

To fix the leak, we need to ensure that we delete the Expression instance in the destructor of the view class:

```
CChap3View::~CChap3View()
{
   delete m_pExpression;
}
```

When you're developing MFC applications, I recommend that you use all the available features. You're paying for them with the additional overhead, so you should take advantage of what they offer in the way of application debugging. The use of DYNCREATE is a simple example. There are several classes designed just for debugging. When you get a chance, check out the features of the CObject, CMemoryState, and CDumpContext classes.

Summary

In this chapter, we reviewed the benefits of developing software with Visual C++ and Microsoft's Foundation Class libraries. Using Visual C++ and MFC allows us to be more productive as Windows developers, because we can focus on the problems being solved rather than on continually solving old ones. We reviewed the main design features of MFC, and in the process we completed a simple MFC application that tested the Expression class from Chapter 2.

The only way to really understand MFC is to dive into the source code. It is included with the professional edition in the default location **\MSDEV\MFC\SRC**. Next time you're debugging your code, go ahead and step into those MFC functions. It may be confusing at first, but after some time you'll begin to understand what's going on. Then watch your productivity skyrocket (or plummet if you get too enthralled with what's happening).

This book is about developing COM-based components and ActiveX controls, so let's get started.

Chapter *4*

Microsoft's Component Object Model

In Chapter 3 we looked at Visual C++ and the MFC libraries and how they can help in the development of Windows software. In this chapter we will take a detailed look at Microsoft's Component Object Model (COM). Microsoft's COM provides the binary standard that we need to make our software more reusable, and we'll provide much low-level detail about how COM provides a binary standard wrapper for software components. You don't need to know this level of detail to use the technology, but if you understand what's going on at this level, you'll have a much easier time. It will also help when something goes wrong and you must do some low-level debugging. To paraphrase the great physicist Richard P. Feynman, once you understand the universe at the atomic level, everything else is easy. And so it is with COM: once you comprehend it at its lowest level, the rest (OLE, ActiveX) is simple.

The sample code in this chapter, except for the two example applications at the end, is used strictly for illustration and is not expected to be compiled and run. Instead, it's intended to demonstrate various C++ techniques used in building COM-based, binary standard components. After this chapter, we will be using the MFC implementation of COM, OLE, and ActiveX. Chapter 5 will provide a transition from the low-level COM to the higher-level ActiveX and MFC. So hang tight, we'll soon be doing some cool things.

NOTE There is much confusion about what COM, OLE, and ActiveX are and how they are different. COM is a *system*-level standard that provides basic object model services on which to build higher-level services. OLE and ActiveX are examples of a higher-level service. OLE and ActiveX provide application-level features but are built using COM's services. So the terms *COM, OLE,* and *ActiveX* are somewhat interchangeable in that their capabilities and features are closely related. However, each term describes a separate set of technologies. OLE and ActiveX are built using COM, as are other new Microsoft technologies, such as the DirectX game SDK. All its services are accessed through COM-based interfaces. So don't let these terms get in the way of your understanding. We'll discuss COM in this chapter and then move to OLE and ActiveX in the remaining chapters. Just remember that OLE and ActiveX are primarily COM-based interface definitions with a few APIs thrown in to help.

113

A Binary Standard

In previous chapters, we discussed the importance of binary standards to the development of software components. Binary standards allow easy interoperation and reuse of components across language implementations (such as Microsoft and Borland C++), between disparate languages (such as Visual Basic and C++), and across process boundaries. COM is such a standard. We've discussed the benefits of using binary standards and the benefits of developing software applications using them. Now we're ready to dig into the details of how it all works.

In Chapter 2, we developed a C++ class, Expression, that we will continue to use in this chapter. Our design of the Expression class allows for easy reuse within the C++ language environment. Our goal now is to use COM to augment the Expression class so that it can be shared across various languages and processes.

When used within C++, the Expression class is a compile-time construct. We can create instances of Expression at run time, but the definition of Expression and how it behaves cannot change at run time. To use the Expression class in C++, you must include its definition (for example, **EXPRESS.H**). If the implementation for Expression changes, the program using it may need to be recompiled and relinked. COM eliminates this dependency on compile-time definitions by providing run-time mechanisms to query a component's functionality.

We will use the C++ language to implement our COM objects. COM does not require that you use C++ for its implementation, but, as you will see, because of the internal structure of COM objects C++ is the preferred method.

Component Interfaces

One important aspect of a software component is its interface. The component's interface is its contract with the user, and it describes exactly what can be done. As we've discussed, the other important feature of a software component is complete encapsulation of its implementation details. COM provides this capability by defining a standard way of implementing the interfaces of a COM object. Recall the public interface of the Expression class:

```
class Expression : public CObject
{
...
// Here's the interface
public:
   CString  GetExpression();
   void     SetExpression( CString strExp, BOOL bInfix );

   BOOL     Validate();
   long     Evaluate();
};
```

Because the interface is the essence of our component, we need a binary standard way of making it available to non–C++ users. The COM, OLE, and ActiveX specifications are composed mostly of interfaces. Once you understand the concept of a COM interface, the rest is easy. The following example code shows how a simple COM interface is implemented in C++:

```
// public interface definition of our Expression component
// An abstract class
class IExpression
{
public:
   virtual CString GetExpression() = 0;
   virtual void SetExpression( CString str, BOOL bInfix ) = 0;
   virtual BOOL Validate() = 0;
   virtual long Evaluate() = 0;
};

// Inherit from the abstract Interface definition class
class Expression : public IExpression
{
// Class Implementation here, just as before
...
// Here's the interface implementation
public:
   virtual CString  GetExpression();
   virtual void     SetExpression( CString strExp, BOOL bInfix );
   virtual BOOL     Validate();
   virtual long     Evaluate();
};
```

First, we declare a new class that is abstract and contains only the public functions of our class. All interface functions are declared pure virtual. This new class is called IExpression; the *I* indicates that it is an interface declaration. COM uses this nomenclature throughout its implementation. The IExpression class provides an external interface declaration for our Expression object. It also forces the creation of a virtual function table (Vtable) in any derived classes.

This polymorphic use of virtual functions in a base class is central to the design of COM. It provides a Vtable that contains only the public methods (the interface) of the class. The IExpression class contains no data members and no implementation functions. Its only purpose is to force the derived class, Expression, to implement, virtually, the methods of the component interface.

Because we allow access only through a Vtable pointer, access to the members of the component implementation is impossible. Only those functions declared in the interface class are available to the component user. Study the preceding example. It is fairly small and simple, and it contains the core concept of COM: the use of Vtables to hide the implementation of component interfaces. A COM interface is just a pointer to a pointer to a C++-style Vtable. This relationship is illustrated in Figure 4.1.

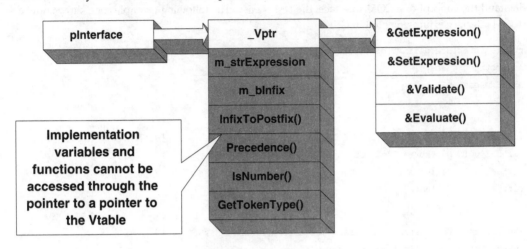

Figure 4.1 COM Vtable usage.

Following is an example of how a client application might use the IExpression interface provided by the Expression class. This example isn't a true implementation of COM but rather is simplified to show, conceptually, how COM works.

```
// An identifier for our Expression class
#define CLSID_Expression 1000

// This provides a standard method of obtaining
// an instance pointer for the specified object
RESULT GetObject( OBJID objId, void** ppv )
{
    if (  objId == CLSID_Expression )
    {
      *ppv = new Expression;
      return ( S_OK );
    }
    else
      return( E_INVALID_OBJECT_ID );
}

void RemoveObject( void* pv )
{
    delete pv;
}
```

```
main()
{
   IExpression* pIExpression;
   if ( GetObject( CLSID_Expression, (void**) &pIExpression ) == S_OK )
   {
      pIExpression->SetExpression( "1 + 2", TRUE );
      cout << pIExpression->Evaluate() << endl;
      RemoveObject( pIExprBAD );
   }
}
```

Given our previous `Expression` declarations, we implement a function, `GetObject`, that takes as a parameter an object ID that identifies the specific component that we need and returns a pointer to that component object. As illustrated in the `main()` section, the user of the component requires knowledge only of the `IExpression` interface to use the object effectively. The `GetObject` function could possible reside outside the client's executable or even outside the client's process. The `RemoveObject` function is called when the client is finished with the component. `RemoveObject` is responsible for deleting the component instance when all clients are finished using it. But we're getting ahead of ourselves.

Standard COM Interfaces

The preceding example is not yet a COM object. COM requires that at least one standard interface be present in an object to qualify it as a COM object. `IUnknown` is the one interface that all COM objects must support. `IUnknown` serves two purposes. The first is to provide a standard way for the component user (or client) to ask for a specific interface within a given component. `QueryInterface`, a method of `IUnknown`, provides this capability. The second purpose is to help in the management of the component's lifetime. The `IUnknown` interface provides two methods—`AddRef` and `Release`—that provide lifetime management of a component instance. Here is the definition of `IUnknown`:

```
class IUnknown
{
   virtual HRESULT   QueryInterface( REFIID riid, void** ppv ) = 0;
   virtual ULONG     AddRef() = 0;
   virtual ULONG     Release() = 0;
};
```

As you can see, `IUnknown` is an abstract class that provides the requirements for all classes that derive from it. It mandates that the three methods be implemented in the deriving class. It also ensures that the deriving class will have a Vtable, just as in the `IExpression` interface we examined earlier.

   `QueryInterface` returns a pointer to a specific interface (such as `IUnknown` or `IExpression`) contained within a COM object. The first parameter, `REFIID`, is a reference to the specific interface ID, which is a unique identifier for the interface we are querying for. The second parameter, `void**`, is the location where the interface pointer will be returned. The return value, an HRESULT, is a handle to a COM-specific error structure that contains any error information. We'll get to the details later; right now we're trying to grasp the big picture.

In our example, if a user requires the services of the Expression class, he or she would request the IExpression interface. This request can be made through an existing IUnknown interface (on an Expression component) or can be requested during the component's instantiation. COM requires that the IUnknown interface be present in any COM object and that all COM interfaces also contain the IUnknown interface. This arrangement allows a component user to obtain an interface pointer to any interface within the component by querying any existing interface on that component. Here's what our example looks like with the IUnknown interface added:

```
// public interface definition
// An abstract class that derives from IUnknown
class IExpression : public IUnknown
{
public:
    virtual CString GetExpression() = 0;
    virtual void SetExpression( CString str, BOOL bInfix ) = 0;
    virtual BOOL Validate() = 0;
    virtual long Evaluate() = 0;
};

// Derive from the abstract Interface definition class
class Expression : public IExpression
{
// Class Implementation here, just as before
...
// Here's the interface implementation
public:
    virtual HRESULT  QueryInterface( REFIID riid, void** ppv );
    virtual ULONG    Release();

    virtual ULONG    AddRef();

    virtual CString  GetExpression();
    virtual void     SetExpression( CString strExp, BOOL bInfix );
    virtual BOOL     Validate();
    virtual long     Evaluate();
};
```

The addition of deriving IExpression from IUnknown requires us to now implement seven methods: three from IUnknown and the four original Expression class methods. We now have a Vtable in our class that looks like Figure 4.2.

Vtable

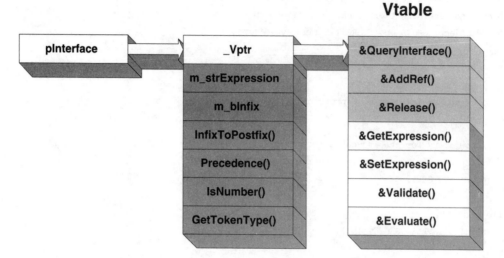

Figure 4.2 Expression class with `IUnknown` added.

Our example now looks like this. We've added the implementation of `IUnknown::QueryInterface`.

```
// The identifier for the COM IUnknown interface
#define IID_IUnknown 1
// An identifier for our Expression class
#define CLSID_Expression 1000
// An identifier for our IExpression interface
#define IID_IExpression 2000

HRESULT Expression::QueryInterface( REFIID riid, void** ppv )
{
   // Our Expression class contains both of these
   // interfaces so returning a pointer to this provides
   // both implementations. The client will cast the returned
   // pointer to the appropriate pointer type.
   switch( riid ) {
     case IID_IUnknown:
     case IID_IExpression:
        *ppv = this;
        return( S_OK );
     default:
        return( E_NOINTERFACE );
   }
}
```

```
// This provides a standard method of creating a component
// object and returning the requested interface on that object
RESULT GetObject( OBJID objId, REFIID riid, void** ppv )
{
    if (  objId == CLSID_Expression )
    {
        // Create an instance of Expression
        *ppv = new Expression;

        // Now query for the requested interface
        ( ( Expression* ) ( *ppv ) )->QueryInterface( riid, ppv );
        return ( S_OK );
    }
    else
      return( E_INVALID_OBJECT_ID );
}

void RemoveObject( void* pv )
{
    delete pv;
}

main()
{
    IUnknown*     pIUnknown;
    IExpression* pIExpression;

    // Create an Expression component and get its
    // IUnknown interface
    GetObject( CLSID_Expression, IID_IUnknown, (void**) &pIUnknown );
    // Now use the IUnknown interface to get the
    // IExpression interface
    pIUnknown->QueryInterface( IID_IExpression, (void**) &pIExpression );

    // Now use the IExpression interface pointer
    pIExpression->SetExpression( "1 + 2", TRUE );
    cout << pIExpression->Evaluate() << endl;

    RemoveObject( pIExpression );
};
```

The implementation of QueryInterface may be a little difficult to comprehend at this point. All it does is to return a pointer to the Vtable pointer for the Expression object. Because IExpression is derived from IUnknown, a pointer to the Expression object provides both interfaces. The preceding code won't actually compile and run—a few things are still missing—but I hope you're getting the idea.

There is a standard way of depicting COM objects and their interfaces. Figure 4.3 depicts our Expression class with its IExpression and IUnknown interfaces. IUnknown is shown on the upper right, because it is always required and so will be present in any COM object. Other interfaces are usually shown on the left-hand side of the component. Remember, though, that every interface on the left contains an IUnknown interface, too. Every COM interface implements IUnknown.

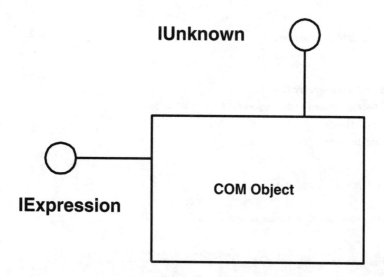

Figure 4.3 COM object representation.

Component Lifetimes

We've learned that access to a component interface is obtained through IUnknown::QueryInterface. The other two functions provided by IUnknown are used to control the lifetime of the component object. This process is termed *reference counting*.

Each component class contains a member variable, usually named m_dwRef, that maintains a count of the outstanding references to (or clients of) its COM interfaces. The interface user has only a pointer to a pointer to the object and so cannot directly delete the object when finished. In reality, the client shouldn't think of deleting the object anyway, because others may be using the same component object. Only the COM object can determine when it can or should be deleted. The object's reference count is controlled by the client using the AddRef and Release functions of IUnknown. This is one reason every COM interface must contain an implementation of IUnknown. Let's use our simple Expression example to describe the reference counting requirements.

```
class IUnknown
{
   virtual HRESULT  QueryInterface( REFIID riid, void** ppv ) = 0;
   virtual ULONG    AddRef() = 0;
   virtual ULONG    Release() = 0;
};

class IExpression : public IUnknown
{
public:
   virtual CString GetExpression() = 0;
   virtual void SetExpression( CString str, BOOL bInfix ) = 0;
   virtual BOOL Validate() = 0;
   virtual long Evaluate() = 0;
};

class Expression : public IExpression
{
// Class Implementation here, just as before.
...

   // Add a new member variable to keep track of the
   // outstanding interface references to an instantiation
   // Initialize to zero during construction
   DWORD m_dwRef;

public:
   // Nothing has changed here
   virtual HRESULT  QueryInterface( REFIID riid, void** ppv );
   virtual ULONG    Release();
   virtual ULONG    AddRef();

   virtual CString  GetExpression();
   virtual void     SetExpression( CString strExp, BOOL bInfix );
   virtual BOOL     Validate();
   virtual long     Evaluate();
};

HRESULT Expression::QueryInterface( REFIID riid, void** ppv )

{
   switch( riid ) {
     case IID_IUnknown:
```

```
      case IID_IExpression:
          *ppv = this;

          // We're returning a new interface pointer
          // so call AddRef on the new pointer
          ( (LPUNKNOWN) *ppv)->AddRef();
          return( S_OK );

      default:
          return( E_NOINTERFACE );
   }
}

Expression::Expression ()
{
      m_dwRef = 0;
      m_bInFix = TRUE;
}

// IUnknown::Release implementation
ULONG Expression::Release()
{
   m_dwRef-;

   // When the reference count reaches zero
   // delete ourselves
   if ( m_dwRef == 0 )
   {
      delete this;
      // Can't return m_dwRef, it's gone
      return 0;
   }
   else
      return m_dwRef;
}

// IUnknown::AddRef implementation
ULONG Expression::AddRef()
{
   m_dwRef++;
   return m_dwRef;
}
```

To support the AddRef and Release functions of IUnknown we added a member variable, m_dwRef, that keeps a count of the current references, or outstanding interface pointers, to our object. The AddRef and Release functions directly affect a COM interface, but an interface is not an instance of the object itself. This object can have any number of users of its interfaces at a given time and must maintain an internal count of its active interfaces. When this count reaches zero, the object is free to delete itself. It is important that object users diligently AddRef and Release the interfaces when appropriate. If they don't, the component will hang around forever (or until a reboot, whichever comes first). The AddRef, Release pair is similar to the new, delete pair used to manage memory in C++. Whenever a user obtains a new interface pointer or assigns its value to another variable, AddRef should be called through the new pointer. You must be careful, though, because many COM interface functions return pointers to interfaces; in these cases, the functions call AddRef through the returned pointer. The most obvious example is QueryInterface. It always calls AddRef after allocating a new interface, so it isn't necessary to call AddRef again. Here are some examples:

```
// The initial CoCreateInstance calls QueryInterface internally.
// We'll study this COM function in a moment. It instantiates a
// COM object of the requested type and returns an interface pointer
// to the created object.
HRESULT hr;
hr = CoCreateInstance( ID_Expression, &lpExpression );
if ( FAILED( hr ) )
   return;

// At this point m_dwRef = 1

// Get an IUnknown pointer (QI calls AddRef internally)
hr = lpExpression->QueryInterface( IID_IUnknown, &lpUnknown );
if ( FAILED( hr ))
{
   // The call failed, so decrement m_dwRef to 0 by calling
   // release through the initial pointer and return.
   lpExpression->Release();
   return;
}

// If everything worked, m_dwRef = 2

// Make a local copy of the interface
LPUNKNOWN lpU2 = lpUnknown;
lpU2->AddRef();

// Now m_dwRef = 3

// use lpU2
// free the interface
```

```
luU2->Release();
// The release decrements m_dwRef so it is now 2
// No longer valid, set to NULL
lpU2 = NULL;

{
   Expression* lpExp2 = lpExpression;
   lpExp2->AddRef();  // m_dwRef = 3
   ... Use lpExp2
}
// We screwed up here. lpExp2 was destroyed as
// it went out of scope, but we did not call
// Release() so the reference count is still 3.

lpUnknown->Release();    // m_dwRef = 2
lpExpression->Release(); // m_dwRef = 1
// The object lives forever
```

Like the C++ new and delete operators, AddRef and Release calls should "match up." The exception is QueryInterface. Treat a call to QueryInterface as a call to AddRef. QueryInterface allocates a new interface internally and so must call AddRef.

Multiple Interfaces

COM objects nearly always contain multiple interfaces. If a COM object had only one interface, it would have to be IUnknown, and that wouldn't provide very much functionality. Some of the interfaces implemented by an object (such as IUnknown) are there to support COM's purpose of providing the binary standard wrapper around the component's functionality. By exposing the component's distinct behavior, the other interfaces are what make the component useful. In many cases, these interfaces are already defined by the COM, OLE, or ActiveX standard. Your job is to provide a distinct implementation of the interface. In other cases, you will create your own custom interfaces to provide specific behavior. We will discuss both approaches in the next few chapters.

In C++, there are three ways to implement multiple interfaces in a COM object: multiple inheritance, interface implementation, and C++ class nesting. Of the three methods, we will focus on and use C++ class nesting, because that is how MFC implements COM/OLE interfaces. C++ class nesting is the hardest to understand (at first), but it is the most efficient. Let's briefly look at each method. In Chapter 5, we will go into more detail as we discuss MFC's COM/OLE implementation.

Declaring multiple interfaces within a single C++ class doesn't sound very difficult at first, but it can be tricky. Because COM interfaces are really pointers to a C++-style Vtable, a multiple interface class requires multiple Vtables. Another reason that component classes and their interface implementation classes must be closely coupled (via class nesting) is the need to maintain reference counting. When there are multiple interfaces on a COM object, all of them must cooperate in the reference counting scheme. There is only one reference count per object, and the interfaces must share it. This coupling is maintained through multiple IUnknown interfaces.

Multiple Inheritance

First, let's look at how multiple inheritance can solve the multiple Vtable problem. We'll continue the Expression class example by adding an interface, IExpression2. One of the useful features of COM is the ability it gives you to maintain multiple versions of an interface for a particular component class. This arrangement allows easier upgrading and augmenting of components. When developers enhance an existing component, they can provide a new interface that exposes the new functionality. At the same time, the original interface can be maintained. This approach ensures that any applications developed with the original interface will continue to work, and the component user can migrate to the more functional interface as time permits.

The new IExpression2 interface will provide a new feature that IExpression did not. Its declaration follows.

```
class IExpression : public IUnknown
{
    virtual CString GetExpression() = 0;
    virtual void    SetExpression( CString strExp, BOOL bInfix ) = 0;
    virtual BOOL    Validate() = 0;
    virtual long    Evaluate() = 0;
};

// New interface derives from the old one
class IExpression2 : public IExpression
{
    virtual CString ErrorString() = 0;
};
```

The new method, ErrorString, returns a textual description (such as "Too many closing parentheses.") of any errors that occur during the call to Validate. If Validate returns FALSE, the ErrorString method is called to obtain a description of the problem, which is then presented to the user. We would like to provide both interfaces for our COM object so that the user can choose the more appropriate one. We can deploy the new component without breaking any existing applications that use it. Using multiple inheritance, we would declare something like this:

```
class Expression : public IExpression, public IExpression2
{
    // implementation of all three interfaces
    // IUnknown
    // IExpression
    // IExpression2
};
```

To illustrate one of the difficulties of using multiple inheritance to implement multiple interfaces, I've written the QueryInterface function for our declaration. One of the ambiguities of using multiple inheritance is that the multiple Vtable implementations are handled by typecasting to the appropriate interface declaration. The value of this (and therefore its Vtable pointer) varies depending on the required casting. Both IExpression and IExpression2 contain an IUnknown interface, so either one could be used to return IUnknown.

```
HRESULT Expression::QueryInterface( REFIID riid, void** ppv )
{
    *ppv = NULL;

    if ( riid == IUnknown || riid == IExpression )
       *ppv = (IExpression *) this;
    else if ( riid == IExpression2 )
       *ppv = (IExpression2 *) this;
    else
        return( E_NOINTERFACE );

    ((LPUNKNOWN) *ppv)->AddRef();
    return( S_OK );
}
```

Multiple inheritance may work in some circumstances, but in our case we have a severe "name collision" problem. The two Expression interface classes—IExpression and IExpression2—contain method names that are the same. (For example, GetExpression is contained in both classes.) This ambiguity makes multiple inheritance difficult to use and complex to implement. The IUnknown interface is also ambiguous, making it difficult to implement a COM-based reuse technique called *aggregation*, which we will discuss in a moment. In other circumstances, where there are no name collisions and aggregation is not a requirement, multiple inheritance can be an effective technique.

Interface Implementations

Another option is to use interface implementations, which use multiple classes that contain pointers to the main class that implements the component's behavior. As you will see, the purpose of the interface implementation classes is to provide a Vtable for the interface they define. They delegate all their IUnknown functions to the main class. To promote clarity, error handling is not included.

```
// Classes that implement each COM interface but
// delegate their implementations of IUnknown
class ImpExpression : public IExpression
{
    Expression* m_pExpression;
public:
```

```
    // Constructor
    ImpExpression( Expression* pExp ) { m_pExpression = pExp; }

    // Interface
    virtual HRESULT  QueryInterface( REFIID riid, void** ppv );
    virtual ULONG    Release();
    virtual ULONG    AddRef();

    virtual CString  GetExpression();
    virtual void     SetExpression( CString strExp, BOOL bInfix );
    virtual BOOL     Validate();
    virtual long     Evaluate();
};

// Classes that implement each COM interface but
// delegate their implementations of IUnknown
class ImpExpression2 : public IExpression2
{
    Expression* m_pExpression;
public:
    // Constructor
    ImpExpression2( Expression* pExp ) { m_pExpression = pExp; }

    // Interface
    virtual HRESULT  QueryInterface( REFIID riid, void** ppv );
    virtual ULONG    Release();
    virtual ULONG    AddRef();

    virtual CString  GetExpression();
    virtual void     SetExpression( CString strExp, BOOL bInfix );
    virtual BOOL     Validate();
    virtual long     Evaluate();
    virtual CString  ErrorString();
};

class Expression : public IUnknown

{
...
// All basically the same as before except for the
// addition of pointers for the implementation classes
    ImpExpression*   m_pImpExpression;
    ImpExpression2*  m_pImpExpression2
```

```
...
// Only IUnknown functions are implemented in the base
// or parent class.
   virtual HRESULT  QueryInterface( REFIID riid, void** ppv );
   virtual ULONG    Release();
   virtual ULONG    AddRef();

// Make the Interface Implementation classes
// friends so that they can access protected members
   friend class IExpression;
   friend class IExpression2;
};

// The constructor for Expression
// must create the Interface Implementation objects
Expression::Expression()
{
   // Instantiate the Implementations
   m_pImpExpression = new ImpExpression( this );
   m_pImpExpression2 = new ImpExpression2( this );
}
// Destructor must remove the Interface Implementation instances
Expression::~Expression()
{
   delete m_pImpExpression;
   delete m_pImpExpression2;
}

// QueryInterface is a little special
HRESULT Expression::QueryInterface( REFIID riid, void** ppv )
{
   if ( riid == IID_IUnknown )
      *ppv = this;
   else if ( riid == IID_IExpression )
      *ppv = m_pImpExpression;
   else if ( riid == IID_IExpression2 )
      *ppv = m_pImpExpression2;
   else
      return( E_NOINTERFACE );

   ((LPUNKOWN) *ppv)->AddRef();
   return( S_OK );
}
```

NOTE By declaring another class as a `friend` class, you explicitly give that class access to your class's `private` and `protected` members. In the preceding example, we declare the implementation classes as `friend`s so that they can access the implementation members of the `Expression` class.

The `Expression` class now inherits only from the `IUnknown` interface and delegates to other classes the implementation of the behavior-specific interfaces. These classes are made `friend` classes so they can access the protected variables and methods of `Expression` for implementation of the exposed functionality. `Validate` is implemented in the other classes but still must access `m_strExpression`, `InfixToPostfix`, and so on. `AddRef` and `Release` are the same as before, but `QueryInterface` now returns a pointer to the Vtable of the specified interface implementation class. The lifetimes of the interface implementation objects are controlled by `Expression`. When an `Expression` instance is deleted, its destructor also removes the interface implementation class instances.

```
// Classes that implement each COM interface but
// delegate their implementations of IUnknown.
class ImpExpression : public IExpression
{
    Expression* m_pExpression;

public:
    // Constructor
    ImpExpression( Expression* pExp ) { m_pExpression = pExp; }

    // Interface
    virtual HRESULT  QueryInterface( REFIID riid, void** ppv );
    virtual ULONG    Release();
    virtual ULONG    AddRef();

    virtual CString  GetExpression();

    virtual void     SetExpression( CString strExp, BOOL bInfix );
    virtual BOOL     Validate();
    virtual long     Evaluate();
};

HRESULT ImpExpression::QueryInterface( REFIID riid, void** ppv )
{
    // delegate to the main class
    return m_pExpression->QueryInterface( riid, ppv );
}
DWORD ImpExpression::AddRef()
{
    return m_pExpression->AddRef();
}
```

```
DWORD ImpExpression::Release()
{
    return m_pExpression->Release();
}

BOOL ImpExpression::Validate()
{
    ...
    // Same as all previous examples, but we now must reference the
    // base or parent members explicitly. Because we are friends, we
    // have direct access to the protected members.
    Tokenizer.SetString( m_pExpression->m_strExpression );
    Tokenizer.Tokenize();
    ...
    // Check for validity
    while( Tokenizer.GetToken( strToken ) )
    {
        switch( m_pExpression->GetTokenType( strToken ) )
        {
            ...
        ...
}
```

To maintain a correct reference count for the component object as a whole, the implementation class's IUnknown methods defer to the parent class implementation. This practice ensures that there is only one point where reference counting occurs. QueryInterface also defers to the Expression class implementation, because the Expression class contains all the appropriate Vtable pointers. The only change required to the implementation of the IExpression interface methods is to use the m_pExpression pointer to directly access the needed Expression members. Making them friend classes of the base class makes this change easy.

```
class ImpExpression2 : public IExpression2
{
    // Pointer to controlling object
    Expression* m_pExpression;
public:
    // Constructor
    ImpExpression2( Expression* pExp ) { m_pExpression = pExp; }

    // Interface
    virtual HRESULT  QueryInterface( REFIID riid, void** ppv );
    virtual ULONG    Release();
```

```
    virtual ULONG    AddRef();

    virtual CString  GetExpression();
    virtual void     SetExpression( CString strExp, BOOL bInfix );
    virtual BOOL     Validate();
    virtual long     Evaluate();
    virtual CString  ErrorString();
};

HRESULT ImpExpression2::QueryInterface( REFIID riid, void** ppv )
{
    // delegate to the main class
    return m_pExpression->QueryInterface( riid, ppv );
}
BOOL ImpExpression2::Validate()
{
    ...
    // Same as all previous examples, but we now must reference the
    // base or parent members explicitly. Because we are friends, we
    // have direct access to the protected members.
    Tokenizer.SetString( m_pExpression->m_strExpression );
    Tokenizer.Tokenize();
    ...
    // Check for validity
    while( Tokenizer.GetToken( strToken ) )
    {
        switch( m_pExpression->GetTokenType( strToken ) )
        {
            ...
        ...
}
```

NOTE In practice, you wouldn't typically implement the common interface functions (such as Validate and SetExpression) in both implementation classes. The only difference between the two interfaces is the addition of the ErrorString method, so the shared class methods would be implemented by a common class shared by the two interface implementation classes. This would also be the case in the class nesting example that we will demonstrate next.

The implementation of the second interface is similar to that of the first interface, IExpression, so it isn't detailed here. I've included an implementation of QueryInterface to show that it, too, delegates to the parent class.

Interface implementations are an easily understandable method of providing multiple COM interfaces. Interface implementations are easily managed if you have only a small number of interfaces, but in a class with more than a few interfaces, this approach can become complex. For a more detailed look at multiple inheritance and interface implementations, see Brockschmidt's *Inside OLE*. Our focus is on MFC's method: class nesting.

C++ Class Nesting

Instead of using multiple inheritance or interface implementations, the MFC libraries use a technique called *class nesting*. This approach provides multiple Vtables for the single nesting class by exposing the Vtables of the nested classes. This method also allows for easy management of reference counting. It is similar to interface implementations but does not require the use of forward and back pointers between classes. Class nesting saves eight bytes for each COM interface. Using class nesting, our example now looks like this:

```
class IExpression : public IUnknown
{
public:
    virtual CString GetExpression() = 0;
    virtual void SetExpression( CString str, BOOL bInfix ) = 0;
    virtual BOOL Validate() = 0;
    virtual long Evaluate() = 0;
};

class IExpression2 : public IExpression
{
public:
    virtual CString ErrorString() = 0;
};

class Expression : public IUnknown
{
// Class Implementation here, just as before
...
    // Only IUnknown implemented in main class
    virtual HRESULT  QueryInterface( REFIID riid, void** ppv );
    virtual ULONG    Release();
    virtual ULONG    AddRef();

    class XExpression : public IExpression
    {
    public:
        virtual HRESULT  QueryInterface( REFIID riid, void** ppv );
```

```
    virtual long      Release();
    virtual long      AddRef();

    virtual CString GetExpression();
    virtual void      SetExpression( CString strExp, BOOL bInfix );
    virtual BOOL      Validate();
    virtual long      Evaluate();
} m_xExpression;

friend class XExpression;

class XExpression2 : public IExpression2
{
public:
    virtual HRESULT  QueryInterface( REFIID riid, void** ppv );
    virtual long      Release();
    virtual long      AddRef();

    virtual CString GetExpression();
    virtual void      SetExpression( CString strExp, BOOL bInfix );
    virtual BOOL      Validate();
    virtual long      Evaluate();
    virtual CString ErrorString();
} m_xExpression2;
friend class XExpression2;

};
```

Using nested classes, the implementations of the COM interfaces are contained in classes that are "nested" within the main `Expression` class. Each nested class has a Vtable, so there is a Vtable for each COM interface (just what we need). The implementations of the `IUnknown` methods are similar to the interface implementation technique described earlier. The members `m_xExpression` and `m_xExpression2` are embedded instances of the nested classes. Whenever an instance of the `Expression` class is created, two embedded instances of the nested class are created along with it. The embedded instances can be accessed only within the nesting class, because they exist only within its scope. Here's the `QueryInterface` for the `Expression` class:

```
HRESULT Expression::QueryInterface( REFIID riid, void** ppv )
{
    *ppv = NULL;

    if ( riid == IID_IUnknown )
        *ppv = this;
    else if ( riid == IID_IExpression )
        *ppv = &m_xExpression;
```

```
    else if ( riid == IID_IExpression2 )
        *ppv = &m_xExpression2;
    else
        return( E_NOINTERFACE );

    if ( *ppv )
    {
        ((LPUNKNOWN)*ppv)->AddRef();
        return S_OK;
    }
    return E_NOINTERFACE;
}
```

This technique is relatively straightforward. If the user requests an IUnknown interface, the Vtable pointer for the main class is returned. If either of the IExpression interfaces is required, a pointer to the appropriate nested class instance is returned. The Vtable pointer, _vptr, is the first entry of any C++ instance with virtual functions, so the address of an embedded class instance (such as m_xExpression) is a pointer to a pointer to the Vtable. The AddRef and Release functions for the nesting class are the same as in the interface implementation method, but they are slightly different for the nested classes, as we will see.

To understand the implementation of the nested classes, we need to review a couple of C++ features. To define a nested class member, you use the multiple scoping operators:

```
HRESULT Expression::XExpression::QueryInterface(...);
```

This code enables you to "scope" down to the nested class function. The other item is the C++ offsetof macro. The offsetof macro is used to address the base class members directly from inside the nested classes. The offsetof macro calculates the difference between a class member and the starting address of the class. MFC uses the offsetof macro to eliminate the need for a pointer to the outer class. We will discuss this in more detail in Chapter 5 when we detail MFC's implementation of OLE.

MFC defines a C macro, METHOD_PROLOGUE, that uses the offsetof macro to address back into the main class. It is defined like this:

```
#define METHOD_PROLOGUE(theClass, localClass) \
    theClass* pThis = \
        ((theClass*)((BYTE*)this - offsetof(theClass, m_x##localClass)));

METHOD_PROLOGUE( Expression, Expression )
// Expands to the following
Expression* pThis =
        ((Expression*)((BYTE*)this -
        offsetof( Expression, m_xExpression)));
```

When implementing the methods within the nested classes, you use this macro to initialize the pThis pointer, which allows access to the nesting ("outer") class members. Here is the implementation of XExpression's QueryInterface and AddRef functions:

```
HRESULT Expression::XExpression::QueryInterface( REFIID riid, void** ppv )
{
    METHOD_PROLOGUE( Expression, Expression );
    return pThis->QueryInterface( riid, ppv );
}

ULONG Expression::XExpression::AddRef()
{
    METHOD_PROLOGUE( Expression, Expression );
    return pThis->AddRef();
}
```

pThis behaves like this for the main class, so pThis can be used to access the member functions as well as the member variables of Expression. Figure 4.4 illustrates how the METHOD_PROLOGUE macro calculates the pThis pointer. Here's how we implement the Validate function:

```
long Expression::XExpression::Validate()
{
    CStringStack stack;
    Tokenizer tokenizer;
    CString strToken;
    CString strTop;

    METHOD_PROLOGUE( Expression, Expression );

    tokenizer.SetString( pThis->m_strExpression );
    tokenizer.Tokenize();

    // Check for validity
    while( tokenizer.GetToken( strToken ) )
    {
        ...
    }
    ...
    return FALSE;
}
```

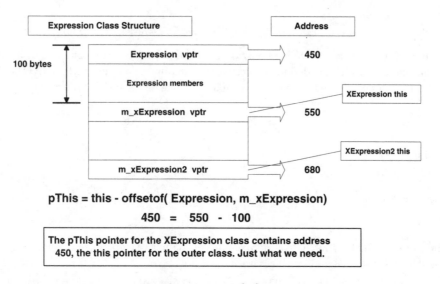

Figure 4.4 pThis calculation.

As you can see, the pThis pointer enables us to directly access the members of the outer, nesting class. Class nesting is the method used by MFC to implement multiple interfaces within one COM object. This is an introduction to the technique that we will cover again in Chapter 5.

GUIDs

With multiple component-based applications running on a component-based operating system, there can be hundreds of different components. In such an environment, it is imperative that there be a way to uniquely distinguish each component. COM uses the method described in the Open Software Foundation Distributed Computing Environment Standard for Remote Procedure Calls. This standard describes a *universally unique identifier* (UUID). Composed of 128 bits, the UUID is statistically guaranteed to be unique in every situation. It combines a unique network address (from your network card) with the then-current date and time. COM calls this value a *globally unique identifier*. GUIDs are used within COM to identify interfaces, component classes, type libraries, and property pages (we'll discuss the last two later). Here's an example of a GUID:

```
a988bd40-9f1a-11ce-8b9f-10005afb7d30
```

There are two primary uses of GUIDs. The first, a CLSID (class ID) is used to uniquely identify a specific COM component class. The second, an IID (interface ID) is used to uniquely identify a specific interface type (such as IUnknown or IExpression). The DEFINE_GUID macro is used to assign a GUID to a variable that is easier to use programmatically.

```
DEFINE_GUID( CLSID_Expression,
        0xA988BD40,0x9F1A,0x11CE,0x8B,0x9F,0x10,0x00,0x5A,0xFB,0x7D,0x30);
```

```
DEFINE_GUID( IID_IExpression,
             0xA988BD41,0x9F1A,0x11CE,0x8B,0x9F,0x10,0x00,0x5A,0xFB,0x7D,0x30);
```

It's important that the identifier be defined only once for the given executable or DLL. At the one point in your program where you intend to define (not declare) the identifier, you must include **INITGUID.H** before the **.H** file that includes the declarations. Here's what it looks like in our `Expression` example:

```
// ExpSvr.cpp

...

#include "stdafx.h"

#include <initguid.h>
#include "ExpSvr.h"

#include <stdio.h>
```

By including **INITGUID.H**, you change the meaning of the `DEFINE_GUID`. It no longer just declares the GUID's variable; it also defines and initializes it.

In our example, we defined two GUIDs: one is a CLSID that uniquely identifies the specific component class `Expression`, and the other is an IID to identify our new interface, `IExpression`. There are a few ways to generate GUIDs for use in your applications. The easiest way is to let MFC's ClassWizard or AppWizard generate a GUID whenever you add a new component or interface. Another way is to use the `CoCreateGuid` function provided by the COM API. But if you're working on a project that will use multiple GUIDs (as most do), you will probably want to generate a range of GUIDs. For the examples in this book, I ran the **UUIDGEN.EXE** utility provided with Visual C++ as follows:

```
c:\msdev\bin\uuidgen -n50 > bookids.txt
```

This produced 50 sequential GUIDs that we're using right now. The primary benefit of using sequential GUIDs is that they're easier to look up in the Registry, which we'll discuss in the next section.

There is one other way to generate GUIDs. Visual C++ provides the GUIDGEN.EXE program, which generates a single GUID at a time. It has a neat feature that formats the GUID as a C++ define so you can quickly paste it into your program code.

The COM API provides functions to make dealing with GUIDs much easier. Table 4.1 gives a quick view of what COM provides. A good reference for these functions and macros is the *OLE 2 Programmer's Reference, Volumes 1 and 2*, which are also available on-line with Visual C++: position the cursor over the function name and press **F1**.

Table 4.1 Useful GUID Helper Functions

Function	Purpose
CoCreateGuid(GUID* pGuid)	Programmatic way of generating one unique GUID
IsEqualGUID(REFGUID, REFGUID)	Compares two GUIDs
IsEqualIID(REFIID, REFIID)	Compares two IIDs
IsEqualCLSID(REFCLSID, REFCLSID)	Compares two CLSIDs
CLSIDFromProgID(LPCOLESTR, LPCLSID)	Returns the CLSID for the given ProgID
ProgIDFromCLSID(REFCLSID, LPOLESTR*)	Returns the ProgID from the CLSID

Note: 16-bit COM uses standard C style strings (LPSTR) and 32-bit OLE uses the Win32 Unicode standard (LPOLESTR) for all of its string handling. We'll discuss converting from ANSI to Unicode strings (and back) in the next few chapters.

We have many functions for manipulating GUIDs within a C or C++ program, but what about developers using Visual Basic (or a similar language)? Must they explicitly provide the 128-bit number to identify the specific component class that they require? No. COM provides a more human-readable method of accessing a component class. It's called the *program ID* (ProgID). ProgIDs are simple text strings that are associated, through the Windows Registry, with a specific CLSID. For our example I've chosen a ProgID of Chap4.Expression.1. This allows a Visual Basic developer to the following:

```
Dim obj as Object
Set obj = CreateObject( "Chap4.Expression.1" )
obj.SetExpression( "10 + 10 * 10" )
text1 = obj.Evaluate()
```

The CreateObject statement takes a ProgID that identifies the specific component. The number following Expression is used to indicate a version-specific component. One of the powerful features of COM is the ability it gives you to expose multiple versions of a component interface, thus making component upgrades and feature additions easy. How does Visual Basic know how to find and create the Expression component? It uses CLSIDFromProgID, which queries the Windows Registry.

The Windows Registry

The Windows Registry in Windows 95 and Windows NT plays a significant role in the management and configuration of the operating system. It includes system configuration information, user-specific information, and information about installed hardware and software. The Registry replaces many of the files that we're familiar with in Windows 3.1: **WIN.INI**, **CONFIG.SYS**, **SYSTEM.INI**, and so on. All these files and the software-specific **.INI** files that typically resided in the Windows directory have been combined into the Registry. This arrangement makes it much easier to manage multiple machines in a LAN environment. Both Windows 95 and Windows NT allow the use of a shared, or networked, Registry, eliminating the accumulation of hundreds of **.INI** files in the Windows directory that occurs under Windows 3.x.

We'll explore the features of the Registry because COM and ActiveX depend heavily on the functionality provided by it. CLSIDs for COM objects and various options associated with them are stored in the Registry. This provides nonvolatile storage of COM information that is required to "bootstrap" various COM executables and DLLs.

There are several ways to update the Registry with the CLSID information of our COM objects. The first approach is to create a text file of the form shown later in this section and then "merge" the information into the Registry using functions provided in the REGEDIT program. The second technique is to programmatically update the Registry using the Win32 Registry API functions. The third method is to manually add and edit the fields. Although this may be necessary when you're fixing a problem, it is not recommended. (A fourth method is to let MFC do it for you, as we'll see in Chapter 5.)

The Registry orders system information in a hierarchical manner, with several predefined top, or root, levels. The one we're interested in is HKEY_CLASSES_ROOT. This section of the Registry stores COM/ActiveX information, shell information such as file extension associations, and other software-related items. Information stored in the Registry is of the form key = value. This arrangement allows easy lookup of a value associated with a key in this hierarchical structure. The value is optional and is sometimes used when only the presence or absence of the key is important. Examples include the Insertable, NotInsertable, and Control keys that we will use.

An important subkey under HKEY_CLASSES_ROOT is CLSID. Under this subkey are all the public component CLSIDs currently registered on your system. All the COM system CLSIDs, any that are installed by third-party software, and those we will use in our projects are registered here. Figure 4.5 shows the NT version of REGEDIT displaying the Registry entries for the Expression component that we will develop shortly.

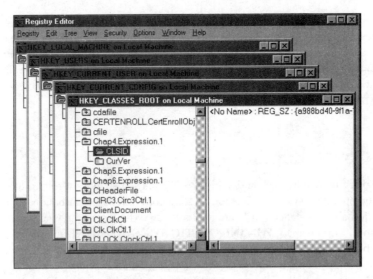

Figure 4.5 Windows NT 4.0 Registry.

NOTE There are several differences between the Windows NT and Windows 95 registries. The differences don't affect COM component information directly, but it is important to understand that the registry implementations are not identical. Here are some of the differences:

1. Windows NT has a different security model from that of Windows 95. The Windows 95 Registry does not contain security information.

2. The Windows 95 Registry does not completely replace the **CONFIG.SYS, WIN.INI**, and **SYSTEM.INI** files. Certain system information is contained in these files.

3. On Windows NT, the older INI API functions support a "pass-through" mechanism that will update the Registry when you're using the INI API functions. This feature is not currently supported in Windows 95.

4. The Registry hierarchy is slightly different between the two operating systems. The differences are most pronounced in Windows NT 3.5x.

The following lines show what is required to register our `Expression` component using the appropriate version of REGEDIT (see the Note). The lines are stored in a standard ASCII text file with an extension of **.REG**.

```
REGEDIT
HKEY_CLASSES_ROOT\CLSID\{a988bd40-9f1a-11ce-8b9f-10005afb7d30} = Chap4 Expression Component
HKEY_CLASSES_ROOT\CLSID\{a988bd40-9f1a-11ce-8b9f-10005afb7d30}\ProgID = Chap4.Expression.1
HKEY_CLASSES_ROOT\CLSID\{a988bd40-9f1a-11ce-8b9f-10005afb7d30}\VersionIndependentProgID =
Chap4.Expression.1
HKEY_CLASSES_ROOT\CLSID\{a988bd40-9f1a-11ce-8b9f-10005afb7d30}\InprocServer32 =
c:\chap4\Server\WinDebug\server.dll
HKEY_CLASSES_ROOT\CLSID\{a988bd40-9f1a-11ce-8b9f-10005afb7d30}\NotInsertable

HKEY_CLASSES_ROOT\Chap4.Expression.1 = Chap4 Expression Component
HKEY_CLASSES_ROOT\Chap4.Expression.1\CLSID = {a988bd40-9f1a-11ce-8b9f-10005afb7d30}
HKEY_CLASSES_ROOT\Chap4.Expression.1\CurVer = Chap4.Expression.1
```

The following line creates the initial CLSID subkey for our component:

```
HKEY_CLASSES_ROOT\CLSID\{a988bd40-9f1a-11ce-8b9f-10005afb7d30} = Chap4 Expression Component
```

The value `Chap4 Expression Component` is not actually necessary, but on a system with a large number of CLSIDs it's nice to quickly associate a CLSID with a particular component. The human-readable value is beneficial, and Registry browsers (such as OLEVIEW) will have something to show in the value field of your component's CLSID.

```
HKEY_CLASSES_ROOT\CLSID\{a988bd40-9f1a-11ce-8b9f-10005afb7d30}\ProgID = Chap4.Expression.1
HKEY_CLASSES_ROOT\CLSID\{a988bd40-9f1a-11ce-8b9f-10005afb7d30}\VersionIndependentProgID =
Chap4.Expression.1
```

```
HKEY_CLASSES_ROOT\CLSID\{a988bd40-9f1a-11ce-8b9f-10005afb7d30}\InprocServer32 =
c:\chap4\Server\WinDebug\server.dll
```

```
HKEY_CLASSES_ROOT\CLSID\{a988bd40-9f1a-11ce-8b9f-10005afb7d30}\NotInsertable
```

The rest of the lines set up various subkeys and values "below" the upper-level { a988bd40...} CLSID key. Which subkeys are needed as well as their specific values depend on the type of component that is being registered. Some of the important CLSID Registry key entries are detailed in Table 4.2.

Table 4.2 Important Registry Key Entries

Entry	Purpose
ProgID	Identifies the ProgID string for the COM class. It must contain 39 characters or fewer and can contain periods.
InprocServer32	Contains the path and filename of the 32-bit DLL. It does not have to contain the path, but if it does not, it can be loaded only if it resides within Windows PATH. 16-bit versions do not include the "32" extension.
LocalServer32	Contains the path and filename of the 32-bit EXE. 16-bit versions do not include the "32" extension.
CurVer	The ProgID of the latest version of the component class.
NotInsertable	Indicates that this component will not display in the OLE standard Insert Object dialog box.

In the previous section, I showed you how a Visual Basic developer can access a specific component class by using its ProgID. For this to work, we need an entry in the Registry that maps the less specific ProgID to the more specific CLSID of the component. The following entries create a Chap4.Expression.1 subkey off of HKEY_CLASSES_ROOT. Under Chap4.Expression.1, two additional subkeys—CurVer and CLSID—are also added. As you can imagine, the CLSID subkey and its value provide a cross-reference to the HKEY_CLASSES_ROOT\CLSID entry, where additional component information can be obtained.

```
HKEY_CLASSES_ROOT\Chap4.Expression.1 = Chap4 Expression Component
```

```
HKEY_CLASSES_ROOT\Chap4.Expression.1\CLSID = {a988bd40-9f1a-11ce-8b9f-10005afb7d30}
```

```
HKEY_CLASSES_ROOT\Chap4.Expression.1\CurVer = Chap4.Expression.1
```

We will use these entries when we register our example later in the chapter.

N O T E

The Registry editor program is **REGEDIT.EXE** in Windows 3.x and Windows 95, and **REGEDT32.EXE** in Windows NT. The method used to merge the file is also different on the three platforms. Under Windows 3.x, there is a **Merge Registration file** item on the File menu. Using Windows NT (3.51 and 4.0), you must invoke File Manager or the Explorer, locate the **.REG** file, and double-click to register the information in the Registry. Windows 95 provides a merge function within the Registry editor, similar to the Window 3.x REGEDIT program.

Class Factories

Because COM objects sometimes are located outside the component user's process space and must be accessed from various languages, a language-independent way of instantiating a component is required. In C++, the new operator is used to dynamically instantiate an object. COM supplies a standard interface, IClassFactory, that all components must provide if they are to be externally instantiated. Following is the definition of IClassFactory. Like all COM interfaces, it must implement IUnknown.

```
class IClassFactory : public IUnknown
{
    virtual HRESULT CreateInstance( LPUNKNOWN pUnk, REFIID riid, void** ppv ) = 0;
    virtual HRESULT LockServer( BOOL fLock ) = 0;
};
```

A *class factory* is a COM object whose sole purpose is to facilitate the creation of other, more useful COM objects. CreateInstance does what it says; it creates an instance of the specified component class and returns the requested interface on that instance. LockServer provides a way for a client to lock a server in memory. We will define the term *server* in detail shortly. Briefly, a server houses one or more COM objects within either a DLL or an executable (EXE). By locking a server in memory, the client ensures that it will be available when needed, even when there are no instantiated components within the server. Typically, a server is locked this way for performance reasons. Here's how the Expression class factory is implemented:

```
class ExpClassFactory : public IClassFactory
{
protected:
    // Reference count for the ClassFactory instance
    DWORD       m_dwRef;

public:
    ExpClassFactory();
    ~ExpClassFactory();

    // IUnknown implementation
    virtual HRESULT   QueryInterface( REFIID riid, void** ppv );
    virtual ULONG     Release();
    virtual ULONG     AddRef();

    // IClassFactory implementation
    virtual HRESULT CreateInstance( LPUNKNOWN pUnk, REFIID riid, void** ppv );
    virtual HRESULT LockServer( BOOL fLock );
};

HRESULT ExpClassFactory::CreateInstance(LPUNKNOWN pUnk, REFIID riid, void** ppv )
{
```

```
    Expression*    pExp;
    HRESULT        hr;
    // Initialize the returned pointer to
    // NULL in case there is a problem.
    *ppv = NULL;

    // Create a new instance of Expression
    pExp = new Expression;
    // Query the requested interface on the
    // new expression instance
    hr = pExp->QueryInterface( riid, ppv );

    if (FAILED( hr ))
        delete pExp;

    return hr;
}


STDMETHODIMP ExpClassFactory::LockServer( BOOLfLock )
{
  if ( fLock )
        g_dwLocks++;
  else
        g_dwLocks-;

  return NOERROR;
}
```

The user of the `Expression` component will first get a pointer to the `Expression` class factory. The user will then use the `IClassFactory` function `CreateInstance` to create an instance of the `Expression` class. If the user requests it, the `CreateInstance` function can also return the `IExpression` interface, which can be used to process algebraic expressions. The component user would do something like this:

```
main()
{
    LPCLASSFACTORY lpCF;
    Expression* lpExp;
    HRESULT hr;
    // Get the class factory for the Expression class
    hr = CoGetClassObject( CLSID_Expression,
                           CLSCTX_INPROC,
                           NULL,
                           IID_IClassFactory,
                           &lpCF );
```

```
    // Using the class factory interface, create an instance of the
    // component and return the IExpression interface.
    lpCF->CreateInstance( NULL, IID_IExpression, &lpExp );
    // Release the class factory
    lpCF->Release();

    // Use the component to do some work
    lpExp->SetExpression( "1+2", TRUE );
    lpExp->Evaluate();

    // Release it when we're finished
    lpExp->Release();
}
```

CoGetClassObject is a COM API function that returns the class factory of the requested component (identified by the CLSID). CoGetClassObject then returns the class factory interface so that we can create an instance of the Expression component class. Once we've used the class factory to create an instance of Expression, we call Release through IClassFactory, and Release then deletes the class factory. This three-step process is performed often, so COM provides a helper function, CoCreateInstance, that encapsulates the steps. By using CoCreateInstance, you avoid dealing with the class factory interface; you just call CoCreateInstance with the specific component interface (such as IExpression) that you require.

Figure 4.6 illustrates what we've built so far. We have two COM components (the Expression component and its class factory), each with two interfaces. This is the minimum number of interfaces to encapsulate our C++ object in a binary standard wrapper.

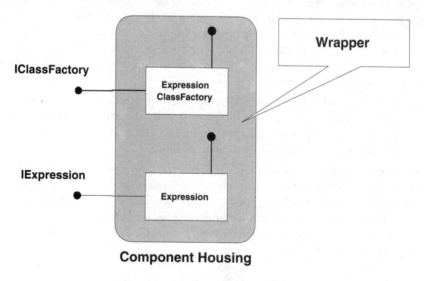

Figure 4.6 Binary standard wrapper for the Expression class.

Where Do Components Live?

COM objects are contained either within a Windows executable (EXE) or a Windows dynamic link library (DLL). Multiple COM objects can be maintained using either method. The user of a component doesn't need to know which technique is used to house the components. The component developer, on the other hand, implements things differently depending on which housing is used.

Most of the COM/OLE components that we will develop will be housed in Windows DLLs. ActiveX controls are almost always implemented as DLLs, because DLLs provide the best performance. OLE automation components are sometimes implemented in DLLs and sometimes in executables. Microsoft Word and Microsoft Excel are two popular Automation servers that are implemented as executables.

A Windows DLL that contains COM objects is called an *in-process*, or *inproc*, server. An executable that contains COM objects is called a *local server*. In the future, when distributed COM is available, an executable that resides on another machine on a network will be called a *remote server*. I'll use this terminology from this point on.

Local servers can be designed to function independently of COM. Many traditional applications have added OLE support by wrapping and exposing their internal methods with COM/OLE interfaces. This technique allows the application to be driven externally by another application or programming language. Visual Basic developers can incorporate these applications within their own VB applications because of Visual Basic's ability (using COM/OLE) to control and interoperate with OLE-compliant applications.

There are three reasons that, as a developer, you might implement your components within a local server. The most important one is that local servers provide easy 16-bit-to-32-bit interoperability. If you develop a 16-bit local server, its functionality can be harnessed, without change, by both 16-bit and 32-bit applications. For example, the 32-bit version of Visual Basic can interoperate with and control the 16-bit version of Microsoft Word. The reverse is also true: you can use 16-bit Visual Basic to drive 32-bit local servers. A second reason to implement your components within a local server applies if you're exposing existing functionality from a large application. This may be the easiest way to provide COM support in an existing legacy or monolithic Windows application. The third reason that you may require a local server applies if your components provide extensive visual or GUI functions that make heavy use of the Windows message queue. In this case, a local server may be the only choice.

In-process servers depend on the process in which they are contained. Their functionality cannot be harnessed without this context of a containing process. Visual Basic custom controls are similar to COM/OLE in-process servers in that they must be placed on a Visual Basic form to be useful. ActiveX controls, the topic of focus in the last half of this book, are very similar.

The primary benefit of implementing COM/OLE components as in-process servers is their small size and speed. The major problem is that they cannot be used in both 16-bit and 32-bit processes. (This issue will become less important as 32-bit operating systems become more common.) If your components require use in both Win16 and Win32 environments, you will need to produce both a 16-bit and a 32-bit implementation. Another drawback of in-process servers is that they do not have a true Windows message loop and must share the one in the containing process.

If you have the option of housing your components in either a local or an in-process server, you should probably choose the in-process type. They are far more efficient and perform significantly faster than local servers. Why? In-process servers require no marshaling, a prime factor in component performance.

NOTE In certain cases, a 16-bit local server may be required if you want to support legacy products within new 32-bit applications. Under Windows NT, there is not an easy-to-use 32-bit-to-16-bit thunking mechanism. One way to overcome this limitation is to implement your 16-bit-dependent services within a 16-bit COM-based Automation server. This method allows 32-bit applications (as well as 16-bit ones) to easily use older 16-bit code. If it's too much work or if you don't have source code to convert your 16-bit applications, this is one solution. I've done a lot of it. If you need help, read Chapter 6 and send me an email.

Marshaling

Marshaling is the process of transferring function arguments and return values across a process boundary. Marshaling requires that you copy the values to shared memory so that the other process can access it. Intrinsic types such as `short` and `long` are easy to marshal, but most others, such as pointers to structures, are a little more difficult. You can't just make a copy of a pointer, because its value (an address) has no meaning in the context of another process. You must copy the whole structure so that the other process can access it. The larger the structure, the greater the decrease in component performance.

We've observed that COM objects are housed in either a Windows executable or a Windows DLL. When the component housing is a DLL, it is called an in-process server to denote that the server component is executing within the context of the client's address space (executable). This is the most efficient method of interacting with a COM object, because no marshaling is necessary (both the client and server can freely exchange pointers).

Our examples so far have been in-process. The Vtables contain the addresses of the COM interface functions. When marshaling is required, these values are, of course, different. COM's marshaling hides this complexity from the developer by using a proxy for the interface's Vtable pointer. Figure 4.7 illustrates this mechanism. Internally, it appears to both processes that the COM object is in-process, but, in reality, COM is managing the proxy object and marshaling the function arguments using Win32's RPC capabilities. This mechanism allows COM objects to be distributed across networked machines. Marshaling is an interesting and complex topic but is beyond our scope. See the Bibliography for more details.

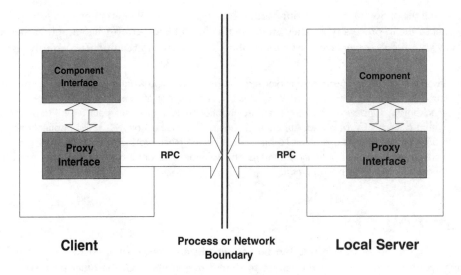

Client   Process or Network Boundary   Local Server

Figure 4.7 Cross-process marshaling with RPC.

Under 16-bit Windows, marshaling across process boundaries is done using LRPC, which means "lightweight" RPC. Using this method, window messages are passed back and forth between the two communicating processes. This is why you should increase you message queue buffer size to 96 to support COM/OLE under Win16.

N O T E

Distributed COM

Figure 4.7 shows how RPC is used to facilitate cross-process communication with COM. Initially, this mechanism worked only between processes that were on the same machine. Today, with the release of Windows NT 4.0, the communicating COM-based processes can now reside on different machines within a network. This means that we can deploy a COM-based component on a machine in New York and access its services on a client machine in Kansas City. The client machine is oblivious to the location of the server component. It could reside locally on the client machine, in the LAN room in Kansas City, or in New York. The COM-client software doesn't care and doesn't need to know in what address space the server is executing.

Years ago, when COM was initially released, Microsoft told developers that if they would develop their components using the COM APIs, their components would eventually work across the network without requiring changes to the implementation. Microsoft has kept its promise. With the addition of one Registry key entry (RemoteServerName), a component that is implemented with marshaling support (such as IDispatch) will now work across distributed machines.

The term *distributed COM* is redundant and will eventually go away. COM was always expected to provide distributed object services, and it took time to implement them. COM now implements this feature, but DCOM will be used for a while for marketing and similar purposes.

N O T E Distributed COM support is provided by Windows NT 4.0. By the time you read this, DCOM support for Windows 95, will be available as an upgrade or service pack. This will allow transparent distributed object support on the two 32-bit Windows platforms. Additional COM parameters and functions have been added to the Win32 API to support the new DCOM features.

Custom COM Interfaces

Most of what COM (and ActiveX, as we'll see in the next chapter) provides are various interfaces that a component must implement to be binary standard and provide application functionality. We've investigated two of these interfaces in detail: IUnknown and IClassFactory. The IExpression interface is classified as a COM custom interface. Custom interfaces do not have COM's standard marshaling support, so we must implement the Expression component as an in-process server because such a server doesn't require marshaling. We could have implemented the Expression component within an executable, making it a local server, but writing a marshaling handler is beyond our scope.

In Chapter 6, when we use the IDispatch interface, you will see that it is easy to implement components within an executable housing when COM provides default marshaling. We will also look at dual interfaces, which combine a custom Vtable interface with a standard IDispatch interface; the client can then choose the most efficient interface to use. But how does a component client determine the type of interfaces a server provides? Good COM-based components advertise such information using standard COM interfaces.

Describing a Component

Once you've developed a COM-based component, there are certain techniques that your component should use to advertise its behavior. COM provides system-level functions and interfaces to allow a standard way of describing a component's behavior. There are two basic techniques. A component belongs to a *component category*, which provides a way to segregate components based on their capabilities. The second technique is to provide a *type library* for your component. A type library provides a granular description of your component: which interfaces it exposes, whether the interfaces are custom or standard, the method signatures, and so on.

Component Categories

The component category standard was introduced recently with the ActiveX SDK. Before its release, the only way of describing a component's gross functionality was through a few Registry keys. We discussed a few of these keys in the previous section on the Windows Registry. An ActiveX control might mark itself with the Control key, and an OLE document server might the Insertable key, indicating its ability to be inserted into an OLE document container.

The proliferation of COM-based components has made this mechanism too broad to describe all the various flavors of components. The component category standard extends the key mechanism, giving a component a comprehensive way of describing its potential services. Component categories still use the Windows Registry, but a number of new keys have been added. The standard also allows a component to declare new, custom categories. In Chapter 7 we will discuss component categories in more detail.

Type Information

Once a component registers its specific category type, it should also provide a type library. A type library is a binary entity that can be shipped separately from the component (as a **.TLB** file) or can be tacked onto the end of the component's housing as a resource. A type library provides explicit details about the interfaces and data types used by a component.

A type information file is initially written using either Microsoft's Object Description Language (ODL) or the Interface Definition Language (IDL). The ODL or IDL script must be compiled with either MKTYPLIB (for ODL) or the MIDL (for IDL) compiler. After the type information is made available and advertised via the system Registry, the client can query for the information and determine how it should interact with the COM-based server. We will cover type information in more detail in Chapter 6.

COM Containment and Aggregation

As we discussed in Chapters 1 and 2, software and component reuse is very important. COM provides two methods for reusing component class objects: *containment* and *aggregation*. Containment and aggregation are similar to the C++ reuse techniques that we discussed in Chapter 2, but COM provides *binary* reuse as opposed to the compile-time, or *source-code–dependent*, reuse provided by C++. We won't cover these methods in detail—each one could easily fill an entire chapter—but we will encounter these terms throughout our discussion of COM, OLE, and ActiveX, so we'll cover them briefly.

COM object containment is similar to the C++ technique of class composition that we covered in Chapter 2. Containment and composition achieve reuse by using the services of a COM object or C++ class internally. The interface of the contained component is exposed only indirectly (if at all) via methods provided by the containing (or "outer") component. The interfaces of the internal (or "inner") COM component are used by the outer COM object in the implementation of its interfaces. The outer object can also, if it chooses, expose the inner object's interfaces. The lifetime of the inner object is controlled completely by the outer component just as in C++. A COM object need not do anything to support its use as an inner or contained object.

COM object aggregation is similar to COM containment except that the interface of the inner, or contained, COM object is directly exposed. The aggregate object doesn't need or use the functionality of the contained object internally; instead, it exposes the inner object's interfaces as if they were its own. The IUnknown interface of the outer aggregate object provides access to all the interfaces of the inner objects. This detail is what makes implementing aggregation a little complicated at times. The management of the lifetimes of the outer and inner objects must be coordinated through the IUnknown implementation. Successful lifetime management of the aggregate object requires that the inner objects provide support for a *controlling unknown*, which is the outer object in aggregation. When an inner COM object is created as part of an aggregate, it is passed a pointer to the outer object's IUnknown implementation. The inner object then defers its IUnknown implementation to that of the outer object, providing a consistent approach to the management of the aggregate object's lifetime. A COM object supports aggregation if it includes support for deferring its IUnknown implementation to that of a controlling unknown.

The COM API

COM is primarily a model for component implementation. It provides only a few low-level functions to "get things going." Most of the true benefits of COM are provided when you build a rich layer on top of COM's services. ActiveX is such a layer. As an application-level implementation of the Component Object Model, ActiveX adds a rich set of interfaces and additional APIs beyond those provided by COM. We'll investigate features of ActiveX in Chapter 5, but first let's take a quick look at the functions provided by COM. At the end of this chapter we will go through some examples and investigate the various API functions. Table 4.3 describes COM functions that are important for our purposes. This is not a comprehensive list, but it includes those that are used most often when you're building software components.

Table 4.3 Useful COM Functions

Function ("Who Calls It")	Purpose
CoBuildVersion (client and server)	Gets the major and minor build numbers of the installed COM libraries. Used only by local servers. (16-bit only.)
CoInitialize (client and server)	Initializes the COM libraries for use by a process. Not used by in-process servers.
CoUninitialize (client and server)	Releases the COM libraries when its services are no longer needed. Not used by in-process servers.
CoGetClassObject (client)	Gets an instance of a class factory for a specific COM object.
CoCreateGUID (client and server)	Creates a new unique GUID.
CoCreateInstance (client), CoCreateInstanceEx (client)	Creates an instance of a specific COM object, which may be on a remote machine.
CoRegisterClassObject (server)	Registers the existence of a class factory for a particular COM object.
DllCanUnloadNow (in-process server)	Called periodically by COM to determine whether the DLL can be unloaded (when no objects are instantiated within the DLL housing). Implemented by in-process servers.
DllGetClassObject (server)	Entry point implemented by in-process servers so that its class factory interfaces can be obtained by client processes.

CoBuildVersion (16-bit Only)

CoBuildVersion is called by both client and server COM applications if the server isn't in-process. It should be called prior to CoInitialize to ensure that the COM libraries and DLLs are of the same major version number as when the client or server application was compiled. The minor version number may differ. If the major version numbers differ, the COM libraries cannot be used. The return value is a 32-bit integer, where the high-order 16 bits are the major build number and the low-order 16 bits are the minor build number. When you're compiling an application, the current build numbers are maintained in the COM system include file **OLE2VER.H**.

CoInitialize

CoInitialize is called after the COM build versions have been validated with CoBuildVersion. CoInitialize initializes the COM libraries and DLLs so that the APIs can be used. In 16-bit COM/OLE, CoInitialize takes one parameter, a pointer to a memory allocator. 32-bit COM and OLE do not allow a user-implemented memory allocator, so NULL should be passed. This approach uses the default IMalloc implementation.

CoUninitialize

CoUninitialize is called to free the use of the COM libraries and DLLs. CoUninitialize should be called only if CoInitialize has been successfully called previously.

CoRegisterClassObject

CoRegisterClassObject is called by a server to register its class factories as available. CoRegisterClassObject should be called for every class factory that a particular housing supports. This should be done as soon as possible, even before the Windows message loop is processed. CoRegisterClassObject is called only by local servers. An in-process server must export the DllGetClassObject function to allow retrieval of its component's class factories. Table 4.4 lists the CoRegisterClassObject parameters.

Table 4.4 CoRegisterClassObject **Parameters**

Parameter	Description
REFCLSID rclsid	The CLSID for the component class being registered.
LPUNKNOWN pUnk	Pointer to a controlling unknown.
DWORD dwClsContext	The requested context for the server housing. This can be one, two, three, or all of the following: CLSCTX_INPROC_SERVER, CLSCTX_INPROC_HANDLER, CLSCTX_LOCAL_SERVER, and CLSCTX_REMOTE_SERVER.

Table 4.4 CoRegisterClassObject Parameters (continued)

Parameter	Description
DWORD flags	REGCLS flags specify how multiple instances of the component should be created. Use one of the following: REGCLS_SINGLEUSE, REGCLS_MULTIPLEUSE, or REGCLS_MULTI_SEPARATE.
LPDWORD lpdwRegister	A value returned that must be used when deregistering the class object using the CoRevokeClassObject function.

The flags parameter of CoRegisterClass controls how requests for multiple instances of your component should be handled. This is important for local server implementations, and we will cover it in Chapter 6.

CoGetClassObject

CoGetClassObject is a low-level function that allows a client to get the IClassFactory interface of a specific COM object, thereby allowing the client to create an instance of a COM object. If the module that contains the component is not loaded (DLL) or is not running (EXE), CoGetClassObject will query the system Registry to determine the pathname for the component housing, either an in-process server (DLL) or a local server (EXE). Then the function loads the DLL and calls the entry point DllGetClassObject to get the requested class factory; or, if it is a local server, CoGetClassObject uses CreateProcess() to invoke a copy of the executable. Once the server is invoked and registers its class factories via CoRegisterClassObject, CoGetClassObject returns a pointer to the requested IClassFactory.

For Windows NT 4.0, the COSERVERINFO parameter is used to allow instantiation on remote servers. Prior to NT 4.0, this parameter was reserved and required a NULL. Table 4.5 lists the CoGetClassObject parameters.

Table 4.5 CoGetClassObject Parameters

Parameter	Description
REFCLSID rclsid	A reference to the CLSID for the specific component.
DWORD dwClsContext	The requested context for the server housing. This can be one, two, three, or all of the following: CLSCTX_INPROC_SERVER, CLSCTX_INPROC_HANDLER, CLSCTX_LOCAL_SERVER, and CLSCTX_REMOTE_SERVER.
COSERVERINFO pServerInfo	Pointer to COSERVERINFO structure.
REFIID riid	A reference to an IID for the specific interface to be returned from the created class object. This interface will normally be IClassFactory so that the client can create an instance of the required component.
VOID** ppvObj	A void pointer to return the specified interface.

CoCreateInstance and CoCreateInstanceEx

CoCreateInstance is used by a component user, or client application, to create an instance of the specified component class. It is a helper function that calls CoGetClassObject to get a class factory for the component and then uses the IClassFactory::CreateInstance method to create the component instance. You should use CoCreateInstance instead of performing the three-step process shown next unless you need to create multiple component instances or you need to explicitly lock the instance by calling IClassFactory::LockServer.

```
// What CoCreateInstance does internally
CoGetClassObject(..., &pCF );
pCF->CreateInstance(..., &pInt );
pCF->Release();
```

CoCreateInstance's parameters (Table 4.6) are similar to those required by CoGetClassObject. The primary difference is that the client using CoCreateInstance will ask for the specific interface on the component (such as IExpression) instead of an IClassFactory pointer. CoGetClassObject creates an instance of a component's class factory, whereas CoCreateInstance creates an instance of the requested component class. As we've discussed, a component and its class factory are separate COM objects.

Table 4.6 CoCreateInstance Parameters

Parameter	Description
REFCLSID rclsid	A reference to the CLSID for the specific component.
IUnknown* pUnkOuter	The controlling outer unknown (when you're using aggregation).
DWORD dwClsContext	The requested context for the server housing. This can be one, two, three, or all of the following: CLSCTX_INPROC_SERVER, CLSCTX_INPROC_HANDLER, CLSCTX_LOCAL_SERVER, and CLSCTX_REMOTE_SERVER.
REFIID riid	A reference to an IID for the specific interface to be returned from the created component object.
VOID** PPVObj	A void pointer to return the specified interface.

CoCreateInstanceEx is used to create an instance of the COM object on a remote machine. The fourth parameter specifies the remote machine. If the parameter is NULL and if there isn't a RemoveServerName Registry entry, the object is created locally. The COSERVERINFO parameter allows you to specify the name of the remote machine in UNC, DNS, or IP format. To improve efficiency, the client can query for multiple interfaces as part of the create. The MULTI_QI structure allows you to provide an array of IIDs. Upon creation, CoCreateInstanceEx returns the array filled with interfaces and the result of the queries. Both new structures are shown next. Table 4.7 lists the parameters of CoCreateInstanceEx.

```
typedef struct  _COSERVERINFO
{
    DWORD dwReserved1;
```

```
    LPWSTR pwszName;
    COAUTHINFO *pAuthInfo;
    DWORD dwReserved2;
}   COSERVERINFO;

typedef struct _MULTI_QI
{
    const IID*    pIID;
    IUnknown *    pItf;
    HRESULT       hr;
}   MULTI_QI;
```

Table 4.7 CoCreateInstanceEx Parameters

Parameter	Description
REFCLSID rclsid	A reference to the CLSID for the specific component.
IUnknown* pUnkOuter	The controlling outer unknown (when you're using aggregation).
DWORD dwClsContext	The requested context for the server housing. This can be one, two, three, or all of the following: CLSCTX_INPROC_SERVER, CLSCTX_INPROC_HANDLER, CLSCTX_LOCAL_SERVER, and CLSCTX_REMOTE_SERVER.
COSERVERINFO* pServerInfo	Information about the remote server machine.
ULONG	Number of QueryInterfaces to perform for the MULTI_QI structure.
MULTI_QI	An array of MULTI_QI structures. This makes it more efficient to retrieve a series of interfaces from the create call.

DllCanUnloadNow

DllCanUnloadNow is implemented by in-process servers. Its purpose is to allow COM to periodically check to determine whether the DLL can be unloaded. DllCanUnloadNow takes no parameters and returns either S_FALSE, indicating to COM that the DLL cannot be unloaded, or S_OK, which indicates to COM that the DLL can be unloaded because there are no current references to it.

DllGetClassObject

DllGetClassObject is implemented by in-process servers to expose the class factories for its component objects. When a client application requests a component housed within an in-process server, COM calls the DllGetClassObject entry point within the DLL with the parameters shown in Table 4.8.

Table 4.8 `DllGetClassObject` Parameters

Parameter	Description
`REFCLSID rclsid`	A reference to the CLSID for the specific component.
`DWORD dwClsContext`	The requested context for the server housing. This can be one, two, or all of the following: CLSCTX_INPROC_SERVER, CLSCTX_INPROC_HANDLER, and CLSCTX_LOCAL_SERVER.
`LPVOID pvReserved`	Reserved. Must be NULL.
`REFIID riid`	A reference to an IID for the specific interface to be returned from the created COM object. This will normally be `IClassFactory` so that the client can create an instance of the requested component.
`VOID** ppvObj`	A `void` pointer to return the specified interface.

Client/Server Flow

Now that we've reviewed the major COM API functions, let's follow the flow of a simple client/server interaction. Table 4.9 describes the flow between a client executable and an in-process server.

Table 4.9 Client/Server Flow for In-Process Server

Client	COM/OS	In-Process Server
Initialize COM (`CoInitialize()`).		
Create an instance of a component's class factory (`CoGetClassObject()`).		
	Check Registry for path and filename of the in-process server DLL. If the DLL is not loaded for the client process, load it.	
		`DllGetClassObject()` is called with the CLSID of the requested component. Create class factory and return an `IClassFactory` pointer.
Use `IClassFactory` to create an instance of the component. Request the specific interface we need, such as `IExpression` ((pCF->CreateInstance().)		

Table 4.9 Client/Server Flow for In-Process Server (continued)

Client	COM/OS	**In-Process Server**
		The component's class factory creates an instance of the component object and returns an interface pointer to `IExpression`.
Release the class factory instance (`pCF->Release()`).		
		`Release()` for the class factory causes the reference count to reach zero, so the class factory instance is deleted.
The interface on the component object is used to perform some tasks. When the tasks are finished, `Release()` is called.		
		`Release()` decrements the internal reference count to reach zero, and the component object destroys itself. The component object count also reaches zero because there are no object instances in the DLL.
At some point (such as at idle time) `CoFreeUnusedLibraries()` is called.		
	COM/OS calls `DllCanUnloadNow()`.	
		`DllCanUnloadNow()` returns `TRUE`.
	`DllCanUnloadNow()` returns `TRUE`, and COM unloads the DLL.	

In the next scenario, (Table 4.10), the server application is implemented as a local server. There are many possible scenarios with local servers. The EXE may or may not be running when the client asks for a component's services, and the REGCLS flags also play a role when multiple instances of a component are required. The scenario in Table 4.10 uses a single instance of the executable, and the executable isn't running when the client requests a component class. It should give you a good idea of what occurs when you're using a local server.

Table 4.10 Client/Server Flow for Local Server (Server Not Running)

Client	COM/OS	Server
Initialize COM (`CoInitialize()`).		
Create an instance of a component's class factory (`CoGetClassObject()`).		
	COM checks to see if the component has been registered within its internal tables. If it is, then the EXE is running. If it isn't, then query the Registry for the pathname of the local server EXE. Start up the EXE and wait for it to register its class factories.	
		COM starts up the EXE.
		Initialize COM (`CoInitialize()`).
		Register all the housed component's class factories as available using `CoRegisterClassObject`.
		A class factory instance is created for the requested component and is returned.
`CoGetClassObject` returns with a pointer to the component's class factory.		
Use `IClassFactory` to create an instance of the component. Request the specific interface we need, such as `IExpression` `pCF->CreateInstance`.		
		The component's class factory creates an instance of the component object and returns an interface pointer.
Release the class factory instance (`pCF->Release()`).		
		`Release()` for the class factory causes the reference count to reach zero, so the class factory instance is deleted.
The interface on the component object is used to perform some tasks. When the tasks are finished, `Release()` is called.		

Table 4.10 Client/Server Flow for Local Server (Server Not Running) (continued)

Client	COM/OS	Server
		`Release()` decrements the internal reference count to reach zero, and the component object destroys itself. The component object count also reaches zero, because there are no object instances in the EXE. The EXE unregisters its class factories by calling `CoRevokeClassObject` and then terminates.

COM C++ Macros, BSTRs, and So On

Until this point, I haven't been using the standard COM/OLE macros when declaring interfaces, because for instructional purposes they get in the way of understanding what's going on. COM, OLE, and MFC use C/C++ macros extensively to hide the implementation details of the various platforms. We're getting ready to write real code, so it's time I explained the macros we'll be using. There are four macros for COM/OLE interface declarations and definitions: STDMETHOD, STDMETHOD_, STDMETHODIMP, and STDMETHODIMP_. In an earlier example of IExpression, we declared it like this:

```
// public interface definition of our Expression component
// An abstract class
class IExpression
{
public:
   virtual CString GetExpression() = 0;
   virtual void SetExpression( CString str, BOOL bInfix ) = 0;
   virtual BOOL Validate() = 0;
   virtual long Evaluate() = 0;
};
```

Using the COM's macros and intrinsic data types, it would be declared as follows:

```
class IExpression
{
public:
   STDMETHOD_(BSTR,GetExpression()) PURE;
   STDMETHOD_(void, SetExpression(BSTR, BOOL)) PURE;
   STDMETHOD_(BOOL, Validate())      PURE;
   STDMETHOD_(long, Evaluate())      PURE;
};
```

The expansion of STDMETHOD_ depends on the target platform and whether you're using C or C++. The expansion for Win32 using C++ is as follows:

```
// OBJBASE.H

#define STDMETHODCALLTYPE          __stdcall
...
#define STDMETHOD(method)          virtual HRESULT STDMETHODCALLTYPE method
#define STDMETHOD_(type,method)    virtual type STDMETHODCALLTYPE method
#define PURE                       = 0

#define STDMETHODIMP               HRESULT STDMETHODCALLTYPE
#define STDMETHODIMP_(type)        type STDMETHODCALLTYPE
```

As you can see, our earlier example is similar to the expanded macro version, with the exception of the additional return type __stdcall. This Microsoft-specific calling convention is used by the Win32 API functions. It specifies that the callee will clean up the stack after the call. It isn't important to our understanding, but it's interesting reading if you have nothing else to do. As you can see, PURE equates to = 0 and is just another way of making a function pure virtual. Most COM interfaces return HRESULT, so the special macro STDMETHOD defaults the return type to HRESULT. We didn't use it in the IExpression interface, but here is a quick example from IClassFactory:

```
STDMETHOD( LockServer(BOOL fLock) )  PURE;
// Expands to this
virtual HRESULT _stdcall LockServer(BOOL fLock) = 0;
```

STDMETHOD is also used in the declaration of interface methods within the implementing class. The only difference is that you don't need the PURE qualifier. The STDMETHODIMP macros are used when you implement the interface function. Here are the declarations of our IExpression methods within the Expression class:

```
class Expression : public IExpression
{
...
   // IExpression
   STDMETHOD_(BSTR, GetExpression());
   STDMETHOD_(void, SetExpression( BSTR, BOOL ));

   STDMETHOD_(BOOL, Validate());
   STDMETHOD_(long, Evaluate());
...
};
```

When we implement the functions in our **.CPP** file, we use the STDMETHODIMP macros as follows:

```
STDMETHODIMP_(BSTR) Expression::GetExpression()
{
   return ::SysAllocString( m_strExpression );
```

```
}

STDMETHODIMP_(void) Expression::SetExpression( BSTR bstrExp, BOOL bInfix )
{
   m_strExpression = bstrExp;
   m_bInfix = bInfix;
}

STDMETHODIMP_(BOOL) Expression::Validate()
{
...
}

STDMETHODIMP_(long) Expression::Evaluate()
{
...
}
```

BSTR

If you look closely, you'll see another difference in the preceding declarations. In the GetExpression function of IExpression, we return something declared as a BSTR. A BSTR is a binary string and is one of the standard data types used within Visual Basic. It is a string that stores its length in the first two or four bytes (depending on the platform) and the string data thereafter. BSTR is a standard data type that is used extensively in Automation. We're using it here to return a copy of the expression as well as to set the expression in SetExpression. The client application may not understand the structure of MFC's CString class, nor should it have to. COM and ActiveX define many standard data types that are provided by COM's standard marshaling support so that clients and servers have a standard way of passing data. We'll talk more about these types in Chapters 6 and 7. Custom data types are also supported within COM and are typically used with custom interfaces, but they're beyond the scope of this book.

One important aspect of COM interoperation between client and server processes is that the client is responsible for deallocating memory allocated by the server. Only the client knows when it will be finished with a piece of data returned through an interface method call, so the client is responsible for the deallocation. COM provides functions to make this fairly easy. MFC also makes it easy as by providing BSTR support within its CString class.

HRESULT and SCODE

Most COM interface methods and API functions return an HRESULT. An HRESULT in Win32 is defined as a DWORD (32 bits) that contains information about the result of a function call. The high-order bit indicates the success or failure of the function, the next 15 bits indicate the facility and provide a way to group related return codes, and the lowest 16 bits provide specific information on what occurred. (If you are an old DEC

VMS programmer, this is how the system error codes work there as well. David Cutler designed them both.) To check the gross success or failure of a function, you need only check the high-order bit of the return, and COM provides some macros to make this easy. The SUCCEEDED macro evaluates to TRUE if the function call was successful, and the FAILED macro evaluates to TRUE if the function failed. These macros aren't specific to COM and ActiveX but are used throughout the Win32 environment and are defined in **WINERROR.H**. Return values in Win32 are prefixed with S_ when they indicate success, and E_ to indicate failure.

```
// From WINERROR.H

...

// Generic test for success on any status value (nonnegative numbers
// indicate success).
//

#define SUCCEEDED(Status) ((HRESULT)(Status) >= 0)

//
// and the inverse
//

#define FAILED(Status) ((HRESULT)(Status)<0)

...
//
// Create an HRESULT value from component pieces
//

#define MAKE_HRESULT(sev,fac,code) \
    ((HRESULT) (((unsigned long)(sev)<<31) | ((unsigned long)(fac)<<16) | ((unsigned
long)(code))) )
#define MAKE_SCODE(sev,fac,code) \
    ((SCODE) (((unsigned long)(sev)<<31) | ((unsigned long)(fac)<<16) | ((unsigned long)(code))) )
```

An SCODE is a special return value used for Win16 COM/OLE functions, but under Win32 an SCODE is really an HRESULT. You should use HRESULT instead of SCODE when developing 32-bit applications.

N O T E   Win16 COM/OLE used the function's GetScode to map an HRESULT to an SCODE and ResultFromScode to map an SCODE to an HRESULT. Our examples will use these functions when providing Win16 support. For example, to return E_NOINTERFACE from QueryInterface, which returns an HRESULT, you would do this: return ResultFromScode(E_NOINTERFACE).

An Example

Now that we've discussed the details of COM, we need some good examples to tie all the concepts together. In the next few sections we will develop two programs. First, we will implement the `Expression` component as an in-process server. We won't implement it as a local server, because the custom interface, `IExpression`, would require special marshaling code. As we'll see in Chapter 6, a standard ActiveX interface, `IDispatch`, provides additional functionality, including marshaling, for the `Expression` class.

Then we will build a simple client application that will use the `Expression` component as an in-process server. We will use MFC but without MFC's COM/OLE support; instead, we will use native COM calls. We've delved into the details of COM so that we have a solid footing on which to continue. Later, when using MFC, we won't probe into the depths of COM again because the details have been nicely abstracted by the MFC libraries.

The Expression Class as a COM Component

Throughout this chapter we've been using the `Expression` class and its public interface for the example code. In this section, we'll develop a COM component that is contained within a DLL. This in-process server will allow the `Expression` object to be used by any COM-compliant client process. In the next section we will develop a C++ client application that uses the `Expression` component.

Start Visual C++, choose **File/New**, and select **New Project Workspace**. From the New dialog box, select **MFC AppWizard (dll)** as the project type and name the project **SERVER**. Then click the **Create** button to continue. Figure 4.8 shows the New Project Workspace dialog box.

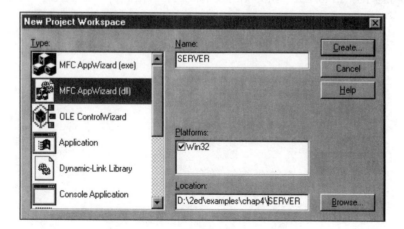

Figure 4.8 The New Project Workspace dialog box.

In the MFC AppWizard Step 1 of 1 dialog box, select the **Regular DLL with MFC statically linked** option and take the defaults on the others. Click **Finish** to create the project files. Make sure the options match those shown in Figure 4.9.

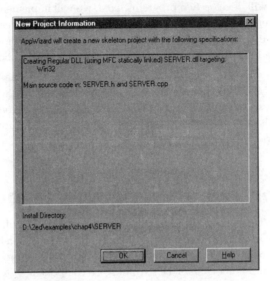

Figure 4.9 Server New Project Information dialog box.

These steps create a template DLL application that uses the MFC libraries. There isn't much code—basically just the include files needed for MFC support. The initial AppWizard-produced code from **SERVER.H** is shown next:

```
// Server.h : main header file for the SERVER DLL
//

#ifndef __AFXWIN_H__
    #error include 'stdafx.h' before including this file for PCH
#endif

#include "resource.h"

/////////////////////////////////////////////////////////////////////////////
// CServerApp
// See server.cpp for the implementation of this class
//

class CServerApp : public CWinApp
{
public:
```

```
        CServerApp();

// Overrides
        // ClassWizard generated virtual function overrides
        //{{AFX_VIRTUAL(CServerApp)
        //}}AFX_VIRTUAL

        //{{AFX_MSG(CServerApp)
            // NOTE - the ClassWizard will add and remove member functions here.
            //    DO NOT EDIT what you see in these blocks of generated code !
        //}}AFX_MSG
        DECLARE_MESSAGE_MAP()
};
```

This code declares our CWinApp-derived application class. As we discussed in Chapter 3, all MFC applications derive an application class from CWinApp that is globally instantiated. The code here declares the application constructor CServerApp. Let's look at **SERVER.CPP**:

```
// Server.cpp : Defines the initialization routines for the DLL.
//

#include "stdafx.h"
#include "Server.h"

#ifdef _DEBUG
#define new DEBUG_NEW
#undef THIS_FILE
static char THIS_FILE[] = __FILE__;
#endif

/////////////////////////////////////////////////////////////////////////////
// CServerApp

BEGIN_MESSAGE_MAP(CServerApp, CWinApp)
    //{{AFX_MSG_MAP(CServerApp)
        // NOTE - the ClassWizard will add and remove mapping macros here.
        //    DO NOT EDIT what you see in these blocks of generated code!
    //}}AFX_MSG_MAP
END_MESSAGE_MAP()

/////////////////////////////////////////////////////////////////////////////
// CServerApp construction

CServerApp::CServerApp()
{
```

```
    // TODO: add construction code here,
    // Place all significant initialization in InitInstance
}

/////////////////////////////////////////////////////////////////////////
// The one and only CServerApp object

CServerApp theApp;
```

There isn't much here either. Under Win32, when DLLs are initially loaded, the entry point `DllMain` is called with the `hInstance` parameter. The MFC libraries encapsulate this entry point and provide the function `InitInstance` to allow the application to perform any initializations. We don't need to initialize anything on startup, so we'll use the AppWizard code as provided. AppWizard has generated a basic DLL in which to implement our COM-specific code.

In-process servers must contain the function `DllGetClassObject`, which provides a standard entry point for clients that instantiate a class factory object for the specified component class (CLSID) and returns its `IClassFactory` interface. If an in-process server supports multiple COM objects, the `DllGetClassObject` function will contain code to identify the specific CLSID and will create the corresponding class factory. Our DLL contains only the `Expression` component and its supporting class factory, so it's pretty simple. `DllGetClassObject` provides the class factories for all the components in our housing, so we should add the following code to the end of **SERVER.CPP**.

```
STDAPI DllGetClassObject( REFCLSID rclsid, REFIID riid, void** ppv )
{
    HRESULT            hr;
    ExpClassFactory    *pCF;

    pCF = NULL;

    // Make sure the CLSID is for our Expression component
    if ( rclsid != CLSID_Expression )
        return( E_FAIL );

    pCF = new ExpClassFactory;

    if ( pCF == NULL )
        return( E_OUTOFMEMORY );

    hr = pCF->QueryInterface( riid, ppv );

    // Check for failure of QueryInterface
    if ( FAILED( hr ) )
    {
        delete pCF;
        pCF = NULL;
    }

    return hr;
}
```

The function checks for CLSID_Expression. If the caller is requesting an unrecognized component class, we return E_FAIL. If the correct CLSID is provided, we instantiate an Expression class factory and query for the requested interface, typically IClassFactory. We then return the HRESULT of QueryInterface.

The second COM function that must be implemented in an in-process server is DllCanUnloadNow. This function provides a way for COM to periodically check to determine whether the DLL can be unloaded. Here's our implementation of DllCanUnloadNow. It also belongs in **SERVER.CPP**.

```
STDAPI DllCanUnloadNow(void)
{
    if ( g_dwObjs || g_dwLocks )
        return( S_FALSE );
    else
        return( S_OK );
}
```

We're responsible for keeping track of how many COM objects are in use at any given time. The global variables g_dwObjs and g_dwLocks keep track of the instantiated Expression objects and the current number of LockServer calls. LockServer, a member of the IClassFactory interface, provides a way for a client to lock a DLL in memory even if it is not currently being used. We declare these variables globally outside any function. (They must hang around even when there are no instantiated objects.)

```
// Server.cpp : Defines the initialization routines for the DLL.
//

#include "stdafx.h"
#include "Server.h"
```

```
#include <initguid.h>
#include "expsvr.h"

DWORD        g_dwObjs = 0;
DWORD        g_dwLocks = 0;
```

```
#ifdef _DEBUG
#define new DEBUG_NEW
#undef THIS_FILE
static char THIS_FILE[] = __FILE__;
#endif
```

These global variables are for a particular instance of the DLL. Under Win32, every process that loads this DLL gets a fresh copy with the global variables initialized to zero. This isn't exactly true under Win16, because DLLs exist at a system level and aren't owned by a particular process, but this method works under Win16 as well. We've also added the include for the **EXPSVR.H** file that contains the definitions and IID for our custom interface, IExpression. I've highlighted the changes from the Chapter 3 implementation of the Expression class (in the file **EXPRESS.H**). It would be beneficial to copy the **EXPRESS.H** from the Chapter 3 project to your Chapter 4 SERVER project directory and rename it **EXPSVR.H**.

```
//
// ExpSvr.h
//

// access to the global variables in SERVER.CPP
extern DWORD g_dwObjs;
extern DWORD g_dwLocks;

DEFINE_GUID( CLSID_Expression,
            0xA988BD40,0x9F1A,0x11CE,0x8B,0x9F,0x10,0x00,0x5A,0xFB,0x7D,0x30);
DEFINE_GUID( IID_IExpression,
            0xA988BD41,0x9F1A,0x11CE,0x8B,0x9F,0x10,0x00,0x5A,0xFB,0x7D,0x30);

//
// A Stack class that supports CStrings
//
class CStringStack : public CObject
{
protected:
    DECLARE_DYNCREATE( CStringStack )
    CStringList m_StringList;

public:

    CStringStack();
    CStringStack( CStringStack& stack );
    ~CStringStack();

    CStringStack& operator=( const CStringStack& lhs );

    virtual void Dump( CDumpContext& );

    void    Push( CString );
    BOOL    Peek( CString& );
    BOOL    Pop( CString& );
    BOOL    IsEmpty();
    void    Clear();
};

//
// Tokenizes an algebraic expression string
//
class Tokenizer : public CObject
{
protected:
```

```
    DECLARE_DYNCREATE( Tokenizer )
    char        m_szBuffer[256];
    CStringList  m_TokenList;

public:
    Tokenizer();
    Tokenizer( const CString& strString );
    ~Tokenizer();

public:
    void     SetString( const CString& str );
    short    Tokenize();
    BOOL     GetToken( CString& str );
    BOOL     PeekToken( CString& str );
    void     ClearTokens();

};

class IExpression : public IUnknown
{
public:
    STDMETHOD_(BSTR,GetExpression()) PURE;
    STDMETHOD_(void, SetExpression(BSTR, BOOL)) PURE;
    STDMETHOD_(BOOL, Validate())       PURE;
    STDMETHOD_(long, Evaluate())       PURE;
};

class Expression : public IExpression
{
protected:
    enum TokenType
    {
        BogusToken,
        OperatorToken,
        OpenParenToken,
        CloseParenToken,
        NumberToken
    };

protected:
    CString          m_strExpression;
    BOOL             m_bInfix;
```

```
    // Reference count
    DWORD           m_dwRef;

public:
    // Constructors
    Expression();
    Expression( CString str, BOOL bInfix );
    // Destructor
    ~Expression();
    // Copy constructor
    Expression( Expression& x );
    // assignment operator
    Expression& operator=( Expression& rhs );

protected:
    BOOL            IsNumber( const CString& strToken );
    TokenType       GetTokenType( const CString& strToken );
    int             Precedence( const CString& strToken );
    BOOL            InfixToPostfix();

public:
    // IUnknown
    STDMETHOD(QueryInterface( REFIID, void** ));
    STDMETHOD_(ULONG, AddRef());
    STDMETHOD_(ULONG, Release());
    // IExpression
    STDMETHOD_(BSTR, GetExpression());
    STDMETHOD_(void, SetExpression( BSTR, BOOL ));
    STDMETHOD_(BOOL, Validate());
    STDMETHOD_(long, Evaluate());
};

class ExpClassFactory : public IClassFactory
{
protected:
    DWORD           m_dwRef;

public:
    ExpClassFactory();
    ~ExpClassFactory();

    // IUnknown
    STDMETHOD( QueryInterface(REFIID, void** ));
```

```
    STDMETHOD_(ULONG, AddRef());
    STDMETHOD_(ULONG, Release());

    // IClassFactory
    STDMETHOD( CreateInstance(LPUNKNOWN, REFIID, void**));
    STDMETHOD( LockServer(BOOL));
};
```

The new items expose our C++ component using COM. We now need to add the implementation of the preceding functions to **EXPSVR.CPP**. Only a few things have changed, so I include only the pertinent code. Items not shown are taken directly from the Chapter 3 implementation in **EXPRESS.CPP**. The original implementations of CStringStack and Tokenizer and the protected member functions InfixToPostfix, Precedence, IsNumber, and GetTokenType have not changed.

```
//
// ExpSvr.cpp
//

#include "stdafx.h"
```

```
// To support Unicode conversion in 4.0
#if ( _MFC_VER >= 0x400 )
    #include <afxpriv.h>
#endif
```

```
#include <stdio.h>

...
```

We first need to include the MFC **AFXPRIV.H** header file. With the release of MFC 4.0, we now must manage all Unicode conversions ourselves. Fortunately, **AFXPRIV.H** provides a number of macros that make the process much simpler.

Remember, all Win32 COM/OLE functions are inherently Unicode. Our project, however, is built using ANSI (or multibyte) strings. As you will see, we will need to use Unicode when passing strings to and from the COM functions. Also, the BSTR type expects Unicode strings. Here are the rest of the changes to **EXPSVR.CPP**:

```
ExpClassFactory::ExpClassFactory()

{
    m_dwRef = 0;
}

ExpClassFactory::~ExpClassFactory()

{
}
```

```
STDMETHODIMP ExpClassFactory::QueryInterface( REFIID riid, void** ppv )
{
    *ppv = NULL;

    if ( riid == IID_IUnknown || riid == IID_IClassFactory )
        *ppv = this;

    if ( *ppv )
    {
        ( (LPUNKNOWN)*ppv )->AddRef();
        return NOERROR;
    }

    return ResultFromScode(E_NOINTERFACE);
}

STDMETHODIMP_(ULONG) ExpClassFactory::AddRef()
{
    return ++m_dwRef;
}

STDMETHODIMP_(ULONG) ExpClassFactory::Release()
{
    if ( --m_dwRef )
        return m_dwRef;
    else
        delete this;

    return 0;
}

STDMETHODIMP ExpClassFactory::CreateInstance
( LPUNKNOWN pUnkOuter, REFIID riid, void** ppvObj )
{
    Expression* pExpression;
    HRESULT     hr;

    *ppvObj = NULL;

    pExpression = new Expression;

    if ( pExpression == NULL )
        return E_OUTOFMEMORY;

    hr = pExpression->QueryInterface( riid, ppvObj );
```

```
    if ( FAILED( hr ) )
        delete pExpression;
    else
        g_dwObjs++;  // Increment the global object count

    return hr;
}

STDMETHODIMP ExpClassFactory::LockServer( BOOL fLock )

{

    if ( fLock )
        g_dwLocks++;
    else
        g_dwLocks-;

    return NOERROR;
}

// Constructors
Expression::Expression()
{
    m_dwRef = 0;
    m_bInfix = TRUE;
}

Expression::Expression( CString strExpression, BOOL bInfix )
{
    m_dwRef = 0;
    m_strExpression = strExpression;
    m_bInfix = bInfix;
}

Expression::~Expression(void)
{
    g_dwObjs-;
}

STDMETHODIMP_(void) Expression::SetExpression( BSTR bstrExp, BOOL bInfix )
{
    m_strExpression = bstrExp;
}

STDMETHODIMP_(BOOL) Expression::Validate()
{
```

```
...
// Implementation the same, only the declaration is different
...
}

STDMETHODIMP_(long) Expression::Evaluate()
{
...
// Implementation the same, only the declaration is different
...
}

STDMETHODIMP Expression::QueryInterface( REFIID riid, void** ppv )
{
    *ppv = NULL;

    if ( riid == IID_IUnknown || riid == IID_IExpression )
        *ppv = this;

    if ( *ppv )
    {
        ( (LPUNKNOWN)*ppv )->AddRef();
        return( S_OK );
    }
    return (E_NOINTERFACE);
}

STDMETHODIMP_(ULONG) Expression::AddRef()
{
    return ++m_dwRef;
}

STDMETHODIMP_(ULONG) Expression::Release()
{
    if ( --m_dwRef )
        return m_dwRef;

    delete this;
    return 0;
}
```

I saved `GetExpression` for last, because we encounter Unicode again. **AFXPRIV.H** includes several macros that make dealing with Unicode easier. The macros are described in detail in *MFC Tech Note 59*, but we're using just one of them here. `T2OLE` converts an ANSI string to Unicode. The required `USES_CONVER-`

SION line declares some local storage for the conversion macros. Once we get a Unicode string, we pass it to the COM SysAllocString function.

Remember, too, that we will allocate storage for the returned string, and the client is responsible for eventually releasing the memory. This is an important rule to understand when you're working with COM.

```
STDMETHODIMP_(BSTR) Expression::GetExpression()
{
#if ( _MFC_VER >= 0x400 )
    USES_CONVERSION
    LPCOLESTR lpOleStr = T2COLE( m_strExpression );
    return ::SysAllocString( lpOleStr );
#else
    return ::SysAllocString( m_strExpression );
#endif
}
```

We need to export the COM API functions so that they can be called outside the DLL. Visual C++ creates a default **.DEF** file as part of the project, but you must export the two COM-specific functions that we added to **SERVER.CPP**. Open **SERVER.DEF** and add the highlighted code:

```
; Server.def : Declares the module parameters for the DLL.

LIBRARY        SERVER
DESCRIPTION    'SERVER Windows Dynamic Link Library'

EXPORTS
    ; Explicit exports can go here
              DllGetClassObject       @2
              DllCanUnloadNow         @3
```

We're almost finished. Next, we add the new **EXPSVR.CPP** file to the project. Click **Insert/Files into Project** and add **EXPSVR.CPP**. After this, go ahead and compile and link the SERVER DLL.

Register the Component

Before we can use the component, it must be registered in the Windows Registry. Later, we'll do this programmatically, but for now we'll need to use **REGEDIT.EXE** (Windows 95), File Manager (NT 3.51), or Explorer (Windows 95 or NT 4.0), depending on your operating system. Included on the accompanying CD-ROM is a **.REG** file (**WIN32.REG**) that you can use to enter the keys into the Registry. Following is the text of the **WIN32.REG** file for the Chap4 Expression Component. You will have to edit **WIN32.REG** and modify the highlighted line with the path of your project.

```
REGEDIT
HKEY_CLASSES_ROOT\CLSID\{a988bd40-9f1a-11ce-8b9f-10005afb7d30} = Chap4 Expression Component
HKEY_CLASSES_ROOT\CLSID\{a988bd40-9f1a-11ce-8b9f-10005afb7d30}\ProgID = Chap4.Expression.1
HKEY_CLASSES_ROOT\CLSID\{a988bd40-9f1a-11ce-8b9f-10005afb7d30}\VersionIndependentProgID =
Chap4.Expression.1
HKEY_CLASSES_ROOT\CLSID\{a988bd40-9f1a-11ce-8b9f-10005afb7d30}\InprocServer32 =
c:\chap4\Server\Debug\server.dll
HKEY_CLASSES_ROOT\CLSID\{a988bd40-9f1a-11ce-8b9f-10005afb7d30}\NotInsertable

HKEY_CLASSES_ROOT\Chap4.Expression.1 = Chap4 Expression Component
HKEY_CLASSES_ROOT\Chap4.Expression.1\CLSID = {a988bd40-9f1a-11ce-8b9f-10005afb7d30}
HKEY_CLASSES_ROOT\Chap4.Expression.1\CurVer = Chap4.Expression.1
```

After we've registered the component, we can quickly test the server with a nice utility: **OLEVIEW.EXE**.

A Quick Test of the In-Process Server

Included with Visual C++ is a program called **OLEVIEW.EXE** (It may instead be named **OLE2VW32.EXE**.) OLEVIEW is also included with the ActiveX SDK. It is good for initially testing COM/OLE components. We will use one of its features here to ensure that our new **SERVER.DLL** can be loaded. We will also verify that it has been successfully entered into the Registry.

Start **OLEVIEW.EXE** using your favorite method (mine is **start oleview** from a command prompt) and locate the entry for our server Chap4 Expression Component. If you can't find it, make sure that you are displaying noninsertable objects. You will also need to set **OLEVIEW.EXE** to **Expert Mode** to locate the component. It will be under the All Objects tree. Once you've located our server, click on it once to highlight it. The Registry information should display as shown in Figure 4.10.

Now, to quickly test to see whether we've done everything right, double-click or expand the entry. This will attempt to perform a CoGetClassObject, which calls our DllGetClassObject function to instantiate a class factory. If this succeeds, you'll see the IUKnown interface displayed under the entry as in Figure 4.10. If it fails, you'll see something like this "CO_E_SERVER_EXEC_FAILURE" on the status bar. This means either that the path to the DLL is wrong or the DLL isn't there. Another possibility is that you forgot to export the DllGetClassObject function from your DLL.

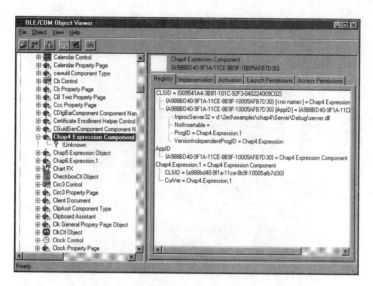

Figure 4.10 Successful call to `CoGetClassObject`.

A COM Client Application

Next we'll build an application that uses the `Expression` in-process server that we developed in the previous section. In Chapter 3, we developed an MFC application that used the original `Expression` C++ class from Chapter 2. Our client application is going to behave, on the surface, just as it did in Chapter 3. The application user types an expression and then validates or evaluates the expression using the command buttons.

We'll provide the same functionality, but instead of incorporating the C++ class into the application, we will access the `Expression` COM object for the needed functionality.

Start Visual C++, go into AppWizard, and create a new project just as we did at the end of Chapter 3. Call this new project **CLIENT**. Make it an SDI application with no OLE support and be sure to derive the `View` class from `CFormView` so that we can easily place our controls. When you get to the last AppWizard screen, check to make sure it matches the screen shown in Figure 4.11.

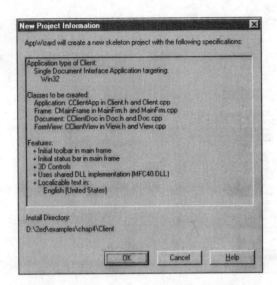

Figure 4.11 Client New Project Information dialog box.

Just as in Chapter 3, edit the **.RC** file and add an entry field and two command buttons to the `IDD_CLIENT_FORM` dialog. Name the command buttons `IDC_VALIDATE` and `IDC_EVALUATE` and the entry field `IDC_EXPRESSION`. Close the resource editor and save the changes. Now start ClassWizard, go to the `CClientView` class, and tie the `IDC_VALIDATE` and `IDC_EVALUATE BN_CLICKED` events to a function. Take the default `OnValidate` and `OnEvaluate`. All this is the same as in Chapter 3. Now compile and link the application and make sure it looks similar to the screen shown in Figure 4.12.

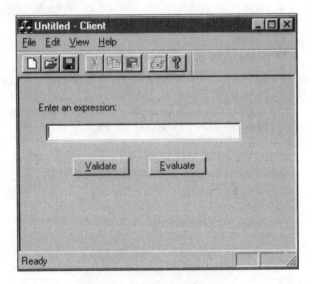

Figure 4.12 Client application.

Before we can access our COM component, we must set up the COM/OLE environment by initializing the various DLLs. COM provides the `CoInitialize` API functions to perform this task. Edit the `InitInstance` member of **CLIENT.CPP**. `InitInstance` is called only once during the startup of the application. This file provides a perfect place to initialize COM.

```
// client.cpp
...
BOOL CClientApp::InitInstance()
{
    // Standard initialization
    // If you are not using these features and wish to reduce the size
    //  of your final executable, you should remove from the following
    //  the specific initialization routines you do not need.

    // Initialize COM
    HRESULT hr = ::CoInitialize( NULL );
    if ( FAILED( hr ) )
    {
        AfxMessageBox( "Unable to Initialize COM, exiting" );
        return FALSE;
    }

    Enable3dControls();
...
}
```

NOTE `CoBuildVersion` is required only for 16-bit applications. Under Win32, this call is not required and is documented as obsolete. If you're writing 16-bit code, you should check the version of the COM/OLE DLLs on the executing system. Here's how:

```
        // Check the version of the COM DLLs
    DWORD dwBV = ::CoBuildVersion();
    if ( HIWORD( dwBV ) != rmm || LOWORD( dwBV ) < rup )
    {
        AfxMessageBox( "COM Version is too old to continue" );
        return FALSE;
    }
```

The symbols `rmm` and `rup` refer to the COM/OLE build number and are defined in the **OLE2VER.H** include file.

```
    // client.cpp
    ...
    #include "view.h"
    #include <ole2ver.h>
    #ifdef _DEBUG
```

We also need to include the **AFXOLE.H** file in **STDAFX.H** so that we have access to the various COM/OLE API functions.

```
// stdafx.h
...
#include <afxwin.h>          // MFC core and standard components
#include <afxext.h>          // MFC extensions

#include <afxole.h>
```

We should terminate and release the COM libraries when our application terminates. MFC provides `ExitInstance`, an overridable member of `CWinApp` that is called just before application termination. Using ClassWizard, select `CClientApp` from the dropdown listbox. Select `CClientApp` in the Objects IDs listbox, and all the overridable members of `CWinApp` are shown. Select `ExitInstance` from the Messages listbox and click the **Add Function** button. Then click **Edit Code** and add the following:

```
int CClientApp::ExitInstance()
{
    // Shutdown COM
    ::CoUninitialize();

    return CWinApp::ExitInstance();
}
```

Now we have added basic COM support to our application. Go ahead and compile, link, and run the application in debug to get a sense of what occurs. Not much, right? COM is easy.

Now let's add the functionality from the `Expression` in-process server. Because the `IExpression` interface is a custom interface not provided by COM, we need to include the interface definition. Open a new file in Visual C++ and call it **IEXP.H**. Either type in or copy the following code from **EXPSRV.H**.

```
//
// iexp.h - contains the IID and interface definition for the
//          IExpression custom interface.

#ifndef IEXP_H_
#define IEXP_H_

#ifdef INITGUID
#include <initguid.h>
#endif

DEFINE_GUID(IID_IExpression,
            0xA988BD41,0x9F1A,0x11CE,0x8B,0x9F,0x10,0x00,0x5A,0xFB,0x7D,0x30);

class IExpression {
public:
```

```
   STDMETHOD(QueryInterface(REFIID, void**)) PURE;
   STDMETHOD_(ULONG, AddRef())           PURE;
   STDMETHOD_(ULONG, Release())          PURE;

   STDMETHOD_(BSTR,GetExpression()) PURE;
   STDMETHOD_(void, SetExpression(BSTR, BOOL)) PURE;
   STDMETHOD_(BOOL, Validate())          PURE;
   STDMETHOD_(long, Evaluate())          PURE;
};

#endif  // inclusion guard
```

The information in **IEXP.H** is all we need to access the functionality of the Expression component. It defines the interface ID (IID) and each of the public methods provided by the component. In Chapter 6, we will implement the Expression component using the standard ActiveX interface IDispatch. Using IDispatch, we eliminate the client's need for any static component information like in the preceding code.

To use the Expression component, we need to instantiate a copy of it and obtain a pointer to the IExpression interface. We will add code to do this in the CClientView class contained in **VIEW.H** and **VIEW.CPP**. First, we need to forward declare the IExpression class; then we declare a member variable, m_pIExp, that will contain the IExpression interface pointer.

```
// view.h : interface of the CClientView class
//
/////////////////////////////////////////////////////////////////////////

class IExpression;

class CClientView : public CFormView
{
protected: // create from serialization only
   CClientView();
   DECLARE_DYNCREATE(CClientView)

   // Add a pointer to IExpression
   IExpression* m_pIExp;

public:
   //{{AFX_DATA(CClientView)
   enum{ IDD = IDD_CLIENT_FORM };
      // NOTE: the ClassWizard will add data members here
   //}}AFX_DATA
   ...
};
```

When the `View` class is instantiated, we create an instance of the `Expression` component using its class factory. To obtain a pointer to the `Expression` class factory interface, we must use `CoGetClassObject`. `CoGetClassObject` requires a CLSID, so we first call `CLSIDFromProgID` to convert `Chap4.Expression.1` to the unique 128-bit CLSID. `CLSIDFromProgID` does the conversion by looking for the `Chap4.Expression.1` key in the Registry and returning the associated CLSID.

CoGetClassObject first looks in COM's table of registered class objects. If the object isn't found, `CoGetClassObject` queries the Registry to determine how to invoke the EXE or DLL. If the component is housed in a DLL, as in our case, it checks to see whether the DLL is loaded. If it is not, the function calls `LoadLibrary` to load the DLL. Once the DLL is loaded, the entry point `DllGetClassObject` is called with the CLSID that is passed. Add the following to **VIEW.CPP**:

```
// view.cpp : implementation of the CClientView class
//

#include "stdafx.h"
#include "client.h"
#include "document.h"
#include "view.h"

// Define INITGUID so that IID_IExpression is defined only once
#define INITGUID
#include "iexp.h"

// To support Unicode conversion in 4.0
#if ( _MFC_VER >= 0x400 )
   #include <afxpriv.h>
#endif

...

CClientView::CClientView()
   : CFormView(CClientView::IDD)
{
   //{{AFX_DATA_INIT(CClientView)
      // NOTE: the ClassWizard will add member initialization here
   //}}AFX_DATA_INIT
   // TODO: add construction code here

   LPCLASSFACTORY lpClassFactory;
   HRESULT hr;
   CLSID Clsid;

   m_pIExp = NULL;

// Convert the file contents to Unicode for ver 4.0
```

```
#if ( _MFC_VER >= 0x400 )
  USES_CONVERSION
  LPCOLESTR lpOleStr = T2COLE( "Chap4.Expression.1" );
  hr = ::CLSIDFromProgID( lpOleStr, &Clsid );
#else
  hr = ::CLSIDFromProgID( "Chap4.Expression.1", &Clsid );
#endif
  if( FAILED( hr ))
  {
    AfxMessageBox( "CLSIDFromProgID failed\n" );

    return;
  }

  hr = ::CoGetClassObject( Clsid,
                           CLSCTX_INPROC_SERVER | CLSCTX_LOCAL_SERVER,
                           NULL,
                           IID_IClassFactory,
                           (LPVOID FAR *) &lpClassFactory );
  if ( FAILED( hr ) )
  {
    AfxMessageBox( "CoGetClassObject failed" );
    return;
  }

  hr = lpClassFactory->CreateInstance( NULL,
                                       IID_IExpression,
                                       (LPVOID FAR *) &m_pIExp );
  if ( FAILED( hr ) )
  {
    m_pIExp = NULL;
    AfxMessageBox( "ClassFactory->CreateInstance failed" );
    return;
  }

  lpClassFactory->Release();
}
```

Once we have a pointer to `IClassFactory`, we call `CreateInstance`, requesting the `IID_IExpression` interface. If all goes well, the interface pointer is returned. We are then finished with the class factory object and call `Release` through its interface, `IClassFactory`. At this point **SERVER.DLL** is loaded, and it contains an instance of the `Expression` class.

When the application terminates, we need to clean up by releasing the IExpression interface, which allows the DLL to unload. Add the following code to the CClientView destructor:

```
CClientView::~CClientView()
{
    if ( m_pIExp )
        m_pIExp->Release();
}
```

When the application user clicks the **Validate** or **Evaluate** button, we need to call the appropriate function in the Expression component. We already have a pointer to the IExpression interface, so this is easy. The code is very similar to that in Chapter 3, where we were using the C++ class directly. The only difference is that we now use an interface pointer instead.

```
void CClientView::OnEvaluate()
{
    CString strExpression;
    char szTemp[128];

    if ( m_pIExp == NULL )
    {
        AfxMessageBox( "No Interface to Expression" );
        return;
    }

    // Get the expression from the entry field
    CWnd* pWnd = GetDlgItem(IDC_EXPRESSION);
    pWnd->GetWindowText( strExpression );

    TRACE1( "OnEvaluate: Expression is %s\n", strExpression );

    BSTR bstrExp = strExpression.AllocSysString();
    m_pIExp->SetExpression( bstrExp, TRUE );
    ::SysFreeString( bstrExp );

    long lResult = m_pIExp->Evaluate();
    sprintf( szTemp, "%ld", lResult );

    pWnd->SetWindowText( szTemp );

    // Set focus back to the entry field

    GetDlgItem( IDC_EXPRESSION )->SetFocus();
}

void CClientView::OnValidate()
```

```
{
    CString strExpression;

    if ( m_pIExp == NULL )
    {
        AfxMessageBox( "No Interface to Expression" );
        return;
    }

    // Get the expression from the entry field
    CWnd* pWnd = GetDlgItem( IDC_EXPRESSION );
    pWnd->GetWindowText( strExpression );

    TRACE1( "OnValidate: Expression is %s\n", strExpression );

    BSTR bstrExp = strExpression.AllocSysString();
    m_pIExp->SetExpression( bstrExp, TRUE );
    ::SysFreeString( bstrExp );

    if (! m_pIExp->Validate() )
        AfxMessageBox( "Invalid Expression, try again" );

    //Set focus back to the entry field
    GetDlgItem(IDC_EXPRESSION)->SetFocus();
}
```

After adding all the preceding code, compile and link the CLIENT application.

Debugging the Client Application

Because our server is in-process, it is easy to debug both the client and server pieces. When running the client executable, you can step into the IExpression interface calls and go directly into the server code. Debugging a local server process is more difficult, but with Windows NT you can load multiple copies of the Visual C++ debugger and debug two processes simultaneously.

Summary

In this chapter our goal was to understand what Microsoft's Component Object Model is, what it can provide, and how it is implemented. We learned that COM provides a binary standard way for various languages and processes to interoperate and that this is done primarily through component interfaces. Component class interfaces are best developed using C++ because COM's internal structure is heavily dependent on a structure called a Vtable; Vtables are built using the virtual function mechanisms of C++. All

COM objects must implement an interface called IUnknown that provides the ability for a client process to query for an interface on a given component. IUnknown also provides methods that help with the management of a component object's lifetime.

Almost all COM objects expose multiple interfaces. To provide multiple interfaces in C++, we need to provide multiple Vtables for our class. We looked at three methods of implementing multiple interfaces in C++: multiple inheritance, interface implementations, and class nesting. Class nesting is the method used by MFC.

GUIDs are 128-bit unique identifiers that are used to identify COM object classes as well as the interfaces that these classes expose. The Windows Registry is used by COM to register component classes and provides a mechanism to locate a component by its unique CLSID or by a ProgID, which is a less unique, readable string that also identifies a component class.

Each COM object also must provide a class factory. The class factory is itself a COM object whose sole purpose is to create instances of another component class. These two components—the component class and its associated class factory—are the minimum requirements to provide a COM binary standard wrapper. These objects must be implemented within a component housing so that the components can be executed within the operating system.

There are two methods of housing components. In-process servers are implemented as DLLs and are typically faster than the other housing type, the local server or executable, because in-process servers don't require marshaling. Marshaling, the process of copying function arguments across these process or network boundaries, can greatly affect the performance of a component.

COM is a robust, system-level system standard on which higher-level application standards, such as ActiveX, can be built.

Chapter 5

COM, OLE, ActiveX, and the MFC Libraries

In Chapter 4 we discussed Microsoft's Component Object Model (COM). In this chapter, we will investigate the relationship of COM, OLE, and ActiveX. Once we understand that, we will look deep into the MFC libraries to see how MFC implements its abstracted view of these technologies. As we go along, we will convert the client and server applications of Chapter 4 to use MFC's COM-based classes instead of going directly to the COM/OLE APIs.

Our purpose in this chapter is to understand how MFC implements its COM support. With this knowledge, we can then move forward with a solid understanding of MFC-based COM technologies. In particular, we will answer two questions: what exactly are OLE and ActiveX? How are they related and how are they different?

This chapter focuses on the low-level details of how MFC implements support for COM, OLE, and ActiveX. You don't really need to master this low-level detail to build software components, but if you understand the low-level implementation, it's much easier to understand the how to effectively implement software based on these technologies.

What Is COM?

As the "Model" part of its name indicates, COM is a model for binary standard software development. Other vendors are free to implement the model using whatever mechanisms they choose, as long as the resulting implementation adheres to the model. Microsoft has provided an implementation of COM within its Windows operating systems. Windows provides COM-based system-level services that all software developers can use.

What Is OLE?

That's a difficult question to answer. A few years ago, OLE was an acronym for Object Linking and Embedding. OLE version 1.0 (circa 1991) was focused only on the linking and embedding of word process- ing and spreadsheet documents, but OLE version 2.0 (circa 1993) added many features that had nothing to do with *compound* documents. After the release of OLE 2.0, Microsoft stated that OLE was no longer an acronym for Object Linking and Embedding but instead was an umbrella term to describe all the features provided by OLE. These features include OLE automation, OLE controls, and several others—technologies that don't fit into the compound document area. The concept of a version number was also dropped. The technology can be, and is, constantly updated without affecting existing software.

In short, OLE is a well-defined set of COM-based interfaces (and a set of API functions that facilitate the use of these interfaces). That's it. OLE provides a robust, application-level implementation of COM that gives developers a new tool in the struggle to provide reusable software. The COM API functions we looked at in Chapter 4 provide the foundation on which to build this robust implementation on all the Windows platforms.

As an architecture, OLE is highly extensible. If new features are needed within OLE or in an operating system (such as Windows) that uses COM or OLE internally, it is easy to define a new OLE interface to pro- vide the functionality. It can be delivered to users by providing a new in-process server or by adding the interface (and its supporting COM object and so on) to an existing system DLL (such as **OLE32.DLL**). This arrangement makes it easy to augment the OLE system environment and provides easy upgrading of exist- ing capabilities. Windows 95 and Windows NT 4.0 make extensive use of OLE within their GUI shells. You extend the shell by writing DLLs, which are OLE in-process servers. And because of OLE's ability to expose additional interfaces on the same object, this addition of functionality in no way harms or affects existing software that may use the augmented interface. Once the COM infrastructure is in place, extension of vari- ous operating system functions is rather easy. Future Windows operating systems will make extensive use of this capability as Microsoft continues its quest to evolve Windows into a true object-oriented operating system.

What Is ActiveX?

Another difficult question. Before 1996, the term *OLE* was used to describe nearly all of the COM-based Windows development technologies. In April 1996, Microsoft unveiled its new Internet-based technology and changed many of the terms it had previously used to describe various COM-based technologies. The implementation and use of the technologies didn't change, but their names changed. ActiveX became the term used to describe Microsoft's Web-based technologies. Instead of OLE controls, we had ActiveX con- trols. Instead of OLE automation, the term was now Automation.

These technologies existed before April 1996, and their implementations still contain all the OLE inter- faces from before; only the name has been changed. In addition, several new technologies were announced. ActiveX scripting is a new technology, although it is a collection of COM-based interfaces and possibly a few new APIs.

In a nutshell, COM is a system-level service provided by the Windows operating systems. OLE is a series of well-defined COM-based interfaces and a few APIs that provide a standard way of providing compound document support to applications. Similarly, ActiveX is a series of COM-based interfaces and a few APIs that provide a large number of application-level services to applications developers, especially those who focus on Web-based development. In many cases, the OLE and ActiveX interfaces intersect. Both technologies may define and use the same set of interfaces.

In other words, OLE and ActiveX (and DirectX) are a way of categorizing the technologies. In reality, they are just a collected group of COM-based interfaces and maybe a few APIs. That's it. Figure 5.1 illustrates the relationships among these technologies.

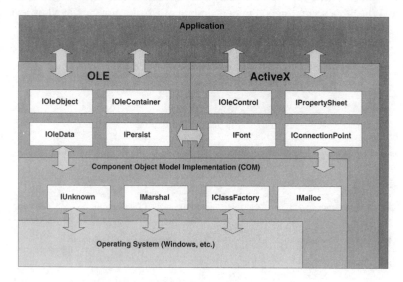

Figure 5.1 COM, OLE, and ActiveX relationships.

To make things simple, throughout the rest of the book I will use the term *ActiveX* because the technologies that we're focusing on come from this category. Automation and ActiveX controls are our primary focus. If I regress and use *OLE*, I'll explain why. I will also use the term *COM* when discussing functionality that supports both OLE and ActiveX. It is a good general term when you're discussing COM-based software. Also, the use of *ActiveX* can be confusing, because many of the interfaces and API calls are prefixed with "OLE" and not "ActiveX." Just keep in mind that, in most occurrences, OLE = ActiveX.

MFC and ActiveX

Even though ActiveX is a collection of COM-based interfaces, their large number and implementation requirements can make ActiveX a complex technology to grasp. The MFC libraries provide a way for a developer to start using ActiveX without having to understand all the details of what's going on "under the covers." As we discussed in Chapter 3, one of the primary purposes of application frameworks is to provide an abstracted view of the low-level implementation of system technologies. MFC does this, and in this chapter I'll show you how MFC does it. We'll look under the covers of MFC so that we can use what we learned in Chapter 4.

Chapters 4 and 5 concern the low-level implementation details of COM, ActiveX, and MFC. You may not understand everything at first, but these chapters are here when you need them. After this chapter, we'll focus more on how to use ActiveX. As you gain experience with ActiveX, you will see more and more opportunities to use the technology in many areas of the software you develop. It is a powerful technology.

You will also find that MFC may not provide an abstraction or encapsulated class for the ActiveX features you require. When this occurs, a good understanding of what is going on at a low level will allow you to implement the technology yourself, with or without the help of MFC.

Figure 5.2 shows some of the important ActiveX classes provided by MFC. We will discuss the highlighted ones in this chapter. In later chapters we will discuss some of the others.

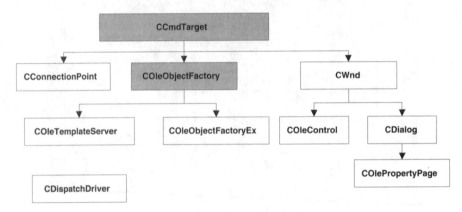

Figure 5.2 Important MFC ActiveX classes.

Interfaces and Grouped Functionality

The OLE and ActiveX technologies contain several hundred interfaces, and the number continues to grow as new capabilities are added. Many of these interfaces are grouped to describe various application technologies. Examples include compound documents, structured storage, drag and drop, Automation, ActiveX documents, and others. Most developers are familiar with OLE's compound document technology but may not be familiar with all the new things added in the latest ActiveX specification. We will focus on two technologies: Automation and ActiveX controls. As you'll see, they use many of the interfaces currently described by ActiveX. Figure 5.3 shows a view of some of the ActiveX interfaces we'll deal with when developing Automation servers and ActiveX controls.

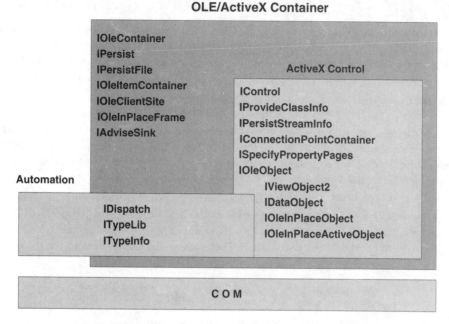

Figure 5.3 COM-based interfaces and application functionality.

Converting the Expression Examples to Use MFC

To illustrate how MFC implements COM/ActiveX, we will convert the CLIENT and SERVER applications from Chapter 4 to use the MFC libraries. Instead of using the native COM API functions and straight C++ constructs for the implementation, we will use MFC's abstracted implementation. This arrangement will illustrate the differences in the techniques and provide a better understanding of how MFC implements its ActiveX support.

Because we were doing certain things at a very low level, not everything will convert directly to MFC. MFC currently does not provide a wrapped ActiveX class for every ActiveX technology. This applies only to certain functions in the CLIENT module; everything in the SERVER will convert right over. As with all application frameworks, MFC cannot implement changes as quickly as they are added to the OS environment. There are areas of ActiveX that are not implemented in MFC, so the developer must use C++ and the APIs explicitly. When we encounter such situations, we will know enough to implement them ourselves.

Converting the Chapter 4 Client Application

There isn't much work involved in converting the CLIENT application from Chapter 4. The most difficult part is probably in deciding how you want to go about doing it. The changes are so minor you might simply modify the chapter CLIENT project as the following sections demonstrate. Or you could build a new CLIENT project following the steps in Chapter 4 and then continue with the items in the following section.

I've changed the CLSID and ProgID of the Chapter 5 server application so that we can distinguish it from the other servers that we will create or have created. In our client application we have hard coded the specific ProgID that we want to use. What I'm recommending is that we add a modal dialog box that allows us to enter the ProgID before we attempt to call the CLSIDFromProgID function. Using this method, we can modify the existing CLIENT application and continue to use it with both the Chapter 4 and Chapter 5 server examples. Here's what we need to do.

Open the Chapter 4 CLIENT project, click the **Resource** tab, select **Insert/Resource**, and add a new DIA-LOG resource. Use **IDD_DIALOG** as the ID. Add a combo box with an ID of **IDC_PROGID** and a static field that says something like **Please select the ProgID to use:**. The combo box should have a style of **Drop List**, but first you need to set it to **Simple** to size it. Then remove the **Cancel** button. The dialog box should look something like Figure 5.4.

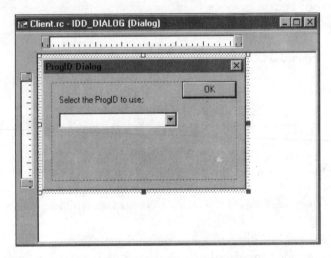

Figure 5.4 Server selection dialog box.

Now we need to create a class that encapsulates the dialog box we just built. We can easily do this using ClassWizard. If you invoke ClassWizard when editing a dialog resource, you will get a screen like that in Figure 5.5. Click **OK** to get the New Class dialog box. Add a new class with the name **CProgIDDlg**, deriving it from CDialog, and name the implementation files **PROGDLG.H** and **PROGDLG.CPP**. Then press **Create a new class**. Figure 5.6 depicts the screen before you click **Create**.

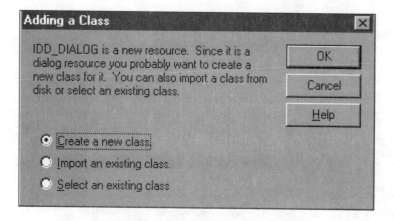

Figure 5.5 Adding a Class dialog box.

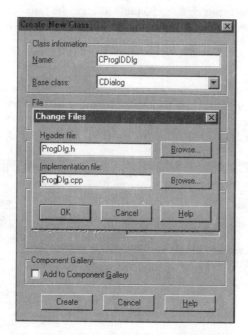

Figure 5.6 Adding a class with ClassWizard.

We've added a new class to the CLIENT project. Now we need to fill the combo box with valid ProgIDs when the dialog box is initially loaded. Go back into ClassWizard, select the **Message Map** tab, and choose **CProgIDDlg** as the class name. Override the WM_INITDIALOG message by selecting it and clicking the **Add**

Function button. This action adds a function called `OnInitDialog`. Add the following code to **PROGDLG.CPP** to load our combo box.

```
BOOL CProgIDDlg::OnInitDialog()
{
    CDialog::OnInitDialog();

    // TODO: Add extra initialization here
    CComboBox* pCB = (CComboBox*) GetDlgItem( IDC_PROGID );
    // Add the valid strings to the combo box
    pCB->AddString( "Chap4.Expression.1" );
    pCB->AddString( "Chap5.Expression.1" );

    return TRUE;  // return TRUE unless you set the focus to a control
                  // EXCEPTION: OCX Property Pages should return FALSE
}
```

Drop list–style combo boxes can also be prefilled using the resource editor. After choosing the drop list style, switch to the General Properties page and you can enter the strings in a listbox on the right. Using this method, you won't have to override `OnInitDialog` just to prefill the list.

N O T E

We need a variable in the `CProgIDDlg` class to contain the combo box selection when the user presses the **OK** button. Go into ClassWizard again and select the **Member Variable** tab with **CProgIDDlg** as the class name. Select **IDC_PROGID** and click the **Add Variable** button. Name the variable **m_strProgID** and select a category of **Value** and a type of **CString**. Click **OK**. Your screen should look like Figure 5.7.

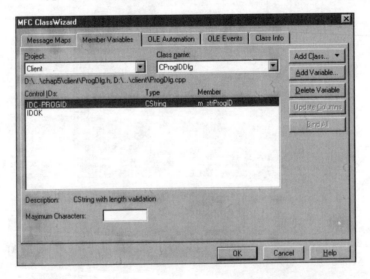

Figure 5.7 ClassWizard Member Variables dialog box.

Now add the following code to **VIEW.CPP**. This creates an instance of the CProgIDDlg class and then calls its DoModal method to display the dialog box. After the user presses **OK**, the DoModal method returns with the m_strProgID variable containing the combo box selection. We then use that value to get our CLSID.

```cpp
//
// View.cpp : implementation of the CClientView class
//

...

// Define INITGUID so that IID_IExpression is defined only once
#define INITGUID
#include "iexp.h"
// To support Unicode conversion in 4.0
#if ( _MFC_VER >= 0x400 )
    #include <afxpriv.h>
#endif

// Include the definition of our new dialog
#include "progdlg.h"

...

CClientView::CClientView() : CFormView(CClientView::IDD)
{
...

    // Create an instance of our new dialog class
    CProgIDDlg Dlg;
    // Invoke it modally
    Dlg.DoModal();

// To support Unicode conversion in 4.0
#if ( _MFC_VER >= 0x400 )
    USES_CONVERSION;
    hr = ::CLSIDFromProgID( T2COLE( Dlg.m_strProgID ), &Clsid );
#else
    hr = ::CLSIDFromProgID( Dlg.m_strProgID, &Clsid );
#endif
    if (FAILED( hr ))
    {
        AfxMessageBox( "CLSIDFromProgID failed" );
        return;
    }
...
}
```

We can now use our CLIENT application to connect to either the Chapter 4 or Chapter 5 server example. Compile, link, and run the application to make sure that you can connect to the Chapter 4 server. You can try to connect to the Chapter 5 server, but because we haven't built it yet, you'll most likely get an error.

Initializing the ActiveX Environment

In Chapter 4, our CLIENT application had to initialize the COM libraries before using any COM components. As we've discussed, ActiveX is the technology that provides most of the application-level functionality we need when we're developing software components. Instead of initializing the COM environment, from now on we will initialize the ActiveX environment. The OLE/ActiveX API function `OleInitialize` is very similar to `CoInitialize`. `OleInitialize` initializes not only COM but also the ActiveX libraries. MFC provides a helper function, `AfxOleInit`, that checks the version of the ActiveX DLLs and initializes the environment by calling `OleInitialize`. In **CLIENT.CPP**, we comment out the explicit COM API calls and use MFC's `AfxOleInit` function instead.

```
// Initialize COM
//HRESULT hr = ::CoInitialize( NULL );
//if ( FAILED( hr ) )
//{
//    AfxMessageBox( "Unable to Initialize COM, exiting" );
//    return FALSE;
//}

// Call this MFC function instead
if ( AfxOleInit() == 0 )
{
    AfxMessageBox( "Unable to Initialize OLE, exiting" );
    return FALSE;
}
```

We also terminated the use of the COM environment by calling `CoUninitialize`. We no longer need to worry about this when we use the MFC `AfxOleInit` function. MFC ensures that the appropriate uninitialize functions are called when the application terminates, so we comment out the `CoUninitialize` call.

```
int CClientApp::ExitInstance()


{

    // Shutdown COM
        // No need to do this if we use MFC's AfxOleInit()
    //::CoUninitialize();
    return CWinApp::ExitInstance();

}
```

That does it for the client piece. Because we are accessing a COM object with an ActiveX custom interface, little is required in the client code to use an ActiveX component. Most of the work required is in the implementation of the ActiveX server, be it an in-process server or a local server. Let's convert the server application from Chapter 4 to use MFC exclusively.

Converting the Chapter 4 Server Application

In the next few sections we will convert the Chapter 4 server application. In the process, we will investigate how MFC implements COM and ActiveX. The first MFC class that we will encounter is CCmdTarget, which provides much of the ActiveX functionality we need when dealing with ActiveX interfaces. The second MFC class that we'll explore is COleObjectFactory. Aptly named for what it does, COleObjectFactory implements COM's IClassFactory interface as well as MFC's implementation of the class factory. MFC takes care of instantiating our MFC ActiveX objects, so we don't have to write very much code to get class factory capabilities.

Following is the **EXPSVR.H** file from the Expression component of Chapter 4.

```
//
// ExpSvr.h
//

DEFINE_GUID( CLSID_Expression,
            0xA988BD40,0x9F1A,0x11CE,0x8B,0x9F,0x10,0x00,0x5A,0xFB,0x7D,0x30);
DEFINE_GUID( IID_IExpression,
            0xA988BD41,0x9F1A,0x11CE,0x8B,0x9F,0x10,0x00,0x5A,0xFB,0x7D,0x30);

// implementation class declarations...
// Token, CStringStack, etc.

...

class IExpression : public IUnknown {
public:
    STDMETHOD_(BSTR,GetExpression()) PURE;
    STDMETHOD_(void, SetExpression(BSTR, BOOL)) PURE;
    STDMETHOD_(BOOL, Validate())       PURE;
    STDMETHOD_(long, Evaluate())       PURE;
};

class Expression : public IExpression
{
protected:
    enum TokenType
```

```
    {
        BogusToken,
        OperatorToken,
        OpenParenToken,
        CloseParenToken,
        NumberToken
    };

protected:
    CString         m_strExpression;
    BOOL            m_bInfix;

protected:
    DWORD           m_dwRef;

public:
    Expression();
    ~Expression();

protected:
    BOOL            IsNumber( const CString& strToken );
    TokenType       GetTokenType( const CString& strToken );
    int             Precedence( const CString& strToken );
    BOOL            InfixToPostfix();

public:
    STDMETHOD( QueryInterface( REFIID, void** ));
    STDMETHOD_(ULONG, AddRef());
    STDMETHOD_(ULONG, Release());

    STDMETHOD_(BSTR, GetExpression());
    STDMETHOD_(void, SetExpression( BSTR, BOOL ));
    STDMETHOD_(BOOL, Validate());
    STDMETHOD_(long, Evaluate());
};

class ExpClassFactory : public IClassFactory
{
protected:
    DWORD           m_dwRef;

public:
    ExpClassFactory();
    ~ExpClassFactory();
```

```
// IUnknown
STDMETHOD( QueryInterface(REFIID, void** ));
STDMETHOD_(ULONG, AddRef());
   STDMETHOD_(ULONG, Release());
// IClassFactory
STDMETHOD( CreateInstance(LPUNKNOWN, REFIID, void**));
STDMETHOD( LockServer(BOOL));
};
```

We need to do quite a few things here to convert the interface, the implementation, and the class factory so that they use MFC's ActiveX classes. You will see that much of our original code is not required when we use MFC's implementation. Let's go through each line of code and convert it to MFC.

```
//
// ExpSvr.h
//
//DEFINE_GUID( CLSID_Expression,
//            0xA988BD40,0x9F1A,0x11CE,0x8B,0x9F,0x10,0x00,
//            0x5A,0xFB,0x7D,0x30);

DEFINE_GUID( IID_IExpression,
            0xA988BD41,0x9F1A,0x11CE,0x8B,0x9F,0x10,0x00,
            0x5A,0xFB,0x7D,0x30);
```

We comment out the DEFINE_GUID macro that defines our CLSID. We will use MFC's method of defining a CLSID later when we convert our class factory. The IID_IExpression DEFINE_GUID macro will stay the same, because we are implementing a custom ActiveX interface and MFC has no knowledge of the IID of the component.

```
class IExpression : public IUnknown {
public:
   STDMETHOD_(BSTR,GetExpression()) PURE;
   STDMETHOD_(void, SetExpression(BSTR, BOOL)) PURE;
   STDMETHOD_(BOOL, Validate())      PURE;
   STDMETHOD_(long, Evaluate())      PURE;
};
```

Nothing changes here, either, for the same reasons. This is a custom interface, and the IExpression class provides the Vtable definition for use by the component user.

The majority of the changes are to the Expression component class. The declaration for the class changes from this:

```
class Expression : public IExpression
```

to this:

```
class Expression : public CCmdTarget
```

This change—deriving from CCmdTarget instead of IExpression—automatically provides significant functionality for the Expression component class. Let's take a closer look at CCmdTarget.

CCmdTarget

The CCmdTarget class is a workhorse when it comes to the implementation of ActiveX within MFC. Not only does it provide a great deal of ActiveX functionality, but it also provides the message mapping mechanism we discussed in Chapter 3 and the Automation IDispatch mapping features that we will discuss in Chapter 6. CCmdTarget provides basic mapping support for MFC in general. What we need to understand about CCmdTarget for now is how it implements the IUnknown interface and its functions: QueryInterface, AddRef, and Release.

Following is a partial list of the CCmdTarget class declaration from **AFXWIN.H**:

```
class CCmdTarget : public CObject
{
...
// ActiveX interface map implementation
public:
    // data used when CCmdTarget is made ActiveX aware
    DWORD      m_dwRef;
    LPUNKNOWN m_pOuterUnknown;  // external controlling unknown if != NULL
    DWORD      m_xInnerUnknown;  // place-holder for inner controlling unknown

    DECLARE_INTERFACE_MAP()

public:
    // these versions do not delegate to m_pOuterUnknown
    DWORD InternalQueryInterface(const void*, LPVOID* ppvObj);
    DWORD InternalAddRef();
    DWORD InternalRelease();
    // these versions delegate to m_pOuterUnknown
    DWORD ExternalQueryInterface(const void*, LPVOID* ppvObj);
    DWORD ExternalAddRef();
    DWORD ExternalRelease();

    // implementation helpers
    LPUNKNOWN GetInterface(const void*);
...
};
```

There are a few things in CCmdTarget that we recognize; the reference count variable (m_dwRef) and some methods that look similar to what we need for the IUnknown interface except that they are prefixed with Internal and External. What's this all about? We'll see in a moment. CCmdTarget supports reference counting and the IUnknown interfaces using a technique called *interface maps*. Each class derived from CCmdTarget inherits this capability, but to use it certain steps must be followed. Did you notice the macro DECLARE_INTERFACE_MAP? It expands (via the preprocessor) to this:

```
private: \
  static const AFX_INTERFACEMAP_ENTRY _interfaceEntries[]; \
protected: \
  static AFX_DATA const AFX_INTERFACEMAP interfaceMap; \
  virtual const AFX_INTERFACEMAP* GetInterfaceMap() const; \
```

The DECLARE_INTERFACE_MAP macro provides a static array of interface IDs (IIDs) for a given class that is derived from CCmdTarget. This table is used by QueryInterface to look up the interface asked for in the REFIID parameter. CCmdTarget itself has a base interfaceMap table that is queried if the derived class does not provide an implementation. I'm sure this is a little confusing at this point, but we had to start somewhere. Back to the Expression class.

```
class Expression : public CCmdTarget
{
...
public:
    STDMETHOD( QueryInterface( REFIID, void** ));
    STDMETHOD_(ULONG,  AddRef());
    STDMETHOD_(ULONG,  Release());

    STDMETHOD_(BSTR, GetExpression());
    STDMETHOD_(void, SetExpression( BSTR, BOOL ));
    STDMETHOD_(BOOL, Validate());
    STDMETHOD_(long, Evaluate());
};
```

To provide an interface map for the Expression class, we need to use DECLARE_INTERFACE_MAP so that we have an interface table that contains our IUnknown and IExpression interfaces. Because every interface must also contain an IUnknown interface, MFC provides some easy-to-use macros for declaring interfaces. These macros use the C++ nested class idiom that we described in the Chapter 4. The preceding interface declaration becomes:

```
DECLARE_INTERFACE_MAP()

BEGIN_INTERFACE_PART( Expression, IExpression )
  STDMETHOD_(BSTR, GetExpression());
  STDMETHOD_(void, SetExpression( BSTR, BOOL ));
  STDMETHOD_(BOOL, Validate());
```

```
    STDMETHOD_(long, Evaluate());
END_INTERFACE_PART( Expression )
```

This code declares a nested class with the name XExpression and provides the declaration for the three methods of IUnknown. Here we derive from our IExpression interface class to ensure that our Vtable is present in the nested class. MFC's macros tend to obscure my understanding at times, so I've "preprocessed" them for you. Here's what's really going on:

```
#define BEGIN_INTERFACE_PART(localClass, baseClass) \
    class X##localClass : public baseClass \
    { \
    public: \
        STDMETHOD_(ULONG, AddRef)(); \
    STDMETHOD_(ULONG, Release)(); \
    STDMETHOD(QueryInterface)(REFIID iid, LPVOID* ppvObj); \
```

BEGIN_INTERFACE_PART declares the nested class and provides the declaration for the IUnknown members. It also builds the nested class name by prepending an X to the outer class name. In this case, it becomes XExpression.

Then you declare your own interface methods using the standard COM STDMETHOD_ macro as before:

```
    STDMETHOD_(BSTR, GetExpression());
        STDMETHOD_(void, SetExpression( BSTR, BOOL ));
    STDMETHOD_(BOOL, Validate());
    STDMETHOD_(long, Evaluate());
```

```
#define END_INTERFACE_PART(localClass) \
    } m_x##localClass; \
    friend class X##localClass; \
```

Once all the interface methods are declared, you use the MFC macro END_INTERFACE_PART(localClass) to end the class declaration, nest an instance of the class, and finally make the nested class a friend of the parent class, just as we did in Chapter 4 when implementing multiple COM interfaces. MFC always uses class nesting even if there is only one interface (not counting IUnknown). Following is declaration before and after preprocessing:

```
// Before
BEGIN_INTERFACE_PART( Expression, IExpression )
    STDMETHOD_(BSTR, GetExpression());
    STDMETHOD_(void, SetExpression( BSTR, BOOL ));
    STDMETHOD_(BOOL, Validate());
    STDMETHOD_(long, Evaluate());
END_INTERFACE_PART( Expression )

// After preprocessing
```

```
class XExpression : public IExpression
{
    STDMETHOD_(ULONG, AddRef)();
    STDMETHOD_(ULONG, Release)();
    STDMETHOD(QueryInterface)(REFIID iid, LPVOID* ppvObj);

    STDMETHOD_(BSTR, GetExpression());
    STDMETHOD_(void, SetExpression( BSTR, BOOL ));
    STDMETHOD_(BOOL, Validate());
    STDMETHOD_(long, Evaluate());
} m_xExpression;
friend class XExpression;
```

There you have it. We have declared our new MFC-compatible COM interface. The declaration for the IUnknown methods comes from our earlier, unchanged declaration of IExpression. We're not quite finished with the Expression class. As we will see, CCmdTarget takes care of our reference counting, so we can remove the member variable that was responsible for that.

```
class Expression : public CCmdTarget
{
...
protected:
    // Remove the reference count variable
    //DWORD          m_dwRef;

...
};
```

We've almost completed the conversion of the Expression class declaration to MFC. Now let's look at the implementation.

In **EXPSVR.H** we declared an interface map using DECLARE_INTERFACE_MAP. This macro declared interfaceMap and InterfaceEntries, two static member variables of Expression. Because these variables were declared static, they must be initialized at compile time. We do this in **EXPSVR.CPP**:

```
// ExpSvr.cpp
...
BEGIN_INTERFACE_MAP( Expression, CCmdTarget )
    INTERFACE_PART( Expression, IID_IExpression, Expression )
END_INTERFACE_MAP()
```

That's all there is to it. The BEGIN_INTERFACE_MAP macro defines the GetInterfaceMap member function and begins the table entry for our interface map. BEGIN_INTERFACE_MAP also defines our interfaceMap member, which points to CCmdTarget (the parent class) and to Expression (the derived class). This makes it easy to search through the derivation hierarchy looking for a particular COM interface when a client uses the `QueryInterface` function.

```
#define BEGIN_INTERFACE_MAP(theClass, theBase) \
    const AFX_INTERFACEMAP* theClass::GetInterfaceMap() const \
        { return &theClass::interfaceMap; } \
    const AFX_DATADEF AFX_INTERFACEMAP theClass::interfaceMap = \
        { &theBase::interfaceMap, &theClass::_interfaceEntries[0], }; \
    const AFX_DATADEF AFX_INTERFACEMAP_ENTRY theClass::_interfaceEntries[] = \
    { \
```

Each `INTERFACE_PART` macro defines one COM interface entry in our map. The `offsetof` macro is used to directly access the address of the Vtable of the nested class instance, `m_xExpression`, within `Expression`.

```
#define INTERFACE_PART(theClass, iid, localClass) \
    { &iid, offsetof(theClass, m_x##localClass) }, \
```

Finally, the `END_INTERFACE_MAP` macro terminates the interface map with an identifiable signature.

```
#define END_INTERFACE_MAP() \
    { NULL, (size_t)-1 } \
    }; \
```

After preprocessor expansion, we get the following:

```
const AFX_INTERFACEMAP* Expression::GetInterfaceMap() const
{ return &Expression::interfaceMap; }
const AFX_DATADEF AFX_INTERFACEMAP Expression::interfaceMap =
{ &CCmdTarget::interfaceMap, &Expression::_interfaceEntries[0], };
const AFX_DATADEF AFX_INTERFACEMAP_ENTRY Expression::_interfaceEntries[] =
{
    { &IID_IExpression, offsetof( Expression, m_xExpression ) },
    { NULL, (size_t) - 1 }
};
```

For debugging purposes it's nice to go ahead and preprocess the code by hand so that you can step through it much more easily. In the example programs for this chapter, I've provided the preprocessed output and have commented out the MFC macro. This makes debugging much more understandable. But once you understand what's going on, you need to use the macros provided by MFC, because their implementation may change with newer versions of the libraries.

Figure 5.8 illustrates what the `INTERFACE_MAP` macros have created for our `Expression` class.

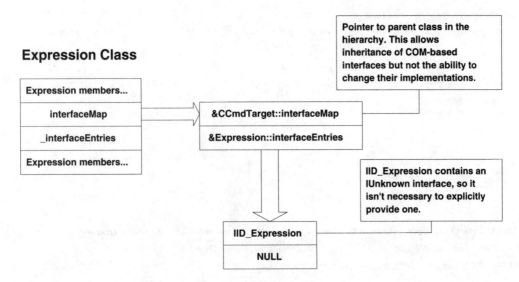

Figure 5.8 Interface maps.

To get a sense of how this works, let's look at CCmdTarget's implementation of QueryInterface. The following code provides the gist of CCmdTarget's implementation. (Some of the details have been left out to protect the innocent.) As you will see in the next section, your class will implement the true QueryInterface method, but it will defer to one of CCmdTarget's InternalQueryInterface or ExternalQueryInterface methods:

```
// The QueryInterface that is exported to normal clients
// This is the method we will use when implementing our
// our QueryInterface
DWORD CCmdTarget::ExternalQueryInterface(const void* iid, LPVOID* ppvObj)
{
    // delegate to controlling unknown if aggregated
    if (m_pOuterUnknown != NULL)
        return m_pOuterUnknown->QueryInterface(*(IID*)iid, ppvObj);

    // If we're not part of an aggregate, call the
    // InternalQueryInterface method below
    return InternalQueryInterface(iid, ppvObj);
}

// real implementation of QueryInterface
DWORD CCmdTarget::InternalQueryInterface(const void* iid, LPVOID* ppvObj)
{
    // check local interfaces. If the IID is found
```

```
   // assign it to the provided void** pointer
   if ((*ppvObj = GetInterface(iid)) != NULL)
   {
      // interface was found — add a reference
      ExternalAddRef();
      return NOERROR;
   }

...

   // interface ID not found, fail the call
   return (DWORD)E_NOINTERFACE;
}


// This function spins through the InterfaceEntries of all of the classes
// derived from CCmdTarget looking for the requested interface.
LPUNKNOWN CCmdTarget::GetInterface(const void* iid)
{
...

   // Get the InterfaceMap of the most derived class
   // GetInterfaceMap was implemented by the BEGIN_INTERFACE_MAP macro
   const AFX_INTERFACEMAP* pMap = GetInterfaceMap();
...

   // Walk the interface map to find the IID
   do
   {
      // Walk through each interface entry for the class
      const AFX_INTERFACEMAP_ENTRY* pEntry = pMap->pEntry;
      while (pEntry->piid != NULL)
      {
         if (*(IID*)pEntry->piid == *(IID*)iid)
         {
            // check INTERFACE_ENTRY macro
            LPUNKNOWN lpUnk = GetInterfacePtr(this, pEntry);

            // check vtable pointer (can be NULL)
            if (*(DWORD*)lpUnk != 0)
               return lpUnk;
         }

         // entry did not match — keep looking
         ++pEntry;
      }
```

```
    // While there are more entries in the map
    // This walks "backwards" in the map from the most derived
    // class up the hierarchy eventually to CCmdTarget itself.
    } while ((pMap = pMap->pBaseMap) != NULL);

    // interface ID not found, fail the call
    return NULL;
}
```

Let's look into the implementation of each method of Expression. Following are the default constructor and destructor for Expression. Only a default constructor is supplied, because MFC will dynamically create an instance of Expression whenever IClassFactory::CreateInstance is called. We'll discuss IClassFactory in a moment. CCmdTarget provides the AfxOleLockApp and AfxOleUnlockApp functions, which are similar to the IClassFactory::LockServer method. Microsoft recommends that you call AfxOleLockApp in the constructor, and AfxOleUnlockApp in the destructor, of a COM component class. The CCmdTarget method OnFinalRelease is called when the reference count of an object reaches zero. The default implementation in CCmdTarget calls delete this to destroy the object.

```
Expression::Expression()
{
    // Increment the active object count
    AfxOleLockApp();
    m_bInFix = TRUE
}
```

```
Expression::~Expression()
{
    // decrement the active object count
    AfxOleUnlockApp();
}
```

The BEGIN_INTERFACE_PART macro created a nested class named XExpression and declared the IUnknown members, so let's implement them:

```
STDMETHODIMP_(ULONG) Expression::XExpression::AddRef()
{
    METHOD_PROLOGUE( Expression, Expression )
    return pThis->ExternalAddRef();
}

STDMETHODIMP_(ULONG) Expression::XExpression::Release()
{
    METHOD_PROLOGUE( Expression, Expression )
    return pThis->ExternalRelease();
```

```
}

STDMETHODIMP Expression::XExpression::QueryInterface( REFIID iid, LPVOID far *pvvObj )

{

    METHOD_PROLOGUE( Expression, Expression )
    return (HRESULT) pThis->ExternalQueryInterface( &iid, pvvObj );

}
```

This code should look familiar. In Chapter 4, we discussed the use of nested classes. The METHOD_PRO-LOGUE macro uses the offsetof macro to calculate the this pointer of the nesting class. In Chapter 4 we delegated the IUnknown methods to the nesting class just as we are doing here, but now we're delegating to CCmdTarget's External functions. CCmdTarget provides two implementations of each IUnknown method: an internal and an external function. These differences concern the support of component aggregation. In most cases, it's beneficial to provide aggregation ability—it doesn't cost much—so you should use the External methods provided by CCmdTarget.

We also need to change the implementation of our exposed interface methods. Some of the implementation of the expression functionality is in the outer, or nesting class, but the interface is provided via the nested class. So we have to scope down using multiple scope resolution operators when implementing the methods, just as we did above with the IUnknown interface. We also need to use the METHOD_PRO-LOGUE macro to access the implementation members in the nesting Expression class. Here are the changes for our four IExpression interface methods:

```
STDMETHODIMP_(BSTR) Expression::XExpression::GetExpression()

{

    METHOD_PROLOGUE( Expression, Expression )

// To support Unicode conversion in 4.0 and above
#if ( _MFC_VER >= 0x400 )
    USES_CONVERSION;
    return ::SysAllocString( T2COLE( pThis->m_strExpression ) );
#else
    return ::SysAllocString( pThis->m_strExpression );
#endif
}

STDMETHODIMP_(void) Expression::XExpression::SetExpression( BSTR bstrExp, BOOL bInfix )

{

    METHOD_PROLOGUE( Expression, Expression )
    pThis->m_strExpression = bstrExp;
    pThis->m_bInfix = bInfix;

}
```

```
STDMETHODIMP_(BOOL) Expression::XExpression::Validate()
{
    METHOD_PROLOGUE( Expression, Expression )
...
    tokenizer.SetString( pThis->m_strExpression );
    // Tokenize our expression
    tokenizer.Tokenize();

    // Check for validity
    while( tokenizer.GetToken( strToken ) )
    {
        switch( pThis->GetTokenType( strToken ) )
        {
        ...
        }
        ...
    }
...
}


STDMETHODIMP_(long) Expression::XExpression::Evaluate()
{
    METHOD_PROLOGUE( Expression, Expression )
...
    if ( pThis->m_bInfix )
    {
        pThis->InfixToPostfix();
    }

    tokenizer.SetString( pThis->m_strExpression );
    tokenizer.Tokenize();

    // While there are tokens to process
    while( tokenizer.GetToken( strToken ) )
    {
        switch( pThis->GetTokenType( strToken ) )
        {
        ...
        }
    }
...
}
```

By deriving from CCmdTarget, we no longer need to keep track of our reference counts inside the implementing class. We also no longer need to keep track of a controlling unknown for aggregation. Now let's turn our attention to the class factory, ExpClassFactory.

Class Factories

As you may recall from Chapter 4, each COM object requires the services of a class factory (which itself is a COM object). This arrangement allows client applications to create instances of your COM object. Client applications gain access to the class factory by using the function CoGetClassObject, which uses one of two methods. If the component object is housed within an in-process server, CoGetClassObject calls the DllGetClassObject entry point within the DLL. If the component object is housed in a local server, COM queries the active object table to determine whether the component's class factory is already running and therefore registered. If it is, COM returns the class factory, and so on. The important thing is that the class factories for a given housing, be it in-process or executable, are always available for a client process to access.

In our Chapter 4 server example, we provided a C++ class, ExpClassFactory, that implemented the CreateInstance function of IClassFactory that created instances of our Expression class. Here's the declaration from **EXPSVR.H**:

```
// Expsvr.h
...
class ExpClassFactory : public IClassFactory
{
protected:
    DWORD           m_dwRef;

public:
    ExpClassFactory();
    ~ExpClassFactory();

    // IUnknown
    STDMETHODIMP           QueryInterface(REFIID, void** );
    STDMETHODIMP_(ULONG) AddRef();
    STDMETHODIMP_(ULONG) Release();
    // IClassFactory
    STDMETHODIMP           CreateInstance(LPUNKNOWN, REFIID, void**);
    STDMETHODIMP           LockServer(BOOL);
};
```

MFC implements the class factory for a component by adding a static class member for each component class in your server application. This static member is an instance of the MFC class COleObjectFactory. Adding a class factory to your component is easy; you just use a few MFC macros. When you're using MFC, it isn't necessary to explicitly declare and implement a separate class factory class for each of your components as we did in Chapter 4. Let's look at COleObjectFactory in more detail.

COleObjectFactory

COleObjectFactory implements each component's class factory, provides facilities to register each class factory with COM, and provides a mechanism for programmatically updating the system Registry (so that you don't have to distribute a **.REG** file with your component).

As we discussed earlier, MFC implements its COM/ActiveX interface classes by deriving from CCmdTarget. Such is the case with the COleObjectFactory class. Its declaration goes something like this:

```
class COleObjectFactory : public CCmdTarget
{
...
    DECLARE_DYNAMIC(COleObjectFactory)
...
public:
    COleObjectFactory* m_pNextFactory;   // list of factories maintained

protected:
    DWORD m_dwRegister;               // registry identifier
    CLSID m_clsid;                    // registered class ID
    CRuntimeClass* m_pRuntimeClass;   // runtime class of CCmdTarget derivative
    BOOL m_bMultiInstance;            // multiple instance?
    LPCTSTR m_lpszProgID;             // human readable class ID

// Interface Maps
public:
    BEGIN_INTERFACE_PART(ClassFactory, IClassFactory)
        INIT_INTERFACE_PART(COleObjectFactory, ClassFactory)
        STDMETHOD(CreateInstance)(LPUNKNOWN, REFIID, LPVOID*);
        STDMETHOD(LockServer)(BOOL);
    END_INTERFACE_PART(ClassFactory)

    DECLARE_INTERFACE_MAP()

    ...
};
```

The MFC COleObjectFactory provides a great deal of functionality for the developer. One purpose of COleObjectFactory is to maintain a list of all the COM component classes within a given component housing (EXE or DLL). We'll get to some of the details in a minute. For now let's focus on those aspects of COleObjectFactory that are important to our conversion of the SERVER example.

The COleObjectFactory constructor takes four arguments. Each argument is described in Table 5.1.

Table 5.1 `COleObjectFactory` Parameters

Parameter	Description
`REFCLSID riid`	A reference to the CLSID for the component that this class factory will support.
`CRuntimeClass* pRuntimeClass`	A pointer to the run-time class. This provides the class factory with the ability to dynamically create instances of the associated component class.
`BOOL bMultiInstance`	This flag indicates whether the component class supports multiple instances within the same housing. If it is `FALSE`, which is the MFC default, the housing supports multiple instances. If this flag is `TRUE`, multiple instances of the housing will be launched for each new instance of a component class.
`LPCSTR lpszProgID`	The ProgID for the component class. The ProgID is a readable string that makes it easier for client applications to create instances of the component object.

You won't use the `COleObjectFactory` constructor directly, because it is implemented by the IMPLE-MENT_OLECREATE() macro, which is used to provide a class factory within your component class.

MFC provides a global class factory in that all the COM objects within a housing use the same method to expose their `IClassFactory` interface to client applications. This is done by using a set of (guess what?) MFC macros. So, for starters, we need to remove the `ExpClassFactory` declaration in **EXPSVR.H** and the implementation in **EXPSVR.CPP**. In its place we'll add the following code to the `Expression` class declaration in **EXPSVR.H**:

```
class Expression : public CCmdTarget
{
    DECLARE_DYNCREATE( Expression )
...
};

// macro definitions from AFX.H
#define DECLARE_DYNCREATE(class_name) \
        DECLARE_DYNAMIC(class_name) \
        static CObject* PASCAL CreateObject();
#define DECLARE_DYNAMIC(class_name) \
public: \
    static AFX_DATA CRuntimeClass class##class_name; \
    virtual CRuntimeClass* GetRuntimeClass() const; \
```

The `DECLARE_DYNCREATE( classname )` macro provides MFC with a way to dynamically create classes whenever required during the execution of your application. The macro also includes the `DECLARE_DYNAMIC( classname )` macro. This macro also provides certain dynamic capabilities that all classes derived from `CObject` inherit. In particular it provides a nonstandard run-time type information (RTTI) capability within MFC.

NOTE

What is RTTI? It's a new addition to the proposed C++ standard that allows C++ developers to easily determine the type of an object at run time. For example, all MFC classes that derived from `CObject` and include `DECLARE_DYNAMIC()` can use the `IsKindOf` function of `CObject`. This allows a developer to determine at run time the identity of a class instance. For example, dynamic classes derived from `CObject` can do something like this:

```
Expression* pExp = new Expression;
...
// At run time check the explicit type of the class
if ( pExp->IsKindOf( RUNTIME_CLASS( Expression ) ))
    // do something
```

The preferred and object-oriented method would be to use the polymorphism capabilities of C++ so that explicit checking isn't required. That's why RTTI is debatable. RTTI is currently part of the draft C++ standard. It is expected to be approved and is currently implemented in most commercial compilers, including Visual C++.

After we ensure that a class instance can be created by MFC, we need to declare a class factory for our component. We use the `DECLARE_OLECREATE( classname )` macro, adding the declaration after `DECLARE_DYNCREATE()` in **EXPSVR.H**.

```
// Expsvr.h
...
class Expression : public CCmdTarget
{
   DECLARE_DYNCREATE( Expression )
   DECLARE_OLECREATE( Expression )
...
};

// macro definition from AFXDISP.H
#define DECLARE_OLECREATE(class_name) \
protected: \
  static AFX_DATA COleObjectFactory factory; \
  static AFX_DATA const GUID AFX_CDECL guid; \
```

The `DECLARE_OLECREATE` macro declares two static members within the `Expression` class: a `COleObjectFactory` variable (`factory`) and a `GUID` variable called (appropriately) `guid`. Because these variables are declared static, there is only one instance and they exist outside the scope of any particular `Expression` instance.

That completes the modifications to **EXPSVR.H**. We now need to define the static variables within **EXPSVR.CPP**.

As you're probably beginning to realize, MFC uses various macros to declare static members of your classes. You use the DECLARE macros in the declaration of your class in the **.H** file, and you must also define or initialize the members using MFC's IMPLEMENT macros in your **.CPP** file.

```
// Expsvr.cpp

#include "stdafx.h"
#include "expsvr.h"
```

```
IMPLEMENT_DYNCREATE( Expression, CCmdTarget )
```

```
// macro definition from AFXDISP.H
#define IMPLEMENT_DYNCREATE(class_name, base_class_name) \
  void PASCAL class_name::Construct(void* p) \
      { new(p) class_name; } \
  _IMPLEMENT_RUNTIMECLASS(class_name, base_class_name, 0xFFFF, \
      class_name::Construct)
```

The IMPLEMENT_DYNCREATE(class, baseclass) macro initializes the run-time class information needed for dynamic construction. You can see how the Construct method is implemented in the macro expansion using the new operator. Next, we initialize our COleObjectFactory variable. Here's the use of the COleObjectFactory constructor:

```
#define IMPLEMENT_OLECREATE(class_name, external_name, l, w1, w2, \
                            b1, b2, b3, b4, b5, b6, b7, b8) \
  AFX_DATADEF COleObjectFactory class_name::factory(class_name::guid, \
    RUNTIME_CLASS(class_name), FALSE, _T(external_name)); \
    const AFX_DATADEF GUID AFX_CDECL class_name::guid = \
    { l, w1, w2, { b1, b2, b3, b4, b5, b6, b7, b8 } }; \
```

The IMPLEMENT_OLECREATE macro takes three parameters. The first one is the class name Expression. This identifies the class whose class factory object we're going to initialize. The second parameter is the ProgID for the class. You remember ProgIDs. They provide a readable identifier for accessing the CLSID of a component object. The third parameter is the CLSID broken up into 11 long, word, and byte chunks. I've changed the CLSID slightly from the one that we used in Chapter 4, so we can have distinct Chapter 4 and Chapter 5 versions of the Expression component and our client application can access either one. The first parameter of the GUID assignment is now 0xA988BD42 instead of the 0xA988BD40 in Chapter 4.

```
// Expsvr.cpp
```

```
IMPLEMENT_OLECREATE( Expression, "Chap5.Expression.1", 0xA988BD42,
                     0x9F1A,0x11CE,0x8B,0x9F,0x10,0x00,0x5A,0xFB,0x7D,0x30 )
```

```
//AFX_DATADEF COleObjectFactory Expression::factory( Expression::guid,
//           RUNTIME_CLASS( Expression ),
//           FALSE,
```

```
//              _T( "Chap5.Expression.1" ));
//const AFX_DATADEF GUID AFX_CDECL Expression::guid = { 0xA988BD42, 0x9F1A, //0x11CE, 0x8B, 0x9F,
0x10, 0x00, 0x5A, 0xFB, 0x7D, 0x30 };
```

COleObjectFactory::Register

The `Register` method registers a particular class factory with the COM environment so that client applications can access it. `Register` calls the COM API function `CoRegisterClassObject` for local-server implementations. Run-time registration isn't necessary for in-proc servers, but MFC still requires a call to the `Register` function; it sets an internal variable, `m_dwRegister`, that indicates the factory is registered. This requirement also provides consistency, from the developer's viewpoint, between local-server and in-process implementations (you always call it).

COleObjectFactory::RegisterAll

The `RegisterAll` method is similar to the `Register` function except that it registers all known class factories within an MFC application. Again, this is required for both local-server and in-process server implementations. `RegisterAll` should be called as soon as possible after an application is launched, usually in the `InitInstance` method of your `CWinApp`-derived application class.

To do this in our converted server application, we add a call to `RegisterAll` in our `InitInstance`. In Chapter 4, we didn't need to do anything during startup, so we didn't override `InitInstance`, but we need to now. To do that, go into ClassWizard (**Ctrl-W**), select the **Message Map** tab, and double-click on the **InitInstance Message** to add the function to the `CServerApp` class. Then add the following highlighted code:

```
//
// server.cpp : Defines the initialization routines for the DLL.
//

#include "stdafx.h"
#include "server.h"

...

BOOL CServerApp::InitInstance()
{
    // TODO: Add your specialized code here and/or call the base class
    COleObjectFactory::RegisterAll();

    return CWinApp::InitInstance();
}
```

Now when our server is initially loaded, all its contained class factories will be registered with COM. In the case of an in-process server, this call initializes MFC's internal variables, because it does not need to directly register with COM.

COleObjectFactory::Revoke and RevokeAll

Local servers that register their class factories with the COM environment are required to `Revoke` them as the application terminates. MFC handles this automatically for your application by calling `RevokeAll`, which in turn calls `Revoke` for each class factory that is registered. For in-process servers, this method does nothing.

COleObjectFactory::UpdateRegistry and UpdateRegistryAll

The `Register` and `Revoke` methods involve the dynamic updating of the COM running object table. `UpdateRegistry` and `UpdateRegistryAll` allow your application to easily update the Windows Registry. By using these functions, you don't need to build **.REG** files to distribute with your applications. MFC makes it easy to populate the Registry with all the pertinent component information. Depending on your component housing, you must use different techniques of performing this automatic updating. Local servers should call `UpdateRegistryAll` whenever they are executed. In-process servers must export the function `DllRegisterServer`. Let's update our server to use this new capability. Our Chapter 4 server required the use of a **.REG** file to register our CLSID and ProgID in the Windows Registry. If we implement and export the function `DllRegisterServer` and call `UpdateRegistryAll`, the component registration can be handled by a standard utility such as **REGSVR32.EXE**. Here's the implementation that we add to **SERVER.CPP**, and the new export for the **.DEF** file:

```
// Add this to SERVER.CPP
// by exporting DllRegisterServer, you can use regsvr32.exe
STDAPI DllRegisterServer(void)
{
   COleObjectFactory::UpdateRegistryAll();
   return ( S_OK );
}
```

```
; Server.def : Declares the module parameters for the DLL.
LIBRARY        "SERVER"
DESCRIPTION  'SERVER Windows Dynamic Link Library'

EXPORTS
       ; Explicit exports can go here
            DllGetClassObject        @2
            DllCanUnloadNow          @3
            DllRegisterServer        @4
```

If your application is an in-process server, you can use **REGSVR32.EXE** like this:

```
c:>regsvr32 server.dll
```

REGSVR32.EXE is a simple application (supplied with VC++ and the ActiveX SDK) that calls the DLL's `DllRegisterServer` entry point. The DLL does the work of registering itself in the Registry. You can also register your new server by using the Visual C++ **Tools/Register Control** menu item. The preceding command calls REGSVR32 with the project's DLL as a parameter. It's a quick way to register in-process servers. As you'll see in a later chapter, ActiveX controls are really just in-process servers with a number of standard interfaces.

REGSVR32 isn't a very complicated program. If you're having problems registering a component housed within a DLL and you want to really understand what REGSVR32 is doing, here's some code that may help.

N O T E

```
//
// RegisterServer takes as a parameter the
// explicit path and filename of the OLE
// server that you want to register.
// E.g., c:\winnt\system32\clock.ocx
// This function loads the DLL/OCX and calls
// the DllRegisterServer function.
//
DWORD RegisterServer( char* szPath )
{
    HINSTANCE hInstance = ::LoadLibrary( szPath );
    if ( 0 == hInstance )
    {
        return ::GetLastError();
    }

    typedef void (FAR PASCAL *REGSERVER)(void);
    REGSERVER RegServer = (REGSERVER)
        ::GetProcAddress( hInstance, _T( "DllRegisterServer" ));

    if ( 0 == RegServer )
    {
        return ::GetLastError();
    }

    RegServer();

    ::FreeLibrary( hInstance );
```

```
        return 0;
}
```

If a server application is implemented as a local server, COM standards recommend that the local server update the Registry every time the application is run. This is easy to do using MFC. You would do something like the following. (MFC will add this function automatically when building a local server that has COM support, but we're doing it the hard way right now.)

```
BOOL CMFCApp::InitInstance()
{
...
    // When a server application is launched stand-alone, it is a good idea
    //  to update the system registry in case it has been damaged.
    COleObjectFactory::UpdateRegistryAll();
}
```

We'll discuss this in more detail in Chapter 6 when we build a local-server application that uses Automation.

MFC COM Helper Functions

MFC has certain "helper" functions that aren't members of any class but provide COM-specific functionality for your application's use. We need to use two of these functions to complete our server application.

AfxDllGetClassObject provides the implementation of COM's DllGetClassObject function. MFC internally maintains a pointer to a list of all class factories in your application. As we saw earlier, COleObjectFactory contains a member variable, m_pNextFactory, that implements a linked list of your COleObjectFactory instances. MFC maintains a pointer to the beginning of this list. AfxDllGetClassObject searches this list for the requested CLSID, creates an instance of the internal class factory, and returns a pointer to the requested Interface ID (IID), just as we did in Chapter 4. We need to change our implementation of DllGetClassObject in **SERVER.CPP** as follows:

```
//
// Server.cpp
//
...
STDAPI DllGetClassObject( REFCLSID rclsid, REFIID riid, void** ppv )
{
    //HRESULT              hr;
    //ExpClassFactory      *pCF;
    // pCF = 0;
    //if ( rclsid != CLSID_Expression )
    //    return( E_FAIL );
```

```
//pExpression = new ExpClassFactory();
//if ( pCF == NULL )
//   return( E_OUTOFMEMORY );
//hr = pCF->QueryInterface( riid, ppv );
//if ( FAILED( hr ) )
//   delete pExpression
//return( hr );

// Let MFC do the work
return AfxDllGetClassObject( rclsid, riid, ppv );
}
```

AfxDllCanUnloadNow is the other MFC helper function that we need to use in our application. Because we now let MFC keep track of the reference counts on our component objects, we don't have the knowledge to implement the COM DllCanUnloadNow function. So we need to change our implementation of DllCanUnloadNow in **SERVER.CPP**.

```
STDAPI DllCanUnloadNow(void)
{
//if ( g_dwObjs || g_dwLocks )
//   return( S_FALSE );
//else
//   return( S_OK );

// Let MFC do the work
return AfxDllCanUnloadNow();
}
```

After making all the changes to the server, build it and test it using the client application we developed earlier in the chapter. You should be able to access both the Chapter 4 and Chapter 5 server programs.

A Recap of the Example Applications

We've been working with our heads down in this chapter, and I think we need an overview of what we've done. First, we added a modal dialog box to our Chapter 4 client application that lets us choose a specific ProgID on startup. We then removed the COM initialization functions and replaced them with a call to MFC's AfxOleInit function. The rest of the COM/ActiveX code we left alone, because there wasn't a direct MFC replacement.

The server application required more changes. We first derived our component class, Expression, from CCmdTarget instead of IExpression. In the process, we learned quite a bit about the mother of all ActiveX classes in MFC: CCmdTarget. It provides the IUnknown interface plus an interface mapping mechanism that makes it easy to provide `QueryInterface`. `CCmdTarget` uses nested classes and encapsulates the reference counting of our components classes, so we don't have to.

Next, we explored the MFC `COleObjectFactory` class and how it provides class factories for our component classes. `COleObjectFactory` automatically keeps track of all the class factories and provides a function, `AfxDllGetClassObject`, to use to expose them to client processes. `COleObjectFactory` provides other features, including the ability to automatically update the Registry with a component's **.REG** information. Throughout this discussion, we learned a great deal about how MFC provides COM/ActiveX support.

Summary

In this chapter, we have looked at how the MFC libraries implement COM and ActiveX support. In particular, we looked at various MFC helper functions—`AfxOleInit`, `AfxDllGetClassObject`, `AfxDllCanUnloadNow`, and so on—that make implementing ActiveX applications easier. We also investigated two important MFC classes that provide COM functionality: `COleObjectFactory` and `CCmdTarget`. In doing so we converted our client and server examples to use MFC's COM support. From this point on, we will use MFC to develop all of our software components.

These first five chapter have provided a solid base for building ActiveX software using the MFC libraries. In the next chapter, we'll use Automation. Automation and MFC make it very easy to wrap existing C++ functionality so that it can be accessed by various other languages.

Chapter 6

Automation

Now it's time to start using this wonderful technology called ActiveX. In this chapter, we'll investigate Automation, an ActiveX technology that is a boon for developers. Automation makes it easy to wrap existing software modules for use outside C and C++ and provides a powerful mechanism to expose an application's functionality to programmatic users. This makes the application an ActiveX component.

What Is ActiveX Automation?

Automation is many things, but it provides two broad techniques that we will explore in this chapter. The first one, which we've been working toward since the first chapter, is the ability to wrap C++ classes and expose their functionality to other, non-C++ language users. This feature alone provides a significant new ability in the development of Windows software.

We will also explore the other technique: using Automation to drive another application or process. This was one of Microsoft's original uses for automation, and it makes it easy to build a generic macro language that will work with many different application products. Microsoft's Visual Basic for Applications is an example of using automation for this purpose.

The ability to expose an application's functionality in a standard way makes an application a software component. If you need the services of a good word processor in your application, you can purchase a word processor that exposes its capabilities via Automation and use it within your application. Microsoft Word, Microsoft Project, and Internet Explorer provide access to nearly all their capabilities through automation.

Automation is one of the most important technologies in ActiveX. It allows for a truly dynamic method whereby two applications can interoperate. In our previous examples, the user or client application had to know just a little about the Expression component—namely, the declaration of the IExpression interface.

Automation removes this last constraint and provides dynamic determination and invocation of a component's interface methods. Automation provides a true *late-binding* mechanism not only within a single language but also between languages and between local or remote processes. This late-binding mechanism is implemented by adding a level of indirection to a component's Vtable pointer implementation. I promised that in these later chapters we wouldn't spend as much time covering the low-level details, and I'm going to keep my promise, but occasionally we will drop down to investigate how MFC implements various features.

Automation Controllers

In earlier chapters we described the user of a component as the *client*. Clients that use and interact with Automation components are called *automation controllers*. This term implies that the client is controlling the component, and in many ways this is correct. Before the specification for ActiveX controls was complete, Automation using the `IDispatch` interface allowed only one-way interaction between client and server applications. This one-way communication constraint explains the use of the term *controller*.

The ActiveX controls specification added the concept (and implementation) of an "outgoing" interface where events that occur within a component can be communicated to the controlling component. In this realm, the concept of who is controlling the interaction blurs, as both components communicate as equals. With the addition of ActiveX events, the relationship between controller and server becomes peer-to-peer instead of the earlier master-slave.

In this chapter, we will use the master-slave type of automation. We will use the `IDispatch` interface to build an application that also contains our `Expression` component class. At first the idea of one-way interoperation may seem constrictive, but in reality that is how we typically develop programs. A normal function call in C++ is synchronous and occurs with one-way communication. You call the function, and your program waits until it returns. The only communication coming back is the value of the return code and any parameters that were passed by reference.

A C++ example of two-way communication is the use of a callback Function, which allows an event to be communicated "out of band" of the normal flow of your application. A callback function takes as a parameter a pointer to a function that you write. As the function executes, it "calls back" into your function with specific information. This arrangement also provides a notification mechanism. A simple example of a callback is the C run-time function `qsort`. For the typical use of an `IDispatch` interface, when only one process is in control of the interaction, the term *controller* describes the use of the interface quite effectively.

The archetypal Automation controller is Visual Basic, which provides a robust controller environment. Visual Basic isn't the only controller available, nor is its use required. The MFC libraries make it easy to develop an application that acts as a controller and drives other applications, although MFC doesn't currently provide the dynamic invocation capabilities of Visual Basic unless you write the code yourself. We'll take a look at what is required in all these circumstances.

NOTE

Actually, the event mechanism is implemented using a reverse (or incoming) dispatch interface. However, I don't want to add too much complexity here as we begin discussing the `IDispatch` interface. We will explore the concept of an ActiveX event in later chapters.

Visual versus Nonvisual Components

The `Expression` class is an example of a nonvisual component. The services it provides have little to do with any GUI aspect of an application. We've been using its capabilities within a Windows entry field, but that need not be the case. The class could be used internally by any number of applications that need the ability to parse and evaluate algebraic expressions. Nonvisual components are usually best implemented as Automation servers. Visual components are probably best implemented as ActiveX controls. There are exceptions, of course, but this is a good general rule to follow.

The IDispatch Interface

Automation is based on an ActiveX interface called `IDispatch`, which provides the ability to dynamically invoke methods on a component within a server. This arrangement differs slightly from the earlier COM custom interface technique of our `Expression` component. When you're using custom interface implementations, the client application requires the `IExpression` declaration to use the component. The `IExpression` declaration (its Vtable structure) is used at compile time to define the Vtable structure of the `Expression` interface. This implements *early binding* of the component's interface. If a new method is added to `IExpression`, the client application must be recompiled to use the new capability.

A server component that implements its methods using `IDispatch` instead of using a custom interface provides a number of additional capabilities. By using `IDispatch`, the interaction between the client and server applications uses late binding of the component's interface methods. The client doesn't require compile-time declarations of the server's component interface. This makes it easy for a server component to change its interface (even at run time!) without requiring the client application to be recompiled or relinked. Of course, any changes to the interface methods should be communicated to the client application so that it can take advantage of the new features. To understand how `IDispatch` provides language-independent late binding, we need to look at its implementation.

Another significant feature added by using `IDispatch` is that of standard marshaling. The default Windows COM implementation contains a number of data types that can be used by components that use `IDispatch`. Intrinsic support for these data types makes it easy to build components that work across local and remote processes.

Most COM interfaces are like the `IExpression` example. They provide a structure that requires a rigid implementation of an abstract class. COM defines the abstract class (interface), but the application developer must provide a unique implementation of that abstract class. `IDispatch` is a little different, because it adds a level of indirection to the Vtable-style interfaces that we've studied so far. One term for this new interface type is *dispinterface*, for dispatch interface. That term succinctly describes how `IDispatch` differs from the standard Vtable implementation. The client does not access a component's functionality through the Vtable pointer, as we did with `IExpression`. Instead, the client first looks up the function, provides a key to the desired function, and finally invokes or dispatches the function (see Figure 6.1).

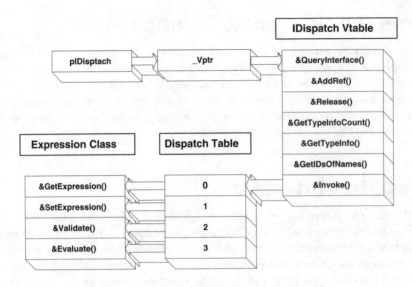

Figure 6.1 IDispatch Vtable and dispatch table.

As you can see from Figure 6.1, there's a bit more going on here with the IDispatch interface than there was with a custom COM interface in the previous chapters. The client still gets a Vtable pointer, but now that the Vtable doesn't have direct access to the Expression methods, the request must first go through the IDispatch::Invoke method. Invoke contains a parameter that maps the method call to a specific entry in the dispatch map. This additional level of indirection is what provides for late binding to the component's methods. Let's take a quick look at IDispatch's methods.

Remember, the server component implements the IDispatch methods, and the controller (or client) calls that implementation through the IDispatch server's pointer. Our next example will describe this process in detail.

N O T E

Invoke

Invoke provides most of the functionality of the IDispatch interface. It takes eight parameters, the most important of which is the DISPID. The DISPID is mapped to a specific offset within the dispatch table and determines which component class method is invoked. Table 6.1 lists the parameters of Invoke. We aren't going to study them in detail yet. We just need to understand that the controller calls Invoke with these parameters instead of calling a component's methods directly through a Vtable implementation.

Table 6.1 `IDispatch::Invoke` Parameters

Parameter	Purpose
DISPID dispidMember	The numeric ID of the specific member within the dispatch table that the controller wants to access.
REFIID riid	Reserved; must be `IID_NULL`.
LCID lcid Support.	A locale ID that indicates the locale if the component supports National Language
USHORT wFlags	The type of `Invoke` call. This flag indicates which type of operation it wants to perform (access a property, invoke a method, and so on). It must be one of the following: `DIS-PATCH_METHOD`, `DISPATCH_PROPERTYGET`, `DISPATCH_PROPERTYPUT`, and `DISPATCH_PROPERTYPUTREF`.
DISPPARMS FAR* pdispparms	The parameter structure that contains an array of parameters for the function.
VARIANT FAR* pvarResult	Where to store the result of the call. `NULL` if the method returns `void`. Ignored on `PROPERTY_PUT`s.
EXCEPINFO FAR* pexcepinfo	Storage for any exception information if an exception occurs.
UINT FAR* puArgErr	Indicates the array element that contains an invalid type when a type mismatch occurs.

As you can see, the controller must provide a great deal of information about the function call to the server's component object. This is one of the drawbacks of late binding. Because the controller doesn't have this information at compile time, it must provide it at run time to use the component's methods. This requirement adds overhead to every method call made on a component and directly affects performance.

Late binding is great, but how can the controller obtain enough information about the component's methods to use the `Invoke` method? The three other methods of `IDispatch` help in this regard.

GetIDsOfNames

`GetIDsOfNames` provides a facility for the controller to map the textual automation server property or method name, such as `GetExpression`, to its numeric DISPID. The DISPID can then be used with the `Invoke` function to access the property or method of the server. Calling `GetIDsOfNames` before every call to `Invoke` can get rather expensive. It is recommended that the controller call `GetIDsOfNames` only once for each property or method and cache the returned DISPID. This technique will speed the interaction. Table 6.2 lists the parameters of `GetIDsOfNames`.

Table 6.2 `IDispatch::GetIDsOfNames` Parameters

Parameter	Purpose
`REFIID riid`	Reserved, must be `IID_NULL`.
`OLECHAR** rgszNames`	An array of member names for which the caller wants the corresponding DISPID. The first element is the name of the member property or method, and the subsequent names are for named parameters.
`unsigned int cNames`	The number of member names in the array.
`LCID lcid`	A locale ID that indicates the locale if the component supports National Language Support.
`DISPID* rgdispid`	An array of DISPIDs. The first element returned is the DISPID of the property or method, and the subsequent elements contain DISPIDs of any named parameters.

GetTypeInfo

Typically, a controller that provides dynamic lookup and calling of automation methods won't have all the type information necessary to populate the `Invoke dispparams` structure. An automation server should call `GetTypeInfoCount` to determine whether the component can provide type information and, if it can, should then call `GetTypeInfo` to get the type information.

For a component to be useful in various development tool implementations, it should provide type information. The type information can be provided by creating an ODL file that describes each property and method along with its return types and parameter types. This file can be compiled into a binary form that makes it easy for client applications to obtain detailed type information for the component. We will discuss this in more detail later in this chapter.

MFC's current implementation of Automation support (aside from ActiveX controls) does not provide type information and returns `E_NOTIMPL`.

GetTypeInfoCount

`GetTypeInfoCount` is used by the controller to determine whether the component object contains type information that can be provided to the controller. Setting the passed-in parameter to 1 indicates that type information is available, and zero indicates that no type information is available. In either case, the method should return `S_OK`. Even without type information, the controller can use the other `IDispatch` methods.

Automation Properties and Methods

The concept of an Automation *property* is very similar to the concept of a C++ member variable. To the user of an Automation property, it will behave and act like a variable in the implementing language. Property values can easily be assigned and retrieved. You would normally use a property if there is an internal C++ variable that it can be associated with. Here's how an Automation property is used within Visual Basic:

```
Dim btn as object
Dim szCaption as String
' Create an instance of a "Button" class
Set btn = CreateObject( "AutoButton" )
' The button has a Caption property
' Set the caption
btn.Caption = "Cancel"
' Get the caption value
szCaption = btn.Caption
```

As you can see, the syntax for working with the Caption property is similar to the syntax you use when you're using an intrinsic data type. In Automation, properties can also have parameters. The parameters typically are used as indexes into an ordered data type. Here's an example of a property with parameters:

```
Dim lbx as object
Dim szString as String
' Create an instance of a "Listbox" class
Set lbx = CreateObject( "AutoListbox" )
' The listbox has a "Text" property
' Fill the list box
For i = 0 to 9
    ' Set the item text
    lbx.Text(i) = "Item " + i
Next
' Get the 5th listbox item text
szString = lbx.Text(4)
```

Automation methods are analogous to C++ class methods. They perform some action within the component when invoked by a controller. The addition of parameters somewhat blurs how Automation properties are different from Automation methods. The primary syntactic difference is that you can't assign a value to an Automation method.

```
Dim lbx as object
Dim szString as String
' Create an instance of a "Listbox" class
Set lbx = CreateObject( "AutoListbox" )
' Empty the Listbox with the clear method
lbx.Clear
' The following makes no sense, and generates an error
lbx.Clear = 10
```

Automation Data Types

Automation provides standard marshaling of parameters and return values across process boundaries. This arrangement makes it easy to implement your components within a local server. To provide marshaling for Automation, COM defines and limits the data types that can be used. I've outlined these data types in Table 6.3. Not all of these types are supported by Visual C++'s ClassWizard, but most of them are.

Table 6.3 Automation-Compatible Data Types

Type	Description
BSTR	A binary string that stores the length of the string in the first two or four bytes of the structure and stores the actual string directly following.
Byte, int, short, long, BOOL, float, double, char*	Intrinsic types.
CY	A currency value stored in eight-byte integer. Used for fixed-point representation of a number. The integer represents the value multiplied by 10,000.
DATE	A date stored in a double, where January 1, 1900, is 2.0, January 2 is 3.0, and so on. Functions are provided by ActiveX to help in the manipulation of the date type.
SCODE	A 32-bit error code.
LPUNKNOWN	A pointer to an IUnknown interface.
LPDISPATCH	A pointer to an IDispatch interface.
Safe Array	An array of one of the preceding data types, including an array of Variants.
VARIANT	A union containing any one of the preceding types.

In certain cases, the supported types in Table 6.3 can be passed by reference, thus allowing the callee to modify the parameter value. In many cases, the values are stored in Automation's VARIANT data type structure. The VARIANT data type allows the controller and the server to communicate.

The VARIANT Data Type

The VARIANT data type is the most important Automation data type. It provides a convenient and effective technique for passing parameters between COM-based components. Also, because of its implementation, a variant can be used to overload Automation methods. Sometimes it's easiest to describe something by showing the code. Here's a condensed definition of the VARIANT structure.

```
struct tagVARIANT
{
    VARTYPE vt;
    union
    {
```

```
        LONG lVal;

        BYTE bVal;

        SHORT iVal;

        FLOAT fltVal;

        DOUBLE dblVal;

        VARIANT_BOOL boolVal;

        SCODE scode;

        CY cyVal;

        DATE date;

        BSTR bstrVal;

        IUnknown *punkVal;

        IDispatch *pdispVal;

        SAFEARRAY *parray;

        BYTE *pbVal;

        SHORT *piVal;

        LONG *plVal;

        FLOAT *pfltVal;

        DOUBLE *pdblVal;

        SCODE *pscode;

        CY *pcyVal;

        DATE *pdate;

        BSTR *pbstrVal;

        IUnknown **ppunkVal;

        IDispatch **ppdispVal;

        SAFEARRAY **pparray;

        VARIANT *pvarVal;

        PVOID byref;

        CHAR cVal;

    }

};


typedef tagVARIANT VARIANT;
typedef VARIANT VARIANTARG;
```

A VARIANT is just a big union of different types and an identifier indicating which type is within the union. The vt member indicates the actual data type, thereby allowing the receiver to extract the data from the appropriate union element. Several COM APIs and macros make working with variants easier. Table 6.4 shows the most useful API calls. For a look at the macros, peruse the **OLEAUTO.H** file in the \MSDEV\INCLUDE directory. MFC also provides a COleVariant class that makes using the variant data type a little easier.

Table 6.4 Useful Variant-Based APIs

Function	Purpose
`VariantInit( VARIANT* )`	Initializes a variant to `VT_EMPTY`.
`VariantClear( VARIANT* )`	Initializes a variant by first freeing any memory used within the variant. This is useful when client-side applications need to clear a variant passed from a server.
`VariantChangeType( … )`	Coerces a variant from one type to another. For example, this method will change a `long` (I4) to a `BOOL` and even an `IDispatch` pointer to a `BSTR`.
`VariantCopy( VARIANT*, VARIANT* )`	Makes a copy of a variant and frees any existing memory in the destination before making the copy.

I mentioned that variants can be used to overload Automation methods. Here's an example in a Visual Basic–like language:

```
objCollection.Add( "Jessica" )
' objName is an automation object
objCollection.Add( objName )
' txtControl is an edit control
objCollection.Add( ByRef txtControl.Text )
```

The `Add` Automation method takes one parameter, which is a variant. Because the method takes a variant, the method user can pass different variant-supported data types to the method. The preceding example first passes a `BSTR`, and then an Automation object, which is an `IDispatch` pointer, and finally a `BSTR` by reference. The `Add` method is implemented to handle all these types, thus making the method easy to use. This concept gives the server developers access to the powerful object-oriented technique of overloading.

The Safe Array

The safe array data type and its associated APIs let you move arrays of Automation-compatible types between local and remote processes. A number of safe array functions are provided by COM. For more information, take a look at the on-line documentation or the *OLE Programmer's Reference Guide, Volume Two.*

A Native IDispatch-Based Component

Now it's time for an example to solidify our understanding of the `IDispatch` interface. We've used the `Expression` class to build a COM-based component with a custom interface, using native API calls and then using MFC. Now let's implement the `Expression` class using native Automation, implementing both the server and client sides of the `IDispatch` interface. After that, we'll do it again using MFC. First, let's build the server.

The Expression Class as an ActiveX Component

In Chapter 4, we turned the Expression class into a COM component. We used a COM custom interface to expose the Expression functionality. Now we'll expose its functionality via a standard ActiveX interface: IDispatch. We've discussed the benefits of using IDispatch, so we'll focus primarily on its implementation. The changes are based on using the **EXPSVR.H** and **EXPSVR.CPP** files from the Chapter 4 SERVER project. As you'll see, only slight modifications are necessary to convert a component that uses a custom COM interface into one that uses a standard ActiveX interface. Later, when we discuss dual interfaces, you'll see how to build a component that exposes both interfaces, providing a component user with tremendous implementation flexibility.

Building the Visual C++ Project

We'll house our new component in a DLL, making it a COM in-process server. In the MFC-based version of the project, we will implement it within an EXE housing. By implementing a component within an EXE, you gain cross-process and cross-network capabilities without any additional work. By using IDispatch, we automatically get cross-process marshaling. That's one of its major benefits.

We've used Visual C++ quite a bit by now, so I'll just hit the high points of building a project. Start VC++ and perform the following steps to create our initial Automation server:

1. Create a new Project Workspace and specify an **MFC AppWizard (dll)** project.

2. Name the project **Server** and take the provided defaults. Select **Regular DLL using Shared MFC DLL,** but no **OLE Automation** or **Windows Sockets** support.

3. After you click the **Create** button, your screen should be similar to Figure 6.2.

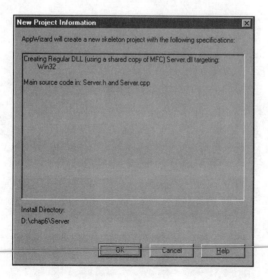

Figure 6.2 SERVER project information dialog box.

Copy the **EXPSVR.H** and **EXPSVR.CPP** files from your Chapter 4 SERVER project or from the accompanying CD-ROM. What follows are changes required to convert the `Expression` component from implementing a custom `IExpression` interface to use `IDispatch` instead.

Updating SERVER.H and SERVER.CPP

The initial **SERVER.CPP** file does not have the COM support that we added in Chapter 4. For a quick review, here's what you need to add to **SERVER.CPP**:

```
//
// Server.cpp : Defines the initialization routines for the DLL.
//

#include "stdafx.h"
#include "server.h"

#include <initguid.h>
#include "expsvr.h"

DWORD       g_dwObjs = 0;
DWORD       g_dwLocks = 0;
...
```

We need to include **EXPSVR.H** to define the `Expression` class factory and the `Expression` class, because `DllGetClassObject`, the COM function that exposes our component, needs them. The two global variables keep track of the number of instantiated objects within the housing and the number of `LockServer` calls made by the client. Here are the changes for **SERVER.CPP**:

```
STDAPI DllGetClassObject( REFCLSID rclsid, REFIID riid, void** ppv )
{
    HRESULT             hr;
    ExpClassFactory     *pCF;

    pCF = 0;

    // Make sure the CLSID is for our Expression component
    if ( rclsid != CLSID_Expression )
        return( E_FAIL );

    pCF = new ExpClassFactory;

    if ( pCF == NULL )
        return( E_OUTOFMEMORY );

    hr = pCF->QueryInterface( riid, ppv );
```

```
    // Check for failure of QueryInterface
    if ( FAILED( hr ) )
    {
        delete pCF;
        pCF = NULL;
    }

    return hr;
}

STDAPI DllCanUnloadNow(void)
{
    if ( g_dwObjs || g_dwLocks )
        return( S_FALSE );
    else
        return( S_OK );
}
```

DllGetClassObject and DllCanUnloadNow are part of Chapter 4's SERVER application. COM requires that a DLL housing support these two functions. They allow the client (through COM) to create an instance of our component. Also, don't forget to export these functions in you **.DEF** file:

```
; Server.def : Declares the module parameters for the DLL.

LIBRARY        "SERVER"
DESCRIPTION    'SERVER Windows Dynamic Link Library'
EXPORTS
    ; Explicit exports can go here
    DllGetClassObject
    DllCanUnloadNow
```

Modifying EXPSVR.H and EXPSVR.CPP

That was pretty easy. Now let's do the difficult part: implement IDispatch within the Expression class. Here are the changes to make to **EXPSVR.H**:

```
//
// ExpSvr.h - Expression header
//

// access to the global variables in SERVER.CPP
extern DWORD g_dwObjs;
extern DWORD g_dwLocks;
```

```
DEFINE_GUID( CLSID_Expression,
              0xA988BD40,0x9F1A,0x11CE,0x8B,0x9F,0x10,0x00,0x5A,0xFB,0x7D,0x30);
//DEFINE_GUID( IID_IExpression,
//              0xA988BD41,0x9F1A,0x11CE,0x8B,0x9F,0x10,0x00,0x5A,0xFB,0x7D,0x30);

const DISPID_GETEXPRESSION = 1001;

const DISPID_SETEXPRESSION = 1002;
const DISPID_EVAL = 1003;
const DISPID_VALIDATE = 1004;
```

We don't need the GUID for the custom interface; we need only a CLSID to identify the Automation object. Next, we've added some constants that we'll use later as the DISPIDs for the Expression object. The Automation specification already has a DISPID_EVALUATE definition so we use DISPID_EVAL instead.

```
//class IExpression : public IUnknown
//{
//public:
//    STDMETHOD_(BSTR,GetExpression()) PURE;
//    STDMETHOD_(void, SetExpression(BSTR, BOOL)) PURE;
//    STDMETHOD_(BOOL, Validate())      PURE;
//    STDMETHOD_(long, Evaluate())      PURE;
//};

class Expression : public IDispatch // public IExpression
{
protected:
...
```

We're now implementing the IDispatch interface so we can comment out the IExpression declaration and derive our Expression class interface from IDispatch. Like all other COM interfaces, IDispatch derives from IUnknown. Because we derive Expression from IDispatch, we must declare and implement seven public methods (our interface) in the Expression class: QueryInterface, AddRef, Release, GetTypeInfoCount, GetTypeInfo, GetIDsOfNames, and Invoke. Here are the changes:

```
public:
    // IUnknown
    STDMETHOD(QueryInterface( REFIID, void** ));
    STDMETHOD_(ULONG, AddRef());
    STDMETHOD_(ULONG, Release());

    // IDispatch
    STDMETHOD(GetTypeInfoCount( UINT* pctinfo ));
    STDMETHOD(GetTypeInfo( UINT itinfo,
```

```
                                LCID lcid,
                                ITypeInfo** pptinfo ));
    STDMETHOD(GetIDsOfNames( REFIID riid,
                             OLECHAR** rgszNames,
                             UINT cNames,
                             LCID lcid,
                             DISPID* rgdispid ));
    STDMETHOD(Invoke( DISPID dispid,
                      REFIID riid,
                      LCID lcid,
                      WORD wFlags,
                      DISPPARAMS FAR* pDispParams,
                      VARIANT FAR* pvarResult,
                      EXCEPINFO FAR* pExcepInfo,
                      unsigned int FAR* puArgErr ));

    // IExpression
    //STDMETHOD_(BSTR, GetExpression());
    //STDMETHOD_(void, SetExpression( BSTR, BOOL ));
    //STDMETHOD_(BOOL, Validate());
    //STDMETHOD_(long, Evaluate());

protected:
    // Here's the classes true functionality. It is now
    // exposed only through our new IDispatch methods.
    BSTR      GetExpression();
    void      SetExpression( BSTR bstr, BOOL bInFix );
    BOOL      Validate();
    long      Evaluate();
```

The IUnknown declarations are unchanged, but we now declare the four IDispatch methods instead of the custom IExpression methods that we used previously. The class must provide its Expression functionality, but the methods are not part of its public interface and so are moved to a protected section. That completes the **EXPSVR.H** file. Now let's modify **EXPSVR.CPP**.

```
STDMETHODIMP Expression::QueryInterface( REFIID riid, void** ppv )
{
    *ppv = NULL;

//    if ( riid == IID_IUnknown || IID_IExpression )
    if ( riid == IID_IUnknown || riid == IID_IDispatch )
        *ppv = this;
```

```
    if ( *ppv )
    {
        ( (LPUNKNOWN)*ppv )->AddRef();
        return( S_OK );
    }
    return (E_NOINTERFACE);
}
```

The first change is in the implementation of QueryInterface. Instead of supporting IExpression, we now support IDispatch. That's easy enough. What else needs to be done?

```
STDMETHODIMP Expression::GetTypeInfoCount( UINT* pctinfo )
{
    // Indicate that we don't expose any type information
    *pctinfo = 0;
    return S_OK;
}
```

Here's our implementation of the GetTypeInfoCount method. To simplify the example, we don't support exposing our type information. We indicate this by setting the pctinfo parameter to zero and returning S_OK.

```
STDMETHODIMP Expression::GetTypeInfo( UINT itinfo,
                                      LCID lcid,
                                      ITypeInfo** pptinfo )
{
    // Not implemented
    if ( pptinfo )
        *pptinfo = 0;
    return( E_NOTIMPL );
}
```

GetTypeInfo is just as easy. We set the pptinfo parameter to zero and return E_NOTIMPL to indicate that type information is not supported. Here comes the essence of Automation.

```
STDMETHODIMP Expression::GetIDsOfNames( REFIID riid,
                                        OLECHAR** rgszNames,
                                        UINT cNames,
                                        LCID lcid,
                                        DISPID* rgdispid )
{
    // To make things simple, we only support 1 name at a time
    if ( cNames > 1 )
```

```
        return( E_INVALIDARG );

// Convert the member name to regular ANSI
USES_CONVERSION;
char* szAnsi = OLE2T( rgszNames[0] );

// Compare the member name to see if it's one that we have
// and return the correct DISPID
if ( strncmp( "GetExpression", szAnsi, 14 ) == 0 )
    rgdispid[0] = DISPID_GETEXPRESSION;
else if ( strncmp( "SetExpression", szAnsi, 14 ) == 0 )
    rgdispid[0] = DISPID_SETEXPRESSION;
else if ( strncmp( "Validate", szAnsi, 8 ) == 0 )
    rgdispid[0] = DISPID_VALIDATE;
else if ( strncmp( "Evaluate", szAnsi, 8 ) == 0 )
    rgdispid[0] = DISPID_EVAL;
else
    return( DISPID_UNKNOWN );

// Everything worked!
return S_OK;
}
```

In Automation the client application need not have any knowledge of a server's methods at compile and link time. As we discussed earlier, Automation enables late binding of methods and their parameters. To provide this capability, we've implemented the GetIDsOfNames method.

The client can now call GetIDsOfNames at run time to get the specific DISPID for a method within the Expression component. We defined our DISPIDs earlier. Our job now is to map the member name to a specific DISPID. This is easy. The rgszNames parameter is an array of member names provided by the calling application. The array consists of a method or property name in the first element, optionally followed by named parameter elements. I won't complicate the issue by discussing named parameters, but that's why we are provided an array of member names.

All COM interface calls use native Unicode, so we convert the Unicode string to ANSI to facilitate the comparison. Then we do a simple string comparison. If we get a match, we return the respective DISPID. If we don't get a match, we return the required DISPID_UNKNOWN error.

```
STDMETHODIMP Expression::Invoke( DISPID dispid,
                                 REFIID riid,
                                 LCID lcid,
                                 WORD wFlags,
                                 DISPPARAMS FAR* pDispParams,
                                 VARIANT FAR* pvarResult,
```

```
                        EXCEPINFO FAR* pExcepInfo,
                        unsigned int FAR* puArgErr )
{
  switch( dispid )
  {
    case DISPID_GETEXPRESSION:
        if ( pvarResult )
        {
            VariantInit( pvarResult );
            V_VT( pvarResult ) = VT_BSTR;
            V_BSTR( pvarResult ) = GetExpression();
        }
        return S_OK;

    case DISPID_SETEXPRESSION:
        if ( !pDispParams ||
                pDispParams->cArgs != 2 )
            return( DISP_E_BADPARAMCOUNT );

        // We don't support named arguments
        if ( pDispParams->cNamedArgs > 0 )
            return( DISP_E_NONAMEDARGS );

        HRESULT hr;
         // Coerce the variant into the desired type
         // In this case we would like a BSTR
         hr = VariantChangeType(  &(pDispParams->rgvarg[1]),
                             &(pDispParams->rgvarg[1]),
                             0,
                             VT_BSTR );

        // If we can't get a BSTR return type mismatch
         if ( FAILED( hr ))
            return( DISP_E_TYPEMISMATCH );

        // Coerce the variant into the desired type
         // In this case we would like an I4 or long
         hr = VariantChangeType( &(pDispParams->rgvarg[0]),
                             &(pDispParams->rgvarg[0]),
                             0,
                             VT_I4 );
```

```
        if ( FAILED( hr ))
            return( DISP_E_TYPEMISMATCH );

    // Finally call our method with the correct parameters
      // Remember the parameters come in right to left
      SetExpression( pDispParams->rgvarg[1].bstrVal,
                        pDispParams->rgvarg[0].iVal );

    return( S_OK );

case DISPID_VALIDATE:
    if ( pvarResult )
    {
        VariantInit( pvarResult );
        V_VT( pvarResult ) = VT_I4;
        V_I4( pvarResult ) = Validate();
    }
    else
        Validate();

    return S_OK;

case DISPID_EVAL:
    if ( pvarResult )
    {
        VariantInit( pvarResult );
        V_VT( pvarResult ) = VT_I4;
        V_I4( pvarResult ) = Evaluate();
    }
    else
        Evaluate();
    return S_OK;

default:
    return( DISP_E_MEMBERNOTFOUND );
    }
}
```

The Invoke method provides most of the functionality of the IDispatch interface. First, we determine which member was invoked by the client, as indicated by the specific DISPID. Our simple server doesn't expose any type information, so the only way for the client to get the DISPID is to explicitly call the GetIDsOfNames method.

Based on the DISPID passed, we call the appropriate `Expression` method. The only difficulty is in how to interpret and handle all those parameters used in the `Invoke` method. Let's examine each one in detail.

```
case DISPID_GETEXPRESSION:
   if ( pvarResult )
   {
      VariantInit( pvarResult );
      V_VT( pvarResult ) = VT_BSTR;
      V_BSTR( pvarResult ) = GetExpression();
   }
   return S_OK;
```

The `GetExpression` method takes no parameters and returns a `BSTR` containing the current `Expression` value. The sixth parameter of `Invoke` is a `VARIANT` allocated by the caller for the purpose of passing the return value of the call. The client need not provide this parameter, so we check to ensure that it is a nonzero pointer before we do our work. `GetExpression` has no side effects, so there is no need to process the call if the caller does not provide storage to return the result. If a variant is provided, we initialize it, set the variant type, and assign its value with a call to `GetExpression`.

Two of the other `Expression` methods do not take parameters and return a result. `Evaluate` and `Validate` are very similar.

```
case DISPID_VALIDATE:
   if ( pvarResult )
   {
      VariantInit( pvarResult );
      V_VT( pvarResult ) = VT_I4;
      V_I4( pvarResult ) = Validate();
   }
   else
      Validate();
   return S_OK;

case DISPID_EVAL:
   if ( pvarResult )
   {
      VariantInit( pvarResult );
      V_VT( pvarResult ) = VT_I4;
      V_I4( pvarResult ) = Evaluate();
   }
   else
      Evaluate();
   return S_OK;
```

The primary difference between these two implementations is that they must perform some action even if the caller does not provide storage for the result. The two methods can be called in two ways using a controller language such as Visual Basic:

```
nResult = objExpression.Evaluate()
```
` or
```
objExpression.Evaluate
```

The first method uses the result and the second one does not. Make sure that you handle all the various conditions when mapping your methods.

```
case DISPID_SETEXPRESSION:

  if ( !pDispParams ||
          pDispParams->cArgs != 2 )
      return( DISP_E_BADPARAMCOUNT );

  // We don't support named arguments
  if ( pDispParams->cNamedArgs > 0 )
      return( DISP_E_NONAMEDARGS );

  HRESULT hr;
  // Coerce the variant into the desired type
  // In this case we would like a BSTR
  hr = VariantChangeType(  &(pDispParams->rgvarg[1]),
                           &(pDispParams->rgvarg[1]),
                           0,
                           VT_BSTR );

  // If we can't get a BSTR return, invalidate argument
  if ( FAILED( hr ))
      return( DISP_E_TYPEMISMATCH );

  // Coerce the variant into the desired type
  // In this case we would like an I4 or long
  hr = VariantChangeType( &(pDispParams->rgvarg[0]),
                          &(pDispParams->rgvarg[0]),
                          0,
                          VT_I4 );

  if ( FAILED( hr ))
      return( DISP_E_TYPEMISMATCH );

  // Finally call our method with the correct parameters
  SetExpression( pDispParams->rgvarg[1].bstrVal,
                 pDispParams->rgvarg[0].iVal );

  return( S_OK );
```

Calling the `SetExpression` method is the most complicated case. It does not return a value, but it takes two parameters. The `DISPPARAMS` structure is allocated and passed by the caller. It contains an array of parameters, each stored in a `VARIANTARG` structure. We first check to make sure that we have two parameters. If we don't, we return `DISP_E_PARAMCOUNT`. Next, we make sure that the caller has not passed any named arguments. We don't support them in our simple example. We then coerce the parameters into types that our internal `SetExpression` method supports.

`VariantChangeType` takes a variant type and coerces it into a type that you specify. In our first case, we need the actual `Expression` string as a binary string (`BSTR`). Automation controllers can pass this value in a number of ways. `VariantChangeType` does all the work for you. For example, here are some ways that Visual Basic might call `SetExpression`:

```
Dim objExp As Object
Dim v As Variant
Dim str As String

Set objExp = CreateObject("Chap6.Expression.1")
v = "100 * 500"
str = "100 * 600"
objExp.SetExpression str, 1
objExp.SetExpression (str), 1
objExp.SetExpression v, 1
' txtExpression is a standard Windows entry field
objExp.SetExpression txtExpression, 1
```

Each one of the preceding calls to `SetExpression` passes a different variant type for the `BSTR` parameter. The first one passes a `BSTR` by reference (`ByRef`). The second one passes it as we would typically expect, just a simple `BSTR`. The third call passes a variant by reference, and the fourth call passes a pointer to the `IDispatch` interface of Visual Basic's standard ActiveX Edit control. Thankfully, `VariantChangeType` handles the complexity of converting all these different types into the one we would like: a straight `BSTR`.

You might wonder how `VariantChangeType` can convert an `IDispatch` pointer into a `BSTR`. An Automation server can specify a default `Value` property that provides the value most appropriate for the server. Servers need not specify this default, but many of them do. `VariantChangeType` will attempt to obtain the type that you're trying to convert to by calling the `Value` property through the passed-in `IDispatch`. In the preceding example, the standard Visual Basic Edit control has a value property that returns the string within the edit field. This is exactly what we need, so everything works.

We've finished the hard work. All that remains is to change the return types of our previously exposed `Expression` class methods. Because they are no longer directly exposed, we don't need to treat them as COM interface functions. We only need remove the `STDMETHOD` macros from the declarations in **EXPSVR.H** and remove the definitions in **EXPSVR.CPP**. Here's an example from the CPP file.

```
//STDMETHODIMP_(BOOL) Expression::Validate()
BOOL Expression::Validate()
//STDMETHODIMP_(long) Expression::Evaluate()
long Expression::Evaluate()
```

Once we've made all the changes, we rebuild the project. We now have an `Expression` component that can be used from a variety of development environments, one of which is Visual Basic. Let's test our component with Visual Basic.

However, before we move on and test our new IDispatch-based server, we need to register the component. We're not using MFC, so we have to use a .REG file like we did with the Chapter 4 server. The CD-ROM contains the WIN32.REG file. Modify the InprocServer32 entry to include the path to the SERVER.DLL on your local machine. Then use Explorer or REGEDIT.EXE to add the entries to the Registry. Here's how it looks on my machine.

```
HKEY_CLASSES_ROOT\CLSID\{a988bd40-9f1a-11ce-8b9f-10005afb7d30}
    \InprocServer32 = d:\examples\chap6\Server\Debug\server.dll
```

Using Visual Basic as an Automation Controller

Visual Basic is easy to use. If you've never developed an application with Visual Basic, you should give it a try. Many developers dismiss it because it has "Basic" in its name, but our focus as developers should be on providing solutions to problems and not on a philosophical debate about which language is best. Visual Basic is the de facto Automation controller, and in this section we'll demonstrate why. Visual Basic eases the task of harnessing the functionality of ActiveX servers.

If you don't have Visual Basic, don't worry. Visual C++ comes with an OLE/ActiveX test program that provides all the functionality we need to test our component. The file **DISPTEST.EXE** is in the \MSDEV\BIN directory. To run it, just type **start DISPTEST** from the command line.

N O T E

Start Visual Basic and build a form that looks like the screen in Figure 6.3. It's easy—just drag and drop an entry field and two buttons from the tool palette. Name the entry field **txtExpression**, the **Validate** button **cmdValidate**, and the **Evaluate** button **cmdEvaluate**. To set these values, set focus to the control and then modify the value of the Name property in the Property window. You should also set the default Text property to a null string.

Figure 6.3 Visual Basic form.

Visual Basic has many built-in data types, most of which map directly to the standard Automation types. The one we're interested in is `Object`, which encapsulates an `IDispatch` pointer and so allows you to call the various methods on that `IDispatch`. The first step is to define an object. We do this in the form's globals section, which is the area outside any function or procedure.

```
Dim objExp As Object
```

At application startup, one of the first things to happen is the loading of the form, so we create an instance of the `Expression` object and assign it to the `objExp` pointer. The Visual Basic command `CreateObject` internally calls COM's `CoCreateInstance` method to create an instance of the COM object and then requests the default `IDispatch` for that object. Visual Basic stores this pointer in the `objExp` variable.

```
Sub Form_Load ()
    Set objExp = CreateObject("Chap6.Expression.1")
End Sub

Sub Form_Unload (Cancel As Integer)
    Set objExp = Nothing
End Sub
```

Visual Basic's version of `QueryInterface::Release` is to set the `objExp` variable to `Nothing`. This frees the connection to the Automation object. You need not do this explicitly (as we've done here), because Visual Basic will do it whenever the object goes out of scope. Still, it's good programming practice.

To use the object, we add the following lines of code. These methods should look familiar; we added them to our Automation wrapper earlier in this chapter. To add code for the button click event in Visual Basic, double-click on the button. Add the following code for each button.

```
Sub cmdEvaluate_Click ()
    Dim szExp As String
    szExp = txtExpression.Text
    objExp.SetExpression szExp, True
    txtExpression = objExp.Evaluate()
End Sub

Sub cmdValidate_Click ()
    Dim szExp As String
    szExp = txtExpression.Text
    objExp.SetExpression szExp, True
    If objExp.Validate() = False Then
        MsgBox ("Invalid Expression, try again")
    End If
End Sub
```

The syntax for calling object methods in Visual Basic is `object.Method parameters` if there isn't a return value, or `retValue = object.Method( parameters )` if there is a return value. As you can see, it's easy to use our Automation wrapped component. We've used Visual Basic to build an application around our C++ `Expression` class with just 13 lines of code. Press **F5** and run the application. You can step through each line of code using the **F8** key.

A Non-MFC Automation Controller

We've taken a look at what it takes to implement an Automation server, and we then tested it by using Visual Basic as the Automation controller. Next, let's take a quick look at what is required to implement the controller (or client) side in C++. We'll do this initially without the help of MFC's Automation support, but later we'll use MFC. I don't want to spend very much time in this section, but I think it's important for a solid understanding of what Automation is all about.

The accompanying CD-ROM contains the source for this simple client application in the \Examples\Chap6\Client directory. The example is built using a simple dialog-based Visual C++ application. It is similar to the examples in Chapter 3 through Chapter 5 except that it is dialog-based and does not use MFC's document-view architecture. To follow along and build the application as we go, first build a Visual C++ application with the following options:

1. Name the application **Client**.

2. Build an **MFC AppWizard (EXE)** project.

3. In AppWizard Step 1, choose a **Dialog based** application.

4. In AppWizard Step 2, accept the defaults of **About box** and **3D controls** and check the **OLE automation** support button. This action adds the OLE include files and the call to `AfxOleInit` for us. We know what these options do, so we'll let AppWizard do it for us.

5. In AppWizard Step 3, choose to use the MFC library as a **Shared DLL**.

6. In AppWizard Step 4, change the names of the **CClientDlg** class to **DIALOG.H** and **DIALOG.CPP**.

7. Click the **Finish** button. You should have a screen similar to Figure 6.4.

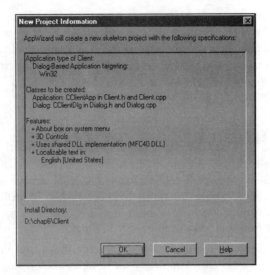

Figure 6.4 Non-MFC client application generation.

> **NOTE** If you forget to add **OLE Automation** support to the application, you will get an error in the `CoCreateInstance` call. The `HRESULT` will be something like `0x800401F0`, which by itself doesn't mean much. When you get a `FAILED` status on a COM-based function call, you can look up a textual rendition of the error in the **WINERROR.H** include file. The `0x800401F0` error maps to "CoInitialize has not been called," a much clearer error message.

Just as we've done in previous versions of the CLIENT application, we'll add two buttons and an entry field to the dialog resource. The button IDs are `IDC_EVALUATE` and `IDC_VALIDATE`, and the entry field has an ID of `IDC_EXPRESSION`. Using ClassWizard, we then add, for both buttons, handlers for the `BN_CLICKED` event.

Once we've done all that, we start adding the code. There a few additions to **DIALOG.H**:

```
//
// Dialog.h : header file
//

class CClientDlg : public CDialog
{
...

// Implementation
protected:
    HICON        m_hIcon;
```

```
    LPDISPATCH    m_pDispatch;
    HRESULT       GetDispID( const char* szName, DISPID& dispid );
    BOOL          SetExpression( CString& strExpression );
    BOOL          Evaluate( long& lValue );
    BOOL          Validate( BOOL& bValid );
...
};
```

The m_pDispatch member will hold the IDispatch to the Expression component, and the other methods help implement the client-side IDispatch functionality. When the dialog box is created, the OnInitDialog method is called. This is a good place to create an instance of the Expression component, much as we did in Chapters 4 and 5. We use CoCreateInstance to create an instance of the Expression class, but this time we ask for the IDispatch interface instead of IExpression. The modifications below are to **DIALOG.CPP**:

```
//
// Dialog.cpp
//
...
// Use MFC's Unicode conversion functions
#include <afxpriv.h>
...

CClientDlg::CClientDlg(CWnd* pParent /*=NULL*/)
    : CDialog(CClientDlg::IDD, pParent)
{
    ...
    m_pDispatch = 0;
}

BOOL CClientDlg::DestroyWindow()
{
    // Release the dispatch interface
    if ( m_pDispatch )
        m_pDispatch->Release();

    return CDialog::DestroyWindow();
}

BOOL CClientDlg::OnInitDialog()
{
    CDialog::OnInitDialog();
    ...
```

```
// Create the dispatch to our expression component
// It must be a Unicode string
USES_CONVERSION
LPCOLESTR lpOleStr = T2COLE( "Chap6.Expression.1" );
CLSID Clsid;
HRESULT hr = ::CLSIDFromProgID( lpOleStr, &Clsid );
if( FAILED( hr ))
{
    AfxMessageBox( "CLSIDFromProgID failed\n" );
    return TRUE;
}

hr = CoCreateInstance( Clsid,
                       0,
                       CLSCTX_INPROC_SERVER,
                       IID_IDispatch,
                       (LPVOID FAR *) &m_pDispatch );
if (FAILED( hr ))
{
    AfxMessageBox( "CoCreateInstance failed" );
    return TRUE;
}
```

```
    return TRUE;  // return TRUE  unless you set the focus to a control
}
```

We added a handler for the DestroyWindow message so that we can release the dispatch when the dialog box is closed. Most of the preceding code should be familiar by now. All the work is done in OnInitDialog. First, we convert our ProgID to Unicode and then retrieve the associated CLSID. We then call CoCreateInstance and ask for the IDispatch of the component. If all goes well, we have all we need to call the component's methods directly.

Notice that we do not have any compile-time definition of the Expression component. We did not include **EXPSVR.H**. Instead, we will dynamically query for the DISPIDs of the methods and invoke them dynamically using the Invoke method of IDispatch. Here's a helper function to return a DISPID of the provided method name:

```
HRESULT CClientDlg::GetDispID( const char* szName, DISPID& dispid )
{
    HRESULT hr;
    // Get a Unicode version of the string
    USES_CONVERSION
    LPOLESTR lpOleStr = T2OLE( szName );
```

```
hr = m_pDispatch->GetIDsOfNames( IID_NULL,
                    &lpOleStr,
                    1,
                    LOCALE_SYSTEM_DEFAULT,
                    &dispid );

if (FAILED( hr ))
{
    char szTemp[128];
    sprintf( szTemp, "GetIDsOfNames for '%s' failed, HRESULT is %x", szName, hr
          );
    AfxMessageBox( szTemp );
    return hr;
}

return S_OK;
}
```

This is straightforward. We pass a Unicode version of the member name (such as SetExpression) and a pointer to a DISPID variable. We call the GetIDsOfNames implemented by the server, and, if everything works, we get back the DISPID of the member.

We need the DISPID because we use the Invoke method to access the functionality in the Expression component, and Invoke requires a DISPID. We could have obtained the DISPID from the type information of the server, but we didn't implement type information. We'll cover this later. For now, the client application must call GetIDsOfNames to get the DISPID. Here's how we call SetExpression in the server. I've added a SetExpression method to our dialog class:

```
BOOL CClientDlg::SetExpression( CString& strExpression )
{
    // OK, here we go. Get the DISPID of the SetExpression method
    DISPID dispid;
    if ( FAILED( GetDispID( "SetExpression", dispid )))
        return TRUE;

    // Now that we have the DISPID, call the method using IDispatch::Invoke

    DISPPARAMS dispparms;
    memset( &dispparms, 0, sizeof( DISPPARAMS ));
    dispparms.cArgs = 2;

    // allocate memory for all VARIANT parameters
    VARIANTARG* pArg = new VARIANTARG[dispparms.cArgs];
    dispparms.rgvarg = pArg;
```

```
    memset(pArg, 0, sizeof(VARIANT) * dispparms.cArgs);

    // The parameters are entered right to left
    dispparms.rgvarg[0].vt = VT_I4;
    dispparms.rgvarg[0].lVal = 1;
    dispparms.rgvarg[1].vt = VT_BSTR;
    dispparms.rgvarg[1].bstrVal = strExpression.AllocSysString();

    // Invoke the Start method in the local server
    HRESULT hr = m_pDispatch->Invoke( dispid,
                            IID_NULL,
                            LOCALE_SYSTEM_DEFAULT,
                            DISPATCH_METHOD,
                            &dispparms,
                            0,          // No return value
                            0,          // No exception support
                            NULL );

    // Free up our variantargs
    delete [] pArg;

    if ( FAILED( hr ))
    {
        char szTemp[128];
        sprintf( szTemp, "Unable to Invoke 'SetExpression'. HR is %x", hr );
        AfxMessageBox( szTemp );
        return TRUE;
    }

    return FALSE;
}
```

First, we get the DISPID of `SetExpression`. `SetExpression` takes two parameters and returns `void`. Once we have the DISPID, we build the parameter list for the call. The `DISPPARAMS` structure houses the parameters that we will pass via the `Invoke` method. Here's what it looks like:

```
typedef struct FARSTRUCT tagDISPPARAMS
{
    VARIANTARG FAR* rgvarg;              // Array of arguments.
    DISPID FAR* rgdispidNamedArgs;       // Dispatch IDs of named arguments.
    unsigned int cArgs;                  // Number of arguments.
    unsigned int cNamedArgs;             // Number of named arguments.
} DISPPARAMS;
```

We set the number of arguments to 2 and allocate storage for two VARIANTARG structures. Next, we clear the structures, and finally we initialize the variants with the parameter data. Arguments are stored right-to-left in the DISPPARAMS structure, so we first pass a long with a value of 1. We then set up a BSTR with the string value by calling CString's AllocSysString member.

Once everything is set up, we call Invoke through our IDispatch pointer. The server then unpacks everything in the DISPPARAM structure and executes the method. We implemented that code earlier, so you should see how it all fits together. The other methods are very similar.

```
BOOL CClientDlg::Evaluate( long& lValue )
{
  DISPID dispid;
  if (FAILED( GetDispID( "Evaluate", dispid )))
     return TRUE;

  // Now that we have the DISPID, call the method using IDispatch::Invoke
  DISPPARAMS dispparms;
  memset( &dispparms, 0, sizeof( DISPPARAMS ));

  // This method returns a value, so we need a VARIANT to store it in

  VARIANTARG vaResult;
  VariantInit( &vaResult );

  HRESULT hr = m_pDispatch->Invoke( dispid,
                      IID_NULL,
                      LOCALE_SYSTEM_DEFAULT,
                      DISPATCH_METHOD,
                      &dispparms,
                      &vaResult,
                      0,
                      NULL );

  if ( FAILED( hr ))
  {
     char szTemp[128];
     sprintf( szTemp, "Unable to Invoke 'Evaluate'. HR is %x", hr );
     AfxMessageBox( szTemp );
     return TRUE;
  }

  lValue = vaResult.lVal;
  return FALSE;
}
```

```
BOOL CClientDlg::Validate( BOOL& bValid )
{
  DISPID dispid;
  if (FAILED( GetDispID( "Validate", dispid )))
    return TRUE;

  // Now that we have the DISPID, call the method using IDispatch::Invoke
  DISPPARAMS dispparms;
  memset( &dispparms, 0, sizeof( DISPPARAMS ));

  // This method returns a value, so we need a VARIANT to store it in
  VARIANTARG vaResult;
  VariantInit( &vaResult );

  hr = m_pDispatch->Invoke( dispid,
                            IID_NULL,
                            LOCALE_SYSTEM_DEFAULT,
                            DISPATCH_METHOD,
                            &dispparms,
                            &vaResult,
                            0,
                            NULL );

  if ( FAILED( hr ))
  {
    char szTemp[128];
    sprintf( szTemp, "Unable to Invoke 'Validate'. HR is %x", hr );
    AfxMessageBox( szTemp );
    return TRUE;
  }

  bValid = vaResult.lVal;
  return FALSE;
}
```

The code in the Evaluate and Validate methods is very similar to the earlier SetExpression, with one exception: these methods return values and do not take parameters. We pass a blank DISPPARAMS structure and provide a VARIANT in which the server can store a return value. After Invoke returns, we extract the value from the VARIANT and pass it to the local caller.

After coding these methods, all that remains is to add the calls to the button handlers.

```
void CClientDlg::OnEvaluate()
{
```

```
   if (! m_pDispatch )
   {
      AfxMessageBox( "There is no dispatch" );
      return;
   }

   // Get the expression from the entry field
   CString strExpression;
   CWnd* pWnd = GetDlgItem( IDC_EXPRESSION );
   pWnd->GetWindowText( strExpression );

   if ( SetExpression( strExpression ))
   {
      AfxMessageBox( "Unable to 'SetExpression'" );
      return;
   }

   long lResult;
   if ( Evaluate( lResult ))
   {
      AfxMessageBox( "Unable to 'Evaluate' Expression" );
      return;
   }

   // Set the returned value in the entry field
   char szTemp[128];
   sprintf( szTemp, "%ld", lResult );
   pWnd->SetWindowText( szTemp );

   // Set focus back to the entry field
   GetDlgItem( IDC_EXPRESSION )->SetFocus();
}

void CClientDlg::OnValidate()
{
   if (! m_pDispatch )
   {
      AfxMessageBox( "There is no dispatch" );
      return;
   }

   // Get the expression from the entry field
   CString strExpression;
```

```
CWnd* pWnd = GetDlgItem( IDC_EXPRESSION );
pWnd->GetWindowText( strExpression );

if ( SetExpression( strExpression ))
{
    AfxMessageBox( "Unable to 'SetExpression'" );
    return;
}

BOOL bValid;
if ( Validate( bValid ) )
{
    AfxMessageBox( "Enable to 'Validate' expression" );
    return;
}

if (! bValid )
    AfxMessageBox( "Invalid Expression, try again" );

// Set focus back to the entry field

GetDlgItem(IDC_EXPRESSION)->SetFocus();

}
```

Except for the new technique of calling the methods in the `Expression` component, this code is nearly identical to that used in the earlier CLIENT examples. Now build the application. It should behave just like the examples in Chapters 3, 4, and 5 and the Visual Basic example that we developed earlier in this chapter.

MFC and IDispatch

Next, we'll focus on the MFC facilities that help in the development of component applications that need Automation support. Initially, we'll focus on the server side of `IDispatch`. Later, we'll build an Automation controller similar to the one we built earlier, this time using Visual C++'s shortcut technique. MFC provides the ability to act as an Automation controller but only in a static way. ClassWizard's Automation tab has a **Read Type Library** button that reads a type library from an existing Automation server and provides an MFC wrapper class derived from `COleDispatchDriver`, which wraps each Automation property or method with a C++ method. If the component class adds methods, you must rebuild the `COleDispatchDriver`-derived class in order to use them. Currently, there is no MFC class that encapsulates the ability to dynamically query and invoke functions (as Visual Basic does) within an Automation server, although it wouldn't be hard to implement one yourself.

MFC implements the `IDispatch` interface as part of the main COM class `CCmdTarget`. `CCmdTarget` maintains a *dispatch map* in much the same way that it maintains a COM interface map and the Windows message map structures. Implementing an Automation component class is easy in MFC. The only requirement is that the class be derived from `CCmdTarget` so that it will contain a hierarchy of dispatch maps. Dispatch maps implement the dispatch table (shown previously in Figure 6.1) and provide the mapping from a DISPID to a specific method of an Automation class.

We will discuss the MFC `IDispatch` implementation further as we develop the examples.

An Example MFC-Based Automation Server

I know you must be getting tired of our `Expression` class example, but I promise this is the second-to-last time you will see it. In Chapter 10, we'll finish the `Expression` example by developing an expression evaluation ActiveX control. For now, we're focusing on how COM and ActiveX work instead of actually using it. In the rest of the chapters we'll develop some neat examples.

What we'll do first with our example is to wrap the `Expression` class with an Automation wrapper. This is quick and easy, and it lets us access the `Expression` functionality from Visual Basic, C++, and other languages that support Automation. All our previous examples have been in-process servers, but we'll make this one a local server, for two reasons. First, we haven't learned this yet, and we need to understand the differences between the two implementations. Second, we'll use the marshaling capabilities of COM, which allow the interoperation of 16-bit and 32-bit applications.

Start Visual C++ and follow these steps to create the initial project:

1. Name the application **AutoSvr**.
2. Build an **MFC AppWizard (EXE)** project.
3. In AppWizard Step 1, choose a **Multiple documents** application.
4. In AppWizard Step 2 of 6, accept the default of **None** for database support.
5. In AppWizard Step 3 of 6, select **None** for **OLE Container support** and enable **OLE automation** support.
6. In AppWizard Step 4 of 6, take the default features but turn off **Print Preview** support.
7. In AppWizard Step 5 of 6, take the default **Regular DLL using Shared MFC DLL**.
8. In AppWizard Step 6 of 6, derive the view from **CFormView** and change the implementation file's name to **VIEW.H** and **VIEW.CPP**. Also, change the document class implementation files to **DOCUMENT.H** and **DOCUMENT.CPP**.
9. Click the **Finish** button. You should have a screen similar to Figure 6.5.

Figure 6.5 AUTOSVR project information dialog box.

Now we copy **EXPRESS.CPP** and **EXPRESS.H** from the Chapter 3 project into the working directory of our AUTOSVR project. After doing this, select **Insert/Files into project** and add **EXPRESS.CPP** to our project.

In Chapter 3, we used the `Expression` class directly in our project to provide algebraic expression capabilities. In Chapters 4 and 5, we used COM and ActiveX to separate the `Expression` class into a component that was accessed through a custom COM interface, and earlier in this chapter we implemented the component using a native `IDispatch` interface. Now we'll wrap the existing C++ class inside an Automation (`IDispatch`-based) wrapper class. This technique will expose the class's capabilities without modifying the implementation at all. The `Expression` class will be just as useful to C++ developers as it will be to developers who use Automation–capable tools (such as Visual Basic). Go ahead and compile, link, and run the application before we add the wrapping.

Wrapping the Expression Class

Start ClassWizard (**Ctrl-W**) and select the **OLE Automation** tab. Click the **Add Class** button to add a new class to our project. In the Class Name entry field, type **OExpression**. The default header and implementation filenames are fine. However, for this example I'm using the 8.3 names of **OEXPRESS.H** and **OEX-PRESS.CPP**. In the Base class dropdown listbox, select **CCmdTarget**, the class from which our new class will be derived. As we discussed before, MFC's `CCmdTarget` provides the base COM functionality for all the MFC classes. Our Automation wrapper class will be derived from it.

When we chose to derive from `CCmdTarget`, three additional options were enabled in the OLE Automation frame. The second checkbox, **OLE Automation**, asks whether we want to enable this feature for our class. We do, so check it. When **OLE Automation** is checked, the **Createable by type ID** option is enabled. This option, when checked, causes ClassWizard to create a CLSID and ProgID for our new Automation class. When your component class is to be directly exposed without going through the main OLE class for the application, you should check this option. If you do, the entry field will allow you to enter the ProgID for your Automation class. We want to allow direct access to the Expression class, so we check the **Createable by type ID** box and enter **Chap6.MFCExpression.1** in the entry field. See Figure 6.6.

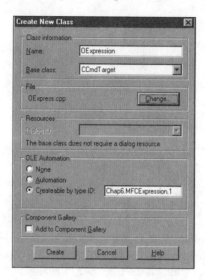

Figure 6.6 ClassWizard Create New Class dialog box.

Click the **Create** button and then press **OK** in the ClassWizard dialog box. This adds two new files to our application: **OEXPRESS.H** and **OEXPRESS.CPP**. Let's take a look at what they do. Here's **OEXPRESS.H**:

```
//
// Oexpress.h : header file
//

class OExpression : public CCmdTarget
{
    DECLARE_DYNCREATE(OExpression)
protected:
    OExpression();        // protected constructor used by dynamic creation

// Overrides
    // ClassWizard generated virtual function overrides
    //{{AFX_VIRTUAL(OExpression)
public:
    virtual void OnFinalRelease();
```

```
    //}}}AFX_VIRTUAL
// Implementation
protected:
    virtual ~OExpression();

    // Generated message map functions
    //{{AFX_MSG(OExpression)
    // NOTE - the ClassWizard will add and remove member functions here.
    //}}}AFX_MSG

    DECLARE_MESSAGE_MAP()
    DECLARE_OLECREATE(OExpression)

    // Generated OLE dispatch map functions
    //{{AFX_DISPATCH(OExpression)
    // NOTE - the ClassWizard will add and remove member functions here.
    //}}}AFX_DISPATCH
    DECLARE_DISPATCH_MAP()
};
```

Most of this code should look familiar. In Chapter 5, we explored in detail most of the macros in **OEX-PRESS.H**. We have the requisite macros that allow for dynamic creation. There's the class factory macro DECLARE_OLECREATE. The only new thing is the DECLARE_DISPATCH_MAP macro, we'll look at it in more detail in a moment. First, we'll add some Automation properties and methods:

```
// oexpress.cpp : implementation file
//
...

IMPLEMENT_DYNCREATE(OExpression, CCmdTarget)

BEGIN_DISPATCH_MAP(OExpression, CCmdTarget)
    //{{AFX_DISPATCH_MAP(OExpression)
        // NOTE - the ClassWizard will add and remove mapping macros here.
    //}}}AFX_DISPATCH_MAP
END_DISPATCH_MAP()

IMPLEMENT_OLECREATE(OExpression, "Chap6.Expression.1", 0x9b027266, 0xb3e4, 0x11ce, 0xb6, 0xe, 0xf2,
0xbd, 0x12, 0x2b, 0xbc, 0x9)

OExpression::OExpression()
{
    EnableAutomation();

    // To keep the application running as long as an ActiveX Automation
```

```
   //    object is active, the constructor calls AfxOleLockApp.

   AfxOleLockApp();
}

OExpression::~OExpression()
{
   // To terminate the application when all objects created with
   //       with ActiveX Automation, the destructor calls AfxOleUnlockApp.

   AfxOleUnlockApp();
}

void OExpression::OnFinalRelease()
{
   // When the last reference for an automation object is released
   //    OnFinalRelease is called.  This implementation deletes the
   //    object.  Add additional cleanup required for your object before
   //    deleting it from memory.

   delete this;
}
```

Except for the call to EnableAutomation in the constructor, all the code in the implementation file, **OEX-PRESS.CPP**, should also be familiar. All we need to do now is to add the methods and properties from the Expression class. We'll use (guess what?) ClassWizard to do this. Start ClassWizard and select the **OLE Automation** tab. Make sure that you have the **OExpression** class selected as well.

Using the **Automation** tab of ClassWizard allows you to add and remove Automation methods and properties. For the Expression class, we'll add four methods. Click the **Add Method** button, type **GetExpression** in the External Name field, and choose a return type of **BSTR**. Then press **OK**. This adds the GetExpression method to the OExpression class. We need to do this for each of the four methods of Expression. The SetExpression method takes two parameters. You add parameters by clicking in the Parameter list listbox and typing the parameter name in the left-hand side, and the parameter type on the right. Figure 6.7 shows the SetExpression method being added.

The two remaining methods—Validate and Evaluate—take no parameters. When you're finished adding all four methods, the **OLE Automation** tab should look like Figure 6.8.

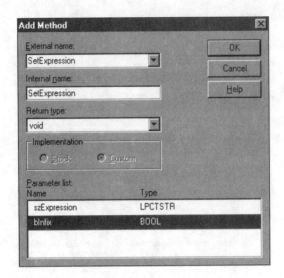

Figure 6.7 Adding the `SetExpression` method.

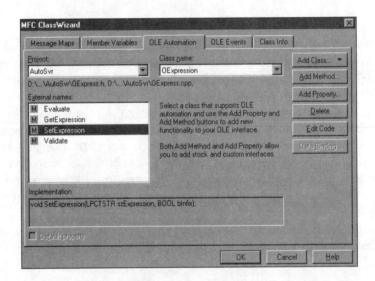

Figure 6.8 Adding Automation methods with ClassWizard.

ClassWizard has added four new methods to the `OExpression` class. It is now our responsibility to make them do something. All we are doing is wrapping the `Expression` class, so we include its declarations in **OEXPRESS.CPP**:

```
//
// oexpress.cpp : implementation file
//

#include "stdafx.h"
#include "autosvr.h"

#include "express.h"

#include "oexpress.h"
```

We also include a member of the Expression class within OExpression so that each instance of the Expression component has its own instance of Expression. Add the following to **OEXPRESS.H**:

```
class OExpression : public CCmdTarget
{
      DECLARE_DYNCREATE(OExpression)
protected:
      OExpression();           // protected constructor used by dynamic creation

// Attributes
public:
      Expression   m_Expression;

// Operations
public:
      ...
};
```

Now we need to access the m_Expression instance in the exposed Automation methods. This is easy—it's a one-to-one mapping of the methods and their parameters.

```
/////////////////////////////////////////////////////////////////////////
// OExpression message handlers

BSTR OExpression::GetExpression()
{
   // TODO: Add your dispatch handler code here

   CString s = m_Expression.GetExpression();
   return s.AllocSysString();
}

void OExpression::SetExpression(LPCTSTR szExpression, BOOL bInfix)
{
   // TODO: Add your dispatch handler code here
```

```
    m_Expression.SetExpression( szExpression, bInfix );
}

BOOL OExpression::Validate()
{
    // TODO: Add your dispatch handler code here

    return m_Expression.Validate();
}

long OExpression::Evaluate()
{
    // TODO: Add your dispatch handler code here

    return m_Expression.Evaluate();
}
```

We're finished. That's all there is to wrapping an existing C++ class with Automation. We designed the class from the beginning to be compatible with Automation controllers by not passing structures, references, or pointers and using only native or Automation-supported data types. The specification for Automation supports passing certain types by reference, but currently there aren't any controllers that provide this functionality. I imagine, though, that this feature will soon be available.

Compile, link, and run the application. It doesn't do much, but running the application causes MFC to automatically update the Windows Registry with the OExpression component information. Any Automation controller can now access the Expression component.

MFC's Dispatch Macros

Now we'll take a look at how MFC built the dispatch table for the four methods that we added to OExpression. The following code was added by ClassWizard as we added the methods for the OExpression class:

```
// From oexpress.h
class OExpression : public CCmdTarget
{
...
    // Generated OLE dispatch map functions
    //{{AFX_DISPATCH(OExpression)
    afx_msg BSTR GetExpression();
    afx_msg void SetExpression(LPCTSTR szExpression, BOOL bInfix);
    afx_msg BOOL Validate();
    afx_msg long Evaluate();
    //}}AFX_DISPATCH
    DECLARE_DISPATCH_MAP()
};
```

The preceding code is used by ClassWizard to declare, and keep track of, the internal methods used to implement the Automation properties and methods. The `DECLARE_DISPATCH_MAP` macro declares a few static member variables in the class to store and retrieve the dispatch map and its entries. Once the member functions are declared in the **.H** file, they are placed in the dispatch map in our **.CPP** file (also done for us by ClassWizard):

```
// From oexpress.cpp
..
BEGIN_DISPATCH_MAP(OExpression, CCmdTarget)
   //{{AFX_DISPATCH_MAP(OExpression)
   DISP_FUNCTION(OExpression, "GetExpression", GetExpression, VT_BSTR, VTS_NONE)
   DISP_FUNCTION(OExpression, "SetExpression", SetExpression, VT_EMPTY, VTS_BSTR
                 VTS_BOOL)
   DISP_FUNCTION(OExpression, "Validate", Validate, VT_BOOL, VTS_NONE)
   DISP_FUNCTION(OExpression, "Evaluate", Evaluate, VT_I4, VTS_NONE)
   //}}AFX_DISPATCH_MAP
END_DISPATCH_MAP()
...
```

The `DISP_FUNCTION` macro and its companions, `DISP_PROPERTY` and `DISP_PROPERTY_EX`, define the Automation property or method name, the implementing function or member variable, the return type, and the parameters for the entry in the dispatch map.

```
#define DISP_FUNCTION(theClass, szExternalName, pfnMember, vtRetVal, vtsParams) \
   { _T(szExternalName), DISPID_UNKNOWN, vtsParams, vtRetVal, \

     (AFX_PMSG)(void (theClass::*)(void))pfnMember, (AFX_PMSG)0, 0 }, \

#define DISP_PROPERTY(theClass, szExternalName, memberName, vtPropType) \
   { _T(szExternalName), DISPID_UNKNOWN, NULL, vtPropType, (AFX_PMSG)0, (AFX_PMSG)0, \
     offsetof(theClass, memberName) }, \

#define DISP_PROPERTY_EX(theClass, szExternalName, pfnGet, pfnSet, vtPropType) \
   { _T(szExternalName), DISPID_UNKNOWN, NULL, vtPropType, \
     (AFX_PMSG)(void (theClass::*)(void))pfnGet, \
     (AFX_PMSG)(void (theClass::*)(void))pfnSet, 0 }, \
```

ClassWizard does all this for us. At first the idea of ClassWizard mucking around in your code can be a little disconcerting, but after you get used to it you'll think it's great.

Let's take a look at how MFC uses the dispatch map to process requests from a controller application. When `CCmdTarget::EnableAutomation` is called in the constructor of the `OExpression` class, `EnableAutomation` creates an instance of the MFC class `COleDispatchImp`, which contains the implementation of the `IDispatch` interface. `EnableAutomation` copies the Vtable of `COleDispatchImp` to m_xDispatch, an internal variable within CCmdTarget. The following code, from CCmdTarget, illustrates this:

```
// enable this object for ActiveX Automation, called from derived class ctor
void CCmdTarget::EnableAutomation()
{
    ASSERT(GetDispatchMap() != NULL);    // must have DECLARE_DISPATCH_MAP

    // construct an COleDispatchImpl instance just to get to the vtable
    COleDispatchImpl dispatch;

    // vtable pointer should be already set to same or NULL
    ASSERT(m_xDispatch.m_vtbl == NULL||
        *(DWORD*)&dispatch == m_xDispatch.m_vtbl);

    // sizeof(COleDispatchImpl) should be just a DWORD (vtable pointer)
    ASSERT(sizeof(m_xDispatch) == sizeof(COleDispatchImpl));
    // copy the vtable (and other data) to make sure it is initialized
    m_xDispatch.m_vtbl = *(DWORD*)&dispatch;
    *(COleDispatchImpl*)&m_xDispatch = dispatch;
}
```

Once this is set up, a client application's QueryInterface call for IDispatch will return a pointer to the m_xDispatch.m_vtbl member. The client now has an IDispatch pointer that contains the methods: Invoke, GetIDsOfNames, GetTypeInfoCount, and GetTypeInfo. All these methods are implemented in the COleDispatchImp class. For an example, let's follow the sequence where the client initially calls the SetExpression Automation method. MFC doesn't provide an implementation of the GetTypeInfoCount and GetTypeInfo methods, so the client should call GetIDsOfNames to convert the string "SetExpression" to the appropriate DISPID. The following code shows the nonimplementation of the GetTypeInfo functions and the implementation of GetIDsOfNames:

```
STDMETHODIMP COleDispatchImpl::GetTypeInfoCount(UINT* pctinfo)
{
    *pctinfo = 0;
    return E_NOTIMPL;
}

STDMETHODIMP COleDispatchImpl::GetTypeInfo(UINT /*itinfo*/, LCID /*lcid*/,
    ITypeInfo** pptinfo)
{
    METHOD_PROLOGUE_EX(CCmdTarget, Dispatch)
    ASSERT_VALID(pThis);

    *pptinfo = NULL;
    return E_NOTIMPL;
}
```

```
STDMETHODIMP COleDispatchImpl::GetIDsOfNames( REFIID riid, LPTSTR* rgszNames, UINT cNames, LCID
/*lcid*/, DISPID* rgdispid )
{
    METHOD_PROLOGUE_EX(CCmdTarget, Dispatch)
    SCODE sc = S_OK;

    // fill in the member name
    const AFX_DISPMAP* pDerivMap = pThis->GetDispatchMap();
    rgdispid[0] = pThis->MemberIDFromName(pDerivMap, rgszNames[0]);
    if (rgdispid[0] == DISPID_UNKNOWN)

      sc = DISP_E_UNKNOWNNAME;

    // argument names are always DISPID_UNKNOWN (for this implementation)
    for (UINT nIndex = 1; nIndex < cNames; nIndex++)
        rgdispid[nIndex] = DISPID_UNKNOWN;

    return sc;
}
```

I've highlighted the preceding code that finds the DISPID for the given method or property name.
CCmdTarget::MemberIDFromName does the work. Here it is:

```
MEMBERID PASCAL CCmdTarget::MemberIDFromName(
    const AFX_DISPMAP* pDispMap, LPCTSTR lpszName)
{
    // search all maps and their base maps
    UINT nInherit = 0;
    while (pDispMap != NULL)
    {
        // search all entries in this map
        const AFX_DISPMAP_ENTRY* pEntry = pDispMap->lpEntries;
        // How many entries in the dispatch map
        UINT nEntryCount = GetEntryCount(pDispMap);
        for (UINT nIndex = 0; nIndex < nEntryCount; nIndex++)
        {
            if (pEntry->vt != VT_MFCVALUE &&
                lstrcmpi(pEntry->lpszName, lpszName) == 0)
            {
                if (pEntry->lDispID == DISPID_UNKNOWN)
                {
                    // the MEMBERID is combination of nIndex & nInherit
                    return MAKELONG(nIndex+1, nInherit);
                }
```

```
            // the MEMBERID is specified as the lDispID
            return pEntry->lDispID;
    }
    ++pEntry;
    }
  pDispMap = pDispMap->pBaseMap;
  ++nInherit;
  }

  return DISPID_UNKNOWN;  // name not found
}
```

The preceding code spins through the dispatch map, maps the external name to the internal DISPID, and returns it to the client application (the Automation controller). The implementation of dispatch maps is similar to the implementation of MFC's COM interface maps that we covered in Chapter 5. You may have noticed the code that uses the `nInherit` flag. You can easily derive new classes from existing Automation-enabled MFC classes and then override or leave intact the Automation properties and methods from the base class. This is explained in *MFC Tech Note 39*.

When the client wants to invoke an Automation method or manipulate an Automation property, it calls the `COleDispatchImp::Invoke` method with the DISPID (which it obtained through `GetIDsOfNames`) and any required parameters. MFC maps the DISPID to a specific method (or property) and calls it on behalf of the client application. The code for `Invoke` is rather long, so I haven't included it here. Most of the MFC implementation of Automation is in **OLEDISP1.CPP** in the standard MFC source path \MSDEV\MFC\SRC.

Local Server Differences

In Chapters 4 and 5 we housed our components in DLLs because they used custom COM interfaces and therefore could not be marshaled across process boundaries. Now that we are using a standard COM interface, this is no longer necessary. Most of the differences between local and in-process servers occur in the `InitInstance` method of the derived `CWinApp` class.

When we built our application with AppWizard and answered **Yes, please** to the question concerning Automation, AppWizard generated quite a bit of Automation specific code for us. Our application now supports ActiveX Automation. AppWizard generated a unique CLSID for our application as well as a ProgID based on the project name. The component class within our application is the `CDocument`-derived class, so the generated ProgID is `AutoSvr.Document`. It's easy to change this ID; all you need to do is to modify the sixth substring of the `IDR_AUTOSVR_TYPE` string in the string table of the **.RC** file. (It's easy to identify. It's the only one with a period in it.) Following are selected lines from the `InitInstance` method in **AUTOSVR.CPP**.

```
// This identifier was generated to be statistically unique for your app.
// You may change it if you prefer to choose a specific identifier.
```

```
static const CLSID BASED_CODE clsid =
{ 0x77fc5ac3, 0xb494, 0x11ce, { 0xb6, 0xe, 0xfd, 0x5d, 0x8a, 0xfc, 0x39, 0x75 } };
```

This is the AppWizard-generated CLSID for our CDocument class. You will find it in the Registry associated with our application's ProgID. CDocument is the only (default) application class that derives from CCmdTarget, so it is the only class that can expose Automation methods and properties. As you will see in our next example, this is where you will typically add methods and properties to allow your application to be automated by an external Automation controller.

```
/////////////////////////////////////////////////////////////////////////////
// CAutosvrApp initialization

BOOL CAutosvrApp::InitInstance()
{
    // Initialize ActiveX libraries
    if (!AfxOleInit())
    {
        AfxMessageBox(IDP_OLE_INIT_FAILED);
        return FALSE;
    }
```

Initialize the ActiveX libraries, just as we did in Chapter 5:

```
    // Connect the COleTemplateServer to the document template.
    //   The COleTemplateServer creates new documents on behalf
    //   of requesting OLE containers by using information
    //   specified in the document template.
    m_server.ConnectTemplate(clsid, pDocTemplate, FALSE);
```

This is a little more complicated. You can ignore the comment about "requesting OLE containers." The member variable, m_server, is an instance of COleTemplateServer and is declared within the CAutosvrApp class. COleTemplateServer is derived from COleObjectFactory and provides a class factory for the CDocument-derived class. The ConnectTemplate method attaches the server to the document template class. The third parameter, bMultiInstance, is an important one. It indicates whether an application instance should be invoked for every new document that is created. For MDI applications, this flag is set to FALSE to indicate that the application can support multiple client connections within a single EXE. For SDI applications, this flag is set to TRUE, which indicates that a new EXE will be launched for every client that creates an instance of the CDocument class.

```
    // Register all COM server factories as running.  This enables the
    //   COM libraries to create objects from other applications.
    COleTemplateServer::RegisterAll();
    // Note: MDI applications register all server objects without regard
    //   to the /Embedding or /Automation on the command line.
```

Here's where all the class factories for our local server are registered with COM. This call is the same as our previous chapter example of COleObjectFactory::RegisterAll. As the comment indicates, if this is an MDI application, the RegisterAll method is called regardless of the /Automation flag on the command line. This is because the application supports access by multiple controllers within the same EXE. In an SDI application, the RegisterAll method is called only if the EXE is started with the /Automation flag. The /Automation flag tells the EXE that it was launched on behalf of a controller, as opposed to being launched by an application user.

```
// Parse the command line to see if launched as ActiveX server
if (RunEmbedded() || RunAutomated())
{
    // Application was run with /Embedding or /Automation.  Don't show the
    //  main window in this case.
    return TRUE;
}
```

When COM starts an executable on behalf of a requesting client (or controller) via the CoGetClassObject function, COM uses the LocalServer32 entry in the Registry. The entry should have the /Automation command-line option tacked on the end of the pathname. This arrangement enables the application to start without showing its main window. When you're using an Automation server, it isn't always necessary to see what the server is doing, so the default local server behavior is to not show its main window when started by an Automation controller.

```
// When a server application is launched stand-alone, it is a good idea
//  to update the system registry in case it has been damaged.
 m_server.UpdateRegistry(OAT_DISPATCH_OBJECT);
COleObjectFactory::UpdateRegistryAll();

...
}
```

The preceding code updates the Registry with all the information that would normally be included in the **.REG** file for a server. When you add component classes to an MFC application, as we did with the OExpression class, this information will automatically be added to the Registry the next time the application is run without the /Automation switch. Let's see whether all this works by quickly building an application to test the OExpression component.

Type Information

In our discussions so far, the controller (or client) application has required certain information about the component before the application can access the component's functionality. In our examples, we've hard coded the names of the members in the server and have had to know the number of parameters and their types. In a component-based environment, this is hardly a good situation. A client application shouldn't have to know the specifics of a component's services at compile time. A better approach would be for the server application to somehow advertise its functionality through some well-specified technique. In this way, generic clients could query a server programmatically for all the information needed to use a certain piece of functionality. COM provides such a mechanism, and it's called *type information*.

A component's type information describes, in a binary standard way, the capabilities of the server. The component's Automation methods and property names, their return values, and the number and types of their parameters can all be described using type information.

The type information for a component is described using Microsoft's Object Description Language. Visual C++ automatically maintains a file, **PROJNAME.ODL**, with the definition of all your control's methods, properties, and events. An exhaustive discussion of the structure of an ODL file is beyond our scope, but I've included a partial listing of the ODL file for the AUTOSVR example that we just developed. Whenever we added a method using ClassWizard's **OLE Automation** tab, ClassWizard wrote a line to the project's ODL file. Table 6.5 contains some of the important keywords used in an ODL.

```
//
// AutoSvr.odl : type library source for AutoSvr.exe
//
// This file will be processed by the Make Type Library (mktyplib) tool to
// produce the type library (AutoSvr.tlb).

[ uuid(A7699974-0060-11D0-A61D-E8F97D000000), version(1.0) ]
library AutoSvr
{
    importlib("stdole32.tlb");

    ...

    // Primary dispatch interface for OExpression

    [ uuid(32CE8D20-0129-11D0-A61F-6C5374000000) ]

    dispinterface IOExpression
    {
        properties:
            // NOTE - ClassWizard will maintain property information here.
            //    Use extreme caution when editing this section.
            //{{AFX_ODL_PROP(OExpression)
            //}}AFX_ODL_PROP

        methods:
            // NOTE - ClassWizard will maintain method information here.
            //    Use extreme caution when editing this section.
            //{{AFX_ODL_METHOD(OExpression)
```

```
        [id(1)] void SetExpression(BSTR szExpression, boolean bInfix);
        [id(2)] BSTR GetExpression();
        [id(3)] long Evaluate();
        [id(4)] boolean Validate();
    //}}AFX_ODL_METHOD
};

    // Class information for OExpression

    [ uuid(32CE8D21-0129-11D0-A61F-6C5374000000) ]
    coclass MFCExpression
    {
        [default] dispinterface IOExpression;
    };

    //{{AFX_APPEND_ODL}}
};
```

Table 6.5 ODL Keywords

Keyword	Purpose
interface	Standard COM-based, Vtable interface definition.
dispinterface	Defines an IDispatch interface. This includes the DISPIDs, properties, and methods for the interface.
coclass	Describes an implementation of a component object class.
default	Indicates that the interface is the default IDispatch interface. This is the one that is returned when a client queries for IDispatch.
bindable	The property supports being bound from the client and supports notification via the IPropertyNotifySink::OnChange method.
requestedit	The property supports the OnRequestEdit notification of IPropertyNotifySink.
hidden	When used as an attribute of a property, it indicates that the property should not be displayed by type library browsers.
library	Begins the definition of a type library. This gives its name and GUID. The GUID is listed in the Registry and provides a way for tools and components to locate the library's TLB file.
source	Indicates that the IDispatch interface is an outgoing one. This means that the IDispatch is not implemented by the control but instead is called by the control. This keyword is used for the control's event set.
id(num)	Defines the DISPID for the associated property or method.
version	Version of the library, interface, or class implementation.
uuid(uuidval)	The GUID that identifies the library or interface.

As you can see, the ODL describes the Automation methods that our Expression component exposes. The DISPID, name, and parameter types are all described using ODL keywords.

The ODL file must be compiled into a binary form for other OLE components to use. Visual C++ contains a utility, MKTYPLIB, that compiles the ODL file and produces a binary file with an extension of **TLB**. This file can be distributed as is, or it can be appended to a DLL or EXE file as a resource. Visual C++ automatically invokes the MKTYPLIB utility whenever the ODL file changes. It then binds the .TLB file into the resources of your server's housing file (either a DLL or EXE).

Once the type information is in a binary form, it can easily be queried by OLE tools and other components. The OLEVIEW utility can display the type information of a component. Just double-click on the IDispatch interface to display the details of the interface.

A client application can obtain and iterate over a server's type information in one of several ways. As we've seen, the IDispatch interface provides two methods—GetTypeInfoCount and GetTypeInfo—that provide access to the type information. However, this approach requires the client to instantiate a component before scanning a server's capabilities. This requirement can be expensive if the only reason for instantiating the component is to query type information. A client application (such as a component browser) that is interested only in a component's capabilities and does not want to use the component can scan the type information by accessing it directly in the housing. The **TypeLib** Registry entry provides the location of a component's type information.

Dual Interfaces

We now have the pieces to understand the concept of a *dual interface*. Dual interfaces are implemented by a server component and give the client application two different ways to access its functionality. We studied custom COM interfaces in Chapter 4, and in this chapter we took a look at IDispatch, a very useful ActiveX interface. A dual interface combines a custom interface with the standard IDispatch interface. This technique allows the client to choose which interface it wants to use.

Figure 6.9 depicts what the Expression component would look like with a dual interface. It is a combination of our custom interface (IExpression) and the IDispatch that we implemented earlier in this chapter. The Expression methods are now exposed directly through our Vtable and through the IDispatch.

Why should we expose two interfaces that provide basically the same functionality? The primary reason is performance. If the server has an in-process (DLL) implementation, then no marshaling is required. The client can directly bind to the custom interface methods and make very efficient calls. The performance with this method is nearly identical to that of direct C or C++ function bindings: very fast. However, if the client requires a local-server implementation of the server because of 32-bit-to-16-bit interoperation or another cross-process requirement, the client can use the IDispatch implementation. This method is slower because of marshaling requirements and the added time required to use the Invoke method and possibly GetIDsOfNames.

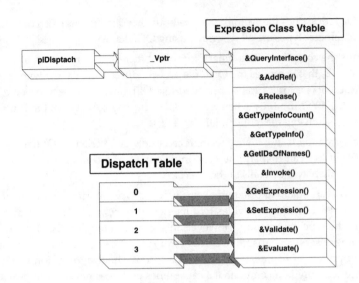

Figure 6.9 Expression class with a dual interface.

I say "possibly" because there are really three ways a client can bind to a dual interface server: late binding, ID binding, and early binding. Each one has specific type checking and performance characteristics. Here's a look at each one.

Late Binding

The examples that we've developed so far in this example have used late binding. We have ignored any type information provided by the server and have dynamically, at run time, determined the DISPID of the method to call; we have called Invoke through the IDispatch interface. Basically, everything occurred at run time. This is the most expensive technique and provides virtually no type checking. Any type checking is performed at run time by the server. Although this technique is the slowest, it is also the most flexible because everything is determined at run time. If the server interface changes, the client need not be recompiled to take advantage of the changes.

ID Binding

ID binding is very similar to late binding. The only difference is that the call to GetIDsOfNames is not made at run time. This approach saves a significant amount of time and dramatically improves performance. This technique requires that the server provide type information. At compile time, the controller application reads the type library and retrieves the DISPIDs of the called members. It can then statically store these values for use at run time.

ID binding also provides better compile-time type checking, because the compiler can determine the parameter types from the server's type library. However, if the members are rearranged in the server or if additional members are added, you must recompile to access the new functionality. Our next Visual C++ example will illustrate ID binding.

Early Binding

Early binding also requires that the server provide type information. It is the most efficient and the least flexible of the three techniques. As always, there is a trade-off. Early binding provides good type checking, because the controller uses the type information to verify the parameters as it builds them, which is done at compile time and not at run time. The binding is directly through the Vtable, so no DISPIDs or calls to Invoke are required. If the server is implemented in a DLL, the speed of early binding is the same as that of a direct DLL-type function call. However, as with ID binding, early binding requires a rebuild whenever the server component's interface is changed.

A Visual C++ Automation Controller

Actually, we've already built an Automation controller using Visual C++, but we did it without using MFC. Visual C++'s ClassWizard makes it easy to access the methods and properties of an Automation server. MFC uses ID binding in its implementation. Let's build a quick application to demonstrate how to access the functionality of the MFC-based server that we built in the previous example.

First, start Visual C++ and use AppWizard to create an application with the following options:

1. Name the application **VCClient**.
2. Build an **MFC AppWizard (EXE)** project.
3. In AppWizard Step 1, choose a **Single document** application.
4. In AppWizard Step 2 of 6, accept the default of **None** for database support.
5. In AppWizard Step 3 of 6, select **None** for **OLE Container support**, and be sure to enable **OLE automation** support.
6. In AppWizard Step 4 of 6, take the default features, but turn off **Print Preview** support.
7. In AppWizard Step 5 of 6, take the default Regular DLL using Shared MFC DLL.
8. In AppWizard Step 6 of 6, derive the view from **CFormView** and change the implementation file's name to **VIEW.H** and **VIEW.CPP**. Also, change the document class implementation files to **DOCU-MENT.H** and **DOCUMENT.CPP**.
9. Click the **Finish** button.

Just as we've done in previous versions of the CLIENT application, we add two buttons and an entry field to the dialog resource (IDD_VCCLIENT_FORM). The button IDs are IDC_EVALUATE and IDC_VALIDATE, and the entry field has an ID of IDC_EXPRESSION. Using ClassWizard, we add, for both buttons, handlers for the BN_CLICKED event.

Next, we'll use ClassWizard to create a wrapper class for our Automation-enabled `Expression` component that we added to the AUTOSVR example. Start ClassWizard and follow these steps:

1. Go to the **OLE Automation** tab.
2. Click the **Add Class** button and choose **From an OLE TypLib**.
3. From the Import from TypLib file dialog box, select the **AUTOSVR.TLB** file from the \DEBUG directory of the AUTOSVR project.
4. In the Confirm Classes dialog box shown in Figure 6.10, change the names of the header and implementation files to **SVR.H** and **SVR.CPP**, respectively. This will remove any confusion with the AUTOSVR files from the previous project. Click **OK** to add the files to our project.

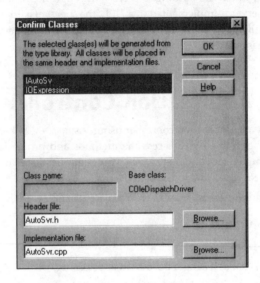

Figure 6.10 Confirm Classes dialog box.

What did all that do? Visual C++ opened the type library file of our AUTOSVR local-server application and created two classes that will make it easy to access any functionality housed in the **AUTOSVR.EXE** application. ClassWizard created two classes: `IAutoSvr` and `IOExpression`. Every AppWizard-based application gets a default Automation-enabled document class, and that is what the `IAutoSvr` class refers to. We didn't add any functionality to that class, but we will in the next section. For now, we'll focus on the `IOExpression` class. It provides an `IDispatch`-based interface to our `Expression` component within the AUTOSVR application. Here is the definition from **SVR.H**:

```
//
// svr.h
// Machine generated IDispatch wrapper class(es) created with ClassWizard
//
```

```
...

/////////////////////////////
// IOExpression wrapper class

class IOExpression : public COleDispatchDriver
{
public:
    IOExpression() {}              // Calls COleDispatchDriver default constructor
    IOExpression(LPDISPATCH pDispatch) : COleDispatchDriver(pDispatch) {}
    IOExpression(const IOExpression& dispatchSrc) : COleDispatchDriver(dispatchSrc) {}

// Attributes
public:

// Operations
public:

    void SetExpression(LPCTSTR szExpression, BOOL bInfix);
    CString GetExpression();
    long Evaluate();
    BOOL Validate();
};
```

Here are those methods that we're familiar with. ClassWizard read the type library and created prototypes for the OExpression methods in the AUTOSVR application. Nearly all the work is done by MFC's COleDispatchDriver class, but before we look at it, here is the code from the **SVR.CPP** file:

```
//
// svr.cpp
// Machine generated IDispatch wrapper class(es) created with ClassWizard
//

#include "stdafx.h"
#include "svr.h"

...

void IOExpression::SetExpression(LPCTSTR szExpression, BOOL bInfix)
{
    static BYTE parms[] =
        VTS_BSTR VTS_BOOL;
    InvokeHelper(0x1, DISPATCH_METHOD, VT_EMPTY, NULL, parms,
        szExpression, bInfix);
}
```

```
CString IOExpression::GetExpression()
{
    CString result;
    InvokeHelper(0x2, DISPATCH_METHOD, VT_BSTR, (void*)&result, NULL);
    return result;
}

long IOExpression::Evaluate()
{
    long result;
    InvokeHelper(0x3, DISPATCH_METHOD, VT_I4, (void*)&result, NULL);
    return result;
}

BOOL IOExpression::Validate()
{
    BOOL result;
    InvokeHelper(0x4, DISPATCH_METHOD, VT_BOOL, (void*)&result, NULL);
    return result;
}
```

This code is similar to the code that we developed at the beginning of this chapter in the CLIENT example. MFC, however, has a set of routines that make it easy to call Automation methods with various parameter types. MFC's implementation of the Automation client uses the ID binding technique that we just discussed. The first parameter of the `InvokeHelper` function is the DISPID of the method or property. This value is hard coded and is determined when the Automation wrapper class is generated. This technique eliminates the need for `COleDispatchDriver` to call `GetIDsOfNames`, but if the server's implementation is changed—say, by the addition of other methods—the whole class must be regenerated and the application recompiled and relinked. Remember, that's one of the drawbacks of the ID binding technique. Let's take a quick look at the `COleDispatchDriver` class.

COleDispatchDriver

MFC's `COleDispatchDriver` class provides a basic implementation of the client side of an Automation interface. It basically encapsulates the functionality that we developed in the non-MFC CLIENT example at the beginning of this chapter. Table 6.6 lists some useful members of the `COleDispatchDriver` class. We'll use some of them as we finish the VCCLIENT examples.

Table 6.6 Important `COleDispatchDriver` Members

Parameter	Purpose
`m_lpDispatch`	The `IDispatch` pointer that the instance is using.
`CreateDispatch( LPCSTR ProgID )`	Creates an instance of an automation object and attaches it to the wrapper class instance.
`AttachDispatch( LPDISPATCH )`	Attaches an existing `IDispatch` pointer to the wrapper class. Use this method if you have a dispatch pointer to an existing object.
`ReleaseDispatch( void )`	Releases any attached dispatch pointer.
`InvokeHelper( ... )`	A help method used to call `IDispatch::Invoke`. This makes it a little easier to call members in the automation server component.
`SetProperty( DISPID, VT, value )`	Sets a property of the provided type and value.
`GetProperty( DISPID, VT, value* )`	Retrieves a property value of the described DISPID and type.

The `IOExpression` wrapper class uses the `InvokeHelper` method to call the `Expression` component's methods. This code was generated automatically for us; all we need to do is to create an instance of the wrapper class and use either the `CreateDispatch` or `AttachDispatch` method to create or attach an instance of an `Expression` component. We'll use `CreateDispatch`. The `AttachDispatch` method "attaches" an existing `IDispatch` pointer to the wrapper class, which assigns the pointer to the internal `m_pDispatch` member.

We will use the component in our view class, so make the following modifications to **VIEW.H**:

```
//
// View.h : interface of the CVCClientView class

#include "svr.h"

class CVCClientView : public CFormView
{
...

// Implementation
protected:
    IOExpression    m_IOExpression;
...

};
```

We include the wrapper class definition (**SVR.H**) and add an instance of the class as a member of our view class. When the view is created, we need to create an instance of the `Expression` component housed in the AUTOSVR application. Later, when we shut down our application, we will release our connection to the component. We can handle these steps in the view's constructor and destructor.

```
CVCClientView::CVCClientView()
    : CFormView(CVCClientView::IDD)
{
    //{{AFX_DATA_INIT(CVCClientView)
        // NOTE: the ClassWizard will add member initialization here
    //}}AFX_DATA_INIT
    m_IOExpression.CreateDispatch( "Chap6.MFCExpression.1" );
}

CVCClientView::~CVCClientView()
{
    m_IOExpression.ReleaseDispatch();
}
```

We create an instance using `CreateDispatch` and pass the ProgID of our component. `CreateDispatch` uses `CoCreateInstance` and queries for an `IDispatch` pointer, just as we did in the non-MFC CLIENT example. When we're finished, we call `ReleaseDispatch`, which releases the interface.

Now that we have a dispatch to our `Expression` component, we can use all the wrapper methods in the `IOExpression` class. First, though, we need to add handlers for the `IDC_VALIDATE` and `IDC_EVALU-ATE` buttons, just as we've done several times before. After you've done that, add the following code to the handlers:

```
void CVCClientView::OnEvaluate()
{
    // Get the expression from the entry field
    CString strExpression;
    CWnd* pWnd = GetDlgItem( IDC_EXPRESSION );
    pWnd->GetWindowText( strExpression );

    m_IOExpression.SetExpression( strExpression, TRUE );

    long lResult = m_IOExpression.Evaluate();

    // Set the returned value in the entry field
    char szTemp[128];
    sprintf( szTemp, "%ld", lResult );
    pWnd->SetWindowText( szTemp );

    // Set focus back to the entry field
    GetDlgItem( IDC_EXPRESSION )->SetFocus();
}

void CVCClientView::OnValidate()
{
```

```
// Get the expression from the entry field

CString strExpression;
CWnd* pWnd = GetDlgItem( IDC_EXPRESSION );
pWnd->GetWindowText( strExpression );

m_IOExpression.SetExpression( strExpression, TRUE );

if (! m_IOExpression.Validate() )
    AfxMessageBox( "Invalid Expression, try again" );

// Set focus back to the entry field
GetDlgItem(IDC_EXPRESSION)->SetFocus();
}
```

The code is nearly identical to what we've coded before; the only difference is the way that we're accessing the `Expression` component. We're now using MFC, and the `Expression` component resides in the AUTOSVR application.

When we call `CreateDispatch` in the view's constructor, COM starts the AUTOSVR executable. Because we're just using the services of AUTOSVR, we don't actually see the application. It's not in the task list, but if you use a utility such as PVIEW you'll see that it is running. When we shut down and release the `IDispatch` pointer, AUTOSVR shuts down as well.

Automating an MFC Application

At the beginning of the chapter, I mentioned that there are two uses of Automation that are important to the reuse of software. We've explored the first approach: using Automation to wrap existing code and exposing it for other applications and languages to use. The second technique is to turn an existing application into a component. That's what we'll do next. We'll allow our AUTOSVR application to be driven externally. In doing so, we will implement many of the Automation properties and methods that Microsoft recommends be exposed when an application provides Automation support. We'll also allow the controlling application to use our `Expression` functionality, although a little differently from the techniques we've discussed previously.

The first thing we need to do is to update the `CFormView` dialog box so that it has the `IDC_EXPRESSION` entry field and the `IDC_VALIDATE` and `IDC_EVALUATE` buttons that we've used before. I won't lead you through that again. Just edit the `IDD_AUTOSVR_FORM` dialog box and make it look like the one in Figure 6.11.

We're not going to use the `IExpression` method to implement the `Expression` class functionality; we've already exposed it for other applications to use. We will use the `Expression` class internally, just as we would any C++ object. Our focus now is to allow an external client to drive the behavior of our application.

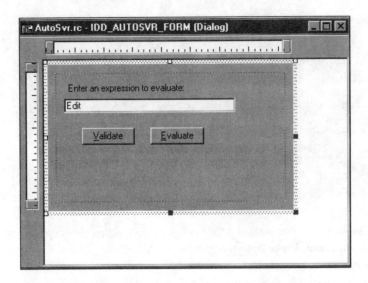

Figure 6.11 Building the AUTOSVR form dialog box.

When automating or allowing an external application to drive your application, you must expose properties and methods that are similar to ones that you use internally. The MFC document/view architecture makes it easy to allow your application to be automated, but only through the CDocument-derived class. Of the standard application classes provided by AppWizard in our project, only CDocument and its derivatives are derived from CCmdTarget. (Actually, the CWnd class is derived from CCmdTarget. Any true window classes in your application can support Automation, but they're not directly exposed by ClassWizard.) As you may recall, only classes derived from CCmdTarget have COM support within MFC. So we expose all our application's methods and properties through the CDocument-derived class, which in our application is CAutosvrDoc.

AUTOSVR is an MDI application and so can support multiple Automation clients simultaneously. Our first step is to allow an Automation controller to set the expression in our entry field and act as though it is pressing the **Validate** and **Evaluate** command buttons. To do this, we need to look at the document/view architecture again. Within an MFC MDI application, whenever a new document is created, a new frame/document/view tuple is created. This arrangement makes it easy to manage each MDI child window or view. There is one document instance and one or more view instances associated with each MDI child. So we need to add an instance of the Expression class to the document class. Why not the view class? It could also go there, but the Expression class contains the data of our application and so belongs within the document. As you'll see, this technique makes things fairly easy to implement. Add the following code to **DOCUMENT.H**:

```
// document.h : interface of the CAutosvrDoc class
//
/////////////////////////////////////////////////////////////////////
```

```
class Expression;

class CAutosvrDoc : public CDocument
{
protected: // create from serialization only
    CAutosvrDoc();
    DECLARE_DYNCREATE(CAutosvrDoc)

// Attributes
protected:
Expression* m_pExpression;

public:
Expression* GetExp() const { return m_pExpression; }

...
```

Here we've added a pointer to the Expression class and have included a forward declaration for the Expression class. This arrangement reduces the dependencies on the **EXPRESS.H** file. Most of the MFC application classes include **DOCUMENT.H** but don't need access to the definition of the Expression class. Because we've forward declared the class and have implemented it using a pointer, only **DOCUMENT.CPP** and **VIEW.CPP** need to include **EXPRESS.H**. We've also added a GetExp function that returns the expression pointer. This pointer will be useful when we need to access the Expression instance from within the view class. Here's the instantiation and destruction code for **DOCUMENT.CPP**:

```
// document.cpp : implementation of the CAutosvrDoc class
//

#include "stdafx.h"
#include "autosvr.h"
#include "express.h"
#include "document.h"

...
/////////////////////////////////////////////////////////////////////////////
// CAutosvrDoc construction/destruction

CAutosvrDoc::CAutosvrDoc()
{
    // TODO: add one-time construction code here

    EnableAutomation();
    AfxOleLockApp();

    m_pExpression = new Expression;
}
```

```
CAutosvrDoc::~CAutosvrDoc()
{
    AfxOleUnlockApp();
    delete m_pExpression;
}
```

Now go into ClassWizard and add the two functions for the BN_CLICKED event. Take the defaults OnValidate and OnEvaluate. Add the following code to **VIEW.CPP**:

```
// view.cpp : implementation of the CAutosvrView class
//

#include "stdafx.h"
#include "autosvr.h"
#include "document.h"
#include "express.h"
#include "view.h"
...
void CAutosvrView::OnEvaluate()
{
    // TODO: Add your control notification handler code here
    CString strExpression;
    char szTemp[128];

    // Get the expression from the entry field
    CWnd* pWnd = GetDlgItem(IDC_EXPRESSION);
    pWnd->GetWindowText( strExpression );

    TRACE1( "OnEvaluate: Expression is %s\n", strExpression );

    CAutosvrDoc* pDoc = GetDocument();
    pDoc->GetExp()->SetExpression( strExpression, TRUE );

    long lResult = pDoc->GetExp()->Evaluate();
    sprintf( szTemp, "%ld", lResult );

    pWnd->SetWindowText( szTemp );

    // Set focus back to the entry field
    GetDlgItem( IDC_EXPRESSION )->SetFocus();

}

void CAutosvrView::OnValidate()
{
```

```
// TODO: Add your control notification handler code here
CString strExpression;

// Get the expression from the entry field
CWnd* pWnd = GetDlgItem( IDC_EXPRESSION );
pWnd->GetWindowText( strExpression );

TRACE1( "OnValidate: Expression is %s\n", strExpression );

CAutosvrDoc* pDoc = GetDocument();
pDoc->GetExp()->SetExpression( strExpression, TRUE );

if (! pDoc->GetExp()->Validate() )
    AfxMessageBox( "Invalid Expression, try again" );

// Set focus back to the entry field
GetDlgItem(IDC_EXPRESSION)->SetFocus();
}
```

This is a little different from our previous implementations. We now must get the document associated with our view in order to access the `Expression` instance. This is how typical MFC development is done. The data is stored in the document and the view must go and get it.

We've done enough that we should probably compile, link, and run. When you do, you should see something like the screen in Figure 6.12. It shows three active documents, each with an instance of the `Expression` class. On application startup, you only will see one MDI child window. You must explicitly create the others either through the **File/New** menu item or by using multiple Automation controllers.

Everything should be working from the perspective of the application user, so now we can allow the process to be automated by an external application. To do this, we expose some methods that correspond to user actions within the application. Start ClassWizard, go to the **OLE Automation** tab, select the `CAutosvrDoc` class, and add an `Expression` property. You should have a screen like that in Figure 6.13.

The External Name field holds the name that the controller will use to manipulate the property (or method). The type will change depending on which implementation method you choose. The **Stock** implementation is used for ActiveX controls, so we will see it shortly. The **Member Variable** implementation adds a member variable to your class and directly exposes it to the controller. If you don't really care what the controller is doing with the property, this may be the method to use. The **Get/Set Methods** implementation provides C++-style `Get` and `Set` methods to wrap around the member variable. This is probably the most typical technique used. The controller must go through the `Get` and `Set` methods to access the internal variable, so the application knows when it changes.

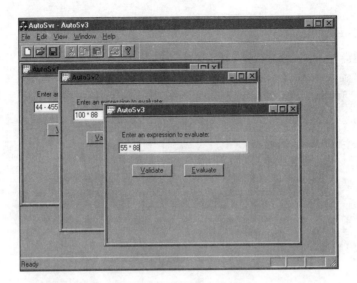

Figure 6.12 AUTOSVR application with three documents.

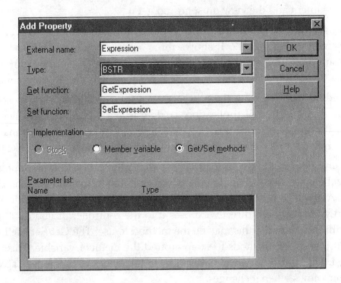

Figure 6.13 ClassWizard Add Property dialog box.

For our example, we'll choose a type of **BSTR** and an implementation of **Get/Set Methods**. If you don't want to allow the controller to set the property, clear out the **Set Function** entry field. This will put in its place a `SetNotSupported` method; if the controller attempts to set the function, it will throw an OLE exception. For this example, we want to allow the property to be set, so don't clear the Set function's name. Click **OK** to add the property. Click **Edit Code** in the ClassWizard dialog box and add the following code:

```
/////////////////////////////////////////////////////////////////////////////
// CAutosvrDoc commands

BSTR CAutosvrDoc::GetExpression()
{
    // TODO: Add your property handler here

    // Get the expression and return it to the Controller
    CString s = m_pExpression->GetExpression();
    return s.AllocSysString();
}

void CAutosvrDoc::SetExpression(LPCTSTR lpszNewValue)
{
    // TODO: Add your property handler here

    // Update the Expression instance with the new
    // expression, default the type to infix
    m_pExpression->SetExpression( lpszNewValue, TRUE );

    // Update the dialog form associated with the view
    // by sending it a hint as to what changed
    UpdateAllViews( NULL, VIEW_HINT_SETEXPRESSION );
}
```

The last section of code, which calls UpdateAllViews, needs some explanation. Now that we're using MFC's document/view architecture—in which the data is stored in the document class and the view is responsible for the display of this data—we must inform the views whenever any document data has changed. UpdateAllViews causes the View::OnUpdate function to be called for each view associated with the document. When the document calls UpdateAllViews, the document can pass a hint that helps the view determine what data has changed. I've set up three different hints that the view uses to determine what to do. These hints need to be defined in **DOCUMENT.H**:

```
// document.h : interface of the CAutosvrDoc class
//

class Expression;

const VIEW_HINT_SETEXPRESSION = 1;
const VIEW_HINT_VALIDATE      = 2;
const VIEW_HINT_EVALUATE      = 3;
```

The hints are used by the OnUpdate method of our view class. Here's the code that updates the appropriate view item, depending on the hint provided by the document class. You must override the OnUpdate method of CAutosvrView using ClassWizard and then add the following code to **VIEW.CPP**:

```
void CAutosvrView::OnUpdate(CView* pSender, LPARAM lHint, CObject* pHint)
{
    // TODO: Add your specialized code here and/or call the base class

    switch( lHint )
    {
        // The Automation controller called the
        // validate function. Simulate a push
        // of the "Validate" button.
        case VIEW_HINT_VALIDATE:
            OnValidate();
            break;

        // The Automation controller called the
        // Evaluate function. Simulate a push
        // of the "Evaluate" button.
        case VIEW_HINT_EVALUATE:
            OnEvaluate();
            break;

        case VIEW_HINT_SETEXPRESSION:
            CWnd* pWnd = GetDlgItem(IDC_EXPRESSION);
            CAutosvrDoc* pDoc = GetDocument();
            pWnd->SetWindowText( pDoc->GetExp()->GetExpression() );
            break;
    }
}
```

As you can see, we either simulate a press of one of the buttons or set the text of the entry field. This technique makes it easy for the Automation class, CAutosvrDoc, to update the user's view as a controller invokes these methods.

We need to add Automation methods that allow an external application to simulate the press of our two buttons: **Validate** and **Evaluate**. Use ClassWizard to add two Automation methods—Validate and Evaluate—that take no parameters and return void. Then add the following code:

```
void CAutosvrDoc::Validate()
{
    // TODO: Add your dispatch handler code here
```

```
    UpdateAllViews( NULL, VIEW_HINT_VALIDATE );
}

void CAutosvrDoc::Evaluate()
{
    // TODO: Add your dispatch handler code here
    UpdateAllViews( NULL, VIEW_HINT_EVALUATE );
}
```

There isn't much to do here. We just route the update to the view class with the specific hint, and the view simulates actions of a user. That was too easy. We need to add a little more to the AUTOSVR application.

Standard Application Properties

When we're providing Automation capabilities for a full application, as we're doing here with the AUTOSVR project, Microsoft recommends that certain standard properties and methods be supplied for the external application user. Microsoft also recommends a specific hierarchy for the Automation objects that are contained with the application. At the root is the `Application` object. An application contains a list of document objects, and so on. This hierarchy is consistent with the structure of typical MFC applications. It provides consistency among applications developed by various vendors and makes it easier for developers when they begin using the Automation capabilities of an application; the naming and object hierarchy are consistent. This standard is detailed in the *OLE 2 Programmer's Reference, Volume Two*. Table 6.7 lists some of the recommended `Application` object properties in AUTOSVR to add a few more options when we're driving our application via an Automation controller.

Table 6.7 Application Object Properties

Type/Property	Purpose
LPDISPATCH Application (Read-only)	Returns the `IDispatch` for the application object.
BSTR Name (Read-only)	Returns the name of the application.
BSTR FullName (Read-only)	Returns the complete pathname and filename for the application.
long Top	Sets or returns the distance from the top of the display to the top of the main application window.
long Left	Sets or returns the distance from the left edge of the display to the left edge of the main application window.
long Height	Sets or returns the height of the application's main window.
long Width	Sets or returns the width of the application's main window.
BOOL Visible	Toggles the visibility of the application windows.

The Chapter 6 AUTOSVR project on the accompanying CD-ROM implements all the standard `Application` properties described in Table 6.7. They're all fairly easy to implement, and you might try them yourself before checking what's on the CD-ROM. As you're developing the properties for the AUTOSVR project, you need a way to easily test the new properties and methods you've added. We need another Visual Basic application.

Driving the Autosvr Example

Now that we have added properties and methods to AUTOSVR, we need a controller to test what we've done. We'll be using the DISPTEST tool provided with Visual C++. If you have a current version of Visual Basic, it will work, too. Figure 6.14 shows the Visual Basic form of our VBDRIVER example, which we will use to control AUTOSVR.

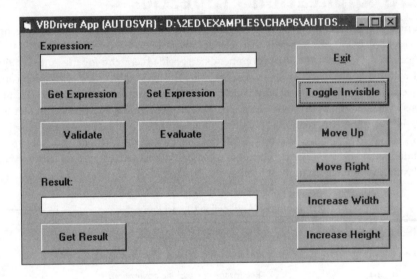

Figure 6.14 Visual Basic driver application.

The form has buttons that map to the various Automation methods and properties that we have added to AUTOSVR. To get things going, we connect to the main application object when we initially start the Visual Basic application.

```
' Global Form declaration
' Declared outside of any form procedure
Dim obj as Object

Sub Form_Load ()
    Dim objApp As object
```

```
Set obj = CreateObject("Autosvr.Document")
Set objApp = obj.Application
Form1.Caption = "VBDriver App (" + objApp.Name + ") - " + objApp.FullName
Set objApp = Nothing
End Sub
```

Here we are creating an instance of AUTOSVR. The `CreateObject` function will start the application if it isn't running and will create a new document if the application is running. MFC MDI applications allow multiple concurrent clients to access its document component. Whenever a new instance is created, a new document/view/template structure is created to service the controller.

I've added some code to test the various `Application` object properties we added. The `obj.Application` property returns an `LPDISPATCH` that we test by calling the `Name` and `FullName` properties. The rest of the code is fairly simple. Following is some of the code. It would be best to get the source from the accompanying CD-ROM, load Visual Basic (or **DISPTEST.EXE**), and experiment with the properties.

```
' Toggle the visibility of the main application window
' as well as the caption of the command button
Sub cmdVisible_Click ()
    If obj.Visible Then
        obj.Visible = False
        cmdVisible.Caption = "Toggle Visible"
    Else
        obj.Visible = True
        cmdVisible.Caption = "Toggle Invisible"
    End If
End Sub

' Increate the width of the application window
Sub cmdWidth_Click ()
    obj.Width = obj.Width + 5
End Sub
```

Summary

In this chapter, we investigated a powerful feature of ActiveX called Automation. Automation can be used to encapsulate a C++ language class in a binary standard wrapper that can easily be accessed by non-C++ languages. Automation also provides facilities that make it easy to control an application externally by another application or programming tool such as Visual Basic.

The backbone of Automation is the IDispatch interface and its four methods: Invoke, GetIDsOfNames, GetTypeInfoCount, and GetTypeInfo

Chapter 7

ActiveX Controls

Now it's time to change gears a little. In the first half of the book we concentrated on the whys and hows of developing reusable software components. We focused primarily on the COM and OLE technologies that provide us with the ability to build software components. We now understand what COM, OLE, and ActiveX are all about. We investigated using C++, custom COM interfaces, and Automation in the creation of software components, and now we're ready to develop the ultimate software components: ActiveX controls.

In this chapter we'll investigate what it takes to implement an ActiveX control. We'll look at the history of the OLE and ActiveX control standards and discuss various ways ActiveX controls can be used in conjunction with visual development tools, such as Microsoft's Visual Basic and Visual C++. Once we have a broad understanding of the technology used to implement controls, we'll use the remaining chapters to focus on the development of various types of ActiveX controls. This chapter provides an introduction to the technology. After this, it will be all coding.

OLE's Compound Document Architecture

The initial goal of OLE was to provide software users with a *document-centric* environment. OLE defines COM-based interfaces that enable applications to embed software objects developed by various vendors. This important capability has added significantly to the ease of use of various software products.

Figure 7.1 shows Microsoft Word with a Visio drawing embedded within the Word document. If I want to edit the Visio drawing, I can do so within Word by double-clicking on the embedded drawing; Visio executes "in-place," and the Word menu changes to a Visio one. This arrangement allows me to use Visio's functionality completely within Word. The benefit of this technology is that the user doesn't have to switch between applications to get work done. The focus is on the creation of the document and not on the assembling of different application "pieces" into a complete document, explaining the origin of the term *document-centric*. The document, and not the applications needed to combine and produce it, is the user's focus.

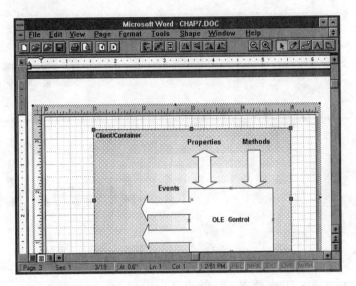

Figure 7.1 Visio drawing embedded in a Word document.

There are some problems with this shift in paradigms. Many users initially get confused when the Word menu changes to Visio's or Excel's. Also, most applications are large and cumbersome and experience significant performance problems when users attempt to launch several large applications at once. These problems will be overcome as users assimilate the changes and as developers restructure their applications to include smaller modules of functionality that operate independently (and as a whole).

ActiveX controls are built using many of the techniques of OLE compound documents. Plenty of material is available that explains OLE as a compound document standard, so I won't spend much time on it here except when it directly pertains to the development of ActiveX controls.

Compound Document Containers and Embedded Servers

Compound document containers are those applications that allow the embedding of OLE-compliant compound document servers. Examples of containers include Microsoft's Word and Excel, Corel's WordPerfect, and others.

Applications such as Visio are embedded servers that support being activated in-place within a compound document container application. This technique of being invoked within another application and merging its menus is called *visual editing*. The user double-clicks on the server's *site*—its screen location within the container—and the embedded server is launched and becomes activated in-place.

Compound document servers are typically implemented as executables and therefore are large. They include the complete functionality of the application that is being embedded within the container application. This is one reason that the effective use of compound document technology was initially viewed as requiring extensive system resources. But with advances in hardware and the move to 32-bit operating systems, this is no longer a serious problem.

Many compound document containers are also compound document servers. You can embed a Word document in an Excel spreadsheet as well as embed an Excel spreadsheet within a Word document. (This is one reason they are such large applications.) Most ActiveX controls are embedded servers that are designed to perform quite differently from compound document servers.

ActiveX Controls

ActiveX controls incorporate, or use, much of the technology provided by COM, OLE, and ActiveX—in particular, those technologies pioneered in compound documents. Many COM-based interfaces must be implemented by both the client (or container) and the control to provide this powerful component-based environment. Figure 7.2 illustrates the communication between a control and its client.

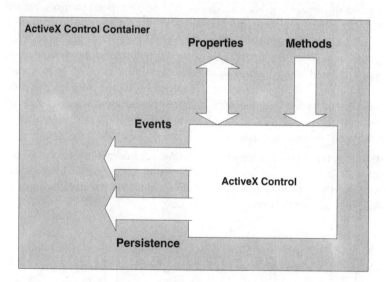

Figure 7.2 Interaction between a control and its client.

In Chapter 1, we discussed the importance of discrete software components to the future of software development. The underlying technology required to build robust software components is provided by COM and the ActiveX control specification. Problems must be overcome, but today ActiveX controls provide the most comprehensive solution.

In Chapter 6, we used Automation to encapsulate a nonvisual software component, our `Expression` class. The ActiveX control architecture provides a robust method of building visible software components. In addition to the visible aspect, ActiveX controls also provide a way to communicate events externally so that users of the control can use these events to signal other programmatic actions. A simple example is a timer control whose only purpose is to provide a consistent series of events that the control user can tie to some other programmatic action.

Another important capability of ActiveX controls is their ability to save their state. This quality of persistence allows a control user to initially define a control's characteristics knowing that they will persist between application design, running, and distribution. This capability is not intrinsically supported by the Automation servers discussed in Chapter 6.

Types of ActiveX Controls

There are three basic ActiveX control types. Graphical controls provide significant functionality by their visual representation and manipulation of data. An example might be an image display control. The second type is also graphical, but it implements or extends a standard Windows control. Its behavior is based on, and uses, the functionality of an existing control provided by Windows. An example is a standard listbox that has been enhanced to contain checkboxes. The third type, nonvisual controls, provides all their functionality without any graphical requirements. Examples of nonvisual controls include a timer control, a Win32 API control, and a network services control. Their main purpose is to expose Automation methods, properties, and events for a visual developer. Except for the timer control (whose purpose is to provide a uniform timer event and would be prohibitively expensive to implement using Automation), most nonvisual controls can function as Automation servers. However, providing an implementation using ActiveX controls makes them easier to use within graphical development environments, provides persistence of state, and supports an event mechanism to communicate with the container. We will develop examples of all three control types in the remaining chapters.

An additional control type is the Internet-aware control. An Internet-aware control can take the form of any of the three control types but has additional environmental requirements. Internet-aware controls must be designed to work effectively in low-bandwidth environments and to carefully implement user services. We will discuss these requirements in detail in Chapter 12.

ActiveX Controls as Software Components

We've come a long way in our quest for a technique to build robust and reusable software components, and we've finally reached a comprehensive destination. In Chapter 6, we saw how effective Automation is at providing reusable components by wrapping C++ classes and exposing their functionality. We also found three limitations of Automation. First, it provides only limited outgoing notification capabilities. Automation components are inherently synchronous and provide only one-way communication in their basic configuration. This is one reason that Automation objects are driven by Automation controllers. The second limitation involves the lack of a visual aspect to Automation components. Third, Automation, in contrast to controls, lacks a persistence mechanism. Persistence of control properties is an important feature not provided through Automation.

From now on we will focus exclusively on the design, development, and use of ActiveX controls. They provide a sophisticated event mechanism so that they can notify their users of events. Events are fired asynchronously, notifying the user of an important occurrence within the component and allowing the control user to harness the event and perform other actions in a larger component-based application. ActiveX controls also allow easy implementation of the visual or GUI aspect of a software component. This and other features of ActiveX controls provide a rich environment on which to build visually oriented development tools. And remember, the COM standard is an open one, and its design is completely documented for all to use. This arrangement creates an environment where vendors will develop tools for using this technology. The availability of third-party tools can only benefit those who develop software components.

The creation of rich, control-based development environments is important to the ultimate success of the component-based development paradigm. One of the problems of component development is the application's dependency on many different system-level and application-level components. The ultimate success of component-based software depends on robust tools that ease the tasks of distribution and management of the application and its components. Today, ActiveX controls are supported by nearly all major development tools. They have become the de facto software component.

Another important feature of ActiveX controls is that Microsoft has placed them at the center of its new Internet-based software focus. ActiveX controls are used throughout Microsoft's new Web-based technologies. Internet Explorer itself is implemented using a robust and feature-laden ActiveX control. ActiveX controls can be embedded within HTML-based Web pages to add tremendous application-like functionality to static Web-based documents. Thousands of ActiveX controls are available, and the market will only grow as the Internet and corporate intranets continue to flourish.

Some Terminology

A lot of terminology is associated with the OLE compound document standard, so I'll provide you with some short definitions to help as we move forward. The terminology for OLE changes often, and some of the terms are equivalent. Some of the definitions are cyclical, so you may have to loop through twice.

UI-Active Object

Embeddable objects are UI-active when they have been activated in-place and are being acted upon by the user. The UI-active server merges its menus with that of the containing application (such as Word). Only one server can be UI-active within a container at a time.

Active Object

When embeddable objects are not UI-active, they are active, loaded, or passive. (Local server objects have an additional state: running.) Most ActiveX controls prefer to remain in the active state, because it provides the control with a true HWND in which to render itself. In the loaded state, an embeddable object typically provides a metafile representation of itself for the container to display and lies dormant waiting to be in-place activated.

Embeddable Object

An embeddable object supports enough of the OLE document interfaces that it can be embedded within an OLE container. This doesn't mean that it supports in-place activation, only that it can render itself within the container. The object is said to be "embedded" because it is stored in the container's data stream. For example, in our previous Visio demonstration, the Visio object, which Microsoft Word knows nothing about, is actually stored or embedded within Word's **.DOC** file, which is a compound document file.

Passive Object

A passive object exists only in the persistent storage stream, typically on disk. To be modified, the object must be "loaded" into memory and placed in the running state. A passive object is just a string of bits on a storage device. Software is required to load, interpret, and manipulate the object.

Visual Editing and In-Place Activation

These terms describe the capability of an embeddable object to be activated in-place. In-place activation is the process of transitioning the object to the active state. In most compound document container applications, this process also forces the object into the UI-active state if it is an outside-in object. Once the object is activated, the user can interact with the embedded object. When the object is in-place active, the server and container can merge their menus.

Outside-In Object

Outside-in objects become active and UI-active at the same time. Outside-in objects are activated and immediately become UI-active by a double-click of the mouse. Compound document servers are outside-in objects. You must double-click the Visio object to invoke Visio when editing within Microsoft Word.

Inside-Out Object

Inside-out objects become UI-active with a single mouse click. They are typically already in the active state within the container. ActiveX controls are inside-out objects, although this option can be controlled by the control developer. With the creation of the OLE Controls 96 specification, which we will discuss in detail shortly, controls are not required to support any in-place activation interfaces.

ActiveX Control Containers

ActiveX controls are discrete software elements that are similar to discrete hardware components and are of little use by themselves. You need a control container to actually use an ActiveX control. Control containers make it easy to tie together various ActiveX controls into a more complex and useful application. An important feature of an ActiveX control container is the presence of a scripting language that is used to allow programmatic interaction with the various controls within the container.

ActiveX control containers are similar to the compound document containers that we described earlier, but the older compound document containers lack a few new interfaces specified for ActiveX controls. ActiveX controls can still function within compound document containers (if they're designed properly), but many of their most discerning features will not be accessible.

Although compound document containers and ActiveX control containers share many internal characteristics, their ultimate goals differ. As we've discussed, compound document containers focus on the assembly of documents for viewing and printing and are typically complete applications. ActiveX control containers are usually used as "forms" that contain controls that are tied together with a scripting language to create an application. Figure 7.3 shows two Visual Basic forms, each containing some ActiveX controls. Contrast this with the Word and Visio example in Figure 7.1.

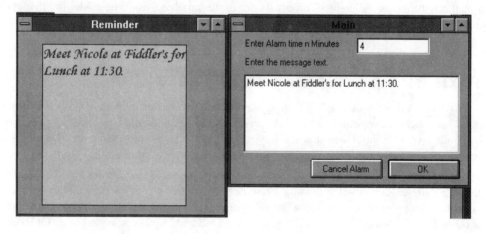

Figure 7.3 Two Visual Basic forms, each with some ActiveX controls.

Container Modalities

In typical visual development environments, the container operates in various *modes*. When the developer is designing a form (control container) or Web page, the control should behave differently than when it is actually being executed. To use Visual Basic as an example, when a Visual Basic developer needs a listbox control, the developer clicks the listbox icon on the tool palette, drags a representation of the listbox control, and drops it on a form. The listbox representation is merely a rectangle with a name in the top left corner. During design time, there is no need to create a window just to provide a representation of the control. When the Visual Basic form and its associated code are executed by a user of the application, the listbox control window is actually created and therefore needs to behave like a listbox and perform any special functions through its exposed properties, methods, and events. These two modes are referred to as the *design-phase* and *run-time* modes.

Visual Basic also allows a developer to single-step through the application. At each break-point, you can examine variables, check the call stack, and so on. When Visual Basic is in this mode—debug mode—the listbox control is frozen and doesn't act on any window events.

I used Visual Basic for this example, but there are a large number of other control containers, including Visual C++, Borland's Delphi, Microsoft's Internet Explorer, and so on. The ActiveX control standard provides two *ambient* properties that can be implemented by the container to indicate its various modes. Ambient properties are container states that can be queried by the contained controls. If the ambient property `UserMode` is `TRUE`, it indicates that the container is in a mode in which the application user can interact with a control. This mode would normally equate to a run-time mode in the Visual Basic example. If `UserMode` is `FALSE`, the container is in a design-type mode. The `UIDead` property indicates, when `TRUE`, that the control should not respond to any user input. This is similar to the debug mode of Visual Basic.

Throughout the rest of the chapters, I'll use the terms design phase, run-time mode, and debug mode to distinguish the differences in a container's states.

Control and Container Interfaces

Although we haven't directly covered OLE compound document servers in this book, we understand how the technology works. Compound document servers can be implemented as local servers, in-process servers, or both. ActiveX controls are almost always implemented as in-process servers. Most of the components that we've developed so far have been in-process servers, so we're comfortable with them.

The primary difference between the `Expression` in-process server of Chapter 5 and an ActiveX control is that the `Expression` object is missing a few ActiveX control–based interfaces. Many of these interfaces are required for a control to be classified as a compound document server and concern themselves with the control's visual aspect and its ability to be embedded and in-place activated in an OLE compound document container.

The act of building a component or a container amounts to a process of implementing and exposing a series of COM-based interfaces. A control implements a series of interfaces that a container expects and vice versa. Figure 7.4 shows the large number of interfaces that a control typically implements. I say "typically," because the requirements for implementing an ActiveX control have recently been loosened significantly. The basic concept of an ActiveX control has changed from its being a hybrid compound document server to being a small and nimble COM-based component. The newer control specifications reduce to one the number of interfaces a control must implement. We'll discuss these new standards shortly.

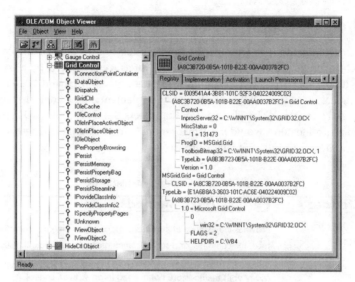

Figure 7.4 Control-implemented interfaces.

ActiveX Controls and Containers: A History

ActiveX controls—called OLE controls at the time—were introduced as an OLE-based technology in early 1994 as a replacement for the aging Visual Basic custom control (VBX). However, the technology was new, and very few development tools supported the use of OLE controls. Visual Basic 4.0, the version that provided support for OLE controls, would not be delivered until late 1995. Microsoft Access version 2.0 provided minimal support, as did Microsoft FoxPro version 3.0. You could develop ActiveX controls starting with the late 1994 release of Visual C++ version 2.0. However, even though you could develop controls, you could not use them within Visual C++. This capability had to wait for the late 1995 release of Visual C++ 4.0.

The initial version of the OLE control specification, now called the OLE Controls 94 spec, required an ActiveX control to implement a large number of COM-based interfaces. Most of these interfaces were part of the compound document specification, because ActiveX controls were really in-process compound document servers with a couple of new interfaces (such as `IOleControl`). During this period, OLE control containers were just compound document containers that implemented a few additional, control-specific interfaces (such as `IOleControlSite`).

In early 1996, after more than a year's experience with implementing and using OLE controls, Microsoft modified the specification significantly and called it the OLE controls 96 specification. The new specification addresses a number of performance issues inherent with controls implemented using the 1994 specification. The new specification also adds significant new features and capabilities for controls and containers.

The OLE Controls 94 Specification

The original OLE control architecture was specified as an extension to the existing compound document specification. An OLE control had to implement all the interfaces required by a compound document embedded server with in-place activation capabilities (such as `IOleObject` and `IOleInPlaceObject`). In addition to these original interfaces, OLE controls had to implement all the control-specific interfaces (such as `IDispatch` and `IOleControl`). In all, a control that meets the OLE controls 94 specification and provides support for all control features would implement more than 15 interfaces. These interfaces are listed in Table 7.1 along with a short description of their purpose.

Table 7.1 OLE Controls 94 Interfaces

Control-Side Interface	Purpose/MFC Methods
`IOleObject`	Provides the essence of the OLE compound document architecture. Through this interface, the container and server communicate to negotiate the size of the embedded object (the control, in our case) as well as get the `MiscStatus` bits for the control. Many of its methods are not needed in an ActiveX control.
`IOleInPlaceObject`	A control must implement `IOleInPlaceObject` to support the ability to be activated and deactivated in-place within the container. The interface also provides a method to notify the control when its size changes or it is moved within the container.
`IOleInPlaceActiveObject`	A control must implement `IOleInPlaceActiveObject` to provide support for the use, and translation of, accelerator keys within the control. Many of `IOleInPlaceActiveObject`'s methods are not required for ActiveX controls.
`IOleControl`	A new interface added to support ActiveX controls. It provides methods to enhance the interaction with the control's container. `IOleControl` primarily adds functionality so that the control and container can work together when handling keyboard input.
`IDataObject`	A control implements this interface to provide graphical renderings to the container.
`IViewObject2`	Implemented by controls that provide a visual aspect. `IViewObject2` provides the container with methods to tell the control to render itself within the container's client area.
`IPersistStream,` `IPersistStreamInit,` `IPersistStorage`	The persist interfaces are implemented by the control so that they may persist their values within the container's structured storage. A control's properties can persist between instantiations.
`IProvideClassInfo`	Implemented by an ActiveX control to allow a client application (usually a container) to efficiently obtain the type information for the control. It contains only one method, `GetClassInfo`, which returns an interface pointer that provides access to the control's binary representation of its type library.

Table 7.1 OLE Controls 94 Interfaces (continued)

Control-Side Interface	Purpose/MFC Methods
ISpecifyPropertyPages	Provides a way for the container to query the control for its list of property pages. ISpecifyPropertyPages has only one method: GetPages. The GetPages method is called by the container. The container provides a pointer to a CAUUID structure that returns a counted array of CLSIDs. This enumerates all the property page CLSIDs used by the control. The container uses these CLSIDs with a COM function, typically CoCreateInstance, to instantiate the page objects.
IPerPropertyBrowsing	Provides a way for the control to furnish additional information about its properties.
IPropertyPage2	Implemented by each property page component, it provides the container with methods to get the size, move, create, destroy, activate, and deactivate the component's property page windows.
IConnectionPointContainer	Used to provide the container with an outgoing IDispatch interface. This enables the control to communicate events to the container.
IConnectionPoint	A control can support several event sets. For each one, the control must provide an implementation of the IConnectionPoint interface.
IDispatch	A control's properties and methods are provided through its IDispatch interface.

As you can imagine, implementing a control without the help of MFC would be an arduous task at best. Implementation of a control container is even more difficult. It also requires a large number of interfaces, and a container must manage multiple controls within it.

Shortly after the release of the OLE Controls 94 specification, Microsoft released a document that described how a container and its controls should interact with each other. Much of this coordination was already specified via the compound document specification, but there was still a need for a document that would help developers understand the complex relationship between a control and its container. The resulting document, OLE Controls and Container Guidelines Version 1.1, was released in late 1995.

The guidelines put forth the minimum requirements of a control or control container. They describe the interfaces that are mandatory and those that are optional. It basically provides a set of guidelines for control and container developers. The large number of interfaces, methods, and techniques and the inherent limitations of human language made it difficult to get all containers and controls to work together. This was to be expected with a new and complex technology. However, the guidelines gave developers a good set of rules to follow when developing a control or container.

OLE Controls 96 Specification

Although OLE controls were a wonderful new technology that validated the concept of component-based development, they weren't perfect. The large number of interfaces and methods that a control had to implement, coupled with the requirement that most controls display a window when running, made them somewhat "heavy." Building an application with a large number of OLE controls could be problematic; there were also some functionality holes that needed to be filled. To address these issues, Microsoft released, in early 1996, the OLE Controls 96 specification.

The full text of the specification is part of the ActiveX SDK and is available from Microsoft. Following are some of the new features.

- **Mouse interaction for inactive objects.** The previous control specification stated that most controls should stay in the active state by setting the OLEMISC_ACTIVATEWHENVISIBLE flag. This arrangement required the container to load and activate a control whenever it was visible. Activating a control required the creation of a window to handle any user interaction (such as mouse clicks and drag-and-drop) with the control. The new specification adds a new interface, IPointerInactive, that allows a control to interact with the user while in the inactive state. The presence of this capability is communicated to the container with the OLEMISC_IGNOREACTIVATEWHENVISIBLE flag.

- **Drawing optimizations.** The old control specification required a control to reselect the old font, brush, and pen into the container-supplied device context whenever it was finished processing the IOleView::Draw call. The new specification adds a parameter to the Draw method that indicates whether the control must reset the state of the device context. It is up to the container to support this new feature, but the control can determine whether it is supported by checking the pvAspect parameter for the DVASPECTINFOFLAG_CANOPTIMIZE flag. If this flag is set, the control does not have to take the steps required to restore the state of the container-supplied device context after drawing its representation.

- **Flicker-free activation and deactivation.** When a control is activated in-place by a container, the control does not know whether its display bits are in a valid state. A new interface, IOleInPlaceSiteEx, communicates to the control whether or not a redraw is necessary. The new interface adds three methods to IOleInPlaceSite.

- **Flicker-free drawing.** Another new interface has been added to the OLE Controls 96 specification to support flicker-free drawing, nonrectangular objects, and transparent objects. As we'll see in Chapter 9, flicker-free drawing can be achieved by using an off-screen device context, but it consumes additional resources. The new IViewObjectEx interface adds methods and parameters to make flicker-free drawing easier to implement at the control. Nonrectangular and transparent controls were supported in the previous control specification, but they required a great deal of drawing work on the part of the control developer. The new specification provides additional drawing aspects (such as DVASPECT_TRANSPARENT) that make implementation of nonrectangular and transparent controls easier and more efficient.

- **Windowless controls.** The previous specification required in-place active objects to maintain a window when active. This requirement was necessary, as we mentioned earlier, to support user interaction within the control. This issue has now been addressed with the IPointerInactive interface. Controls that require a window also make nonrectangular and transparent regions difficult to implement. Windowless controls draw their representation directly on a device context provided by the container. There is no need for a true HWND. To support this capability, though, several issues must be handled. User interaction beyond mouse clicks and drag-and-drop, such as keystrokes, must be handled by the container and passed to the control. Another new interface, IOleInPlaceSiteWindowless, which is derived from IOleInPlaceActiveObject, supports these new requirements. It provides methods to handle focus, mouse capture, and painting of a control without a window.

- **In-place drawing for windowless controls.** A windowless control draws directly on a device context provided by the container. Several methods in IOleInPlaceSiteWindowless enable the control to get and release a device context, invalidate regions, and scroll the area in which it draws.

- **Hit detection for nonrectangular controls.** The new IViewObjectEx interface has two methods that support hit detection within nonrectangular controls. The container calls these methods to determine whether the area clicked by the user is within the extents of a nonrectangular control.

- **Quick activation.** The process of loading a control into a container can affect performance. The negotiation that occurs during this process can take some time. For this reason, a new interface, IQuickActivate, streamlines the control loading process. The new interface encapsulates many of the calls and callbacks that are required when a control is loaded.

- **Undo.** The undo section is container-specific. It allows a container to implement a multilevel undo mechanism.

- **Control sizing.** In the Controls 94 specification, control sizing is managed by a series of calls and callbacks while the control and container negotiate the sizing of the control. Several interfaces and methods are involved in this process. The new specification provides an additional method in the new IViewObjectEx interface that makes this process more efficient. It also provides several control sizing options.

- **Translation of event coordinates.** The Controls 94 specification required controls to use HIMETRIC units when passing coordinates to the container. The Controls 96 specification uses device units or points, a technique that's more consistent with the values used in methods and properties. Translations are necessary for containers that support both control types.

- **Textual persistence.** Certain containers (such as Visual Basic) store control properties in a text format. This arrangement makes it easy for control users to modify property values using a simple text editor. Before the Controls 96 specification, the interfaces that are used to implement this efficient mechanism of saving properties were not documented. The new specification documents a new interface that lets you efficiently save a control's properties in a *property bag* by implementing the IPersistPropertyBag interface.

That summarizes the enhancements added by the OLE Controls 96 specification. As you can see, most of the changes focus on making ActiveX controls more efficient to implement and use. It will take some time for the development tool vendors to incorporate these changes into their containers, but it will eventually happen. Also, with the release of Visual C++ version 4.2, many of these features are supported at the control development level. We'll cover some of them as we build the example controls. Table 7.2 lists the new interfaces added by the Controls 96 specification.

Table 7.2 New Control Interfaces

Control-Side Interface	Purpose/MFC Methods
IPointerInactive	Provides a way for the control to respond to user interaction when the control is not in the active state.
IOleInPlaceSiteEx	Adds flicker-free redrawing methods.
IOleInPlaceSiteWindowless	Supports the creation of windowless controls.
IQuickActivate	Provides a more efficient way of initially loading a control.
IViewObjectEx	Adds drawing optimizations, support for nonrectangular objects, and new control sizing options.
IPersistPropertyBag	Adds more efficient ways of storing and retrieving text-based control properties.
IProvideClassInfo2	The new IProvideClassInfo2 interface provides an additional method, GetGUID, that returns the GUID specified in the GUIDKIND parameter. This is useful when the container is implementing a control's outgoing, or event, interface.

Control and Container Guidelines Version 2.0

Along with the OLE Controls 96 specification, Microsoft released a document that provides guidelines for control and container developers. By following the guidelines, developers can help make their controls and containers work together reliably. The ActiveX control is becoming ubiquitous within development tools and applications. The large number of controls and containers, with their specialized functionality, makes it imperative for certain guidelines to be followed. By following the guidelines, a developer makes the control or container useful within the maximum number of development environments.

The guideline document is currently part of the ActiveX SDK. You can look there for detailed information on each guideline. Following is a summary of the key control–specific aspects of the guidelines. Some of the concepts presented in this summary are covered in detail later in the chapter.

- **A COM object.** An ActiveX control is just a specialized COM object. The only basic requirements for a control is that it support self-registration and the IUnknown interface. These are the only true requirements of a control. However, such a control could not provide much functionality. The guidelines show how a developer can add only those interfaces that the control needs. The ultimate purpose is to make the control as lightweight as possible.

- **Self-registration.** control must support self-registration by implementing the DllRegisterServer and DllUnregisterServer functions and must add the appropriate embeddable objects and Automation server entries in the Registry. A control must also use the component categories API to indicate which services are required to host the control.

- **Interface support.** If a control supports an interface, it must support it at a basic level. The document provides guidelines for each potential ActiveX control and container interface. It describes which methods must be implemented within an interface if that interface is implemented.

- **Persistence support.** If a control needs to provide persistence support, it must implement at least one IPersist* interface and should, if possible, support more than one. This requirement makes it easier for a container to host the control. Support for IPersistPropertyBag is highly recommended, because most of the major containers provide a "Save as text" capability.

- **Ambient properties.** If a control supports ambient properties, it must respect certain ambient properties exposed by the container. They are LocaleID, UserMode, UIDead, ShowGrabHandles, ShowHatching, and DisplayAsDefault.

- **Dual interfaces.** The guidelines strongly recommend that ActiveX controls and containers support dual interfaces. If you recall from Chapter 6, an Automation server implements a dual interface by providing both an IDispatch interface and a COM custom interface for its methods and properties.

- **Miscellaneous.** ActiveX controls should not use the WS_GROUP or WS_TABSTOP window flags, because it may conflict with the container's use of these flags. A control should honor a container's call to IOleControl::FreezeEvents. When events are frozen, a container will discard event notifications from the control.

ActiveX Controls for the Internet

ActiveX controls are a perfect solution to many of the problems facing Web developers. Web pages are small applications. They need controls, such as edit boxes and listboxes, and in most regards can be developed as regular Windows applications, especially now that most of Microsoft's technologies (such as VBScript and ActiveX controls) are supported within a Web browser. Internet Explorer is a highly functional ActiveX control container. It implements much of the new Controls 96 functionality as well as many other ActiveX technologies. ActiveX controls can be used within the Web environment, but there are some additional requirements for controls that have large amounts of data. We'll cover Internet-based ActiveX controls in detail in Chapter 12.

ActiveX controls can be contained within Web browsers that support the ActiveX container architecture. Today, the most prevalent example is Microsoft's Internet Explorer. A control is typically thought of as a button or edit box, but a control can also be a much larger entity, basically a whole application. Most of Internet Explorer's functionality is contained within one ActiveX control. For most controls, operating within the Web environment is not a problem. However, some controls manipulate large amounts of data. The major difference between a local machine environment and the Web is bandwidth. The OLE-Controls-COM Objects for the Internet specification describes new techniques and interfaces to facilitate working in low-bandwidth environments.

ActiveX Control Functional Categories

A fully functional ActiveX control typically implements around 15 interfaces. Now, with the additional interfaces described in the OLE Controls 96 specification, a large, full-featured control might implement 20 or more interfaces. Such a control, however, would be complex to implement, at least without the help of MFC.

The *Control and Container Guidelines* document reduces control requirements by requiring controls to implement only those interfaces that they need. If a control does not want to support events, it need not implement the interfaces (such as `IConnectionPointContainer`) needed for events. By following the guidelines, a control developer is now free to implement only those interfaces that are necessary. The guideline document categorizes the possible control-implemented interfaces by function. The next several sections describe the major ActiveX functional categories according to the interfaces that they must implement.

Standard COM Object Interfaces

An ActiveX control is a typical COM object. It must provide the most basic COM service: the `IUnknown` interface. To create an instance of a control, it must also have a class factory, which requires the implementation of one of the `IClassFactory` interfaces. The `IClassFactory2` interface provides additional, license-oriented features for components that implement it. We'll discuss this in more detail in Chapter 8.

Compound Document Interfaces

ActiveX controls are typically compound document servers. The compound document interfaces provide support for important features such as displaying a visual representation of the control, user interaction with the control, and in-place activation. Several interfaces are needed to support this functionality.

The `IOleObject` interface provides basic embedded object support so that the control (compound document server) can communicate with the container. There are a number of methods in the `IOleObject` interface, but only a few are of interest to ActiveX controls. The `SetExtent` and `GetExtent` methods are used to negotiate a control's extent or size, and the `GetMiscStatus` method returns the various `OLEMISC_*` status bits set for the control. We'll cover each of these methods in the section on control Registry key entries.

The `IOleView[x]` interfaces provide a way for the container to obtain a graphical rendering of the control. The control implements this interface and draws its representation onto a device context provided by the container. The initial version of this interface, `IOleView`, was part of the original compound document specification. The OLE Controls 94 specification added `GetExtent`, which allowed the container to get a server's extents through this interface instead of `IOleObject`. Then, as part of the OLE Controls 96 specification, the `IOleViewEx` interface was added. This interface includes five new methods that facilitate flicker-free drawing, nonrectangular objects, hit testing, and additional control sizing options. MFC versions 4.2 and higher support the new `IOleViewEx` interface.

The `IDataObject` interface is used by compound document servers to provide the container with a method of rendering data to a device other than a device context. ActiveX controls typically use the `IOleView[x]` interface instead of `IDataObject`, but it can be implemented if needed.

A control must implement the compound document `IOleInPlaceObject` interface to support the ability to be activated and deactivated in-place within the container. This interface also provides a method to notify the control when its size changes or is moved within the container.

A control must implement `IOleInPlaceActiveObject` to provide support for the use, and translation of, accelerator keys within the control. Many of `IOleInPlaceActiveObject`'s methods are not needed for ActiveX controls.

The compound document interface, `IOleCache2`, can be implemented by a control to provide caching of its representation, improving performance in some situations.

Most ActiveX controls provide a graphical representation, so most controls should provide support for the compound document interfaces. However, this is no longer a requirement. If a control is nonvisual and does not require these interfaces, it is free to not implement them. A well-behaved container should still be able to handle the control.

Automation Support

For a control to provide basic functionality, it needs to implement some properties and methods. As we discussed in Chapter 6, Automation is a standard way of exposing member variables and member functions from a COM-based server. A control provides services by providing an implementation of the `IDispatch` interface. Once implemented, a control becomes an Automation server.

A control's Automation interface is one of its most important features. The control standards provide a number of standard properties and methods. When designing a control, you will typically spend much of your time working with properties and methods. Let's look at the different types implemented by ActiveX controls.

Properties

A control property is basically a characteristic of the control. Examples include color, height, font, and so on. In a software component sense, the properties of a control enable a developer to affect the appearance and behavior of a control. In most cases, a property maps to a C++ class member variable that maintains the value of a property.

Control developers can implement custom properties that are specific to the control being developed (such as "Count") as well as use the stock properties provided by the ActiveX control standard. Certain properties may be valid only during the execution or run-time phase of a container. An example is a property that contains the number of elements in a listbox or one that contains the HWND of the control. During the design phase, this property has no meaning to the control user. It is useful only during the execution of the application. Other properties may be read-only at run time or even write-only at design time.

Standard and Stock Properties

The ActiveX Control standard provides a set of standard properties that should be used instead of implementing custom properties for similar functionality. This arrangement provides a standard or uniform interface for the component user. All ActiveX controls that expose a particular functionality will use the same property name. Examples include BackColor, Caption, and hWnd. These are properties that almost all visual ActiveX controls should provide. Table 7.3 lists the standard properties currently defined by the standard. We will also use the term *stock* properties, which are ActiveX control standard properties whose implementation is provided by MFC.

Table 7.3 Standard Control Properties

Property	Purpose
Appearance*	Appearance of the control (e.g., 3-D).
AutoSize	If TRUE, the control should size to fit within its container.
BackColor*	The background color of the control.
BorderStyle*	The style of the control's border. A short that currently supports only two values. A zero indicates no border, and 1 indicates to draw a normal, single-line border around the control. More styles may be defined in the future.
BorderColor	The color of the border around the control.
BorderWidth	The width of the border around the control.
DrawMode	The mode of drawing used by the control.
DrawStyle	The style of drawing used by the control.
DrawWidth	The width of the pen used for drawing.
FillColor	The fill color.
FillStyle	The style of the fill color.
Font*	The font used for any text in the control.
ForeColor*	The color of any text or graphics within the control.
Enabled*	TRUE indicates that the control can accept input.
hWnd*	The hWnd of the control's window.
TabStop	Indicates whether the control should participate in the tab stop scheme.
Text*, Caption*	A BSTR that indicates the caption or text of the control. Both properties are implemented with the same internal methods. Only one of the two may be used.
BorderVisible	Show the border.

* Indicates stock implementation provided by MFC

Ambient Properties

The definition of *ambient* is "surrounding or encircling," and this precisely describes the relationship between ActiveX control containers and the ActiveX controls contained therein. The ActiveX control standard defines a set of ambient properties that are read-only characteristics of the control container. These characteristics define the ambiance surrounding each of the controls. A good example is the container's ambient font. To provide a uniform visual interface to the application user, the container may define an ambient font that each control should consider using. If a control in the container uses a font to display text information, it would be nice if it would use the font that all the other controls are using.

Ambient properties are also useful from a development perspective. The developer can quickly change the ambient property of a container and affect all the controls within it. Instead of changing the property for every control, the developer has to change it only at the container level.

Ambient properties are provided by the default `IDispatch` of the client site provided to a control by a control container. When a control is loaded, MFC calls `QueryInterface` for the default `IDispatch` on its client site. To retrieve an ambient property, the control calls `IDispatch::Invoke` with the DISPID of the ambient property. These are standard, known DISPIDs, so there is no need to use `IDispatch::GetIDsOfNames` beforehand.

Not all ambient properties pertain directly to the GUI aspects of a container and its controls. Other properties are used by the container to indicate its current state to the enclosed controls. The `UserMode` ambient property is used to indicate the state of the container. Is it currently in design, run, or debug mode? The `DisplayName` property conveys to the control its external name used by the container. The correct use of ambient properties is important to the development of ActiveX controls, and we will cover each one in detail in later chapters. The ambient properties are shown in Table 7.4.

Table 7.4 Ambient Properties

Property	Purpose/ MFC Method to Access
BackColor	Background color of the control. OLE_COLOR COleControl::AmbientBackColor
DisplayName	The name of the control as given by the container. This name should be used when the control needs to display information to the user. CString COleControl::AmbientDisplayName
Font	The recommended font for the control. LPFONTDISP COleControl::AmbientFont
ForeColor	Foreground color for text. OLE_COLOR COleControl::AmbientForeColor
LocaleID	The container's locale ID. LCID COleControl::AmbientLocaleID
MessageReflect	If this property is TRUE, the container supports reflecting messages back to the control. BOOL COleControl::ContainerReflectsMessages
ScaleUnits	A string name for the container's coordinate units (such as "twips" or "cm"). CString COleControl::AmbientScaleUnits
TextAlign	Indicates how the control should justify any textual information. 0 = numbers to the right, text to the left, 1 = left justify, 2 = center justify, 3 = right justify, 4 = fill justify. short COleControl::AmbientTextAlign
UserMode	Returns TRUE if the container is in run mode; otherwise, the container is in design mode. BOOL COleControl::AmbientUserMode
UIDead	The UIDead property indicates to the control that it should not accept or act on any user input directed to the control. Containers may use this property to indicate to the control that it is in design mode or that it is running, but the developer has interrupted processing during debugging. BOOL COleControl::AmbientUIDead

Table 7.4 Ambient Properties (continued)

Property	Purpose/ MFC Method to Access
ShowGrabHandles	If TRUE, the control should show grab handles when UI-active. BOOL COleControl::AmbientShowGrabHandles
ShowHatching	If TRUE, the control should show diagonal hatch marks around itself when UI-active. BOOL COleControl::AmbientShowHatching
DisplayAsDefault	The container sets this property to TRUE for a button style control when it becomes the default button within the container. This occurs when the user tabs to the specific control or the control is actually the default button on the form, and the focus is on a nonbutton control. The button should indicate that it is the default button by thickening its border.
SupportsMnemonics	If TRUE, the container supports the use of mnemonics within controls.
AutoClip	If TRUE, the container automatically clips any portion of the control's rectangle that should not be displayed. If FALSE, the control should honor the clipping rectangle passed to it in IOleInPlaceObject's SetObjectRects method.

Control Methods

In Chapter 6, we discussed Automation methods. ActiveX control methods are basically the same and are implemented via the IDispatch interface. One of the new features of ActiveX controls (in contrast to Visual Basic custom controls) is the ability they give you to implement custom methods. These methods allow the control user to call specific functionality within the control. This is no different from our Automation server examples of Chapter 6.

The ActiveX control standard currently provides two standard methods that should be implemented in your control if it supports the behavior (Table 7.5). The Refresh method causes an immediate redraw of the control, and the DoClick method causes the control to fire the standard Click event. (We'll cover events in a moment.) Implementing these methods requires just two mouse clicks, and we will do so in the controls that we develop.

Table 7.5 Standard Control Methods

Method	Purpose/MFC Method
Refresh	Redraw the control. COleControl::OnRefresh
DoClick	Generate a Click event. COleControl::OnDoClick

Property Pages

Controls that support the concept of properties should also provide support for property pages. ActiveX controls need a standard way to visually present their properties to the user of the control (the visual developer). The ActiveX control standard added *property page* technology as part of its implementation. Each control has associated with it one or more property pages that allow visual manipulation of its properties. As its property values change, the control is notified and can act on the request.

A property page is similar (visually) to a single tab of the tabbed dialog boxes that have become popular in Windows applications. Tabbed dialog boxes allow presentation of large amounts of data within a small space and allow the grouping of related application features within a tab. A dialog box containing multiple tabs is similar to a Windows 95 property sheet.

Windows 95 uses property sheets throughout its new interface. Property sheets are part of the Windows 95 API and are one of the new common controls. Windows 95 has added many new full-featured common controls, and we will use one of them to build an ActiveX control in a later chapter.

OLE property pages are different from the Windows 95 common control and provide additional capabilities. Each OLE property page is itself a component, or COM object, as we will see. Currently there are three stock property pages that ActiveX controls can use: Font, Color, and Picture. They provide standard implementations for properties that many controls will use. A control developer can also provide one or more custom property pages for a control.

The control container is responsible for managing the design and run-time environment of which many controls may be a part. Implementing each control's property pages as distinct COM objects allows the container to invoke or instantiate the pages independent of the control. This is important, because the user may choose multiple controls, either of the same or of different types, and may want to modify the properties that are common to the selected controls. It is the responsibility of the container to filter through the property pages and display only those that are common among the selected controls. Once this is done, the property page component is responsible for notifying its respective control. In other words, the container knows when to display a control's property pages (at the request of a user) and is responsible for querying each selected control to obtain its respective property pages. The container then assembles them into a *property sheet* that frames the property pages. Once this property sheet is complete, the user can modify and apply the changes to the underlying controls. As this occurs, the property page communicates directly with the control, requiring no help from the container (Figure 7.5).

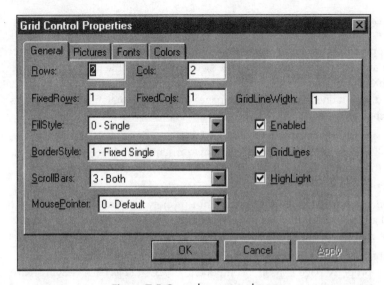

Figure 7.5 Control property sheet.

The container creates the property sheet frame that contains the **OK**, **Cancel**, **Apply**, and **Help** buttons. The property pages within this frame are individual COM objects and are manipulated by the container using Automation. These capabilities are provided by new OLE interfaces specified in the ActiveX control standard, although they can be used outside ActiveX controls. Let's briefly look at each one.

ISpecifyPropertyPages

The `ISpecifyPropertyPages` interface is implemented by the control. It provides a way for the container to query the control for its list of property pages. `ISpecifyPropertyPages` has only one method: `GetPages`. The `GetPages` method is called by the container. The container provides a pointer to a `CAUUID` structure that returns a counted array of CLSIDs. This enumerates all the property page CLSIDs used by the control. The container uses these CLSIDs with a COM function, typically `CoCreateInstance`, to instantiate the page objects.

```
typedef struct tagCAUUID
{
    ULONG cElems;
    GUID FAR* pElems;

} CAUUID;

// ISpecifyPropertyPages
BEGIN_INTERFACE_PART(SpecifyPropertyPages, ISpecifyPropertyPages)
    INIT_INTERFACE_PART(COleControl, SpecifyPropertyPages)
```

```
STDMETHOD(GetPages)(CAUUID FAR*);
END_INTERFACE_PART(SpecifyPropertyPages)
```

IPropertyPageSite

`IPropertyPageSite` facilitates communication between the property page component and the property sheet frame as implemented by the container. An `IPropertyPageSite` pointer is provided to each property page after it has been instantiated through `IPropertyPage::SetPageSite`. The `OnStatusChange` method is used by the property page to indicate to the frame that one or more properties have been modified. The frame then enables the **Apply** button.

The `GetLocaleID` method is used by the property page to retrieve the appropriate language identifier from the property frame. The `GetPageContainer` method currently has no defined behavior but may be used in the future to obtain an interface on the property sheet frame itself. The `TranslateAccelerator` method helps in the management of accelerator keys used by the property pages.

IPropertyPage2

The `IPropertyPage2` interface is implemented by each property page component and provides the container with methods to get the size of as well as move, create, destroy, activate, and deactivate the component's property page window. The container creates a frame for each property page and uses these methods to manage the display of the property sheet. This arrangement allows the property sheet to appear and behave as if driven by one application, when, in fact, a property sheet comprises individual components housed within a frame window created by the container. Each method is detailed in Table 7.6.

Table 7.6 `IPropertyPage2` Methods

Methods	Purpose/MFC Method
SetPageSite	Initializes the property page by providing a pointer to the `IPropertyPageSite`. `COlePropertyPage::OnSetPageSite`
Activate	Causes creation of the dialog box based on the property page dialog resource specified by the control developer.
Deactivate	Destroys the dialog window created by the preceding method.
GetPageInfo	Returns to the property frame a `PROPPAGEINFO` structure that contains the title, size, and help information for the property page.
SetObjects	Passes to the property page a list of `IDispatch` interfaces for each of the controls that will be affected by changes made via the property page.
Show	Called by the frame with a nCmdShow parameter. This usually either shows or hides the property page window. MFC passes the nCmdShow parameter to the `ShowWindow` method.
Move	Called by the frame to move the property page window. An `LPRECT` structure is provided and is passed to the `MoveWindow` method by MFC.

Table 7.6 `IPropertyPage2` Methods (continued)

Methods	Purpose/MFC Method
IsPageDirty	Called by the frame to determine whether the **Apply** button should be enabled.
Apply	The **Apply** button was pressed, and all changes need to be propagated to all the affected controls. MFC calls the `DoDataExchange` method implemented in the property sheet.
Help	The **Help** button on the frame was pressed. MFC calls the property page's `OnHelp` method. The default implementation does nothing.
TranslateAccelerator	The frame passes keystrokes to the page so that it can act on the message. MFC passes the keystroke to `PreTranslateMessage` if it is not intercepted by the property page.
EditProperty	Called by the frame with the DISPID of the property that is requesting edit. The default MFC implementation, `OnEditProperty`, does nothing.

Property Persistence

A control that provides property support through the `IDispatch` and property page interfaces may also want to support persistence of those properties. Not all properties require persistence, but from a user's perspective, persistence of properties makes development of applications easier.

During the container's design phase (when building an application using a visual tool), the developer typically modifies various properties of a control. To save the resulting state of the control's properties, the development tool and its containers ask each control to save the state of its properties. This process, called *serialization*, provides persistence of a control's state. Persistence allows a control to have a unique initial state, set during the design phase, when loaded and activated within a container. The `IPersistStorage` and `IPersistStreamInit` interfaces provide this capability.

`IPersistStorage` is supported by OLE compound document containers. `IPersistStorage` accesses OLE's structured storage technology, which provides a hierarchical storage mechanism above the operating system's file system. OLE embedded servers implement this interface so that the container can ask each embedded object to serialize itself within the container's structured storage file. For compound document objects, this requires the storage of a large and complex set of data (such as a Word document or an Excel spreadsheet). This interface provides more functionality (and therefore larger files) than is usually required for lighter weight ActiveX control objects.

The `IPersistStreamInit` interface was added with the ActiveX control specification and provides a simpler, stream-based approach to serialization. ActiveX control containers typically support this interface in addition to `IPersistStorage`. To support embedding within both container types, controls should implement both interfaces.

Another persistence interface, `IPersistPropertyBag`, was added by the Controls 96 specification. `IPersistPropertyBag` and the container-side interface, `IPropertyBag`, provide an efficient method of saving and loading text-based properties. The control implements `IPersistPropertyBag`, through which the container calls `Load` and `Save`, thereby notifying the control to either initialize itself or save its property values. It does this through the `IPropertyBag::Read` and `IPropertyBag::Write` methods provided by the container. The property bag persistence mechanism is very effective in a Web-based environment, where a control's property information may be stored within the HTML document.

A control should support as many of these persistence interfaces as possible to provide the most flexibility to the container. Likewise, a container should support as many as possible. The more persistence interfaces are implemented, the greater the chance that a container and control will work together efficiently.

Connectable Objects and Control Events

A major improvement provided by the ActiveX control architecture is the addition of an outgoing event mechanism. In Chapter 6, we described Automation as a primarily one-way technique of communicating (programmatically) with another component. This technique was sufficient for using or driving components or applications, but it does not provide the robust feedback needed when multiple components are interacting or when a higher-level entity is used to tie controls together.

Events provide a way for a control to notify its container that something is about to occur or has occurred. The container typically provides a way for a user to perform certain actions whenever it is notified of these events. There is no requirement that the container actually implement or perform any actions when it receives control event notifications. As we described earlier, a container is usually a part of a larger development environment in which there is either an interpreted script-like language (such as Visual Basic) or a compiled language such as Visual C++. This language is used to perform programmatic actions when a control fires an event.

Event communication between COM-based components is a major addition to the technology and is used extensively by ActiveX controls. The technology is termed *connectable objects*, because it provides true peer-to-peer communication between cooperating components. Events are implemented within ActiveX controls using the `IDispatch` interface and the *connectable objects* interfaces: `IConnectionPoint` and `IConnectionPointContainer`.

ActiveX controls implement the `IConnectionPointContainer` interface to indicate to the container that they support one or more outgoing (or event) interfaces. These outgoing interfaces allow the control to invoke Automation methods within the container. The `IConnectionPointContainer` interface provides a mechanism to establish this link.

The `IConnectionPointContainer` interface contains two methods. `EnumConnectionPoints` provides a way for the container to iterate through all the connection points within the control. The `FindConnectionPoint` method uses an interface ID (IID) to identify the specific interface that a container is looking for. Each of these methods provides a way to obtain pointers to the `IConnectionPoint` interface.

`IConnectionPoint` is also implemented by the control, but not as part of its main interface. (It's not available via `QueryInterface`.) `IConnectionPoint` is implemented on a different object and is used to set up the outgoing connection with the container.

`IConnectionPoint` provides five methods, but we'll discuss only two of them. The other methods provide more functionality than we need for our purposes. The `Advise` method is used by the container to establish a connection with the control. The container passes an interface pointer to one of its interfaces to the control. (For events, this interface is an `IDispatch`.) The control then calls methods implemented by the container by calling through this interface. The `Unadvise` method is used to terminate this connection. This process is fairly complex, but Table 7.7 details the use of these interfaces to set up event notification between the control and its container. The interface that we are setting up is a pointer to the container's implementation of our control's event set. The Automation methods are specified by the control but implemented in the container.

Table 7.7 Event Set `IDispatch` Setup

Container	Control
Inserts and loads the control.	Contains the definition of the event `IDispatch`.

Upon load, it queries for the control's type information. The control must provide a primary event set `IDispatch`:
`pPCI = QueryInterface( IProvideClassInfo[x] )`
`pPCI->GetClassInfo()`
	Returns the type information for the control. This is a binary version of the definitions from the **.ODL** file. The control should implement `IProvideClassInfo2`, because it makes it easier for the container to determine the IID of the control's default event set.

From the type information, determine the IID for the default event set. For our example, we will use `IID_EventSet`. If the control implements `IProvideClassInfo2`, the container can call `GetGUID` with the `GUIDKIND_DEFAULT_SOURCE_IID` parameter to quickly determine the event set IID.	

Get the `IConnectionPointContainer` interface:
`pICPC = QueryInterface`
`( IConnectionPointContainer )`
	Return its `IConnectionPointContainer` implementation.

Get the `ConnectionPoint` interface for the default event set:
`pICP = pICPC->FindConnectionPoint`
`( IID_EventSet )`
	Return an `IConnectionPoint` pointer for the specified IID.

The container must now implement the event set as an automation interface. It then calls through the connection point to set the control's pointer to the container's implementation of the event `IDispatch`:
`pICP->Advise( pEventDispatch)`
`m_pEventDispatch = pEventDispatch`
	Set an internal pointer equal to the container's (event) `IDispatch` implementation:

	When the control fires an event, it does something like this: `m_pEventDispatch->Invoke( myDispID...)` The control knows the DISPID as well as all the parameters and types, because it defines them.

A control's methods provide a way for the container to perform actions within the control. Control events provide a way for the control to perform actions within the container. As we've discussed, controls are Automation servers that expose their methods and properties using the IDispatch interface. This arrangement allows client to obtain the control's IDispatch and then the DISPIDs of each method and property (using IDispatch::GetIDsOfNames). The client can then call these methods within the control using IDispatch::Invoke.

Control events are implemented in a similar way except in reverse. As you add events to a control, it builds code that will call an Automation method for each event with its parameters. The definition of this interface is provided to the container (via IProvideClassInfo[x]) as the control is being loaded. The new IProvideClassInfo2 interface adds the GetGUID method to make it easier for the container to find the correct event set. By passing the dwGuidKind parameter of DEFAULT_SOURCE_IID, the control returns the default event IID.

The container then implements the IDispatch interface based on the type information provided by the control. The IDispatch pointer is then returned to the control through the IConnectionPoint::Advise method. Later, when a control needs to fire an event, it calls through this IDispatch::Invoke with the DISPID of the event method. (The control knows the DISPID because it defined it, so there is no need to call GetIDsOfNames.) This call invokes the method within the container (i.e., the event fires).

Standard Events

To present a uniform event set for users of ActiveX controls, the ActiveX control standard currently provides nine *standard* events that can be used to develop an ActiveX control. These events are ones that visual controls usually provide to notify the control user when they occur. They are listed in Table 7.8. The only one that requires more explanation, in this short overview, is the stock Error event, which provides a simple mechanism to report errors that occur within your control. You should follow specific rules when using the Error event, and we will cover them in one of our example controls. As with the standard properties, the events implemented by MFC are called *stock* events.

Table 7.8 Standard Events

Event	Purpose/Stock MFC Function
Click	Fired by a BUTTONUP event for any of the mouse buttons. COleControl::FireClick
DblClick	Fired by a BUTTONDBLCLK message. COleControl::FireDblClick
Error	Fired by the control when an error occurs. COleControl::FireError
KeyDown	Fired by the WM_SYSKEYDOWN or WM_KEYDOWN message. COleControl::FireKeyDown
KeyPress	Fired by the WM_CHAR message. COleControl::FireKeyPress
KeyUp	Fired by the WM_SYSKEYUP or WM_KEYUP message. COleControl::FireKeyUp
MouseDown	Fired by the BUTTONDOWN event. COleControl::FireMouseDown
MouseMove	Fired by the WM_MOUSEMOVE message. COleControl::FireMouseMove
MouseUp	Fired by the BUTTONUP event. COleControl::FireMouseUp

Custom Events

MFC allows you to define custom events for your controls. The return values and parameters are the same as those for Automation methods. The primary difference between stock and custom events is that MFC provides an implementation for each stock event that automatically fires when the event occurs. For custom events, the developer must implement the code that fires the event.

Keystroke Handling

ActiveX controls are typically visual components that provide some kind of interaction with the control user. If a control needs to process keystrokes, it should implement the IOleControl interface. It contains four methods, of which two are specific to keystroke processing.

GetControlInfo fills in a caller-supplied CONTROLINFO structure. This structure defines the keyboard mnemonics implemented in the control and contains a dwFlags variable that describes how the control will behave if the user presses the **Esc** or **Return** key when the control is UI-active.

The container calls OnMnemonic when a keystroke matches one in the control's mnemonic table set by a previous GetControlInfo call. A button control can handle accelerators and other button-type details by using these two methods and the OLEMISC_ACTSLIKEBUTTON flag. The container should also expose the DisplayAsDefault ambient property and provide an implementation of the IOleControlSite::TranslateAccelerator method. A control has first crack at keystrokes when it's UI-active, but it can call this method if it does not use the message:

```
interface IOleControl : IUnknown
{
    HRESULT    GetControlInfo(CONTROLINFO *pCtrlInfo);
    HRESULT    OnMnemonic(LPMSG pMsg);
    HRESULT    OnAmbientPropertyChange(DISPID dispID);
    HRESULT    FreezeEvents(BOOL fFreeze);
}

typedef struct tagCONTROLINFO
{
    ULONG  cb;
    HACCEL hAccel;
    USHORT cAccel;
    DWORD  dwFlags;
} CONTROLINFO;
```

The other two methods of IOleControl are important for most controls. The container calls OnAmbientPropertyChanged to inform the control that one or more ambient properties have changed. The only parameter is the DISPID of the property that changed. If more than one property changed, DISPID_UNKNOWN is passed to the control.

FreezeEvents is called by the container to freeze and unfreeze the control's event mechanism. If FreezeEvents passes TRUE, the container will ignore any events fired by the control until the container unfreezes the control by calling this method with a FALSE parameter. Some containers may, for example, want to freeze events while the other controls in the container are still being initialized.

Control Containment

The ActiveX control architecture allows a control to contain other ActiveX controls without making the parent control implement all the required container-side interfaces. The controls are "contained" in the usual Windows sense of parent and child windows and not in the compound document sense. To support simple control containment, the container must implement the ISimpleFrameSite interface. The control must call the methods when processing its window messages. Here's the definition for ISimpleFrameSite:

```
interface ISimpleFrameSite : public IUnknown
{
    PreMessageFilter(HWND hwnd, UINT msg, WPARAM wp, LPARAM lp,
                    LRESULT FAR* lplResult, DWORD FAR* lpdwCookie);
    PostMessageFilter(HWND hwnd, UINT msg, WPARAM wp, LPARAM lp,
                    LRESULT FAR* lplResult, DWORD dwCookie);
}
```

To support simple frame containment, a control must do all of the following:

1. It must call the container's PreMessageFilter method before processing any window messages and must call the container's PostMessageFilter method after processing the message. The message should not be processed if the PreMessageFilter returns S_FALSE.
2. The control must be implemented as an in-process server.
3. The control should set the OLEMISC_SIMPLEFRAME flag.
4. The control must properly handle painting of subclassed controls. This requires treating the wParam in the WM_PAINT message as the handle to a device context.

MFC and ActiveX Controls

Visual C++ and the MFC libraries provide a feature-rich environment for implementing and using ActiveX controls. Most of the functionality is contained in two MFC classes: COleControl and COlePropertyPage. We'll cover both classes in detail in the next few chapters. However, I'd like to briefly discuss COleControl in the context of all the interfaces we've described in this chapter.

The base COleControl class implements 22 COM-based interfaces. The default behavior of COleControl is full featured. It provides all the functionality described in the "Control Functional

Categories" section and supports nearly all the new features described in the Controls 96 specification as well as those discussed in *ActiveX Controls—COM Objects for the Internet*. This means that, by default, any controls you build with MFC must always carry around this weight even if the functionality isn't used. This isn't necessarily bad, because using tools such as MFC is a trade-off. There are, however, other alternatives for developing controls.

The ActiveX SDK gives you a lightweight control framework that provides a small subset of MFC's control functionality. For developers who want to build small, efficient controls, this tool gets them started. It does require a good understanding of the implementation of ActiveX controls.

Visual C++ also provides an tool that makes it easy to create basic ActiveX controls. ControlWizard is very similar to AppWizard. It provides a skeletal control project based on answers to a few questions. ControlWizard allows a developer to write his or her first control in a matter of minutes.

Visual C++ and ActiveX Control Support

Along with the specification of ActiveX controls, Microsoft's tools have provided various levels of development support. The following sections provide a brief look into the history of Microsoft's support for control development within Visual C++.

Visual C++ Version 2.0 (MFC 3.0)

Visual C++ version 2.0 (32-bit), released in the fall of 1994, was the first version to provide support for building ActiveX controls using MFC. The CD-ROM contained the Control Development Kit (CDK), a separately installable set of components. They included a modified version of ClassWizard and a new control-based AppWizard called, appropriately, ControlWizard, that made it easy to build a "shell" control with the desired base functionality.

The CDK contained two new MFC classes—COleControl and COlePropertyPage—that provided most of the CDK functionality. The CDK also included a subset of the other MFC classes to use in building controls. The important point about the version 2.x releases is this: using Visual C++ version 2.x, you could only *build* ActiveX controls; you could not actually *use* them within Visual C++. There were several ActiveX control hosting environments (such as Visual Basic and Visual FoxPro), but you could not host controls within Visual C++ dialogs or views. This capability would have to wait until version 4.0 and higher.

The latest 16-bit version of Visual C++ (version 1.51) was also provided on the CD-ROM. A 16-bit version of the CDK was provided that was installed separately. Control projects that were initially started using the 32-bit version of ControlWizard would easily move between the two environments: Visual C++ 2.0 and Visual C++ 1.51. This arrangement made it simple to target both 16-bit and 32-bit platforms.

Visual C++ Version 2.1 (MFC 3.1)

Visual C++ version 2.1, released in early 1995, basically fixed some of bugs in the previous version CDK that made it difficult to build usable controls. Version 2.1 was a very stable release and made it rather easy to build effective ActiveX controls. Visual Basic 4.0, which was a great ActiveX control container, had been out for a few months, and most development tool vendors were hard at work to provide tools to facilitate the use and development of ActiveX controls. This support made developing ActiveX controls a worthwhile endeavor.

The latest 16-bit version of Visual C++, version 1.52b, was also shipped on the CD-ROM. The CDK was updated with minor fixes.

Visual C++ Version 2.2 (MFC 3.2)

Visual C++ version 2.2 was released in the summer of 1995. It added a few new features and bug fixes for the CDK. It shipped with version 1.52c of the 16-bit Visual C++ environment, which is basically the same version available today (September 1996).

Visual C++ Version 4.0 (MFC 4.0)

Visual C++ version 4.0, a major release (October 1995), added significant features for ActiveX control developers and users. Visual C++ now provided control hosting capabilities, making it easy to incorporate ActiveX controls within Visual C++ dialog boxes. ActiveX controls could be created dynamically and added to MFC-based views. Finally, all the features of ActiveX controls could be used by Visual C++ developers.

As part of the major 4.0 release, the earlier CDK was integrated within the rest of MFC. The full complement of MFC classes could now be used within ActiveX controls. ActiveX controls became simply MFC-based DLLs. They were no different from any other MFC-based COM server.

However, Version 4.0 removed some of the previous functionality. ControlWizard lost the ability to import a VBX header definition and build a skeleton project. Also, ControlWizard no longer would generate both 16-bit and 32-bit projects, so multiplatform support became harder to manage. These changes were necessary because parallel upgrades to the 16-bit compiler were discontinued. The 16-bit version (1.52c) shipped with Visual C++ 2.2 was the last upgrade to the 16-bit version of Visual C++. The primary focus was now 32-bit development.

Visual C++ Version 4.1 (MFC 4.1)

Visual C++ version 4.1 added little, except for bug fixes, that was specific to ActiveX control development. An example and Tech Note (65) were added that showed how to convert an MFC-based Automation server to support both the IDispatch interface and a custom interface, thereby providing dual interface support.

Visual C++ Version 4.2 (MFC 4.2)

Visual C++ version 4.2 added support for many of the enhancements outlined in the OLE Controls 96 specification. These features include windowless controls, flicker-free controls, nonrectangular controls, and other control optimizations. Internet-based enhancements were also added. `CAsyncMonikerFile`, `CDataPathProperty`, and other classes were added to support this new Internet functionality.

 As this book was going to press, Microsoft released the beta of Visual Basic 5.0 Control Creation Edition. You can now use Visual Basic to develop ActiveX controls. The Control Creation Edition is free, so you should definitely download it and give it a try. For details, check out my web site at http://www.WidgetWare.com.

NOTE

Win32 versus Win16 Control Development

The last version of Visual C++ to make it easy to move between 16-bit and 32-bit platforms was version 2.2. The 32-bit version also came with the 16-bit Visual C++ version 1.52c. If you built your controls initially with version 2.2, they could easily be moved back and forth between version 2.2 and version 1.52c. However, these versions lack some of the important new ActiveX features. If you need to support both platforms, you basically have three choices. You can use the older versions of Visual C++ and place a few `#ifdef WIN32` lines around the bit-specific code. Another good alternative is to use the non-MFC control framework provided with the ActiveX SDK, which we'll discuss in Chapter 12. The third option is to write your own framework. Right now, I think the best option is to use the non-MFC framework from the ActiveX SDK.

Extended Controls

The control container is responsible for and manages the control's site, or location. There is information about the control that only the container knows. Examples include the control's position within the container and the control's external name. The control user may wish to modify these values. The best way to present this information to the user would be to secretly add these container-specific properties to each control within the container, giving the user a seamless property interface. Each control would have a `top`, `left`, and `name` property. To provide this capability, a container needs a way to "wrap" a control and augment its property list. *OLE aggregation* makes this task easy.

The ActiveX control standard describes an *extended* control that is created by the container and is aggregated with the original control (Figure 7.6). The container-specific properties, or extended properties, are implemented by the container in the aggregate object. Containers may also want to implement container-wide properties that, if modified, affect all the controls within the container. An example is the extended `visible` property. If the container's `visible` property is `FALSE`, it would indicate that each control within the container is not visible. Extended controls make this easy. Although the extended control can hide the implementation of properties for a given control if necessary, the standard recommends that control developers not use the extended control properties that are currently defined. These properties are listed in Table 7.9. Although the standard does not specify any extended methods or events, a container could add them using the extended control.

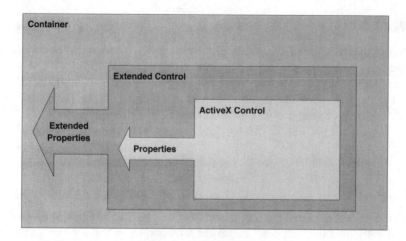

Figure 7.6 Extended control.

Table 7.9 Extended Control Properties

Type/Name	Purpose
BSTR Name	The name given to the control by the user.
BOOL Visible	The visibility of the control.
IDispatch Parent	An IDispatch for the container's extended properties.
BOOL Cancel	Is the control the default **Cancel** button for the container?
BOOL Default	Is the control the **Default** button for the container?

Control-Specific Registry Entries

Just like all the OLE components we've studied so far, ActiveX controls require specific entries in the system Registry. These entries describe attributes of the control that potential containers will use when loading it. Each of the following entries is a subkey under the control's CLSID. Each control typically has a ProgID registered that points back to the specific CLSID, as do all the components that we developed in previous chapters.

Control

The Control entry indicates that the component is an ActiveX control. This entry allows containers to easily identify the ActiveX controls available on the system by searching through the Registry looking only for CLSIDs with a Control subkey. There is no value for the control entry. Its existence is all that is required.

InprocServer32

This entry indicates that the control is a 32-bit in-process server. We used this subkey for the in-process servers that we developed in earlier chapters. The only difference is that the filename of an ActiveX control has an extension of OCX. The OCX extension isn't a requirement—16-bit MFC leaves it as DLL—but use of it is recommended so that it is easy to distinguish between a DLL and a control. Here's the entry for the control that we will develop in Chapter 8.

```
InprocServer32 = c:\postit\objd32\postit.ocx
```

Insertable

The `Insertable` entry indicates that the component can be embedded within a compound document container. This is the entry used by compound document servers such as Visio, Word, and Excel. Compound document containers populate the Insert Object dialog box by spinning through the Registry looking for the `Insertable` key. ActiveX controls should add this subkey only if they can provide functionality when embedded within a compound document container. Because ActiveX controls are a superset of visual servers, they can always be inserted within a compound document container, and this is one way to test the robustness of your controls.

MiscStatus

The `MiscStatus` entry specifies various options of interest to the control container. These values can be queried before the control is loaded, and in some cases they indicate to the container how the control should be loaded. The value for this entry is an integer equivalent of a bit mask value composed of optional `OLEMISC_*` flags. Many of these values were added with the ActiveX control specification and so are specific primarily to ActiveX controls. Table 7.10 details `OLEMISC` bits of interest to control developers.

Table 7.10 Control `OLEMISC` Status Bits

Name	Purpose
ACTIVATEWHENVISIBLE	This bit is set to indicate that the control prefers to be active when visible. This option can be expensive when there are a large number of controls. The Controls 96 specification makes it possible for controls to perform most functions even when not active. This flag should be set so that the control will work in containers that do not support the new specification.
IGNOREACTIVATEWHENVISIBLE	Added by the Controls 96 specification. If a control supports the new optimized control behavior, it should set this flag to inform new containers that they can safely use the Controls 96 specification enhancements.

Table 7.10 Control OLEMISC Status Bits (continued)

Name	Purpose
INVISIBLEATRUNTIME	Indicates that the control should be visible only during the design phase. When running, the control should not be visible. Any control that provides only nonvisual services will fit in this category.
ALWAYSRUN	The control should always be running. Controls such as those that are invisible at run time may need to set this bit to ensure that they are loaded and running at all times. In this way, their events can be communicated to the container.
ACTSLIKEBUTTON	The control is a button and so should behave differently if the container indicates to the control that it should act as a default button.
ACTSLIKELABEL	The container should treat this control like a static label. For example, the container should always set focus to the next control in the tab order.
NOUIACTIVE	Indicates that the control does not support UI activation. The control may still be in-place activated, but it does not have a UI-active state.
ALIGNABLE	Indicates that the container should provide a way to align the control in various ways, usually along a side or the top of the container.
IMEMODE	Indicates that the control understands the input method editor mode, which is used for localization and internationalization within controls.
SIMPLEFRAME	The control uses the ISimpleFrameSite interface (if supported by the container). ISimpleFrameSite allows a control to contain instances of other controls. This is similar to group box functionality.
SETCLIENTSITEFIRST	A control sets this bit to request that the container set up the control's site before the control is constructed. In this way, the control can use information from the client site (particularly ambient properties) during loading.

ProgID

The value of the ProgID entry is set to the current, version-specific ProgID for the control. This is no different from the entries for our components in earlier chapters.

ToolbarBitmap32

The ToolbarBitmap32 entry value specifies the filename and resource ID of the bitmap used for the toolbar of the container. MFC stores the control's bitmap within the OCX file's resources, so a typical entry looks like this:

```
ToolbarBitmap32 = c:\postit\objd32\postit.ocx, 1
```

TypeLib

The `TypeLib` entry value specifies the GUID of the type library for the control. The container uses this GUID to look up the location of the type library. The type libraries installed on the system are listed as sub-keys under the `TypeLib` key in the Registry. The type library information for the control is in the resources of the OCX file, so the path and filename are the same as the `InprocServer32` entry.

Version

The value of this subkey indicates the current version of the control.

Component Categories

As we discussed earlier, the ActiveX Controls 96 specification requires that ActiveX controls support the concept of component categories. The control Registry entries that we just discussed are still useful and necessary for support of containers that have not moved to the new specification. However, as a control developer you should also provide component category support for your controls. First, let's take a look at what component categories are.

Why Component Categories?

Early in the days of ActiveX controls, a few Registry entries were all that were needed to specify the functionality of a control. The `Control` Registry key indicated the existence of a control, and the `Insertable` key indicated whether the control could function as a simple OLE embedded visual server. Today, however, the functional capabilities of all COM-based components (especially controls) continues to expand rapidly. A more efficient and useful mechanism for categorizing the capabilities of these objects is needed.

Today, my NT machine has several hundred COM-based components installed. My Registry is filled with CLSIDs and ProgIDs of these components, and there are only a few ways to distinguish the differences in capabilities between these objects. Only a few Registry entries indicate their purpose. Wouldn't it be great if I could sift through these components and get a specific view of the functionality of each one? That's where the new component categories specification comes in. Thanks to component categories, the OLE-VIEW utility now shows me a more understandable view of the components on my system (see Figure 7.7).

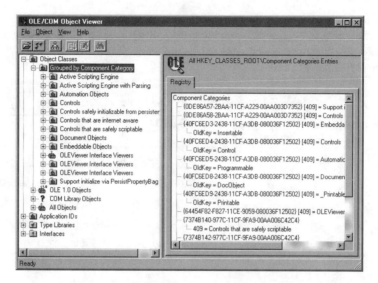

Figure 7.7 OLEVIEW with component categories.

The CATID

Categories are identified using a category ID. A CATID is another name for the 128-bit GUID used throughout COM. Along with the CATID there is a locale ID, which is specified by a string of hexadecimal digits and a human-readable string. The known CATIDs are stored in the Registry under the HKEY_CLASSES_ROOT\Component Categories key. Figure 7.8 shows some of the Registry entries under this key.

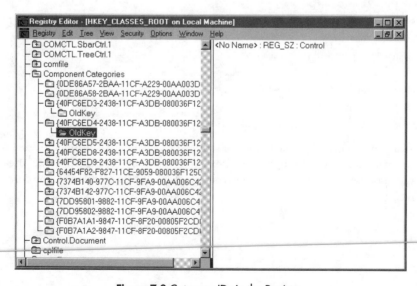

Figure 7.8 Category IDs in the Registry.

The old Registry entries that were previously used to categorize components are supported for backward compatibility. As you can see in Figure 7.8, some Registry entries have an `OldKey` entry, which provides a way to map the older Registry mechanism to the new component categories one. Table 7.11 lists the CATIDs associated with the old Registry entries.

Table 7.11 Category IDs for Old Registry Entries

Old Registry Entry	CATID Symbol from COMCAT.H	GUID
Control	CATID_Control	40FC6ED4-2438-11cf-A3DB-080036F12502
Insertable	CATID_Insertable	40FC6ED3-2438-11cf-A3DB-080036F12502
Programmable	CATID_Programmable	40FC6ED5-2438-11cf-A3DB-080036F12502
DocObject	CATID_DocObject	40FC6ED8-2438-11cf-A3DB-080036F12502
Printable	CATID_Printable	40FC6ED9-2438-11cf-A3DB-080036F12502

Categorizing Your Controls

You categorize a control in two ways: first, by the control's capabilities and, second, by the capabilities required by its potential container. Two new Registry entries are used to communicate this information. The `Implemented Categories` entry lists those category capabilities that your control provides, and the `Required Categories` entry lists those categories that your control requires from a container. These subkeys are added below the CLSID of a control. Here's an example:

```
HKEY_CLASSES_ROOT\CLSID\{12345678-...}
        ; CATID for "Insertable"
        \Implemented Categories\{40FC6ED3-2438-11cf-A3DB-080036F12502}
        ; CATID for "Control"
        \Implemented Categories\{40FC6ED4-2438-11cf-A3DB-080036F12502}
        ;The CATID for an internet aware control
        \Implemented Categories\{...CATID_InternetAware...}
        ;Our control requires ISimpleFrame support
        \Required Categories\{...CATID_SimpleFrameControl...}
```

Currently, the component categories specification describes a few standard categories. Additional categories will be added as the technologies require them. For example, the ActiveX scripting model uses two component categories to indicate scripting support within controls. Table 7.12 shows some of the defined categories as of this writing.

Table 7.12 ActiveX Component Categories

CATID Symbol from COMCAT.H	Purpose

`CATID_PersistsToMoniker,`
`CATID_PersistsToStreamInit,`
`CATID_PersistsToStream,`
`CATID_PersistsToStorage,`
`CATID_PersistsToMemory,`
`CATID_PersistsToFile,`
`CATID_PersistsToPropertyBag`
	Used by Internet-aware controls to indicate which persistence methods they support. These can be used to indicate that an interface is required if the control supports only one persistence method.

`CATID_SimpleFrameControl`	The control implements or requires the container to provide `ISimpleFrameSite` interface support.
`CATID_PropertyNotifyControl`	The control supports simple data binding.
`CATID_WindowlessObject`	The control implements the new windowless feature of the Controls 96 specification.
`CATID_InternetAware`	The control implements or requires some of the Internet-specific functionality, in particular the new persistence mechanisms for Web-based controls.
`CATID_VBFormat, CATID_VBGetControl`	The control uses one or both of these Visual Basic–specific interfaces.
`CATID_VBDataBound`	The control supports the advanced data binding interfaces.

As part of the ActiveX SDK, Microsoft provides the component categories specification. It describes how to implement component categories within your COM-based components and provides (guess what?) two new interface definitions to help with the management of component categories: ICatRegister and ICatInformation. An implementation of these interfaces is provided by a new DLL that is part of the ActiveX SDK. It is called the Component Categories Manager.

The Component Categories Manager

To make it somewhat easy to add component category support to your ActiveX controls, Microsoft provides the Component Categories Manager (CCM). This simple in-process server implements the ICatRegister and ICatInformation interfaces. Component categories are defined Registry entries, and the CCM provides a simple way to maintaining these entries within the Registry. To create an instance of the CCM, you use the COM CoCreateInstance method and pass the defined CCM CLSID: CLSID_StdComponentCategoriesMgr.

ICatRegister

The ICatRegister interface provides methods for registering and unregistering specific component categories. Here's its definition:

```
interface ICatRegister : IUnknown
{
    HRESULT RegisterCategories(
        ULONG cCategories,
        CATEGORYINFO rgCategoryInfo[]);

    HRESULT UnRegisterCategories(
        ULONG cCategories,
        CATID rgcatid[]);

    HRESULT RegisterClassImplCategories(
        REFCLSID rclsid,
        ULONG cCategories,
        CATID rgcatid[]);

    HRESULT UnRegisterClassImplCategories(
        REFCLSID rclsid,
        ULONG cCategories,
        CATID rgcatid[]);

    HRESULT RegisterClassReqCategories(
        REFCLSID rclsid,
        ULONG cCategories,
        CATID rgcatid[]);

    HRESULT UnRegisterClassReqCategories(
        REFCLSID rclsid,
        ULONG cCategories,
        CATID rgcatid[]);
};
```

There are six registration methods, three of which are used to reverse the registration process. The unregister methods do the opposite of the register methods, so we'll cover only the three registration methods.

RegisterCategory takes the count and an array of CATEGORYINFO entries and ensures that they are registered on the system as valid component categories. This means placing them below the HKEY_CLASSES_ROOT\Component Categories entry. In most cases, the category will already be in the Registry, but it doesn't hurt to make sure. Here's the definition of the CATEGORYINFO structure and some simple code that shows how to use the RegisterCategory method:

```
typedef struct  tagCATEGORYINFO
{
    CATID catid;
    LCID lcid;
    OLECHAR szDescription[ 128 ];
} CATEGORYINFO;
```

```
#include "comcat.h"
HRESULT CreateComponentCategory( CATID catid, WCHAR* catDescription )
{
    ICatRegister* pcr = NULL ;
    HRESULT hr = S_OK ;

    // Create an instance of the category manager.
    hr = CoCreateInstance( CLSID_StdComponentCategoriesMgr,
                           NULL,
                           CLSCTX_INPROC_SERVER,
                           IID_ICatRegister,
                           (void**)&pcr );
    if (FAILED(hr))
        return hr;

    CATEGORYINFO catinfo;
    catinfo.catid = catid;
    // English locale ID in hex
    catinfo.lcid = 0x0409;

    // Make sure the description isn't too big.
    int len = wcslen(catDescription);
    if (len>127)
        len = 127;
    wcsncpy( catinfo.szDescription, catDescription, len );
    catinfo.szDescription[len] = '\0';

    hr = pcr->RegisterCategories( 1, &catinfo );
    pcr->Release();

    return hr;
}
```

The preceding code creates an instance of the Component Category Manager using its defined CLSID, `CLSID_StdComponentCategoriesMgr`, while asking for the `ICatRegister` interface. If everything works, a `CATEGORYINFO` structure is populated with the information provided by the caller, and the `RegisterCategory` method is called. However, we haven't yet added anything for a specific component.

To add the `\Implemented Categories` Registry entries for a control, we use the `RegisterClassImplCategories` method. It takes three parameters: the CLSID of the control, a count of the number of CATIDs, and an array of CATIDs to place under the `\Implemented Categories` key. Here's some code to mark a control as implementing the `Control` category.

```
    ICatRegister* pcr = NULL ;
    HRESULT hr = S_OK ;
```

```
// Create an instance of the category manager.
hr = CoCreateInstance( CLSID_StdComponentCategoriesMgr,
                       NULL,
                       CLSCTX_INPROC_SERVER,
                       IID_ICatRegister,
                       (void**)&pcr );
if (SUCCEEDED(hr))
{
    // Register that we support the  "Control" category
    CATID rgcatid[1];
    rgcatid[0] = CATID_Control;
    hr = pcr->RegisterClassImplCategories(clsid, 1, rgcatid);
}

if (pcr != NULL)
    pcr->Release();
```

To add `\Category Required` entries for a control, you use the `RegisterClassReqCategories` method. It takes the same parameters as `RegisterClassImplCategories`, and the example code is nearly identical to the preceding code, so there's no need to demonstrate it. You would register required categories only if your control required some specific container capability such as `ISimpleFrameSite` support.

The *Container and Control Guidelines* document requires that a control support both registering and unregistering of categories. The other three methods take the same parameters but reverse the registration process. If you provide component category registration for your controls you must also support unregistering them. All the controls that we will develop will provide this support.

ICatInformation

The `ICatInformation` interface provides methods that enumerate over the available categories on the system, get the description associated with a given CATID, retrieve a list of components that support a set of categories, and determine whether a specific class supports or requires a specific category. Two methods return enumerators for the implemented and required categories for a specific component. Here's the definition of `ICatInformation`:

```
interface ICatInformation : IUnknown
{
    HRESULT EnumCategories(
        LCID lcid,
        IEnumCATEGORYINFO** ppenumCategoryInfo);

    HRESULT GetCategoryDesc(
```

```
        REFCATID rcatid,
        LCID lcid,
        OLECHAR* ppszDesc);

    HRESULT EnumClassesOfCategories(
        ULONG cImplemented,
        CATID rgcatidImpl[],
        ULONG cRequired,
        CATID rgcatidReq[],
        IEnumCLSID** ppenumClsid);

    HRESULT IsClassOfCategories(
        REFCLSID rclsid,
        ULONG cImplemented,
        CATID rgcatidImpl[],
        ULONG cRequired,
        CATID rgcatidReq[]);

    HRESULT EnumImplCategoriesOfClass(
        REFCLSID rclsid,
        IEnumCATID** ppenumCatid);

    HRESULT EnumReqCategoriesOfClass(
        REFCLSID rclsid,
        IEnumCATID** ppenumCatid);
};
```

The `ICatInformation` interface isn't really needed by a control, but containers use it extensively within their Insert Control dialog boxes. The categories provide a useful mechanism to filter the components available on the system. The container user is presented with an effective way of determining which component provides the needed capabilities.

Summary

In this chapter we've described the technology used to implement ActiveX controls. The ActiveX control standard provides a solid foundation on which to build software components. ActiveX controls provide Automation properties, methods, and events. They also allow implementation of the visual aspect of a component. There are three basic types of ActiveX controls: graphical controls, controls subclassed from existing windows controls, and nonvisual controls.

ActiveX controls use much of the existing technology provided by OLE, including the OLE document standard and the interfaces used to implement in-place-capable embedded servers. ActiveX controls must reside within a container application in order to be used. To support embedding and activation within a container, controls must implement a number of COM-based interfaces.

Although compound document containers typically support the embedding of ActiveX controls, their purpose is different from that of typical ActiveX control containers. Compound document containers support the embedding of large applications that provide significant functionality and are used in the process of document creation. Control containers support the embedding of smaller components that are tied together to form applications. Typically, a control container exists within a visually oriented development environment or tool. A good example is Visual Basic. Another example of an ActiveX control container is Microsoft's Internet Explorer.

Initially, it was necessary for ActiveX controls to implement a large number of COM-based interfaces. However, with the introduction of the OLE Controls 96 specification and the *Control and Container Guidelines 2.0*, ActiveX controls can now implement only those interfaces whose functionality they use. The OLE Controls 96 specification also provides a number of enhancements that make controls more efficient.

ActiveX controls that provide a visual representation should implement a number of compound document interfaces. ActiveX controls implement properties, methods, and events based on the Automation and connectable objects standards. Events provide an additional capability within ActiveX controls and allow the container to tie programmatic actions to a control's events.

Control containers can provide the control with information about its surrounding environment through ambient properties. Ambient properties allow controls to adapt their appearance and some behaviors to those of the container. Control containers can also implement an extended control that aggregates with a control to present additional properties to the control user. This approach provides a uniform, container-specific property set for all controls within the container. The container also provides the control with a way of serializing its properties. In this way, the control can be destroyed and re-created while maintaining its characteristics.

Controls allow modification of their properties through custom and stock property pages. Property pages are independent COM objects that are typically instantiated by the control's container. Visual C++ provides a number of classes and tools that make the development of ActiveX controls easier. ControlWizard initially builds a skeletal control project with a great deal of basic functionality.

An extended control is provided by the container. It aggregates with the control and exposes additional properties and events implemented by the container. For COM to identify controls, specific Registry entries are defined by the standard. Recently, because the simple Registry entries do not provide a granular enough indication of a component's requirements and capabilities, the concept of a component category was add to the COM specification.

Chapter 8

A Simple Control

To help you get to know Visual C++ and ControlWizard and learn how MFC implements ActiveX controls, in this chapter we'll develop a fairly simple control. The control provides functionality similar to that of the Windows label control. Our sample contains text that you can modify (during design time and run time), and it has attributes such as font and color and events such as `Click`. As we develop this control, we will delve into the details of ControlWizard and the source code it produces for us. We will then augment the generated source to include stock and custom properties, stock and custom methods, stock and custom events, and ambient properties. When we are finished with this chapter, you should have a solid grounding in ActiveX controls. Each of the remaining chapters will focus on developing specific control types. Our purpose here is to introduce many of the topics that we will investigate thoroughly in later chapters.

Our First Control

Our first control is a simple visual implementation of the ubiquitous Post-it note. We will implement as many of the stock properties, methods, and events as we can, showing how each one is used within a control. We will also build a custom property page and use two of the stock property pages provided by MFC. Using the POSTIT control, we will also investigate MFC's implementation of ActiveX controls so that we can do more neat things in the chapters to come. To give you an idea of where we are going, Figure 8.1 shows the POSTIT control and its property pages within a container.

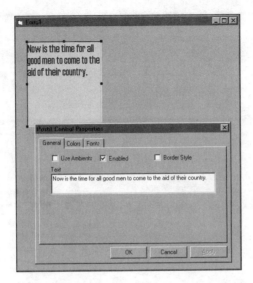

Figure 8.1 The POSTIT control and its property pages.

ControlWizard

ControlWizard is similar to AppWizard in that it generates the project files for a skeletal control based on the options you choose. After you use ControlWizard to generate the initial files for a control, you will not use it again on that specific project. Instead, you will use ClassWizard to add features to your control, just as we have in the past with projects created by AppWizard. To summarize, in Visual C++ you use AppWizard or ControlWizard to initially generate a project. After that, you use ClassWizard to manage the addition of features to the project.

Start Visual C++ and create a new project. Select **OLE ControlWizard** from the New Project Workspace dialog box. Select a root directory for the project and name the project **POSTIT**. Your dialog box should like the one shown in Figure 8.2.

Click the **Create** button to create the project. In the next dialog box, Step 1 of 2, set the **Runtime license** check box to **Yes, please** to indicate that we want to use this feature in the POSTIT project. Take the defaults on the other two options. Click **Next** after ensuring that your dialog box looks similar to the one in Figure 8.3.

The second ControlWizard dialog box allows you to choose various options for your control. For our fist project, we'll choose **Activates when visible**, **Available in "Insert Object" dialog**, and **Has an "About" box**. Let's take a look at the possible options in Figure 8.4.

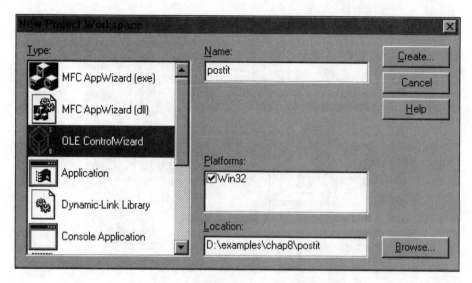

Figure 8.2 New Project dialog box.

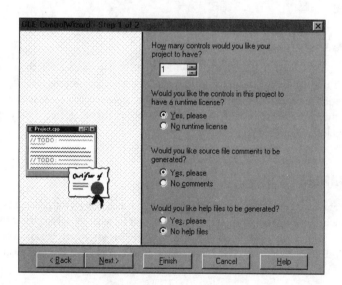

Figure 8.3 OLE ControlWizard Step 1 of 2.

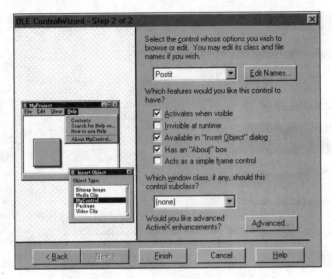

Figure 8.4 OLE ControlWizard Step 2 of 2.

Activate When Visible

For most controls, you should check the **Activate when visible** flag. This adds the OLEMISC_ACTIVATE-WHENVISIBLE flag to the MiscStatus entry within the Registry. By setting this flag, you indicate to the container that you want the control to be active, which means that you have a true hWnd whenever the control is visible within the container. Containers need not support this flag, but if they don't, they won't be very good control containers (and so won't last very long).

Invisible at Runtime

Certain controls do not require a visible representation at run time. These controls are typically called nonvisual controls. MFC includes an example, TIME, that needs to be visible only during the design process. If you check this option, ControlWizard will not create a window for your control, and you will need to implement only the design-time drawing functions within the framework. We will develop a nonvisual control later in the book.

Available in "Insert Object" Dialog

As we've discussed, a control is identified in the Registry by the existence of a Control subkey below its CLSID entry. If you check this option, ControlWizard will also register the control with the Insertable subkey. This option will allow the control to be accessed from applications as if it were a compound document server. If you want to try your control in a noncontrol container, go ahead and check this option. It's easy to change later.

Has an "About" Box

Choosing this option will provide a custom method, `AboutBox`, a dialog resource, and the code to invoke the About box dialog for your control. Most containers provide a way for this method to be invoked during design mode so that the control user can obtain version information.

Acts as Simple Frame Control

If you select this option, ControlWizard will set the `OLEMISC_SIMPLEFRAME` flag. This option is typically used for controls that group other controls and treat them all as one tab stop. The simple frame control acts as the parent window of a group of contained, or child, controls. The Windows group box is an example of this kind of control.

Which Window Class, If Any, Should This Control Subclass?

One of the quickest and most effective ways to develop an ActiveX control is to subclass the functionality of an existing Windows control. Much of the functionality will already be provided by the Windows control. It is then relatively easy to augment this basic behavior. This option allows you to select the control that you will subclass. We will cover this option in another chapter.

Advanced...

The **Advanced** button opens a dialog box that contains a number of new options. The optimization options presented in this dialog box are part of the OLE Controls 96 specification that we discussed in Chapter 7. It will take some time for most control containers to support these options, but we should try to use them if possible. For our first control, we won't use any of these special options (Figure 8.5).

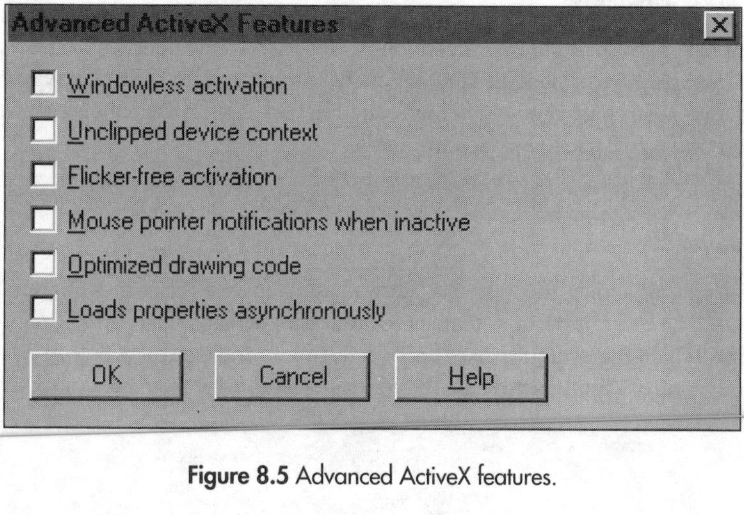

Figure 8.5 Advanced ActiveX features.

WINDOWLESS ACTIVATION

If your control does not require a window to provide its services, you should check this option. A control typically needs a window to call many of the Windows API functions. However, the container can provide a window handle to facilitate making function calls within your control. Using a window will increase the memory requirements of your control and will also require additional load time when instantiated by a container. If you choose windowless activation, the **Unclipped device context** and **Flicker-free activation** options will be disabled. They relate only to controls with windows.

UNCLIPPED DEVICE CONTEXT

The container passes controls a device context on which to draw. The container may set up a clipping region to ensure that the control does not draw outside its boundaries. By checking this option, you inform the container that your control is well behaved and will not draw outside its client rectangle. The container can then act more efficiently by not setting up a clipping context to pass to the control.

FLICKER-FREE ACTIVATION

If your control represents itself the same way when in the active and inactive states, this option will help eliminate flicker when the control is switched between states.

MOUSE POINTER NOTIFICATIONS WHEN INACTIVE

This option provides an implementation of the `IPointerInactive` interface. Your control will receive mouse move messages when in the inactive state.

OPTIMIZED DRAWING CODE

If you click this option, the control will indicate that it can take advantage of the new OLE Controls 96 optimized drawing options. However, the container must support the new optimizations.

LOADS PROPERTIES ASYNCHRONOUSLY

As an enhancement to support low-bandwidth environments such as the Internet, ActiveX controls can have some of their persistent properties loaded asynchronously. For example, a control may have a property that is a GIF file, which may take some time to load over the Internet. This option allows the control to load the image in the background. We'll use this option in Chapter 12.

Edit Names...

The Edit Names dialog box, shown in Figure 8.6, allows you to change the names of your C++ classes, their filenames, and so on. The most important items here are the **Type ID**, which is the ProgID for our control, and the **Type Name**, which the container uses when referring to the control. ControlWizard produces two main classes for your control's implementation: the control class and the property page class.

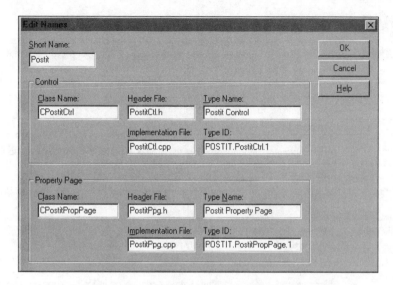

Figure 8.6 Edit Names dialog box.

Click **OK** in the Edit Names dialog box and then **Finish** in the OLE ControlWizard Step 2 of 2 dialog box. The final dialog box is shown in Figure 8.7. Click **OK**, and ControlWizard will generate the control's project files. Then go ahead and compile and link the project.

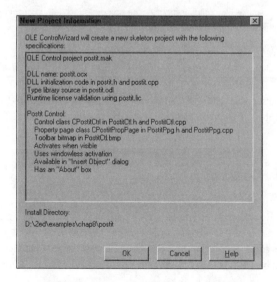

Figure 8.7 New Project Information dialog box.

ControlWizard-Generated Files

Just like AppWizard, ControlWizard generates all the files needed for a typical ActiveX control project. Table 8.1 describes the files generated by ControlWizard.

Table 8.1 ControlWizard-Generated Files

File	Purpose
ReadMe.txt	A file containing information about the project. It details the files created and their purpose.
Postit.cpp, Postit.h	`CWinApp`-derived class that provides the default MFC DLL implementation.
PostitCtl.cpp, PostitCtl.h	Contains the declaration and implementation of the control object. This is a class derived from `COleControl`.
PostitPpg.cpp, PostitPpg.h	Contains the declaration and implementation of the control's property page component. As we described in Chapter 7, a property page is itself a COM object.
Postit.odl	An ODL file that contains the type information for our control.
PostitCtl.bmp	Bitmap for your control that the container can use on its toolbar, and elsewhere.
Postit.ico	This is the icon used in the About box for our control.
Postit.mak	The project's make file.
Postit.def	The Windows definition file for our control. This file exports the four functions (such as `DllRegisterServer`) that we need as a COM in-process server.
Postit.rc, Resource.h	Resource file containing our About box dialog, a default property page dialog definition, and the string table for our control.
Postit.lic	A default license file for our new control.
StdAfx.cpp, StdAfx.h	Standard MFC include and implementation files. These files provide support for the MFC classes.

Before we start adding functionality to the POSTIT control, let's take a detailed look at the source code that ControlWizard generated for us. As we do this, we'll also review the new MFC control classes.

COleControlModule

`COleControlModule` is derived from `CWinApp`. `CWinApp` provides the framework for a basic Windows application for both DLL and EXE implementations, as we've seen in previous chapters. The **POSTIT.H** file inherits all the functionality of `CWinApp` and overrides only the `InitInstance` and `ExitInstance` methods. The only interesting thing in this file is the declarations of the version number variables that are available in all your control modules. These variables are useful for maintaining different versions of your controls.

```
// postit.h : main header file for POSTIT.DLL

#if !defined( __AFXCTL_H__ )
   #error include 'afxctl.h' before including this file
```

```
#endif

#include "resource.h"       // main symbols

////////////////////////////////////////////////////////////////////////
// CPostitApp : See postit.cpp for implementation.
class CPostitApp : public COleControlModule
{
public:
   BOOL InitInstance();
   int ExitInstance();
};

extern const GUID CDECL _tlid;
extern const WORD _wVerMajor;
extern const WORD _wVerMinor;
```

The **POSTIT.CPP** file, which implements the CPostitApp class, is a little more interesting. This file contains the exported DLL functions that support programmatic registration of the control within the Registry. As we learned in Chapter 5, COM recommends that the DllRegisterServer function be implemented within in-process server applications to provide easy registration of components. The ActiveX control standard goes one step further and recommends the use of another function, DllUnregisterServer, that makes it easy to remove all your component-specific information from the Registry. This is a great idea. If applications don't provide an easy removal mechanism, the Registry can easily become cluttered with applications and components that you've previously removed.

 I imagine that future versions of Visual C++ will also handle the steps necessary to register a control's component categories. The 4.x versions, however, do not. Later in this chapter we will add component category support to our control. The DllRegister* functions provide a perfect place to

N O T E   perform this task.

Two functions are missing from **POSTIT.CPP** that are important to our COM-based implementation. As you may recall, COM-based components implemented in DLLs must export two functions: DllGetClassObject and DllCanUnloadNow. In Chapter 5, we implemented them in our main CWinApp-derived class file, **SERVER.CPP**. Where are they? MFC has once again encapsulated some of the complexity for us. These required entry points are provided by an MFC DLL. The code is in **OLEEXP.CPP**:

```
/////////////////////////////////
// DllGetClassObject
extern "C"
STDAPI DllGetClassObject(REFCLSID rclsid, REFIID riid, LPVOID* ppv)
{
   AFX_MANAGE_STATE(AfxGetStaticModuleState());
   return AfxDllGetClassObject(rclsid, riid, ppv);
```

```
}

///////////////////////////////
// DllCanUnloadNow
extern "C"
STDAPI DllCanUnloadNow(void)
{
    AFX_MANAGE_STATE(AfxGetStaticModuleState());
    return AfxDllCanUnloadNow();
}
```

As we described in Chapter 5, the MFC-provided `AfxDllGetClassObject` looks through a list of `COleObjectFactory` objects within the DLL. Once the object is found, it constructs an instance of the object and returns the `IClassFactory` interface. So don't worry, they're still there. They've just been hidden for our convenience. We'll cover the `AFX_MANAGE_STATE` call shortly.

```
// postit.cpp : Implementation of CPostitApp and DLL registration.

#include "stdafx.h"
#include "postit.h"

#ifdef _DEBUG
#undef THIS_FILE
static char BASED_CODE THIS_FILE[] = __FILE__;
#endif

CPostitApp NEAR theApp;

const GUID CDECL BASED_CODE _tlid =
{ 0xbbf8b099, 0xbe9e, 0x11ce, { 0xa4, 0x3c, 0xac, 0xe7, 0x1f, 0x16, 0xdb, 0x7f } };

const WORD _wVerMajor = 1;
const WORD _wVerMinor = 0;

/////////////////////////////////////////////////////////////////////////////
// CPostitApp::InitInstance - DLL initialization

BOOL CPostitApp::InitInstance()
{
    BOOL bInit = COleControlModule::InitInstance();

    if (bInit)
    {
        // TODO: Add your own module initialization code here.
    }
```

```
    return bInit;
}

/////////////////////////////////////////////////////////////////////////
// CPostitApp::ExitInstance - DLL termination
int CPostitApp::ExitInstance()
{
    // TODO: Add your own module termination code here.

    return COleControlModule::ExitInstance();
}

/////////////////////////////////////////////////////////////////////////
// DllRegisterServer - Adds entries to the system registry
STDAPI DllRegisterServer(void)
{
    AFX_MANAGE_STATE(_afxModuleAddrThis);

    if (!AfxOleRegisterTypeLib(AfxGetInstanceHandle(), _tlid))
        return ResultFromScode(SELFREG_E_TYPELIB);

    if (!COleObjectFactoryEx::UpdateRegistryAll(TRUE))
        return ResultFromScode(SELFREG_E_CLASS);

    return NOERROR;
}

/////////////////////////////////////////////////////////////////////////
// DllUnregisterServer - Removes entries from the system registry
STDAPI DllUnregisterServer(void)
{
    AFX_MANAGE_STATE(_afxModuleAddrThis);

    if (!AfxOleUnregisterTypeLib(_tlid))
        return ResultFromScode(SELFREG_E_TYPELIB);

    if (!COleObjectFactoryEx::UpdateRegistryAll(FALSE))
        return ResultFromScode(SELFREG_E_CLASS);

    return NOERROR;
}
```

There are a few items that we need to cover in **POSTIT.CPP**. The DllRegisterServer and DllUnregisterServer functions first call the AFX_MANAGE_STATE macro, so let's look at it.

AFX_MANAGE_STATE

Even though ActiveX controls are small components, they depend heavily on many aspects of the MFC libraries. To maintain a small size, controls use the shared library (DLL) implementation of MFC. Because the MFC code can be shared among all the control, this saves a great deal of code space when an application uses many controls in its implementation.

MFC, when implemented in a DLL, needs to keep track of various internal variables and states that pertain to its internal implementation. This state information must be maintained for every module (such as a DLL) that accesses the MFC DLLs. When the MFC DLLs (such as **MFC40.DLL**) are being used by a number of user DLLs, the MFC internal state data must reflect the process that is currently using MFC. That's what AFX_MANAGE_STATE is for. It ensures that the internal state of MFC is set to reflect that of the calling module. Your control functions must follow three rules to make sure that the MFC state information is correct:

- If the function is exported or exposed externally, you must call the AFX_MANAGE_STATE macro before anything else in the function. This is exemplified by the DllRegisterServer call.
- If your control contains another window's control as a child window, your control should call AFX_MANAGE_STATE when processing any messages for the child window.
- If the function is a member of a COM interface, it should use the METHOD_MANAGE_STATE macro.

COleControl

The COleControl class provides the bulk of the MFC implementation. COleControl is derived from MFC's CWnd class, which encapsulates the functionality of a window. As you can imagine, there is tremendous functionality in the CWnd class, and we will focus on methods of this class in the remaining chapters as we develop various types of ActiveX controls. Our purpose now is to understand a little about COleControl.

COleControl contains more than 100 methods, and this number doesn't include the hundreds that are inherited from the parent CWnd class. Table 8.2 describes some of the more important methods of COleControl. The methods deal with control initialization, persistence, ambient properties, events, stock properties, data binding, and drawing. They are documented completely in MFC's on-line help.

Table 8.2 Important COleControl Members

Method	Purpose
SetInitialSize	Sets the initial size of the control, specified in device units (pixels). This method is usually called in your control's constructor.
SetModifiedFlag	Indicates that a persistent property within the control has been changed.
ExchangeExtent	Serializes the size of the control.

Table 8.2 Important `COleControl` Members (continued)

Method	Purpose
ExchangeVersion	Serializes the control's current version. The `_wVerMinor` and `_wVerMajor` variables are provided by Control Wizard, and can be used to identify the current version of the control.
ExchangeStockProperties	Serializes all of the control's defined stock properties.
DoPropertyExchange	Called to save or restore the persistent properties of the control.
OnReset	Resets the control's properties to their initial state.
InvalidateControl	Forces a redraw of the control.
TranslateColor	Converts an `OLE_COLOR` value into a `COLORREF` value.
ThrowError	Throws an error from within a control. Used to communicate a failure during the execution of code outside a method or property handler function.
AmbientBackColor, AmbientForeColor, AmbientUserMode, AmbientUIDead, **etc.**	Returns the current value of the named ambient property.
FireClick, FireDblClick, FireMouseDown, **etc.**	Fires the specific stock event.
FireEvent[Name]	Fires a custom event.
GetBackColor, SetBackColor	Gets or sets the stock `BackColor` property.
SetFont	Sets the stock font.
SelectStockFont	Selects the stock font into the current device context.
GetHwnd	Returns the `HWND` of the control's window or `NULL`.
GetText, InternalGetText, SetText	Gets or sets the `Text` or `Caption` stock property. `InternalGetText` should be used internally by the control's methods.
DoSuperclassPaint	Called in `OnDraw` to paint a control that has subclassed a Windows control.
OnDraw	Called by the framework to render the control on the passed DC.
OnDrawMetafile	Called by the framework when it wants a metafile representation of the control. This will typically occur when printing or in design or nonuser mode and the control doesn't have a valid `HWND`.
OnAmbientPropertyChange	Called when a container's ambient property or properties have changed.
OnTextChanged	Called when the stock `Text` or `Caption` property has changed.
OnSetExtent	Called when the container has changed the control's extents.

POSTITCTL.H and **POSTITCTL.CPP** implement our control's `COleControl`-derived class: `CPostitCtrl`. Let's take a look at what we initially get from ControlWizard. (I haven't included everything—just the items that are interesting.)

```
// PostitCtl.h : Declaration of the CPostitCtrl ActiveX control class.

/////////////////////////////////////////////////////////////////////////////
// CPostitCtrl : See PostitCtl.cpp for implementation.
class CPostitCtrl : public COleControl
{
    DECLARE_DYNCREATE(CPostitCtrl)

...

// Overrides
    // ClassWizard generated virtual function overrides
    //{{AFX_VIRTUAL(CPostitCtrl)
    public:
        virtual void  OnDraw(CDC* pdc, const CRect& rcBounds, const CRect& rcInvalid);
        virtual void  DoPropExchange(CPropExchange* pPX);
        virtual void  OnResetState();
        virtual DWORD GetControlFlags();
    //}}AFX_VIRTUAL

// Implementation
    protected:
    ~CPostitCtrl();

    BEGIN_OLEFACTORY(CPostitCtrl)          // Class factory and guid
    virtual BOOL VerifyUserLicense();
    virtual BOOL GetLicenseKey(DWORD, BSTR FAR*);
    END_OLEFACTORY(CPostitCtrl)

    DECLARE_OLETYPELIB(CPostitCtrl)        // GetTypeInfo
    DECLARE_PROPPAGEIDS(CPostitCtrl)       // Property page IDs
    DECLARE_OLECTLTYPE(CPostitCtrl))       // Type name and misc status

// Message maps, etc.
...
};
```

I've left out all the message maps, dispatch maps, event maps, and so on. We will cover them a little later. What's left are the four default overrides: `OnDraw`, `DoPropExchange`, `OnReset`, and `GetControlFlags`. These are the only methods that are required to be implemented by the new control, but to make a control do much of anything we'll have to override a few more.

The BEGIN_OLEFACTORY and END_OLEFACTORY macro pair provides our control with the licensing capability that we chose in ControlWizard. This macro pair provides the declaration of the additional methods in the IClassFactory2 interface that we discussed in Chapter 7. Because we chose the licensing option, we are required to implement the VerifyLicenseKey and GetLicenseKey methods in our **.CPP** file.

The DECLARE_OLETYPELIB macro provides a static method that will return a pointer to the control's type library information. The DECLARE_PROPPAGEIDS macro sets up a static function that will return an array of CLSIDs for the property pages defined for the control. These CLSIDs will be defined later in **POSTITCTL.CPP**. The DECLARE_OLECTLTYPE macro provides two static functions for our class that let us access the ID of the type library within the resource file and return the OLEMISC status bits used by the control.

Now let's go through what ControlWizard generated for us in **POSTITCTL.CPP**. We will skip the message, dispatch, and event maps, but we will get to them shortly.

```
// PostitCtl.cpp : Implementation of the CPostitCtrl ActiveX control class.
...
/////////////////////////////////////////////////////////////////////////
// Initialize class factory and guid

IMPLEMENT_OLECREATE_EX(CPostitCtrl, "POSTIT.PostitCtrl.1",
    0xbbf8b096, 0xbe9e, 0x11ce, 0xa4, 0x3c, 0xac, 0xe7, 0x1f, 0x16, 0xdb, 0x7f)
```

This macro implements our class factory functions and should look similar to what we covered in earlier chapters. The following code declares the ProgID for the control and initializes the class factory for our control. The implementation for ActiveX controls tacks on some additional functionality. The _EX adds an override of a virtual method to return the CLSID of the control.

```
/////////////////////////////////////////////////////////////////////////
// Type library ID and version

IMPLEMENT_OLETYPELIB(CPostitCtrl, _tlid, _wVerMajor, _wVerMinor)

/////////////////////////////////////////////////////////////////////////
// Interface IDs

const IID BASED_CODE IID_DPostit =
{ 0xbbf8b097, 0xbe9e, 0x11ce, { 0xa4, 0x3c, 0xac, 0xe7, 0x1f, 0x16, 0xdb, 0x7f } };
const IID BASED_CODE IID_DPostitEvents =
{ 0xbbf8b098, 0xbe9e, 0x11ce, { 0xa4, 0x3c, 0xac, 0xe7, 0x1f, 0x16, 0xdb, 0x7f } };
```

The IMPLEMENT_OLETYPELIB macro defines the static class methods that load the type library from the control's resources and return it to the caller. The interface ID definitions are for the control's (incoming) method and property IDispatch implementation and for the (outgoing) event IDispatch interface. These IDs are also declared in the control's ODL file.

...

```
//  Primary dispatch interface for CPostitCtrl
[ uuid(BBF8B097-BE9E-11CE-A43C-ACE71F16DB7F),
   helpstring("Dispatch interface for Postit Control"), hidden ]
   dispinterface _DPostit
...
//  Event dispatch interface for CPostitCtrl
[ uuid(BBF8B098-BE9E-11CE-A43C-ACE71F16DB7F),
   helpstring("Event interface for Postit Control") ]
   dispinterface _DPostitEvents
```

These IIDs provide a way for the container to specify a specific interface within the control after it gets the control's type information through the `IProvideClassInfo` interface.

```
//////////////////////////////////////////////////////////////////////
// Control type information

static const DWORD BASED_CODE _dwPostitOleMisc =
      OLEMISC_ACTIVATEWHENVISIBLE |
      OLEMISC_SETCLIENTSITEFIRST |
      OLEMISC_INSIDEOUT |
      OLEMISC_CANTLINKINSIDE |
      OLEMISC_RECOMPOSEONRESIZE;

IMPLEMENT_OLECTLTYPE(CPostitCtrl, IDS_POSTIT, _dwPostitOleMisc)

#define IMPLEMENT_OLECTLTYPE(class_name, idsUserTypeName, dwOleMisc) \
   UINT class_name::GetUserTypeNameID() { return idsUserTypeName; } \
   DWORD class_name::GetMiscStatus() { return dwOleMisc; }
```

When we used ControlWizard to create our control, we answered various questions concerning the behavior of the control. ControlWizard used our answers to initialize the `dwPostitOleMisc` variable. This information is provided to the container through the control's `IOleObject::GetMiscStatus` method. The framework calls the virtual class methods implemented by the `IMPLEMENT_OLECTLTYPE` macro.

Control Licensing

ActiveX controls are small software components that must be distributed along with the applications developed using them. Commercial developers need ways to ensure that these components are licensed so that users won't be tempted to copy the components from machine to machine without paying for their use. Licensing is similar to copy protection but works a little differently. The distribution of the component with an application that uses it should be easy: just distribute the appropriate .OCX files that the application depends on. This is fine, but the developer or marketer of the ActiveX control will normally allow distribution of the control only for use as a run-time component. Instead of providing two different OCX files, the same OCX handles both environments. The design-time capabilities of a component are reserved for those who purchase it for use in the development of specific applications; users shouldn't be allowed to distribute a design-time–capable OCX.

The ActiveX control standard provides a way to add licensing capability to a control. This is an optional feature that commercial developers will use, but it can also be used for internally developed components. An additional interface was added to the OLE specification to provide this control licensing facility.

The `IClassFactory2` interface was added to provide licensing support for ActiveX controls. Three additional methods were added: `RequestLicKey`, `GetLicInfo`, and `CreateInstanceLic`. During the development cycle using an ActiveX container-based tool, the `GetLicInfo` method ensures that the control can be used during the design process. When the tool is building a distributable version of the application that uses the control, a call is made to `RequestLicKey`, which returns an implementation-defined key that is stored within the application. Later, after the application and the run-time version of the control are installed on a user's machine, the application will pass the stored key to `CreateInstanceLic` when an instance of the control is created.

The new methods provided in `IClassFactory2` only specify a licensing API; they do not specify how the licensing should be implemented. The keys that are passed back and forth between the container and the control can be as simple as a text string or as complex as using a secure encryption method that requires a licensing server. The MFC implementation provides a simple default method that depends on the existence of a **.LIC** file and a text string contained within it. The MFC implementation can be extended, as always, if you require a more stringent licensing model. Control licensing support through the `IClassFactory2` interface is provided by MFC with an enhancement of the `COleObjectFactory` class.

COleObjectFactoryEx

The `BEGIN_OLEFACTORY` macro added a nested class to `CPostitCtrl` called `CPostitCtrlFactory`. ControlWizard provides the implementation of the `UpdateRegistry` method that either registers or unregisters the control's entries within the Registry with the help of the `AfxOle*` Registry functions. Each of the parameters supplies the information to store within the Registry. I've commented each parameter with its matching Registry entry.

```
/////////////////////////////////////////////////////////////////////////////
// CPostitCtrl::CPostitCtrlFactory::UpdateRegistry -
// Adds or removes system registry entries for CPostitCtrl
BOOL CPostitCtrl::CPostitCtrlFactory::UpdateRegistry(BOOL bRegister)
{
    // TODO: Verify that your control follows apartment-model threading rules.
    // Refer to MFC TechNote 64 for more information.
    // If your control does not conform to the apartment-model rules, then
    // you must modify the code below, changing the 6th parameter from
    // afxRegInsertable | afxRegApartmentThreading to afxRegInsertable.

    if (bRegister)
```

```
      return AfxOleRegisterControlClass(
              AfxGetInstanceHandle(),
              m_clsid,              // CLSID
              m_lpszProgID,         // ProgID
              IDS_POSTIT,           // Textual control name
              IDB_POSTIT,           // ToolboxBitmap32
              // Threading model used by the control
              afxRegInsertable | afxRegApartmentThreading,
              _dwPostitOleMisc,     // MiscStatus
              _tlid,                // TypeLib
              _wVerMajor,
              _wVerMinor);          // Combined to create version
   else
      return AfxOleUnregisterClass(m_clsid, m_lpszProgID);
}
```

The following two methods provide the default MFC implementation of the control licensing feature. This is a fairly simple implementation, but it can be easily enhanced by replacing the Afx functions with ones of your own. The default implementation creates a **.LIC** file with the name of your control project (such as POSTIT.LIC) that contains a copyright in the initial line and then a paragraph about "severe criminal punishment" and so on. The two methods that ControlWizard implemented are methods of the IClassFactory2 interface.

```
/////////////////////////////////////////////////////////////////////////
// Licensing strings

static const TCHAR BASED_CODE _szLicFileName[] = _T("POSTIT.LIC");

static const TCHAR BASED_CODE _szLicString[] = _T("Copyright (c) 1996 ");

/////////////////////////////////////////////////////////////////////////
// CPostitCtrl::CPostitCtrlFactory::VerifyUserLicense -
// Checks for existence of a user license
BOOL CPostitCtrl::CPostitCtrlFactory::VerifyUserLicense()
{
   return AfxVerifyLicFile( AfxGetInstanceHandle(), _szLicFileName,
                            _szLicString);
}

/////////////////////////////////////////////////////////////////////////
// CPostitCtrl::CPostitCtrlFactory::GetLicenseKey -
// Returns a run-time licensing key
BOOL CPostitCtrl::CPostitCtrlFactory::GetLicenseKey(DWORD dwReserved,
     BSTR FAR* pbstrKey)
```

```
{
   if (pbstrKey == NULL)
      return FALSE;

   *pbstrKey = SysAllocString(_szLicString);
   return (*pbstrKey != NULL);
}
```

When the control is inserted into a container during design mode, the container calls `VerifyUserLicense`. As you can see, `VerifyUserLicense` calls the helper function, `AfxVerifyLicFile`, which checks for the instance of the **.LIC** file in the same directory as the control's DLL. Once the file is found, the text of the first line in the file is compared with the text in `_szLicString`. If any of these functions fail, the function returns `FALSE`, indicating that the control is not licensed. A nonzero return indicates that the control is licensed.

Later, the container (or tool) user creates a distributable version of an application that contains the control. The container calls `GetLicenseKey` to obtain a key from the control; the key is stored along with the application distribution files (including the **.OCX** file). After installation, when the application is executed (in user mode), the container calls `VerifyLicenseKey` with its saved internal key. The control verifies that this key is valid and returns `TRUE` if the key is valid and `FALSE` otherwise.

ControlWizard did not provide us with a version of `VerifyLicenseKey`. Its base implementation calls `GetLicenseKey` and compares the return with that provided by the container. To provide a more secure approach, you would need to override and implement your own `VerifyLicenseKey` method as well as modify `GetLicenseKey` and `VerifyUserLicense`. When overriding these functions, you must use multiple scope operators because your `COleObjectFactoryEx`-derived class is nested within the `COleControl`-derived class. Useful methods provided by `COleObjectFactoryEx` are listed in Table 8.3.

Table 8.3 Useful `COleObjectFactoryEx` Methods

Method	Purpose
`UpdateRegistry( BOOL )`	If the parameter is `TRUE`, the Registry is updated with the control's information. If `FALSE`, all control-specific information is removed from the Registry.
`GetLicenseKey( DWORD, BSTR *)`	The container calls this function to retrieve a unique key to store with the distributed application. When the application is run, the container calls `VerifyLicenseKey` to ensure that the control is licensed.
`VerifyLicenseKey( BSTR )`	Called by the container during run-time mode to ensure that the control is licensed.
`VerifyUserLicense( void )`	Called by the container to verify the use of the control in a design-time mode.

That sums up the basic functionality provided by the ControlWizard-generated files, except for the property page files, which we'll cover shortly. Now let's add some real functionality to the POSTIT control.

N O T E Starting with Visual C++ version 4.0, the `IClassFactory2` interface functionality was moved into the `COleObjectFactory` class. However, ControlWizard still generates code that expects the existence of the `COleObjectFactoryEx` class. MFC solves this dilemma by doing this:
`#define COleObjectFactoryEx COleObjectFactory`

Drawing the Control

The container provides a control site in which the control renders itself. There are various conditions under which the container will request that the control draw itself: when the control is created, when the control is hidden by another window and then uncovered, when the container switches from design mode to user mode, and so on. The default MFC implementation calls COleControl::OnDraw for all these actions. It is our job, as implementors of the control, to render the control whenever OnDraw is called. There are other COleControl methods that pertain to drawing, and we will cover them in later chapters.

Following is the default implementation from **POSTITCTL.CPP**. ControlWizard provides a default rendering that fills the background of the control and then draws an ellipse.

```
/////////////////////////////////////////////////////////////////////////////
// CPostitCtrl::OnDraw - Drawing function
void CPostitCtrl::OnDraw(CDC* pdc, const CRect& rcBounds, const CRect& rcInvalid)
{
    // TODO: Replace the following code with your own drawing code.
    pdc->FillRect(rcBounds, CBrush::FromHandle((HBRUSH)GetStockObject(WHITE_BRUSH)));
    pdc->Ellipse(rcBounds);
}
```

The OnDraw method has three parameters. The first parameter is a pointer to an MFC CDC object, which encapsulates a Windows device context. We'll cover the details of device contexts and the methods provided by the CDC class in Chapter 9. For now, a *device context* is an area of the screen that has default brushes, pens, colors, and fonts that are used when drawing the control.

The second parameter, rcBounds, is an instance of MFC's CRect class that contains the bounding rectangle of our control within the container. The third parameter provides a hint as to what part of rcBounds has changed. This information can be used to update only a part of your control if it requires a lot of intensive drawing. We'll use the first two parameters in this chapter.

When our control is constructed, MFC sets its initial size to 50 by 100 device units (or pixels). To override this default, we call COleControl::SetInitialSize in the control's constructor. A square of 200 pixels is fine for our POSTIT control, so add the following code to the constructor:

```
/////////////////////////////////////////////////////////////////////////////
// CPostitCtrl::CPostitCtrl - Constructor
CPostitCtrl::CPostitCtrl()
{
    InitializeIIDs(&IID_DPostit, &IID_DPostitEvents);

    // TODO: Initialize your control's instance data here.
    SetInitialSize( 200, 200 );
}
```

When the control is initially created, the container will provide a control site of 200 by 200 units. Add the following code to draw the control into the device context provided:

```
//////////////////////////////////////////////////////////////////////
// CPostitCtrl::OnDraw - Drawing function
void CPostitCtrl::OnDraw( CDC* pdc, const CRect& rcBounds, const CRect& rcInvalid)
{
    // Create a yellow brush for the background of the control
    CBrush bkBrush;
    bkBrush.CreateSolidBrush( RGB( 0xff, 0xff, 0x00 ));

    // Fill the background with BackColor
    pdc->FillRect( rcBounds, &bkBrush );

    // Draw the text
    pdc->SetBkMode( TRANSPARENT );
    // Set the text color to black
    pdc->SetTextColor( RGB( 0x00, 0x00, 0x00 ));

    // Draw some text
    pdc->DrawText( "This is a simple POSTIT control",
                   -1, CRect( rcBounds ),
                   DT_LEFT | DT_WORDBREAK );
}
```

To draw our simple control, we create a yellow brush. We then fill the control's bounding rectangle with this background brush. To provide a little functionality, we next draw some text in the control using DrawText. Prior to that, we set the drawing mode to TRANSPARENT and set the text color to black. DrawText does much of the drawing work for us; it will automatically word-wrap and left-justify our text within the bounding rectangle. Compile and link the project, and we'll do a little testing.

Registering the Control

Before we can do anything with the control, we need to register it in the Windows Registry just as we register all other COM-based components. The default behavior of Visual C++ is to register the control after every build. A **Custom Build** option in Project/Settings calls REGSVR32 with the path and filename of your control. REGSVR32 calls DllRegisterServer, which updates the Registry with the control information. If you get tired of this action being performed by Visual C++ after every build, remove the lines in the **Custom Build** section in Project/Settings. Later, if you need to register the control, you can use the **Tools/Register Control** option.

Testing the Control

MFC provides a rudimentary testing facility for the controls that you create. I say "rudimentary" because it doesn't provide all the features of a commercial control container such as Visual Basic 4.0. The primary deficiency of MFC is that it lacks an easy-to-use scripting language to manipulate a control's methods and events. Its method of allowing the user to modify the container's ambient properties and the control's stock properties is also lacking, but the Test Container allows us to test basic control functionality. Later in this chapter we will look at the features provided by commercial control containers.

The Test Container can be started from the Visual C++ environment by selecting **Test Container** from the Tools menu. Start it and insert the POSTIT control using the **Edit/Insert OLE Control** menu item. You should see something like the screen in Figure 8.8.

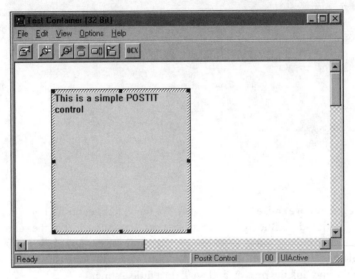

Figure 8.8 Control inserted into the Test Container.

N O T E

If you get an error such as "Unable to Insert Control" when attempting to insert the control into the Test Container, it probably indicates that the **.LIC** file isn't in the same directory as the **.OCX** file. Visual C++ initially places the **.LIC** file into the main project path but creates the debug version of the **.OCX** file in the \PROJNAME\DEBUG directory. To quickly get around this problem, copy the **PROJNAME.LIC** file, which in our case is **POSTIT.LIC**, to the DEBUG directory.

Go ahead and play around with the control. When you move and resize the control, the container calls the OnDraw method and the control is completely redrawn. Notice that as you resize the control, the text within it word-wraps. You can do these things with the control only when it is outlined with a hatched border. This indicates that the control is UI-active, which is similar to a typical window getting focus. Only one control within a container can be UI-active at a given time. Try this by inserting a few more copies of the POSTIT control. (Click the toolbar button marked **OCX**. That's the default toolbar bitmap provided by MFC for our control, but we will change it to something more representative in a moment.)

After inserting a few more copies of the control, you can single-click on a control to make it UI-active. When you do so, any other control that is UI-active will go to the active state and lose its hatched border. This single-click activation indicates that the control is an OLE *inside-out* object. This differs from older visual servers, where you were required to double-click.

Modifying the Default Toolbar Bitmap

The default toolbar bitmap contains the text "OCX." Let's change this to something that better represents our control's purpose. Within Visual C++, change to the resource view, open the Bitmap folder, and double-click on the IDB_POSTIT bitmap. Edit the bitmap to resemble a yellow notepad, as we've done in Figure 8.9.

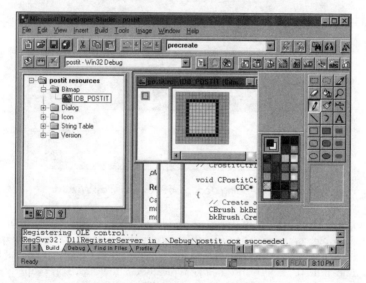

Figure 8.9 Editing the control's bitmap.

Save the changes. The next time we test the control, we'll have a nice toolbar button representation. Our control still doesn't do much, so let's add the stock properties provided by MFC.

Adding Stock Properties

As detailed in Chapter 7, the ActiveX control standard specifies 17 standard properties that controls may typically implement. These standard properties provide generic functionality and provide a way to present a uniform set of properties that most controls will typically implement. MFC currently supplies stock implementations for nine of these standard properties. We'll add eight of them to our POSTIT control. Most of the stock properties affect the appearance of the control.

Control properties are implemented using automation (`IDispatch`). Each control has an `IDispatch` interface for its stock and custom properties and its methods. To implement them for our control, we'll use ClassWizard just as we did in Chapter 6. Fire up ClassWizard and go to the **OLE Automation** tab. Make sure the **Class Name** is `CPostitCtrl`, and click the **Add Properties** button. You will get a dialog box like the one in Figure 8.10.

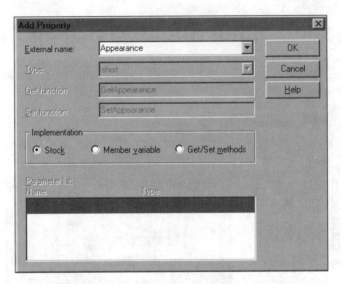

Figure 8.10 Adding stock properties with ClassWizard.

Add every stock property available except `Caption` and `ReadyState`. The `Caption` and `Text` properties use the same internal implementation. The only difference is the external name of the property. Controls should use the `Caption` property to represent small amounts of textual information that typically does not change during run time. Buttons, labels, and the like typically use the `Caption` property. Controls (such as a multiline edit field) that have a lot of text that will be modified at run time should use the `Text` property. We're implementing a control that may contain a lot of textual information, so we will expose the `Text` property. After adding eight of the stock properties, the **OLE Automation** tab should look like Figure 8.11.

The stock properties are implemented with get and set functions. Each stock property has a `Get` and a `Set` method within `COleControl` that allow these properties to be modified externally, usually via the container's property interface or your control's custom property pages. The only current exception is `Hwnd`. It has only a `Get` method for obvious reasons. Whenever a stock property is modified through its `Set` method, the `Set` method will call an `OnPropertyChanged` method, where "Property" is the actual name of the property (such as `OnBackColorChanged`). The default implementation calls `InvalidateControl`, forcing a redraw of the control. You can easily modify this behavior by overriding any of the `OnPropertyChanged` methods within your control class.

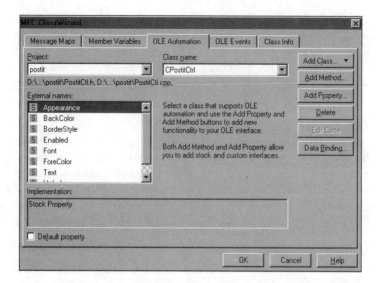

Figure 8.11 Stock properties added by ClassWizard.

Most of the stock properties affect the look of a control: its background and foreground color, the font, the caption, and so on. Next, we'll modify our control's OnDraw method to use these stock properties when drawing. The following sections deal with each stock property and how it is used when you're drawing a control. The last section provides the complete source for OnDraw, so don't worry about typing in until we're finished.

Appearance

The stock appearance property provides the control developer with a standard property that controls the appearance of a control. MFC's current implementation provides just two different options: draw the control using 3-D or not. The implementation uses the Win32 Windows style, WS_EX_CLIENTEDGE, to control the 3-D style.

BackColor

The BackColor property can be used to specify the background of a control. The background typically covers the entire area of a control; the salient features of a control are drawn *on top* of the background. Our control currently creates a yellow background and fills the control with it. By implementing the stock BackColor property, we make it easy for the control user to modify this attribute. To draw the control using the BackColor property, use the COleControl::GetBackColor method:

```
// Get the stock BackColor
CBrush bkBrush;
bkBrush.CreateSolidBrush( TranslateColor( GetBackColor() ));
```

GetBackColor retrieves the current value of the BackColor property. The default value of the BackColor property is the ambient property of the container. If the user does not select a specific background color, the container's background color will be used. The COleControl::TranslateColor method converts an OLE_COLOR type into the COLORREF type needed by the CDC class methods.

ForeColor

The stock ForeColor property can be used in various ways. Controls that contain text typically use this color for the text. This doesn't have to be the case. If the control contains many items that you want the user to be able to customize via a color property, you can choose whatever attribute you feel indicates the foreground color of your control. If you need additional color properties, it is easy to define custom properties for this purpose. We will do this in Chapter 9. ForeColor is similar to the BackColor property in that it defaults to the ambient property of the container if not explicitly set. Here's the new code for the text in the POSTIT control:

```
// Set the text color to the stock ForeColor
pdc->SetBkMode( TRANSPARENT );
pdc->SetTextColor( TranslateColor( GetForeColor() ));
```

If you need to set a stock property programmatically, based on some internal state change or event, Set functions are available for most of the stock properties. In this case, it is SetForeColor.

Caption or Text

As we've discussed, the Caption and Text properties are basically the same. The internal methods to manipulate them are GetText, SetText, and InternalGetText. The InternalGetText method should be used to get the text within your control class. It returns a CString reference instead of an automation BSTR. To draw our text, we need only change one parameter of the DrawText method. It now calls InternalGetText to obtain the value of the Text property:

```
// Draw the text
pdc->DrawText( InternalGetText(),
               -1, CRect( rcBounds ),
               DT_LEFT | DT_WORDBREAK );
```

BorderStyle

The stock BorderStyle property affects the drawing of the border around the control. The current MFC implementation provides only two settings. A zero indicates no border, and a value of 1 denotes drawing of a border around the control. The COleControl class supports both settings, so we don't have to modify our drawing code to support this property.

Font

The stock Font property provides an easy way to expose a font property for your control. If your control uses text in its representation or in any way needs a font, the stock font property makes this easy to manage. COleControl provides a method, SelectStockFont, for selecting the stock font into the current device context (DC). The stock font initially contains the ambient font of the container. You can easily change its value with COleControl::SetFont, or the user can change it through the container's property browser, which will call OnSetFont. The default implementation of OnSetFont updates the stock font and invalidates the control. This is fine for most situations. The following code illustrates how to use SelectStockFont in your OnDraw code:

```
CFont* pOldFont = SelectStockFont( pdc );
...
// Use the font
...
// Restore the old font back into the DC
pdc->SelectObject( pOldFont );
```

This example also demonstrates how the **Drawing Optimization** option can make a control more efficient. If drawing optimization is supported by a container, there is no need to select the old font back into the device context, thus saving a little time. We'll cover this in more detail in Chapter 9.

Hwnd

The stock Hwnd property is a read-only property that exposes the HWND (handle of the window) of the control. This property should also be a run-time–only property, because some containers may not create a window for your control when the container is in design mode. The Hwnd property wouldn't have much use at design time any way, because it is typically used at run time to allow the container's scripting language to directly access, and thus provide, a way to send Windows messages directly to a control's Hwnd. I expect that most containers will not expose this property during the design phase. A control developer need not do anything to handle this stock property; COleControl handles it completely.

Enabled

The stock Enabled property is used to indicate, using either TRUE or FALSE, whether a control is enabled. The Windows operating system provides an API function, EnableWindow, that controls the behavior and appearance of a standard window. When a window is enabled, it functions normally. When a window is not enabled, or is disabled, it does not accept user input and typically changes its appearance as an indication to the user. An example is the standard Windows checkbox control. When it is disabled, the checkbox and the text associated with it are "grayed out" to indicate that it does not accept input.

We'll change the background style of our control to use a diagonal hatching to indicate that it is disabled. We will check the Enabled property before drawing the background of our control:

```
// Create a brush using the stock BackColor
CBrush bkBrush;
// If the control is enabled use a solid brush
// otherwise use a hatched brush to indicate the disabled state
if ( GetEnabled() )
   bkBrush.CreateSolidBrush( TranslateColor( GetBackColor() ));
else
   bkBrush.CreateHatchBrush( HS_DIAGCROSS, TranslateColor( GetBackColor() ));

// Fill the background with BackColor
pdc->FillRect( rcBounds, &bkBrush );
```

Not much is new here except that we've added the check of the Enabled property and have created a hatched brush to fill the control's background.

As promised, here's the complete OnDraw method with the new code that uses the stock properties:

```
///////////////////////////////////////////////////////////////////////////
// CPostitCtrl::OnDraw - Drawing function
void CPostitCtrl::OnDraw(CDC* pdc, const CRect& rcBounds, const CRect& rcInvalid)
{
   // Create a brush with the stock BackColor
   CBrush bkBrush;
   if ( GetEnabled() )
      bkBrush.CreateSolidBrush( TranslateColor( GetBackColor() ));
   else
      bkBrush.CreateHatchBrush( HS_DIAGCROSS, TranslateColor( GetBackColor() ));

   // Fill the background with BackColor
   pdc->FillRect( rcBounds, &bkBrush );

   pdc->SetBkMode( TRANSPARENT );

   // Set the text color to the ForeColor
   // If the control is disabled, draw the
   // text in the background color
   if ( GetEnabled() )
      pdc->SetTextColor( TranslateColor( GetForeColor() ));
   else
      pdc->SetTextColor( TranslateColor( GetBackColor() ));

   // Select the font. SelectStockFont
   // is a method of COleControl that uses the stock
   // font property for the control
```

```
    CFont* pOldFont = SelectStockFont( pdc );

    // Get the text and draw it
    pdc->DrawText( InternalGetText(),
                    -1, CRect( rcBounds ),
                    DT_LEFT | DT_WORDBREAK );

    // Restore the old font of the DC
    pdc->SelectObject( pOldFont );
}
```

Add the preceding code to **POSTITCTL.CPP** and compile and link the project.

NOTE

When you add or remove a property, method, or event to a control, you must update the type library before attempting to build the project. The 16-bit version of Visual C++ requires that you explicitly make the type library apart from the build, so be sure to do this first.

Testing Stock Properties in the Test Container

Now that we've added support for the stock properties and have modified the OnDraw code to use them, we should give them a try. The Test Container works fine for testing these changes. The stock properties initially default to the ambient properties of the container. Start the Test Container and select the **Edit/Ambient properties** menu item. Set the BackColor and ForeColor properties to gray and red. Now insert a POS-TIT control. The control will use the ambient colors when rendering itself. It's hard to determine whether the ForeColor property worked, because we haven't specified the text for the control, but this is easy to do.

To access the properties for a specific control in the container, make sure the control is UI-active by single-clicking on it. Then invoke the **View/Properties** menu item. This pops up a modeless Properties dialog box that allows you to modify the stock properties that we added. This isn't the actual property page created for your control; instead, it's the container's property browser. We'll define and use our own property pages in a moment. As you modify these properties and apply them to the control, it will redraw the control using the new values.

Add some text to the control using the Text property, and change the background and foreground colors. Set the BorderStyle property to 1, and a border will be drawn around the control. Set the Enabled property to zero and watch what happens. There are many things you can do with this control even with just the stock properties. Play with the control until you are comfortable with what's going on in the code. Next, we will add a custom property page to our control.

COlePropertyPage

Property pages provide a way for a control to graphically present custom and stock properties to the control user. The user can then modify the properties and apply the changes to the control. This manipulation usually is done when the user configures the control during the container's design phase.

MFC provides the `COlePropertyPage` class to make it easy to implement property pages for your control. The container usually provides a way for the control user to modify stock properties, which are known to exist within most controls. But some containers, such as Visual C++'s Resource editor do not supply this capability, so it is important to provide an interface to all the properties used in your control. This is easy to do by implementing a combination of custom and stock property pages for your control. Let's take a quick look at the `COlePropertyPage` class and the initial files produced by ControlWizard.

Each property page is itself a COM-based component with a CLSID. This arrangement makes it easy for the container to load and activate a control's property page without bothering the control. When a control is initially loaded, the container retrieves a list of the property page CLSIDs that should be invoked for the control. When the user wants to modify a control's properties, the container instantiates each property page and frames it to create a property sheet. We discussed this in Chapter 7. The important thing to understand is that each property page is a distinct COM-based component object. The `COlePropertyPage` class does almost all the work for us. Here's the initial **POSTITPPG.H** file:

```
// PostitPpg.h : Declaration of the CPostitPropPage property page class.

/////////////////////////////////////////////////////////////////////////
// CPostitPropPage : See PostitPpg.cpp for implementation.
class CPostitPropPage : public COlePropertyPage
{
    DECLARE_DYNCREATE(CPostitPropPage)
    DECLARE_OLECREATE_EX(CPostitPropPage)

// Constructor
public:
    CPostitPropPage();

// Dialog Data
    //{{AFX_DATA(CPostitPropPage)
    enum { IDD = IDD_PROPPAGE_POSTIT };
    //}}AFX_DATA

// Implementation
protected:
    virtual void DoDataExchange(CDataExchange* pDX);    // DDX/DDV support

// Message maps
protected:
    //{{AFX_MSG(CPostitPropPage)
    // NOTE - ClassWizard will add and remove member functions here.
    //    DO NOT EDIT what you see in these blocks of generated code !
    //}}AFX_MSG
    DECLARE_MESSAGE_MAP()

};
```

There's nothing special here except the enum { IDD_PROPPAGE_POSTIT } and the DoDataExchange declaration. The enum value contains the dialog resource for the property page. We'll modify this dialog box in the next section. The DoDataExchange method provides an easy mechanism for moving data between controls within a dialog box and class member variables.

COlePropertyPage derives from CDialog, which derives from CCmdTarget, so we have COM support built into our new class. And the DECLARE_OLECREATE_EX macro provides a class factory for our property page. All the pieces are there for making this class a COM-based component:

```
// PostitPpg.cpp : Implementation of the CPostitPropPage property page class.

...

IMPLEMENT_DYNCREATE(CPostitPropPage, COlePropertyPage)

...

/////////////////////////////////////////////////////////////////////////
// Initialize class factory and guid
IMPLEMENT_OLECREATE_EX(CPostitPropPage, "POSTIT.PostitPropPage.1",
    0xbbf8b09a, 0xbe9e, 0x11ce, 0xa4, 0x3c, 0xac, 0xe7, 0x1f, 0x16, 0xdb, 0x7f)

/////////////////////////////////////////////////////////////////////////
// CPostitPropPage::CPostitPropPageFactory::UpdateRegistry -
// Adds or removes system registry entries for CPostitPropPage
BOOL CPostitPropPage::CPostitPropPageFactory::UpdateRegistry(BOOL bRegister)
{
    if (bRegister)
        return AfxOleRegisterPropertyPageClass(AfxGetInstanceHandle(),
                            m_clsid, IDS_POSTIT_PPG);
    else
        return AfxOleUnregisterClass(m_clsid, NULL);
}

/////////////////////////////////////////////////////////////////////////
// CPostitPropPage::CPostitPropPage - Constructor
CPostitPropPage::CPostitPropPage() :
    COlePropertyPage(IDD, IDS_POSTIT_PPG_CAPTION)
{
    //{{AFX_DATA_INIT(CPostitPropPage)
    //}}AFX_DATA_INIT
}

/////////////////////////////////////////////////////////////////////////
// CPostitPropPage::DoDataExchange - Moves data between page and properties
```

```
void CPostitPropPage::DoDataExchange(CDataExchange* pDX)
{
   //{{AFX_DATA_MAP(CPostitPropPage)
   //}}AFX_DATA_MAP
   DDP_PostProcessing(pDX);
}
```

POSTITPPG.CPP looks very similar to **POSTITCTL.CPP**. The IMPLEMENT_OLECREATE_EX macro contains the ProgID and CLSID for our property page and the UpdateRegistry method. The DoDataExchange method is implemented but currently doesn't do anything. We will add to and discuss it in the next section. Table 8.4 provides a list of useful COlePropertyPage methods.

Table 8.4 Useful COlePropertyPage Methods

Method	Purpose
COlePropertyPage	The constructor takes the ID of a dialog resource and an ID of a string resource for the caption of the page.
IsModified	Indicates whether the user has modified any items on the property page.
SetModifiedFlag	Indicates that an item on the page has been modified.
OnHelp	Called when the user presses the help key on the property sheet, when the page is the current tab.
OnInitDialog	Called when the property page is initialized.
OnEditProperty	Called when the user edits a specific property on the page.
OnSetPageSite	Called when the container loads the page to display it within its property page frame.

Modifying the Custom Property Page

ControlWizard provides us with a custom property page that we can use to let control users modify our control's stock or custom properties. The COlePropertyPage class is derived from CDialog and uses a dialog resource to describe its appearance. We need to add a custom property that allows toggling the use of the container's ambient properties. To add this property to the resources tab, click the Dialog folder and then double-click the **IDD_PROPPAGE_POSTIT** dialog resource. Add a checkbox with the text **Use Ambients** and with an ID of **IDC_USEAMBIENTS**. While you're at it, add a checkbox for our stock Enabled (**IDC_ENABLED**) and BorderStyle (**IDC_BORDER**) properties and a multiline edit field (**IDC_TEXT**) for our Text property. See Figure 8.12.

We now need to create the custom UseAmbients property. Using ClassWizard, select the **OLE Automation** tab, add a property of type **BOOL** using **Get/Set** methods, and call it **UseAmbients**. Now add the following code to **POSTITCTL.H** and **POSTITCTL.CPP**. It adds a member variable to our control class for maintaining the UseAmbients property. We also call InvalidateControl to force a redraw when the property changes.

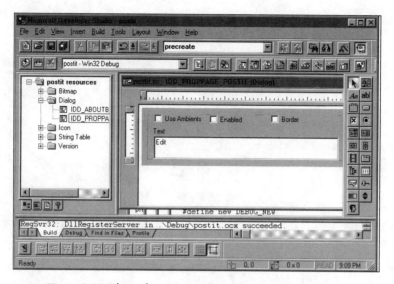

Figure 8.12 Editing the custom property page dialog resource.

```cpp
// PostitCtl.h
class CPostitCtrl : public COleControl
{
    DECLARE_DYNCREATE(CPostitCtrl)

    // Implementation members
    BOOL      m_bUseAmbients;

    ...
};

// PostitCtl.cpp
...
CPostitCtrl::CPostitCtrl()
{
    InitializeIIDs(&IID_DPostit, &IID_DPostitEvents);

    // TODO: Initialize your control's instance data here.
    m_bUseAmbients = FALSE;

    SetInitialSize( 200, 200 );
}
...
/////////////////////////////////////////////////////////////////////////////
// CPostitCtrl message handlers
```

```
BOOL CPostitCtrl::GetUseAmbients()
{
    // TODO: Add your property handler here
    return m_bUseAmbients;
}

void CPostitCtrl::SetUseAmbients(BOOL bNewValue)
{
    // TODO: Add your property handler here
    m_bUseAmbients = bNewValue;
    SetModifiedFlag();

    // Redraw the control
    InvalidateControl();

    // Update any property browser
    BoundPropertyChanged( dispidUseAmbients );
}
```

The call to `BoundPropertyChanged` is an important one. It notifies any associated object, usually the container, that a property has changed within the control. It does this through the `IPropertyNotifySink` interface. For example, this one call will ensure that Visual Basic's property browser will always be in sync with both the control and the control's custom property pages.

For our custom property page to access our custom property, we must create a variable for it in the `CPostitPropPage` class. Start ClassWizard and select the **Member Variables** tab. From the Class Name dropdown, select **CPostitPropPage**. Click the **Add Variable** button and add a variable for the **IDC_USE-AMBIENTS** checkbox. When adding the variable, be sure to type the name of the associated property (within the control) in the Optional OLE Property Name field. Adding a property name here forces the property to be retrieved from the control. It adds a `DDP_Check` entry for the property. In a moment you will see exactly what this does. The dialog box is shown in Figure 8.13.

While you're at it, go ahead and add member variables for the other three stock properties that we placed on the custom property page. When adding these variables, be sure to select the correct stock property name from the Optional OLE Property Name field. The `Text` property is shown being added in Figure 8.14.

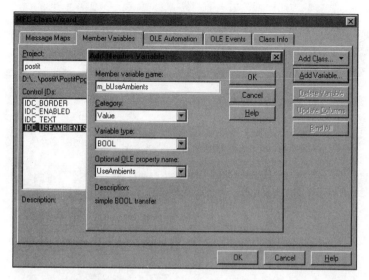

Figure 8.13 Adding a member variable for the UseAmbients property.

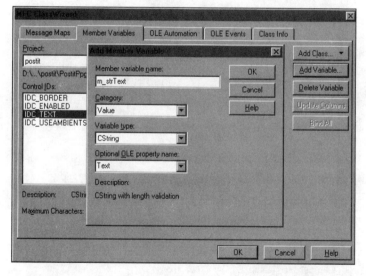

Figure 8.14 Adding a member variable for the stock text property.

The value of m_bUseAmbients is modified when the property page user changes the value of its checkbox. This is done using the normal dialog data exchange macros. ClassWizard adds the following highlighted code to the CPostitPropPage class:

```
// PostitPpg.h
class CPostitPropPage : public COlePropertyPage
{
...
// Dialog Data
    //{{AFX_DATA(CPostitPropPage)
    enum { IDD = IDD_PROPPAGE_POSTIT };
    BOOL        m_bEnabled;
    CString     m_strText;
    BOOL        m_bBorderStyle;
    BOOL        m_bUseAmbients;
    //}}AFX_DATA...
};

// PostitPpg.cpp
...
/////////////////////////////////////////////////////////////////////////////
// CPostitPropPage::CPostitPropPage - Constructor
CPostitPropPage::CPostitPropPage() :
      COlePropertyPage(IDD, IDS_POSTIT_PPG_CAPTION)
{
    //{{AFX_DATA_INIT(CPostitPropPage)
    m_bEnabled = FALSE;
    m_strText = _T("");
    m_bBorderStyle = FALSE;
    m_bUseAmbients = FALSE;
    //}}AFX_DATA_INIT
}

/////////////////////////////////////////////////////////////////////////////
// CPostitPropPage::DoDataExchange - Moves data between page and properties
void CPostitPropPage::DoDataExchange(CDataExchange* pDX)
{
    //{{AFX_DATA_MAP(CPostitPropPage)
    DDP_Check(pDX, IDC_ENABLED, m_bEnabled, _T("Enabled") );
    DDX_Check(pDX, IDC_ENABLED, m_bEnabled);
    DDP_Text(pDX, IDC_TEXT, m_strText, _T("Text") );
    DDX_Text(pDX, IDC_TEXT, m_strText);
    DDP_Check(pDX, IDC_BORDER, m_bBorderStyle, _T("BorderStyle") );
    DDX_Check(pDX, IDC_BORDER, m_bBorderStyle);
    DDP_Check(pDX, IDC_USEAMBIENTS, m_bUseAmbients, _T("UseAmbients") );
```

```
DDX_Check(pDX, IDC_USEAMBIENTS, m_bUseAmbients);
//}}AFX_DATA_MAP
DDP_PostProcessing(pDX);
}
```

The `DoDataExchange` method moves property values between the dialog controls, identified with their IDs, and the member variables of the `CPostitProgPage` class. The direction of the transfer, either from the member variables to the dialog controls or from the dialog controls to the member variables, is indicated by the `m_bSaveAndValidate` member of the `CDataExchange` class. `FALSE` indicates a transfer to the controls.

The DDX functions actually exchange the dialog data. The DDP functions were added for controls and extend MFC's data exchange mechanism to support synchronization of properties across automation-based components. The DDP functions use automation to either get or set the control's property values. The fourth parameter of the DDP function is the name of the automation property that is being affected.

When the container loads a control's property page, `DoDataExchange` is called with the `m_bSaveAndValidate` flag set to `FALSE` to indicate that the dialog's controls should be loaded. Each DDP function, as it is encountered, uses `IDispatch::Invoke` to obtain the associated property value from the control; in other words, the control's `GetProperty` method is called. The `Invoke` may be preceded by a call to `IDispatch::GetIDsOfNames` if the property does not have a standard DISPID (e.g., stock properties). The control's property value is then stored in the property page object's member variable (such as `m_bUseAmbients`). Next, the DDX method is called to transfer the property value to the dialog control. This process is repeated for each DDP/DDX pair. Once this process is finished, the property page is displayed.

When the user modifies a property value and clicks the property sheet's **Apply** or **OK** button, the reverse occurs. `DoDataExchange` is called with `m_bSaveAndValidate` set to `TRUE`. This time the DDP functions update an internal map of the property values, and the `Invoke` call is deferred until the `DDP_PostProcessing` method is called. This is because the appropriate value hasn't yet been transferred from the dialog control to the property page member via the DDX function. Once the transfer has occurred, the `DDP_PostProcessing` method updates each property that was changed via the property sheet by calling the control's appropriate `Set` function using `IDispatch::Invoke`.

The DDP functions currently support most of the automation types. Depending on the property type, you use the appropriate DDP function. For example, if your property is stored in a `short`, you could use the `DDP_CBIndex` to map the value of the property to a position within a combo box. We will do this in a later chapter. The various DDP functions are as follows:

```
DDP_Text(CDataExchange*pDX, int id, BYTE& member, LPCTSTR pszPropName);
DDP_Text(CDataExchange*pDX, int id, int& member, LPCTSTR pszPropName);
DDP_Text(CDataExchange*pDX, int id, UINT& member, LPCTSTR pszPropName);
DDP_Text(CDataExchange*pDX, int id, long& member, LPCTSTR pszPropName);
DDP_Text(CDataExchange*pDX, int id, DWORD& member, LPCTSTR pszPropName);
DDP_Text(CDataExchange*pDX, int id, float& member, LPCTSTR pszPropName);
DDP_Text(CDataExchange*pDX, int id, double& member, LPCTSTR pszPropName);
```

```
DDP_Text(CDataExchange*pDX, int id, CString& member, LPCTSTR pszPropName);

DDP_Check(CDataExchange*pDX, int id, int& member, LPCTSTR pszPropName);

DDP_Radio(CDataExchange*pDX, int id, int& member, LPCTSTR pszPropName);

DDP_LBString(CDataExchange* pDX, int id, CString& member, LPCTSTR pszPropName);

DDP_LBStringExact(CDataExchange* pDX, int id, CString& member, LPCTSTR pszPropName);

DDP_LBIndex(CDataExchange* pDX, int id, int& member, LPCTSTR pszPropName);

DDP_CBString(CDataExchange* pDX, int id, CString& member, LPCTSTR pszPropName);

DDP_CBStringExact(CDataExchange* pDX, int id, CString& member, LPCTSTR pszPropName);

DDP_CBIndex(CDataExchange* pDX, int id, int& member, LPCTSTR pszPropName);
```

Using Stock Property Pages

MFC provides three stock property pages that you can use to allow users to modify your control's properties. The three property pages provide support for your color, font, and picture type properties. We will use the color and font property pages to allow the user to modify our control's stock BackColor, ForeColor, and Font properties. As mentioned previously, containers normally provide an effective way of modifying standard (and often custom) properties, but to build a control that is useful in all control containers, we need to provide an interface for all the properties of our control. The stock property pages give us an easy way to provide a standard interface to Color, Font, and Picture property types.

The three stock property pages are identified by their CLSIDs. To use them within your control, you add them using the PROPPAGEID macro. This technique adds the CLSIDs to the array of property page CLSIDs that is maintained by the control. When the container invokes the property sheet for the control, it determines which pages to load by asking for this array.

Add the following code to **POSTITCTL.CPP**. Be sure to change the page count in the BEGIN_PROP-PAGEIDS macro from 1 to 3.

```
// TODO: Add more property pages as needed.  Remember to increase the count!
BEGIN_PROPPAGEIDS(CPostitCtrl, 3)
    PROPPAGEID(CPostitPropPage::guid)
    PROPPAGEID(CLSID_CColorPropPage)
    PROPPAGEID(CLSID_CFontPropPage)
END_PROPPAGEIDS(CPostitCtrl)
```

By adding two lines of code, we provide a nice way for the control user to modify the Font, BackColor, and ForeColor properties. The standard property pages determine which properties to display within their dropdowns by iterating through all your control's properties. If the supported property type is found, the property page adds it to its list. To add a custom color property to your control—say HeadingColor—use ClassWizard to add a property of type OLE_COLOR. When the standard property sheet is loaded, it will include your new custom property.

Using Ambient Properties

Earlier, we added a custom property, UseAmbients, that allows the control user to indicate whether the control should use the ambient properties provided by the container or the ones specified by the user. We need to modify our drawing code to check the UseAmbients property to determine which property set to use. The new OnDraw code is as follows:

```
/////////////////////////////////////////////////////////////////////////
// CPostitCtrl::OnDraw - Drawing function
void CPostitCtrl::OnDraw(CDC* pdc, const CRect& rcBounds, const CRect& rcInvalid)
{
    CBrush bkBrush;
    // Use a local color reference for increased efficiency
    COLORREF crBack;
    COLORREF crFore;

    // Use the container's properties if the UseAmbients
    // property is true
    if ( m_bUseAmbients )
    {
        crBack = TranslateColor( AmbientBackColor() );
        crFore = TranslateColor( AmbientForeColor() );
    }
    else
    {
        crBack = TranslateColor( GetBackColor() );
        crFore = TranslateColor( GetForeColor() );
    }

    if ( GetEnabled() )
        bkBrush.CreateSolidBrush( crBack );
    else
        bkBrush.CreateHatchBrush( HS_DIAGCROSS, crFore );

    // Fill the background with BackColor
    pdc->FillRect( rcBounds, &bkBrush );

    pdc->SetBkMode( TRANSPARENT );

    // Set the text color to the ForeColor
    // If the control is disabled, draw the
    // text in the background color
    if ( GetEnabled() )
```

```
         pdc->SetTextColor( crFore );
     else
         pdc->SetTextColor( crBack );

     // Select the font
     CFont* pOldFont;
     if ( m_bUseAmbients )
     {
         CFontHolder font( &m_xFontNotification );
         // Get the ambient font's IDispatch
         LPFONTDISP lpFontDisp = AmbientFont();
         // If the container doesn't have an ambient font
         // use the stock font instead
         if ( lpFontDisp == NULL )
             pOldFont = SelectStockFont( pdc );
         else
         {
             // Initialize the CFontHolder with the
             // ambient font dispatch
             font.InitializeFont( NULL, lpFontDisp );
             pOldFont = SelectFontObject( pdc, font );
             // Release the font dispatch
             lpFontDisp->Release();
         }
     }
     else
         pOldFont = SelectStockFont( pdc );

     // Get the text and draw it
     pdc->DrawText( InternalGetText(),
                     -1, CRect( rcBounds ),
                     DT_LEFT | DT_WORDBREAK );

     // Restore the old font of the DC
     pdc->SelectObject( pOldFont );
}
```

The font selection code needs a little more explanation. To effectively handle changing to and from the ambient Font property, we use the CFontHolder class. We'll cover that in the next section. Before we do that, though, we need to add one more method to our control.

Whenever the container's ambient properties change and the m_UseAmbients flag is TRUE, we need to redraw the control. The COleControl::OnAmbientPropertyChange method is called when any of the container's ambient properties changes. First, we override this method in **POSTITCTL.H**, and then we add the implementation code to **POSTITCTL.CPP**. You can initially override a method by clicking the **Messages** dropdown when editing **POSTITCT.CPP**. Scroll down to OnAmbientPropertyChange and select it. It will be added to both the **.H** and the **.CPP** files.

```
class CPostitCtrl : public COleControl
{
...
// Overrides
...
// Override OnAmbientPropertyChange
virtual void OnAmbientPropertyChange( DISPID );
...
};

// PostitCtl.cpp
...
void CPostitCtrl::OnAmbientPropertyChange( DISPID dispid )
{
   // TODO: Add your specialized code here and/or call the base class

   // If the user does not want ambients just return
   if ( m_bUseAmbients == FALSE )
      return;

   // Redraw the control
   InvalidateControl();

   COleControl::OnAmbientPropertyChange(dispid);
}
```

OnAmbientPropertyChange provides the DISPID of the specific ambient that changed. If more than one property has changed, this function passes DISPID_UNKNOWN. We don't really care which ambient changes, so in all cases we call InvalidateControl, which forces a redraw. If the UseAmbients property is FALSE, there is no need to deal with ambients and we just return.

CFontHolder

The CFontHolder class encapsulates a Windows font object. It contains an implementation of the COM IFont and IFontDisp interfaces that provides methods for communicating font information and font property changes among COM-based components.

We use the CFontHolder class to obtain the ambient Font property. The following code is from OnDraw:

```
if ( m_bUseAmbients )
{
    CFontHolder font( &m_xFontNotification );

    // Get the ambient font's IDispatch
    LPFONTDISP lpFontDisp = AmbientFont();

    // If the container doesn't have an ambient font
    // use the stock font instead
    if ( lpFontDisp == NULL )
        pOldFont = SelectStockFont( pdc );
    else
    {
        // Initialize the CFontHolder with the
        // ambient font dispatch
        font.InitializeFont( NULL, lpFontDisp );

        pOldFont = SelectFontObject( pdc, font );

        // Release the font IDispatch
        lpFontDisp->Release();
    }
}
```

The constructor for the CFontHolder class requires a pointer to an IPropertyNotifySink interface. The COleControl class contains a protected member, m_xFontNotification, that implements an IPropertyNotifySink interface for the handling of ambient fonts. We use this member to construct an instance of CFontHolder. After construction, CFontHolder must be initialized with a call to the InitializeFont method.

InitializeFont takes two parameters: a pointer to a FontDesc structure that specifies the font's characteristics, and a pointer to the ambient font's IDispatch. Only one of the two parameters is required, and in our case we need only a pointer to the ambient font's IDispatch. We're in luck—the AmbientFont method returns an LPFONTDISP—so we pass it to InitializeFont. This action creates a valid CFontHolder object that we then pass to COleControl::SelectFontObject. This function selects the ambient font into the device context. If any of this fails, we use the stock font provided by MFC.

Testing the Ambient Property Changes

We can use the Test Container to test the addition of ambient property support to our control. Start the Test Container and from the Edit menu choose **Set Ambient Properties**. Before inserting the control, change the ForeColor, BackColor, and Font ambient properties from their default values. Now insert the control. When the control first loads, it will use the ambient properties of the container even though the initial value of the UseAmbients property is FALSE. Remember, the initial value of stock properties defaults to the ambient values of the container. Now, invoke the property sheet for the control by selecting **Postit Control Object/Properties** from the Edit menu. This action will bring up the custom and two stock property pages that we added to the control. Add some text for the control, check the **UseAmbients** checkbox, and modify the colors and font. Now click the **Apply** button. Only the text that you entered will change the appearance of the control. To use the new values for the stock properties, we need to "turn off" the use of ambient properties. Do this and press the **Apply** button. The control will now use the values of the stock properties.

The **Apply** button calls IDispatch::Invoke with the DISPID of the changed property. This calls the specific property's Set method (such as SetUseAmbients) with the new property value. After updating the property value within the control, the Set method will typically call InvalidateControl, which will force a redraw of the control.

Continue to play with the UseAmbients as well as all the other stock and ambient properties. Try out the Enabled and BorderStyle properties, too. This experimentation should give you a good sense of what goes on as various properties are changed and what effects they have on the underlying control. But remember that what we are doing with the Test Container is simulating the use of the control in design mode. The behavior is quite different during run mode. During design mode, much of the state, or appearance, of the control is configured, and during run time, methods and events do much of the real work.

Adding a Stock Event

Now let's add a stock event to the POSTIT control. As we've discussed, a control event provides a way for the control to communicate events such as mouse clicks, internal state changes, and so on to the user of the control. Events are communicated through the container, which normally provides a scripting language that makes it easy to harness these events for useful purposes.

Adding events is as easy as adding a method or property. Invoke ClassWizard and choose the **OLE Events** tab. Now click **Add Event** and choose the **Click** stock event. Click the **OK** button, and ClassWizard will add an entry to our dispatch map and our control's ODL file to indicate that we support the Click event. Figure 8.15 shows the Add Event dialog box.

The stock events, with the exception of the Error event, are automatically fired by MFC. By clicking a few buttons we have added an event that will fire each time the user clicks the mouse anywhere within the control. Here's the code added to **POSTITCTL.CPP** and the definition added to **POSTIT.ODL**.

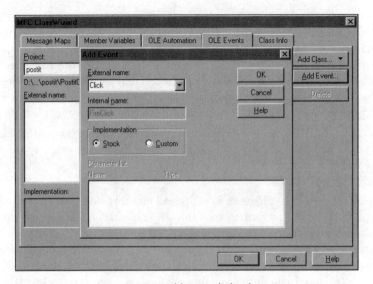

Figure 8.15 Add Event dialog box.

```
// PostitCtl.cpp
...
/////////////////////////////////////////////////////////////////////////
// Event map
BEGIN_EVENT_MAP(CPostitCtrl, COleControl)
    //{{AFX_EVENT_MAP(CPostitCtrl)
    EVENT_STOCK_CLICK()
    //}}AFX_EVENT_MAP
END_EVENT_MAP()

// postit.odl
...
//  Event dispatch interface for CPostitCtrl
[ uuid(BBF8B098-BE9E-11CE-A43C-ACE71F16DB7F),
  helpstring("Event interface for Postit Control") ]
  dispinterface _DPostitEvents
  {
      properties:
          //  Event interface has no properties

      methods:
          // NOTE - ClassWizard will maintain event information here.
          //    Use extreme caution when editing this section.
```

```
//{{AFX_ODL_EVENT(CPostitCtrl)
[id(DISPID_CLICK)] void Click();
//}}AFX_ODL_EVENT
};
```

Event maps are very similar to dispatch maps. Event maps define a table of DISPIDs and their associated member functions. The primary difference is how they are used within a control. As we discussed in Chapter 7, the container will retrieve the control's event IDispatch definition and implement it within the container. The control will then use IDispatch::Invoke to fire its events as they occur. This is easy for the control to do, because the DISPIDs are already known.

Adding the Stock Methods

As we covered in Chapter 7, the ActiveX standard provides two stock methods that controls should implement if it's appropriate. The two methods—Refresh and DoClick—really pertain only to visual controls, so you typically won't implement them in nonvisual controls. The Refresh method might be used for certain nonvisual controls, such as a database or data-feed control in which the concept of refreshing is relevant.

It is easy to provide these two methods for your control. Start ClassWizard, go to the **OLE Automation** tab, and click the **Add Method** button. There are two methods present in the External Name field: Refresh and DoClick. Add each of these by clicking **OK**. That's all there is to it. The default implementation for Refresh is to invalidate the control, forcing a redraw. The default implementation of DoClick is to call the OnClick method, which in turn fires the stock Click event. This arrangement is just fine for our simple control. We will test this behavior later using a commercial container.

Adding a Custom Method

To provide a little functionality for our POSTIT control user, we'll add two custom methods. These methods will allow the control user to set a timer within the control that will go off after a predetermined time interval. Control users can employ this behavior any way they choose, and I'll demonstrate a simple use when building an application with the control later.

Start ClassWizard and add a method to CPostitCtl called SetAlarmTime. This method takes one parameter, a short. SetAlarmTime returns a BOOL to report the success or failure of the method call. Next, add another method and call it StopAlarm. This method returns void and takes no parameters. Next, edit **POSTITCTL.CPP** and add the following code to the methods provided by ClassWizard:

```
#define TIMER_ID 100

BOOL CPostitCtrl::SetAlarmTime(short sSeconds)
{
    // TODO: Add your dispatch handler code here
```

```
    // Set the timer, return TRUE on success, FALSE on error
    if ( GetHwnd() )
        return SetTimer( TIMER_ID, sSeconds * 1000, NULL );
    else
        return FALSE;
}

void CPostitCtrl::StopAlarm()
{
    // TODO: Add your dispatch handler code here
    KillTimer( TIMER_ID );
}
```

Our custom methods provide a way for the control user, during run time, to set an alarm that will fire after the indicated number of seconds has elapsed. The `SetAlarmTime` method first checks to ensure that our control has a valid window handle and then calls the `CWnd::SetTimer` method with the number of seconds provided. We multiply this value by 1000, because `SetTimer` expects the time in milliseconds.

The `StopAlarm` method destroys the timer by calling `CWnd::KillTimer`. After setting the timer, the control user may decide to cancel it later. The Windows timer mechanism will post a `WM_TIMER` message after the time period has elapsed. To trap this message, we use ClassWizard to add the `WM_TIMER` message to our message map. Then ClassWizard adds an `OnTimer` method to **POSTITCTL.CPP**, as shown next. I won't go through each step, because you should be familiar with ClassWizard by now.

```
// PostitCtl.cpp
...
void CPostitCtrl::OnTimer(UINT nIDEvent)
{
    // TODO: Add your message handler code here and/or call default
    COleControl::OnTimer(nIDEvent);
}
```

We now need to add an event so that we can notify the control user when the timer fires.

Adding a Custom Event

Custom events provide a way to inform users that something happened within the control. In our case, this event is the expiration of the timer. Adding a custom event is only slightly different from adding a stock event as we did previously. From ClassWizard's **OLE Events** tab, add an event with an external name of **AlarmFired**, and leave the default internal name, **FireAlarmFired**. Include a `long` parameter and call it `nTimerID`. This parameter will report to the user the ID of the timer that expired. This value isn't useful in our case, but if we wanted to let users maintain multiple timers, it would allow users to identify the specific timer that fired. We would need only add another parameter, for a unique timer ID, to both the `SetAlarmTime` and `StopAlarm` methods. I'll leave this as an exercise.

When the control receives the WM_TIMER message, it will fire the event using our internal method: FireAlarmFired. Once we fire the alarm event, we need to kill the timer so that it won't continue to fire. Add the following code to the OnTimer method in **POSTITCTL.CPP**:

```
void CPostitCtrl::OnTimer(UINT nIDEvent)
{
    // TODO: Add your message handler code here and/or call default
    if ( nIDEvent == TIMER_ID )
    {
        FireAlarmFired( nIDEvent );
        // Cancel the alarm
        KillTimer( TIMER_ID );
    }

    COleControl::OnTimer(nIDEvent);
}
```

Serializing the Properties of a Control

When a user places a control on a container and sets the properties so that the control behaves in the expected manner, the settings should persist. The container is responsible for causing the control to persist between design mode and run time, but the control must decide which properties it wants to persist to the container. This process is called *serialization*, and MFC provides the DoPropExchange method for this purpose. Here's the default implementation provided by ClassWizard:

```
/////////////////////////////////////////////////////////////////////////////
// CPostitCtrl::DoPropExchange - Persistence support
void CPostitCtrl::DoPropExchange(CPropExchange* pPX)
{
    ExchangeVersion(pPX, MAKELONG(_wVerMinor, _wVerMajor));
    COleControl::DoPropExchange(pPX);

    // TODO: Call PX_ functions for each persistent custom property.
}
```

The default implementation serializes all the stock properties that you have defined for your control. It is your responsibility to serialize any custom properties that you have added—in our case, the UseAmbients property. Its type is BOOL, so we use the function PX_Bool. The PX* functions are listed in Table 8.5. The first parameter is a pointer to the property exchange object, the second parameter is the name of the property as you would like it stored, and the third parameter is a reference to the property itself. An optional fourth parameter can be used to set the default value for the property. By providing default parameters for the properties, the control will have an initial state when inserted into a container. Complex property types (such as font) require additional parameters, which are shown in Table 8.5. The table does not show the first three parameters, because they are always the same.

```
/////////////////////////////////////////////////////////////////////////////
// CPostitCtrl::DoPropExchange - Persistence support
void CPostitCtrl::DoPropExchange(CPropExchange* pPX)
{
    ExchangeVersion(pPX, MAKELONG(_wVerMinor, _wVerMajor));
    COleControl::DoPropExchange(pPX);

    // TODO: Call PX_ functions for each persistent custom property.
    PX_Bool( pPX, _T("UseAmbients"), m_bUseAmbients, FALSE );
}
```

Table 8.5 DoPropExchange Functions

Function/Type	Purpose
PX_Blob(HGLOBAL&)	Serializes an object in a binary format.
PX_Bool(BOOL&)	Serializes the property as a Boolean.
PX_Color(OLE_COLOR&)	Serializes the property as an OLE_COLOR type.
PX_Currency(CY&)	Serializes the property as a currency data type.
PX_Double(double&)	Serializes the property as type double.
PX_Font(CFontHolder&, const FONTDESC FAR*, LPFONTDISP)	Serializes the property as a font. This function takes a few more parameters than the others.
PX_Float(float&)	Serializes the property as a float.
PX_IUnknown (LPUNKNOWN&, REFIID)	Serializes the IUnknown pointer.
PX_Long(long&)	Serializes the property as type long.
PX_ULong(ULONG&)	Serializes the property as type unsigned long.
PX_Picture (CPictureHolder&)	Serializes a picture property.
PX_Short(short&)	Serializes the property as type short.
PX_UShort(USHORT&)	Serializes the property as type unsigned short.
PX_String(CString&)	Serializes the property as type CString.

When the container serializes its contents, it calls each control and asks it for its property information. The container then uses its own technique of serializing the property information, usually in some form of file. Visual Basic serializes property information in a textual format that is easy to understand, so the following listing shows our control after it has been serialized within a Visual Basic form. This example illustrates only *property-set* persistence and not the more elaborate *binary* persistence that can be used by a control.

```
Begin PostitLib.Postit Postit1
      Height          =   3135
      Left            =   480
      TabIndex        =   0
      Top             =   240
      Width           =   2895
      _version        =   65536
      _extentx        =   5106
      _extenty        =   5530
      _stockprops     =   125
      text            =   "Meet Nicole for lunch at 11:30 at Fiddler's."
      forecolor       =   255
      backcolor       =   65535
      BeginProperty font {FB8F0823-0164-101B-84ED-08002B2EC713}
         name          =     "Monotype Corsiva"
         charset       =   0
         weight        =   400
         size          =   12
         underline     =   0    'False
         italic        =   -1   'True
         strikethrough =   0    'False
      EndProperty
      borderstyle     =   -1
      useambients     =   0    'False
End
```

We can learn a little about what the container is doing by inspecting its serialization file. You might notice that not all of our properties are listed, in particular the `Enabled` property. If a property's value is the same as its default value, as specified in the `DoPropertyExchange` `PX_` functions, there is no need to store the property value. When the container loads a control, it first sets the control's property values to the defaults provided in `DoPropertyExchange`. It then loads the properties from persistent storage, which overlays only those property values that differ from their default values. This arrangement saves space in the persistent file.

Testing the Final Control in a Real Container

One important aspect of developing ActiveX controls is that you should strive to make them work in all available containers. Because the ActiveX control standard is open and leaves certain aspects of its implementation up to the implementor, there will be differences in the containers provided by various tool vendors. One thing is certain: there will be many products that will support ActiveX controls. As I write this, many vendors have stated publicly that their tools will support ActiveX controls. For commercial control developers, this is wonderful news. The more containers that support ActiveX controls, the more customers there are for useful and unique controls. But the one container that will set the standard for the others is Visual Basic. Why? Visual Basic has a very large installed base and so immediately (via upgrades) will become the most ubiquitous, and standard-setting, container.

What I'm getting at is this: to really test your controls, you should test them in as many containers as you can. Containers typically exist within the context of a development tool. Each tool has different goals, so it is important to test in these divergent environments. The controls in this book have been tested with the Test Container, Visual Basic 4.0, Visual C++ 4.2, and Internet Explorer 3.0.

Figure 8.16 shows our POSTIT control within a Visual Basic 4.0 form. As you can see, from the properties window, Visual Basic has added several new properties to our control. Most containers will provide additional properties in this manner using the extended control method that was described in Chapter 7. Many control properties can be managed only by the container (via an extended control). Only the container knows the position of the control within the container, so it adds the `Top`, `Left`, `Height`, and `Width` properties. It also adds other properties that it can easily manage, such as `Visible`, `TabStop`, and `Index`. The `Index` property is used for control arrays, which provide dynamic creation of controls at run time. The container, again, is best equipped to handle this situation.

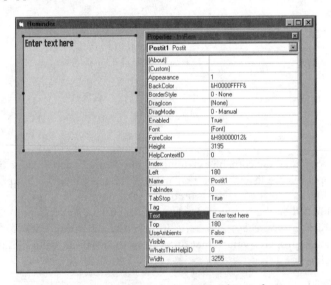

Figure 8.16 POSTIT control in a Visual Basic form.

One thing that the Test Container lacks is a robust way to test our control's methods and events. So we'll develop a simple Visual Basic program to exercise the control. I expect the scripting syntax and techniques to be fairly similar among various control container tools. So although the code here is specific to Visual Basic, it should easily translate to other control environments.

Our simple application is composed of two forms (containers) and a few ActiveX controls. It provides a means to set up an event that will act as a reminder. When the event occurs, a dialog box will pop up and inform the user with the reminder. I won't go through the steps needed to build the application. You can run it yourself with either Visual Basic 4.0 or a 32-bit version of DISPTEST. I'll just show you the two forms and the seven lines of code that tie everything together. The two forms are shown in Figure 8.17.

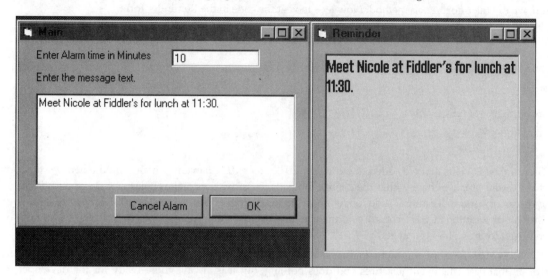

Figure 8.17 Visual Basic application.

When the application runs, the Main form is shown. The user enters the text for the reminder along with the number of minutes. Then the user clicks **OK** and the following code executes:

```
Private Sub cmdOK_Click()
    'Extract the alarm time and multiply by 60
    'to get the number of seconds
    nAlarm = txtTime * 60
    'Call the SetAlarmTime method.
    frmRem.Postit1.SetAlarmTime nAlarm
    'Set the text in postit control on the Reminder form
    frmRem.Postit1.Text = txtText
    'Hide the Reminder form
    frmRem.Hide
End Sub

Private Sub cmdCancel_Click()
    'Stop the timer
    frmRem.Postit1.StopAlarm
End Sub
```

The code is pretty self-explanatory. We call our POSTIT custom method, `SetAlarmTime`, with the number of seconds and also set the stock `Text` property with the text that the user entered. We then ensure that the Reminder form is hidden from view. This code sets everything up. If the user clicks the **Cancel Alarm** button, we call the `StopAlarm` method. Now let's look at the code in the Reminder form.

```
Private Sub Postit1_AlarmFired(ByVal lAlarmID As Long)
    'The alarm fired, make sure the Reminder form is visible
    frmRem.Show
End Sub

Private Sub Postit1_Click()
    Unload Me
End Sub
```

There are two events that we added to our control. The stock `Click` event, which is fired whenever the user clicks the mouse anywhere within the control, unloads the form. This makes it easy for the application user to discard the reminder after it is no longer needed. Our custom event, `AlarmFired`, displays the Reminder form along with the POSTIT control and the contained text of the reminder. Not bad for just seven lines of code (not counting the comments).

The visual developer doesn't usually use many of the methods and events that are provided by the control. In that case, the event just fires and does nothing, but it is always there ready for the developer to employ if needed.

This isn't the most robust or useful application, but remember its purpose is purely didactic. The important thing is that we have tied a few different components together with the Visual Basic language. Most of the work is performed in each control. Visual Basic is just the glue, wiring, or breadboard—however you want to think about it—that ties these discrete components together.

We could easily have developed this simple little application with Visual Basic's label and timer controls instead of our POSTIT control, but we wouldn't have learned anything.

Adding Component Category Support

As we discussed in Chapter 7, the OLE Control 96 specification requires that controls provide component category support in their implementation. Our control doesn't have any special requirements, and it is rather simple to add component category support. **POSTITCTL.CPP** currently does the following when the `DllRegisterServer` function is called:

```
///////////////////////////////////////////////////
// CPostitCtrl::CPostitCtrlFactory::UpdateRegistry -
// Adds or removes system registry entries for CPostitCtrl
///////////////////////////////////////////////////
BOOL CPostitCtrl::CPostitCtrlFactory::UpdateRegistry(BOOL bRegister)
{
```

```
...
   if (bRegister)
      return AfxOleRegisterControlClass(
         AfxGetInstanceHandle(),
            m_clsid,
            m_lpszProgID,
            IDS_POSTIT,
            IDB_POSTIT,
            afxRegInsertable | afxRegApartmentThreading,
            _dwPostitOleMisc,
            _tlid,
            _wVerMajor,
            _wVerMinor);
   else
      return AfxOleUnregisterClass(m_clsid, m_lpszProgID);
}
```

As the comments indicate, `AfxOleRegisterControlClass` updates the system registry with all the control-specific information. These entries, such as `Control`, `TypeLib`, and `InProcServer32`, were described in Chapter 7. COM-based servers must also provide a function to remove a server's Registry entries. MFC maps our control's `DllUnregisterServer` call to the preceding function, which then calls `AfxOleUnregisterClass` to remove the entries. Everything works as planned. Now, however, we need to also provide component category support. Add the following code to **POSTITCTL.CPP**:

```
// PostitCtl.cpp
...
#include <comcat.h>
...
HRESULT CreateComponentCategory( CATID catid, WCHAR* catDescription )
{
   ICatRegister* pcr = NULL ;
   HRESULT hr = S_OK ;

   // Create an instance of the category manager.
   hr = CoCreateInstance( CLSID_StdComponentCategoriesMgr,
                          NULL,
                          CLSCTX_INPROC_SERVER,
                          IID_ICatRegister,
                          (void**)&pcr );
   if (FAILED(hr))
      return hr;
```

```
  CATEGORYINFO catinfo;
  catinfo.catid = catid;
  // English locale ID in hex
  catinfo.lcid = 0x0409;

  int len = wcslen(catDescription);
  wcsncpy( catinfo.szDescription, catDescription, len );
  catinfo.szDescription[len] = '\0';

  hr = pcr->RegisterCategories( 1, &catinfo );
  pcr->Release();

  return hr;
}
```

This code, from Chapter 7, takes a category ID and a description and makes sure the entry exists in the "Component Categories" section of the Registry. We need to make sure that the entry is there before we flag our control. Once we ensure that the category exists, we update our control's Registry entries with the "Implemented Categories" keys. Here's some general code to do this:

```
HRESULT RegisterCLSIDInCategory( REFCLSID clsid, CATID catid )
{
  ICatRegister* pcr = NULL ;
  HRESULT hr = S_OK ;

  // Create an instance of the category manager.
  hr = CoCreateInstance( CLSID_StdComponentCategoriesMgr,
                         NULL,
                         CLSCTX_INPROC_SERVER,
                         IID_ICatRegister,
                         (void**)&pcr );
  if (SUCCEEDED(hr))
  {
     CATID rgcatid[1];
     rgcatid[0] = catid;
     hr = pcr->RegisterClassImplCategories( clsid, 1, rgcatid );
  }

  if ( pcr != NULL )
     pcr->Release();

  return hr;
}

HRESULT UnregisterCLSIDInCategory( REFCLSID clsid, CATID catid )
{
```

```
    ICatRegister* pcr = NULL ;
    HRESULT hr = S_OK ;

    // Create an instance of the category manager.
    hr = CoCreateInstance( CLSID_StdComponentCategoriesMgr,
                           NULL,
                           CLSCTX_INPROC_SERVER,
                           IID_ICatRegister,
                           (void**)&pcr );
    if (SUCCEEDED(hr))
    {
        CATID rgcatid[1];
        rgcatid[0] = catid;
        hr = pcr->UnRegisterClassImplCategories( clsid, 1, rgcatid );
    }

    if ( pcr != NULL )
        pcr->Release();

    return hr;
}
```

Both of the preceding functions take a CLSID and a CATID and update the associated Registry entries. In one case the entries are added, and in the other the entries are removed. All this is easy, because the component category manager does most of the work. After we add these three support functions, the code additions for UpdateRegistry are straightforward:

```
/////////////////////////////////////////////////////////////
// CPostitCtrl::CPostitCtrlFactory::UpdateRegistry -
// Adds or removes system registry entries for CPostitCtrl
/////////////////////////////////////////////////////////////
BOOL CPostitCtrl::CPostitCtrlFactory::UpdateRegistry(BOOL bRegister)
{
    if (bRegister)
    {
        CreateComponentCategory( CATID_Control,
                                 L"Controls" );
        RegisterCLSIDInCategory( m_clsid,
                                 CATID_Control );
        return AfxOleRegisterControlClass(
            AfxGetInstanceHandle(),
            m_clsid,
            m_lpszProgID,
            IDS_POSTIT,
```

```
                IDB_POSTIT,

                afxRegInsertable | afxRegApartmentThreading,

                _dwPostitOleMisc,

                _tlid,

                _wVerMajor,

                _wVerMinor);


        }

    else

    {

    UnregisterCLSIDInCategory( m_clsid,

                                CATID_Control );

    return AfxOleUnregisterClass(m_clsid, m_lpszProgID);

    }

}
```

After we link and register the control, the new "Implemented Categories" entry will be placed in the Registry. Figure 8.18 shows the Registry entries for our POSTIT control.

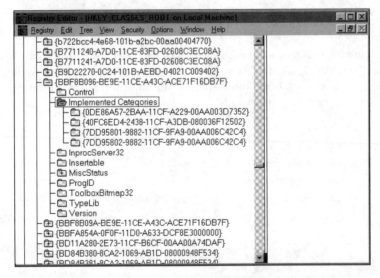

Figure 8.18 Component categories for our control.

The control has three other component categories registered. These categories make it easier to embed the control in Internet Explorer. We'll cover this in more detail in Chapter 12. For now, here's the additional code to support Internet Explorer:

```
#include <objsafe.h>

...

// Add to UpdateRegistry function
```

```
CreateComponentCategory( CATID_SafeForInitializing,
                         L"Controls safely initializable from persistent data" );
RegisterCLSIDInCategory( m_clsid,
                         CATID_SafeForInitializing );
CreateComponentCategory( CATID_SafeForScripting,
                         L"Controls that are safely scriptable" );
RegisterCLSIDInCategory( m_clsid,
                         CATID_SafeForScripting );
CreateComponentCategory( CATID_PersistsToPropertyBag,
                         L"Support initialize via PersistPropertyBag" );
RegisterCLSIDInCategory( m_clsid,
                         CATID_PersistsToPropertyBag );
```

NOTE The component category symbols and **.LIB** files are part of the ActiveX SDK. If you're using Visual C++ 4.x, you will need to install the ActiveX SDK to compile and link the examples. If you don't install the SDK, you can just remove the references to **COMCAT.H**. However, by the time you read this, the later versions of Visual C++ (5.x) will have intrinsic support for component categories. Check out my Web site for the most recent examples and details on newer versions of Visual C++.

Debugging the Control

Visual C++ makes it fairly easy to debug DLL applications. To step through the code for the POSTIT control, we need only set a break-point on the lines we want to debug and press **F5**. This action brings up a dialog box. In **Executable for Debug Session**, enter the path and filename for the Test Container (or any other container). On my machine, it would be **c:\msdev\bin\tstcon32.exe**. After clicking **OK**, you will get a dialog box complaining that **TSTCON32.EXE** doesn't contain any debug information and asking whether it's OK to continue. It is. This will bring up the Test Container. You can then insert your control into the container, and you will eventually break on your break-points.

If you make a mistake typing in the debug executable filename, you can access it from the **Build/Settings/Debug** tab. The first entry field, **Executable for debug session**, contains the path to the executable.

Summary

We've covered a lot of material in this chapter, so let's summarize the topics. Visual C++ and MFC include a number of classes and tools to help in the creation of ActiveX controls. Visual C++ includes a code generation tool called ControlWizard that is similar to AppWizard. ControlWizard builds an ActiveX control project based on answers you supply to various questions. ControlWizard generates the initial control code, and ClassWizard is used thereafter to make additional changes.

A few MFC classes are used exclusively for ActiveX control development. `COleControlModule` provides the application-level class for a control's DLL implementation. This class provides the COM-specific external functions, `DllRegisterServer` and `DllUnregisterServer`. MFC also provides an additional COM-based interface, `IClassFactory2`, that provides component licensing methods. This interface is implemented within MFC with the `COleClassFactoryEx` class and provides a default licensing model for controls.

The `COleControl` class is derived from `CWnd` and contains hundreds of methods. It provides the bulk of the ActiveX control functionality. One of the most important methods in `COleControl` is `OnDraw`, which is called by the container whenever the control requires rendering within its site. Many of the control development details are handled in `OnDraw`. Other important `COleControl` methods include `SetInitialSize`, `OnAmbientPropertyChange`, and `DoDataExchange`.

The ActiveX control standard defines stock properties and methods that control developers should use if appropriate for the control's implementation. We added all of them to our control and explored each one. Font properties require the use of MFC's `CFontHolder` class. This class provides methods to manage OLE's font manipulation interfaces, which allow efficient management of fonts between COM-based components.

ActiveX controls depend on the services of another COM-based component, the property page. Property pages provide a uniform interface to the control's custom and stock properties. Each property page is a distinct component that is used by both the container and the control. The container loads the property pages for a control and frames them within a property sheet. When a user modifies a control's property, the property page, using automation, modifies the property within the control.

Ambient properties are read-only properties exposed by the container. They provide information about the container's environment to the control. There are ambient properties for the container's visual state, such as `Color` and `Font`, as well as ambients that indicate the current mode of the container. These latter properties indicate whether the container is currently in design phase, run mode, or debug mode. This state is important to the control, because its behavior changes depending on the container's state.

Methods and events allow the control user to use the control's functionality as well as to be notified of changes that occur within the control. This two-way communication is an important attribute of controls. The ActiveX control standard defines several standard events, and the stock implementations of these events are provided by the MFC.

Serialization of a control's properties enables the container to maintain the state of a control between the design phase and the running phase. Serialization also provides a way for the control to recognize previous versions of itself and to adjust the loading of properties accordingly. The container is responsible for the representation of the control's property information (when you're using property-set persistence) and ensures that it will be provided to the control in a uniform way.

Controls are COM-based in-process servers and must be added to the system Registry before being used. Visual C++ has a menu item, Register Control, that performs this task. You should also register your control using the new Component Categories specified by the OLE Controls 96 specification. MFC doesn't currently provide this registration by default, but it is easy to do using the provided component categories manager component.

Testing of controls is performed with either the Test Container or with any commercially available container (such as Visual Basic or Internet Explorer). The debugging of controls is similar to debugging other COM-based in-process servers.

Chapter 9

Graphical Controls

In this chapter, we'll concentrate on controls that display information. Most ActiveX controls have a graphical element. We'll focus on what is required to produce a control that draws efficiently and provides a useful representation in the various environments it may encounter. We will also review the MFC classes and techniques that we will use when drawing the ActiveX control.

A Clock Control

Our example control for this chapter is a clock. I know there are hundreds of clock variations available for Windows, but by implementing a clock we'll learn how to effectively draw ActiveX controls. Figure 9.1 shows the completed clock control within a container.

Figure 9.1 The clock control.

We'll use ControlWizard to create the project. We discussed how to use ControlWizard in Chapter 8, so we won't spend much time on it here. Start Visual C++ and use ControlWizard to build a control project with the name CLOCK. Choose the following options:

- In the Step 1 of 2 dialog box, take the defaults of **No License**, **Yes, comments**, and **No help files**.
- In Step 2 of 2, take the defaults.

Click **Finish** and create the control. After the project is created, use ClassWizard to add the following stock properties through the **OLE Automation** tab:

- Appearance
- BackColor
- ForeColor
- Hwnd
- BorderStyle

- Enabled
- Font

Our clock doesn't have a caption or any text, so you might wonder why we need the Font property. You'll see in a moment. We will use it to draw the control's ambient display name during the container's design phase.

MFC's Drawing Classes

Before we jump into the drawing code, let's review some of the techniques used to draw graphics in the Windows operating system. We touched on this in Chapter 8, and I'd like to expound on it a little more before we go further. We'll explore drawing by looking at the classes within MFC that encapsulate the Windows graphical drawing API functions.

The CDC Class

Displaying information within the Windows environment requires the use of the graphical device interface (GDI) functions. GDI provides a device-independent interface to manipulate the devices (such as your video card, monitor, and printer) connected to your computer. Manufacturers provide device drivers for their particular hardware, and we developers use the Windows GDI API to manipulate these devices.

Most of the GDI functions work with or need a *device context* (DC), which provides the connection between your program and the device the DC represents. A device context is usually an area on the screen or printer but may also represent a memory construct called a *metafile*, which we will discuss in a moment. A device context maintains a set of attributes that affect the behavior of the various GDI functions on the DC. Example DC attributes include its default brush, pen, font, background color, and text drawing modes.

The MFC CDC class encapsulates a Windows device context and provides methods to manipulate it. Most of the method names are identical to those of the Windows GDI API, so if you have worked with them before, there shouldn't be much to learn. As we saw in Chapter 8, the COleControl::OnDraw method receives a CDC pointer in which to render the control.

The majority of the methods in the CDC class are for modifying the attributes of a device context or for actually drawing *on* the device context. We can't cover them all, but we'll cover some of the important ones that you will use when drawing your controls. Table 9.1 lists some of the useful members of the CDC class. To get a quick listing of them all from within Visual C++, position the cursor on the text **CDC** and press **F1**.

Table 9.1 Useful CDC Methods

Method	Purpose
FillRect(CRect , CBrush*)	Fills the area indicated by the CRect parameter with the brush provided.
Ellipse(LPRECT)	Draws an ellipse in the rectangle provided. The default pen, fill mode, and brush are used.
Rectangle(CRect)	Draws a rectangle with the default pen, fill mode, and brush.
MoveTo(POINT)	Moves to the point provided.
LineTo(POINT)	Draws a line from the current position to the point provided using the default pen.
SelectObject(CBrush*), SelectObject(CPen*), SelectObject(CFont*)	Selects the GDI object into the device context and returns a pointer to the previously selected object. This object should be selected back into the DC when you're finished.
SelectStockObject(int) WHITE_BRUSH, BLACK_PEN, SYSTEM_FONT, and so on.	Selects a system-provided GDI object into the device context. Examples include:
SetBkColor(COLORREF)	Sets the background color of the device context.
SetBkMode(int)	Sets the background fill behavior.
SetTextColor(COLORREF)	Sets the color of the text for the device context.
TextOut(...), ExtTextOut(...), DrawText(...)	Draws text on the device context
SetTextAlign(UINT)	Sets the default alignment for text output.
CreateCompatibleDC(CDC*)	Creates a memory DC with the characteristics of the DC provided.
SaveDC()	Saves the state of the device context. This includes all the attributes of the DC (brushes, pens, and so on). The method returns an integer identifying the saved DC. This value is later passed to the RestoreDC method.
RestoreDC(int)	Restores that state of a device context previously saved with the SaveDC method. An integer identifying the saved DC is required.
SetMappingMode(int)	Sets the mapping mode for the device context.
GetDeviceCaps(int)	Returns various characteristics of the DC. An example is the logical size of a device unit or pixel.

The DC provided to the OnDraw method is set up by the container, and we cannot make any assumptions about its current attribute set. We must ensure that the DC is set up the way we need it to draw our control. Here are some example CDC methods as they might be used in your control's OnDraw method:

```
pdc->SetBkMode( TRANSPARENT );
pdc->SetTextColor( TranslateColor( AmbientForeColor() ) );
CBrush bkBrush( TranslateColor( GetBackColor() ) );
```

```
CBrush* pOldBrush = (CBrush*) pdc->SelectObject( &bkBrush );
CPen*   pOldPen   = (CPen*)   pdc->SelectStockObject( BLACK_PEN );
pdc->SetTextAlign(TA_CENTER | TA_TOP);

pdc->Ellipse( LPCRECT( rcBounds ));
pdc->ExtTextOut( rcBounds.left, rcBounds.top, ETO_CLIPPED, rcBounds,
                 strCaption, strCaption.GetLength(), NULL );

SelectObject( pOldBrush );
SelectObject( pOldPen );
```

The first five methods set up attributes of the device context. We set the background mode to TRANSPARENT, which indicates that the background will not be redrawn the next time that we use a drawing function. We then set the default text color for drawing text. An instance of a CBrush object is created and initialized to the stock background color. The COleControl::TranslateColor method is used to convert a color value from the OLE_COLOR type to the COLORREF type expected by the CDC method. We then use SelectObject to select the new brush into the device context. We save the old brush so that we can restore it later.

The GDI provides a number of stock objects that are available for the developer to use. The SelectStockObject method selects a system-provided GDI object into the device context. A BLACK_PEN and the control's BackColor property will be used when we use the drawing functions. Next, we set the alignment method for text drawing using SetTextAlign. These five methods modify the DC and provide the default behavior for the drawing methods.

The Ellipse method draws a bounding ellipse inside the rectangle provided. When it draws the ellipse, the device context's attributes are used. ExtTextOut also uses the attributes of the DC when drawing the text. By setting the attributes in the DC, we need not provide a bunch of parameters to the various drawing functions that we use, because they are maintained within the DC itself.

When we're finished drawing, we restore the DC's brush and pen to what they were before we started. We do this because the bkBrush instance was created on the stack and so will go out of scope when the function exits. If we do not select the old brush back into the DC, the DC will be left using an invalid GDI object.

Some of the GDI functions that modify a DC's attributes require the creation of a GDI object to provide as a parameter. When you create the object, it is important to restore the old object and to delete the GDI object when you're finished using it. The C++ language makes it easy to handle this situation. When creating a new GDI object (such as brush, pen, or font), you should create it using the stack as we did in the preceding example for the bkBrush object. When the instance is created on the stack, the compiler will ensure that it is cleaned up when it goes out of scope. The destructor is called, and the GDI object is deleted. Each of MFC's GDI object classes behaves this way.

Creation and destruction of drawing objects every time a control draws can be very expensive. The OLE Control 94 specification, however, required the control to maintain, and thus reset, the state of the device context provided by the container. This meant that the control had to restore the DC to its original state after each call to OnDraw. The OLE Controls 96 specification allows the control and container to coordinate their efforts when drawing. If they both support optimized drawing, the control need not reset the DC every time.

This arrangement makes the drawing process more efficient. When we initially built the clock project, we checked the **Optimize drawing** option. We'll make use of this option later in this chapter.

The CBrush Class

The CBrush class provides methods for creating, destroying, and using a Windows GDI brush object. Brushes are used to fill regions with a particular color. Each device context has a default brush that is used to fill the background when using various GDI functions (or CDC methods).

```
// Create a brush on the stack and initialize it
// to the control's current background color
// When bkBrush goes out of scope its destructor will
// free the GDI resource
CBrush bkBrush( TranslateColor( GetBackColor() ) );

// Create a bright red brush from the heap
// You must delete the brush to free up its resources
CBrush* pBrush = new CBrush( RGB( 0xFF, 0x00, 0x00 ) );
// Use the brush...
delete pBrush;

// Create a blue hatched brush
CBrush hatchedBrush( HS_CROSS, RGB( 0x00, 0x00, 0xFF );
```

In the preceding examples, we used the RGB macro to provide the CBrush constructor with a specific color. The RGB macro constructs a Windows COLORREF value by combining the three parameters. Each parameter specifies the intensity of each specific color—red, green, or blue—in the resulting combined color. Following are example colors that you can produce with the macro. If the device context in which you are selecting the color does not support the particular hue, it will do its best to match the color using a dithering algorithm.

```
RGB( 0x00, 0x00, 0x00 )   // Black
RGB( 0xFF, 0xFF, 0xFF )   // White
RGB( 0xFF, 0x00, 0x00 )   // Red
RGB( 0xC0, 0xC0, 0xC0 )   // Light Gray
RGB( 0xFF, 0xFF, 0 )      // Yellow
```

The CPen Class

The CPen class encapsulates a GDI pen object and provides a convenient method of selecting pens for use within a device context. Pens can be solid, dashed, dot, or even null. Solid pens also support a parameter that allows the pen to be sized. The size is specified in pixels. Here are some example uses of CPen:

```
// Create a solid blue pen 2 pixels wide
CPen penBlue( PS_SOLID, 2, RGB( 0x00, 0x00, 0xFF ) );

// Create a dashed black pen 1 pixel wide
CPen pen;
pen.CreatePen( PS_DASHED, 1, RGB( 0xFF, 0xFF, 0xFF ) );

// Create a Null pen
CPen penNULL( PS_NULL, 1, 0 )
```

The pen and brush objects provide a null implementation. You can select a null brush into a device context to ensure that the bounding area of a CDC method will be treated as TRANSPARENT. A null pen can be selected into a device context so that no border will be drawn when using the various CDC methods (such as Ellipse).

The CFont Class

The CFont class encapsulates a Windows font object. The constructor creates an uninitialized font object that must then be initialized using either the CreateFont or the CreateFontIndirect method. We haven't encountered the need to create a font for our controls to use—we've been using the stock font property—but we have used the CFont class to create a pointer to save the old font when we select our stock font into the DC.

```
// Select the stock font and save the old one
CFont* pOldFont = SelectStockFont( pdc );

// Set up the text drawing modes in the DC
pdc->SetBkMode( TRANSPARENT );
pdc->SetTextAlign( TA_LEFT | TA_TOP );

// Do something with the font
// Draw the text in the upper left corner
pdc->ExtTextOut( rcBounds.left, rcBounds.top, ETO_CLIPPED,
                 rcBounds, strName, strName.GetLength(), NULL );

// Restore the old font
if ( pOldFont )
    pdc->SelectObject( pOldFont );
```

The CBitmap Class

The CBitmap class is similar to the CFont class in that its constructor creates an uninitialized bitmap object that must be initialized later using one of various class methods. LoadBitmap loads a bitmap from an application's resource file. LoadOEMBitmap loads one of the standard, Windows-provided bitmaps, which include checkboxes, arrows, checks, and so on. The method of interest in this chapter is CreateCompatibleBitmap. We will use this method later when we create an off-screen DC to remove flicker from our clock control.

Drawing the Clock

Our clock uses an analog representation, so we initially need to draw a circle to outline the clock's face. This is easy. We just use the CDC:Ellipse method. The following code creates a brush using the stock background color and selects it into the DC. It then creates a solid black pen and selects it into the DC. We then fill the bounding rectangle with the background color and draw the ellipse using the coordinates of the bounding rectangle.

```
CBrush bkBrush( TranslateColor( GetBackColor() ) );
CBrush* pOldBrush = pdc->SelectObject( &bkBrush );

int iPenWidth = 1;
CPen penBlack( PS_SOLID, iPenWidth, RGB( 0x00, 0x00, 0x00 ));
CPen* pOldPen = pdc->SelectObject( &penBlack );

pdc->FillRect( rcBounds, &bkBrush );
pdc->Ellipse( LPCRECT( rcBounds ));
```

The sections that follow describe the process of drawing the clock. Each section has a snippet of code to illustrate the concepts. At the end, I'll present the complete source for the OnDraw method. So if you're typing along, go ahead and add the source that is highlighted, but wait until later to add the source for OnDraw.

We want our clock to be round, so we set its initial size to 200 by 200 pixels in the control's constructor. Later we will add code to ensure that our clock's bounding rectangle is always square.

```
CClockCtrl::CClockCtrl()
{
    InitializeIIDs(&IID_DClock, &IID_DClockEvents);

    // TODO: Initialize your control's instance data here.
    SetInitialSize( 200, 200 );
}
```

Next we need to draw tick marks for the minutes (or seconds) and the hours. This is a little more complicated, and we need to use a little trigonometry.

Drawing the Tick Marks or Calculating the Tick Mark Points

We need to draw tick marks for the second as well as the hour positions on the clock. The hour ticks will be slightly larger than the seconds' ticks. We won't spend much time on the algorithms that we're using to draw the clock. I'll provide a quick overview and an illustration so that you can delve into it if you want to. Figure 9.2 shows a diagram of our control. The outer circle outlines the face of the clock. The inner circle shows how we will calculate and draw the tick marks. By drawing a line connecting the two circles, we will create a "tick." The trick, then, is to calculate the points on the two circles and then connect them.

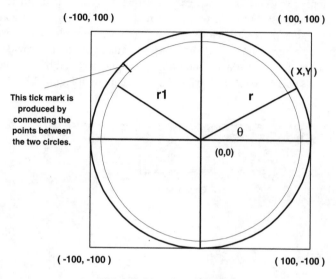

Figure 9.2 Drawing the clock.

To get the points on both circles, we use the cosine and sine functions provided in **MATH.H**. The cos and sin functions take an angle in radians as their parameter, and we all remember that 2π radians equals a full circle (right!). **MATH.H** doesn't provide a symbol for π, so we need the following #defines for our calculations.

```
#define PI 3.141592654
#define START_ANGLE (.5 * PI)
```

Pi to nine digits is just fine. START_ANGLE equates to $\pi/2$ radians (90 degrees), which is the 12:00 position on our clock. We store the tick points in an array, and by starting our calculations at $\pi/2$ radians, we ensure that our array's zero index value will be at the 12:00 position. In other words, array position 10 is equal to 10 minutes after the hour, and so on. To calculate the point on the circle, we use the usual trig functions. The equations are shown next, first in their mathematical form and then in C++ (@ = theta).

```
// to get the x coordinate
cosine@ = x / r or x = cosine@ * r
x = cos( angle ) * r

// To get the y coordinate
sine@ = y / r OR y = sine@ * r
y = sin( angle ) * r
```

rcBounds Upper Left Isn't at (0, 0)

Our calculations are a little more complicated than this, because the `rcBounds` parameter provided to `OnDraw` by the container need not, and probably will not, provide the upper left coordinates as (0,0). If you assume otherwise, you'll probably end up drawing in the container's client area, outside the control's rectangle. For performance reasons, most containers will not provide a clipping region for your control. A clipping region provided by the container would ensure that, even if your control tried to draw outside the container's boundaries, the clipping region would clip it. Most containers do not provide clipping regions, so you need to be careful not to draw outside the bounding rectangle provided by the container. This relationship between the container's client area and the control's site is shown in Figure 9.3.

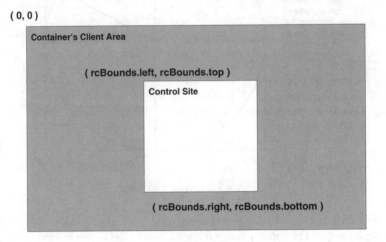

Figure 9.3 Container and control coordinates.

Drawing the Clock Hands

Drawing the hands for our clock is easy once we understand how to draw the ticks. We again use an imaginary circle that is inscribed within the outer circle. The length of each hand is determined by the radius of the smaller circle. The hour hand will be one-half the size of the outer circle, so we divide the outer circle radius by 2. The minute and second hands are the same length and are slightly smaller than the circle used to draw the hour tick marks. Although the minute and second hands are the same length, we will draw them with different thicknesses.

To make drawing the hands fast, we will maintain an array of points within our control class. This array is calculated along with the tick marks array. In our initial implementation, we calculate these points every time we draw the control. This requirement is very expensive, but we will eliminate it in a moment.

Here's the code that handles the ticks and the size and placement of our clock's hands. This code calculates all possible tick and hand positions and stores them in an array. OnDraw then uses the calculated point arrays later to do the drawing. This technique makes the drawing code fairly easy to understand.

```cpp
// ClockCtl.CPP - : Implementation of the CClockCtrl OLE control class.

#include "stdafx.h"
#include "Clock.h"
#include "ClockCtl.h"
#include "ClockPpg.h"

#include <math.h>

#ifdef _DEBUG
...

#define PI 3.141592654
#define START_ANGLE (.5 * PI)
void CClockCtrl::CalcTicksAndHands( CDC *pdc, const CRect& rcBounds )
{
    int nRadius = rcBounds.Width() / 2;
    double r2x, r2y, r1x, r1y;

    // Calculate the size of the hour and
    // minute tick marks. We use a simple
    // scaling method to determine the sizes.
    short sHourTickLen = rcBounds.Width() / 20 + 2;
    short sMinuteTickLen = rcBounds.Width() / 40 + 1;

    // Calculate the minute and second hand arrays
    double angle = START_ANGLE;

    // The inscribing circle must be slightly smaller than the HourTick
    // circle so that we won't "hit" it. We subtract an additional 2 pixels
    // to ensure this.
    // The radius of the circle for the minute and second hand coordinates
    int r2 = nRadius - sHourTickLen - 2;

    // Work ourselves around the circle in 60 unit increments
    // The radian angle changes within the loop
    // r3 is the size of the hour hand. Half the radius
    int r3 = nRadius / 2;
    for ( int i = 0; i < 60; i++ )
    {
        r2x = cos( angle ) * r2 + rcBounds.left;
```

```
    // The direction of the Y axis is reversed
     // when using the MM_TEXT mapping mode. The Y
    // axis increases as you move DOWN instead of up.
    // We reverse the direction by negating the sin
    r2y = -sin( angle ) * r2 + rcBounds.top;
    m_MinSecHands[i].x = short( r2x );
    m_MinSecHands[i].y = short( r2y );

    // Calculate size of hour hand
    r2x = cos( angle ) * r3 + rcBounds.left;
    r2y = -sin( angle ) * r3 + rcBounds.top;

    // Store the hour ticks in an array
    m_HourHands[i].x = short( r2x );
    m_HourHands[i].y = short( r2y );

    angle -= (2 * PI) / 60;
}

// Calculate the tick arrays
// Calculate the small ticks for each minute
angle = START_ANGLE;
r2 = nRadius - sMinuteTickLen;
int r1 = nRadius;
for ( i = 0; i < 60; i++ )
{
    r1x = cos( angle ) * r1 + rcBounds.left;
    r1y = -sin( angle ) * r1 + rcBounds.top;
    r2x = cos( angle ) * r2 +  rcBounds.left;
    r2y = -sin( angle ) * r2 + rcBounds.top;

    // Each tick is composed of two points
    // store them in a 2x60 array of points
    m_MinuteTicks[0][i].x = short( r1x );
    m_MinuteTicks[0][i].y = short( r1y );
    m_MinuteTicks[1][i].x = short( r2x );
    m_MinuteTicks[1][i].y = short( r2y );

    // Get the next radian angle
    angle -= (2 * PI) / 60;
}

// Calculate the hour ticks
```

```
angle = START_ANGLE;
r2 = nRadius - sHourTickLen;
for ( i = 0; i < 12; i++ )
{
    // Get the point on the outer circle
    r1x = cos( angle ) * r1 + rcBounds.left;
    r1y = -sin( angle ) * r1 + rcBounds.top;
    // Get the point on the inner (smaller) circle
    r2x = cos( angle ) * r2 + rcBounds.left;
    r2y = -sin( angle ) * r2 + rcBounds.top;

    // Each tick is composed of two points
    // store them in a 2x12 array of points
    m_HourTicks[0][i].x = short( r1x );
    m_HourTicks[0][i].y = short( r1y );
    m_HourTicks[1][i].x = short( r2x );
    m_HourTicks[1][i].y = short( r2y );

    angle -= (2 * PI) / 12;
}
}
```

Drawing the Clock's Tick Marks and Hands

Once we've calculated everything and stored it in the member arrays, the drawing is straightforward. Here is the code to draw the tick marks. We iterate through our two-dimensional array and use the MoveTo and LineTo drawing primitives.

```
// Draw the minute/second ticks
for ( int i = 0; i < 60; i++ )
{
    pdc->MoveTo( m_MinuteTicks[0][i] );
    pdc->LineTo( m_MinuteTicks[1][i] );
}

// Draw the hour ticks
// with a larger pen
CPen penBlk( PS_SOLID, 2, RGB( 0x00, 0x00, 0x00 ));
pdc->SelectObject( &penBlk );
for ( i = 0; i < 12; i++ )
{
    pdc->MoveTo( m_HourTicks[0][i] );
    pdc->LineTo( m_HourTicks[1][i] );
}
```

Drawing each of the hands is only slightly more complicated. We use the time—minute, hour, or second—as an offset within the appropriate array. The drawing of each hand is very similar, so I've shown only the hour hand code. The only tricky part is calculating the array offset for the hour.

```
// Use the foreground color for the clock hands
// Draw the hour hand
int iPenWidth = 1;
CPen penHour( PS_SOLID, iPenWidth + 3, TranslateColor( GetForeColor() ));
pdc->SelectObject( &penHour );
// Move to the center of the bounding rectangle
pdc->MoveTo( ptCenter );

// An hour spans 5 minute ticks plus the number of minutes divided
// by 12. This provides the gradual movement of the hour hand.
int wHourTick = ( m_wHour * 5 ) + (int) ( m_wMinute / 12 );
// Draw from the center to the array point
pdc->LineTo( m_HourHands[wHourTick] );
```

Getting the Current Time

To have an accurate clock, we need to get the time from the operating system. MFC provides a CTime class that also isolates the platform differences in time functions. So we can write the GetTime function like this:

```
void CClockCtrl::GetTime()
{
   CTime time = CTime::GetCurrentTime();
   m_wHour = time.GetHour();
   if ( m_wHour >= 12 )
      m_wHour -= 12;
   m_wMinute = time.GetMinute();
   m_wSecond = time.GetSecond();
}
```

Before we see the complete OnDraw source, there is one more thing that we need to cover: Windows mapping modes.

Mapping Modes

Figure 9.2 depicts the Cartesian coordinate system that we've all used, but the device context that we get from the container won't provide us with such a coordinate system. We must create it ourselves. To do so, we need a quick review of Windows' mapping modes. For a more detailed treatment, see *Programming Windows 3.1, Third Edition*, by Charles Petzold (Microsoft Press), and the Win32 SDK documentation.

A *mapping mode* is another attribute of the device context. To understand mapping modes, you must first understand the difference between logical coordinates and device coordinates. *Device coordinates* are described in terms of *pixels*, a unit whose size is dependent on the type of display you are using. If you specify an area of 320 by 240 pixels (or device units) and if the program is running on a VGA monitor (640x480), the area will cover one quarter of the screen (half the width and half the height). The true size of a pixel is dependent on the underlying hardware. If you want a control whose size is always 1 inch by 1 inch, you must use *logical coordinates,* and one of Windows' physical unit mapping modes.

Windows' eight mapping modes are listed in Table 9.2. Each mapping mode creates a logical space that is mapped to the physical space of the display or printer.

Table 9.2 Windows Mapping Modes

Mapping Mode	Description
MM_TEXT	Maps one logical unit to one device unit or pixel. The positive y-axis extends downward.
MM_HIMETRIC	Maps one logical unit to 0.01 millimeters. The positive y-axis extends upward.
MM_LOMETRIC	Maps one logical unit to 0.1 millimeters. The positive y-axis extends upward.
MM_HIENGLISH	Maps one logical unit to 0.001 inches. The positive y-axis extends upward.
MM_LOENGLISH	Maps one logical unit to 0.01 inches. The positive y-axis extends upward.
MM_TWIPS	Maps one logical unit to one twentieth of a point, or 1/1440 inches. The positive y-axis extends upward.
MM_ANISOTROPIC	Maps a logical unit to an arbitrary physical unit specified by the developer. Both the x-axis and the y-axis can be arbitrarily scaled. This allows stretching of the coordinate system.
MM_ISOTROPIC	Maps a logical unit to an arbitrary physical unit specified by the developer. The x-axis and y-axis maintain a 1-to-1 ratio.

The easiest mapping mode to work with is MM_TEXT. In this mapping mode, device coordinates and logical coordinates are the same. To put it another way, the logical coordinates map directly to pixels. In MM_TEXT, the upper left corner is point (0,0); Y increases as you move down, and X increases as you move across the screen. The initial view of a DC with an MM_TEXT mapping mode is depicted in Figure 9.4.

The initial setup of our device context will be like Figure 9.4. This is just one quadrant of the Cartesian coordinate system. We need to adjust the coordinate system so that it reflects what we used back when we were learning trig. We adjust the coordinate system by changing the mapping of the logical coordinates to device coordinates with the CDC method SetWindowOrg. SetWindowOrg changes the mapping of logical coordinates to device coordinates. Initially, logical point (0,0) maps to device point (0,0). Device point (0,0) is always the upper left corner of the device. To change the coordinate system for our logical points, we use SetWindowOrg, which takes as a parameter a logical point. After the call, the logical point provided will map to the device point (0,0). This technique changes our logical coordinate system to that of Figure 9.5.

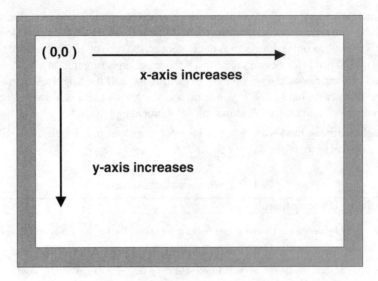

Figure 9.4 Default MM_TEXT settings.

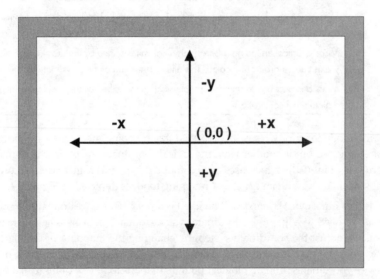

Figure 9.5 New logical coordinates.

This system is slightly different from the coordinate system we're used to. As you can see, the y-axis increases as you move down the axis instead of when moving up. This isn't a serious problem; we just adjust the calculation of the Y point when calculating the arrays for the clock's ticks and hands. The following code, from CalcTicksAndHands, illustrates this change:

```
// Work ourselves around the circle in 60 unit increments
// The radian angle changes within the loop
// r3 is the size of the hour hand. Half the radius
int r3 = nRadius / 2;
for ( int i = 0; i < 60; i++ )
{
    r2x = cos( angle ) * r2 + rcBounds.left;
    // The direction of the Y axis is reversed
    // when using the MM_TEXT mapping mode. The Y
    // axis increases as you move DOWN instead of up.
    // We reverse the direction by negating the sin
    r2y = -sin( angle ) * r2 + rcBounds.top;
    m_MinSecHands[i].x = short( r2x );
    m_MinSecHands[i].y = short( r2y );

    // Calculate size of hour hand
    r2x = cos( angle ) * r3 + rcBounds.left;
    r2y = -sin( angle ) * r3 + rcBounds.top;

    // Store the hour ticks in an array
    m_HourHands[i].x = short( r2x );
    m_HourHands[i].y = short( r2y );

    angle -= (2 * PI) / 60;
}
```

Once we have the device context set to a coordinate system that maps the logical coordinates to what we expect, the calculation of the drawing points is relatively easy. The following code sets up a logical coordinate system like that in Figure 9.5:

```
// Set the coordinate system so that the point
// ( rcBounds.left, rcBounds.top ) is in the
// center of the control's bounding rectangle
pdc->SetWindowOrg( -(nRadius * 2) / 2, -(nRadius * 2) / 2 );

POINT ptCenter;
ptCenter.x = rcBounds.left;
ptCenter.y = rcBounds.top;
```

The OnDraw Source

I promised the complete OnDraw source, and here it is. It uses the other functions that we've investigated: CalcTicksAndHands and GetTime. The source that needs to be added to **CLOCKCTL.H** is also provided.

```cpp
// clockctl.h
class CClockCtrl : public COleControl
{
    DECLARE_DYNCREATE(CClockCtrl)
...
// Implementation
protected:
    ~CClockCtrl();

    void      GetTime();
    void      CalcTicksAndHands( CDC*, const CRect& );
    WORD      m_wHour;
    WORD      m_wMinute;
    WORD      m_wSecond;
    POINT     m_HourHands[60];
    POINT     m_MinSecHands[60];
    POINT     m_MinuteTicks[2][60];
    POINT     m_HourTicks[2][12];
...
};
```

```cpp
// clockctl.cpp
...
void CClockCtrl::OnDraw(CDC* pdc, const CRect& rcBounds, const CRect& rcInvalid)
{
    // Create a brush for the background
    CBrush bkBrush( TranslateColor( GetBackColor() ));
    CBrush* pOldBrush = pdc->SelectObject( &bkBrush );

    // Select a solid black pen 1 pixel wide
    CPen penBlack( PS_SOLID, 1, RGB( 0x00, 0x00, 0x00 ));
    CPen* pOldPen = pdc->SelectObject( &penBlack );

    pdc->FillRect( rcBounds, &bkBrush );
    // draw the face of the clock
    pdc->Ellipse( LPCRECT( rcBounds ));

    int nRadius = rcBounds.Width() / 2;
```

```
// Calculate the tick and hand arrays
CalcTicksAndHands( pdc, rcBounds );

// Set the coordinate system so that the point 0,0 is in the
// center of the control's bounding rectangle (square)
pdc->SetWindowOrg( -(nRadius * 2) / 2, -(nRadius * 2) / 2 );

POINT ptCenter;
ptCenter.x = rcBounds.left;
ptCenter.y = rcBounds.top;

// Draw the minute/second ticks
for ( int i = 0; i < 60; i++ )
{
   pdc->MoveTo( m_MinuteTicks[0][i] );
   pdc->LineTo( m_MinuteTicks[1][i] );
}

// Draw the hour ticks
// with a larger pen
CPen penBlk( PS_SOLID, 2, RGB( 0x00, 0x00, 0x00 ));
pdc->SelectObject( &penBlk );
for ( i = 0; i < 12; i++ )
{
   pdc->MoveTo( m_HourTicks[0][i] );
   pdc->LineTo( m_HourTicks[1][i] );
}

// Get the current time
GetTime();

// Use the foreground color for the clock hands
// Draw the hour hand
int iPenWidth = 1;
CPen penHour( PS_SOLID, iPenWidth + 3, TranslateColor( GetForeColor() ));
pdc->SelectObject( &penHour );
pdc->MoveTo(ptCenter);
int wHourTick = (m_wHour * 5) + (int) ( m_wMinute / 12 );
pdc->LineTo( m_HourHands[wHourTick] );

// Draw the minute hand
CPen penMin( PS_SOLID, iPenWidth + 2, TranslateColor( GetForeColor() ));
pdc->SelectObject( &penMin );
```

```
pdc->MoveTo(ptCenter);
pdc->LineTo( m_MinSecHands[m_wMinute]);

// Draw the second hand
CPen penSecond( PS_SOLID, iPenWidth, TranslateColor( GetForeColor() ));
pdc->SelectObject( &penSecond );
pdc->MoveTo(ptCenter);
pdc->LineTo( m_MinSecHands[m_wSecond] );

// Restore the device context
pdc->SelectObject( pOldBrush );
pdc->SelectObject( pOldPen );
}
```

We've covered almost everything in the source. As you can see, we use several different pen sizes when we draw the clock's outline, tick marks, and hands. We use the ForeColor for the hand color but have hard coded a black pen for the clock's outline and tick marks. A nice exercise would be to provide a custom color property to allow the user to change these. The CLOCK project on the accompanying CD-ROM provides this feature (and others).

Redrawing the Clock Every Second

To make our clock tick, we'll implement a timer that will fire every second. This is similar to what we did in Chapter 8, but we now want the timer to fire continually. Use ClassWizard to add a WM_TIMER handler to the CClockCtrl class and add the following code:

```
void CClockCtrl::OnTimer(UINT nIDEvent)
{
    InvalidateControl();
    COleControl::OnTimer(nIDEvent);
}
```

NOTE
Use of the WM_TIMER message requires a true HWND for our clock control. A window for a control isn't created unless the container activates the control. ControlWizard set the OLEMISC_ACTIVATE-WHENVISIBLE flag for our control, so control containers should provide this functionality.

Whenever the timer fires, we call COleControl::InvalidateControl, forcing a redraw. You should use this method instead of directly calling the OnDraw method, primarily because you don't know which DC to pass to it.

We need to add StartTimer and StopTimer methods to the class just as we did in Chapter 8. Add the declarations to **CLOCKCTL.H** and then add the following code to **CLOCKCTL.CPP**:

```
#define TIMER_ID 100
void CClockCtrl::StartTimer()
{
    SetTimer( TIMER_ID, 1000, NULL );
}

void CClockCtrl::StopTimer()
{
    KillTimer( TIMER_ID );
}
```

We want the clock to run only when the container is in run mode and the control is enabled. To ensure this, we check the `AmbientUserMode` and `Enabled` properties at various places within the control.

When and where should we start the timer? A logical choice might be when the `UserMode` ambient property changes. A new value of `TRUE` would signal a `StartTimer`, and a value of `FALSE` would cause a call to `StopTimer`. Code such as the following would take care of this. We also check to make sure that the control is enabled.

```
void CClockCtrl::OnAmbientPropertyChange( DISPID dispid )
{
    if ( dispid == DISPID_AMBIENT_USERMODE || dispid == DISPID_UNKNOWN )
    {
        if ( AmbientUserMode() && GetEnabled() )
            StartTimer();
        else
            StopTimer();
    }
}
```

The problem is that I've tried the preceding code with many containers, and it doesn't work. Apparently the containers don't call the `IOleControl::OnAmbientPropertyChange` method when switching from design mode to run mode. (Some of the samples included with Visual C++ use this method, but don't be fooled. It doesn't work.) The ActiveX control standard is still young, and it doesn't specify the exact behavior of containers. There are still areas that need a more solid definition.

This code doesn't work because a control's instance is usually deleted and re-created when a container goes from run mode to design mode, and the ambient property has no chance to change. This is an attribute of the container and so may vary. The previous method will work for containers that maintain the instance of a control when switching between design mode and run mode, so we should include it in our control's code.

If a control's instance is deleted and re-created when the container switches modes, we are assured that the control's `HWND` will also be deleted and re-created. To trap this event and possibly start the timer, we override `COleControl::OnCreate`. Using ClassWizard, add a handler for the `WM_CREATE` message. Then add the following code:

```
int CClockCtrl::OnCreate(LPCREATESTRUCT lpCreateStruct)
{
    if (COleControl::OnCreate(lpCreateStruct) == -1)
        return -1;

    if ( AmbientUserMode() && GetEnabled() )
        StartTimer();

    return 0;
}
```

NOTE

The preceding code is again dependent on the creation of a window for the control. As discussed in the previous note, a container that honors the OLEMISC_ACTIVEWHENVISIBLE flag will provide an HWND for the control. In our case, we need the actual window only at run time.

This code works in all the containers that I've tested. When the control's HWND is created, we check the UserMode and Enabled properties. If they are both TRUE, we start the timer. To be safe, you could implement both methods described previously and use a Boolean flag such as m_bTimerStarted to ensure that you don't start the timer twice if both events occur.

To ensure that the timer is stopped when the control is destroyed, we trap the WM_DESTROY message that is generated by Windows whenever a window is destroyed. Use ClassWizard to trap WM_DESTROY and add the following code:

```
void CClockCtrl::OnDestroy()
{
    COleControl::OnDestroy();
    StopTimer();
}
```

We also start and stop the timer when the control's Enabled property is changed at run time. The following code from **CLOCKCTL.CPP**, handles this situation. You must also add the declaration to **CLOCKCTL.H**.

```
void CClockCtrl::OnEnabledChanged()
{
    // Only start the timer if in run mode
    if ( AmbientUserMode() )
    {
        // Only start the timer if the control is enabled
        if ( GetEnabled() )
            StartTimer();
        else
            StopTimer();
    }
}
```

AmbientUIDead

There is one other place where we need to shut down the clock. A container actually has three modes of operation. The `AmbientUserMode` property handles the first two: design mode and run mode. The third mode occurs when a development tool that uses ActiveX control containers runs in *debug* mode. When debugging, the tool user may be single-stepping through its (usually) interpreted language. During this time, it is recommended that controls disable any user input and basically act as if they have been disabled. The `AmbientUIDead` method provides a way to check the container's state. To provide support for this mode as well as the others we've discussed, the `OnAmbientPropertyChange` method looks like this:

```
void CClockCtrl::OnAmbientPropertyChange(DISPID dispid)
{
    if ( dispid == DISPID_AMBIENT_USERMODE ||
         dispid == DISPID_AMBIENT_UIDEAD   ||
         dispid == DISPID_UNKNOWN )
    {
        if ( AmbientUserMode() && GetEnabled() && !AmbientUIDead() )
            StartTimer();
        else
            StopTimer();
    }
    else
        // Just redraw the control
        InvalidateControl();
}
```

In Visual Basic when you press **Ctrl-Break**, the `OnAmbientPropertyChange` method is called with a DISPID of `DISPID_AMBIENT_UIDEAD`. The `AmbientUIDead` method returns `TRUE` and we stop the timer. When the user presses **F5** to run, the method is called again, `AmbientUIDead` returns `FALSE`, and we restart the timer.

Testing the Clock

We've added quite a bit of code, so let's give the clock a test. Compile and link the project and insert it into the Test Container. There isn't much you can do with the clock except let it run (Figure 9.6). You can change the background and foreground colors and so on, but we've done that before. Let's add some more features.

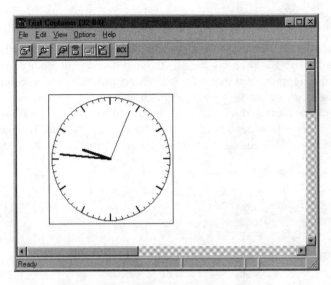

Figure 9.6 Clock control in the Test Container.

Restricting the Size or Shape of the Control

To simplify the drawing of our clock, we'll ensure that the area bounding the control is square. This is easy to do. When the user of the control (usually in design mode) attempts to change its size or extents, the container will notify the control through the COleControl::OnSetExtent method. OnSetExtent receives the new extents for the control. The control can leave the new extents as they are, or it can change them to whatever it wants.

For our purposes, we require only that the resulting area be square. First we override OnSetExtent in our control's class, and then we ensure that the returned SIZEL structure contains a square extent. The SIZEL structure contains a width (cx) and height (cy) of type long:

```
typedef struct tagSIZE
{
    LONG        cx;
    LONG        cy;
} SIZE, *PSIZE, *LPSIZE;

typedef SIZE     SIZEL;
typedef SIZE     *PSIZEL, *LPSIZEL;
```

Add the following code to **CLOCKCTL.H** and **CLOCKCTL.CPP**:

```
// clockctl.h : Declaration of the CClockCtrl OLE control class.

...

class CClockCtrl : public COleControl
{
...
    // Overrides
    virtual BOOL CClockCtrl::OnSetExtent( LPSIZEL lpSizeL );
...
};

// clockctl.cpp

...

BOOL CClockCtrl::OnSetExtent( LPSIZEL lpSizeL )
{
    // Make sure the extent is a square
    // Use the smaller of the sizes for the square
    if ( lpSizeL->cy <= lpSizeL->cx )
        lpSizeL->cx = lpSizeL->cy;
    else
        lpSizeL->cy = lpSizeL->cx;

    // Call the parent implementation
    return COleControl::OnSetExtent( lpSizeL );
}
```

Most of OLE uses HIMETRIC units for all its sizes and measurements. The SIZEL structure provides the new extents in HIMETRIC units. If your control uses some other unit, you must convert it to HIMETRIC before modifying the SIZEL structure. In our case, we don't care about the size. We just want it to be square, so we take the smaller of the two sizes and assign that value to the other.

Calculating HIMETRIC Units

If you want your control to be a certain size, you may need to convert the device units into HIMETRIC units. Here's how to do it. If we wanted our clock to always be 200 by 200 pixels in size, basically not allowing the user to resize the control, we would convert our units (pixels) to HIMETRIC units and return this value in the SIZEL structure. We could do something like this:

```
#define HIMETRIC_PER_INCH   2540      // HIMETRIC units per inch
BOOL CClockCtrl::OnSetExtent( LPSIZEL lpSizeL )
{
    CDC cdc;
    cdc.CreateCompatibleDC( NULL );
```

```
// One way to do it
long lpx = cdc.GetDeviceCaps( LOGPIXELSX );
lpSizeL->cx = MulDiv( 200, HIMETRIC_PER_INCH, lpx );
long lpy = cdc.GetDeviceCaps( LOGPIXELSY );
lpSizeL->cy = MulDiv( 200, HIMETRIC_PER_INCH, lpy );

// Another, easier way to do it
CSize size( 200, 200 );
// Convert the device units to HIMETRIC units
cdc.DPtoHIMETRIC( &size );
lpSizeL->cx = size.cx;
lpSizeL->cy = size.cy;

// Call the parent implementation
return COleControl::OnSetExtent( lpSizeL );
}
```

The preceding code creates a CDC object and then calls CreateCompatibleDC. By passing NULL as the parameter, we get a DC that is compatible with the main display. We then call GetDeviceCaps to determine the number of logical pixels per inch for the display. We use the Windows MulDiv function to multiply HIMETRIC_PER_INCH by 200 and then divide the result by the logical pixels. This calculation gives us the number of HIMETRIC units equal to 200 logical pixels. We do this for both the width (cx) and height (cy). The result is stored in the SIZEL structure, which is passed to the parent's method. This approach ensures that our clock control will always be 200 by 200 logical pixels. I've also shown another way to do it using the CDC::DPtoHIMETRIC method. I included the first method to show you how to get device capabilities using GetDeviceCaps.

If, on the other hand, we want our clock to always be 1 inch by 1 inch independent of the display, the OnSetExtent method could be coded like this:

```
#define HIMETRIC_PER_INCH   2540      // HIMETRIC units per inch
BOOL CClockCtrl::OnSetExtent( LPSIZEL lpSizeL )
{
    // Set the SIZEL structure to be a 1-inch square
    lpSizeL->cx = lpSizeL->cy = HIMETRIC_PER_INCH;

    // Call the parent implementation
    return COleControl::OnSetExtent( lpSizeL );
}
```

The OnSetExtent code is easy, because the SIZEL structure is in logical HIMETRIC units. The SetInitialSize call in the control's constructor would be a just little more complicated, because it expects its dimensions in pixels:

```
CClockCtrl::CClockCtrl()
{
```

```
InitializeIIDs(&IID_DClock, &IID_DClockEvents);

// TODO: Initialize your control's instance data here.
CDC cdc;
cdc.CreateCompatibleDC( NULL );
int cx = cdc.GetDeviceCaps( LOGPIXELSX );
int cy = cdc.GetDeviceCaps( LOGPIXELSY );
// Set the initial control size to a one-inch square
SetInitialSize( cx, cy );
}
```

This code is similar to what we did earlier. We create a CDC object that is compatible with the display, and we use the GetDeviceCaps method to get the logical number of pixels per inch. We then use the result to set the initial size of our control. The actual size of the control will always be physically 1 inch by 1 inch regardless of the resolution of the display device.

Eliminating Control Flicker

As you've probably noticed, the clock "flickers" every time the control is redrawn. The redraw occurs 60 times per minute, and the flicker is annoying. You would have a rough time selling such a control, with its unprofessional appearance. The solution to the flicker problem is to use an "off-screen" device context.

We're familiar with the purpose of a device context. Our control currently draws into the device context provided by the container. It draws directly on the display screen (or printer), and as the control is redrawn each second, this drawing process can be "seen." This redraw causes the flicker. To eliminate the problem and also to simplify the drawing code, we will draw first into a memory device context. Then we will bit-blt the contents of the memory DC to the screen DC. The speed and directness of the bit-blt transfer will eliminate any discernible flicker.

Using a memory DC also makes the drawing more efficient. We will call the CalcHandsAndTicks method only when the size of the control changes. Resizing occurs infrequently anyway, and we shouldn't be calculating the arrays every time we draw the control. We will also eliminate the need for the array calculation routine to adjust its points when the rcBounds upper left corner is not (0,0).

First, we'll add three members to the control class: a CBitmap pointer to hold a bitmap compatible with the control, a CSize member to keep track of the control's current size, and a Boolean switch to indicate whether the control's size has changed:

```
// clockctl.h
...
// Implementation
protected:
    ~CClockCtrl();
...
```

```
   BOOL      m_bResize;
   CBitmap*  m_pBitmap;
   CSize     m_sizeControl;
...
};

// clock.cpp
/////////////////////////////////////////////////////////////////////////
// CClockCtrl::CClockCtrl - Constructor
CClockCtrl::CClockCtrl()
{
...
   m_bResize = TRUE;
   m_pBitmap = NULL;
   m_sizeControl.cy = m_sizeControl.cx = 0;
}

/////////////////////////////////////////////////////////////////////////
// CClockCtrl::~CClockCtrl - Destructor
CClockCtrl::~CClockCtrl()
{
...
   // delete the bitmap for the control
   delete m_pBitmap;
}
```

Next, we move the clock drawing code to another method, DrawClock. This new method does not use the rcInvalid parameter and can also assume that the rcBounds parameter will have an upper left corner of (0,0). We can assume this because we ensure it when we create the memory device context and pass it to the DrawClock method. There is now a check of the m_bResize member variable to determine whether the control's size has changed. We recalculate the clock's tick marks and hand arrays only when the control is resized. The resize event is caught in the new OnDraw code that we will discuss in a moment.

```
void CClockCtrl::DrawClock( CDC *pdc, const CRect& rcBounds )
{
   // Make sure that we don't get an invalid rcBounds
   // It should now always have an upper left of 0,0
   ASSERT( rcBounds.left == 0 );
   ASSERT( rcBounds.top == 0 );

   // Our center will now always be 0,0 after the
   // SetWindowOrg call
   CPoint ptCenter( 0, 0 );
```

```
//ptCenter.x = rcBounds.left;
//ptCenter.y = rcBounds.top;

GetTime();

// Only recalc the arrays when the control's size changes
if ( m_bResize )
{
    m_bResize = FALSE;
    CalcTicksAndHands( pdc, rcBounds );
}

...
}
```

When we call the `CalcTicksAndHands` method in `DrawClock`, we know that the upper left corner of `rcBounds` is (0,0), so we can simplify the code in `CalcTicksAndHands` by removing the addition of `rcBounds.left` and `rcBounds.top` in our calculations:

```
#define PI 3.141592654
#define START_ANGLE (.5 * PI)
void CClockCtrl::CalcTicksAndHands( CDC *pdc, const CRect& rcBounds )
{
...
    // Calculate the hand arrays
    double angle = START_ANGLE;
    double r2x, r2y, r1x, r1y;
    int r2 = nRadius - sHourTickLen - 2;
    // r3 is the hour hand, half the radius
    int r3 = nRadius / 2;
    for ( int i = 0; i < 60; i++ )
    {
        // rcBounds.left is always zero now
//      r2x = cos( angle ) * r2 + rcBounds.left;
//      r2y = -sin( angle ) * r2 + rcBounds.top;
        r2x = cos( angle ) * r2;
        r2y = -sin( angle ) * r2;

        m_MinSecHands[i].x = (short) r2x;
        m_MinSecHands[i].y = (short) r2y;

        // Calculate size of hour hand
//      r2x = cos( angle ) * r3 + rcBounds.left;
//      r2y = -sin( angle ) * r3 + rcBounds.top;
        r2x = cos( angle ) * r3;
        r2y = -sin( angle ) * r3;
```

```
        m_HourHands[i].x = (short) r2x;
        m_HourHands[i].y = (short) r2y;

        angle -= (2 * PI) / 60;
    }
...
}
```

Then we change the OnDraw code to look like this:

```
void CClockCtrl::OnDraw(CDC* pdc, const CRect& rcBounds, const CRect& rcInvalid)
{
    // Our memory DC
    CDC    dcMem;
    // Initialize our memory DC to the characteristics
    // of the DC provided by the container.
    dcMem.CreateCompatibleDC( pdc );

    // If the bounding rectangle has changed
    // We need to re-create our bitmap and
    // recalculate the clock's ticks and hands
    if ( m_sizeControl != rcBounds.Size() )
    {
        // Save the new size of the control
        m_sizeControl = rcBounds.Size();

        // This flag is used by the control drawing
        // routine to determine if it should recalc
        // the clock's ticks, hands, etc.
        m_bResize = TRUE;

        // delete any existing bitmap and create
        // a new one
        if ( m_pBitmap )
            delete m_pBitmap;
        m_pBitmap = new CBitmap;

        // Create a bitmap compatible with the current
        // DC provided by the container
        m_pBitmap->CreateCompatibleBitmap( pdc,
                                           rcBounds.Width(),
                                           rcBounds.Height() );
    }
```

```
// Select the compatible bitmap into our
// memory DC and save the old bitmap.
CBitmap* pOldBitmap = dcMem.SelectObject( m_pBitmap );

// Create a bounding rectangle with upper left corner of 0,0
CRect rcDrawBounds( 0, 0, rcBounds.Width(), rcBounds.Height() );

// Save the memory DC's state
// so that DrawClock can modify it
int iSavedDC = dcMem.SaveDC();
// Draw the clock into our memory DC
DrawClock( &dcMem, rcDrawBounds );
// Restore the DC
dcMem.RestoreDC( iSavedDC );

// BitBlt the memory DC representation
// into the actual screen DC
pdc->BitBlt( rcBounds.left,
             rcBounds.top,
             rcBounds.Width(),
             rcBounds.Height(),
             &dcMem,
             0,
             0,
             SRCCOPY );

// Restore the old bitmap, it will be
// destroyed when the memory DC goes
// out of scope.
dcMem.SelectObject( pOldBitmap );
}
```

I've commented the code, so I'll just hit the high points here. On entry to OnDraw, we create an instance of the CDC class to use as our memory-based DC. By calling CreateCompatibleDC, we initialize the DC to be compatible with the DC provided by the container. The initial DC returned by CreateCompatibleDC cannot be used until it is initialized with an appropriate bitmap for the control (which we will do in a moment). When we're using an off-screen (or memory) DC, the drawing of the control (using various CDC methods) modifies or "draws into" the bitmap of the DC. Later, the CDC::BitBlt method will copy this bitmap into the screen (or printer) device context.

Next, we determine whether the control's size has changed. If it has, we set the m_bResize variable to TRUE to indicate to DrawClock that it needs to recalculate the arrays of clock ticks and hand points. We then save the new size of the control so that we won't execute this code unless the control's size changes again.

Each time the size of the control changes, we re-create our `CBitmap` instance. As described previously, the rendering of the control in the memory DC occurs in the bitmap of the DC. We need to ensure that the bitmap is of the proper size and color depth of the container-provided DC. First, we delete any existing instance of the bitmap and create another `CBitmap` instance. The next call, `CreateCompatibleBitmap`, creates a bitmap for our memory DC that is compatible with the DC provided by the container. (It has the same color depth and so on.) All this occurs only if the user has resized the control during the design phase. At run time, this code is executed only once: when the control is initially created.

Once we have a compatible memory DC and a bitmap that will support the rendering of our control, we use the `SelectObject` method to select the bitmap into the memory DC. Next, we create a temporary `CRect` object with the extents of the control. We also ensure that the upper left coordinates are (0,0). This approach makes the drawing code in `DrawClock` and `CalcHandsAndTicks` less complicated. We save the state of the DC and call `DrawClock` with the memory DC and the `CRect` object. `DrawClock` renders directly into the memory DC (modifying its bitmap). `DrawClock` behaves as if it were drawing with a screen-based DC. When `DrawClock` returns, the memory DC's state is restored and the memory DC (basically its bitmap) is copied to the screen DC using the `BitBlt` method. The first four parameters of `BitBlt` specify the location and size of the transfer within the destination DC (the screen). We use the `rcBounds` left and top values as the starting location of the destination and use the `Width` and `Height` methods to indicate the size of the destination rectangle. The fifth parameter is the source DC (our memory DC). The next two parameters provide the upper left starting points of the source DC. Because our memory DC's bounds start at (0,0), we specify 0,0 as the starting coordinates of the source DC. We're finished. The clock is drawn without any noticeable flicker. All that is left is the cleanup step of selecting the previous bitmap back into our memory DC. If we forget this step, `m_pBitmap`, the compatible bitmap that we are maintaining for our control, would be deleted.

rcInvalid

The `rcInvalid` parameter passed to `OnDraw` is provided by the container, and it indicates the area of the control's image that needs to be rendered. In many cases this parameter will contain the same coordinates that are provided by `rcBounds`, but when the container determines that only a portion of the control needs to be rendered, `rcInvalid` will contain only the invalid region of the control. Use of the `rcInvalid` parameter can provide an alternative way of optimizing drawing of your controls, and you may not need to add the complexity of using a memory-based device context as discussed previously. We can also use it with our memory-based DC approach by copying only the area of the control that the container indicates is invalid. We do this by changing the parameters of the `BitBlt` call in the `OnDraw` method:

```
void CClockCtrl::OnDraw(CDC* pdc, const CRect& rcBounds, const CRect& rcInvalid)
{
...
    // BitBlt the memory DC representation
    // into the actual screen DC
    // By using the rcInvalid rectangle
    // We may only copy a partial image of the
```

```
// clock. This will improve performance
pdc->BitBlt( rcInvalid.left,
             rcInvalid.top,
             rcInvalid.Width(),
             rcInvalid.Height(),
             &dcMem,
             rcInvalid.left - rcBounds.left,
             rcInvalid.top - rcBounds.top,
             SRCCOPY );

    // Restore the old bitmap, it will be
    // destroyed when the memory DC goes
    // out of scope.
    dcMem.SelectObject( pOldBitmap );
}
```

We use the `rcInvalid` rectangle instead of the `rcBounds` rectangle we used previously. Using this technique, the size of the destination area may be different from the size of the bitmap in our memory-based DC. We adjust the source DC coordinates by subtracting the left and top bounding points from the left and top `rcInvalid` points. This technique ensures that the source starting corner maps to the `rcInvalid`-based destination corner. Using this approach, we bit-blt only the area of the control that needs to be repainted.

There is one problem with the memory-based DC approach to drawing controls. Under certain conditions, a control's container may request that the control render itself into a metafile device context. As you'll see in a moment, some of the preceding techniques won't work when we're drawing into a metafile DC. That's the reason we separated the drawing code for the clock.

Metafiles

A *metafile* is a recording of a series of GDI function calls that can be stored in memory or on disk. These metafiles can be "replayed" to reproduce a copy of the original image. Some containers may use a metafile to represent the visual portion of a control. Control containers typically do this only during the design phase, and most containers that I've used employ the metafile representation only when printing an image of the control. Because of the difficulties of rendering to metafiles, I imagine that most control containers will provide a true screen device context during both design mode and run mode and require the control to provide a metafile representation only when printing.

A metafile representation of a visual server's image is used extensively by OLE compound document containers. This arrangement allows the container to display an image without activating the visual editing server. For large visual editing server applications (such as Excel), this is appropriate, but ActiveX controls are much smaller and expect to be active whenever they are visible. This means that they will have an HWND and device context and do not need to provide a metafile representation. But with a little forethought in the design of your controls, it is not difficult to provide a good metafile representation of your control.

OnDrawMetafile

COleControl provides a method, OnDrawMetafile, that is called explicitly when the container requires a metafile representation. The default implementation calls the control's OnDraw method. We've added some CDC methods that are not supported in metafiles, so we need to override OnDrawMetafile for our control. All the code in the OnDraw method deals with setting up and drawing into a memory DC, and the drawing code is in DrawClock. In our OnDrawMetafile method, we pass the provided metafile DC to our DrawClock method:

```
class CClockCtrl : public COleControl
{
    // Overrides
    virtual void OnDrawMetafile( CDC* pdc, const CRect& rcBounds );
};

void CClockCtrl::OnDrawMetafile( CDC* pdc, const CRect& rcBounds )
{
    ASSERT( rcBounds.left == 0 );
    ASSERT( rcBounds.top == 0 );

    DrawClock( pdc, rcBounds );
}
```

The metafile DC's upper left corner will always be (0,0). This is important, because we changed our DrawClock method to require an upper left corner of (0,0). To test this assertion, I've added two ASSERT macros that check the coordinates to ensure that they are always (0,0).

Metafile Restrictions

Metafile device contexts have a few restrictions. Because metafile DCs are not associated with a true device (such as the display), certain DC-related functions will not work properly when used with a metafile DC. The CDC methods that should not be used when you're drawing into a metafile DC can be described as groups of functions that act specifically on a device (Table 9.3). The physical device context is not known when you're drawing into the metafile DC.

Table 9.3 CDC Methods that Shouldn't Be Used with Metafiles

Method Group	Example Methods
Methods that retrieve data from the physical device. This includes most `Get*` and `Enum*` methods.	`GetDeviceCaps, GetTextColor, GetTextMetrics, EnumFonts, EnumObjects, DPtoLP, LPtoDP,` etc.
Methods that appear to be GDI functions but in reality are implemented by other parts of the Windows operating system.	`DrawText, TabbedTextOut, InvertRect, DrawIcon, DrawFocusRect, FrameRect, GrayString,` etc.
Methods that expect the device context to be associated with a physical device.	`SaveDC, RestoreDC, CreateCompatibleDC, CreateCompatibleBitmap,` etc.

You can use most of these methods when drawing in a metafile DC, but they will have no effect when the metafile is subsequently played. The main reason we separated the `OnDraw` and `DrawClock` code is that we wanted to place the code that is not supported by metafiles (all the code needed to draw in an off-screen DC) in a separate routine. The drawing code that works within metafiles is placed in the `DrawClock` routine. When the container needs a metafile representation and therefore calls `OnDrawMetafile`, we pass the DC to the `DrawClock` routine.

Win32 Enhanced Metafiles

The Win32 API removes the metafile restrictions by providing a new metafile format called *enhanced metafiles*. If the container provides an enhanced metafile DC, enhanced metafiles remove the problem of having two different drawing routines for your controls.

In most cases, the container passes the metafile DC to your control in the `OnDrawMetafile` method and so is responsible for providing you with either a standard or an enhanced metafile DC. I expect that 32-bit containers will use the enhanced version of metafiles, because it makes development of the control's code easier.

The container can also request a metafile (`CF_METAFILEPICT`) through the `IDataObject::GetData` interface method. In this case, MFC creates an instance of the `CMetafileDC` class and passes this device context to your control's `OnDrawMetafile` method. The metafile is recorded and passed back to the container as an actual metafile. The container can then play the metafile within whatever device context it chooses.

If your control will be used only in 32-bit environments and you know that the containers that will be used for your control all provide enhanced metafile support, you can probably get away with only one drawing routine. Unfortunately, most control developers do not have this luxury. To be safe, you should probably separate the drawing code that is dependent on a nonmetafile representation as we did with the clock control.

Testing the Metafile

The best way to test whether your control can draw its metafile representation properly is to use the Test Container. With your control UI-active, select the **Edit/Draw Metafile** option. The Test Container will pass your control's OnDrawMetafile a metafile DC and will display the result in a window (Figure 9.7).

Figure 9.7 Test Container's display of the metafile DC.

Drawing the Control in Design Mode

When the container is in design mode, some controls display their name somewhere within their bounding rectangle. The container may provide an ambient property, DisplayName, that controls can display when they draw themselves in design mode. The following code, when added to our control's DrawClock method, will provide this ability (Figure 9.8).

```
void CClockCtrl::DrawClock( CDC *pdc, const CRect& rcBounds )
{
...

    // If the container is in design mode
    if (! AmbientUserMode() )
    {
        // Get the display name from the container
        CString strName = AmbientDisplayName();
        // If it is empty, supply a default name
```

```
        if ( strName.IsEmpty() )
            strName = "Clock";

        // Set the text color to the foreground color
        pdc->SetTextColor( TranslateColor( GetForeColor() ) );

        // Select the stock font and save the old one
        CFont* pOldFont = SelectStockFont( pdc );

        // Set up the text drawing modes in the DC
        pdc->SetBkMode( TRANSPARENT );
        pdc->SetTextAlign( TA_LEFT | TA_TOP );

        // Draw the text in the upper left corner
        pdc->ExtTextOut( rcBounds.left, rcBounds.top, ETO_CLIPPED,
                        rcBounds, strName, strName.GetLength(), NULL );

        // Restore the old font
        if ( pOldFont )
            pdc->SelectObject( pOldFont );
    }
...
}
```

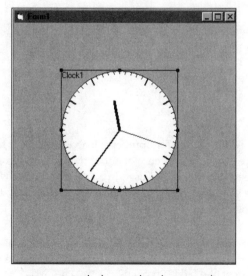

Figure 9.8 Clock control in design mode.

Hiding Properties

We added the stock Font property so that we could use it when drawing the control's name in design mode. Our clock doesn't need or use the font for anything else, so there is no need to expose the property for the control user to modify. The Object Description Language hidden keyword provides a way to hide properties. Container applications and visual tools should check for this attribute and should not display it to the user. We modify our control's ODL file and add the hidden attribute to our stock Font property as follows:

```
// clock.odl : type library source for OLE Custom Control project.
...
//  Primary dispatch interface for CClockCtrl
...
dispinterface _DClock
{
    properties:
        // NOTE - ClassWizard will maintain property information here.
        //    Use extreme caution when editing this section.
        //{{AFX_ODL_PROP(CClockCtrl)
        [id(DISPID_APPEARANCE), bindable, requestedit] short Appearance;
        [id(DISPID_BACKCOLOR), bindable, requestedit] OLE_COLOR BackColor;
        [id(DISPID_BORDERSTYLE), bindable, requestedit] short BorderStyle;
        [id(DISPID_ENABLED), bindable, requestedit] boolean Enabled;
        [id(DISPID_FORECOLOR), bindable, requestedit] OLE_COLOR ForeColor;
        [id(DISPID_FONT), bindable, hidden] IFontDisp* Font;
        [id(DISPID_HWND)] OLE_HANDLE hWnd;
        ...
        //}}AFX_ODL_PROP

...
}
```

Adding the hidden attribute will make the font property inaccessible from tools such as Visual Basic. We don't have to do this, but if we don't, the existence of a font property on a control that doesn't display any text at run time may be confusing for the control user. In a later chapter we will discuss other ways to hide properties from the container's browser. We also shouldn't provide a way to modify the Font property from the control's custom property page.

We could also have used the ambient font property provided by the container when drawing the clock's design time representation in our clock example. Instead, we added a hidden font property to introduce this concept of a hidden property.

N O T E

The SecondChange Event

To add functionality to our control, let's add a custom event. Using ClassWizard, add an event called SecondChange. Then, whenever the control's timer message fires, we should also fire the SecondChange event:

```
void CClockCtrl::OnTimer(UINT nIDEvent)
{
    FireSecondChange();

    InvalidateControl();
    COleControl::OnTimer(nIDEvent);
}
```

We'll use this event in the next example to update an external field.

The Date Property

A control user might also want to obtain the time of day from the control. This is easy to do and will provide an opportunity to use the Automation DATE data type. Invoke ClassWizard and add a custom property with a name of **Date**. Specify a data type of DATE, use the Get/Set implementation method, and clear out the Set method. We will not allow the user to "set" the date property, although it might be a neat feature to add.

After adding the new property, add the following code to the implementation method:

```
DATE CClockCtrl::GetDate()
{
    COleDateTime timeNow;
    timeNow = COleDateTime::GetCurrentTime();

    return (DATE) timeNow;
}
```

COleDateTime

The COleDateTime class encapsulates the Automation DATE data type. A DATE is an eight-byte floating-point value that indicates both the date and the time. The floating-point value can specify any date and time from January 1, 100, to December 31, 9999, with a resolution of about one millisecond. The integer value of the number specifies the date, and the fractional portion specifies the time. The date December 30, 1899, at midnight is represented as 0.0. Table 9.4 gives other examples.

Table 9.4 Example DATE Values

Date	Numeric Representation
December 30, 1899, midnight	0.00
January 1, 1900, midnight	2.00
January 1, 1900, 6 AM	2.25
January 1, 1900, noon	2.50
January 4, 1900, 9 PM	5.875
December 29, 1899, midnight	−1.00
December 18, 1899, noon	−12.50

The DATE type is supported natively by Visual Basic and Visual C++ (through the COleDateTime class) and most other Automation-compatible tools. The COleDateTime class has several useful methods. You've seen one, GetCurrentTime, and we'll use another one in the next example.

Property Pages

We haven't discussed how to build the clock control's property pages, because nothing special is required that we haven't already covered. The custom property page needs the stock properties that we've added to the clock control, with the exception of the Font property discussed previously. The property page for the clock control on the accompanying CD-ROM is shown in Figure 9.9.

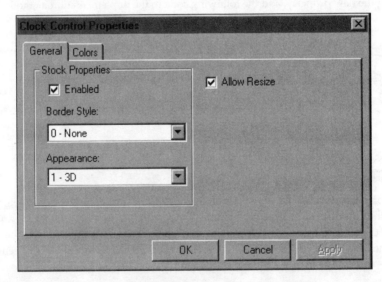

Figure 9.9 Property pages for the clock control.

The control on the accompanying CD-ROM has additional capabilities beyond those described in this chapter. Included are additional color properties for specifying the colors of the clock face, outline, and ticks, and properties that modify the sizing of the control during the design phase.

MFC Control Container Support

Visual C++ version 4.0 and higher supports the use of ActiveX controls within MFC-based applications. This major enhancement to Visual C++ allows C++ developers to take full advantage of this new component technology. With a couple of keystrokes, we can now use ActiveX controls on MFC dialog boxes and views.

The MFC development team added support for control containment by adding functionality to the CWnd class. The new CWnd class is actually a complete ActiveX control container.

The CWnd Class

The CWnd class maintains an embedded instance of the COleControlContainer and COleControlSite classes. These two classes implement the interfaces necessary for the CWnd object to act as an ActiveX control container. However, the classes are not documented because they are only used internally by MFC.

COleControlContainer implements the IOleInPlaceFrame and IOleContainer interfaces. One of the characteristics of a control container is that it can contain any number of embedded objects (controls). To handle this, COleControlContainer maintains a list of COleControlSite objects. COleControlSite implements the interfaces necessary to manage the specific embedded object site. Examples of these interfaces include IOleClientSite, IOleInPlaceSite, IOleControlSite, and the ambient property IDispatch interface.

Table 9.5 lists some of the new CWnd methods that pertain specifically to ActiveX control containment.

Table 9.5 New CWnd Methods

Method	Purpose
CreateControl	Lets you dynamically create an instance of an ActiveX control.
GetControlUnknown	Returns the IUnknown of any associated control.
InvokeHelper	Calls an automation method on the control.
GetProperty, SetProperty	Gets or sets the specified property value in the control.
OnAmbientProperty	Called by MFC to get the specified ambient property value. The control can override this method and set its own ambient properties.
m_pCtrlCont	An embedded instance of the COleControlContainer class.
m_pCtrlSite	An embedded instance of the COleControlSite class. This class gives the control access to its site interfaces. If the value of this member is NULL, then the object is not an ActiveX control.

An Example

To fully understand what's going on when we're using Visual C++ as a control container, let's build a simple application that uses the new CLOCK control. Start Visual C++ and create a new project with the following characteristics:

- MFC AppWizard (exe): Name the project **Contain**.
- MFC AppWizard Step 1: Choose a **Dialog based** application.
- MFC AppWizard Step 2 of 4: Take the defaults, but ensure that **OLE Control** support is included.
- MFC AppWizard Step 3 of 4: Take the defaults.
- MFC AppWizard Step 4 of 4: Take the defaults.

Click **Finish** and create the project.

Clicking the **OLE Control** support checkbox adds a call to `AfxEnableControlContainer` to the `InitInstance` call of our application:

```
// Contain.cpp
...
BOOL CContainApp::InitInstance()
{
    AfxEnableControlContainer();
    ...
}
```

This call initializes the global instance of the `COccManager` class. `COccManager` manages the ActiveX controls within the application. It routes control events, creates and destroys the `COleControlContainer` and `COleControlSite` instances, and generally controls everything about contained ActiveX controls. As with the other new container classes, `COccManager` isn't documented. If you're curious, you can take a look at the **OCCCONT.CPP**, **OCCSITE.CPP**, and **OCCMGR.CPP** files in the \MSDEV\MFC\SRC directory.

Once we have control support for our application, all we have to do next is to start the Component Gallery **Insert/Component** and insert the control that we want to use. For our example, we'll use the CLOCK control that we developed in this chapter. Component Gallery will display a list of all the controls registered on your system. Figure 9.10 shows the Component Gallery dialog box just before insertion of the CLOCK control.

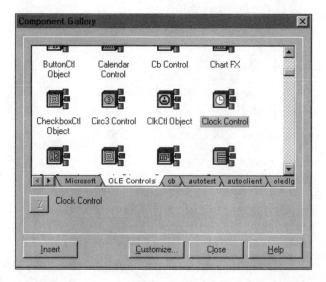

Figure 9.10 Inserting the clock control with Component Gallery.

Select the CLOCK control and click the **Insert** button. A dialog box confirms that you want to generate the indicated classes. Control containment in Visual C++ uses the static Automation wrappering technique that we used in Chapter 6. When you insert the control into our project, Component Gallery will create two new classes, create appropriate header and implementation files, and insert the files into the project. The Confirm Classes dialog box is shown in Figure 9.11.

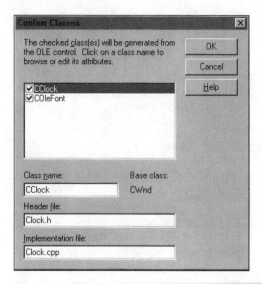

Figure 9.11 Adding the Clock control wrapper classes.

Here's a quick look at the two new classes:

```
// Clock.h

// Machine generated IDispatch wrapper class(es) created by Microsoft Visual C++

// NOTE: Do not modify the contents of this file.  If this class is regenerated by
//  Microsoft Visual C++, your modifications will be overwritten.

// Dispatch interfaces referenced by this interface
class COleFont;

/////////////////////////////////////
// CClock wrapper class
/////////////////////////////////////
class CClock : public CWnd
{
protected:
    DECLARE_DYNCREATE(CClock)
public:
    CLSID const& GetClsid()
    {
        static CLSID const clsid =
            { 0xcc57abb4,
            0xad4e,
            0x11ce,
            { 0xb4, 0x4b, 0x8, 0x0, 0x5a, 0x56, 0x47, 0x18 } };
        return clsid;
    }
    virtual BOOL Create(LPCTSTR lpszClassName,
            LPCTSTR lpszWindowName, DWORD dwStyle,
            const RECT& rect,
            CWnd* pParentWnd, UINT nID,
            CCreateContext* pContext = NULL)
    {
        return CreateControl(GetClsid(),
                            lpszWindowName,
                            dwStyle,
                            rect,
                            pParentWnd,
                            nID);
    }
```

```
    BOOL Create(LPCTSTR lpszWindowName, DWORD dwStyle,
                const RECT& rect, CWnd* pParentWnd, UINT nID,
                CFile* pPersist = NULL, BOOL bStorage = FALSE,
                BSTR bstrLicKey = NULL)
    { return CreateControl(GetClsid(),
                           lpszWindowName,
                           dwStyle,
                           rect,
                           pParentWnd,
                           nID,
                           pPersist,
                           bStorage,
                           bstrLicKey);
    }

// Attributes
public:
    short GetAppearance();
    void SetAppearance(short);
    OLE_COLOR GetBackColor();
    void SetBackColor(OLE_COLOR);
    short GetBorderStyle();
    void SetBorderStyle(short);
    BOOL GetEnabled();
    void SetEnabled(BOOL);
    COleFont GetFont();
    void SetFont(LPDISPATCH);
    OLE_COLOR GetForeColor();
    void SetForeColor(OLE_COLOR);
    OLE_HANDLE GetHWnd();
    void SetHWnd(OLE_HANDLE);
    unsigned long GetFaceColor();
    void SetFaceColor(unsigned long);
    unsigned long GetTickColor();
    void SetTickColor(unsigned long);
    BOOL GetAllowResize();
    void SetAllowResize(BOOL);

// Operations
public:
    void AboutBox();
};
```

Here's the definition for the `CClock` wrapper class. It provides dynamic creation methods (such as `Create`) and Automation wrapper functions for each of the control's properties and methods. Here's the **FONT.H** file:

```
// Font.h
...
//////////////////////////////
// COleFont wrapper class
//////////////////////////////
class COleFont : public COleDispatchDriver
{
public:
    COleFont() {}              // Calls COleDispatchDriver default constructor
    COleFont(LPDISPATCH pDispatch) : COleDispatchDriver(pDispatch) {}
    COleFont(const COleFont& dispatchSrc) : COleDispatchDriver(dispatchSrc) {}

// Attributes
public:
    CString GetName();
    void SetName(LPCTSTR);
    CY GetSize();
    void SetSize(const CY&);
    BOOL GetBold();
    void SetBold(BOOL);
    BOOL GetItalic();
    void SetItalic(BOOL);
    BOOL GetUnderline();
    void SetUnderline(BOOL);
    BOOL GetStrikethrough();
    void SetStrikethrough(BOOL);
    short GetWeight();
    void SetWeight(short);
    short GetCharset();
    void SetCharset(short);

// Operations
public:
};
```

The `COleFont` class provides an Automation interface around the OLE font object. OLE provides an `IFont` interface so that fonts can be marshaled across processes. A similar interface is provided for picture objects with the `COlePicture` object. The implementation files use the Automation property and method manipulation methods of the COleDispatchDriver class to provide access to the clock's properties and methods. Here's a part of **CLOCK.CPP**:

```cpp
// Clock.cpp

// Machine generated IDispatch wrapper class(es) created by Microsoft Visual C++

// NOTE: Do not modify the contents of this file.  If this class is regenerated by
//  Microsoft Visual C++, your modifications will be overwritten.

#include "stdafx.h"
#include "clock.h"

// Dispatch interfaces referenced by this interface
#include "Font.h"

IMPLEMENT_DYNCREATE(CClock, CWnd)

/////////////////////////////////////////////
// CClock properties

short CClock::GetAppearance()
{
    short result;
    GetProperty(DISPID_APPEARANCE, VT_I2, (void*)&result);
    return result;
}

void CClock::SetAppearance(short propVal)
{
    SetProperty(DISPID_APPEARANCE, VT_I2, propVal);
}

OLE_COLOR CClock::GetBackColor()
{
    OLE_COLOR result;
    GetProperty(DISPID_BACKCOLOR, VT_I4, (void*)&result);
    return result;
}

void CClock::SetBackColor(OLE_COLOR propVal)
{
    SetProperty(DISPID_BACKCOLOR, VT_I4, propVal);
}
...
COleFont CClock::GetFont()
{
```

```
   LPDISPATCH pDispatch;

   GetProperty(DISPID_FONT, VT_DISPATCH, (void*)&pDispatch);

   return COleFont(pDispatch);

}


void CClock::SetFont(LPDISPATCH propVal)

{

   SetProperty(DISPID_FONT, VT_DISPATCH, propVal);

}


...


/////////////////////////////
// CClock operations
/////////////////////////////
void CClock::AboutBox()

{

   InvokeHelper(0xfffffdd8, DISPATCH_METHOD, VT_EMPTY, NULL, NULL);

}
```

With the addition of the clock control to our project, it can now be used in the resource editor. Open up the application's main dialog resource, IDD_CONTAIN_DIALOG, make the dialog box a bit larger, and place an instance of the CLOCK control on the dialog box by dragging it from the control pallette and dropping it on the dialog. Give it an ID of IDC_CLOCK. Also, place an entry field below the clock and give it an ID of IDC_TIME. This is shown in Figure 9.12.

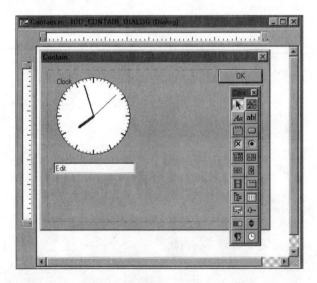

Figure 9.12 Placing the clock control on the dialog box.

Now start ClassWizard and add **Member Variables** for the two controls on our dialog box. Use member names of m_Clock and m_Time. Be sure to add the members using the **Control** category; the default category is **Value**.

MFC provides two ways to create controls: statically and dynamically. Here, we're creating the control statically at design time. The control properties will be stored in the **.RC** file, and the control will be created (deserialized) and displayed when the application is executed. Dynamic creation of controls is also supported in MFC, and we'll do that in a moment. We haven't yet written a line of code, but we can build the project and have a functional application. Figure 9.13 displays the new application.

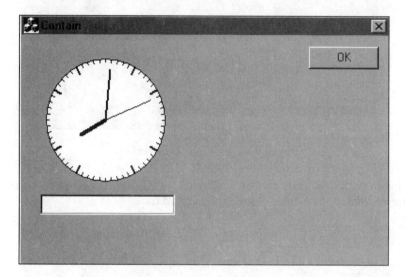

Figure 9.13 The initial application.

Events

To see how MFC supports control event handling, let's perform an action when the clock's SecondChange event fires. Using ClassWizard go to the **Message Maps** tab and select the clock's ID, IDC_CLOCK; the tab will list one "message" in the Messages listbox. Click **Add Function** and add the OnSecondChangeClock method to the **CONTAINDLG.CPP** file. This is shown in Figure 9.14.

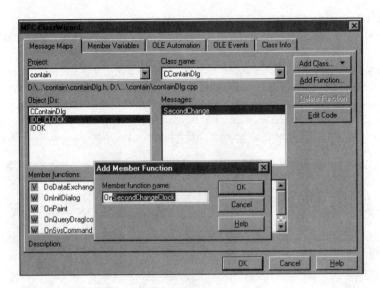

Figure 9.14 Adding an event method.

ClassWizard adds an event handler for the SecondChange event. When the SecondChange event fires, the OnSecondChange method will be called. Add the highlighted code:

```
BEGIN_EVENTSINK_MAP(CContainDlg, CDialog)
    //{{AFX_EVENTSINK_MAP(CContainDlg)
    ON_EVENT(CContainDlg, IDC_CLOCK, 1, OnSecondChangeClock, VTS_NONE)
    //}}AFX_EVENTSINK_MAP
END_EVENTSINK_MAP()

void CContainDlg::OnSecondChangeClock()
{
    COleDateTime date = m_Clock.GetDate();
    m_Time.SetWindowText( date.Format( "%c" ));
}
```

Whenever the control fires the SecondChange event, we get the current date using the Date property and assign it to an instance of the COleDateTime class that we studied earlier. We then use the Format method to get a string representation of the time that we can use to update the text in the edit window.

How does the SecondChange event find its way to the OnSecondChangeClock method? As with most other things in MFC, there's an event map that manages and routes events. An *event map* is almost identical to the dispatch maps we discussed in Chapter 6. MFC's CCmdTarget class has a large number of mapping capabilities. MFC's message maps, interface maps, dispatch maps, and event maps are all handled in much the same way. The macros set up several static class and data members that allow mapping of messages, events, and so on to the appropriate C++ method. In the case of contained control events, the instance of the COccManager class handles looking up events in the event map and calling the right method.

Dynamic Creation

MFC also supports *dynamic creation* of controls. In the preceding scenario, we embedded an instance of a control, which was serialized and stored in the project's resource file. In this section, we'll dynamically create two controls and position them on the dialog box at run time; first, another instance of the Clock control and then an instance of the Postit control from Chapter 8.

When we inserted the Clock control into the CONTAIN project, it created a wrapper class for the control. This arrangement made it easy for us to access the properties and methods specific to the Clock control. The wrapper class contains a Create function that simplifies calling the inherited CWnd::CreateControl method. Here's a look from **CLOCK.H**:

```
CLSID const& GetClsid()
{
    static CLSID const clsid =
        { 0xcc57abb4,
          0xad4e,
          0x11ce,
        { 0xb4, 0x4b, 0x8, 0x0, 0x5a, 0x56, 0x47, 0x18 } };
    return clsid;
}

virtual BOOL Create(LPCTSTR lpszClassName,
          LPCTSTR lpszWindowName, DWORD dwStyle,
          const RECT& rect,
          CWnd* pParentWnd, UINT nID,
          CCreateContext* pContext = NULL)
{
    return CreateControl(GetClsid(),
                         lpszWindowName,
                         dwStyle,
                         rect,
                         pParentWnd,
                         nID);
}
virtual BOOL Create(LPCTSTR lpszWindowName,
             DWORD dwStyle,
             const RECT& rect,
             CWnd* pParentWnd, UINT nID,
```

```
                    CFile* pPersist = NULL,
                    BOOL bStorage = FALSE,
                    BSTR bstrLicKey = NULL)
{
    return CreateControl(GetClsid(),
                         lpszWindowName,
                         dwStyle,
                         rect,
                         pParentWnd,
                         nID,
                         pPersist,
                         bStorage,
                         bstrLicKey);
}
```

Because the wrapper class knows the CLSID of the control, the `Create` method provides a shorthand way of calling `CreateControl`. The best place to create a control for a dialog box is in the handler for the `WM_INITDIALOG` message. `OnInitDialog` is called before the dialog box is displayed. We add a member variable to the dialog class to hold the new clock instance and then create the control:

```
//
// ContainDlg.h : header file
//
class CContainDlg : public CDialog
{
...
// Implementation
protected:
    HICON      m_hIcon;
    CClock*    m_pClock;
...
};

//
// ContainDlg.cpp
///
...
BOOL CContainDlg::OnInitDialog()
{
    CDialog::OnInitDialog();
...
```

```
// TODO: Add extra initialization here
m_pClock = new CClock;
m_pClock->Create( 0, "", WS_VISIBLE,
                CRect( 200, 25, 275, 100 ),
                this,
                100 );

// Make the dynamic clock look a little different
m_pClock->SetAppearance( 1 );
m_pClock->SetFaceColor( RGB( 0, 255, 0 ) );
m_pClock->SetTickColor( RGB( 0, 255, 0 ) );
```

```
    return TRUE;  // return TRUE  unless you set the focus to a control
}
```

We create an instance of the wrapper class, assign it to our member variable, and then call `Create`. `Create` is similar to `CreateControl`, and the details of each parameter are described in Table 9.6. Once the control is created, we modify some of its properties by calling the wrapper class methods. Here we've set the appearance to 3-D and have set the tick and face color to green.

Table 9.6 `CreateControl` Parameters

Parameter	Description
CLSID or ProgID	`CreateControl` is overloaded to take either the CLSID or ProgID of the control to create. In our example, the wrapper class passes the CLSID for us.
lpszWindowName	The name of the window. For controls, this text will be used to set the `Caption` or `Text` property of the control.
dwStyles	Any initial window styles for the control. The most common is `WS_VISIBLE`. Others that can be used for ActiveX controls are `WS_BORDER`, `WS_DISABLE`, `WS_GROUP`, and `WS_TABSTOP`.
Rect	The control's size and position. The rectangle coordinates indicate the left, top, right, and bottom extents (e.g., `CRect( left, top, right, bottom)`).
Parent	The parent window of the control. This must be supplied. In our case, the dialog window (`this`) is the parent.
nId	The ID for the control.
pPersist	A pointer to a CFile object that contains the persistent state of the control. Because the control was created dynamically, we must provide the location and value of the control's persistent data. If they aren't provided, the control will be created without any persistence information.
bStorage	Indicates whether the `pPersist` parameter is stored as `IStream` or `IStorage` data.
bStrLicKey	License key information. If the control requires a license, the key is provided here.

There are a few drawbacks in creating controls dynamically. First, they won't, by default, have any persistent data. Unless we fill out the pPersist parameter, the control will be created as is. We could provide persistence support, but this would require a mechanism for storing the data prior to the control's creation. That mechanism, however, is the responsibility of control containers. If you need to implement a full ActiveX control container, MFC provides a great place to start.

Another problem is that the dynamic approach makes it harder to tie the control's events to a specific handler. If you know which events you want to handle, you can write the handler and then manually enter the events in the event map. To do this for our dynamic clock control, we create a new handler function, OnSecondChangeDyn, and manually add it to the event map:

```
//
// ContainDlg.h : header file
//
class CContainDlg : public CDialog
{
...
    // Generated message map functions
    //{{AFX_MSG(CContainDlg)
    virtual BOOL OnInitDialog();
    afx_msg void OnSysCommand(UINT nID, LPARAM lParam);
    afx_msg void OnPaint();
    afx_msg HCURSOR OnQueryDragIcon();
    afx_msg void OnSecondChangeClock();
    DECLARE_EVENTSINK_MAP()
    //}}AFX_MSG
    afx_msg void OnSecondChangeClockDyn();
    DECLARE_MESSAGE_MAP()
};

//
// ContainDlg.cpp
//
...
```

```
BEGIN_EVENTSINK_MAP(CContainDlg, CDialog)
    //{{AFX_EVENTSINK_MAP(CContainDlg)
    ON_EVENT(CContainDlg, IDC_CLOCK, 1, OnSecondChangeClock, VTS_NONE)
    //}}AFX_EVENTSINK_MAP
    ON_EVENT(CContainDlg, 100, 1 , OnSecondChangeClockDyn, VTS_NONE)
END_EVENTSINK_MAP()
```

```
void CContainDlg::OnSecondChangeClockDyn()
{
    COleDateTime date = m_pClock->GetDate();

    m_EditDyn.SetWindowText( date.Format( "%X" ));
}
```

You must place the ON_EVENT macro outside ClassWizard's area, or ClassWizard will get confused. In the preceding example, we've also added a second entry field to the dialog box to hold the time from our dynamically created control.

MFC allows you to create any control dynamically, even without the wrapper class generated by the Component Gallery. To demonstrate this, let's place an instance of the Postit control from Chapter 8 on our dialog box at run time. The only control-specific information required is the CLSID or ProgID of the control. When generating a control, ControlWizard creates a default ProgID of "Project.ProjectCtrl.1." So our Postit's ProgID is "Postit.PostitCtrl.1." That's all we need to create an instance and add it to our dialog box. Here's the code for OnInitDialog:

```
//
// ContainDlg.h : header file
//
class CContainDlg : public CDialog
{
...
// Implementation
protected:
    HICON       m_hIcon;
    CClock*     m_pClock;
    CWnd*       m_pPostit;
...
```

```
};

//
// ContainDlg.cpp
///
...
BOOL CContainDlg::OnInitDialog()
{
  CDialog::OnInitDialog();
...
  // Make the dynamic clock look a little different
  m_pClock->SetAppearance( 1 );
  m_pClock->SetFaceColor( RGB( 0, 255, 0 ));
  m_pClock->SetTickColor( RGB( 0, 255, 0 ));

  m_pPostit = new CWnd;
  m_pPostit->CreateControl( "Postit.PostitCtrl.1",
                "A dynamically created POSTIT control!",
                WS_VISIBLE,
                CRect( 300, 75, 375, 175 ),
                this,
                101 );

  // Set some of the stock properties
  m_pPostit->SetProperty( DISPID_APPEARANCE, VT_I2, 1 );
  m_pPostit->SetProperty( DISPID_BACKCOLOR, VT_I4, RGB( 255, 255, 255 ));

  return TRUE;  // return TRUE  unless you set the focus to a control
}
```

In this case, we've added a CWnd* member variable to maintain the control instance. We create a new CWnd object and call the CreateControl method, passing in the ProgID of the control to create. For ActiveX controls, the lpszWindowName parameter is used to set the control's caption or text property. The other parameters include the size and position of the control within the dialog box, the parent window (this), and the ID of the control.

Because we don't have a wrapper class for this control, we must use the basic control manipulation methods supplied by CWnd. We set the Appearance property to 3-D and set the background color to white using SetProperty.

When creating controls dynamically, we are responsible for destroying them when the application shuts down. In dialog-based applications, it's best to do this in the dialog's DestroyWindow method. Override it in the CContainDlg class and add the following code:

```
BOOL CContainDlg::DestroyWindow()
{
    // Destroy our dynamic controls
    m_pClock->DestroyWindow();
    delete m_pClock;

    m_pPostit->DestroyWindow();
    delete m_pPostit;

    return CDialog::DestroyWindow();
}
```

Now build the project. When we're finished, we get an application that looks like Figure 9.15.

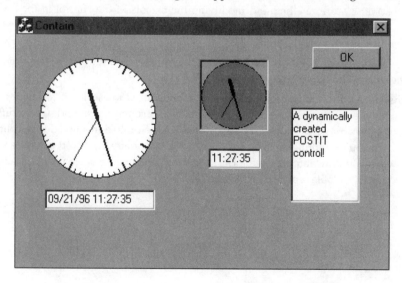

Figure 9.15 CONTAIN dialog box with all of the controls.

Summary

In this chapter we covered the graphical drawing classes provided by MFC. These classes—CBrush, CPen, and so on—encapsulate the Windows graphical device interface API functions. They provide a layer above the GDI and make it a little easier to work with the GDI.

We also described how to build a clock control that uses many of the MFC drawing classes. When rendering your controls, remember that the rcBounds parameter provided to the OnDraw method typically does not provide an upper left corner of (0,0). Your control's drawing code must be adjusted to account for this, or you may inadvertently draw on the container's client area. Another important item to remember is that the device context provided to your control by the container is in an undefined state, and you must set it up the way you need it before rendering your control.

We briefly discussed the Windows mapping modes and the differences between logical and device coordinates. We used the MM_TEXT mapping mode when drawing our clock control, because it is the easiest to understand initially. The coordinate system for the control's rendering area is an attribute of the device context and can be changed.

The size of device units, or pixels, is dependent on the hardware device on which your control is rendered. You specify the initial size of your control in device units in the control's constructor using the SetInitialSize method. You can control the size and shape of your control by overriding the COleControl::OnSetExtent method and modifying the extents of the control in the provided SIZEL structure. The SIZEL structure's extent sizes are in HIMETRIC units, and we discussed ways to convert between device units and HIMETRIC units.

The container uses the ambient property UIDead to notify the control that it is in some sort of debug mode and so the control should not allow user input.

Controls that often draw and update their appearance may need to use an off-screen or memory device context to eliminate flicker. Because the clock control redraws itself every second, we modified it to use a memory DC. Containers may require that the control render itself into a metafile device context at various times, such as when you're printing an image of the control. We briefly discussed metafiles and the restrictions to follow when you draw into a metafile DC. COleControl::OnDrawMetafile is called whenever the container requests a metafile representation.

If you need to use a property within your control but do not want to expose it to visual tool users, you can mark the property as hidden in the control's ODL file. This indicates to property browsers that the property should not be displayed.

Finally, we looked at using ActiveX controls in Visual C++ applications. In MFC version 4.0, the `CWnd` class was enhanced to provide ActiveX container support. Several methods, such as `CreateControl`, `SetProperty`, and `OnAmbientProperty`, were added to make if easy to manage ActiveX controls within MFC applications. Other useful, but undocumented, classes (such as `COleContainer`) were also added. MFC provides a great deal of support for embedding ActiveX controls in dialogs as well as in view-derived classes. Controls can be placed on dialogs at design time or created and placed dynamically at run time.

Chapter 10

Subclassing Windows Controls

In this chapter, we'll look at the details of developing ActiveX controls by subclassing existing Windows standard (non-ActiveX) controls. Subclassing is an effective way of reusing existing control functionality within Windows. By subclassing an existing control, you automatically gain its capabilities. I was tempted to say you "inherit" capability from the control, but subclassing a control is different from deriving a new class based on another class (as in C++).

The Windows operating system provides many controls, and there are even more now that Windows 95 provides additional full-featured *common* controls. Examples of common controls include the Rich Text Format (RTF) control and the tree-list view control. In this chapter we will cover the basics of subclassing, and some of the issues involved, by subclassing a Windows EDIT control and one of the Windows 95 common controls. Understanding the basics of this control will allow you to subclass the other controls as well.

Subclassing a Windows Control

In the SDK/C world of Windows development, subclassing a standard control is a common occurrence. It is similar to object-oriented inheritance in that you acquire the features of the control and are able to augment only those capabilities that you need to. If the control already provides exactly the feature you need, you just pass the message (method) to the original implementation. One major difference is that Windows subclassing can be performed only on an instance of a control. Inheritance in C++ is done using classes and not instances of the classes.

You subclass a control because you want to provide functionality that is similar to that already provided by a standard control. An edit field that accepts only numbers, a listbox that contains icons and text, a 3-D static field—the possibilities are endless. When you subclass an existing control, much of the drawing code and control structures are already implemented for you. However, this is not the case when you imple-

453

ment an *owner-draw* control. Owner-draw controls provide an effective way to represent information in a familiar Windows format (such as a listbox).

A simple Windows control (such as EDIT) is actually just a window. All controls have a window procedure that processes messages sent to the window. Standard windows, such as the EDIT control, have a window procedure that is part of the Windows operating system. Although we don't have access to the source code for the window procedure, the design of Windows makes it easy to subclass, and use the features of, an existing window.

A window is subclassed by replacing its default window procedure with one written by the developer. The new window procedure modifies the behavior of the window by discarding messages intended for the original window procedure, performing some additional actions and forwarding the message, or modifying the contents of the message and passing it on. To remind you what it looks like in C, the following code demonstrates this technique. It subclasses an EDIT control window and allows the entry only of uppercase alpha characters.

```
WNDPROC pfnOriginalEditProcedure;

// Create an EDIT window
HWND hwndEdit = CreateWindowEx( "EDIT", ... );

// Subclass the window by setting the address of its window
// procedure to that of the new subclass procedure. Save the old procedure's
// address so we can call it too.
pfnOriginalEditProcedure = SetWindowLong( hwndEdit,
                                          GWL_WNDPROC,
                                          (LONG) SubclassEditProcedure );

// Subclass procedure. All messages are now processed first by
// this procedure
LRESULT APIENTRY SubclassEditProcedure( HWND hwnd,
                                        UNIT uMsg,
                                        WPARAM wParam,
                                        LPARAM lParam )
{
   switch( uMsg )
   {
     case WM_CHAR:
         // If it's an alpha character make it uppercase
         if ( isalpha( wParam ) )
            wParam = toupper( wParam );
         // otherwise ignore the character
         else
            return 0;
```

```
        break;

    case default:
        break;
    }

    return CallWindowProc( pfnOriginalEditProcedure, hwnd, uMsg, wParam, lParam );
}
```

If an existing Windows control provides a capability that you need within your control and if there are no special requirements that preclude your use of the control, you should probably subclass it. If not, as in the clock example of Chapter 9, you can always implement all the functionality and drawing yourself.

The Expression Class Again

It was in Chapter 6 that we last saw the `Expression` class, and I promised you then that we would see it one more time. In this chapter, our goal is to encapsulate the functionality of the `Expression` component in an ActiveX control. We'll subclass the Windows Edit control and enhance it to provide numeric expression evaluation. This arrangement will make it easy for the user of a visual tool (such as Visual Basic) to drag-and-drop the control in a container and instantly gain expression evaluation capabilities.

Creating the EEdit Project

Use AppWizard to build a ControlWizard-based project with the name EEdit. Follow these steps to specify each of ControlWizard's options:

- In the OLE Control Wizard Step 1 of 2 dialog box, take the defaults **No runtime license**, **Yes, comments**, and **No help files**.
- In OLE Control Wizard Step 2 of 2, take the defaults **Activate when visible** and **Has "About" box**. From the **Which window class, if any, should this control subclass?** dropdown, choose the **EDIT** control.
- Click **Finish** and create the control project.

There is an option that you use when creating an ActiveX control that subclasses an existing Windows control. When you subclass an existing Windows control, ControlWizard adds the needed code. Figure 10.1 shows the Control Options dialog box.

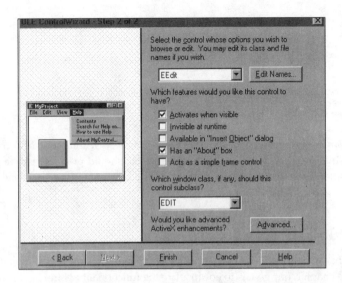

Figure 10.1 Subclass Windows control option.

ControlWizard allows you to choose to subclass any of the standard Windows controls listed in Table 10.1. ControlWizard also allows you to subclass any of the new Windows 95 common controls. Later in this chapter, we will look at subclassing other Windows controls, including the new Windows 95 common controls.

Table 10.1 Standard Windows Controls

Standard Control	Windows Class Name and Use
Button	BUTTON: a Windows push button.
Static	STATIC: provides the ability to display text in various ways.
Edit	EDIT: provides either a single-line entry field or a multiline entry field that has useful editor-like features.
Listbox	LISTBOX: a standard Windows listbox. Listbox controls can operate in different modes (multiselect, single select, and so on). To modify the mode of a listbox, appropriate style bits are applied during creation.
Combo box	COMBOBOX: a standard Windows combo box. It also supports various modes by specifying different style bits during creation.
Scroll bar	SCROLLBAR: the horizontal and vertical scroll bars that you use in most Windows applications.

After the project is created, start ClassWizard and add the following stock properties through the **OLE Automation** tab as we did in Chapter 9. When developing a visual control, you will almost always use at least some of the stock properties.

- Appearance
- BackColor
- ForeColor
- hWnd
- BorderStyle
- Enabled
- Text
- Font

Because we're using the stock font and color properties, go ahead and add the stock font and color property pages. Here's the new code needed for **EEDITCTL.CPP**:

```
// TODO: Add more property pages as needed.  Remember to increase the count!
BEGIN_PROPPAGEIDS(CEEditCtrl, 3)
    PROPPAGEID(CEEditPropPage::guid)
    PROPPAGEID(CLSID_CColorPropPage)
    PROPPAGEID(CLSID_CFontPropPage)
END_PROPPAGEIDS(CEEditCtrl)
```

Compile and link the project, register the control, and insert it into a container. Right away you will see that the control provides significant functionality. You can type text directly into the control, and you can even change the font that it uses. It's a basic Windows edit control, but not everything works yet (from an ActiveX control perspective). Try changing the background and foreground color properties of the control. No luck? In the remaining sections, we'll solve this problem and add functionality in the process.

Code Added by ControlWizard

In Chapter 8 we went through the code generated by ControlWizard. When we chose to subclass a Windows control, ControlWizard generated some additional code. In particular, it automatically provided an override of `COleControl::PreCreateWindow`. The following code is from **EEDITCTL.CPP**:

```
/////////////////////////////////////////////////////////////////////
// CEEditCtrl::PreCreateWindow - Modify parameters for CreateWindowEx

BOOL CEEditCtrl::PreCreateWindow(CREATESTRUCT& cs)
{
    cs.lpszClass = _T("EDIT");
    return COleControl::PreCreateWindow(cs);
}
```

This method provides most of what is required to subclass an existing control. The PreCreateWindow method is called just before the creation of the (OLE) control's window. A reference to the window's CRE-ATESTRUCT is passed to allow you to modify the parameters used in the creation of the window. As you can see, ControlWizard added a line that sets the window class to EDIT. When PreCreateWindow returns, the framework will use the CreateWindowEx function to create an instance of the new EDIT window (or control) using the parameters of the CREATESTRUCT structure. The members of CREATESTRUCT are parameters of the CreateWindowEx function.

```
typedef struct tagCREATESTRUCT {
    LPVOID      lpCreateParams;
    HANDLE      hInstance;
    HMENU       hMenu;
    HWND        hwndParent;
    int         cy;
    int         cx;
    int         y;
    int         x;
    LONG        style;
    LPCSTR      lpszName;
    LPCSTR      lpszClass;
    DWORD       dwExStyle;
} CREATESTRUCT;
```

When you're subclassing a control, MFC needs to keep track of the original window procedure so that you can call it to pass messages through. For subclassed controls, ControlWizard adds a function to your control's implementation file that indicates to the framework that the control has been subclassed. It's called IsSubclassedControl:

```
/////////////////////////////////////////////////////////////////////
// CEEditCtrl::IsSubclassedControl - This is a subclassed control
BOOL CEEditCtrl::IsSubclassedControl()
{
    return TRUE;
}
```

NOTE It is no longer necessary to override GetSuperWndProcAddr in controls that subclass Windows controls. The CWnd class now does this automatically for each control class. Versions of MFC prior to 4.0 required this override in the COleControl-derived class.

The OnDraw code provided by ControlWizard is also different when you subclass a control. It contains only a call to COleControl::DoSuperclassPaint:

```
/////////////////////////////////////////////////////
// CEEditCtrl::OnDraw - Drawing function
void CEEditCtrl::OnDraw( CDC* pdc,
                             const CRect& rcBounds,
                             const CRect& rcInvalid)
{
   DoSuperclassPaint(pdc, rcBounds);
}
```

DoSuperclassPaint sets up the device context and sends a WM_PAINT message to the default window procedure for the subclassed control, as shown next. If you look closely at the following code, you'll see that the framework sends the WM_PRINT message instead of WM_PAINT when running on Windows 95 and Windows NT version 4.x:

```
void COleControl::DoSuperclassPaint(CDC* pDC, const CRect& rcBounds)
{
   if (m_hWnd == NULL)
      CreateWindowForSubclassedControl();

   if (m_hWnd != NULL)
   {
      CRect rcClient;
      GetClientRect(&rcClient);

      if (rcClient.Size() != rcBounds.Size())
      {
         pDC->SetMapMode(MM_ANISOTROPIC);
         pDC->SetWindowExt(rcClient.right, rcClient.bottom);
         pDC->SetViewportExt(rcBounds.Size());
      }
      pDC->SetWindowOrg(0, 0);
      pDC->SetViewportOrg(rcBounds.left, rcBounds.top);

      BOOL bWin4 = afxData.bWin4;
      _AfxFillPSOnStack();
      ::CallWindowProc(
            *GetSuperWndProcAddr(),
            m_hWnd, (bWin4 ? WM_PRINT : WM_PAINT),
            (WPARAM)(pDC->m_hDC),
            (LPARAM)(bWin4 ? PRF_CHILDREN | PRF_CLIENT : 0));
   }
}
```

This technique works fine when the control is in the running state, but it doesn't provide a good representation when the container requests a metafile representation or when the container is in design mode. We will discuss this problem in more detail in a later section.

Selecting the subclass option also provides a default reflected message OCM_COMMAND handler to our control code. We will look at this message handler in detail later when we discuss a subclassed control's reflector window.

The Windows Edit Control

The standard EDIT control provided by Windows has a great deal of built-in functionality. It can function as a single-line entry field that supports copy, cut, and paste (via the clipboard) or as a multiline edit control that provides many of the features of an editor. Much of the functionality of the Windows Notepad utility is provided via an EDIT control.

A standard control's functionality is defined by the messages it sends and receives. Table 10.2 shows some of the messages handled by the EDIT control. This information is available for all the standard controls and the Windows 95 common controls via on-line help or in the Win32 SDK manuals. Our focus is on the EDIT control, but the techniques we will use are also applicable to the others.

Table 10.2 Useful EDIT Control Messages

Message	Purpose
EM_GETLIMITTEXT (Win32)	Returns the current text limit.
EM_GETLINE	Retrieves a line of text from the control.
EM_GETLINECOUNT	Returns the number of lines of text in the control.
EM_GETSEL	Returns the currently selected text.
EM_REPLACESEL	Replaces the selected text with the provided text.
EM_LINELENGTH	Returns the length of the line specified.
EM_SETLIMITTEXT (Win32), EM_LIMITTEXT (Win16)	Sets the maximum number of characters that can be entered into the edit control.
EM_SETREADONLY	Sets the control's read-only mode. No input is accepted from the user.
EM_SETSEL	Selects a range of characters in the control.
EN_CHANGE	Sent to the parent when the control identifies that the control's content has changed.
EN_KILLFOCUS	Sent to the parent when the control loses focus.
EN_MAXTEXT	Sent to the parent when the number of characters trying to be inserted is larger than the maximum text limit.
EN_SETFOCUS	Sent to the parent when the control gains focus.

Table 10.2 Useful EDIT Control Messages (continued)

Message	Purpose
EN_UPDATE	Sent to the parent when the contents of the control are about to be changed. The EN_CHANGE event is sent after the change has occurred.
WM_COMMAND	Sent to the parent window with one of the control's notification messages encoded in the WPARAM parameter.
WM_COPY	Copies the contents of the control to the clipboard with the CF_TEXT format.
WM_CTLCOLOREDIT (Win32), WM_CTLCOLOR (Win16)	Sent to the parent by the control to allow the parent window to select the color of the control when it is to be drawn.
WM_PASTE	Pastes the contents of the clipboard into the control.

The messages prefixed with EN_ are called *notification* messages. These messages are sent from the control to its parent and are used to notify the parent of events or changes within the control. For example, the EN_CHANGE notification message is sent to the parent window when text within the edit control is modified.

The EM_ messages are sent to the control to force it to change its state or to set various characteristics of the control. For example, the EM_SETLIMITTEXT message sets the maximum number of characters that the control will accept. To find out the current text limit, you send the EM_GETLIMITTEXT message.

N O T E

The EM_GETLIMITTEXT and EM_SETLIMITTEXT messages are provided only in Win32. The Win16 implementation provides only the EM_LIMITTEXT message and so gives you no way to retrieve the LIMITTEXT value of an edit control.

The standard controls also support various standard window messages, such as WM_COPY and WM_PASTE, which copy and paste text in the control to the clipboard. The WM_CTLCOLOR message is important for standard controls, because it plays a role in the drawing and coloring of the control. The WM_COMMAND message is used to pass the EN_ notification messages to the control's parent. The EN_ notification messages are passed as parameters of a WM_COMMAND message. We will cover these messages in more detail later as we use them within our ActiveX control.

Window Style Bits

Each of the standard Windows controls has various *style bits* that affect the controls' behavior or appearance. Depending on your requirements, you specify style bits by ORing them with the style member of the CREATESTRUCT in the PreCreateWindow method of your control. Each control has both general (e.g., WM_BORDER) and specific (e.g., ES_LEFT) style bits. We're focusing on the EDIT control here, so I've listed the EDIT control–specific style bits in Table 10.3.

Table 10.3 EDIT Control Style Bits

EDIT Control Style	Purpose
ES_MULTILINE	Indicates that the window will support the control's multiline features.
ES_LEFT*	Left-justify the text in the control.
ES_RIGHT*	Right-justify the text in the control.
ES_CENTER*	Center the text in the control.
ES_LOWERCASE	As text is entered in the control, make it all lowercase.
ES_UPPERCASE	As text is entered in the control, make it all uppercase.
ES_AUTOHSCROLL	If this bit is set, the control will allow the text to scroll when the number of characters in the edit control exceeds the number that can be displayed. If this flag is not set, the entry field will allow only a fixed number of characters.
ES_AUTOVSCROLL*	If set, will allow the text to scroll vertically when used with a multiline entry field.
ES_NOHIDESEL	When set, the text that is selected will continue to show selected when the control loses focus.
ES_READONLY	The entry field is read-only. No text can be entered.
ES_PASSWORD	All characters entered will display as asterisks.
ES_WANTRETURN*	A carriage return will be inserted when the user presses the **Enter** key in a multiline edit field.

* Indicates multiline feature only

Changing a Window's Style Bits before Window Creation

One of the style bits that would be useful for our control is ES_AUTOHSCROLL. If we set this style bit, the text will scroll left if the user types in a text string that is larger than the entry field. If this flag is not set, the control will beep and will not allow any input if the text cannot be displayed completely within the entry field.

To support this ability, we add the ES_AUTOHSCROLL flag to the CREATESTRUCT *style field* in the PreCreateWindow method:

```
/////////////////////////////////////////////////////////////////////////////
// CEEditCtrl::PreCreateWindow - Modify parameters for CreateWindowEx
BOOL CEEditCtrl::PreCreateWindow(CREATESTRUCT& cs)
{
    cs.lpszClass = _T("EDIT");
    cs.style |= ES_AUTOHSCROLL;
    return COleControl::PreCreateWindow(cs);
}
```

Changing a Window's Style Bits at Run Time

You can also change some style bits after a window has been created. To change the style bits of a created window, you use the `GetWindowLong` and `SetWindowLong` functions. The style bits of a window are stored in a `DWORD` that is part of every window structure. The following code shows how to change a window's style bit after it has been created:

```
void SetSomeProperty( BOOL bNewValue )
{
    // Get the current style bits
    DWORD dwStyle = ::GetWindowLong( GetSafeHwnd(), GWL_STYLE );

    // If the user turned on the property
    if ( m_bProperty )
    {
        dwStyle |= WS_WINDOWSTYLEBIT;
    }
    // Turn off the style bit
    else
    {
        dwStyle &= ~WS_WINDOWSTYLEBIT;
    }

    // Update the style for the window
    ::SetWindowLong( GetSafeHwnd(), GWL_STYLE, dwStyle );
}
```

OleControl::RecreateControlWindow

Most of the style bits that are specific to a standard control cannot be changed unless you destroy and re-create the window. `COleControl` provides a function, `RecreateControlWindow`, that makes this easy.

As part of our EEdit implementation, we decided that the `ES_AUTOHSCROLL` flag would provide additional functionality. For instructional purposes, we'll allow the control user to either enable or disable the `AUTOHSCROLL` functionality. We'll add a property that can be changed during the design phase and at run time. Run-time support will require that we destroy and re-create the window.

Using ClassWizard, add an `AutoScroll` property of type `BOOL` with `Get` and `Set` methods as the implementation of the EEdit control. We also need a member variable—call it `m_bAutoScroll`—to store the property's value. The default value will be `TRUE`, because we want the `AUTOHSCROLL` capability enabled by default. Add the new member variable to **EEDITCTL.H** and add the following code for `DoPropExchange`, `PreCreateWindow`, and the `Get` and `Set` methods for the new property to **EEDITCTL.CPP**:

```
// EEditctl.h
...
class CEEditCtrl : public COleControl
{
...
// Implementation
protected:
    ~CEEditCtrl();
    BOOL    m_bAutoScroll;
...
};

// EEditCtl.cpp
...
CEEditCtrl::CEEditCtrl()
{
    InitializeIIDs(&IID_DEedit, &IID_DEeditEvents);

    // TODO: Initialize your control's instance data here.
    m_bAutoScroll = TRUE;
}
...
//////////////////////////////////////////////////////////////////////
// CEEditCtrl::DoPropExchange - Persistence support
void CEEditCtrl::DoPropExchange(CPropExchange* pPX)
{
    ExchangeVersion(pPX, MAKELONG(_wVerMinor, _wVerMajor));
    COleControl::DoPropExchange(pPX);

    // TODO: Call PX_ functions for each persistent custom property.

    // Store/retrieve the AutoScroll property value
    // The default is TRUE
    PX_Bool( pPX, "AutoScroll", m_bAutoScroll, TRUE );
}

//////////////////////////////////////////////////////////////////////
// CEEditCtrl::PreCreateWindow - Modify parameters for CreateWindowEx
BOOL CEEditCtrl::PreCreateWindow(CREATESTRUCT& cs)
{
    cs.lpszClass = _T("EDIT");
```

```
    if ( m_bAutoScroll )
        cs.style |= ES_AUTOHSCROLL;
    return COleControl::PreCreateWindow(cs);
}

BOOL CEEditCtrl::GetAutoScroll()
{
    return m_bAutoScroll;
}

void CEEditCtrl::SetAutoScroll(BOOL bNewValue)
{
    m_bAutoScroll = bNewValue;
    if ( AmbientUserMode() )
        RecreateControlWindow();
    SetModifiedFlag();
}
```

We now check and set the appropriate style bits before the creation of the window in `PreCreateWindow`. Because the control's window is nonexistent or will be destroyed and re-created when the user switches to run mode, the `PreCreateWindow` method will handle design-time modification of the property.

When the ActiveX control is operating at run time, the user can now modify the `AUTOHSCROLL` behavior at run time with a call similar to this:

```
'Turn autoscroll off
EEdit1.AutoScroll = False
```

This code will call `SetAutoScroll`, which sets the new value of `m_bAutoScroll` to `FALSE` and calls `RecreateControlWindow`. `RecreateControlWindow` calls `PreCreateWindow`, and the window is created without the `ES_AUTOHSCROLL` bit. The framework maintains the state of the control throughout this process. A side effect is that the user may see the control quickly disappear and reappear as it is destroyed and re-created.

NOTE   The `COleControl` class maintains only the "text" of our EEdit window. Other Windows control state information, such as the `m_sMaxLength` property (which we will cover next), is not maintained during the call to `RecreateControlWindow`. We can manage this by maintaining the `MaxLength` value within our control's class and resetting the value when the `WM_CREATE` message is received for the newly re-created window. Other subclassed controls, such as listboxes, also require that you maintain certain control state information if you use the `RecreateControlWindow` method.

Go ahead and compile and link the project and insert the control into your favorite container (not the Test Container). Add a few of the EEdit controls and change their `AutoScroll` properties during the design phase and during run time to get a sense of exactly what is going on.

Modifying Control Behavior with Messages

You can also modify the behavior a standard Windows control by sending it messages that are defined by the control. The standard EDIT control allows you to limit the number of characters that can be entered into the entry field. You do this by sending it an EM_SETLIMITTEXT message. The control must exist before you send it the message, so modifying a control's behavior in this manner requires a different approach from that used above.

Add a new property to the control—call it m_sMaxLength—of type short. The control must have a valid HWND before we can initialize the control with the property value. The best time to initialize this value is when the control's window is initially created. Right after a window is created, it receives the WM_CREATE message. Open ClassWizard and add a handler for the WM_CREATE message. We will use this event to set the MaxLength for the control. Add the following highlighted code:

```
// eeditctl.h
class CEEditCtrl : public COleControl
{
...
// Implementation
protected:
    ~CEEditCtrl();
    BOOL    m_bAutoScroll;
    short   m_sMaxLength;
...
};

// EEditctl.cpp
...
CEEditCtrl::CEEditCtrl()
{
    InitializeIIDs(&IID_DEedit, &IID_DEeditEvents);

    // TODO: Initialize your control's instance data here.
    m_bAutoScroll = TRUE;
    m_sMaxLength = 0;
}
...
void CEEditCtrl::DoPropExchange(CPropExchange* pPX)
{
    ExchangeVersion(pPX, MAKELONG(_wVerMinor, _wVerMajor));
    COleControl::DoPropExchange(pPX);

    // TODO: Call PX_ functions for each persistent custom property.
```

```
    PX_Bool( pPX, "AutoScroll", m_bAutoScroll, TRUE );
    PX_Short( pPX, "MaxLength", m_sMaxLength, 0 );
}

...

#ifdef _WIN32
#define LIMITMSG EM_SETLIMITTEXT
#else
#define LIMITMSG EM_LIMITTEXT
#endif
int CEEditCtrl::OnCreate(LPCREATESTRUCT lpCreateStruct)
{
    if (COleControl::OnCreate(lpCreateStruct) == -1)
        return -1;

    if ( m_sMaxLength )
        SendMessage( LIMITMSG, m_sMaxLength, 0 );

    return 0;
}

short CEEditCtrl::GetMaxLength()
{
    return m_sMaxLength;
}

void CEEditCtrl::SetMaxLength(short nNewValue)
{
    m_sMaxLength = nNewValue;

    if ( AmbientUserMode() )
    {
        if ( m_sMaxLength )
            SendMessage( LIMITMSG, m_sMaxLength, 0 );
        else
            SendMessage( LIMITMSG, 32000, 0 );
    }

    SetModifiedFlag();
}
```

There are differences between the Win16 and Win32 implementations of the WM_LIMIT message, so we use the _WIN32 symbol to isolate the differences between the platforms. Once that is done, the implementation of the new property is easy. When the control's window is created, we check the value of the property. If it is nonzero, we use the SendMessage method to modify the behavior of the control. If the control user wants to change the `MaxLength` of the control at run time, the `SetMaxLength` method handles this. If `m_sMaxLength` is set to zero, a limit of 32000 is sent to the control, effectively allowing unlimited text entry.

Added Expression Capabilities with ActiveX Controls

When we last used the `Expression` class in Chapter 6, we provided an automation interface so that its capabilities could be used from non-C++ languages. By developing an ActiveX control implementation, we are making the `Expression` component's functionality more accessible to developers who use visual tools. We also provide a feedback, or event, mechanism so that the tool user can easily tie additional actions to the control's features.

Adding the Stock Events

Because our EEdit control is primarily a visual one, it should provide the stock MFC events. Using ClassWizard, add the following stock events to the `CEEditCtrl` class:

- Click
- DblClick
- KeyDown
- KeyUp
- KeyPress
- MouseDown
- MouseUp
- MouseMove

Adding these stock events provides the control user with the ability to perform actions when one of the events is fired by the default implementation of `COleControl`. We didn't add any code at all, but the control user can now add behavior based on the user clicking or double-clicking within the edit field.

Reflected Window Messages

Standard Windows controls are usually associated with a parent window. That's one of the reasons that they're called *child* windows. In most cases, the parent window is a Windows dialog box. The dialog window acts a lot like an ActiveX control container, because it coordinates the behavior of its child windows. It controls the tabbing order of the controls, notifies them of changes in the environment, and accepts messages, or notifications, from the child controls when something occurs.

When a control is subclassed for use within an ActiveX control, this dialog-based environment does not necessarily exist. ActiveX controls have their own techniques of interacting with the container. The container and controls work together to establish the tabbing order, ambient properties provide a way for the control to retrieve information from the container, and the control can fire events to notify the container of internal changes. The functionality is similar to that in a parent/child window environment, but the implementation is quite different. Instead of Window messages going back and forth, we use automation.

What I'm getting at is this; there is no *parent* window for the subclassed controls to post and receive the Windows messages that define their behavior. To solve this problem, the ActiveX control standard describes a *reflector* window. The reflector window is created by the COleControl implementation, but a reflector window can instead be provided by the container. The container technique would reduce overhead, because it could use only one window that could act as the parent for all contained ActiveX controls that use subclassing. If the control container provides this feature, it must set the MessageReflect ambient property to TRUE. If the container does not support message reflection, the framework will create its own reflector window for each ActiveX control that subclasses a Windows control. This is done by the COleControl base class.

The purpose of the reflector window is to reflect back to the ActiveX control certain Windows messages that would otherwise go to the parent (Figure 10.2). A control notification message such as BN_CLICKED, EN_CHANGED, and so on will be reflected back to the ActiveX control so that it can be implemented as an OLE event. For example, the WM_CTLCOLOR message is sent to the parent to get information about how the child window should paint itself but instead is now reflected back to the ActiveX control for handling. The ActiveX control can then get the container's ambient color properties and paint itself appropriately. Table 10.4 shows the messages that are reflected back to the ActiveX control.

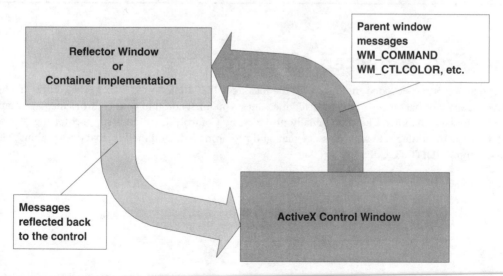

Figure 10.2 A control's reflector window.

Table 10.4 Windows Messages Reflected Back to an ActiveX Control

Message from Control	Message Reflected Back to Control
WM_COMMAND	OCM_COMMAND
WM_CTLCOLOR (Win16)	OCM_CTLCOLOR
WM_CTLCOLOREDIT (Win32)	OCM_CTLCOLOREDIT
WM_CTLCOLORBTN (Win32)	OCM_CTLCOLORBTN
WM_CTLCOLORDLG (Win32)	OCM_CTLCOLORDLG
WM_CTLCOLORLISTBOX (Win32)	OCM_CTLCOLORLISTBOX
WM_CTLCOLORMSGBOX (Win32)	OCM_CTLCOLORMSGBOX
WM_CTLCOLORSCROLLBAR (Win32)	OCM_CTLCOLORSCROLLBAR
WM_CTLCOLORSTATIC (Win32)	OCM_CTLCOLORSTATIC
WM_DRAWITEM	OCM_DRAWITEM
WM_MEASUREITEM	OCM_MEASUREITEM
WM_DELETEITEM	OCM_DELETEITEM
WM_VKEYTOITEM	OCM_VKEYTOITEM
WM_CHARTOITEM	OCM_CHARTOITEM
WM_COMPAREITEM	OCM_COMPAREITEM
WM_HSCROLL	OCM_HSCROLL
WM_VSCROLL	OCM_VSCROLL
WM_PARENTNOTIFY	OCM_PARENTNOTIFY

Handling Reflected Messages

By default, COleControl does nothing with the messages that are reflected back to the control. To fire an event or in any way act on one of the reflected messages, you must add it to your control's message map and provide a message handler. The code initially provided by ControlWizard adds support for the OCM_COMMAND message by adding it to your message map and providing a default method that does nothing. Here is the code from **EEDITCTL.CPP**:

```
// EEditctl.cpp
...
BEGIN_MESSAGE_MAP(CEEditCtrl, COleControl)
    //{{AFX_MSG_MAP(CEEditCtrl)
    ON_MESSAGE(OCM_COMMAND, OnOcmCommand)
    //}}AFX_MSG_MAP
    ON_OLEVERB(AFX_IDS_VERB_EDIT, OnEdit)
    ON_OLEVERB(AFX_IDS_VERB_PROPERTIES, OnProperties)
END_MESSAGE_MAP()
...
/////////////////////////////////////////////////////////////////////////
// CEEditCtrl::OnOcmCommand - Handle command messages
LRESULT CEEditCtrl::OnOcmCommand(WPARAM wParam, LPARAM lParam)
{
#ifdef _WIN32
    WORD wNotifyCode = HIWORD(wParam);
#else
    WORD wNotifyCode = HIWORD(lParam);
#endif

    // TODO: Switch on wNotifyCode here.

    return 0;
}
```

ControlWizard provides a default handler for the OCM_COMMAND message, because you typically fire events when your control receives notification messages. For example, when subclassing a BUTTON control, you will trap the BN_CLICKED message and fire the stock Click event.

Processing a Control's Notification Messages

For our EEdit control, we will process the EN_CHANGED notification message and fire an event that notifies the control user that text in the edit control has changed. First, using ClassWizard, add a custom event called FireChange. The event requires no parameters. Figure 10.3 shows the addition of the custom event.

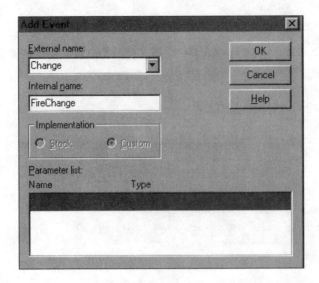

Figure 10.3 Adding a custom event.

Once the event is added, we need to fire it when appropriate. The EEdit control sends a notification message to its parent, which is reflected back to the ActiveX control via the OCM_COMMAND message handler. This message handler calls the OnOcmCommand method with the parameters of the notification message. We check the notify code of the message, and, if it is EN_CHANGE, we fire the change event. Add the following code to **EEDITCTL.CPP**:

```
/////////////////////////////////////////////////////////////////////////
// CEEditCtrl::OnOcmCommand - Handle command messages
LRESULT CEEditCtrl::OnOcmCommand(WPARAM wParam, LPARAM lParam)
{
#ifdef _WIN32
    WORD wNotifyCode = HIWORD(wParam);
#else
    WORD wNotifyCode = HIWORD(lParam);
#endif

    // TODO: Switch on wNotifyCode here.
    switch( wNotifyCode )
    {
      case EN_CHANGE:
          FireChange();
          break;
    }
    return 0;
}
```

As you can see, the code generated by ControlWizard takes care of breaking out the notification parameter from either the wParam or the lParam depending on the platform we are compiling for. We are interested only in the EN_CHANGE notification, so we add a switch statement to identify it and to fire the custom event that we added earlier. Rather painless, isn't it? Setting the colors of a subclassed control is slightly more involved.

Setting the Colors of a Subclassed Control

When you subclass a control, it's important to get the colors to draw correctly. We've briefly discussed the WM_CTLCOLOR message, which a standard control sends to its parent when it needs to draw itself. The WM_CTLCOLOR message contains the DC of the child control, so when the parent receives the message it sets the attributes of the provided DC to those appropriate for the drawing of the child window. The return value of WM_CTLCOLOR is a handle to the brush that is used for the control's background color.

This sounds great, but who is the parent? As we've discussed, the parent of a subclassed control will be the control's reflector window. Depending on the environment in which the control is running, the framework may provide the reflector window, or the container may provide a similar mechanism. In both cases, the control itself becomes the "parent" of the subclassed control. By using the reflected message handler for the OCM_CTLCOLOR message, we provide ourselves with the brushes for coloring the control.

ClassWizard doesn't currently let you add reflected message handlers. You must add them yourself, but it's easy. ControlWizard initially added a handler for our notification messages, so we add another line with the new handler. Add the following highlighted code to **EEDITCTL.CPP**:

```
///////////////////////////////////////////////////////////////////////
// Message map
//
BEGIN_MESSAGE_MAP(CEEditCtrl, COleControl)
    //{{AFX_MSG_MAP(CEEditCtrl)
    ON_MESSAGE(OCM_COMMAND, OnOcmCommand)
    ON_MESSAGE(OCM_CTLCOLOREDIT, OnOcmCtlColor)
    //}}AFX_MSG_MAP
    ON_OLEVERB(AFX_IDS_VERB_EDIT, OnEdit)
    ON_OLEVERB(AFX_IDS_VERB_PROPERTIES, OnProperties)
END_MESSAGE_MAP()
```

Notice that we added a handler for an OCM_CTLCOLOREDIT message and not one for OCM_CTLCOLOR. We'll get to that in a moment. Next, we need to add the declaration for OnOcmCtlColor to **EEDITCTL.H** and then implement it in **EEDITCTL.CPP**:

```
// EEditctl.h

...

class CEEditCtrl : public COleControl
```

```
{
...
// Implementation
protected:
    ~CEEditCtrl();
  BOOL      m_bAutoScroll;
  short     m_sMaxLength;
  CBrush*   m_pBackBrush;
...
  // Subclassed control support
  BOOL PreCreateWindow(CREATESTRUCT& cs);
  BOOL IsSubclassedControl();
  LRESULT OnOcmCommand(WPARAM wParam, LPARAM lParam);
  LRESULT OnOcmCtlColor( WPARAM wParam, LPARAM lParam);
...
};

// EEditctl.cpp
...
CEEditCtrl::CEEditCtrl()
{
  InitializeIIDs(&IID_DEedit, &IID_DEeditEvents);

  // TODO: Initialize your control's instance data here.
  m_pBackBrush = NULL;
  m_bAutoScroll = TRUE;
  m_sMaxLength = 0;
}
...
LRESULT CEEditCtrl::OnOcmCtlColor( WPARAM wParam, LPARAM lParam )
{
  if ( m_pBackBrush == NULL )
    m_pBackBrush = new CBrush( TranslateColor( GetBackColor() ));

  CDC* pdc = CDC::FromHandle( (HDC) wParam );
  pdc->SetBkMode( TRANSPARENT );
  pdc->SetBkColor( TranslateColor( GetBackColor() ));
  pdc->SetTextColor( TranslateColor( GetForeColor() ));

  HBRUSH far* hbr = (HBRUSH far*) m_pBackBrush->GetSafeHandle();
  return ((DWORD) hbr);
}
```

The code in `OnOcmCtlColor` is what you would typically see in the parent (such as a dialog box) of many child controls. When the message is received, we set the background mode and color and the text color just as we would in a normal `OnDraw` method. The tricky part involves the handling of the background color brush.

When processing the `WM_CTLCOLOR` message, we return either a handle to a valid brush or `NULL`. If `NULL` is returned, the default system background color is used. We need to return a handle to a brush that is the current background color, so to process this message we need to maintain an instance of the `CBrush` class with the current background color of our control. We need a `CBrush` pointer member in our control class, and we call it `m_pBackBrush`. We also need to be notified when the `BackColor` property is changed so that we can update our brush with the new color. Override the `OnBackColor` method by declaring it in **EEDITCTL.H** and add the following implementation code. You can also add it through ClassWizard.

```
class CEEditCtrl : public COleControl
{
...
    // Overrides
    virtual void OnBackColorChanged();
...
// Implementation
protected:
    ~CEEditCtrl();
    CBrush*      m_pBackBrush;
...
};

// eeditctl.cpp
...
void CEEditCtrl::OnBackColorChanged()
{
    delete m_pBackBrush;
    m_pBackBrush = new CBrush( TranslateColor( GetBackColor() ) );
    InvalidateControl();
}
```

Whenever the user changes the `BackColor` property, we delete the old brush and create a new one with the new color. We also need to ensure that the brush is deleted when a control's instance is destroyed. Add the following code to the control's destructor:

```
CEEditCtrl::~CEEditCtrl()
{
    // TODO: Clean up your control's instance data here.
    delete m_pBackBrush;
}
```

WM_CTLCOLOR and Win32

The WM_CTLCOLOR message is used only in Win16. Here is its definition:

```
WM_CTLCOLOR
  hdcChild = (HDC) wParam;              // DC of the child window
  hwndChild = (HWND) LOWORD( lParam );  // hwnd of the child window
  nCtlType = (int) HIWORD( lParam );    // type of the control
```

The nCtlType parameter contains the control type: CTLCOLOR_BTN, CTLCOLOR_DLG, CTLCOLOR_EDIT, and so on. When Microsoft moved the Windows messages from Win16 to Win32, the WM_CTLCOLOR message was one that did not make the transition. In Win16, WM_CTLCOLOR's wParam, a WORD, contained the child's 16-bit device context, and the lParam, a DWORD, contained both the child window's HWND (16 bits) and the child control type (16 bits).

In Win32, the size of a HANDLE went from 16 bits to 32 bits, so the HWND and HDC parameters increased to 32 bits. Although the wParam and lParam parameters in Win32 are both 32-bit, this did not leave room for the control type to be passed within the message. To rectify this, the WM_CTLCOLOR message was broken into seven different messages (one for each control type) in Win32.

This arrangement isn't really a big problem, and MFC does a pretty good job of hiding these differences within the framework. The only exception occurs when we handle the reflected window messages using the OCM_* macros.

Because of the differences between the Win16 and Win32 implementations of the reflected message macros (OCM_*), we would like to code the message map as follows:

```
//////////////////////////////////////////////////////////////////////
// Message map
//
BEGIN_MESSAGE_MAP(CEEditCtrl, COleControl)
   //{{AFX_MSG_MAP(CEEditCtrl)
   ON_MESSAGE(OCM_COMMAND, OnOcmCommand)
#ifdef _WIN32
   ON_MESSAGE(OCM_CTLCOLOREDIT, OnOcmCtlColor)
#else
   ON_MESSAGE(OCM_CTLCOLOR, OnOcmCtlColor)
#endif
      //}}AFX_MSG_MAP
   ON_OLEVERB(AFX_IDS_VERB_EDIT, OnEdit)
   ON_OLEVERB(AFX_IDS_VERB_PROPERTIES, OnProperties)
END_MESSAGE_MAP()
```

But ClassWizard parses the message map without any C++ preprocessing, so this code won't work. One way to overcome this problem is to #undefine the OCM_CTLCOLOREDIT symbol under Win16 and redefine it to OCM_CTLCOLOR. This technique allows us to use one source file for both platforms.

```
//////////////////////////////////////////////////////////////////////
// Message map
//
// Because of the differences between the Win16 and
// Win32 WM_CTLCOLOR message, we need to modify the
// #define for the OCM_CTLCOLOREDIT symbol under Win16
//
#ifndef _WIN32
#undef OCM_CTLCOLOREDIT
#define OCM_CTLCOLOREDIT OCM_CTLCOLOR
#endif
BEGIN_MESSAGE_MAP(CEEditCtrl, COleControl)
    //{{AFX_MSG_MAP(CEEditCtrl)
    ON_MESSAGE(OCM_COMMAND, OnOcmCommand)
    ON_MESSAGE(OCM_CTLCOLOREDIT, OnOcmCtlColor)
    //}}AFX_MSG_MAP
    ON_OLEVERB(AFX_IDS_VERB_EDIT, OnEdit)
    ON_OLEVERB(AFX_IDS_VERB_PROPERTIES, OnProperties)
END_MESSAGE_MAP()
```

We've made quite a few modifications to our control, so let's go ahead and compile, link, and test the control within a container. Figure 10.4 shows a simple Visual Basic application that uses the control. When you modify the control's stock color properties, it will affect the control's run-time representation. But it doesn't draw right when you're in design mode. What's going on?

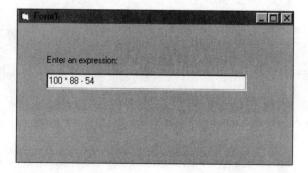

Figure 10.4 EEdit control on a Visual Basic form.

Some Problems with Control Subclassing

The major problem with subclassing windows is that you must provide some form of representation during the container's design phase. The DoSuperclassPaint method doesn't do a very good job of drawing the control without a true window and without the reflector window that is needed to process the WM_CTL-COLOR messages. Another problem is that DoSuperclassPaint may not work at all for containers that require a metafile representation of the control. What can we do?

For one thing, the design-phase representation of a control is not nearly as important as its representation at run time. In Visual Basic 3.0, a listbox was represented as a rectangle with its name in the upper left corner in the design phase. That was it. Because of the various requirements of control containers, it is probably best to render the design-time representation of your subclassed control yourself. It can be as simple or as complex as you would like, but don't let the problem of a design-phase representation stop you from gaining the advantages of subclassing an existing Windows control.

As we discussed in Chapter 9, it is important to provide a drawing routine that will work with a metafile device context. When drawing a subclassed control, as a metafile or in the design phase, I've taken the following approach. Develop a drawing routine that best represents the control. Typical controls will provide the name of the control in the upper left corner during the design phase, just as we did with the clock control in Chapter 9. Represent the control with a shape that is representative of its size and location. Use as many of the stock and custom properties as possible when drawing the control. This includes the color, font, and border properties.

Using this approach, here are the OnDrawMetafile and OnDraw methods for our EEdit control:

```
void CEEditCtrl::OnDrawMetafile( CDC* pdc, const CRect& rcBounds )
{

   DrawDesign( pdc, rcBounds );

}

void CEEditCtrl::OnDraw(
        CDC* pdc, const CRect& rcBounds, const CRect& rcInvalid)

{
   // If the container is in design mode
   // Draw the design representation
   if (! AmbientUserMode() )
      DrawDesign( pdc, rcBounds );
   else
      DoSuperclassPaint( pdc, rcBounds );

}
```

As you can see, if the container is asking for a metafile representation or it is in design mode, we call a new method, DrawDesign. When the control is running, the DoSuperclassPaint method draws the control its native way: by processing the WM_CTLCOLOR* messages and so on. The only purpose of the

DrawDesign method is to provide a good representation of the control the rest of the time (either during design or when it is being printed by the container). This approach is fairly straightforward:

```
void CEEditCtrl::DrawDesign( CDC* pdc, const CRect& rcBounds )
{
    CBrush bkBrush( TranslateColor( GetBackColor() ));
    pdc->FillRect( rcBounds, &bkBrush );

    // Get the stock "text" property value
    CString strName = InternalGetText();

    // Set the textcolor to the foreground color
    pdc->SetTextColor( TranslateColor( GetForeColor() ));

    // Select the stock font and save the old one
    CFont* pOldFont = SelectStockFont( pdc );

    // Set up the text drawing modes in the DC
    pdc->SetBkMode( TRANSPARENT );
    pdc->SetTextAlign( TA_LEFT | TA_TOP );

    // Draw the text in the upper left corner
    pdc->ExtTextOut( rcBounds.left + 1, rcBounds.top + 1, ETO_CLIPPED,
                     rcBounds, strName, strName.GetLength(), NULL );

    // Restore the old font
    if ( pOldFont )
        pdc->SelectObject( pOldFont );
}
```

This code is similar to the drawing code that you've seen before. The only thing is the use of the InternalGetText method to get the text to draw in the control. The value of the Text property is initially set in the control's OnResetState method, which is called when a control is placed within a container for the first time. This is a good spot to initialize our default Text property to the ambient DisplayName property:

```
/////////////////////////////////////////////////////////////////////////////
// CEEditCtrl::OnResetState - Reset control to default state
void CEEditCtrl::OnResetState()
{
    COleControl::OnResetState();  // Resets defaults found in DoPropExchange

    // TODO: Reset any other control state here.
    SetText( AmbientDisplayName() );
}
```

The preceding code sets the initial value of the control's Text property to the ambient DisplayName property provided by the container. Many controls that expose the Text property default its value in this way. For our purposes here, though, a default value of EEdit1 for a control that accepts only numeric expressions doesn't make sense. A more appropriate default value would be zero (I just wanted to show you how to do it).

```
/////////////////////////////////////////////////////////////////////////
// CEEditCtrl::OnResetState - Reset control to default state
void CEEditCtrl::OnResetState()
{
    COleControl::OnResetState();  // Resets defaults found in DoPropExchange

    // TODO: Reset any other control state here.
    SetText( "0" );
}
```

Setting Default Values for Your Control's States

When your control is initially placed in a container, COleControl::OnResetState is called. This method, in turn, calls your control's OnPropertyExchange method with IsLoading() set to TRUE. The CPropExchange::IsLoading method indicates the direction of the property exchange. When it is TRUE, the container is loading the properties; when it is FALSE, the properties are being saved. Because this is the first time that the control has been loaded by the container and because there is no persistent data that has been previously stored, the default values of the PX_ functions are used.

If you haven't provided default values for your PX_ functions, garbage will be returned for each of your properties. It is important to either set the default values of your control's properties by providing the defaults in the PX_ functions or set them in the OnResetState method. Use the following guidelines for help in determining where you should initialize data used in your control.

In the Control's Constructor

Control instance data that is used internally by the control and isn't directly exposed (for example, by a property) should be initialized here.

In the Control's DoPropertyExchange Method

As I mentioned earlier, you can provide a default value for your control's properties as the last parameter of the CPropertyExchange PX_* functions. Here is an example from the AutoScroll property that we added earlier:

```
///////////////////////////////////////////////////////////////////////////
// CEEditCtrl::DoPropExchange - Persistence support
void CEEditCtrl::DoPropExchange(CPropExchange* pPX)
{
    ExchangeVersion(pPX, MAKELONG(_wVerMinor, _wVerMajor));
    COleControl::DoPropExchange(pPX);

    // TODO: Call PX_ functions for each persistent custom property.

    // Store/retrieve the AutoScroll property value
    // The default is TRUE
    PX_Bool( pPX, "AutoScroll", m_bAutoScroll, TRUE );
}
```

There's another good reason to provide default values for your control's properties here. If the property's value is the default value, there will be no need to store it when serializing the control's state. This technique may save storage space in the container's persistence file.

In the Control's OnResetState Method

You can also initialize your control's properties in the OnResetState method. This is a good place to provide defaults for stock properties that are different from those provided by the COleControl::DoPropExchange(pPX) method. COleControl provides the default values for the stock properties, but you can override them when the control is initially loaded by changing their values in OnResetState after it has called COleControl::OnResetState. For example, if you want your control to default to having a border, you can set its value in OnResetState as follows:

```
///////////////////////////////////////////////////////////////////////////
// CEEditCtrl::OnResetState - Reset control to default state
void CEEditCtrl::OnResetState()
{
    COleControl::OnResetState();  // Resets defaults found in DoPropExchange

    // TODO: Reset any other control state here.
    // Turn off any border and make the control 3D
    m_sBorderStyle = 0;
    m_sAppearance = 1;
}
```

You could also use the SetBorderStyle method to set the initial border style, but in this case it's rather expensive. SetBorderStyle calls RecreateControlWindow to destroy and re-create our control's window, because the WS_BORDER style can be set only before the window is created. The same goes for the appearance style.

`OnResetState` is called before your control's window is created, so this is an effective way of initializing your control properties that can't be effectively defaulted using the default values in the `PX_` functions of `DoPropertyExchange`, as described earlier.

Adding the Expression Functionality

We're halfway through the chapter, and we haven't discussed the addition of the `Expression` class. The addition of expression evaluation is fairly trivial compared with what we've done to get the EEdit control to behave in a civilized manner. Before we begin using the `Expression` class, be sure to copy the **EXPRESS.H** and **EXPRESS.CPP** files from the Chapter 2 directory on the accompanying CD-ROM and then insert the **.CPP** file to the project. Also, add the `include` to the top of **EEDITCTL.CPP**.

Our goal is to provide an entry field that accepts only a simple algebraic expression. This includes digits, operators, and the parenthesis characters. The user will enter an expression into the entry field, and the expression will be evaluated when the control loses focus.

To add this functionality, we need to add message handlers for the appropriate control messages: `WM_KILLFOCUS` and `WM_CHAR`. Using ClassWizard, add handlers for these two messages and add the following code to the `OnKillFocus` method:

```
// EEditCtl.cpp : Implementation of the CEEditCtrl OLE control class.

#include "stdafx.h"
#include "EEdit.h"
#include "EEditCtl.h"
#include "EEditPpg.h"

#include "Express.h"

#ifdef _DEBUG
#define new DEBUG_NEW

...
/////////////////////////////////////////////////////////////////////////
// CEEditCtrl message handlers
void CEEditCtrl::OnKillFocus(CWnd* pNewWnd)
{
    COleControl::OnKillFocus(pNewWnd);

    if ( AmbientUserMode() == FALSE || AmbientUIDead() )
        return;

    // Get the value of the "text" property and
    // use it to construct our expression object
    Expression exp( InternalGetText(), TRUE );
```

```
if ( exp.Validate() == FALSE )
{
    SetFocus();
}
else
{
    char szTemp[128];
    long lResult = exp.Evaluate();
    sprintf( szTemp, "%ld", lResult );

    // Set the new value of the "text" property
    // This will also update the edit control
    SetText( szTemp );
}
}
```

Whenever the application user tabs out of the Edit control or clicks on another control, it receives a WM_KILLFOCUS message. We first check to make sure that we are not in design mode and that the container has not set the ambient UIDead property. Next, we retrieve the text from the control using the GetWindowText method. Using the entered text, we construct an instance of our Expression class. If the expression is invalid, we call the SetFocus method; otherwise, we evaluate the expression and place the result into the control using the SetWindowText method.

By returning focus to the control when an invalid expression is entered, we require users to always enter a valid expression. Users cannot tab to a different control within the application or even exit the application without entering a valid expression. This type of validation is called *field-level* validation and may not be the behavior we want. Using the SetFocus method within a focus handler such as OnKillFocus is not recommended. We'll provide alternative solutions in a moment.

One thing that we can do to help ensure that the application user enters a valid expression is to disallow the entry of invalid (expression) characters. We trap the WM_CHAR message for this reason. By subclassing the Edit control, we have an opportunity to inspect and possibly ignore any message destined for the control. We allow the majority of the messages to pass through to the original window procedure. The exceptions are WM_KILLFOCUS and WM_CHAR. We intercepted the kill focus message to perform some action, but we intercept the WM_CHAR message to filter, or remove, certain characters that are entered by the user. Add the following code:

```
void CEEditCtrl::OnChar(UINT nChar, UINT nRepCnt, UINT nFlags)
{
    if ( AmbientUserMode() == FALSE || AmbientUIDead() )
        return;

    if ( isdigit( nChar ) || IsOperator( nChar ) || nChar == ' ' || nChar == '\b' )
    {
        COleControl::OnChar( nChar, nRepCnt, nFlags );
```

```
    }
#ifdef _WIN32
    else
        ::Beep( 100, 100 );
#endif

}
```

```
#define LEFT_PAREN   '('
#define RIGHT_PAREN  ')'
#define MULTIPLY     '*'
#define SUBTRACT     '-'
#define PLUS         '+'
#define DIVIDE       '/'
static BOOL IsOperator( UINT nChar )
{
    switch( nChar )
    {
        case LEFT_PAREN:
        case RIGHT_PAREN:
        case MULTIPLY:
        case SUBTRACT:
        case PLUS:
        case DIVIDE:
            return TRUE;
    }
    return FALSE;
}
```

Again we check the `UserMode` and `UIDead` ambients and return if the container is in a state in which we should not process messages. If it is not, we check to see whether the character entered is either a digit, an operator, a space, or the backspace character. If it is not one of these, we use the Win32 `Beep` function to inform the user that the character cannot be entered into the entry field. If the character is valid, we pass it to the edit control and it is processed normally.

How to Handle an Invalid Entry Condition

Whenever you are validating the entry within an edit field, things get a little tricky. When the user enters an invalid expression in our control, what should we do? Here are some of the options:

- Set focus back to the control. This technique ensures that a valid expression is entered by not allowing the user to tab out of the control.

- Display a message box with a warning message that the expression is invalid. Either continue or set focus back to the control.

- Leave the invalid expression in the control, but fire an event that allows users to perform their own action.

- Replace the invalid expression with a textual error message and continue or set focus back to the control.

One of our goals as control developers is to give the control user flexible options for using the control. So let's add a property, called `ValidateAction`, whose value will determine our action when an invalid expression is entered. We will provide the control user with the first three options described earlier. Using ClassWizard, add the `ValidateAction` property; its type is `short`. Be sure to use the Get/Set-style of implementation. The three possible values of the property will be handled with an C++ enumerated type structure as follows. Add the following enumerated type to **EEDIT.H** so that we can use it in the property page and control files.

```
typedef enum
{
    ActionSetFocus = 0,
    ActionMsgBox = 1,
    ActionEvent = 2
} enumAction;
```

Our new `OnKillFocus` code now checks for the value of the `ValidateAction` property and acts accordingly. Depending on the value of `ValidateAction`, we either return focus to the control, pop up a message box to indicate an error, or fire the `ExpressionInvalid` event. The following code provides this implementation:

```
// eeditctl.h
class CEEditCtrl : public COleControl
{
...
// Implementation
protected:
    ~CEEditCtrl();
    BOOL        m_bAutoScroll;
    short       m_sMaxLength;
    CBrush*     m_pBackBrush;
    short       m_sValidateAction;
    void        DrawDesign( CDC*, const CRect& );
```

```
    DECLARE_OLECREATE_EX(CEEditCtrl)     // Class factory and guid
    DECLARE_OLETYPELIB(CEEditCtrl)       // GetTypeInfo
...
};

// eeditctl.cpp
...
CEEditCtrl::CEEditCtrl()
{
    InitializeIIDs(&IID_DEedit, &IID_DEeditEvents);

    // TODO: Initialize your control's instance data here.
    m_pBackBrush = NULL;
    m_bAutoScroll = TRUE;
    m_sMaxLength = 0;
    m_sValidateAction = short( ActionSetFocus );
}
...
void CEEditCtrl::DoPropExchange(CPropExchange* pPX)
{
    ExchangeVersion(pPX, MAKELONG(_wVerMinor, _wVerMajor));
    COleControl::DoPropExchange(pPX);

    // TODO: Call PX_ functions for each persistent custom property.
    PX_Bool( pPX, "AutoScroll", m_bAutoScroll, TRUE );
    PX_Short( pPX, "MaxLength", m_sMaxLength, 0 );
    PX_Short( pPX, "ValidateAction", m_sValidateAction, short( ActionSetFocus ));
}
...
void CEEditCtrl::OnKillFocus(CWnd* pNewWnd)
{
    COleControl::OnKillFocus(pNewWnd);

    if ( AmbientUserMode() == FALSE || AmbientUIDead() )
        return;

    // Get the value of the "text" property and
    // use it to construct our expression object
    Expression exp( GetInternalText(), TRUE );

    if ( exp.Validate() == FALSE )
    {
```

```
        switch( m_sValidateAction )
        {
            case ActionSetFocus:
                // You cannot get out of this without
                // fixing the expression. Including out of the
                // application!
                SetFocus();
                break;

            case ActionMsgBox:
                // Maybe use a Validate on LostFocus property
                // or instead fire an "Invalid Expression" event
                AfxMessageBox( "Error in Expression, please re-enter", MB_OK );
                break;

            case ActionEvent:
                FireExpressionInvalid();
                break;
        }
    }
    else
    {
        char szTemp[128];
        long lResult = exp.Evaluate();
        sprintf( szTemp, "%ld", lResult );

        // Set the new value of the "text" property
        // This will also update the edit control
        SetText( szTemp );
    }
}
...
short CEEditCtrl::GetValidateAction()
{
    return m_sValidateAction;
}

void CEEditCtrl::SetValidateAction(short nNewValue)
{
    m_sValidateAction = nNewValue;
    BoundPropertyChanged( dispidValidateAction );
    SetModifiedFlag();
}
```

We haven't yet added the `ExpressionInvalid` event, so go ahead and use ClassWizard to add this event. It passes no parameters. Its only purpose is to notify the control user that an invalid expression was entered.

Enumerating Property Values

So far, the properties we have used in our controls have been either textual (`BSTR`), Boolean (`BOOL`), or one of the other OLE supported types (such as `OLE_COLOR`). Textual property values are easily presented to the control user for modification, as are the stock and Boolean types. Most container applications provide support for your properties if they are represented by one of the standard automation types.

But what do you do if you need to represent a property value as a `short` internally and want to provide a range of values to the control user? For our `ValidateAction` property, using the methods that we've investigated so far, the user would be required to enter either a 0, 1, or 2 value to indicate the appropriate validate action. There is no way of ensuring that the user won't enter 195. MFC provides a mechanism for *enumerating* property values to ensure that only valid property values are entered. This method is supported by the `COlePropertyPage` DDX and DDP functions, but you must do some of the work yourself.

First, you add a property of type `short`. Then you edit your control's ODL file and create an enumerated type that enumerates all the possible values of the property. Here's how to do this for our new `ValidateAction` property in **EEDIT.ODL**. I've also added an enumerated property for the stock `BorderStyle` and `Appearance` properties.

```
// EEdit.odl : type library source for OLE Custom Control project.

// This file will be processed by the Make Type Library (mktyplib) tool to
// produce the type library (eedit.tlb) that will become a resource in
// eedit.ocx.

#include <olectl.h>

[ uuid(D5F64C96-D2F1-11CE-869D-08005A564718), version(1.0),
  helpstring("Eedit OLE Custom Control module"), control ]
library EEditLib
{
    importlib(STDOLE_TLB);
    importlib(STDTYPE_TLB);

    typedef enum
    {
        [helpstring("Flat")] Flat = 0,
        [helpstring("3D")]   ThreeD = 1
    } enumAppearance;

    typedef enum
    {
```

```
    [helpstring("None")] None = 0,
    [helpstring("Single")] Single = 1
} enumBorderStyle;

typedef enum
{
    [helpstring("SetFocus")] SetFocus = 0,
    [helpstring("DisplayMsgBox")] DisplayMsgBox = 1,
    [helpstring("FireEvent")] FireEvent = 2
} enumValidateAction;

// Primary dispatch interface for CEEditCtrl

[ uuid(D5F64C94-D2F1-11CE-869D-08005A564718),
  helpstring("Dispatch interface for Eedit Control"), hidden ]
dispinterface _DEedit
{
  properties:
    // NOTE - ClassWizard will maintain property information here.
    //    Use extreme caution when editing this section.
    //{{AFX_ODL_PROP(CEEditCtrl)
    [id(DISPID_APPEARANCE), bindable, requestedit] enumAppearance Appearance;
    [id(DISPID_BACKCOLOR), bindable, requestedit] OLE_COLOR BackColor;
    [id(DISPID_BORDERSTYLE), bindable, requestedit] enumBorderStyle BorderStyle;
    [id(DISPID_ENABLED), bindable, requestedit] boolean Enabled;
    [id(DISPID_FONT), bindable] IFontDisp* Font;
    [id(DISPID_FORECOLOR), bindable, requestedit] OLE_COLOR ForeColor;
    [id(DISPID_HWND)] OLE_HANDLE hWnd;
    [id(DISPID_TEXT), bindable, requestedit] BSTR Text;
    [id(1)] enumValidateAction ValidateAction;
    [id(2)] short MaxLength;
    [id(3)] boolean AutoScroll;
//}}AFX_ODL_PROP
...
};
```

The ODL enum keyword is similar to the one used with C and C++ except that each value can have associated with it additional attributes. For our purposes, the helpstring attribute provides a way to associate a textual description with the property value. Good property browsers will query these values from the control (from its type information) and display them to the control user when selecting a value for an enumerated property. Figure 10.5 shows our ValidateAction property and its enumerated types in Visual Basic's properties window.

Figure 10.5 `ValidateAction` property and its enumerated types.

We also need to provide this enumerated property functionality in our control's custom property page. We'll do that next.

Property Pages Revisited

As we discussed in Chapter 8, not all development environments that support ActiveX controls will provide a nice property browser. We need to provide, via our control's custom and stock property pages, the necessary interface to allow a user to change all our control's properties. The ActiveX control standard specifies that property pages for controls can be either 250x62 dialog units (DLU) or 250x110 DLUs in size. The default size provided by Visual C++ is the smaller: 250x62 DLUs. For the EEdit control, we need to increase the size of our custom property page to 250x110 by modifying it in the Visual C++ dialog editor. Double-click on **EEDIT.RC** and change the size of the control's `IDD_PROPPAGE_EEDIT` dialog to 250x110 DLUs.

Next, add the following controls to the dialog for our stock and custom properties:

- `IDC_ENABLED`: checkbox
- `IDC_APPEARANCE`: droplist combo box
- `IDC_BORDERSTYLE`: droplist combo box
- `IDC_TEXT`: multiline edit field
- `IDC_VALIDATEACTION`: droplist combo box
- `IDC_MAXLENGTH`: single-line edit field
- `IDC_AUTOSCROLL`: checkbox

When you're finished, you should have something that looks like Figure 10.6.

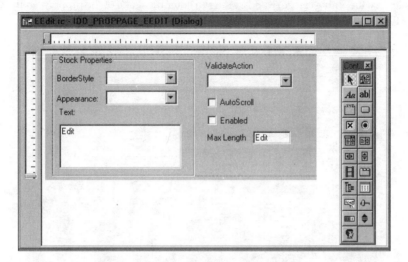

Figure 10.6 Editing the custom property page.

We now need a way to list the enumerated property values that we defined in our ODL file. Because we used droplist combo boxes, this is easy. When editing the styles of the droplist combo boxes, you can enter the default items that will be displayed when the dialog box is loaded. All we need to do is to list the enumerated values in the same order that they are declared. In other words, the item number within the combo box should equate to the associated property value. Figure 10.7 shows the values as entered for our `ValidateAction` property.

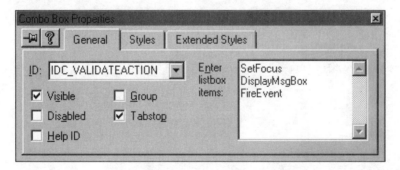

Figure 10.7 Setting the combo box list values.

You should also do this for the `IDC_BORDERSTYLE` combo box. Now that we have the enumerated types defined in the dialog box, we need to ensure that the value is properly transferred to and from the control when the property is being edited via the property page.

ClassWizard will do all this for you. On the **Member Variables** tab, for each control add an appropriate member variable. Use the **Value** category and be sure to enter the name of the property in the **Optional OLE property name** file. This is shown in Figure 10.8.

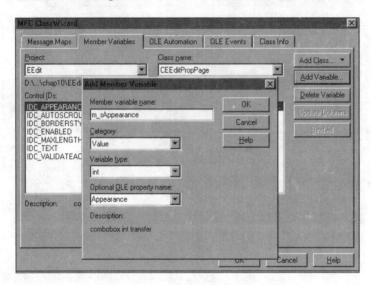

Figure 10.8 Adding member variables for the property page.

The following highlighted code shows the changes that ClassWizard makes to **EEDITPPG.H** and **EED-ITPPG.CPP**.

```
// EEditppg.h
...
///////////////////////////////////////////////////////////////////////////
// CEEditPropPage : See eeditppg.cpp for implementation.
class CEEditPropPage : public COlePropertyPage
{
...
// Dialog Data
  //{{AFX_DATA(CEEditPropPage)
  enum { IDD = IDD_PROPPAGE_EEDIT };
  int    m_sAppearance;
  BOOL   m_bAutoScroll;
  int    m_sBorderStyle;
  BOOL   m_bEnabled;
  int    m_sMaxLength;
  CString m_strText;
  int    m_sValidateAction;
```

```
    //}}AFX_DATA

// Implementation
protected:
    virtual void DoDataExchange(CDataExchange* pDX);    // DDX/DDV support
...
};

/////////////////////////////////////////////////////////////////////////////
// CEEditPropPage::CEEditPropPage - Constructor
CEEditPropPage::CEEditPropPage() :
    COlePropertyPage(IDD, IDS_EEDIT_PPG_CAPTION)
{
    //{{AFX_DATA_INIT(CEEditPropPage)
    m_sAppearance = -1;
    m_bAutoScroll = FALSE;
    m_sBorderStyle = -1;
    m_bEnabled = FALSE;
    m_sMaxLength = 0;
    m_strText = _T("");
    m_sValidateAction = -1;
    //}}AFX_DATA_INIT}

/////////////////////////////////////////////////////////////////////////////
// CEEditPropPage::DoDataExchange - Moves data between page and properties

void CEEditPropPage::DoDataExchange(CDataExchange* pDX)
{
    //{{AFX_DATA_MAP(CEEditPropPage)
    DDP_CBIndex(pDX, IDC_APPEARANCE, m_sAppearance, _T("Appearance") );
    DDX_CBIndex(pDX, IDC_APPEARANCE, m_sAppearance);
    DDP_Check(pDX, IDC_AUTOSCROLL, m_bAutoScroll, _T("AutoScroll") );
    DDX_Check(pDX, IDC_AUTOSCROLL, m_bAutoScroll);
    DDP_CBIndex(pDX, IDC_BORDERSTYLE, m_sBorderStyle, _T("BorderStyle") );
    DDX_CBIndex(pDX, IDC_BORDERSTYLE, m_sBorderStyle);
    DDP_Check(pDX, IDC_ENABLED, m_bEnabled, _T("Enabled") );
    DDX_Check(pDX, IDC_ENABLED, m_bEnabled);
    DDP_Text(pDX, IDC_MAXLENGTH, m_sMaxLength, _T("MaxLength") );
    DDX_Text(pDX, IDC_MAXLENGTH, m_sMaxLength);
    DDV_MinMaxInt(pDX, m_sMaxLength, 0, 32000);
    DDP_Text(pDX, IDC_TEXT, m_strText, _T("Text") );
    DDX_Text(pDX, IDC_TEXT, m_strText);
```

```
DDP_CBIndex(pDX, IDC_VALIDATEACTION, m_sValidateAction, _T("ValidateAction") );
DDX_CBIndex(pDX, IDC_VALIDATEACTION, m_sValidateAction);
//}}AFX_DATA_MAP

DDP_PostProcessing(pDX);
}
```

Most of this code should look familiar. The only new items are the `DDP_CBIndex`, `DDX_CBIndex`, and `DDV_MinMaxInt` functions in the `DoDataExchange` method. The `DDP_CBIndex` function transfers (either to or from) the value of the property page's `m_sValidateAction` variable to the `ValidateAction` property in the control. `DDX_CBIndex` uses the value to set or get the index of the combo box to that of the enumerated property value. These functions make it easy to handle enumerated properties as strings in the property page and as `shorts` in the control. The `DDV_MinMaxInt` function restricts the values that can be entered into the `MaxValue` property's entry field. Figure 10.9 shows the finished page.

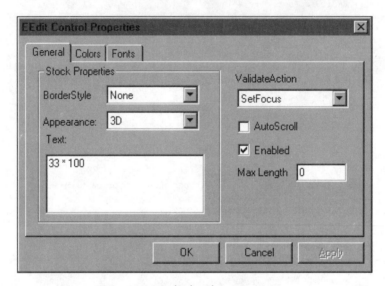

Figure 10.9 Finished EEdit property page.

Using the Control

With our new EEdit control, it is easy to write an application that provides similar functionality as that of the application we built with Visual C++ in Chapter 3. Using Visual Basic, we can create a similar application with almost zero lines of code. On the accompanying CD-ROM, an application is provided that allows you to test the various configurations of the EEdit control. Figure 10.10 shows the test application.

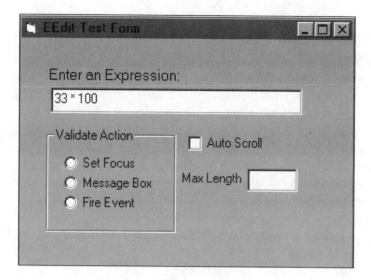

Figure 10.10 Test application.

Drawing Your Controls the 3-D Windows 95 Way

Drawing your controls with the 3-D look of Windows 95 is fairly easy. When drawing the control during the design phase, you can use the Win32 DrawEdge function. For our EEdit control, the addition of the following code to the DrawDesign method will draw a 3-D edge around the control during the design phase:

```
#ifdef _WIN32
   ::DrawEdge( pdc->GetSafeHdc(),
             CRECT(rcBounds),
             EDGE_SUNKEN,
             BF_RECT | BF_ADJUST );
#endif
```

If you want your control to have a 3-D appearance at run time (and if it's a control that has a window), include the new WS_EX_CLIENTEDGE extended Windows style bit in the PreCreateWindow method. This bit is recognized only in Windows 95 and Windows NT 4.0. If you're developing windowless controls, the DrawEdge function makes it easy to draw 3-D–style images during the design phase and at run time.

```
///////////////////////////////////////////////////////////////////////////
// CEEditCtrl::PreCreateWindow - Modify parameters for CreateWindowEx
BOOL CEEditCtrl::PreCreateWindow(CREATESTRUCT& cs)
{
```

```
cs.lpszClass = _T("EDIT");
cs.style |= ES_AUTOHSCROLL;

// Add 3-D support under Windows 95
cs.dwExStyle |= WS_EX_CLIENTEDGE;

return COleControl::PreCreateWindow(cs);
}
```

If you need 3-D support on other platforms, the easiest way to add it is to use the standard 3-D support DLLs (such as **CTL3DV2.DLL** and **CTL3D32.DLL**). This technique is described in detail in the Microsoft Developer Network article "Adding 3-D Effects to Controls." You should also read *MFC Tech Notes 51 and 52*, because you should not add 3-D effects to controls when running on operating systems that already provide this functionality (such as Windows 95 and Windows NT 4.0).

NOTE Visual C++ versions 4.0 and higher handle drawing 3-D controls with the new Appearance property. It checks the version of the operating system and uses the appropriate method, either WS_EX_CLIENTEDIT or DrawEdge, to provide 3-D support.

Subclassing Windows 95 Common Controls

Subclassing the new Windows 95 common controls is just a little more involved that what we've done here with the Windows standard controls. The primary trick is to know the Windows class names for the new common controls. As we discussed previously, ControlWizard modifies the CREATESTRUCT class in the PreCreateWindow method. A list of control names and functionality is provided in Table 10.5. You can obtain additional information by studying the **COMMCTRL.H** and **RICHEDIT.H** files.

```
BOOL CYourCtrl::PreCreateWindow(CREATESTRUCT& cs)
{
    cs.lpszClass = _T( "SysTreeView32" );

    return COleControl::PreCreateWindow(cs);
}
```

Table 10.5 Windows 95 Common Controls

Common Control Name	Windows Class Name to Subclass
Toolbar: A standard toolbar control. Provides tooltip support, dockability, and automatic sizing.	`ToolbarWindow32`
Tooltips: A control that makes it easy ot implement tooltips not only for your toolbar but also for all the controls in your application.	`tooltips_class32`
Status bar: A control that provides status information. The status bar also acts as a progress indicator.	`msctls_statusbar32`
Progress: A simple progress control. Used to display the progress of a lengthy process.	`msctls_progress32`
Track bar: Another name for a slider control. UpDown:	`msctls_trackbar32`
The UpDown control is similar to a spin button control. It's basically an entry field with up and down buttons.	`msctls_updown32`
Header: An easier way to do headings for lists of items. A much better way than using tabs in a listbox.	`SysHeader32`
List view: An icon-container–like control that supports drag-and-drop.	`SysListView32`
Tree view: Provides a hierarchical and graphical view of your data.	`SysTreeView32`
Rich text edit: A control that is similar to the standard EDIT control but provides RTF functionality.	`RICHEDIT` or `RichEdit20A`
HotKey: Allows a user to enter a hot-key by typing it on the keyboard (e.g., **Ctrl+Shift+X**).	`msctls_hotkey32`
Tab: Provides the strip of tabs at the top of a standard tabbed dialog, but doesn't provide help with the page-switching, and so on.	`SysTabControl32`
Animate: A control that plays simple AVI files.	`SysAnimate32`

Subclassing the Tree View Control

To demonstrate how to subclass one of the new Windows 95 common controls, we'll subclass the tree view control. It provides a hierarchical view of whatever the control user wants to provide. An example of a tree view control is the Project Workspace viewer of Visual C++'s Developer Studio. The class, file, and resource views all use the tree view control.

Our implementation won't have all the features of the tree view ActiveX control that comes with Visual Basic, but it will demonstrate all the techniques to create such a control. It won't be hard to add more functionality to our basic control. You should be comfortable with ControlWizard by now, so create a new control project with the following characteristics:

- Name the project **TreeV**.
- Take the default options, but be sure to subclass the tree view control. The class name is **SysTreeView32**.
- Add the `Appearance`, `Enabled`, `Font`, and `hWnd` stock properties through ClassWizard.

MFC provides classes that make it a bit easier to access the functionality of the Windows 95 common controls. Instead of remembering all the Windows messages (such as `TVM_INSERTITEM`), you can use a method within the class (such as `InsertItem`). In the EEdit example, we used `CWnd::SendMessage` with the window messages to affect the behavior of the EDIT control. In this example, we'll use MFC's `CTreeCtrl` class.

Using the MFC Control Classes

Using MFC classes sounds like a perfect solution. However, Visual C++ doesn't make it as easy as it should be. First, the project created with ControlWizard doesn't include the common control header file, so we must add it before we get started. Edit **STDAFX.H** and include **AFXCMN.H**:

```
// stdafx.h : include file for standard system include files,
//      or project-specific include files that are used frequently,
//      but are changed infrequently

#define VC_EXTRALEAN           // Exclude rarely used stuff from Windows headers

#include <afxctl.h>        // MFC support for OLE Controls

// Add common control support
#include <afxcmn.h>

// Delete the two includes below if you do not wish to use the MFC
//   database classes
#ifndef _UNICODE
#include <afxdb.h>               // MFC database classes
#include <afxdao.h>              // MFC DAO database classes
#endif //_UNICODE
```

Second, using the MFC control class within `COleControl` isn't straightforward. When you're subclassing a control within `COleControl`, the `HWND` of the `COleControl`-derived class is actually the `HWND` of the subclassed control. In our case, this is the `HWND` of the tree view control. However, `COleControl` does not contain the tree view–specific methods, so we can't directly use them. We could do something sneaky like this:

```
hItem = ((CTreeCtrl*) this)->InsertItem( &tvStruct );
```

Casting the `COleControl`-derived class to the appropriate control class works, but only because we're lucky. It works because the `CTreeCtrl` implementation uses C++ inline methods. If MFC ever changes its implementation to use standard C++ methods instead of inline, the preceding code will cause run-time protection faults. If casting is the only way to solve a problem, you should question whether there's something wrong with the approach. There usually is. We need another technique.

The best solution I've found is to add a `CTreeCtrl` member to our `CTreeVCtrl` class. Then, if we can somehow attach our subclassed HWND to this new member, everything will work great. There's just one problem: MFC maintains a list of HWNDs that are attached to CWnd-derived objects. The HWND for our control was added to the list when the `CTreeVCtrl` instance was created. We, therefore, can't do this:

```
int CTreeVCtrl::OnCreate(LPCREATESTRUCT lpCreateStruct)
{
    if (COleControl::OnCreate(lpCreateStruct) == -1)
        return -1;

    // TODO: Add your specialized creation code here
    m_TreeCtrl.Attach( this );
...
}
```

Because the map already contains the HWND of the control, this code will cause an ASSERT. Here's the best workaround I can find. First, add a handler for the WM_CREATE method. Then add the following code to **TREEVCTL.H** and **TREEVCTL.CPP**:

```
//
// TreeVCtl.h : Declaration of the CTreeVCtrl OLE control class.
//
class CTreeVCtrl : public COleControl
{
...

// Implementation
protected:
    ~CTreeVCtrl();

    CTreeCtrl    m_TreeCtrl;
...
};

//
// TreeVCtl.cpp
//
...
CTreeVCtrl::~CTreeVCtrl()
{
    // TODO: Clean up your control's instance data here.
    m_TreeCtrl.m_hWnd = 0;
}
...
```

```
int CTreeVCtrl::OnCreate(LPCREATESTRUCT lpCreateStruct)
{
    if (COleControl::OnCreate(lpCreateStruct) == -1)
        return -1;

    // TODO: Add your specialized creation code here
    m_TreeCtrl.m_hWnd = m_hWnd;

    return 0;
}
```

We add an instance of CTreeCtrl, but we don't use the Attach or Create method to create the window. Instead, we assign the HWND of the COleControl-derived class to the m_hWnd member of our CTreeCtrl instance. This works just fine. However, we must ensure that the control won't be destroyed twice, so we set the m_hWnd member to zero in the control's destructor. Now that we've fixed that problem, we can start adding some functionality through our new CTreeCtrl member.

We won't spend much time on the specifics of the tree view control. You can read the MFC documentation for the details. Instead, we'll focus on the issues of subclassing as we build the control. A tree view control needs an image list. An image list is a new Windows 95 common control that maintains a list of images, either bitmaps or icons. Each item in the tree view is typically associated with one of the images maintained in the list view.

The accompanying CD-ROM contains the six **.ICO** files that we'll use in our control. You need to add these to your project with the IDs listed in Table 10.6. You can quickly do this through Developer Studio's **Insert/Resource/Import** menu item. Be sure to add the icons in the order shown in Table 10.6. The image list insertion code requires that the icon IDs are consecutive.

Table 10.6 .ICO Files in the Tree View Control

Resource Symbol	Filename
IDI_AUTHOR	AUTHOR1.ICO
IDI_AUTHOR2	AUTHOR2.ICO
IDI_NOTE	NOTE.ICO
IDI_BOOKS	BOOKS.ICO
IDI_BOOK	BOOK.ICO
IDI_CARDFILE	CARDFILE.ICO

We need an instance of MFC's image list control, CImageList, within our CTreeVCtrl class. We fill the image list with our icons and then pass the list to the tree view control. The following code demonstrates this:

```
//
// TreeVCtl.h : Declaration of the CTreeVCtrl OLE control class.
//
...
class CTreeVCtrl : public COleControl
{
...

// Implementation
protected:
   ~CTreeVCtrl();

   CTreeCtrl     m_TreeCtrl;
   CImageList    m_ImageList;
   void          CreateImageList();
...
};

//
// TreeVCtl.cpp : Implementation of the CTreeVCtrl OLE control class.
//
...
void CTreeVCtrl::CreateImageList()
{
   m_ImageList.Create( 32, 32, FALSE, 6, 0 );

   // Set the background mask color to white
   m_ImageList.SetBkColor( RGB( 255, 255, 255 ));

   for( int i = 0; i < 6; i++ )
   {
      HICON hIcon = ::LoadIcon( AfxGetResourceHandle(),
                             MAKEINTRESOURCE( IDI_AUTHOR + i ));
      m_ImageList.Add( hIcon );
   }

   ASSERT( m_ImageList.GetImageCount() == 6 );

   // Set the image list for the tree
   m_TreeCtrl.SetImageList( &m_ImageList, TVSIL_NORMAL );
}

int CTreeVCtrl::OnCreate(LPCREATESTRUCT lpCreateStruct)
{
```

```
if (COleControl::OnCreate(lpCreateStruct) == -1)
    return -1;

// TODO: Add your specialized creation code here
// Set up the HWND for our embedded CTreeCtrl instance
m_TreeCtrl.m_hWnd = m_hWnd;
CreateImageList();

return 0;
}
```

In the preceding code, we create an instance of the image list control, setting the image size to 32x32 pixels. We specify that no mask will be used and indicate that the initial size of the list is six images. The call to `CImageList::SetBkColor` sets the background color of the images to white, which is the color I used for the background of the images. Next, we loop through and load the six icons and add each one to the image list. Finally, we associate the image list with the tree view control.

Our simple tree view control has only four custom properties. Using ClassWizard, add the following custom properties. Use the `Get` and `Set` implementation technique and add the appropriate implementation variables to **TREEVCTL.H**.

- **HasLines**: Boolean, `m_bHasLines`
- **HasLinesAtRoot**: Boolean, `m_bHasLinesAtRoot`
- **HasButtons**: Boolean, `m_bHasButtons`
- **IndentSize**: long, `m_lIndentSize`

Here's the code from **TREEVCTL.H**:

```
//
// TreeVCtl.h : Declaration of the CTreeVCtrl OLE control class.
//

class CTreeVCtrl : public COleControl
{
    DECLARE_DYNCREATE(CTreeVCtrl)
...
// Implementation
protected:
    ~CTreeVCtrl();

    CTreeCtrl    m_TreeCtrl;
    CImageList   m_ImageList;
```

```
void        CreateImageList();
long        m_lIndentSize;
BOOL        m_bHasLines;
BOOL        m_bHasButtons;
BOOL        m_bHasLinesAtRoot;
...
};
```

When we initially created the control with ControlWizard, it added the following code:

```
BOOL CTreeVCtrl::PreCreateWindow(CREATESTRUCT& cs)
{
    cs.lpszClass = _T("SysTreeView32");
    return COleControl::PreCreateWindow(cs);
}
```

As you may recall from the EEdit example, we can set up any additional window styles here in PreCreateWindow. There are several styles specific to the tree view control, and I've listed them in Table 10.7. To start, we'll use the TVS_LINESATROOT, TVS_HASBUTTONS, and TVS_HASLINES styles, which map directly to three of the properties we added.

```
BOOL CTreeVCtrl::PreCreateWindow(CREATESTRUCT& cs)
{
    if ( m_bHasLinesAtRoot )
        cs.style |= TVS_LINESATROOT;
    if ( m_bHasButtons )
        cs.style |= TVS_HASBUTTONS;
    if ( m_bHasLines )
        cs.style |= TVS_HASLINES;

    cs.lpszClass = _T("SysTreeView32");
    return COleControl::PreCreateWindow(cs);
}
```

Table 10.7 Styles of the Tree View Control

Style	Description
TVS_HASLINES	Display lines linking children to their parents.
TVS_LINESATROOT	Display lines attached to the root item.
TVS_HASBUTTONS	Show plus sign "buttons" to expand and contract the hierarchy.
TVS_EDITLABELS	Allow the user to edit the text associated with each item in the control.
TVS_SHOWSELALWAYS	Show the selected item even after the control loses focus.
TVS_DISABLEDRAGDROP	Disable begin drag notifications.

We set the appropriate window styles based on the value of our properties. The default value for each property is TRUE. Here's the code needed to make the property values persistent. The PX function for the IndentSize property is also provided.

```
void CTreeVCtrl::DoPropExchange(CPropExchange* pPX)
{
    ExchangeVersion(pPX, MAKELONG(_wVerMinor, _wVerMajor));
    COleControl::DoPropExchange(pPX);

    // TODO: Call PX_ functions for each persistent custom property.
    PX_Bool( pPX, _T( "HasLines" ), m_bHasLines, TRUE );
    PX_Bool( pPX, _T( "HasLinesAtRoot" ), m_bHasLinesAtRoot, TRUE );
    PX_Bool( pPX, _T( "HasButtons" ), m_bHasButtons, TRUE );
    PX_Long( pPX, _T( "IndentSize" ), m_lIndentSize, 0 );
}
```

The newer Windows 95 controls support changing styles at run time using the SetWindowLong API function. For each of our "Has" properties, we'll use this function to update the control at run time. It's simple. Here's the code for the HasLines property:

```
BOOL CTreeVCtrl::GetHasLines()
{
    return m_bHasLines;
}

void CTreeVCtrl::SetHasLines(BOOL bNewValue)
{
    if ( GetSafeHwnd() == 0 )
        return;

    m_bHasLines = bNewValue;

    DWORD dwStyle = ::GetWindowLong( m_hWnd, GWL_STYLE );
```

```
if (! m_bHasLines )
{
   dwStyle &= ~TVS_HASLINES;
   ::SetWindowLong( m_hWnd, GWL_STYLE, dwStyle );
}
else
{
   dwStyle |= TVS_HASLINES;
   ::SetWindowLong( m_hWnd, GWL_STYLE, dwStyle );
}

// Force a redraw and update any browser
SetModifiedFlag();
BoundPropertyChanged( dispidHasLines );
}
```

When the property is updated, we first make sure that we can get a valid HWND. If we can't get an HWND, we're probably in design mode, which isn't a problem. Then we use the GetWindowLong function to retrieve the existing window style bits. We check the new value of the property and either turn on or turn off the TVS_HASLINES style. Next, we invalidate the control to force a repaint and call BoundPropertyChanged to update any attached browsers. This same approach is used for each of the "Has" properties. With a few **Copy/Paste** commands, you should have the other methods working in no time. The IndentSize property isn't much different:

```
void CTreeVCtrl::SetIndentSize(long nNewValue)
{
   if ( GetSafeHwnd() == 0 )
      return;

   m_lIndentSize = nNewValue;
   m_TreeCtrl.SetIndent( m_lIndentSize );

   // Force a redraw and update any browser
   SetModifiedFlag();
   BoundPropertyChanged( dispidIndentSize );
}
```

Instead of setting window style bits, we call the SetIndent method of CTreeCtrl to set the new indent value. Now the control user can change the style of our tree control at both design time and run time. Because the new controls support changing these styles at run time, there's no need to worry about saving the state of the control, calling RecreateControl, and then restoring the earlier state. This approach makes changing styles much more efficient.

To finish the control, let's add some items to the tree view. Typically, you would expose a method from the control that would allow the control user to add items to the view, but for our example we'll add them within the control. First, we need an `AddItem` method:

```
HTREEITEM CTreeVCtrl::AddItem( HTREEITEM hParent,
                               HTREEITEM hAfter,
                               LPSTR szText,
                               int  iImage,
                               int  iSelImage)
{

   HTREEITEM hItem;
   TV_INSERTSTRUCT tvStruct;

   tvStruct.item.mask = TVIF_TEXT | TVIF_IMAGE | TVIF_SELECTEDIMAGE;
   tvStruct.hParent = hParent;
   tvStruct.hInsertAfter = hAfter;

   tvStruct.item.iImage = iImage;
   tvStruct.item.iSelectedImage = iSelImage;
   tvStruct.item.pszText = szText;
   tvStruct.item.cchTextMax = strlen( szText );

   hItem = m_TreeCtrl.InsertItem( &tvStruct );

   return( hItem );
}
```

This method takes as a parameter the parent item, the item after which it should be inserted, the text associated with the item, the nonselected image, and finally the image to use when the item is selected. The implementation is straightforward. We fill out the tree view `TV_INSERTSTRUCT` structure and call the `InsertItem` method. This action adds the specific item to the tree view.

Earlier, we added the item icons to the project and inserted them into an image list control. Whenever we add an item, we provide the index value of the image that we want associated with that particular item. This is tricky, because when a resource is added by Visual C++, it assigns the ID. I've added an enumerated type to the `CTreeVCtrl` class to ease the task of managing the IDs:

```
//
// TreeVCtl.h : Declaration of the CTreeVCtrl OLE control class.
//

class CTreeVCtrl : public COleControl
{
...
// Constructor
public:
   CTreeVCtrl();
```

```
  enum
  {
    ICON_AUTHOR,
    ICON_AUTHOR2,
    ICON_NOTE,
    ICON_BOOKS,
    ICON_BOOK,
    ICON_CARDFILE,
  };
  ...
};
```

The next method inserts a series of items into the control using the AddItem method. For each item that we insert, we provide the following:

- A handle to the parent item or zero if there isn't one.
- A handle to the item to insert before. In our case, we use the TVI_SORT symbol, which indicates that the control should just sort the items.
- The text to display for the item.
- An index into the image list control specifying the image to associate with the item.
- An index into the image list control specifying the image to use when the item is selected.

```
//////////////////////
// Add some test items
//////////////////////
BOOL CTreeVCtrl::TestItems()
{
    HTREEITEM       hParent, hChild1, hChild2;

    // Insert the root object
    hParent = AddItem( 0, TVI_SORT,
                       "Authors", ICON_CARDFILE,
                       ICON_CARDFILE );

    // Insert the authors, their books, and magazines
    hChild1 = AddItem( hParent, TVI_SORT,
                       "Charles Petzold", ICON_AUTHOR,
                       ICON_AUTHOR2 );

    hChild2 = AddItem( hChild1, TVI_SORT,
                       "Books", ICON_BOOKS, ICON_BOOKS );
```

```
AddItem( hChild2, TVI_SORT,
         "Programming Windows 3.1, Third Edition",
         ICON_BOOK, ICON_BOOK );
AddItem( hChild2, TVI_SORT,
         "Programming The OS/2 Presentation Manager",
         ICON_BOOK, ICON_BOOK );

AddItem( hChild1, TVI_SORT,
         "Articles", ICON_NOTE, ICON_NOTE );

hChild1 = AddItem( hParent, TVI_SORT,
                   "Mark Nelson", ICON_AUTHOR,
                   ICON_AUTHOR2 );
hChild2 = AddItem( hChild1, TVI_SORT,
                   "Books", ICON_BOOKS, ICON_BOOKS );
AddItem( hChild2, TVI_SORT,
         "C++ Programmers Guide to the STL",
         ICON_BOOK, ICON_BOOK );
AddItem( hChild1, TVI_SORT,
         "Articles", ICON_NOTE, ICON_NOTE );

hChild1 = AddItem( hParent, TVI_SORT,
                   "Jeffrey Richter", ICON_AUTHOR,
                   ICON_AUTHOR2 );
hChild2 = AddItem( hChild1, TVI_SORT,
                   "Books", ICON_BOOKS, ICON_BOOKS );
AddItem( hChild2, TVI_SORT,
         "Windows 3.1: A Developer's Guide",
         ICON_BOOK, ICON_BOOK );
AddItem( hChild1, TVI_SORT,
         "Articles", ICON_NOTE, ICON_NOTE );

return TRUE;
}
```

Once you've added these methods, build the project and insert it into your favorite container. You should see something like Figure 10.11.

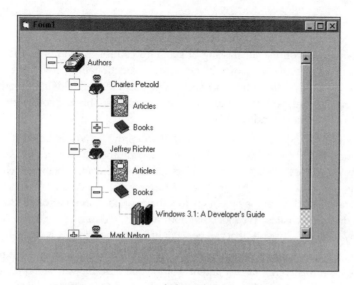

Figure 10.11 Our subclassed tree view control.

The Property Page

Adding the code for the property page is easy, and we've done it several times before. Take a look at Figure 10.12 and build one similar to that. Actually, there isn't any code to write. ClassWizard does everything for you. However, you need to add the enumerated properties for the appearance property to **CTREEV.ODL** in order make your property page more robust. You may also want to add component category support so that you can embed the control in Internet Explorer. All this is implemented in the example control on the accompanying CD-ROM.

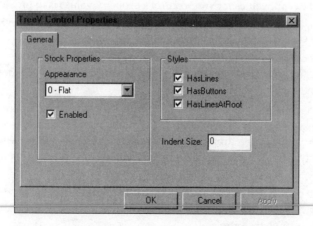

Figure 10.12 Our tree view control's property sheet.

Summary

Our focus in this chapter was on the subclassing of standard controls provided by the Windows operating system. Subclassing is an effective way of reusing existing functionality provided by standard controls. Reuse by subclassing works by intercepting messages meant for the original window procedure of the standard control and then either discarding or modifying the messages. This is a common technique for developing applications in C using the Windows SDK.

Windows provides six standard controls and Windows 95 provides an additional 10 common controls, all of which can be subclassed. To subclass a control, we override the `COleControl::PreCreateWindow` method and modify the `CREATESTRUCT` with the class name of the control being subclassed. We can make additional modifications to the control in the `PreCreateWindow` method. A control's style bits affect the behavior of the control. Certain style bits can be set only before the creation of the control window, and others can be modified after the window is created. We looked at both types. `COleControl::RecreateControlWindow` provides an easy way to modify style bits that can be set only before the window is created.

Subclassed controls expect to have a parent window that helps in the management of the child control's environment. ActiveX controls do not have a parent window, because they are stand-alone windows inserted within a container. The ActiveX control standard specifies the need for a reflector window to reflect messages intended for the parent window back to the child window. In this regard, the child window acts also as its parent and so is in control of all its messages. One set of messages sent by a subclassed control is its notification messages, which signify that events have occurred. When a notification message is reflected back to the control, it fires an OLE event to alert the control user. Handling the coloring of the control also requires working with reflected messages, particularly the `WM_CTLCOLOR*` messages. These messages, normally sent to a parent dialog window, contain instructions on the colors to use for painting the child control. By responding to the reflected `WM_CTLCOLOR*` messages, an ActiveX control tells itself how it should be colored.

One of the problems of control subclassing is the difficulty of providing a good design-phase representation of the control. With a little thought, you can handle this problem. In many situations, a control's design-phase representation is not nearly as important as its run-time representation. You may also need to provide your own metafile representation of the control.

The best way to set default values for your control's property values is to provide a default value to the property exchange functions in the `DoPropertyExchange` method. In some cases, you may also have to set default values in the control's `OnResetState` method.

After you have subclassed a standard control, it is easy to intercept messages using the MFC message map functionality. To intercept a message, use ClassWizard to add a handler for the message. Then discard, handle, or modify the message in the handler code.

You can enumerate property values for property browsers by adding an enumerated type with the associated `helpstrings` to your control's **.ODL** file. To add support for enumerated properties in your control's custom property page, use a droplist combo box that is prefilled with the textual representation of the enumerated property. The `DDP_CBIndex` function makes it easy to convert and transfer the property values to and from the control.

Property pages can be one of two sizes: either 250x62 or 250x110 dialog units (DLUs). You can use the `DrawEdge` function, the `WS_EX_CLIENTEDGE` window style, and MFC's stock `Appearance` property to provide a 3-D appearance for your controls.

Using MFC's Windows 95 control classes within your own controls is fairly easy to do. By subclassing the new common controls, you can quickly take advantage of the features provided by these controls.

Chapter 11

Nonvisual Controls

We've covered two of the three broad types of ActiveX controls: graphical controls and controls that subclass existing Windows controls. In this chapter we will investigate the design and use of nonvisual ActiveX controls, which provide their functionality without providing a visual element.

To illustrate how easy it is to build a simple client/server application with ActiveX controls, we will develop a control that provides Win32 named pipes services, allowing a visual tool user to create applications using Win32 named pipes. The details of interacting with the API functions will be contained within the ActiveX control, and the control user will need just a handful of properties and methods to build applications using named pipes.

Goals of Nonvisual Controls

The goals of a nonvisual control are similar to those that we've described for components in general. The goal is to build controls that encapsulate the complexity of a problem and expose a more user-friendly way of interacting with that problem. We demonstrated this in the first half of the book by converting the `Expression` C++ class to an automation component. By exposing only four expression methods, we made it easy for a component user to harness the expression evaluation capabilities of our C++ class. In Chapter 10, we converted the `Expression` component to work as an ActiveX control. We could also convert the `Expression` component to a nonvisual control, but let's do something a little more interesting.

A Win32 Pipe Control

The example control we'll develop uses the Win32 pipes API. *Pipes* provide a way for processes to share information easily. Interprocess communication with pipes can be used between processes on a single, local machine or between processes that are on separate, or remote, machines. We'll briefly cover the features of Win32 pipes. For a more detailed look at pipes and other interprocess communication and networking techniques available under Win32, see Mark Andrews's book, C++ *Windows NT Programming* (second edition, M&T Books, 1996).

Two fundamental pipe types are supported by Win32. *Anonymous* pipes provide only one-way communication between processes, do not support network communication, and are typically used by processes that have a parent-child relationship. *Named* pipes allow both one-way and two-way communication between processes and support communication between processes on local and networked machines. Our example control will use named pipes.

Named Pipes

Named pipes provide client/server–style communication techniques. The *server* process initially creates a named pipe by calling the `CreateNamedPipe` function. This action creates a named pipe instance with a unique name and allows *client* processes that know the name of the pipe to connect to, and begin conversing with, the server process. The client process uses either the `CreateFile` or the `CallNamedPipe` function to connect to the pipe created by the server process. Many pipe-based applications support the connection of multiple client processes to a single server process, the typical configuration of client/server applications. For our example control, the server will allow a connection only from one client process at a time.

Message Types

Named pipes support two different message-processing models. A message between processes can be handled as a byte stream or as message unit. The various pipe API functions take parameters that specify the read and write mode for the specified pipe. For our purposes, we will use the message-based mode of operation for our pipe control. Data sent via the `WriteFile` function will be sent and read as a unit by both the server and the client processes. This is the most effective method of sending messages that have an inherent structure. The byte stream mode is useful for passing unstructured data between processes.

Asynchronous versus Synchronous I/O

Named pipes support two methods of performing I/O. *Asynchronous* I/O allows the process to start a read or write operation and then to continue with other tasks. When the read or write operation completes, the process is notified, usually via a semaphore, that the operation has completed. The process can then obtain and use the data from the read operation or free the data used in the write operation. Asynchronous operation requires the use of threads under Win32. Supporting multiple threads in an ActiveX control is beyond the scope of this book, so we will use a hybrid approach for our control.

Synchronous operation is easier to understand and is how we typically develop programs. When we make a function call, the program waits until the function operation is completed before returning. This is the single-thread-of-execution model that we use when we develop most programs. To provide support for pipes in our control, we'll simulate the existence of a thread for our server's pipe. We will use a Windows timer and the `PeekNamedPipe` function to simulate this process.

Pipe Names

Pipe names must be unique to distinguish them from other named pipes in the system. They do not have to be unique networkwide, because pipe names are qualified with the server's name in a networked environment. Pipe names are not case-sensitive and can be as many as 256 characters in length. Here is the format of a pipe name:

```
\\servername\pipe\this.is.a.pipe.name
```

The first part of the pipe name is the network name of the server's machine. On Windows NT and Windows 95, the name of a networked machine begins with "\\" followed by the machine's name. The "\pipe" part of the name is required and specifies the global area for pipe names on the machine being addressed. Finally, the text following "\pipe\" gives the unique name of the specific pipe: "this.is.a.pipe.name."

A fully qualified pipe name for a pipe on a local machine is as follows:

```
\\.\pipe\this.is.a.pipe.name
```

The single dot (".") is shorthand for the local machine name. When you're developing applications that use pipes for local machine interprocess communication, this is all that is required. This approach is much better than hard coding the local machine's name, because it will change as you move your applications to other machines. Table 11.1 lists the named pipe functions that we will use in our PIPE control.

Table 11.1 Win32 Named Pipe API Functions

Function	Purpose
CreateNamedPipe	Used by the server process to create an instance of a named pipe. The name of the pipe is provided as a parameter. Clients cannot connect to a named pipe until it has been explicitly created by the server process.
CreateFile	Used by client processes to connect to a named pipe. The pipe name passed may contain a network pathname allowing the intermachine communication.
ConnectNamedPipe	Used by the server process to wait for a client process to connect to the pipe.
CallNamedPipe	This function is a helper function for client processes. It encapsulates multiple calls into one. It connects to a pipe, waiting if necessary, and then writes to and reads from the pipe. It then closes the pipe.
WaitNamedPipe	Used by the client to wait for an instance of the pipe to become available. The wait time can be infinite or the default value used in the CreateNamedPipe function.
DisconnectNamedPipe	Closes the server end of the pipe. If a client is still connected to the pipe, an error will occur when it next accesses the pipe.

Table 11.1 Win32 Named Pipe API Functions (continued)

Function	Purpose
PeekNamedPipe	Copies data from a pipe without actually removing it and also returns information about the pipe.
ReadFile	Reads data from a pipe.
WriteFile	Writes data to a pipe.
CloseHandle	Closes a pipe handle, which closes the pipe.

Creating the Pipe Control Project

Start Visual C++ and ControlWizard and create a new control project. Call it **Pipe** and use these options:

- In the Step 1 of 2 dialog box, take the defaults of **No License**, **Yes, comments**, and **No help files**.
- In Step 2 of 2, take all the defaults except one. Be sure to check the **Invisible at runtime** option.
- Click **Finish** and create the control.

The only new item that we checked is the **Invisible at runtime** option. This option adds the OLEMISC_INVISIBLEATRUNTIME flag to the control's MiscStatus flags stored in the Registry. This flag tells the container that the control will be visible only during the design phase.

Drawing the Control during the Design Phase

All that's needed during the design phase is a simple representation of the control. It's easy for the control user to select the control by clicking on its representation, gaining access to the control's properties, events, and methods. Add the following code to the **PIPECTL.CPP** file. We set the initial size of the control and initialize the pipe's handle in the control's constructor.

```
/////////////////////////////////////////////////////////////////////
// CPipeCtrl::CPipeCtrl - Constructor
CPipeCtrl::CPipeCtrl()
{
   InitializeIIDs(&IID_DPipe, &IID_DPipeEvents);

   // Set the control's initial size
   SetInitialSize( 28, 26 );
}

/////////////////////////////////////////////////////////////////////
```

```
// CPipeCtrl::OnDraw - Drawing function
void CPipeCtrl::OnDraw(
                CDC* pdc, const CRect& rcBounds, const CRect& rcInvalid)
{
    CBitmap bitmap;
    BITMAP  bmp;
    CPictureHolder picHolder;
    CRect rcSrcBounds;

    bitmap.LoadBitmap( IDB_PIPE );
    bitmap.GetObject( sizeof(BITMAP), &bmp );
    rcSrcBounds.right = bmp.bmWidth;
    rcSrcBounds.bottom = bmp.bmHeight;

#ifdef _WIN32
    ::DrawEdge( pdc->GetSafeHdc(),
            CRect( rcBounds ),
            EDGE_RAISED,
            BF_RECT | BF_ADJUST );
#endif

    picHolder.CreateFromBitmap( (HBITMAP)bitmap.m_hObject, NULL, FALSE );
    picHolder.Render( pdc, rcBounds, rcSrcBounds );
}
```

N O T E The preceding technique could be made more efficient by maintaining an instance of the control's bitmap in our class and using the Bit-Blt functions, as we did in Chapter 9, but I'm using this method for two reasons. First, it introduces you to the CPictureHolder class. Second, the rendering of a nonvisual control occurs only during the design phase (hopefully a small percentage of its lifetime), so its rendering doesn't really require the techniques used in Chapter 9.

We discussed in Chapter 10 most of what is shown here, with the exception of the CPictureHolder class that we will discuss in a moment. To provide a design-phase representation of the control, we use the control's tool palette bitmap image. We use the CBitmap::LoadBitmap method to load the bitmap from the control's resource file. The GetObject method retrieves information about a GDI object, and we use it to fill this BITMAP structure:

```
typedef struct tagBITMAP {
    LONG    bmType;
    LONG    bmWidth;
    LONG    bmHeight;
    LONG    bmWidthBytes;
    WORD    bmPlanes;
```

```
  WORD   bmBitsPixel;
  LPVOID bmBits;
} BITMAP;
```

We then draw a 3-D border around the control using the `DrawEdge` function. The `EDGE_RAISED` flag draws the control as a raised button on the container. Next, we get the true size of the bitmap and store it in `rcSrcBounds`. Using our instance of `CPictureHolder`, we use its `CreateFromBitmap` method to initialize the picture object with our control's bitmap. We then render the control into the container's device context using the `Render` method. Figure 11.1 shows the PIPE control in the Test Container. You will need to modify the control's tool palette image in the **PIPE.RC** file.

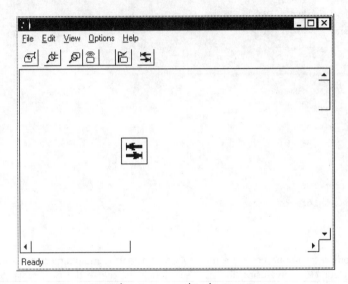

Figure 11.1 The pipe control in the Test Container.

CPictureHolder

The `CPictureHolder` class provides methods that make it easy to manipulate and display bitmaps, icons, and metafiles. It supplies an implementation of the OLE `IPicture` interface that provides a uniform way of working with picture type objects.

A `CPictureHolder` instance must be initialized to empty using the `CreateEmpty` method or using one of the three picture type initialization methods: `CreateFromBitmap`, `CreateFromIcon`, or `CreateFromMetafile`. Once initialized, the item can be rendered into a DC by using the `Render` method.

The `CPictureHolder` class can be used to provide `Picture` properties for your controls. When you're adding a property with ClassWizard, one of the automation property types is `LPPICTUREDISP`. This property allows you to include in your control an instance of `CPictureHolder` that can be easily modified by the control user. Visual C++ also provides a stock property page, `PROPPAGEID(` `CLSID_CPicturePropPage)`, that you can use in controls that use `Picture` properties.

OnSetExtent

Although the preceding code allows rendering of our control's bitmap to various sizes, expanding a bitmap image doesn't always produce a nice representation of the original bitmap. We'll override the `OnSetExtent` method, as we did in previous chapters, to fix the size of the control's representation. Not all containers will honor the return of `OnSetExtent`, but the preceding rendering code handles the situation in which the control user may size the control larger than we would like; it renders the image correctly, only larger. Add the following code for the `OnSetExtent` method. We'll cover the changes to **PIPECTL.H** shortly.

```
// pipectl.cpp

...

BOOL CPipeCtrl::OnSetExtent( LPSIZEL lpSizeL )
{
    CDC cdc;
    cdc.CreateCompatibleDC( NULL );

    CSize size( 28, 26 );
    cdc.DPtoHIMETRIC( &size );

    lpSizeL->cx = size.cx;
    lpSizeL->cy = size.cy;

    // Call the parent implementation
    return COleControl::OnSetExtent( lpSizeL );
}
```

Adding the Pipe Functionality

The next few sections describe the various properties, methods, and events that we will add to the PIPE control's implementation. To give you an idea of what you will see, we'll take a look at what we need to add to **PIPECTL.H**. This will be quicker than showing a snippet of the **.H** file every time we need to add a new member variable or overriding prototype, and you'll get a quick introduction to what we'll be doing. Following are the pertinent sections of **PIPECTL.H**:

```
// pipectl.h : Declaration of the CPipeCtrl OLE control class.

/////////////////////////////////////////////////////////////////////////////
// CPipeCtrl : See pipectl.cpp for implementation.

class CPipeCtrl : public COleControl
```

```
{
    DECLARE_DYNCREATE(CPipeCtrl)

// Constructor
public:
    CPipeCtrl();

// Overrides
    virtual BOOL OnSetExtent( LPSIZEL lpSizeL );
    virtual void OnSetClientSite();
    virtual void OnFreezeEvents( BOOL bFreeze );

...

// Implementation
protected:
    ~CPipeCtrl();

    void StartTimer();
    void StopTimer();
    BOOL CreatePipe();
    void ClosePipe();
    void ReadPipe();

    HANDLE   m_hPipe;
    CString  m_strPipeName;
    short    m_sPipeType;
    int      m_iFreeze;
    CString  m_strError;
...
};

// PipeCtrl.cpp
...
CPipeCtrl::CPipeCtrl()
{
        InitializeIIDs(&IID_DPipe, &IID_DPipeEvents);

    // Set the control's initial size
    SetInitialSize( 28, 26 );

    m_hPipe = 0;
    m_iFreeze = 0;
}
```

We override the `OnSetClientSite` method to create a window for our control. The `OnFreezeEvents` method provides indications from the container about whether the control should fire events. We already covered why we override `OnSetExtent`.

The member methods—`StartTimer`, `StopTimer`, `CreatePipe`, `ClosePipe`, and `ReadPipe`—are helper functions used by the control's exposed methods. `m_hPipe` is a handle to the pipe instance for the control. `m_strPipeName`, `m_sPipeType`, and `m_strError` are variables for properties exposed by the control, and `m_iFreeze` holds the current state of the container's `Freeze` state. All these will be discussed in more detail as we build the control.

Adding the Properties

Our PIPE control requires only three properties. We don't need any of the MFC stock properties, because they are used primarily by visually oriented controls. Using ClassWizard, add the three properties discussed next. The first, `ErrorMsg`, contains a text string of any errors that occur during processing. The second, `PipeName`, contains the name of the pipe. The third, `PipeType`, indicates the mode of the control. Our control will have two general modes of operation, as indicated by the `PipeType` property. Each instance of the control will operate as either a pipe server or a pipe client process.

ErrorMsg

The `ErrorMsg` property, type `BSTR`, is used to report to the user of the control a text error message. The property is read-only, because it can only be queried and cannot be `Set`. The property is meaningful only during the run phase of the container and so is also considered a run-time–only property.

To make a property read-only when using ClassWizard, you must choose the **Get/Set** method of implementation (which we always do) and then clear out the Set Function entry field. ClassWizard will add the address of the `SetNotSupported` function in the dispatch map:

```
/////////////////////////////////////////////////////////////////////
// Dispatch map
BEGIN_DISPATCH_MAP(CPipeCtrl, COleControl)
    //{{AFX_DISPATCH_MAP(CPipeCtrl)
    DISP_PROPERTY_EX(CPipeCtrl, "ErrorMsg", GetErrorMsg, SetNotSupported, VT_BSTR)
    ...
END_DISPATCH_MAP()
```

The `COleControl::SetNotSupported` method is actually a helper function for the `COleControl::ThrowError` method, which we will discuss in more detail later. The `SetNotSupported` method is implemented like this:

```
void COleControl::SetNotSupported()
{
```

```
    ThrowError(CTL_E_SETNOTSUPPORTED, AFX_IDP_E_SETNOTSUPPORTED);
}
```

This code reports the error to the container using the automation exception mechanism. You can also use SetNotSupported to provide a run-time–only implementation of a property:

```
void CYourControl::SetAProperty(short sNewValue)
{
    // If not running report an error
    if (! AmbientUserMode() )
    {
        // Throw the CTL_E_SETNOTSUPPORTED error
        SetNotSupported();
    }
    // Go ahead and set the property value
}
```

In a previous chapter we discussed the use of the ODL hidden keyword as a way of hiding properties from property browsers. Another method is to check the UserMode of the container and, if it is not in run mode, disallow the getting of a property's value. As we described earlier, the ErrorMsg property should not be displayed during the design phase and is valid only during run time. The code for our GetErrorMsg method uses the GetNotSupported method to enforce this requirement:

```
BSTR CPipeCtrl::GetErrorMsg()
{
    // Most containers that provide property browsers (e.g. VB)
    // will trap this exception and will not display the property
    // in the property browser. This is just what we want.
    // If we're not in run mode don't allow anyone to get the
    // property's value.
    if ( AmbientUserMode() == FALSE )
        GetNotSupported();

    return m_strError.AllocSysString();
}
```

GetNotSupported is implemented just like the SetNotSupported method. It throws a CTL_E_GETNOT-SUPPORTED exception.

PipeName

The `PipeName` property is of type `BSTR` and contains the fully qualified pipe name that the control uses when creating or connecting to a pipe instance. It is the responsibility of the control user to provide the control with a valid pipe name. We could easily add rudimentary syntactic checking (such as ensuring the existence of "\pipe\" in the name), but I'll leave that as an exercise.

```
BSTR CPipeCtrl::GetPipeName()
{
    return m_strPipeName.AllocSysString();
}

void CPipeCtrl::SetPipeName(LPCTSTR lpszNewValue)
{
    // If the pipe name is modified during run time
    // it will only take effect the next time that either
    // a server calls "Create" or a client calls "Connect"
    m_strPipeName = lpszNewValue;

    BoundPropertyChanged( dispidPipeName );
    SetModifiedFlag();
}
```

PipeType

The `PipeType` property indicates the current mode of operation for the control. Its type is `short` but can contain only two values: zero and 1. As we did in Chapter 10, we need to set up an enumerated type in **PIPE.ODL** and modify the property's type so that we can present a nice interface for containers whose property browsers support enumerated property types.

```
// pipectl.cpp
...
short CPipeCtrl::GetPipeType()
{
    return m_sPipeType;
}

void CPipeCtrl::SetPipeType(short nNewValue)
{
    // Don't allow setting of the property at run time
    // This isn't absolutely necessary, but it's an example
    // of a property that cannot be modified when running.
```

```
   // If you were to allow modification of the control's mode
   // during run time, we would have to ensure that any active
   // pipe connections were cleaned up, and so on.
   if ( AmbientUserMode() )
      ThrowError( CTL_E_SETNOTSUPPORTEDATRUNTIME,
                  "You can't change the PipeType property at runtime" );

   m_sPipeType = nNewValue;

   BoundPropertyChanged( dispidPipeType );
   SetModifiedFlag();
}

// pipe.odl
...
typedef enum
{
   [helpstring("Server")] Server = 0,
   [helpstring("Client")] Client = 1
} enumPipeType;

[ uuid(96612B01-D79F-11CE-86A3-08005A564718),
  helpstring("Dispatch interface for Pipe Control"), hidden ]
dispinterface _DPipe
{
   properties:
      // NOTE - ClassWizard will maintain property information here.
      //    Use extreme caution when editing this section.
      //{{AFX_ODL_PROP(CPipeCtrl)
      [id(1)] BSTR PipeName;
      [id(2)] enumPipeType PipeType;
      [id(3)] BSTR ErrorMsg;
      //}}AFX_ODL_PROP
...
};
```

For containers that don't provide a nice interface to a control's properties, we need to provide one of our own via the control's custom property page. Just as we did in Chapter 10, we'll use a dropdown combo box to present the PipeType enumerated options in the control's custom property page. A simple entry field will suffice for the PipeName property.

The following code shows the additions to the property page implementation files. It's best to add these using ClassWizard, but you can add individually if you want to. We've also added an enumerated type to **PIPE.H** so that we can use it throughout the project.

```
// pipe.h
...
#include "resource.h"        // main symbols

typedef enum
{
   TypeServer = 0,
   TypeClient = 1
} enumPipeType;

// pipeppg.h
...
/////////////////////////////////////////////////////////////////////////////
// CPipePropPage::CPipePropPage - Constructor
CPipePropPage::CPipePropPage() :
     COlePropertyPage(IDD, IDS_PIPE_PPG_CAPTION)
{
   //{{AFX_DATA_INIT(CPipePropPage)


   //}}AFX_DATA_INIT
}

// pipectl.h
...
/////////////////////////////////////////////////////////////////////////////
// CPipePropPage::DoDataExchange - Moves data between page and properties
void CPipePropPage::DoDataExchange(CDataExchange* pDX)
{
   //{{AFX_DATA_MAP(CPipePropPage)



   //}}AFX_DATA_MAP
   DDP_PostProcessing(pDX);
}
```

We need not include the `ErrorMsg` property on our control's custom property page, because it is a run-time–only property and does not need to be accessed during the design process (Figure 11.2).

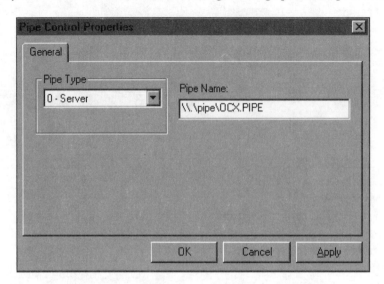

Figure 11.2 The pipe control's custom property page.

Whenever you add properties to your controls, you should also ensure that they have default values and are serialized using the `DoPropExchange` method in the control's implementation file. In our case, this is **PIPECTL.CPP**:

```
/////////////////////////////////////////////////////////////////////////////
// CPipeCtrl::DoPropExchange - Persistence support
void CPipeCtrl::DoPropExchange(CPropExchange* pPX)
{
    ExchangeVersion(pPX, MAKELONG(_wVerMinor, _wVerMajor));
    COleControl::DoPropExchange(pPX);

    // TODO: Call PX_ functions for each persistent custom property.

    // Default to "TypeServer"
    PX_Short( pPX, "PipeType", m_sPipeType, TypeServer );
    // Provide a default pipe name
    PX_String( pPX, "PipeName", m_strPipeName, "\\\\.\\pipe\\OCX.PIPE" );
}
```

Again, because our `ErrorMsg` property is needed only at run time and has no default value or any persistent state, there is no need to serialize it.

Adding the Pipe Methods

Because our PIPE control doesn't have a visual element, most (if not all) of its functionality is provided through the methods that it exposes to the control user. One of our goals is to hide the complexity of the underlying API calls by doing much of the work within the control and exposing only a small number of abstracted, high-level methods.

Our control's `PipeType` property indicates whether it should act as a pipe server or a pipe client. To make this interface easy to use, we provide methods that are specific to the mode of the control. If the control is configured to act as a server, the user must use the server-specific methods, and if it is configured as a pipe client, the user must use the client-specific set of methods. The five PIPE methods—two for a server instance and three for a client instance—are listed in Table 11.2.

Table 11.2 PIPE Control Methods

Method/Applicable Mode	Purpose
`Create` (Server)	The `Create` method is used by a pipe server to create an instance of a pipe. The name of the pipe is provided by the `PipeName` property. Only one instance of a pipe is supported per control.
`Destroy` (Server)	The `Destroy` method is used by a pipe server to destroy the previous instance of a pipe.
`Connect` (Client)	The `Connect` method is used by a pipe client to connect to a server's pipe instance. The name of the pipe to connect to is provided by the `PipeName` property.
`Disconnect` (Client)	The `Disconnect` method is used by a pipe client to disconnect from a server's pipe instance.
`Write` (Client)	The `Write` method is used by a pipe client to send data to a server's pipe instance. A `Write` is not valid until the client has successfully connected to a server's pipe via the `Connect` method.

Using ClassWizard, add the five methods listed in Table 11.2 to the PIPE control. All the methods return `BOOL`, and only the `Write` method requires a parameter. `Write` sends a message to the pipe server and takes a parameter of type `LPCTSTR`. After you have added the methods, add the implementation code described in the next few sections.

Create

The `Create` method creates an instance of a pipe. A pipe control that is configured to behave as a server uses this method to create a pipe that can be accessed by a client process. The name of the pipe is provided by the `PipeName` property. Only one instance of a pipe is supported per control. The following code implements the `Create` method:

```
BOOL CPipeCtrl::Create()
{
    // Clear any error message
    m_strError.Empty();

    // Make sure we're the right type
    if ( m_sPipeType != TypeServer )
    {
        m_strError = "'Create' should not be called from a pipe Client";
        return FALSE;
    }

    // We've already create a pipe instance
    if ( m_hPipe )
    {
        m_strError = "A Pipe has already been created, use 'Destroy', and try again";
        return FALSE;
    }

    // If CreatePipe fails, it will set
    // the ErrorMsg property, so all we have
    // to do is return FALSE indicating the error
    if ( CreatePipe() == FALSE )
        return FALSE;

    // Start a timer to check for connections
    // and writes to the pipe
    StartTimer();

    return TRUE;
}
```

The Create method first clears the ErrorMsg string. As you will see, we do this at the beginning of all the automation methods of our control. This technique ensures that the error string is cleared every time the user calls a method within the control. All our methods return a BOOL that indicates the success or failure of the method. If the method returns FALSE, the control user should check or display the ErrorMsg property, which will contain the specific error. The following Visual Basic code illustrates the error checking technique that should be used:

```
If Not Pipe.Create Then
    MsgBox Pipe.ErrorMsg
End If
```

After initializing the error string, we check to ensure that the PipeType property is consistent with the method being called. We also will do this in all the subsequent methods that we discuss. If that check succeeds, we check to see whether we already have a valid pipe handle. If we do, we again return FALSE along with an appropriate error message.

Finally, we get to some functionality. We call the CreatePipe helper method that we will discuss in a moment. If it is successful, we start a timer that we will use to periodically check the pipe for both connections and data. We will also discuss this timer in a later section.

Destroy

The Destroy method is used by a pipe server to destroy the previous instance of a pipe. A control configured as a server typically calls this method before shutting down.

```
BOOL CPipeCtrl::Destroy()
{
    // Clear any error message
    m_strError.Empty();

    // Make sure we're the right type
    if ( m_sPipeType != TypeServer )
    {
        m_strError = "'Destroy' should not be called from a pipe Client";
        return FALSE;
    }

    ClosePipe();
    StopTimer();

    return TRUE;
}
```

The Destroy method contains mostly error-checking code, which we've discussed previously. If all goes well, we use the ClosePipe helper method and stop the timer. The Create and Destroy methods provide the interface for a control configured to act as a server. The next three methods are specific to a control that is configured as a pipe client.

Connect

The Connect method is used by a pipe client to connect to a server's pipe instance. The name of the pipe to connect to is provided by the PipeName property.

```
BOOL CPipeCtrl::Connect()
{
    // Clear any error message
    m_strError.Empty();
```

```
// Make sure we're the right type
if ( m_sPipeType != TypeClient )
{
    m_strError = "'Connect' should not be called with type set to pipe Server";
    return FALSE;
}

if ( m_hPipe )
{
    m_strError = "A pipe is already Connected";
    return FALSE;
}

// Attempt a connect to the server's pipe
m_hPipe = ::CreateFile( LPCTSTR( m_strPipeName ),
                        GENERIC_WRITE,
                        0,
                        NULL,
                        OPEN_EXISTING,
                        FILE_FLAG_WRITE_THROUGH,
                        NULL );

// An error returns INVALID_HANDLE_VALUE
if ( m_hPipe == INVALID_HANDLE_VALUE )
{
    DWORD dwError = ::GetLastError();
    switch( dwError )
    {
        case ERROR_FILE_NOT_FOUND:
            m_strError.Format(
                    "Unable to open the specified pipe %s. Error is FILE_NOT_FOUND",
                    LPCTSTR( m_strPipeName ) );
            break;

        default:
            m_strError.Format(
                "Unknown Error trying to open the specified pipe %s. LastError is %d",
                LPCTSTR( m_strPipeName ),
                dwError );
            break;
```

```
        }
        // Reset the pipe handle to zero
        m_hPipe = 0;

        // Indicate an error occurred
        return FALSE;
    }

    // Success
    return TRUE;
}
```

Almost all the code is for error checking. The real work occurs in the `CreateFile` function call. See the Win32 help file for specifics concerning the parameters of the `CreateFile` function. If `CreateFile` succeeds, we have a valid connection between a server's pipe instance and our client control.

Disconnect

The `Disconnect` method is used by a pipe client to disconnect from a server control's pipe instance. As mentioned previously, the client control can maintain only one connection to a pipe at a time and must disconnect before attempting to connect to another pipe instance.

```
BOOL CPipeCtrl::Disconnect()
{
    // Clear any error message
    m_strError.Empty();

    // Make sure we're the right type
    if ( m_sPipeType != TypeClient )
    {
        m_strError = "'Disconnect' should not be called from a pipe Server";
        return FALSE;
    }

    // Close the pipe
    ClosePipe();

    return TRUE;
}
```

This code contains the usual error checking and finally a call to the helper function, `ClosePipe`, which does all the work. For a client control, `ClosePipe` calls `CloseHandle` with the pipe's handle.

Write

The `Write` method is used by a pipe client to send data to a server's pipe instance. A `Write` is not valid until the client has successfully connected to a server's pipe via the `Connect` method.

```
BOOL CPipeCtrl::Write( LPCTSTR Message )
{
    // Clear any error message
    m_strError.Empty();

    // Make sure we're the right type
    if ( m_sPipeType != TypeClient )
    {
        m_strError =  "'Write' should not be called from a pipe Server";
        return FALSE;
    }

    // Make sure we have a valid pipe
    if ( m_hPipe == 0 )
    {
        m_strError = "Pipe is not 'Connected'";
        return FALSE;
    }

    // Number of bytes written to the pipe
    DWORD dwWritten;

    // Write to the pipe
    BOOL bRet = ::WriteFile( m_hPipe,
                             Message,
                             strlen( Message ),
                             &dwWritten,
                             NULL );

    // A FALSE return indicates an error
    if (! bRet )
    {
        // Get the error number and fire the error event
        DWORD dwError = ::GetLastError();
        m_strError.Format( "Unable to write to pipe. LastError = %d",
```

```
                    dwError );

    // Close the pipe
    ClosePipe();

    return FALSE;
  }

  return TRUE;
}
```

Again, this code is mostly error checking followed by the work. The `WriteFile` function takes the data passed through the `LPCTSTR  Message` parameter and writes to the pipe. If an error occurs during the write, indicated by a `FALSE` return, we build an error message and assign it to the `ErrorMsg` property. We then close the pipe and return `FALSE`. If all goes well, we return `TRUE`, indicating success.

Helper Methods

The preceding automation methods depend on a few internal helper functions. The `CreatePipe` and `ClosePipe` methods are described next.

The `CreatePipe` method is called by the control's `Create` method and also from the `OnTimer` method that we will discuss in a moment. `CreatePipe` calls the named pipe API function `CreateNamedPipe` with parameters that are appropriate for single pipe instance server. Parameters of note include `PIPE_TYPE_MESSAGE`, which indicates that the pipe will treat the data exchanges as type messages, and `PIPE_ACCESS_INBOUND`, which indicates that the pipe will only be receiving messages from client processes and will not transfer any data to the client.

If `m_hPipe` contains the symbol `INVALID_HANDLE_VALUE`, indicating an error, the Win32 `GetLastError` function is called to retrieve the specific error that occurred. This return value, along with a textual error message, is later passed to the container via our `FirePipeError` event.

```
BOOL CPipeCtrl::CreatePipe()
{
  // Create an instance of a named pipe
  // Use the name provided by the control user
  m_hPipe  = ::CreateNamedPipe( LPCTSTR( m_strPipeName ),
              PIPE_ACCESS_INBOUND | FILE_FLAG_OVERLAPPED,
              PIPE_WAIT | PIPE_TYPE_MESSAGE | PIPE_READMODE_MESSAGE,
              1,
              BUFFER_SIZE,
              BUFFER_SIZE,
              100,
              NULL );
```

```
// Check for an error return
if ( m_hPipe == INVALID_HANDLE_VALUE )
{
    char szTemp[128];
    DWORD dwError = ::GetLastError();
    sprintf( szTemp, "Unable to CreatePipe LastError = %d\n", dwError );

    // Set the error property
    m_strError = szTemp;
    m_hPipe = 0;

    // Return an error
    return FALSE;
}

// Success
return TRUE;
}
```

The `ClosePipe` method is called by many methods, including those that support the server and those that support the client. If the pipe handle is valid, `ClosePipe` checks the mode of the control, and if the control is acting as a server, it disconnects any clients from the pipe. Independent of the control's mode, `ClosePipe` then closes the pipe handle. It completes its function by setting the `m_hPipe` member to zero.

```
void CPipeCtrl::ClosePipe()
{
    // Close the pipe if there is a valid handle
    if ( m_hPipe )
    {
        // Disconnect if we are a server
        if ( m_sPipeType == TypeServer )
            ::DisconnectNamedPipe( m_hPipe );
        ::CloseHandle( m_hPipe );

        m_hPipe = 0;
    }
}
```

Adding the Supporting Events

We also need two events for our PIPE control. One event reports that a control, acting as a server, has received data from a client. The other is used to report pipe-specific errors to the control user. Using

ClassWizard, add two events. The first, `MessageReceived`, passes a `BSTR` parameter to the container. The second, `PipeError`, passes both a `long` and a `BSTR` parameter.

MessageReceived

The `MessageReceived` event is used to communicate the reception of a message from a client (control) process. The `MessageReceived` event is sent only to an instance of a control that is acting as a pipe server. A control configured as a pipe client uses the `Write` method to send data, and when the data is received by the server, it is passed on via the `MessageRecieved` event. You will see how `MessageReceived` is used in a moment, when we discuss the `ReadPipe` method.

PipeError

The `PipeError` event provides a way of reporting errors that occur outside the scope of a control's automation methods. In a moment, when we discuss control error handling, you will see that there is a certain protocol that must be followed when you're handling errors within your control. The `PipeError` event passes the result of the Win32 `GetLastError` function along with a text description of the error.

Visual C++ also provides the stock `Error` event, which can be used to communicate error information back to the container.

Freezing Events

ActiveX control containers may not always be in a state that allows them to receive events from controls. When the container is initially loading its contained controls, when the container is re-creating and destroying control instances, or when the container is processing an event from another control, it may not be able to handle the firing of multiple simultaneous events.

The ActiveX control standard provides an interface method, `IOleControl::FreezeEvents`, that the container can use to notify the control when it should and should not fire events. This method is mapped to the `COleControl::OnFreezeEvents` method for your controls to use. The default implementation provided by `COleControl` does nothing. The `OnFreezeEvents` method passes a `boolean` parameter that indicates whether the control should fire events. If the parameter is `TRUE`, the control should not fire events, and if it is `FALSE`, the control can process events normally.

This sounds fine, but what should a control do if it needs to fire an event and the container won't let it? The control can do one of three things. It can fire the event normally (and the container will ignore it), it can throw the event away by not firing it, or it can queue the event using an internal mechanism and fire it later, when the container again allows the firing of events. The first two methods—firing or throwing the event away—are simple to do. The third method isn't hard to implement but requires that you maintain a list of events along with any contextual information needed to fire the event later. Some controls may even require a priority queuing mechanism that maintains synchronization of the control's events. We will use the second method. If the container indicates that the control should not fire events and if the control has an event to fire, it will ignore the event and continue processing.

First, we override the OnFreezeEvents method. Then we maintain the state of the container's FreezeEvent flag. This isn't difficult. Add the following code to **PIPECTL.CPP**:

```
void CPipeCtrl::OnFreezeEvents( BOOL bFreeze )
{

  if ( bFreeze )
    m_iFreeze++;
  else
    m_iFreeze—;
}
```

Whenever the container changes the FreezeEvent state, we either increment or decrement the value of a member variable in our control's implementation class. We must maintain a count of the OnFreezeEvents calls, because the container can nest FreezeEvents calls.

Now, when we need to fire an event, we check our member variable to determine whether the event can be fired. It looks something like this:

```
// Fire the MessageReceived event
// If the container says it's OK
if ( m_iFreeze == 0 )
    FireMessageReceived( szBuffer );
```

You could queue events within your controls using something similar to this. This method requires a class that contains the type and state of a given event. The control class also maintains a list of these event instances using the MFC CObList class:

```
void CYourCtrl::OnFreezeEvents( BOOL bFreeze )
{

  if ( bFreeze )
    m_iFreeze++;
  else
    m_iFreeze—;

  // If events allowed
  if ( m_iFreeze == 0 )
  {
    // check the queue
    POSITION pos = m_EventList.GetHeadPosition();
    while( pos )
    {
      CEvent* pEvent = (CEvent*) m_EventList.GetNext( pos );
```

```
            pEvent->Fire();
        }
    }
}
...
void CYourControl::SomeMethod()
{
    // If we can't fire the event, queue it
    if ( m_iFreeze )
    {
        // Build event object
        // and add it to the tail of the event list
        CEvent* pEvent = new CEvent( type );
        m_EventList.AddTail( pEvent );
    }
    else
        FireEvent(...);
}
```

The complexity is in the design of the CEvent class, ensuring that the events still have meaning after the code that would have fired them has already executed.

Using a Timer to Check the Pipe

Applications that use Win32 pipes to provide client/server services typically implement the server side using multiple threads. The named pipes API makes it easy for a server process to provide a thread for each client that connects to an instance of a pipe. As I mentioned earlier, it is beyond the scope of this chapter to investigate the complexities of implementing an ActiveX control that uses multiple threads. Without the ability to start a thread for each client connection, we must limit to one the number of client connections for each instance of the control. We also must simulate the existence of an executing thread for the server side of the pipe. We simulate this thread with the help of a timer message.

Using ClassWizard, add a handler for the WM_TIMER message and add methods to **PIPECTL.H** and **PIPECTL.CPP** to support the starting and stopping of the timer. This code is identical to that used in the CLOCK control of Chapter 9.

```
// pipectl.h
...
// Implementation
protected:
    ~CPipeCtrl();
```

```
   void StartTimer();
   void StopTimer();
...

// pipectl.cpp

...
```

```
#define TIMER_ID 100
void CPipeCtrl::StartTimer()
{
   SetTimer( TIMER_ID, 200, NULL );
}

void CPipeCtrl::StopTimer()
{
   KillTimer( TIMER_ID );
}
```

As you can see from the preceding timer code, we fire the timer every 200 milliseconds. Every time the timer fires, we check the status of the pipe using the `PeekNamedPipe` function. Add the following code to the `OnTimer` message handler:

```
// pipectl.cpp

...

void CPipeCtrl::OnTimer(UINT nIDEvent)
{
   if ( m_hPipe )
   {
      BOOL bRet;
      DWORD dwAvailable;
      // Peek the pipe to determine if there
      // is any data in the pipe. Also, we can
      // determine if a client is connected to
      // the pipe by the return code from PeekNamedPipe
      bRet = ::PeekNamedPipe( m_hPipe,
                              NULL,
                              NULL,
                              NULL,
                              &dwAvailable,
                              NULL );
      if (! bRet )
      {
         DWORD dwError = ::GetLastError();
```

```
    // Depending on the error do different things
    // These error codes are defined in WINERROR.H
    switch( dwError )
    {
        // This error indicates that there is
        // no client connected to the pipe
        // so ignore it, and continue
        case ERROR_BAD_PIPE:
            break;

        // This error occurs when a client
        // disconnects from the pipe. We close
        // the current instance of the pipe
        // and re-create a new one.
        case ERROR_BROKEN_PIPE:
            ClosePipe();
            if( CreatePipe() == FALSE )
            {
                // Error during create, shut down
                StopTimer();
                if ( m_iFreeze == 0 )
                    FirePipeError( dwError,
                        "Unable to Create a new Pipe after a client disconnect" );
            }
            break;

        // If we get an error that we don't expect
        // we close the pipe, stop the timer, and
        // report the error. This stops us from
        // getting into an endless timer loop.
        default:
            StopTimer();
            ClosePipe();
            if ( m_iFreeze == 0 )
                FirePipeError( dwError, "Unknown error in 'PeekNamedPipe'" );
            break;
    }
}
else
{
    // If there is data in the pipe
```

```
      // call the read function
    if ( dwAvailable )
        ReadPipe();

    }

  }

}
```

The preceding code executes only when the control is acting as a pipe server. It continually checks the status of the server's pipe using the `PeekNamedPipe` function. The return code of `PeekNamedPipe` indicates whether a client process is connected to the pipe. If there is a valid connection, we check the `dwAvailable` flag, and, if there is data available in the pipe, we call the `ReadPipe` function.

If we encounter an error while processing the `WM_TIMER` message, we fire the `PipeError` event. We use an event because when processing the `WM_TIMER` message, we are not executing in the context of an automation method or property. The control user has not actually made a synchronous call to the control, so there is no other way to report an error except to fire an event. We will discuss this further in a moment. As you can see, if the container is not accepting events, we continue with the normal processing of the method.

If `PeekNamedPipe` returns successfully and if the `dwAvailable` parameter indicates that there is data in the pipe, the `ReadPipe` helper method is called:

```
#define BUFFER_SIZE 512
void CPipeCtrl::ReadPipe()
{
   BOOL bRet;
   char szBuffer[BUFFER_SIZE + 1];
   unsigned long  ulRead;
   // Read the pipe
   bRet = ::ReadFile( m_hPipe,
                  szBuffer,
                  BUFFER_SIZE,
                  &ulRead,
                  NULL );

   // A TRUE return indicates success
   if ( bRet )
   {
       // ulRead contains the number of bytes in
       // the pipe message.
       if ( ulRead )
       {
           szBuffer[ulRead] = '\0';
           // Fire the MessageReceived event
           // If the container says it's OK
```

```
        if ( m_iFreeze == 0 )
            FireMessageReceived( szBuffer );
    }
}
// A FALSE return indicates failure
else
{
    // Use the ::GetLastError function to get
    // the actual error number
    DWORD dwError = ::GetLastError();
    // Pass back the error number and a message to the container
    if ( m_iFreeze == 0 )
        FirePipeError( dwError, "Error while reading the pipe" );
    ClosePipe();
}
}
```

The `ReadPipe` code is straightforward. It is called only when `PeekNamedPipe` has indicated that there is data to read from the pipe. `ReadPipe` uses the Win32 `ReadFile` function, and, if the return is successful, `ReadPipe` zero terminates the buffer. If the container allows events, `ReadPipe` calls the `MessageReceived` event with the data read from the pipe. If an error occurs, `ReadPipe` gets the error number and passes it along with a text message to the container via the `PipeError` event.

Certain nonvisual controls need the services of a true `HWND` when working as an ActiveX control. In this case, you need to explicitly create a window for your control.

Invisible Controls That Require a Window

Our PIPE control needs the services of a window. The default implementation provided by ControlWizard does not create a window for the control. This is appropriate, because we told ControlWizard that our control would be invisible at run time so there is no apparent need for a window. Still, there are reasons to have a window for a control. Our reason is that we want to use a window to handle the `WM_TIMER` message.

If your nonvisual control needs the services of a window when loaded and running in a container, the `COleControl::RecreateControlWindow` method will create a default window for your control when called. To ensure that the control's window is created as soon as possible, the best place to put this is the `COleControl::OnSetClientSite` method. `OnSetClientSite` is called as the container loads the control within the container. It is a good place to initially create the default window. We need a true `HWND` only when the container is in run mode, so we check the ambient property `UserMode` before calling `RecreateControlWindow`.

```
// This ensures that our control has a valid HWND
// as soon as it is placed on a container at run time
```

```
void CPipeCtrl::OnSetClientSite()
{

    if ( AmbientUserMode() )

        RecreateControlWindow();

}
```

Handling Errors in Controls

There are three basic ways to handle errors that occur in your controls. The first is the typical procedural way that we are all familiar with: a return value from your class methods. The second method is to use the automation exception mechanism. This technique is useful in automation properties, because the value returned from a property method is the value of the property and you can't return an "error." The third approach uses an event to communicate the error to the container. This technique should be used when the container is not executing in the context of your control's methods or properties (it's doing something else).

The automation methods and properties that are exposed by our control are called synchronously by the container. When you're using a scripting language such as Visual Basic, a method call like the following one does not return until the method is complete:

```
' Call the pipe control's Create method
If Not Pipe1.Create then
      MsgBox Pipe1.ErrorMsg
End If
```

The preceding code executes synchronously, so the most effective and efficient way of reporting errors is to return a value from the call, as we have done. This is the preferred method of reporting errors when you're using automation methods. In this case, the error is encountered while executing code within the control, and the container code (such as Visual Basic) is waiting on the return from the automation call.

Automation properties return the value of the property, so the preceding method of returning an error value won't work. Get/Set methods are typically used to implement the assignment and retrieval of a control's properties, and automation provides an exception mechanism to report error conditions to the container. We have used this technique in most of the controls we have developed. The SetNotSupported method is an example of the use of this exception mechanism. It uses the COleControl::ThrowError method and is similar to the C++ method of handling exceptions. For example, a run-time property uses the automation exception mechanism to inform the container that the property can be accessed only at run time. The following code illustrates this technique:

```
void CPipeCtrl::SetPipeType(short nNewValue)
{
    // Don't allow setting of the property at run time
    // This isn't absolutely necessary, but it's an example
    // of a property that cannot be modified when running.
    // If you were to allow modification of the control's mode
```

```
    // during run time, we would have to ensure that any active
    // pipe connections were cleaned up, and so on.
    if ( AmbientUserMode() )
        ThrowError( CTL_E_SETNOTSUPPORTEDATRUNTIME,
                    "You can't change the PipeType property at runtime" );

    m_sPipeType = nNewValue;

    SetModifiedFlag();
}
```

The `SetPipeType` method returns a `void`, but we are still able to communicate to the container that the property cannot be modified during run time. This technique of using an automation exception to communicate with the container can be used only when the control is executing in the context of an automation property or method.

There are times, however, when an error may occur in your control's code when the container is not waiting for a return from an automation call. For example, the `OnTimer` method in our PIPE control executes every 200 milliseconds and is never explicitly called by the container. In this case, errors that occur cannot be reported using the techniques described earlier. Instead, an event must be used.

The event technique should be used in any control code that is executed outside an automation method or property. In this case, the automation content is not present, and the `ThrowError` method will not work properly. Instead, your control should fire an event to inform the container that an error has occurred. We used this technique in our `OnTimer` and `ReadPipe` methods, because they execute asynchronously and are never called directly by the container. Here's a snippet of the code:

```
void CPipeCtrl::ReadPipe()
{
    // A TRUE return indicates success
    if ( bRet )
    {
    ...
    }
    // A FALSE return indicates failure
    else
    {
        // Use the ::GetLastError function to get
        // the actual error number
        DWORD dwError = ::GetLastError();
        // Pass back the error number and a message to the container
        if ( m_iFreeze == 0 )
            FirePipeError( dwError, "Error while reading the pipe" );
        ClosePipe();
    }
}
```

This code informs the container of the problem by firing the `PipeError` event with the error information.

The automation exception mechanism is used to implement run-time–only, read-only, and design-time–only properties.

Run-Time–Only Properties

Run-time–only properties are those properties that can be accessed and modified only when the container is in run mode. An example of this type is the `ErrorMsg` property that is used in our PIPE control. To enforce the use of the property only at run time, we used the `SetNotSupported` and `GetNotSupported` methods. Each of these methods uses `COleControl::ThrowError` to notify the container that the property cannot be accessed at various times. Here is the code for the `ErrorMsg` property:

```
BSTR CPipeCtrl::GetErrorMsg()
{
    // Most containers that provide property browsers (e.g., VB)
    // will trap this exception and will not display the property
    // in the property browser. This is just what we want.
    // If we're not in run mode don't allow anyone to get the
    // property's value.
    if ( AmbientUserMode() == FALSE )
        GetNotSupported();

    return m_strError.AllocSysString();
}
```

If the container is not in run mode, we throw the `CTL_E_GETNOTSUPPORTED` exception. To enforce run-time–only setting of a property, you would do this:

```
void CYourControl::SetAProperty(short sNewValue)
{
    // If not running report an error
    if (! AmbientUserMode() )
    {
        // Throw the CTL_E_SETNOTSUPPORTED error
        SetNotSupported();
    }
    // Go ahead and set the property value
}
```

Design-Time–Only Properties

To implement properties that can be modified only during the container's design phase, you would do the opposite of what we've just discussed. There are a number of standard error messages that can be thrown from within your control's code. Two of them are specific to not allowing the modification of properties at run time:

```
void CYourControl::SetAProperty(short sNewValue)
{
    // If not design phase report an error
    if ( AmbientUserMode() )
    {
        ThrowError( CTL_E_SETNOTSUPPORTEDATRUNTIME,
                    "Property cannot be set at runtime" );
    }

    // Go ahead and·set the property value
    sProperty = sNewValue;
}

short CYourControl::GetAProperty()
{
    // If not design report an error
    if ( AmbientUserMode() )
    {
        ThrowError( CTL_E_GETNOTSUPPORTEDATRUNTIME,
                    "Get not allowed at runtime" );
    }

    // Go ahead and return the property value
    return sProperty;
}
```

Containers can look for these specific exceptions and report them consistently.

Using the Control

To test the controls, let's develop a Visual Basic application that uses our new PIPE control. Actually, we'll develop three application. The first one will demonstrate how to use the PIPE control by using two instances of the control within one application. The next example will contain two Visual Basic applications: one that will act as the server application and another that will act as the client. These applications can be run on separate machines in a networked environment.

Figure 11.3 shows our first application, a Visual Basic form that contains two instances of the PIPE control. One of the controls acts as a pipe server, and the other acts as a pipe client. This application shows how easy it is to use the PIPE control and provides a simple way to test the control. This application basically talks to itself.

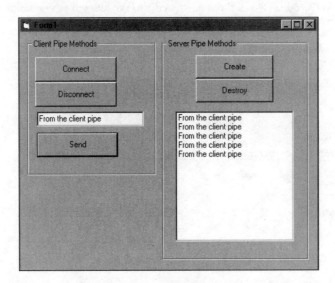

Figure 11.3 Visual Basic form with two instances of the PIPE control.

The PIPE control instances can't be seen on the form—they are invisible at run time—but they provide the majority of the functionality of the application. First, the **Create** button is clicked to create an instance of the server pipe, and then the **Connect** button is clicked to connect the client pipe control to the server's instance. You can then enter text in the entry field and send it to the server's pipe. As the server receives messages from the client, it logs them in the listbox. Here is the Visual Basic source code for the complete application, all of about 30 lines of code:

```
Private Sub cmdConnect_Click()
    If Not ClientPipe.Connect Then
        MsgBox ClientPipe.ErrorMsg
    End If
End Sub

Private Sub cmdCreate_Click()
    If Not ServerPipe.Create Then
        MsgBox ServerPipe.ErrorMsg
    End If
End Sub

Private Sub cmdDisconnect_Click()
```

```
    If Not ClientPipe.Disconnect Then
        MsgBox ServerPipe.ErrorMsg
    End If
End Sub

Private Sub cmdSend_Click()
    If Not ClientPipe.Write(Text1) Then
        MsgBox ClientPipe.ErrorMsg
    End If
End Sub

Private Sub Destroy_Click()
    If Not ServerPipe.Destroy Then
        MsgBox ServerPipe.ErrorMsg
    End If
End Sub

Private Sub ServerPipe_PipeError(ByVal dwError As Long, ByVal szError As String)
    MsgBox "Error occurred " & dwError & " " & szError
End Sub

Private Sub ClientPipe_PipeError(ByVal dwError As Long, ByVal szError As String)
    MsgBox "Error occurred " & dwError & " " & szError
End Sub

Private Sub ServerPipe_MessageReceived(ByVal szMessage As String)
    List1.AddItem szMessage
End Sub
```

The next application contains two Visual Basic executables that run on separate machines in a networked environment. It is similar to the previous application but allows communication to occur across machines. Figure 11.4 shows the server application.

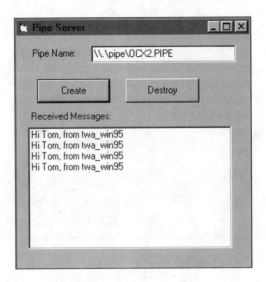

Figure 11.4 The server application.

The only difference is that you are allowed to modify the `PipeName` property before you create the pipe instance. As you can see, the `PipeName` contains a local pipe filename. The messages received are from an instance of the client application running on another machine (Figure 11.5).

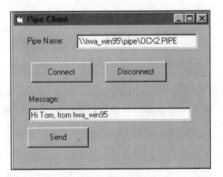

Figure 11.5 Message received from another machine.

The combined number of Visual Basic lines of code is again around 30. By encapsulating the Win32 API calls and providing an easy-to-use interface to our ActiveX control, we have made it easy for a visual tool user to develop useful applications. That is the goal of building software components: provide robust functionality that is easy to use.

Summary

Nonvisual controls provide functionality by exposing properties and methods that supply an abstraction of a more complex technology. Uses for nonvisual controls are numerous: wrapping a C++ class to provide its functions to a visual tool user, abstracting a group of operating system functions, or providing an easy-to-use interface for business-specific problem. In these examples, nonvisual controls can make it easy for a visual tool user to gain access to functionality.

Win32 named pipes provide a way to test this theory. They supply a mechanism for communication between processes on local and remote machines. Named pipes can be used to implement basic client/sever techniques between processes.

Nonvisual controls require the developer to provide a design-phase–only representation of the control, because it will not be visible when the container is in run mode. An easy way to represent a nonvisual control at design time is to use its toolbar bitmap image. The `CPictureHolder` class provides a way to allow the bitmap to be manipulated.

An ActiveX control container can inform its contained controls that they either can or cannot fire events. There are various reasons that a container may disable the firing of a control's events, and it is important that the control honor this request. `COleControl` provides a method, `OnFreezeEvents`, that is called whenever the container requests a change in the `FreezeEvents` status. A simple way to implement this behavior in your controls is to maintain a flag that mirrors the setting of the last `OnFreezeEvents` call. Whenever your control needs to fire an event, you should check this flag. If it is `TRUE`, the simplest thing to do is to not fire the event, effectively throwing the event away. A more sophisticated method would be to save the events and fire them later.

Nonvisual controls are instantiated without a true window. If your control requires the use of a window, you can call the `COleControl::RecreateControlWindow` method. The best time to do this is when the control is initially placed within a container. The `OnSetClientSite` method is called when this occurs.

There are three ways to handle errors in your control code. For automation methods and properties, you should use a standard return value if possible. You can also use the `COleControl::ThrowError` method to cause an automation exception. This technique is used to implement the `SetNotSupported` and `GetNotSupported` methods that are used to implement run-time–only, read-only, and design-time–only properties. The `ThrowError` method should be used only within an automation method. When errors occur in your control outside an automation call, you must use an event to communicate the problem to the container. MFC provides a stock error event for this case.

Chapter *12*

Internet-Aware Controls

ActiveX controls can be used as is in web-style applications. In most cases, this means applications (HTML-based Web pages) that use a Web browser. However, several new ActiveX specifications provide additional techniques that can be used to make ActiveX controls more Internet-aware. In this chapter, we will explain these new techniques, build a control that uses them, and discuss some of the tools that can be used to build and test Internet-aware ActiveX controls.

What Are Internet-Aware Controls?

Internet-aware controls differ only slightly from the controls we've developed. Internet-aware controls are concerned with two additional issues: lack of bandwidth and the need for security. The ActiveX SDK includes new technologies that enable controls to operate effectively in low-bandwidth environments and provides security techniques to help with the management of component software in the Internet (or intranet) environment.

The issue of bandwidth is addressed with a new URL and Asynchronous Moniker specification, which allows a control to handle large property values (such as an image) more efficiently. *Asynchronous monikers* provide a mechanism for the control to download large amounts of property information asynchronously. Before the asynchronous moniker specification, the container was forced to wait while a control's properties were loaded. In a low-bandwidth environment, such as the Internet, this wait is not acceptable.

ActiveX controls have full access to the machine on which they are executing. In an Internet-type environment, where controls are part of Web documents, a number of security issues arise. The new component download specification allows transparent download and registration of controls to machines browsing Web documents. In this environment, security issues must be addressed. ActiveX provides several techniques to make ActiveX components secure and safe in Internet-type environments.

Web Terminology

This chapter contains many new terms that you may not be familiar with. Internet-based technologies are becoming important in all aspects of development. Even if you don't write Web-based software, it is radically changing the tools you use. Microsoft is rapidly changing the focus of its commercial software, operating systems, and development tools to make use of Web-based technologies. What follows is a quick introduction to some of the terms that we will encounter. This book is about component software development, so it is impossible to cover all the technologies that are used in Web-based environments. Several books are listed in the Bibliography for those who need information on technologies such as HTML, Java, HTTP, and so on. The following definitions will help introduce you to these technologies.

HTML

Hypertext Markup Language (HTML) is *the* language of the Web environment. The development of HTML along with a standard protocol (HTTP) to transport HTML documents is the primary reason for the tremendous growth of the Web. HTML makes it easy to describe static documents for publishing in Web-based environments.

A Web page begins as an ASCII-based HTML document. The document describes its contents using various *elements*. An element is demarcated with a set of *tags*, usually a begin-tag and an end-tag. Here's an example:

```
<P>This sentence is centered.</P>
```

Here we have an example of the paragraph element. Its begin tag is `<P>` and its end tag is `</P>`. An element can also have zero or more *attributes* that modify the effect of an element. Here's an example of the `ALIGN` attribute in our paragraph example:

```
<P ALIGN = CENTER>This sentence is centered.</P>
```

One of the most important elements in HTML is the *anchor*. An anchor supplies a jumping point, or go to, within a Web page, thus providing its hypertext capabilities. The anchor element is specified with the `<A></A>` tag pair. Here's an example:

```
<A HREF = "http:\\www.cnn.com">Click here to go to CNN</A>
```

As you can imagine, there are a large number elements specified by HTML. We're just taking a quick look. Here's a minimal HTML version 3.2 document:

```
<!DOCTYPE HTML PUBLIC "-//W3C//DTD HTML 3.2//EN">
<HTML>
<HEAD>
<TITLE>A Minimal Web Page</TITLE>
</HEAD>
<BODY>
</BODY>
</HTML>
```

The primary purpose of HTML is to specify text- and image-based documents in a machine- and display-independent way. HTML describes the formatting characteristics of a document. Later, we'll take a look at the `OBJECT` element, which allows the embedding of ActiveX controls. By adding ActiveX controls to HTML documents, you add dynamic capabilities to Web documents.

VBScript

VBScript is a subset of both Visual Basic and Visual Basic for Applications. Visual Basic is a full implementation of the language and is integrated into a full-featured development environment. Visual Basic for Applications is a subset of Visual Basic that is used as the macro language for many of Microsoft's high-end applications. VBScript is a subset that removes any commands (such as `CreateObject, FileCopy,` and `Open`) that provide unsecure access to the local machine.

VBScript is used to add logic to HTML-based documents. To do this, however, the logic must be tied to a component such as an ActiveX control. Internet Explorer provides an object model that allows a VBScript developer to access most browser functionality. For example, here's a quick VBScript program that displays information about the viewing browser. This program is quite different from a static HTML document, because it is actually executed each time it is viewed. The HTML code is generated and interpreted dynamically.

```
<!DOCTYPE HTML PUBLIC "-//W3C//DTD HTML 3.2//EN">
<HTML>
<HEAD>
<TITLE>Our First Script</TITLE>
<SCRIPT LANGUAGE="VBScript">
  <!—
    document.write "<CENTER>"
    document.write "<H2>" & "Here's some information about your browser" & "</H2>"
    document.write "Name:   " & Window.Navigator.AppName & "<BR>"
    document.write "Version: " & Window.Navigator.AppVersion & "<BR>"
    document.write "Code name: " & Window.Navigator.AppCodeName & "<BR>"
    document.write "User agent: " & Window.Navigator.UserAgent
    document.write "</CENTER>"
    document.close
  —>
</SCRIPT>
</HEAD>
<BODY>
</BODY>
</HTML>
```

URL

A uniform resource locator (URL) specifies the exact location of a resource within a Web-based environment. It comprises four parts: the specific protocol of accessing the resource (such as HTTP), the address of the machine that contains the resource (such as www.microsoft.com), the resource location on the machine (usually a filename), and any parameters that should be passed to the resource. Here are some typical URLs:

```
http://www.sky.net/~toma/faq.htm
mailto:toma@sky.net
news://msnews.microsoft.news
```

A URL is an important and powerful attribute of Web-based environments. It specifies everything that a browser needs to work with the given resource: the encoded data type and the exact, unique location in a network of several million machines.

Embedding Controls in HTML-Based Documents

ActiveX controls are important to Microsoft's Web-based software strategy. Microsoft's Web browser, Internet Explorer, is a capable ActiveX control container. By allowing the embedding of controls, a browser can now provide access to all the capabilities of the local machine. This feature, complete access to the Win32 API, is what makes the use of ActiveX controls so compelling in Web-based applications.

Building Web-based applications by embedding controls and connecting them with a script language such as VBScript is similar to building other, non-Web applications. By moving its Visual Basic and ActiveX technologies to the Web, Microsoft has made it easy for developers to leverage their existing expertise. We've already written a few Visual Basic applications that use ActiveX controls, and writing a browser-based application using VBScript and ActiveX controls is only slightly different.

OLE Controls/COM Objects for the Internet

The primary ActiveX SDK document that describes the requirements for providing Internet-aware support for ActiveX controls is titled *OLE Controls/COM Objects for the Internet*. Most of this document has been incorporated into the ActiveX SDK on-line help. It provides a good comprehensive view of the new technologies that make COM objects, specifically ActiveX controls, useful in low-bandwidth environments. The next few sections describe these new techniques.

The Object Element

The HTML standard provides a special element for embedding object instances within HTML-based pages. It is used to embed images, documents, applets, and, in our case, ActiveX controls. Here's the OBJECT element for the control that we will develop later in this chapter:

```
<OBJECT ID="Async1" WIDTH=280 HEIGHT=324
```

```
CLASSID="CLSID:0C7B4FD3-13C1-11D0-A644-B4C6CE000000"
CODEBASE="http://www.sky.net/~toma/Async.ocx">
    <PARAM NAME="_Version" VALUE="65536">
    <PARAM NAME="_ExtentX" VALUE="7403">
    <PARAM NAME="_ExtentY" VALUE="8567">
    <PARAM NAME="_StockProps" VALUE="173">
    <PARAM NAME="BackColor" VALUE="16777215">
    <PARAM NAME="Appearance" VALUE="1">
    <PARAM NAME="TextPath" VALUE="http://www.sky.net/~toma/log">
</OBJECT>
```

The OBJECT element has several important attributes. The ID attribute is used to specify a name for the embedded object. This name is useful when you're using VBScript to access the component programmatically. The WIDTH and HEIGHT attributes specify the extents of the object.

The next attribute, CLSID, is used by the container (browser) to instantiate a local copy of the embedded ActiveX control. (The control may not reside on the local machine, and this is a problem that the specification solves. We'll discuss this detail in a moment.) All the container must do is call CoCreateInstance with the provided CLSID. After the control is created, the container passes the control its persistent data provided by the PARAM elements.

The PARAM element is valid only within an OBJECT element. Its purpose is to store property values of the embedded object. The NAME attribute provides the property name, and the VALUE attribute provides any value. The TYPE attribute, which isn't shown in our example, indicates the specific Internet media type for the given property.

You should recognize the BackColor and Appearance properties from our previous examples. There are several properties that we have not discussed. Properties prefixed with an underscore are internal properties maintained by MFC. For example, the _StockProps entry is a bit mask that specifies which of MFC's stock properties are used by the control. The TextPath property is a new one. It's actually a new property type, a *data path*, defined for Internet-aware controls. We'll discuss this new property type in detail shortly.

Remember, an ActiveX browser is just an ActiveX control container, and the OBJECT element provides a standard way of serializing the state of an embedded control. If you compare how Visual Basic saves the state of a form (.**FRM**) to the attributes in the OBJECT element, you'll see that they are very similar.

Persistent Control Data

When a control is instantiated by a container, the container provides an interface (such as IPersistPropertyBag) to the control through which it can load its persistent properties. In most cases, this property data is small: a font, a color, or a small string. Each property value is usually less than 100 bytes. In our case, the control is embedded within a Web page, and this property data is stored (and retrieved) via the PARAM element.

This arrangement works fine for most cases, but what if we have a very large property value, such as a 2-MB GIF or BMP image? Should we encode and store the BMP data in-line (via the PARAM element) in the

HTML document? We could, but loading the document in a low-bandwidth environment would be excruci-ating, especially given the fact that a control's properties are loaded synchronously. The browser would be virtually locked while the 2MB+ HTML page was downloaded.

In other cases, a control's persistent data cannot, by definition, be stored locally in the HTML document. If a control provides streaming video or audio, the data is real-time and can be supplied only after instantia-tion by the container. In addition, it must be processed asynchronously or it will never work. A major addi-tion to the ActiveX control architecture is support for these large property values through the new data path property.

Data Path Properties

The data path property is a new property type added by the COM Objects for the Internet specification. A data path property is simple: it is a simple BSTR that contains a *link* (such as a URL) to the property data. Instead of embedding the data for the property within the HTML document, you store a link to the data. This technique isn't new. The concept of maintaining links to document data began with OLE version 1.0. Now, this concept has become important to Web-based documents. Figure 12.1 illustrates how a control's small and large properties are stored within a document.

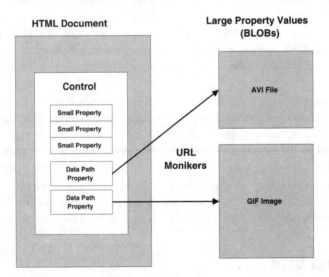

Figure 12.1 Data path properties and links.

Data path properties enable a control to store property data independently of the control itself. This is an important new capability. For example, if you write a control that retrieves and displays a weather map, the weather map image can be accessed through a data path property. When the control is placed in a Web page, only a link, via a URL, is needed. As the weather map is updated throughout the day, updating the image is as easy as changing the file specified in the control's data path property (a URL). The local control can then periodically refresh the image.

There are four key points to remember when you're working with data path properties:

- They enable progressive rendering of images. Asynchronous downloading allows the container to load and instantiate several controls at the same time. This capability is important in the Web environment.
- The control is ultimately responsible for the format of the downloaded data.
- The container, in most cases, tells the control where to retrieve the data. URLs can be specified relative to the container's location, so in many cases only the container can produce the absolute URL.
- Data path properties provide a mechanism to stream continuous data (such as audio data) to a control.

As is usually the case, we'll see that MFC makes it easy to implement data path properties in a control.

Monikers

A *moniker*, in COM at least, is an object that names or identifies a particular instance of a COM object. In Chapter 4, we discussed how to create generic instances of COM objects using the `CoCreateInstance` function. `CoCreateInstance` concerns itself with the creation of an object type but not a specific instance of that object. Monikers provide a way to create a specific instance of an object.

Monikers are themselves COM objects. However, they are small and encapsulate only the data necessary to re-create an instance of the object from some storage mechanism independent of the moniker. In our example of an ActiveX control, a specific control instance embedded within a Web document is identified with a moniker. The moniker encapsulates the CLSID of the control and how and where the control's persistent data is stored. In other words, the container identifies a particular embedded control via a moniker. The container and controls also identify data path properties using monikers.

The act of instantiating, initializing, and returning an interface pointer to the object named by a moniker is called *binding*. Instantiating and initializing an object that contains a large amount of data (such as an object that manipulates images) can take a significant amount of time, especially in a low-bandwidth environment. In this environment we need a new type of moniker.

Asynchronous Monikers

Before the release of the ActiveX specification, binding an object through its moniker occurred synchronously. The Internet's low-bandwidth environment, however, required the ability for this process to occur asynchronously. Instantiating a large object across a 14,400-baud line can take some time. Asynchronous monikers allow the container to instantiate a control, synchronously initialize the control with any small local properties, and then permit asynchronous loading of the control's large properties.

Asynchronous monikers, through the `IBindStatusCallback` interface, also allow a control and container to communicate the progress of an asynchronous download. This technique enables the container to display an indication to the user of how much of the data has been received.

URL Monikers

Currently, the only implementation of an asynchronous moniker is the URL moniker. A URL moniker is named with a URL and is used to instantiate and retrieve the data stored outside the control's small properties. Typically, a COM object and its persistent data are stored together locally. In the case of data path properties, the data is stored somewhere across the network.

A new COM API, `CreateURLMoniker`, takes a URL string and returns an `IMoniker` interface pointer. Because URLs can be specified relative to the current default location of the container, it is preferable that the container create the moniker and pass it to the control. However, if the control is executing in a container that does not support data path properties, it can do the work itself by using the new `MkParseDisplayNameEx` function.

The ReadyState Property and the OnReadyStateChange Event

With the addition of data path properties, a control will now be active and running before all its properties are initialized. For this reason, a new standard property, `ReadyState`, and a standard event, `OnReadyStateChange`, were added.

If a control depends on data contained in its data path properties, it may not be ready to interact with a user or with the container. The `ReadyState` property, whose potential values are listed in Table 12.1, is used by the control user and the container to determine the readiness state of a control. The `OnReadyStateChange` event is fired by the control to inform both the control user and the container of any change in its readiness state. A new return code, `E_PENDING`, has also been added to the control specification. A control can return `E_PENDING` in those methods that depend on properties that have not finished loading. For example, if the control cannot properly render its content, it may return `E_PENDING` from `OnDraw`. However, this behavior will be correctly interpreted only by those containers that support the new Internet-aware control standards.

Table 12.1 Control Readiness States

Control State	Description
`READYSTATE_UNINITIALIZED`	Default state after instantiation of control by the container.
`READYSTATE_LOADING`	Control is loading its local and asynchronous properties.
`READYSTATE_LOADED`	Control is now initialized. All its local, synchronous properties have finished loading.
`READYSTATE_INTERACTIVE`	The control supports user interaction, but some asynchronous data is still loading.
`READYSTATE_COMPLETE`	Control has loaded all its asynchronous property data and is ready to interact fully with the user.

Component Categories

We discussed component categories in detail in Chapter 7. Component categories provide a way for a COM object to describe the functionality it supports and the functionality it requires of its container. Several component categories are specific to Internet-aware controls. Each is listed in Table 12.2. Two of the component categories—CATID_SafeForScripting and CATID_SafeForInitializing—indicate a control's safety level when executing within a browser environment.

Table 12.2 Internet-Specific Component Categories

CATID Symbol from COMCAT.H	Purpose
CATID_PersistsToMoniker, CATID_PersistsToStreamInit, CATID_PersistsToStream, CATID_PersistsToStorage, CATID_PersistsToMemory, CATID_PersistsToFile, CATID_PersistsToPropertyBag	Used by Internet-aware controls to indicate which persistence methods they support. These can be used to indicate that an interface is required if the control supports only one persistence method.
CATID_RequiresDataPathHost	The control expects help from the container with its data path properties. The container must support IBindHost.
CATID_InternetAware	The control implements or requires some of the Internet-specific functionality, in particular the new persistence mechanisms for Web-based controls. The control also handles large property values with the new data path property type. This includes support for asynchronous downloads.
CATID_SafeForScripting	The control is safe for use within scripting environments.
CATID_SafeForInitializing	The control can safely be initialized.

CATID_PersistsTo*

If a control supports only one of the persistent interfaces, it should indicate so by registering the correct CATID_PersistsTo* component category in the Required Categories section. Controls developed with MFC's COleControl class support the majority of these persistence interfaces and do not need to specify this category.

CATID_RequiresDataPathHost

A data path property can contain either a relative or an absolute URL. It is desirable for a control's container to help manage a control's data path properties by creating the appropriate URL moniker and passing the bind context to the control. New control containers such as Internet Explorer support this capability. However, older containers such as Visual Basic 4.0 do not.

A control can actually create a URL moniker and download the remote data without the help of the container as long as the specified URL is absolute. If the URL is specified relative to the path maintained by the container, however, the moniker creation will fail because the control does not have the complete URL.

The `RequiresDataPathHost` category is used by those controls that require a container to help with the moniker creation and asynchronous downloading of data path properties. If a control requires this support, it should register this category under the `Required Categories` section. We will do this for our example control later.

CATID_InternetAware

A control that is Internet-aware implements its large properties with data path properties and also handles downloading these properties asynchronously. The control also uses the `ReadyState` property and its associated `OnReadyStateChange` event so that the control user and container can determine the readiness state of the control. Our example control does this, so we will register this component category.

CATID_SafeForScripting

ActiveX controls have complete access to the machine on which they are executing and potentially can harm the local system or expose capabilities that allow the control user to cause harm. Within Web browsers, such as Internet Explorer, a control's capabilities can be used by the scripting language of the browser (such as VBScript). The control may be safe when executing under normal circumstances, but what about when the control's capabilities are used by an untrustworthy or malicious script?

For example, suppose you develop a control that exposes a `CreateObject` function that allows a script writer to create instances of Automation objects within VBScript. The control is not safe. It would be easy for someone to use the `CreateObject` method to instantiate an external application (such as Microsoft Word) and use it to delete local files, install a virus, and so on.

If your control in any way exposes functionality that can be used by a malicious script to harm the local system, it is not safe for scripting. If the control does not expose potentially malicious functionality, it can register the `SafeForScripting` component category or implement the `IObjectSafety` interface within the control. If a control is safe for scripting, it can be used within ActiveX browsers with their security level set to high.

CATID_SafeForInitializing

In a browser environment, a control can also cause damage to a local system if the data it downloads is from a malicious or untrustworthy source. When the control is instantiated on the local machine, the container provides an `IPersist*` interface to initialize any persistent data. Because the data's location is provided by the script writer, the data is also a potential security problem. If a control's persistent data, even when coming from an unknown source, cannot harm the local machine, it can indicate that it is safe for initializing by registering the `SafeForInitializing` component category or by implementing the `IObjectSafety` interface.

```
IObjectSafety : public IUnknown
{
public:
   virtual HRESULT GetInterfaceSafetyOptions( REFIID, DWORD, DWORD ) = 0;
   virtual HRESULT SetInterfaceSafetyOptions( REFIID, DWORD, DWORD ) = 0;
};
```

Component Download

ActiveX specifies a new component download service that provides a platform-independent way of transporting COM-based components to a user's local machine. As part of the download, the service will also verify the integrity of the component and, once it's downloaded, will register it on the local machine. For our purposes in this chapter, a COM-based component is an ActiveX control and its dependencies (such as DLLs). However, the component download specification provides the ability to download any COM-based component.

Downloading and installing software on a user's machine should not be taken lightly. Security is an important part of the component download service. Before downloading a component, the service uses the code signing and certificate mechanisms provided by the WinVerifyTrust service, which we will discuss in more detail shortly.

When Internet Explorer or another ActiveX-compliant control container encounters the OBJECT element with a CLSID attribute, it attempts to locate and instantiate the object using the new COM API function CoGetClassObjectFromURL. If COM cannot instantiate the component on the local machine, it searches for the component package file specified in the OBJECT element's CODEBASE attribute. The location of the component package can be specified in the CODEBASE value, but the local machine's Internet search path (if defined) is ultimately used to locate the component package.

If the component is found, it is downloaded and verified as safe using the WinVerifyTrust service. If all goes well, the control is registered on the local machine. After registration, the component is instantiated and the requested interface is returned to the client, and finally we see the control within the browser.

A component may require the downloading of multiple files to the local machine. An ActiveX control developed with MFC will require the MFC run-time DLLs. ActiveX provides three techniques for packaging a component file and its dependencies. You can specify the actual executable (such as **POSTIT.OCX**), or you can specify a Windows **.CAB** file or a stand-alone **.INF** file. Each one has certain advantages.

A Single Portable Executable

This is the simplest way to specify the downloading of a component. You need only specify the URL to the executable in the CODEBASE attribute of the OBJECT element. Here's an example for the Asynccontrol that we will develop at the end of this chapter:

```
<OBJECT ID="Async1" WIDTH=291 HEIGHT=303
    CLASSID="CLSID:0C7B4FD3-13C1-11D0-A644-B4C6CE000000"
    CODEBASE="http://www.sky.net/~toma/ASYNC.OCX">
    <PARAM NAME="_Version" VALUE="65536">
    <PARAM NAME="_ExtentX" VALUE="7694">
    <PARAM NAME="_ExtentY" VALUE="7985">
    <PARAM NAME="_StockProps" VALUE="165">
    <PARAM NAME="BackColor" VALUE="16777215">
    <PARAM NAME="Appearance" VALUE="1">
    <PARAM NAME="TextPath" VALUE="http://www.sky.net/~toma/log">
</OBJECT>
```

Because Internet Explorer installs all the MFC DLLs that a control depends on, you can be fairly certain that the MFC DLLs that your control needs will already exist on the target machine. If you specify the explicit location of your OCX file, Internet Explorer will download it and register it on the local machine.

By using the single portable executable (PE) mechanism for component download, you lose some capabilities provided by the following two methods. First, you can specify only one file. If your control depends on DLLs that will not always exist on the target machine, you will need to use one of the other methods. Also, the file cannot take advantage of compression, and platform-independent download is not supported.

A CAB File

Using a **.CAB** file lets you package multiple files for download to the target machine. The format of a **.CAB** file is specified using Lempel-Ziv compression, which allows for quicker downloads. To compress files and store them in a **.CAB** file, you can use the **DIANTZ.EXE** utility provided with the ActiveX SDK.

The primary reason for using a **.CAB** file is to save download time by packaging multiple files in a compressed format. You still need an **.INF** file to actually install the components on the target machine. Here's a sample **.INF** file that uses a **.CAB** file:

```
;
; ASYNC.INF - Demonstrates CAB file support through INF
;
[Add.Code]
ASYNC.OCX=ASYNC.OCX
MFC42.DLL=MFC42.DLL

[ASYNC.OCX]
file=http://www.sky.net/~toma/ASYNC.CAB
clsid={0C7B4FD3-13C1-11D0-A644-B4C6CE000000}
FileVersion=1,0,0,0

[MFC42.DLL]
```

```
file=http://www.sky.net/~toma/ASYNC.CAB
FileVersion=4,2,0,0
```

The preceding example illustrates storing two files—**ASYNC.OCX** and **MFC42.DLL**—in the **ASYNC.CAB** file. The **ASYNC.INF** file is specified in the CODEBASE attribute:

```
<OBJECT ID="Async1" WIDTH=291 HEIGHT=303
    CLASSID="CLSID:0C7B4FD3-13C1-11D0-A644-B4C6CE000000"
    CODEBASE="http://www.sky.net/~toma/ASYNC.INF">
    <PARAM NAME="_Version" VALUE="65536">
    <PARAM NAME="_ExtentX" VALUE="7694">
    ...
```

ASYNC.INF is downloaded first, and then **ASYNC.CAB** is downloaded and the components are installed on the local machine.

A Stand-Alone INF File

In the previous example, we used an **.INF** file to install the components. By using a stand-alone **.INF** file, you gain cross-platform capabilities. You specify an **.INF** file in the CODEBASE attribute as shown previously, but you add platform-specific entries to the file. After the browser downloads the **.INF** file, it downloads the platform-specific binaries based on the options provided in the **.INF** file. Here's an example:

```
;
; Sample ASYNC.INF for ASYNC.OCX where multiple platforms are supported
;
[Add.Code]
ASYNC.OCX=ASYNC.OCX

[ASYNC.OCX]
file-win-x86=http://www.sky.net/~toma/x86/ASYNC.OCX
file-win-mips=http://www.sky.net/~toma/mips/ASYNC.OCX
file-win-alpha=http://www.sky.net/~toma/alpha/ASYNC.OCX
clsid={0C7B4FD3-13C1-11D0-A644-B4C6CE000000}
FileVersion=1,0,0,0
```

Only the target machine knows its platform. After downloading the **.INF** file, it can download the platform-specific binary. For more information regarding component download, check out the ActiveX SDK.

Internet Search Path

Even though the CODEBASE attribute specifies the location of a component, there is another step involved. When CoGetClassObjectFromURL determines that the component must be downloaded before instantiation, it first searches the Internet search path (ISP). A machine's Internet search path is located in the Registry under the HKEY_LOCAL_MACHINE key.

```
HKEY_LOCAL_MACHINE\Software\Microsoft\Windows
            \CurrentVersion\InternetSettings\CodeBaseSearchPath
```

First searching the ISP makes available additional administration options to the local machine administrators. In local area or intranet environments, the ISP can be used to specify the location of an object store server, where most components can be found. Using this technique, components can be located and downloaded without specification of the CODEBASE attribute. This behavior can also be used to disallow the downloading of components from unknown or untrusted servers.

The search path takes this form:

```
<URL1>;<URL2>;CODEBASE;<URL3>...
```

The position of the CODEBASE keyword within the ISP affects how components are located. The component download service searches the ISP in the order specified. If CODEBASE is not specified in the ISP, code will not be downloaded from sources other than those explicitly indicated in the ISP. This approach is helpful in those environments where additional security is needed.

ActiveX Controls and Security

In the previous section we discussed how controls are located, downloaded to the local machine, and executed. In such an environment, security is of major concern. An ActiveX control has full access to the Win32 API. This arrangement provides the highest degree of functionality for control writers, but it also creates a potential security problem. Java takes the sandbox approach of not allowing direct access to the local hardware. This technique helps with security, but it reduces functionality significantly. To maintain a high level of functionality, Microsoft uses the new WinVerifyTrust service to protect local machines from malicious components.

Microsoft's approach to security in the Web environment is like that used in software retail channels. There is no guarantee that the software you buy from a local retailer is benign. There is no guarantee, but there is significant *trust*. When you purchase a software package from a vendor, such as Microsoft, you know where the software came from, and you're pretty confident that it will not harm your machine.

Microsoft has taken the steps to set up such an environment of trust on the Web by providing technologies that ensure the authenticity and integrity of a component. A component is marked with a digital signature based on Microsoft's Authenticode technology. The component's signature is then maintained and verified by a trusted authority.

Digital Signatures

To ensure authenticity and integrity, each component is marked using a public-private key mechanism. This *digital signature*, which you can view as a complex checksum, is attached to a component. If the component is compromised in any way, the digital signature will become invalid.

Code Signing

To sign your components using Authenticode so that they can be trusted in the Internet environment, you must register and obtain a certificate from one of the certification authorities such as VeriSign or GTE. After receiving your certificate, you can use the MAKECERT, SIGNCODE, and CHKTRUST utilities provided with the ActiveX SDK to sign your controls.

Internet Explorer Security Levels

Internet Explorer will not download components that have not been properly signed. Internet Explorer allows the user to specify the security level. If the security level is set to high, your controls must be signed (if they do not already reside on the local machine) and they must be safe for scripting and safe for initializing (Figure 12.2). Your control specifies these characteristics through the component categories that we discussed earlier.

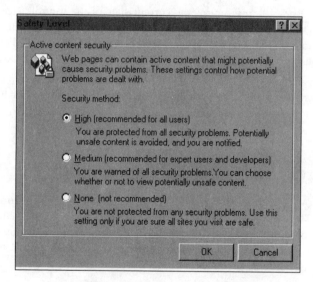

Figure 12.2 Internet Explorer security levels.

Obtaining a Certificate

Individual software developers can obtain certificates for $20 per year through VeriSign. The charge for software development companies is $400 per year. VeriSign can be reached at www.verisign.com.

MFC Support for Internet-Aware Controls

Selecting the **Load properties asynchronously** option in ControlWizard does three things. ControlWizard adds the stock `ReadyState` property to your control, implements the `ReadyStateChange` event for you, and initializes the ready state of your control to `READYSTATE_LOADING` in the control's constructor. This setup sets up your control to use MFC's support for data path properties

ReadyState Support

`COleControl` contains a member, `m_lReadyState`, that maintains the current ready state of your control. By default, this member is set to `READYSTATE_COMPLETE`. In our case, we indicated that our control loads properties asynchronously, so AppWizard set our control's state initially to `READYSTATE_INITIALIZED`. We're now responsible for updating the readiness state of our control as it moves through its various states. MFC provides three new methods pertaining to `ReadyState` and asynchronous download support.

`COleControl::GetReadyState` returns the current state of the control. Because the control's state can be modified through the asynchronous arrival of data, you should check the current state of the control when performing operations that depend on the existence of certain property data. For example, if your control downloads and displays an image, you may want to check the current ready state in your `OnDraw` code.

You use the `InternalSetReadyState` method to update the current readiness state of the control. You will typically call this method in the asynchronous download code, as you'll see in a moment. The `Load` method is used to force downloading of an asynchronous property. The `Load` method takes as a parameter the URL for the property.

CDataPathProperty

The `CDataPathProperty` class is derived from MFC's new asynchronous moniker class: `CAsyncMonikerFile`. The `CDataPathProperty` class is specifically used for ActiveX controls to encapsulate the asynchronous download process. Most of the functionality is provided by `CAsynMonikerFile`, and the control developer need only implement the `OnDataAvailable` method. Table 12.3 details some of the important `CDataPathProperty` members.

Table 12.3 `CDataPathProperty` Members

Member	Description
CDataPathProperty(pControl),	The constructor takes an optional pointer to the associated control. If you do not provide the control instance in the constructor, you must later call `SetControl` to set up the association.
SetControl(pControl)	Associates a control with the data path instance.
Open(szPath, pControl)	Opens a file (usually specified as a URL) for asynchronous downloading.
SetPath(szPath) / GetPath()	Sets or gets the path, usually a URL.

Table 12.3 `CDataPathProperty` Members (continued)

Member	Description
`COleControl* GetControl()`	Returns the ActiveX control instance associated with the data path property.
`ResetData()`	Notifies the container that the data associated with this property is no longer valid. The default behavior is to restart the download process.

An Example Control

To demonstrate some of the techniques discussed in this chapter, let's build a simple Internet-aware control. The control subclasses the `RichEdit` common control. It uses the `ES_MULTILINE` style so that it can display a large amount of data. The control will retrieve and display the contents of any data specified via its data path property. The data is downloaded asynchronously using the new data path property and MFC's `CDataPathProperty` class. It also demonstrates the use of the new `ReadyState` property and `OnReadyStateChange` event.

Create the Async Project

Use AppWizard to build a ControlWizard-based project with the name Async. Follow these steps to specify each of ControlWizard's options:

- In the OLE Control Wizard Step 1 of 2 dialog box, take the defaults of **No runtime license**, **Yes, comments**, and **No help files**.
- In OLE Control Wizard Step 2 of 2, take the defaults of **Activate when visible** and **Has "About" box**. From the **Which window class, if any, should this control subclass?** dropdown, choose the **EDIT** control.
- In OLE Control Wizard Step 2 of 2, click the **Advanced** button and enable the **Loads Properties Asynchronously** option.
- Click **Finish** and create the control project.
- Using ClassWizard, add the following four stock properties: **Appearance**, **BorderStyle**, **BackColor**, and **Font**.
- Add the stock color and font property pages to the control.

The RichEdit Control

In Chapter 10, we focused on useful techniques for subclassing existing Windows controls. Toward the end of the chapter we also discussed subclassing the new Windows 95 common controls. ControlWizard lets you subclass most of them, but conspicuously absent from the list is the new RichEdit control. In our example, we'll use this new control, but a few additional steps are required to get everything to work. We'll cover this first.

The RichEdit control is a big improvement over the basic EDIT control. RichEdit provides an edit-type control with complete font, paragraph, bullet, text color, and embedded OLE object support. Using RichEdit you can implement a good editor without much effort. Actually, Microsoft did—WordPad uses the RichEdit control. It's also written in MFC, and the source is included on the Visual C++ CD-ROM.

To subclass the RichEdit control, we first fix the code added by ClassWizard:

```
BOOL CAsyncCtrl::PreCreateWindow(CREATESTRUCT& cs)

{
    cs.lpszClass = _T("RICHEDIT");
    cs.style |= ES_AUTOHSCROLL | ES_MULTILINE |
                ES_AUTOVSCROLL | ES_READONLY |
                WS_VSCROLL | WS_HSCROLL;

    return COleControl::PreCreateWindow(cs);

}
```

You've seen this before. We change the window class name and set the appropriate styles for our control. To use the RichEdit control, you must load the RICHED32 DLL. You might expect MFC's call to `InitCommonControls` to do this, but there must be some reason that it doesn't. This extra step is probably why Microsoft omitted the RichEdit control from the subclass window option, but it's easy, so let's do it. Here's the code to add to **ASYNCCTL.H** and **ASYNCCTL.CPP**:

```
// AsyncCtl.h

...

/////////////////
// CAsyncCtrl : See AsyncCtl.cpp for implementation.
/////////////////

class CAsyncCtrl : public COleControl

{

...

// Implementation

protected:

    ~CAsyncCtrl();

    HINSTANCE   m_hRTF;

...

};

// AsyncCtl.cpp

...
```

```
CAsyncCtrl::CAsyncCtrl()
{
    InitializeIIDs(&IID_DAsync, &IID_DAsyncEvents);
    m_lReadyState = READYSTATE_LOADING;
    // TODO: Call InternalSetReadyState when the readystate changes.

    // TODO: Initialize your control's instance data here.
    m_hRTF = LoadLibrary( "RICHED32.DLL" );
}

CAsyncCtrl::~CAsyncCtrl()
{
    // Release the richedit dll
    if ( m_hRTF )
    {
        FreeLibrary( m_hRTF );
        m_hRTF = 0;
    }
}
```

Once we've finished that, we can focus on making this control Internet-aware. Our control is fairly simple. To demonstrate how to use a data path property, our control will download and display a remote file whose filename is specified using a URL. The file can be big or small. Either way, the data will be downloaded asynchronously and eventually displayed within the RichEdit control.

Implementing a Data Path Property

Using ClassWizard, add a data path property to the control. The type is BSTR. Name it **TextPath** and use the Get/Set method of implementation. The implementation of a data path property requires you to derive a class from CDataPathProperty and implement the OnDataAvailable method. You must then contain an instance of this class within your COleControl-derived class. First, we create the class.

Using ClassWizard, click **Add Class**, and add the CAsyncText class. Be sure to derive it from CDataPathProperty. You should specify the files as **ASYNCTXT.H** and **ASYNCTXT.CPP**. We will need two member variables to manage the downloading, so let's add them next:

```
//
// AsyncTxt.h : header file
//
...
class CAsyncText : public CDataPathProperty
{
    DECLARE_DYNAMIC(CAsyncText)
```

```
// Attributes
public:

// Operations
public:
    CAsyncText(COleControl* pControl = NULL);
    virtual ~CAsyncText();

...

// Implementation
protected:
    CString      m_strText;
    DWORD        m_dwReadBefore;
};
```

Next, we embed an instance of the new class within the COleControl-derived class (CAsyncText) and associate the two instances by passing a pointer to the control class to our CDataPathProperty-derived member. We then use the CAsyncText instance in the Get and Set methods for our TextPath property:

```
//
// AsyncCtl.h
//
...
class CAsyncCtrl : public COleControl
{

    DECLARE_DYNCREATE(CAsyncCtrl)
...
// Implementation
protected:
    ~CAsyncCtrl();
    CAsyncText     m_ddpText;
    HINSTANCE      m_hRTF;

//
// AsyncCtl.cpp
//
...
#include "Async.h"
// Include our new CDataPathProperty-derived class
#include "AsyncTxt.h"
#include "AsyncCtl.h"
#include "AsyncPpg.h"
```

```
...
CAsyncCtrl::CAsyncCtrl()
{
    InitializeIIDs(&IID_DAsync, &IID_DAsyncEvents);

    m_lReadyState = READYSTATE_LOADING;
    // TODO: Call InternalSetReadyState when the readystate changes.

    // TODO: Initialize your control's instance data here.
    // Associate our control with our CDataPathProperty member
    m_ddpText.SetControl( this );
    m_hRTF = LoadLibrary( "RICHED32.DLL" );
}
...
BSTR CAsyncCtrl::GetTextPath()
{
    CString strResult = m_ddpText.GetPath();
    return strResult.AllocSysString();
}

void CAsyncCtrl::SetTextPath(LPCTSTR lpszNewValue)
{
    Load( lpszNewValue, m_ddpText );
    SetModifiedFlag();
}
```

The CAsyncText class will manage the downloading of the asynchronous data. We expose the Get/Set methods for the TextPath property, which sets and retrieves the path property of CAsyncText. When the control is instantiated, the smaller, synchronous properties are loaded first. Once they are loaded, the container creates an asynchronous moniker with the URL specified through the TextPath property and passes the data to the CAsyncText member. To retrieve the data and store it within our control, we override the CDataPathProperty::OnDataAvailable method. Do this with ClassWizard and then add the following code:

```
void CAsyncGetText::OnDataAvailable(DWORD dwSize, DWORD bscfFlag)
{
    // TODO: Add your specialized code here and/or call the base class
    if ( bscfFlag & BSCF_FIRSTDATANOTIFICATION )
    {
        m_strText = "";
        m_dwReadBefore = 0;
        GetControl()->InternalSetReadyState( READYSTATE_LOADING );
    }
}
```

```
if ( dwSize )
{

    DWORD dwArriving = dwSize - m_dwReadBefore;

    if ( dwArriving > 0 )
    {
        int nLen = m_strText.GetLength();
        LPTSTR psz = m_strText.GetBuffer(nLen + dwArriving);
        Read( psz + nLen, dwArriving );
        m_strText.ReleaseBuffer(nLen + dwArriving);
        m_dwReadBefore = dwSize;

        if ( GetControl()->GetReadyState() < READYSTATE_INTERACTIVE )
        {
            GetControl()->SetText( m_strText );
            GetControl()->InternalSetReadyState( READYSTATE_INTERACTIVE );
        }
    }
}

// Tell the control and the container that
// all of the data is here.
if ( bscfFlag & BSCF_LASTDATANOTIFICATION )
{
    GetControl()->SetText( m_strText );
    GetControl()->InternalSetReadyState( READYSTATE_COMPLETE );
}
```

```
    CDataPathProperty::OnDataAvailable( dwSize, bscfFlag );
}
```

Here's where most of the work gets done. OnDataAvailable is called periodically as data arrives from the remote system. OnDataAvailable signals the arrival. You then read the data using Read, which is inherited from CFile.

The data will arrive in chunks, and the preceding code manages the arrival and storage of the data. The first parameter contains the number of bytes that have been received, including the count of the data currently in the buffer. The second parameter specifies one of three potential states of the download. BSCF_FIRSTDATANOTIFICATION indicates that this is the first piece of data, BSCF_INTERMEDIARYNOTI-FICATION indicates that we're in the middle of the transfer, and BSCF_LASTDATANOTIFICATION tells us that the transfer is finished.

When we're notified that the transfer is starting, we set the m_strText member to null, set the byte counter to zero, and inform the container that the control is in the loading state. Then, as the data arrives, we calculate its size and call the Read method, storing the data in the m_strText buffer.

If this is our first time through and if we have some data, we call SetText, which is a method in our control that places the data in the RichEdit control. This approach quickly provides some data for the user to view. By setting the control's ready state to interactive, we indicate that the control can handle keystrokes.

When all the data has been received, as indicated by the LASTDATANOTIFICATION flag, we update the RichEdit control with all the text and notify the container that the control has completed downloading and is fully operational.

There are a few miscellaneous functions that I've not shown you yet. First, we have a method to set the text in the RichEdit control. I've also implemented the BackColor property for our control. Setting colors for some of the newer common controls is different from what we did in Chapter 10. The RichEdit control uses a message to set its color, so we override OnSetBackColor and send the new color to the control. We need to set the color right after the control is created, so we trap the WM_CREATE message and set the color there, too. Here are the required methods:

```
void CAsyncCtrl::SetText( CString& str )
{
    SetWindowText( str );
    InvalidateControl();
}

void CAsyncCtrl::OnBackColorChanged()
{
    // If we're running, set the background color
    if ( AmbientUserMode() )
    {
        SendMessage( EM_SETBKGNDCOLOR,
                    FALSE,
                    TranslateColor( GetBackColor() ));
    }

    COleControl::OnBackColorChanged();
}

int CAsyncCtrl::OnCreate(LPCREATESTRUCT lpCreateStruct)
{
    if (COleControl::OnCreate(lpCreateStruct) == -1)
        return -1;

    // Set the background color of the edit control
    SendMessage( EM_SETBKGNDCOLOR,
                FALSE,
                TranslateColor( GetBackColor() ));

    return 0;
}
```

Drawing the Control

We also need to modify the control's OnDraw code to draw a simple design-phase representation, as we've done in earlier chapters:

```
void CAsyncCtrl::OnDraw(
    CDC* pdc, const CRect& rcBounds, const CRect& rcInvalid)
{
    // If the container is in design-mode
    // Draw the design representation
    if (! AmbientUserMode() )
       DrawDesign( pdc, rcBounds );
    else
       DoSuperclassPaint( pdc, rcBounds );
}

void CAsyncCtrl::DrawDesign( CDC* pdc, const CRect& rcBounds )
{
    CBrush bkBrush( TranslateColor( GetBackColor() ));
    pdc->FillRect( rcBounds, &bkBrush );

    CString strName = AmbientDisplayName();

    // Set the textcolor to the foreground color
    pdc->SetTextColor( TranslateColor( GetForeColor() ));

    // Select the stock font and save the old one
    CFont* pOldFont = SelectStockFont( pdc );

    // Set up the text drawing modes in the DC
    pdc->SetBkMode( TRANSPARENT );
    pdc->SetTextAlign( TA_LEFT | TA_TOP );

    // Draw the text in the upper left corner
    pdc->ExtTextOut( rcBounds.left + 1, rcBounds.top + 1, ETO_CLIPPED,
                     rcBounds, strName, strName.GetLength(), NULL );

    // Restore the old font
    if ( pOldFont )
       pdc->SelectObject( pOldFont );
}
```

More Component Categories

There are several component categories that pertain to Internet-aware controls. We discussed them previously in the "Component Categories" sections of this chapter. All that remains is to write the code to mark our control as being Internet-aware, safe for scripting, and safe for initializing. We developed code in Chapter 7 that makes it easy to register control-implemented control categories. However, we also need to mark our control as *requiring* the `RequiresDataPathHost` category. Our control requires the services of the container to initiate the download of the `TextPath` property.

You should recall that a control can specify its component categories under two different subkeys: `Implemented` and `Required`. All our controls so far have added categories under the `Implemented` subkey. We now need to add a category under the required section. Here is the new code:

```
HRESULT RegisterCLSIDInReqCategory( REFCLSID clsid, CATID catid )
{
    ICatRegister* pcr = NULL ;
    HRESULT hr = S_OK ;

    // Create an instance of the category manager.
    hr = CoCreateInstance( CLSID_StdComponentCategoriesMgr,
                           NULL,
                           CLSCTX_INPROC_SERVER,
                           IID_ICatRegister,
                           (void**)&pcr );
    if (SUCCEEDED(hr))
    {
        CATID rgcatid[1];
        rgcatid[0] = catid;
        hr = pcr->RegisterClassReqCategories( clsid, 1, rgcatid );
    }

    if ( pcr != NULL )
        pcr->Release();

    return hr;
}

HRESULT UnregisterCLSIDInReqCategory( REFCLSID clsid, CATID catid )
{
    ICatRegister* pcr = NULL ;
    HRESULT hr = S_OK ;

    // Create an instance of the category manager.
    hr = CoCreateInstance( CLSID_StdComponentCategoriesMgr,
```

```
                        NULL,
                        CLSCTX_INPROC_SERVER,
                        IID_ICatRegister,
                        (void**)&pcr );
if (SUCCEEDED(hr))
{
    CATID rgcatid[1];
    rgcatid[0] = catid;
    hr = pcr->UnRegisterClassReqCategories( clsid, 1, rgcatid );
}

if ( pcr != NULL )
    pcr->Release();

return hr;
}
```

This code is similar to the `RegisterCLSIDInCategory` that we've used before. The only difference is that we call `ICatRegister::RegisterClassReqCategories`. Using the functions that we developed previously plus the preceding two functions, we can now code our update Registry function:

```
/////////////////////////
// CAsyncCtrl::CAsyncCtrlFactory::UpdateRegistry -
// Adds or removes system Registry entries for CAsyncCtrl
/////////////////////////
BOOL CAsyncCtrl::CAsyncCtrlFactory::UpdateRegistry(BOOL bRegister)
{
    if ( bRegister )
    {
        CreateComponentCategory( CATID_Control,
                                 L"Controls" );
        RegisterCLSIDInCategory( m_clsid,
                                 CATID_Control );

        CreateComponentCategory( CATID_SafeForInitializing,
                                 L"Controls safely initializable from persistent data" );
        RegisterCLSIDInCategory( m_clsid,
                                 CATID_SafeForInitializing );

        CreateComponentCategory( CATID_SafeForScripting,
                                 L"Controls that are safely scriptable" );
        RegisterCLSIDInCategory( m_clsid,
                                 CATID_SafeForScripting );
```

```
        CreateComponentCategory( CATID_PersistsToPropertyBag,
                                 L"Support initialize via PersistPropertyBag" );
        RegisterCLSIDInCategory( m_clsid,
                                 CATID_PersistsToPropertyBag );

        CreateComponentCategory( CATID_RequiresDataPathHost,
                                 L"Requires Data Path Host" );
        RegisterCLSIDInReqCategory( m_clsid,
                                 CATID_RequiresDataPathHost );

        CreateComponentCategory( CATID_InternetAware,
                                 L"Internet-Aware" );
        RegisterCLSIDInCategory( m_clsid,
                                 CATID_InternetAware );

        return AfxOleRegisterControlClass(
                AfxGetInstanceHandle(),
                m_clsid,
                m_lpszProgID,
                IDS_ASYNC,
                IDB_ASYNC,
                afxRegApartmentThreading,
                _dwAsyncOleMisc,
                _tlid,
                _wVerMajor,
                _wVerMinor);
    }
    else
    {
        UnregisterCLSIDInCategory( m_clsid,
                                   CATID_Control );
        UnregisterCLSIDInCategory( m_clsid,
                                   CATID_SafeForInitializing );
        UnregisterCLSIDInCategory( m_clsid,
                                   CATID_SafeForScripting );
        UnregisterCLSIDInCategory( m_clsid,
                                   CATID_PersistsToPropertyBag );
        UnregisterCLSIDInCategory( m_clsid,
                                   CATID_InternetAware );
        UnregisterCLSIDInReqCategory( m_clsid,
                                   CATID_RequiresDataPathHost );

        return AfxOleUnregisterClass(m_clsid, m_lpszProgID);
    }
}
```

Build the project, and let's test our new Internet-aware control using ActiveX Control Pad and Internet Explorer.

Testing the Control

The best way to test the control is to embed it in a Web page and set the `TextPath` property to point to a large file on a remote system. If you want, you can point it to http://www.sky.net/~toma/log, which is a text file that logs the hits to my Web site. The quickest way to build a test Web page is to use Microsoft's ActiveX Control Pad.

ActiveX Control Pad

Microsoft's ActiveX Control Pad utility makes it easy to add ActiveX controls to HTML-based Web pages. It allows you to build simple Web pages, embed ActiveX controls, and add code to tie everything together with VBScript.

We'll test the functionality of our Async control by developing a simple Web page. Start ActiveX Control Pad and perform the following steps. Figure 12.3 shows the control within ActiveX Control Pad.

1. Using **Edit/Insert ActiveX Control**, insert an instance of our new Async control.

2. Set the `BackColor` to white using the property editor, and set the `TextPath` property to point to a URL of your choice.

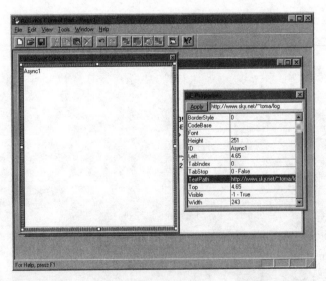

Figure 12.3 Inserting the Async control with ActiveX Control Pad.

When you close the control edit window, Control Pad will insert the OBJECT element code into the new HTML document. When you're finished, you should have something like this in the editor:

```
<HTML>
<HEAD>
<TITLE>New Page</TITLE>
</HEAD>
<BODY>

<OBJECT ID="Async1" WIDTH=324 HEIGHT=335
 CLASSID="CLSID:0C7B4FD3-13C1-11D0-A644-B4C6CE000000">
    <PARAM NAME="_Version" VALUE="65536">
    <PARAM NAME="_ExtentX" VALUE="8573">
    <PARAM NAME="_ExtentY" VALUE="8855">
    <PARAM NAME="_StockProps" VALUE="165">
    <PARAM NAME="BackColor" VALUE="16777215">
    <PARAM NAME="Appearance" VALUE="1">
    <PARAM NAME="TextPath" VALUE="http://www.sky.net/~toma/log">
</OBJECT>

</BODY>
</HTML>
```

This HTML code defines a basic Web page with an embedded instance of our control. Let's make it a bit more intelligent. Using Control Pad, add two listbox controls. A number of basic controls come with Internet Explorer. They are listed under the **Microsoft Forms*** controls. Insert one control before the definition of the Async control and one after the definition. Then use Control Pad to add some VBScript code to the Web page. Select **Tools/Script Wizard** to bring up Script Wizard.

Script Wizard is easy to use. Select the control or window that you want to add code to and start typing the code. We need to add code to the Window OnLoad event, the ListBox1 Change event, and our Async control's ReadyStateChange event. Figure 12.4 shows how to add the OnLoad event code with Script Wizard.

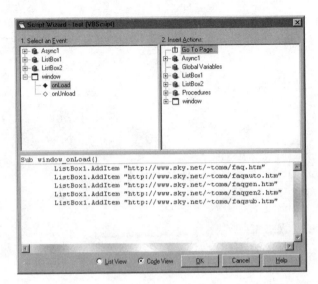

Figure 12.4 Adding VBScript with Script Wizard.

Following is the complete code for our simple example. Notice that we're using a table to house our embedded controls. The HTML specification does not provide a good method of aligning embedded controls, applets, or even images. For our example, we're using a table to align the controls, but a better solution might be to use Microsoft's HTML Layout control. It provides complete 2-D layout capabilities similar to those you have when laying out a Windows dialog box or Visual Basic form.

```
<HTML>
<HEAD>
<TITLE>New Page</TITLE>
</HEAD>
<BODY>
<CENTER>
<H1>Our Async Control in Internet Explorer!</H1>
</CENTER>
    <SCRIPT LANGUAGE="VBScript">
<!-
Sub window_onLoad()
      ListBox1.AddItem "http://www.sky.net/~toma/faq.htm"
      ListBox1.AddItem "http://www.sky.net/~toma/faqauto.htm"
      ListBox1.AddItem "http://www.sky.net/~toma/faqgen.htm"
      ListBox1.AddItem "http://www.sky.net/~toma/faqgen2.htm"
      ListBox1.AddItem "http://www.sky.net/~toma/faqsub.htm"
end sub
```

```
-->
    </SCRIPT>
    <SCRIPT LANGUAGE="VBScript">
<!--
Sub ListBox1_Change()
        Async1.TextPath = ListBox1.Text
end sub
-->
    </SCRIPT>
<TABLE CELLPADDING = 10>
<TR>
<TD>
    <OBJECT ID="ListBox1" WIDTH=199 HEIGHT=264
     CLASSID="CLSID:8BD21D20-EC42-11CE-9E0D-00AA006002F3">
        <PARAM NAME="ScrollBars" VALUE="3">
        <PARAM NAME="DisplayStyle" VALUE="2">
        <PARAM NAME="Size" VALUE="5239;6984">
        <PARAM NAME="MatchEntry" VALUE="0">
        <PARAM NAME="FontCharSet" VALUE="0">
        <PARAM NAME="FontPitchAndFamily" VALUE="2">
    </OBJECT>
<TD>
    <SCRIPT LANGUAGE="VBScript">
<!--
Sub Async1_ReadyStateChange( NewState )
  Select Case NewState
     Case 0
        ListBox2.AddItem "Initialized"

     Case 1
        ListBox2.AddItem "Loaded"

     Case 2
        ListBox2.AddItem "Loading"

     Case 3
        ListBox2.AddItem "Interactive"

     Case 4
        ListBox2.AddItem "Complete"

  End Select
end sub
-->
```

```
  </SCRIPT>
  <OBJECT ID="Async1" WIDTH=291 HEIGHT=303
CLASSID="CLSID:0C7B4FD3-13C1-11D0-A644-B4C6CE000000">
    <PARAM NAME="_Version" VALUE="65536">
    <PARAM NAME="_ExtentX" VALUE="7694">
    <PARAM NAME="_ExtentY" VALUE="7985">
    <PARAM NAME="_StockProps" VALUE="165">
    <PARAM NAME="BackColor" VALUE="16777215">
    <PARAM NAME="Appearance" VALUE="1">
    <PARAM NAME="TextPath" VALUE="http://www.sky.net/~toma/log">
</OBJECT>
<TR>
<TD>
  <OBJECT ID="ListBox2" WIDTH=227 HEIGHT=95
   CLASSID="CLSID:8BD21D20-EC42-11CE-9E0D-00AA006002F3">
      <PARAM NAME="BackColor" VALUE="16777215">
      <PARAM NAME="ForeColor" VALUE="255">
      <PARAM NAME="ScrollBars" VALUE="3">
      <PARAM NAME="DisplayStyle" VALUE="2">
      <PARAM NAME="Size" VALUE="5979;2512">
      <PARAM NAME="MatchEntry" VALUE="0">
      <PARAM NAME="FontCharSet" VALUE="0">
      <PARAM NAME="FontPitchAndFamily" VALUE="2">
   </OBJECT>
</TABLE>
</BODY>
</HTML>
```

After adding all the code, save the HTML document and fire up Internet Explorer. You should see something like Figure 12.5.

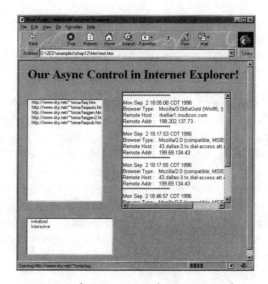

Figure 12.5 The Async control in Internet Explorer.

Notice the progress indicator in the lower right-hand corner. In Figure 12.5, the control is downloading a very large (>500 KB) file. The progress functionality of asynchronous property download provides this feedback to the container.

The ActiveX Control Framework

The ActiveX SDK includes an ActiveX control framework (also known as BaseCtl). This framework is sometimes called the Light Weight Control Framework, because its purpose is to allow the developer to build small ActiveX controls. The framework isn't currently supported by Microsoft but is provided for those developers who have a solid understanding of ActiveX controls and don't want the overhead of MFC when developing their controls. For more information on developing controls using this framework, visit my Web site.

Summary

Internet-aware controls differ only slightly from the controls developed in previous chapters. Internet-aware controls are concerned with two additional issues: low bandwidth and security. The ActiveX SDK provides new technologies that enable controls to operate effectively in low- bandwidth environments and supports security techniques to help with the management of component software in the an Internet (or intranet) environment.

HTML is the language of the Web, and a few HTML elements are useful for ActiveX controls. VBScript is Microsoft's Visual Basic implementation for browser environments. ActiveX browsers, such as Internet

Explorer, are ActiveX control containers. A control is embedded within a Web page using the HTML `OBJECT` element.

Nearly all of the new technologies that allow controls to operate in the low-bandwidth Internet environment are outlined in the OLE controls/COM objects for the Internet specification. The primary new addition for controls is the concept of a data path property. Data path properties use URL monikers to enable asynchronous downloading of a large property value such as an image. During the download process, the control indicates its state through the new `ReadyState` property and `OnReadyStateChange` event.

A number of new component categories were added specifically for Internet-aware controls. A few of them are required for controls to operate safely within the Web environment. When browsing Web pages, a user may not have the embedded ActiveX controls on his or her local machine. In this case, the new component download specification enables a browser to locate, download, register, and execute the component on the local machine.

ActiveX controls have full access to the machine on which they are executing. In an Internet-type environment, where controls are part of Web documents, there are a number of security issues. The new component download specification allows transparent download and registration of controls to machines browsing Web documents. Microsoft has specified a mechanism for ensuring the authenticity and integrity of components in the Web environment. As a software developer, you must register for this service in order to digitally sign your components.

MFC provides support for the new Internet-aware control techniques. The new `CDataPathProperty` class makes it easy to provide asynchronous property download support to your controls. Testing your Internet-aware controls is easy using Microsoft's ActiveX Control Pad.

Chapter *13*

ActiveX Control Frequently Asked Questions

As developers, we sometimes spend hours, even days, trying to determine how to implement a particular feature of our software or to fix a bizarre bug. The software development universe is expanding so fast that it requires long days and nights of study and research just to stay current. That's why collaboration among developers is important. Internet newsgroups, forums, list servers, and FAQs all help increase our productivity. Instead of knocking your head against the wall for two days, you can find an answer, usually with sample code, that will allow you to implement a feature in much less time. It all comes down to collaboration and the management of information. That's what makes the Internet, as embodied in the Web, an important tool for software developers.

I know—you're probably skeptical of all the hype. A year ago, so was I. But after using the Web and building my own Web site, I really believe that it is changing the way we develop software and will also change the way we conduct day-to-day business.

My Web site is devoted to ActiveX development, particularly controls, and contains an ActiveX control FAQ that I maintain. This chapter will answer a few of the most frequently asked questions concerning ActiveX controls. Along the way, I will provide an explanation of what is going on under the hood in hopes of providing you with additional insight into the development of ActiveX controls.

The Sample Control

As part of this chapter I've developed a control that demonstrates the techniques that we will discuss. It even has an appropriate name: **FAQ.OCX**. The control doesn't do anything, but it demonstrates several techniques that you should find useful when developing your own controls.

All the questions are answered in the context of using the Microsoft Foundation Class libraries. A part of Visual C++, the MFC framework makes it rather easy to develop ActiveX controls. However, using MFC can sometimes obscure the understanding you need to solve some of the problems you'll encounter during development. The sample control was developed with Visual C++ version 4.1.

How do I restrict or change the size of my control?

This question, and its variations, is the *most* frequently asked ActiveX control question. I see this question posted regularly to one of the OLE, ActiveX, or control-based newsgroups, so let's address it right away. Regular windows are typically sized using the various Windows API functions (such as `SetWindowPos`). You can restrict the size of a window by trapping the `WM_WINDOWPOSCHANGING` message and modifying the `WINDOWPOS` structure.

ActiveX controls, however, differ from regular windows, because they provide their functionality only when contained within an ActiveX control container. The container endows ActiveX controls with significantly more capabilities than regular windows have, but this power comes at a cost. To reside within an OLE container, a control must implement several COM-based interfaces. If the control wants to muck with its environment (of which size is an attribute), it must negotiate these changes with its container.

The container provides the control with an area in which to work, and the control must respect this area. Changes to the control's size must be negotiated with the container. The MFC `COleControl` class provides four methods to facilitate control sizing: `SetInitialSize`, `SetControlSize`, `OnSetObjectRects`, and `OnSetExtent`.

Developers face two common situations in which control sizing is an issue. First, you may want to restrict your control's size (or its extents) so that users cannot produce an invalid condition during the design phase. You might, for example, have an analog clock that should always be square or a fixed-size icon that serves as the control's representation (typically for a nonvisual control such as a timer). Second, as the control's developer you may need to affect its size based on one of its properties. An example would be an image control that needs to size dynamically based on the extents of the image. We'll cover both scenarios.

Nonvisual controls typically display a small bitmap during the design phase, often the toolbar bitmap that the control provides to containers that support it. The bitmap image is a set size, and there is no need for the user to size the control, but the container provides sizing handles by default. To restrict the size of the bitmap image, we need to do two things. First, we set the initial size of the control to its static size using the `COleControl::SetInitialSize` method. This code should be placed in your control's constructor:

```
/////////////////////////////////////////////////
// CFAQCtrl::CFAQCtrl - Constructor
CFAQCtrl::CFAQCtrl()
{
    InitializeIIDs(&IID_DFAQ, &IID_DFAQEvents);
    SetInitialSize( 28, 28 );
}
```

`SetInitialSize` takes as a parameter the size of the control in pixels. It converts the unit to HIMETRIC (OLE's favorite) and sets the extents maintained within `COleControl`. This technique takes care of the initial size of the control when it is created, but how do we stop the user from sizing the control during the design phase? To do this, we need to understand how the control and its container interact.

The container provides a control with its site, or location within the container. The container is responsible for allowing the user to size the control's site and will inform the control of its new size. If a control, an in-place OLE server, wants to be informed about these size changes, it sets the OLEMISC_RECOMPOSEONRE-SIZE bit in its MiscStatus flags. For AppWizard-generated controls, MFC turns this bit on by default and delivers it to the container via its implementation of IOleObject::GetMiscStatus. If this bit is set, the container will notify the control of any change in size by calling the IOleObject::SetExtent method.

COM-based interfaces are just declarations; *you* must provide the implementation. MFC supplies a default implementation for all the interfaces required of an ActiveX control. The default implementation of IOleObject::SetExtent resizes the control. Actually, it does a bit more—because various things must occur depending on the state of the control—but first it gives us an opportunity to augment the default implementation by calling COleControl::OnSetExtent. We can override OnSetExtent and do one of two things. We can return FALSE, which tells the container that the control cannot be resized, or we can modify the extents passed via the SIZEL structure and return TRUE. For our purposes, we want to disallow any sizing of our iconic representation, so we return FALSE:

```
BOOL CFAQCtrl::OnSetExtent( LPSIZEL lpSizeL )
{
    return FALSE;
}
```

That's all there is to it—just two new lines of code to implement a control of fixed size.

As I mentioned, we can also modify the extents in the SIZEL structure. One option available in the FAQ control is to ensure that the control is always square. To do this, we need only pick one of the extents and assign it to the other:

```
BOOL CFAQCtrl::OnSetExtent( LPSIZEL lpSizeL )
{
    // Make sure the control is a square.
    // Use the smaller of the extents for the sides.
    if ( lpSizeL->cy <= lpSizeL->cx )
        lpSizeL->cx = lpSizeL->cy;
    else
        lpSizeL->cy = lpSizeL->cx;

    return COleControl::OnSetExtent( lpSizeL );
}
```

This is easy, too, but you must remember one thing. The extents provided in the SIZEL structure are in HIMETRIC units. If you are working in something other than HIMETRIC, such as pixels (device units), you will need to convert the unit. The following code ensures that a control's size is always 200x200 pixels:

```
BOOL CFAQCtrl::OnSetExtent( LPSIZEL lpSizeL )
{
   // Ensure that the control is always sized
   // at 200x200 pixels. Get a DC and convert
   // the pixels to HIMETRIC.
   CDC cdc;
   cdc.CreateCompatibleDC( NULL );
   lpSizeL->cx = lpSizeL->cy = 200;
   cdc.DPtoHIMETRIC( lpSizeL );

   return COleControl::OnSetExtent( lpSizeL );
}
```

This method isn't the most efficient way of doing the conversion. A faster implementation, one that does not require a DC, is left as an exercise for the reader.

We understand how to handle situations in which the user or container is manipulating the size of the control, but what about when you need to change the control's extents from within the control? It's easy. MFC provides another size-related method: SetControlSize. The FAQ control demonstrates all these sizing scenarios. It has a property, ControlSize, that allows you to change its sizing behavior and its size. I won't spend much time on the control—you can experiment with it yourself—but you need just a bit of understanding for this section. ControlSize is a dynamic enumerated property (we'll discuss this in a moment) that provides the user with a list of potential control sizes, one of which is "Draw Iconic." Whenever this property is set, the control must negotiate its new size with the container by calling COleControl::SetControlSize:

```
void CFAQCtrl::SetControlSize(short nNewValue)
{
   POSITION pos = m_lstSizes.GetHeadPosition();
   while( pos )
   {
      CCtrlSize* pSize = (CCtrlSize*) m_lstSizes.GetNext( pos );
      if ( nNewValue == pSize->m_sCookie )
      {
         m_pControlSize = pSize;

         // SetControlSize forces a redraw so no need
         // to call SetModifiedFlag or InvalidateControl.
         COleControl::SetControlSize( pSize->m_sizeCtrl.cx,
                                      pSize->m_sizeCtrl.cy );

         BoundPropertyChanged( dispidControlSize );
         break;
      }
   }
}
```

COleControl::SetControlSize does different things depending on the in-place state of the control. If the control is in-place active, SetControlSize calls OnPosRectChange through its IOleInPlaceSite interface, which is implemented by the container. This call informs the container of the new extents, and the container has an opportunity to accept, ignore, or modify the new extents. The container informs the control of any modifications by calling IOleInPlaceObject::SetObjectRects. You can act on this call by overriding COleControl::OnSetObjectRects. This negotiation takes place when your control is in-place active, which typically means at run time, although some containers (such as Delphi) in-place activate controls while in design mode.

During the design phase, a call to SetControlSize resizes the window through OnSetExtent, which changes COleControl-maintained extents. OnSetExtent also calls COleControl::InvalidateControl, which informs the container, through IAdviseSink::OnViewChanged, that the view of the control has changed. The container then calls IOleObject::GetExtent to obtain the control's new size and finally forces the control to redraw through IViewObject::Draw. Whew! I told you that functionality comes with a price, and it's more than just processing time; it is also this complexity thing. That's why frameworks are so popular. They shield us (a little) from this complexity.

That should cover sizing of your controls. I haven't talked about changing the coordinates of a control, but this question comes up much less frequently because the default implementation works fine. Seldom does the control implementation need to manipulate its position within the container. If you need to, though, take a look at COleControl::SetRectInContainer.

One other thing. The behavior I've discussed depends on a solid container implementation. Without it, the sizing scenarios will not work as desired. Both the container and the control must work together. If one of them does not follow the standard, all bets are off. Of course, your control should do its best when it encounters hostile environments. I've tested these techniques with various containers. Visual Basic and Visual C++ support them all; Delphi and Visual FoxPro still need some work. Let's get to some more questions.

Can I access my control from its property page?

This question is posed in different ways, all of them concerned primarily with how to obtain better, more direct communication with a control from its property page. MFC's DDP function mechanism is limited. The DDP functions allow communication only of a small number of automation types. That's it. When you're developing even modestly complex controls, the DDP functions don't provide enough (direct) communication with the control.

An ActiveX control and each of its property pages are implemented as separate COM objects. Property pages can be instantiated independently of any associated control. For this reason, property pages use automation to communicate with controls, most often to get and set property values. This design allows a container to associate a property page with multiple controls. A user can select two or more controls, and the container will intersect their properties and show only those pages included in this intersection. This arrangement allows a control user to quickly set a specific property (say, the font) of a group of controls.

MFC-provided DDP functions, which use automation, do not always provide enough flexibility to effectively manipulate a control's properties. As we'll see in the next question, it would be nice if we could access the associated control instance within the property page. Well, MFC makes this access rather easy.

When the container constructs a property sheet by assembling the control's various property pages, the container provides each page instance with a list of control instances that should be affected. This information is provided through IPropertyPage::SetObjects. Upon construction of a property page, an array of IUnknown pointers is provided to the property page. The property page's implementation of SetObjects will typically call QueryInterface for the IDispatch pointers of any associated controls. The property page can then easily get and set a control's properties through this interface.

MFC's COlePropertyPage::GetObjectArray method makes it easy to access a property page's array of IDispatch pointers. Once you have this pointer, you can use CCmdTarget::FromIDispatch to obtain the actual COleControl-derived instance of your control. FromIDispatch checks to ensure that the IDispatch Vtable pointer that you provide is the same as MFC's IDispatch implementation. In other words, this technique will work only if your control was written using MFC's CCmdTarget-based classes (such as COleControl). This technique also requires MFC version 4.0 and above.

Enough talk. Let's see some code:

```
LPDISPATCH CFAQPropPage::GetControlDispatch()
{
    // Get the property page's IDispatch array
    ULONG ulObjects;
    LPDISPATCH* lpObjectArray = GetObjectArray( &ulObjects );
    ASSERT( lpObjectArray != NULL );

    // I'm assuming there is but one control, ours
    // This is a pretty straightforward assumption
    // Most containers don't even support multi-control
    // selection of custom property pages.
    // Return the dispatch
    return( lpObjectArray[0] );
}
```

The preceding code retrieves the IDispatch pointer of our control by returning the first element of the page's object array. We make the assumption that this is our control's IDispatch, and today this is a fairly easy assumption to make. With just this information, we can now directly interact with our control but only through its IDispatch. The following code sets the Filename property of our FAQ control:

```
void CFAQPropPage::SetControlFilename( const CString& strFilename )
{
    // Needed for Unicode conversion functions
    USES_CONVERSION;

    // Get the dispatch of the control
    LPDISPATCH lpdispControl = GetControlDispatch();

    // Update the control here using automation calls
    COleDispatchDriver PropDispDriver;
```

```
    DISPID dwDispID;
    // Get a Unicode string
    LPCOLESTR lpOleStr = T2COLE( "Filename" );
    if (SUCCEEDED( lpdispControl->GetIDsOfNames(IID_NULL,
                        (LPOLESTR*)&lpOleStr,
                        1, 0, &dwDispID)))
    {
        PropDispDriver.AttachDispatch( lpdispControl, FALSE);
        PropDispDriver.SetProperty( dwDispID, VT_BSTR, strFilename );
        PropDispDriver.DetachDispatch();
    }
}
```

The preceding code could probably use a little explanation. USES_CONVERSION is a macro provided in **AFXPRIV.H** that facilitates the conversion of ANSI strings to Unicode strings. In MFC versions before 4.0, ANSI-to-Unicode string translation was provided by default. In MFC versions 4.0 and higher, you must do the conversions yourself. All Win32 OLE calls expect Unicode strings. T2COLE converts an ANSI string to a const Unicode string. For additional details, check out **AFXPRIV.H** and *MFC Tech Note 59*: "Using MFC MBCS/Unicode Conversion Macros." The rest of the code retrieves the IDispatch of our control and attaches it to an instance of COleDispatchDriver. This makes it easier to use the IDispatch methods.

The preceding steps mimic how the standard DDP functions update and retrieve property values from a control. The DDP functions use the COlePropertyPage::SetPropText methods. Several SetPropText methods are implemented within COlePropertyPage. Each one is overloaded to take a different property type. The SetPropText methods aren't documented, but by using them we can shorten the preceding code to this:

```
void CFAQPropPage::SetControlFilename( CString& strFilename )
{
    SetPropText( "Filename", strFilename );
}
```

If you need to access only the automation properties or methods of your control, the preceding techniques will work fine. However, if you need to access non-automation aspects of your control or would rather use straight C++ bindings (it's faster), you can do this:

```
CFAQCtrl* CFAQPropPage::GetControlInstance()
{
    LPDISPATCH lpdispControl = GetControlDispatch();
    ASSERT( lpdispControl != NULL );

    return (CFAQCtrl*) CCmdTarget::FromIDispatch( lpdispControl );
}
```

The FromIDispatch method of CCmdTarget allows you to retrieve the C++ instance associated with an IDispatch pointer. This technique requires that your property page and control implementation use MFC, but it works. Another requirement is that the COM object be implemented in-process. ActiveX controls are always implemented as in-process servers—I haven't yet found an exception—so this requirement isn't a problem.

By retrieving the instance of our control, we can do just about anything with our control within the property page. In the answer to the next question, we will use this new flexibility to manipulate an array of properties.

How can I implement a property array?

Why, you ask, would I want to access my control instance from its property page? There are a few reasons. One is that the DDP functions provided by MFC don't always give us the functionality we need, especially when it comes to property arrays. A good example of a property array, or parameterized property, is a list-box control that allows the user to prefill the listbox, during the design phase, with strings. This list of strings can be manipulated via one property name and index (the parameter) like this:

```
Dim str as String
str = Listbox.List( 1 )
```

Here, List is a property array that holds the strings contained within the listbox. The DDP functions do not allow you to get and set property values stored within arrays, so we must do something else. We communicate with our control directly using the technique described in the previous section:

```
void CFAQPropPage::DoDataExchange(CDataExchange* pDX)
{
    ...

    // Set or retrieve the string list
    // from the control instance
    if ( pDX->m_bSaveAndValidate )
        UpdateList();
    else
        RetrieveList();

    DDP_PostProcessing(pDX);
}
```

Within our property page implementation, whenever DoDataExchange is called we check the state of the data transfer. If the page is updating the control's properties, as indicated by m_bSaveAndValidate, we update an associated list within the control. When we're retrieving the control's properties, the reverse occurs. The code for each method retrieves the control instance and either queries or updates a multiline edit field within the property page:

```
//
```

```
// Spin through the multiline edit box and update the control's list
//
void CFAQPropPage::UpdateList()
{
    CStringList strList;
    CEdit* pEdit = (CEdit*) GetDlgItem( IDC_PROPERTYLIST );

    // Get the number of lines
    int nLines = pEdit->GetLineCount();
    for ( int line = 0; line < nLines; line++ )
    {
        char szLine[128];
        int nCount = pEdit->GetLine( line, szLine, sizeof( szLine ) - 1 );
        // GetLine doesn't null terminate
        szLine[nCount] = '\0';
        if ( nCount )
            strList.AddTail( szLine );
    }

    // Get the control instance
    CFAQCtrl* pFAQCtrl = GetControlInstance();

    // Pass the list to the control
    pFAQCtrl->SetPropertyArray( strList );
}

//
// Get the property array list from the control
//
void CFAQPropPage::RetrieveList()
{
    CStringList strList;
    CEdit* pEdit = (CEdit*) GetDlgItem( IDC_PROPERTYLIST );

    // Clear any existing data in the edit box
    pEdit->SetSel( 0, -1 );
    pEdit->ReplaceSel( "" );

    // Get the control instance
    CFAQCtrl* pFAQCtrl = GetControlInstance();

    // Get the list from the control
    pFAQCtrl->GetPropertyArray( strList );
```

```
// Fill the entry box
POSITION pos = strList.GetHeadPosition();
while( pos )
{
    // Add a CR/LF pair when inserting into the
    // multiline EDIT.
    CString str = strList.GetNext( pos ) + "\r\n";
    pEdit->ReplaceSel( str );
}

// Clear any selection
pEdit->SetSel( -1, 0 );

}
```

Within the property page, a CStringList instance is maintained that contains a list of strings for the droplist. A private method within the COleControl-derived class, which takes a CStringList reference, is used to pass the data to the control instance. Most of the preceding code deals with getting the control's instance and is described in the property page section. The important part is that we're not using the DDX/DDP functions but instead are doing the work ourselves. A similar approach is needed within the control too:

```
/////////////
// Property array implementation
/////////////
void CFAQCtrl::GetPropertyArray( CStringList& rList )
{
    rList.RemoveAll();
    POSITION pos = m_lstStrings.GetHeadPosition();
    while( pos )
    {
        rList.AddTail( m_lstStrings.GetNext( pos ));
    }
}

void CFAQCtrl::SetPropertyArray( CStringList& rList )
{
    m_lstStrings.RemoveAll();
    POSITION pos = rList.GetHeadPosition();
    while( pos )
    {
        m_lstStrings.AddTail( rList.GetNext( pos ));
    }
```

```
}
```

These methods are called from within the property page to update the control's string list member. Now we can maintain a property array both within the control and within the property page.

But that's only half the problem. Another FAQ is, "How can I serialize (or persist) a property array?" This isn't a straightforward question. The default control persistence (PX) functions don't handle property arrays either, so we do something similar to our property page solution. Again, we check the direction of the property exchange in our control's DoPropExchange method and call the appropriate internal method:

```
void CFAQCtrl::DoPropExchange(CPropExchange* pPX)
{
    ExchangeVersion(pPX, MAKELONG(_wVerMinor, _wVerMajor));
    COleControl::DoPropExchange(pPX);

    // Save or restore the list of strings
    if ( pPX->IsLoading() )
        LoadPropArray( pPX );
    else
        SavePropArray( pPX );
}

void CFAQCtrl::LoadPropArray( CPropExchange* pPX )
{
    // Make sure the list is empty
    m_lstStrings.RemoveAll();

    // Get the size of the list
    short sListSize;
    PX_Short( pPX, "ListSize", sListSize, 0 );

    // Read in the list
    CString strPropName;
    CString strValue;
    for( int i = 0; i < sListSize; i++ )
    {
        strPropName.Format( "%s%d", "List", i );
        PX_String( pPX, strPropName, strValue, "" );
        m_lstStrings.AddTail( strValue );
    }
}

void CFAQCtrl::SavePropArray( CPropExchange* pPX )
{
    short sListSize = m_lstStrings.GetCount();
```

```
// Write out the list size
PX_Short( pPX, "ListSize", sListSize );

// write out the strings
int i = 0;
CString strPropName;
CString strValue;
POSITION pos = m_lstStrings.GetHeadPosition();
while( pos )
{
    strPropName.Format( "%s%d", "List", i++ );
    strValue = m_lstStrings.GetNext( pos );
    PX_String( pPX, strPropName, strValue );
}
}
```

The trick here is to generate appropriate property names and store the strings there. The PX function property name parameter need not be a valid property name for your control; any value will do. I've added a ListSize property name and List0 through Listn property names to store any number of strings that the user may enter during the design phase.

I'll be the first to admit that this method may not be the most efficient way to do this, but it works. A better solution would probably be to use the PX_Blob function and store the strings in a binary format, an approach that would require less storage. This technique adds some complexity though, because MFC-based classes cannot be directly serialized using PX_Blob.

How can I provide a list of valid options for my properties?

Many control properties have a valid range of values. The default ClassWizard implementation does not provide a range limit for your properties. The primary technique of ensuring valid values for your control's properties is to use *enumerated properties,* which provide a way to prevent entry of invalid property values as well as providing a more user-friendly representation. Figure 13.1 is the property page of our FAQ control with three enumerated properties. You should also recognize the multiline entry field from the previous discussion.

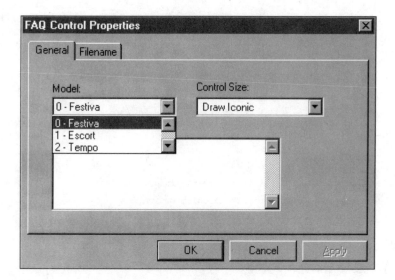

Figure 13.1 FAQ control property page.

There are two ways of implementing enumerated properties: statically and dynamically. Static enumerated properties are the easiest to implement and should be sufficient for most control properties. The control developer basically hard codes the potential property values with the control's type information via the **.ODL** file. The enumerated type's `HelpString` parameters can be queried by property browsers via the `ITypeInfo` interface. You define an enumerated type and then change your property definition to use the enumerated type instead of the default `short` value. Here's a simple definition for the stock `Model` property from **FAQ.ODL**:

```
//
// FAQ.ODL
//
[ uuid(D09D8510-B240-11CF-A58E-0000837E3100), version(1.0),
  helpstring("FAQ ActiveX control module"), control ]
library FAQLib
{
    importlib(STDOLE_TLB);
    importlib(STDTYPE_TLB);

    typedef enum
    {
        [helpstring("Festiva")] Festiva = 0,
        [helpstring("Escort")] Escort = 1,
        [helpstring("Tempo")] Tempo = 2
```

```
    [helpstring("Probe")] Probe = 3
    [helpstring("Taurus")] Taurus = 4
} enumModel;

//   Primary dispatch interface for CFAQCtrl
[ uuid(D09D8511-B240-11CF-A58E-0000837E3100),
  helpstring("Dispatch interface for FAQ Control"), hidden ]
dispinterface _DFAQ
{
    properties:
        // NOTE - ClassWizard will maintain property information here.
        //    Use extreme caution when editing this section.
        //{{AFX_ODL_PROP(CFAQCtrl)
        [id(1)] short ControlSize;
        [id(2)] BSTR Filename;
        [id(3)] enumModel Model;
        //}}AFX_ODL_PROP

    . . .
}
```

In property browsers (such as Visual Basic, Visual C++, and Delphi) that support this technique, only the five enumerated options are shown. The user is able to choose only from this list. You should also use these options in your control's custom property page. (Remember, not all tools provide property browsers, and that's one reason for custom property pages.) You can add the enumerated options using the DDP/DDX_CBIndex functions within the DoDataExchange method:

```
void CFAQPropPage::DoDataExchange(CDataExchange* pDX)
{
    //{{AFX_DATA_MAP(CFAQPropPage)
    DDP_CBIndex(pDX, IDC_MODEL, m_sModel, _T("Model") );
    DDX_CBIndex(pDX, IDC_MODEL, m_sModel);
    . . .
    //}}AFX_DATA_MAP

    DDP_PostProcessing(pDX);
}
```

There are two techniques you can use to initialize the combo box with the valid strings. First, you can override OnInitDialog and add the strings there. Second, you can enter the strings within the Developer Studio resource editor at design time. Combo boxes with the droplist style allow the entry of a default list of strings. To keep things nice, you may also want to add an enum to your control class and use it in your control code. The sample control demonstrates all these techniques.

```
BOOL CFAQPropPage::OnInitDialog()
{
    COlePropertyPage::OnInitDialog();

    // Here's one way to populate the static enumerated
    // property combo box. The other is to add the strings
    // in the resource editor.
    CComboBox* pWnd = (CComboBox*) GetDlgItem( IDC_MODEL );
    pWnd->AddString( "Festiva" );
    pWnd->AddString( "Escort" );
    pWnd->AddString( "Tempo" );
    pWnd->AddString( "Probe" );
    pWnd->AddString( "Taurus" );

    return TRUE;  // return TRUE unless you set the focus to a control
                  // EXCEPTION: OCX Property Pages should return FALSE
}

class CFAQCtrl : public COleControl
{
...
    // Enumerated property members
    short       m_sModel;
    enum
    {
        Festiva = 0,
        Escort = 1,
        Tempo = 2,
        Probe = 3,
        Taurus = 4
    };
...
};
```

You can also provide enumerated property values dynamically. This approach is a little more complicated and is best used when the enumerated values can change or are dependent on other properties within your control, or when a targeted container (or tool) does not support static enumerated properties.

For controls to provide dynamic enumerated properties, they must implement the IPerPropertyBrowsing interface. MFC's COleControl class provides a default implementation and allows your derived-control class to augment this implementation via the OnGetPredefinedStrings, OnGetPredefinedValue, and OnGetDisplayString methods.

We will look at the implementation first from the control side and later from the property page side. To provide dynamic enumerated properties, the three `IPerPropertyBrowsing` methods must be implemented within your control's class. For demonstration purposes, the FAQ control enumerates its `ControlSize` property dynamically. What follows will describe what is required to implement `ControlSize` as a dynamic enumerated property. The following definition describes a small `CCtrlSize` class. Each `CCtrlSize` instance contains a single `ControlSize` property definition.

```
// ControlSize dynamic property support class
class CCtrlSize : public CObject
{
public:
    CCtrlSize( CSize, short, CString );
    CCtrlSize();

public:
    CSize      m_sizeCtrl;
    short      m_sCookie;
    CString    m_strDisplayString;
};
```

The control maintains a linked list of valid `ControlSize` values. The potential property values are dynamic and can be added to this list throughout the lifetime of the control. The control instance also maintains a pointer into the linked list that identifies the current value of the property. This makes it easy to obtain the value in the various control methods. Here's a snippet from **FAQCTL.H**:

```
class CFAQCtrl : public COleControl
{
...
    // Dynamic enumerated property overrides
    virtual BOOL OnGetPredefinedStrings( DISPID dispid,
                                         CStringArray* pStringArray,
                                         CDWordArray* pCookieArray );
    virtual BOOL OnGetPredefinedValue( DISPID dispid,
                                       DWORD dwCookie,
                                       VARIANT FAR* lpvarOut );
    virtual BOOL OnGetDisplayString( DISPID dispid,
                                     CString& strValue );
...
    CCtrlSize*  m_pControlSize;
    CObList     m_lstSizes;
    enum
    {
```

```
            IconicCookie = 0,
            SmallCookie = 1,
            MediumCookie = 2,
            LargeCookie = 3,
            XLargeCookie = 4
        };
    ...
};
```

There are the overrides, a `CCtrlSize` pointer to maintain the current value, and a `CObList` to maintain a list of valid values. When the control is constructed, this list is initialized with potential values.

```
CFAQCtrl::CFAQCtrl()
{
    ...
    // Build a list of valid control sizes
    CCtrlSize* pSize;
    pSize = new CCtrlSize( CSize( 28, 28 ),
                           IconicCookie,
                           " Draw Iconic" );
    m_lstSizes.AddTail( pSize );

    // Default is to draw iconic
    m_pControlSize = pSize;

    pSize = new CCtrlSize( CSize( 100, 100 ),
                           SmallCookie,
                           "100 x 100" );
    m_lstSizes.AddTail( pSize );

    pSize = new CCtrlSize( CSize( 200, 200 ),
                           MediumCookie,
                           "200 x 200" );
    m_lstSizes.AddTail( pSize );

    pSize = new CCtrlSize( CSize( 300, 300 ),
                           LargeCookie,
                           "300 x 300" );
    m_lstSizes.AddTail( pSize );

    pSize = new CCtrlSize( CSize( 400, 400 ),
                           XLargeCookie,
                           "400 x 400" );
    m_lstSizes.AddTail( pSize );
    ...
}
```

The default property setting is to "Draw Iconic," but it is reset if a different persistent value has been set for the control. Also, `COleControl::SetControlSize` is called after the correct `ControlSize` value is obtained, so you must be careful when using dynamic properties. If you set a persistent value, you must ensure that the value is there when you're constructing the control later or that you provide an effective default mechanism for the value.

```
void CFAQCtrl::DoPropExchange(CPropExchange* pPX)
{
    ExchangeVersion(pPX, MAKELONG(_wVerMinor, _wVerMajor));
    COleControl::DoPropExchange(pPX);

    ...

    // If loading the property, find the correct entry in the list
    // and initialize the current property value
    if ( pPX->IsLoading() )
    {
        // Get the cookie value and find the appropriate entry in the list
        m_pControlSize = 0;
        short sCookie;
        PX_Short( pPX, _T( "ControlSize" ), sCookie, IconicCookie );
        POSITION pos = m_lstSizes.GetHeadPosition();
        while( pos )
        {
            CCtrlSize* pSize = (CCtrlSize*) m_lstSizes.GetNext( pos );
            if ( short( sCookie ) == pSize->m_sCookie )
            {
                m_pControlSize = pSize;
                break;
            }
        }
        ASSERT( m_pControlSize != 0 );

        // When loading the size property, update the control's size
        COleControl::SetControlSize( m_pControlSize->m_sizeCtrl.cx,
                                     m_pControlSize->m_sizeCtrl.cy );
    }
    else
    {
        ASSERT( m_pControlSize != 0 );
        // Save cookie value of the dynamic ControlSize property
        PX_Short( pPX, _T( "ControlSize" ),
```

```
        m_pControlSize->m_sCookie,
        IconicCookie );
   }
}
```

Now that we understand the internal management of the potential property values, let's implement the enumerated property methods. The `OnGetPredifinedStrings` method is called by the container, via `IPerPropertyBrowsing::GetPredefinedStrings`, to get a list of potential property values. The DISPID of the specific property is provided along with a pointer to a string array and a DWORD array. If the container is asking for our `ControlSize` property, we fill both lists with values from our `CCtrlSize` list and return TRUE. A TRUE return indicates that the arrays have been filled with values. The cookie array allows the container to later ask for the specific property value associated with the cookie. In our case, the cookie is the position of the value within the list. Later, this approach will make it easier to implement our custom property page, because we will use the cookie as an index into our combo box:

```
BOOL CFAQCtrl::OnGetPredefinedStrings( DISPID dispid,
                                       CStringArray* pStringArray,
                                       CDWordArray* pCookieArray )
{
   if ( dispid == dispidControlSize )
   {
      POSITION pos = m_lstSizes.GetHeadPosition();
      while( pos )
      {
         CCtrlSize* pSize = (CCtrlSize*) m_lstSizes.GetNext( pos );
         pStringArray->Add( pSize->m_strDisplayString );
         pCookieArray->Add( pSize->m_sCookie );
      }
      return TRUE;
   }

   // If it's not ours, let our parent handle the request
   return COleControl::OnGetPredefinedStrings( dispid,
                                               pStringArray,
                                               pCookieArray );
}
```

If a user now selects a specific property value string, the container will ask for its associated value. `OnGetPredefinedValue`, via `IPerPropertyBrowsing::GetPredefinedValue`, provides the DISPID and cookie for the requested value and a VARIANT for the return. All we have to do now is to spin through our list, match the cookies, and return the property value. In our case, the cookie value is the same as the property value, so we fill out the VARIANT and return TRUE, indicating that the value was found.

```
BOOL CFAQCtrl::OnGetPredefinedValue( DISPID dispid,
                                     DWORD dwCookie,
                                     VARIANT FAR* lpvarOut )
{
   if ( dispid == dispidControlSize )
   {
      POSITION pos = m_lstSizes.GetHeadPosition();
      while( pos )
      {
         CCtrlSize* pSize = (CCtrlSize*) m_lstSizes.GetNext( pos );
         if ( short( dwCookie ) == pSize->m_sCookie )
         {
            VariantInit( lpvarOut );
            lpvarOut->vt = VT_I2;
            lpvarOut->iVal = short( dwCookie );
            return TRUE;
         }
      }
   }
   // Call the parent implementation
   return COleControl::OnGetPredefinedValue( dispid, dwCookie, lpvarOut );
}
```

OnGetDisplayString returns the current "string" setting for the DISPID provided. This method is called by the container whenever it needs to update its display. Here is its implementation:

```
BOOL CFAQCtrl::OnGetDisplayString( DISPID dispid, CString& strValue )
{
   if ( dispid == dispidControlSize )
   {
      // This should never happen, we're just being safe.
      if ( m_pControlSize == 0 )
         strValue = "Unknown";
      else
         strValue = m_pControlSize->m_strDisplayString;
      return TRUE;
   }
}
```

That finishes the control-side implementation. Now let's move on to our custom property page. In our solution for static enumerated properties, we used a combo box filled with strings that we defined when compiling the control, or we added them during initialization of the dialog box. For dynamic properties, we need to retrieve the possible values *from the control* at run time. Thanks to the previous discussions, we should be able to do this rather easily. The cookie that we used to identify a specific property value can also be used to indicate the property's index within our combo box. So, within our property page, we will use the technique that a typical property browser would use to retrieve the property's potential values:

```
void CFAQPropPage::GetControlSizeStrings()
{
   // Get the dispatch of the control
   LPDISPATCH lpdispControl = GetControlDispatch();

   // Using IDispatch, query for IPerPropertyBrowsing
   LPPERPROPERTYBROWSING lpBrowse;
   HRESULT hr = lpdispControl->QueryInterface( IID_IPerPropertyBrowsing,
                                               (LPVOID*) &lpBrowse );

   if ( SUCCEEDED( hr ))
   {
      CALPOLESTR      castr;
      CADWORD         cadw;

      // Get the property strings associated with our
      // ControlSize property. This also returns an array
      // of "cookies," but we don't actually need them.
      hr = lpBrowse->GetPredefinedStrings( CFAQCtrl::dispidControlSize,
                                           &castr,
                                           &cadw );

      if ( SUCCEEDED( hr ))
      {
         //
         // Move the strings to our combo box
         //
         CComboBox* pWnd = (CComboBox*) GetDlgItem( IDC_CONTROLSIZE );
         for ( ULONG i = 0; i < castr.cElems; i++ )
         {
            // Must include AFXPRIV.H
            USES_CONVERSION;
            // W2A converts the OLE (Unicode) string to ANSI
            pWnd->AddString( W2A( castr.pElems[i] ) );
         }

         //
         // Free any memory allocated by the server
         //
```

```
        CoTaskMemFree( (void *)cadw.pElems );
        for (i = 0; i < castr.cElems; i++ )
            CoTaskMemFree( (void *)castr.pElems[i] );
        CoTaskMemFree( (void *)castr.pElems );

    }

    // We're finished so release IPerPropertyBrowsing
    lpBrowse->Release();
  }
}
```

We get our control's IDispatch and query through it for IPerPropertyBrowsing. We then call GetPredefinedStrings to get our array of strings and cookies. Next, we iterate over this array and populate our combo box. That's all there is to it. The standard PX_CBIndex function handles updating the control when the user changes a property value. There are some tricky parts. You must deallocate the arrays using COM functions, but once you've done it (and you've now done it once), you've done it a hundred times.

How can I set up a custom property dialog box and access it from Visual Basic's browser using the "…" option?

When developing custom property pages for your controls, you can manipulate and validate those values entered by the control user. However, most visual tools (such as Visual Basic and Delphi) provide their own property browsers. The default behavior of these browsers allows the control user to enter property values that are limited only by the range of the property's intrinsic type. For example, if you have a property that is of type short, the user can enter any value that is within the range of a short. What do you do if you need to provide more stringent property validation? What if you would like to provide a more user-friendly interface that helps the user select the correct property value? One solution, as we discussed earlier, is to provide enumerated properties, but what if the values can't be enumerated? One example of a property that is difficult to enumerate is a filename. To provide a nice, user-friendly interface for these types of properties, you must implement per-property browsing.

From a user perspective, per-property browsing enables modification, via a control-specific property page, of a property from within a tool's browser. In Visual Basic and Visual C++, this additional capability is identified by the appearance of ellipses ("…") beside the property. When the ellipses button is clicked, a control-specific property sheet is displayed. This approach allows custom property manipulation within any tool that supports per-property browsing.

The IPerPropertyBrowsing interface that we described earlier is used to implement per-property browsing—specifically, through an implementation of the MapPropertyToPage method. MapPropertyToPage does basically what it says. The browser passes the DISPID of a specific property, and, if the control wants to provide per-property browsing, it returns the CLSID of the supporting property page.

To demonstrate per-property browsing, let's implement a custom property page for the `Filename` property of our FAQ control. The `Filename` property doesn't do much; it has the usual `Get`/`Set` methods and a `PX_String` function for persistence, but that's it. We'll use it to demonstrate per-property browsing and to answer another FAQ that I often get: "How can I pop up a standard file dialog box from within the property browser?"

I've added a second custom property page to the control (the process for doing this is described in the MFC documentation) and have provided an entry field for the filename. We have placed a button on the page to invoke a standard file dialog box (Figure 13.2).

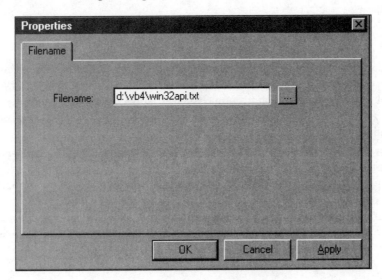

Figure 13.2 Filename property page.

The ellipses button invokes a standard file dialog box that allows the user to browse for a specific filename:

```
void CFAQPropPage2::OnSearch()
{
    CString strExt = "All files (*.*) | *.* ||";

    CFileDialog fileDialog( TRUE,
                            "*.*",
                            NULL,
                            OFN_SHAREAWARE | OFN_LONGNAMES,
                            strExt,
                            this );

    fileDialog.m_ofn.nFilterIndex = 0;
    fileDialog.m_ofn.lpstrTitle = "FAQ Filename Dialog";
```

```
fileDialog.m_ofn.lpstrFile = m_strFilename.GetBuffer(_MAX_PATH);

BOOL bResult = fileDialog.DoModal() == IDOK ? TRUE : FALSE;

m_strFilename.ReleaseBuffer();
if ( bResult == IDOK )
{
    CWnd* pWnd = GetDlgItem( IDC_FILENAME );
    pWnd->SetWindowText( m_strFilename );
    SetControlStatus( IDC_FILENAME, TRUE );
}
}
```

We invoke a modal file dialog box and allow the user to choose a filename. When **OK** is pressed, we update the filename entry field and call `COlePropertyPage::SetControlStatus`, which marks the property as "dirty" and enables the **Apply** button on the property sheet. Now everything is handled just like any other property in a custom property page. When **OK** or **Apply** is pressed, the DDP function is used to update the property within the control instance.

To enable per-property browsing, we override the default implementation of `OnMapPropertyToPage`. When a well-behaved property browser enables editing for a specific property, it calls `IPerPropertyBrowsing::MapPropertyToPage` to see whether the control supports per-property browsing. If per-property browsing is supported, the GUID of the associated property page is returned. When a container calls `MapPropertyToPage`, `COleControl` gives the control a chance to handle the method through `OnMapPropertyToPage`. The DISPID of the specific property is provided. Here's our implementation from the FAQ control:

```
//
// Support for VB's "..." browser option. Displays a specific
//   property page based on the provided dispid. In our case we
//   will pop up our "Filename" property page.
//
BOOL CFAQCtrl::OnMapPropertyToPage( DISPID dispid, LPCLSID lpclsid, BOOL* pbPageOptional )
{
    // Return our custom "Filename" property page if
    // the client asks for it.
    if ( dispid == dispidFilename )
    {
        *lpclsid = CFAQPropPage2::guid;
        *pbPageOptional = FALSE;
        return TRUE;
    }

    return COleControl::OnMapPropertyToPage( dispid, lpclsid, pbPageOptional );
}
```

In Visual Basic, when the user clicks on the ... button, Visual Basic calls `MapPropertyToPage` to get the GUID of the associated property page. If one is provided, the container builds a property frame with the specific property page. This technique allows control-specific editing outside a control's custom property pages.

The `pbPageOptional` flag indicates to the property browser whether or not the property can be edited outside its property page. Our filename property can be edited within an external browser, so we set the flag to `TRUE`.

The three other `IPerPropertyBrowsing` methods that we used earlier to implement dynamic enumerated properties are not needed here. It's not possible for us to enumerate all the valid filenames, although we could check the filename for syntactic validity. Oh well, yet another exercise for the reader.

When I change a property's value through its property page, the tool's property browser isn't updated. Why not?

You've already seen code from the FAQ sample that answers this question. If you want your design-time property changes via your control's property pages to immediately update an external property browser (such as Visual Basic or Delphi), you need only call the `BoundPropertyChanged` method after setting the new value:

```
void CYourCtrl::SetSomeProperty(short nNewValue)
{
   m_sSomeProperty = nNewValue;

   // Update the property browser
   BoundPropertyChanged( dispidSomeProperty );
   SetModifiedFlag();
}
```

`BoundPropertyChanged` informs the browser, via `IPropertyNotifySink::OnChanged`, that a control's property value has changed. The browser then retrieves the new value through the control's `IDispatch`. The parameter provides the dispatch ID of the property that changed. `DISPID_UNKNOWN` can be used to force an update of all known properties.

Why can't I set the colors on my subclassed BUTTON control?

Button controls do not pay attention to the reflected `OCM_CTLCOLORBTN` message. If you want to create a button control that provides custom color capabilities, you will have to use an owner-draw control.

How can I provide F1 support for my properties within Visual Basic's property browser?

To add support for **F1** help within various browsers, you need to modify your control's **.ODL** file. The modifications specify the help context IDs for your control's properties, methods, and events. The steps and keywords required to modify the **.ODL** file are explained in Microsoft Knowledge Base article Q130275.

How do I add support for the Help button in my property page?

First you need to create a **.HLP** file for your properties. Then for each of your custom property pages, add a call to `SetHelpInfo` in the constructor of your property page class. You must provide a short comment for tooltip support, the filename of your **.HLP** file, and the help context ID to be passed during the `WinHelp` call. The default implementation of the **Help** button calls `WinHelp` with the parameters provided via `SetHelpInfo`. If necessary, you can change this default behavior by overriding and implementing the `COlePropertyPage::OnHelp` method.

How do I return an array of items from my control?

To return an array of items, you can use an automation safe array. There isn't room to discuss all the features of safe arrays here, so I'll briefly cover how to use them in an automation method. A tremendous amount of documentation comes with Visual C++ that covers the various safe array APIs and so on.

Add a method to your control that takes a `VARIANT` pointer as a parameter. A variant is a generic data type that can hold values or pointers to other, more specific automation types. One of the data types that can be contained within a variant is a safe array. You can have an array of `shorts`, `longs`, `BSTRs`, `Dates`, and so on. In the method, allocate a `SAFEARRAY`, allocate space for the items, and then populate the array with these values. Then initialize the `VARIANT` structure. The following code creates a `SAFEARRAY` of `BSTR` elements. As with all automation data, the server allocates the storage, and the client (for example, Visual Basic) is responsible for the deallocation.

```
void CMyControl::GetArray( VARIANT FAR* pVariant )
{
    // Get the number of items
    int nCount = GetCount();

    // Create a safe array of type BSTR
    // cElements of the first item indicates the size of the array
    SAFEARRAYBOUND saBound[1];
    SAFEARRAY* pSA;

    saBound[0].cElements = nCount;
    saBound[0].lLbound = 0;
    pSA = SafeArrayCreate( VT_BSTR, 1, saBound );

    for( long i = 0; i < nCount; i++ )
    {
        BSTR bstr;

        // Get the next item, create a BSTR, and
        // stuff it in the array. GetItem returns a CString.
        bstr = GetItem( i ).AllocSysString();
```

```
      SafeArrayPutElement( pSA, &i, bstr );
      ::SysFreeString( bstr );
   }

   // Init the variant
   VariantInit( pVariant );

   // Specify its type and value
   pVariant->vt = VT_ARRAY | VT_BSTR;
   pVariant->parray = pSA;
}
```

The Visual Basic code to access the elements of the array would look something like this:

```
   Dim t As Variant
   Dim i as Integer

   MyControl1.GetArray t

   For i = 0 To MyControl1.Count - 1
       ListBox.AddItem  t( i )
   Next i
```

How can I communicate with other controls in the container?

To communicate with other ActiveX controls within a container, use the `IOleItemContainer::Enum Objects` method. `COleControl` provides a method, `GetClientSite`, that provides access to the `IOleClientSite` interface. Through this method you can get a pointer to the `IOleItemContainer` interface. Once you have a pointer to this interface, you can enumerate over the contained controls:

```
void CMyCtrl::EnumControls()
{
   LPOLECONTAINER pContainer = NULL;
   // Get a pointer to the IOleItemContainer interface
   HRESULT hr = GetClientSite()->GetContainer( &pContainer );
   if ( SUCCEEDED( hr ))
   {
      // Types of objects to enum
      DWORD dwFlags = OLECONTF_ONLYIFRUNNING |
                      OLECONTF_EMBEDDINGS |
                      OLECONTF_ONLYUSER;

      LPENUMUNKNOWN pEnumUnknown = NULL;
      hr = pContainer->EnumObjects( dwFlags, &pEnumUnknown );
```

```
    if ( SUCCEEDED( hr ))
    {
        LPUNKNOWN pNextControl = NULL;
        // Loop through the controls
        while( SUCCEEDED( hr ) && pEnumUnknown->Next( 1, &pNextControl, NULL ) == S_OK)
        {
            LPDISPATCH pDispatch = NULL;

            // Get the IDispatch of the control
            hr = pNextControl->QueryInterface( IID_IDispatch, (LPVOID*) &pDispatch );
            if ( SUCCEEDED( hr ))
            {
                COleDispatchDriver PropDispDriver;
                DISPID dwDispID;

                // Use automation to access various properties and methods
                USES_CONVERSION;
                LPCOLESTR lpOleStr = T2COLE( "SomeProperty" );
                if (SUCCEEDED( pDispatch->GetIDsOfNames(IID_NULL,
                                    (LPOLESTR*)&lpOleStr, 1, 0, &dwDispID)))
                {
                    PropDispDriver.AttachDispatch( pDispatch, FALSE);
                    UINT uiCount;
                    PropDispDriver.GetProperty( dwDispID, VT_I4, &uiCount );
                    PropDispDriver.DetachDispatch();
                    pNextControl->Release();
                }
            }
        }
        pEnumUnknown->Release();
    }
}
}
```

The preceding example demonstrates how to access the IDispatch of all the controls within the container. There are many other things you could do. To identify the controls you're looking for, you could implement a custom interface within the (target) control and then call QueryInterface to find it. You could also look for a specific CLSID of a control after retrieving the IOleObject interface. You should be able to do almost anything once you've found the control you're looking for.

Why does AmbientUserMode *always return True?*

You're probably checking the value of `AmbientUserMode` in your control's constructor, destructor, or `OnSetClientSite` method. The value of `AmbientUserMode` is always `TRUE` if the control hasn't yet set up its ambient `IDispatch` connection to its container. You won't get a valid return from `AmbientUserMode` in either the constructor or destructor of your control, but you can in `OnSetClientSite` if you first ensure that the ambient `IDispatch` has been set up. The following code demonstrates how to check `AmbientUserMode` during the call to `OnSetClientSite`:

```
// Ensure the control has a valid HWND as soon as it
// is placed on the container
void CYourCtrl::OnSetClientSite()
{
  // We only need the window at run time
  // Only call recreate when there is a valid ambient dispatch
  if ( m_ambientDispDriver.m_lpDispatch && AmbientUserMode() )
    RecreateControlWindow();
}
```

The `m_ambientDispDriver` member of `COleControl` maintains the ambient dispatch of the container. Only if `m_lpDispatch` is valid is there an appropriate connection to the container, thus allowing retrieval of ambient properties. The preceding code ensures that `RecreateControlWindow` is only called once, when the control is initially created as the container loads the control.

How do I change the actual Name value of my control (VB's Name property)?

The `Name` property that Visual Basic uses is the control's actual `coclass` name. To quickly change this exposed name, modify your control's `coclass` interface name. The following example shows where this name is located in the **.ODL** file. I've changed the name from `Ccc` to `SomethingElse`.

```
//  Class information for CCccCtrl
[ uuid(3B082A53-6888-11CF-A4EE-524153480001),
  helpstring("Ccc"), control ]
coclass SomethingElse
{
  [default] dispinterface _DCcc;
  [default, source] dispinterface _DCccEvents;
};
```

I'm having trouble registering my control. What can I do?

The most common problem you'll encounter when attempting to register a control is the absence of DLLs that the control depends on (such as **MFC40.DLL**). If you're still having problems after ensuring that the right DLLs are installed, you can simulate what **REGSVR32.EXE** does with the following code. This technique allows you to trace through and see exactly where things are going awry.

```
//
// RegisterServer takes as a parameter the
// explicit path and filename of the OLE
// server that you want to register.
// E.g., c:\winnt\system32\clock.ocx
// This function loads the DLL/OCX and calls
// the DllRegisterServer function.
//
DWORD RegisterServer( char* szPath )
{
   HINSTANCE hInstance = ::LoadLibrary( szPath );
   if ( 0 == hInstance )
   {
      return ::GetLastError();
   }
   typedef void (FAR PASCAL *REGSERVER)(void);
   REGSERVER RegServer =
           (REGSERVER) ::GetProcAddress( hInstance,
                              _T( "DllRegisterServer" ));
   if ( 0 == RegServer )
   {
      ::FreeLibrary( hInstance );
      return ::GetLastError();
   }
   RegServer();

   ::FreeLibrary( hInstance );
   return 0;
}
```

Can I create an instance of my control with Visual Basic's CreateObject function?

I've included this question because it was asked four times in a matter of days. It's also nice to know that you can use your ActiveX controls as automation servers if necessary. The main attraction of this approach is that it provides dynamic creation of the control. Using most tools, your control must be placed on a form during the design phase. If you use Visual Basic's `CreateObject` function, there are no design-time dependencies within your Visual Basic project. This flexibility, however, comes with a significant cost. Using your control as an automation server will negate two of the most important features of ActiveX controls: events and persistence.

Visual Basic's `CreateObject` function creates an instance of an automation server. It uses the standard COM APIs to create the instance and then query for the server's `IDispatch`. ActiveX controls are automation servers. However, they also implement a number of other COM-based interfaces and expect to be active within a container. The primary difference between a standard automation server and an ActiveX control is that the control natively supports events and provides a persistence mechanism for its properties (through its container).

By default, a control expects to have a control site containing various interfaces, but `CreateObject` cannot provide them. `COleControl` does, however, provide a way for a control to behave as just an automation server; you need only override `COleControl::IsInvokeAllowed` and return `TRUE`. This technique allows you to use `CreateObject` on your control, although you must be sure that everything will still work without any persistence or event support. You can check for this condition by testing the state of the `m_bInitialized` flag. If it is `FALSE`, the control has not been initialized via the standard container persistence mechanism. The following code allows your control to behave as an automation server and exposes a property, `IsControl`, that indicates its state:

```
BOOL CFAQCtrl::IsInvokeAllowed( DISPID dispid )
{
    return TRUE;
}

BOOL CFAQCtrl::GetIsControl()
{
    // If in design mode don't display the property
    // in the property browser. Throw the
    // CTL_E_GETNOTSUPPORTED exception instead.
    if (! AmbientUserMode() )
    {
        GetNotSupported();
    }

    // m_bInitialized indicates whether the container's
    // persistence mechanism was used to load the control.
    // If it is FALSE, we are acting as an automation server.
    return m_bInitialized;
}
```

Once you've set up your control to work as an automation server, you need to instantiate it. By default, ControlWizard creates a ProgID for controls as `PROJECT.PROJECTCtrl.1`. This is specified in the IMPLE-

MENT_OLECREATE_EX macro, so it's easy to change. To create an instance of your control in Visual Basic, you would do something like this:

```
Dim objFAQCtrl as Object
Set objFAQCtrl = CreateObject( "FAQ.FAQCtrl.1" )

' Do something with the control instance
objFAQCtrl.IsControl

' Now release it
Set objFAQCtrl = Nothing
```

More Answers

If you have other ActiveX control questions, be sure to check out the FAQ I maintain at http://www.sky.net/~toma/faq.htm. If the answer isn't there, send your question to me at toma@sky.net or tom@widgetware.com. I'll do my best to answer it in a timely manner. I also encourage you to contribute any specific issues that you've encountered or special tricks that you've learned while grappling with ActiveX control development. As product development timelines continue to shrink and the technologies that we use become more complex, we must do what we can to maintain our productivity.

Appendix A

CD-ROM Instructions

The CD-ROM contains the source code for all the example programs discussed in the book. The structure of the CD-ROM is illustrated in Figure A.1. I have not included a setup program to copy the files from the CD-ROM; a simple **XCOPY** command will allow you to select those items that you are interested in. For example, to copy the complete CD-ROM contents to your hard drive, create a directory (e.g., XBOOK), and issue the following **XCOPY** command. Of course, you will have to substitute your actual hard drive and CD-ROM device letter.

```
c:\Xbook\XCOPY d:\*.* /s
```

This will create the directory structure shown in Figure A.1 under your XBOOK directory. The contents of each directory are detailed here.

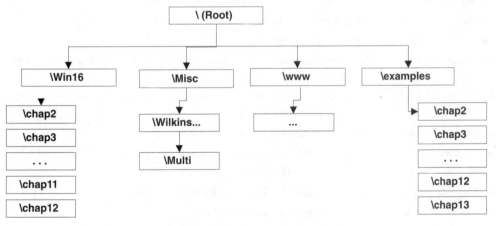

Figure A.1 CD-ROM hierarchy.

\Win16 Directory

I've included the source files and projects from the first edition of the book for those interested in developing 16-bit ActiveX controls. Each chapter directory contains a Visual C++ version 1.52b **make** file for the example projects and controls.

\Examples Directory

The \examples subdirectories contain all the Visual C++ project files for the example programs. Table A.1 details the contents of each directory.

Table A.1 \Example Directory Contents

Path	Description
\examples\chap2\express	Contains the initial **EXPRESS.H** and **EXPRESS.CPP** files. The **make** file included here works with Visual C++ and is built as a Win32 console application.
\examples\chap3	Visual C++ project files for the Chapter 3 project.
\examples\chap4\server	Visual C++ project files for the Chapter 4 SERVER project.
\examples\chap4\client	Visual C++ project files for the Chapter 4 CLIENT project.
\examples\chap5\server	Visual C++ project files for the Chapter 5 SERVER project.
\examples\chap5\client	Visual C++ project files for the Chapter 5 CLIENT project.
\examples\chap6\Autosvr	The project files for the MFC-based automation server we developed in Chapter 6.
\examples\chap6\server	The project files for the non-MFC automation server.
\examples\chap6\client	The project files for the non-MFC automation client.
\examples\chap6\VcClient	MFC-based automation client.
\examples\chap6\vbclient	Visual Basic automation client example. This Visual Basic example uses the non-MFC automation server.
\examples\chap6\vbdriver	Visual Basic automation client driver example. This Visual Basic example demonstrates accessing the MFC-based local server.
\examples\chap8\postit	Visual C++ project files for the POSTIT control.
\examples\chap8\vb	Project files for the Visual Basic example program that uses the POSTIT control.
\examples\chap9\clock	Visual C++ project files for the analog CLOCK control.
\examples\chap9\contain	Visual C++ project files for the CONTAIN container example.
\examples\chap10\eedit	Visual C++ project files for the EEDIT control.
\examples\chap10\vb	Visual Basic project that uses the EEDIT control.
\examples\chap10\treev	Visual C++ project files for the TREEV control.
\examples\chap11\pipe	Visual C++ project files for the PIPE control.

Table A.1 \Example Directory Contents (continued)

Path	Description
\examples\chap11\vb	Project files for the three Visual Basic example programs that use the PIPE control.
\examples\chap12\async	Visual C++ project files for the ASYNC control.
\examples\chap12\htm	HTML files using the sample control.
\examples\chap13\FAQ	Visual C++ project files for the FAQ control.

\WWW Directory

The \WWW directory contains an HTML-based page that contain references to ActiveX resources on the Web. Just load up the **DEFAULT.HTM** file in your browser.

\Misc Directory

The \misc directory contains additional sample control source not directly discussed in the text. For starters, there is great example of a control acting as a container for other controls in the \Misc\Wilkins hierarchy. Bob Wilkins (bob@havana.demon.co.uk) developed this example, and it demonstrates several useful techniques for embedding controls within another control. For the latest information on this example, check out his Web site at: http://www.netlink.co.uk/users/havana/projects.html.

The \Multi directory contains a control that demonstrates embedding multiple Windows controls within one ActiveX control.

Table A.2 \Misc Directory Contents

Path	Description
\Misc\Wilkins\xwdcell, \Misc\Wilkins\xwdgrid, \Misc\Wilkins\vbtest	The XWDCELL directory contains Bob's cell control. The XWDGRID directory contains the grid control that is actually a control container that contains a number of XWDCELL controls. The VBTEST directory contains a Visual Basic executable that implements a crossword puzzle.
\Misc\Multi	A simple control that demonstrates how to embed multiple Windows controls within one ActiveX control. The control contains a multiline EDIT control and a BUTTON control.

Appendix *B*

Bibliography

ActiveX SDK Documentation

The ActiveX SDK contains several documents that are instrumental to understanding ActiveX control and related technologies. Following is a list of the major documents:

OLE Controls/COM Objects for the Internet

Internet Component Download Specification

Asynchronous Moniker Specification

Component Categories Specification

OLE Controls 96 Specification

OLE Control and Container Guidelines Version 2.0

URL Monikers Specification

ActiveX SDK On-line Help

Other Publications

Armstrong, Tom, "Frequently Asked Questions—With Answers—About ActiveX Controls," *Component Builder*, (July and August 1996).

Andrews, Mark, C++ *Windows NT Programming*, New York, NY: M&T Books, 1994.

Blaszczak, Mike, "Implementing OLE Control Containers with MFC and the OLE Control Developer's Kit," *Microsoft Systems Journal* (April 1995).

Blaszczak, Mike, *MFC 4 Programming with Visual C++*, Chicago, IL: Wrox Press Ltd., 1996.

Brockschmidt, Kraig, *Inside OLE*, second edition, Redmond, WA: Microsoft Press, 1995.

Brockschmidt, Kraig, "OLE Integration Technologies," *Dr. Dobb's Special Report: The Interoperable Objects Revolution* (Winter 1994/1995).

Cargill, Tom, *C++ Programming Style*, Reading, MA: Addison-Wesley, 1992.

Chappell, David, *Understanding ActiveX and OLE*, Redmond, WA: Microsoft Press, 1996.

Cilwa, Paul, and Duntemann, Jeff, *Windows Programming Power with Custom Controls*, Scottsdale, AZ: The Coriolis Group, 1994.

DiLascia, Paul, "OLE Made Almost Easy: Creating Containers and Servers Using MFC 2.5," *Microsoft Systems Journal* (April 1994).

Eckel, Bruce, *C++ Inside & Out*, Berkeley, CA: Osborne McGraw-Hill, 1993.

Entsminger, Gary, *The Tao of Objects*, New York, NY: M&T Books, 1990.

Goodman, Kevin J., *Windows NT: A Developer's Guide*, New York, NY: M&T Books, 1994.

Harris, Lawrence, *Teach Yourself OLE Programming in 21 Days*, Indianapolis IN: Sams Publishing, 1995.

Helman, Paul, and Veroff, Robert, *Intermediate Problem Solving and Data Structures*, Menlo Park, CA: The Benjamin/Cummings Publishing Company, Inc., 1986.

Kruglinski, David J., *Inside Visual C++*, second edition, Redmond, WA: Microsoft Press, 1994.

Lang, Eric, "Building Component Software with Visual C++ and the OLE Control Developer's Kit," *Microsoft Systems Journal* (September 1994).

Meyers, Scott, *Effective C++*, Reading, MA: Addison-Wesley, 1992.

Microsoft Developer Network (MSDN) CD-ROM, Redmond, WA: Microsoft, 1995.

The MSDN CD-ROM is produced every quarter and distributed to MSDN members. It contains a tremendous amount (600 MB) of developer-oriented material: white papers, complete books, numerous program examples, back issues of *MSJ*, and so on. Every serious Windows developers should subscribe to this service. Following are some example items:

- Blaszczak, Mike, *Advanced MFC Architecture*
- Blaszczak, Mike, *Beginner MFC Architecture*
- Crane, Dennis, *Enhanced Metafiles in Win32*
- Marsh, Kyle, *Adding 3-D Effects to Controls*
- Rodent, Herman, *Flicker-Free Displays Using an Off-Screen DC*
- Rogerson, Dale, *OLE Controls: Top Tips*
- Rogerson, Dale, *OLE Controls: Registration*
- *Component Object Model (COM) Specification*
- *OLE 2.0 Design Specification*
- Thompson, Nigel, *MFC/COM Objects 4: Aggregation*

OLE Control Developer's Kit: User's Guide & Reference, Redmond, WA: Microsoft Press, 1994.

OLE Programmer's Reference Volume One, Redmond, WA: Microsoft Press, 1996.

OLE Automation Programmer's Reference Volume Two, Redmond, WA: Microsoft Press, 1996.

Petzold, Charles, *Programming Windows 3.1*, third edition, Redmond, WA: Microsoft Press, 1992.

Prosise, Jeff, "Wake Up and Smell the MFC: Using the Visual C++ Classes and Application Framework," *Microsoft Systems Journal* (June 1995).

Richter, Jeffrey M., *Windows 3.1: A Developer's Guide*, New York, NY: M&T Books, 1992.

Williams, Sara, and Kindel, Charlie, "The Component Object Model," *Dr. Dobb's Special Report: The Interoperable Objects Revolution* (Winter 1994/1995).

Index

About the CD-ROM

With the ever increasing pace of change in the software development industry, there comes the difficulty of providing samples program that are current as of the latest release of the compiler, SDK, and so on. Luckily, we now have the Web to make distribution of software rather easy. Please check out my Web site for the most recent samples at:

http://www.WidgetWare.com

If you need assistance with the samples included on the CD-ROM, or have other questions, check out the ActiveX control FAQ that I maintain at the URL above. You can contact me with questions and comments at: tom@WidgetWare.com. I'll do my best to respond promptly.

Tom Armstrong,
November, 1996